COLLECTIVE BARGAINING IN CANADA

Contributors

Carol A. Beatty, Queen's University
John Crispo, University of Toronto
Stuart J. Dimmock, University of Maryland (European Division)
Brian M. Downie, Queen's University
Loren Falkenberg, University of Calgary
Jeffrey Gandz, University of Western Ontario
John Kervin, University of Toronto
Maurice Lemelin, Haut Etude Commerciale, Montreal
Michael MacNeil, Carleton University
Allen M. Ponak, University of Calgary
Felix Quinet, Université du Québec à Hull
Robert Rogow, Simon Fraser University
Bob Sass, University of Saskatchewan
Amarjit S. Sethi, University of Ottawa
Gene Swimmer, Carleton University
Mark Stobbe, Saskatoon
James Thwaites, Laval University

COLLECTIVE BARGAINING IN CANADA

Edited by
Amarjit S. Sethi

© Nelson Canada,
A Division of International Thomson Limited, 1989

Published in 1989 by
Nelson Canada,
A Division of International Thomson Limited
1120 Birchmount Road
Scarborough, Ontario M1K 5G4

Canadian Cataloguing in Publication Data

Main entry under title:

Collective bargaining in Canada

Bibliography: p.
Includes index.
ISBN 0-17-603417-X

1. Collective bargaining–Canada.   I. Sethi,
Amarjit Singh.

HD6524.C65 1989   331.89′0971   C88-094018-2

Printed and bound in Canada

1   2   3   4   89   93   92   91   90

Contents

List of Figures

Figure 1.2 In vertical strabismus (upgaze), covered by _____
distance in _____
one at time. In alternating cover, the eye is _____
the eye.

Figure 1.3 Continuous _____ fixation with one eye at _____

PART I

INDUSTRIAL RELATIONS THEORY

1

Introduction

AMARJIT S. SETHI

This book will examine key themes, issues and concerns that beset collective bargaining in Canada in the 1980s and beyond. Our aim in adopting a thematic approach arises from the rapid and seemingly inevitable changes taking place in industrial relations. These changes include a redefinition of values in light of the new Charter of Human Rights, increasing state intervention, the continuing effects of recession and unstable economic environments, economic restraints, deregulation, information technology and other technological changes, foreign competition and an internationalized marketplace. The present transition in industrial relations has been the subject of much recent discussion in Canada and particularly in the United States. At a theoretical level, it has been argued that the nature of these changes is so radical as to require a thorough re-examination of existing industrial relations theory (Kochan, McKersie and Cappelli, 1984b). At the practical level, collective bargaining faces tremendous challenges to survive and grow as a human institution.

The industrial relations system includes collective bargaining as a method to determine working conditions, wages, job security, and other considerations of interest to employees and management. According to Arthurs et al. (1981: 30), "collective bargaining is the process whereby an employer and a trade union seek to negotiate a collective agreement." And a collective agreement "is a document recording the terms and conditions of employment and the rights and duties of the employer, trade union and employees in a bargaining unit."

The industrial relations system is a broader concept that, in addition to collective bargaining, includes the rules of law by which unions are formed, strikes are settled, and the contract provisions are enforced (Mills and McCormick, 1985). The industrial relations system is in turn influenced by the wider environment comprising legal, economic and sociopolitical subsystems (Figure 1.1).

Labour–management relations refers to the whole set of exchanges between management and labour—political, economic and legal. "Collective bargaining is a part of that relationship and refers to the making and administration of a contract for terms and conditions of employment by management and labor" (Mills and McCormick, 19–20).

Figure 1.1
Industrial Relations System

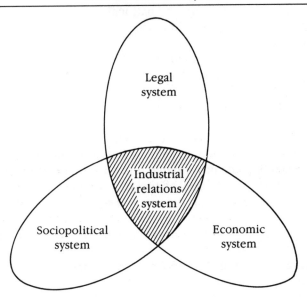

Source: Mills and McCormick, 1985: 9, reprinted by permission.

OVERVIEW OF CHAPTERS

Sethi and Dimmock examine the basic elements of a transactional approach to industrial relations and collective bargaining, and have provided critical appraisal of industrial relations theory. The transactional model of industrial relations focuses on:

1. Structure of industrial relations;
2. Transactional elements, processes, and strategic choices within that structure; and
3. Transactional environmental influences on industrial relations.

The authors examine the theoretical foundations of industrial relations theory and its relationship to collective bargaining.

Rogow examines the specific aspects of legislative/judicial policies and decisions that affect different aspects of collective bargaining. Following a generalized discussion of labour law, Rogow documents recent trends in labour legislation and looks at the future (Chapter 3).

Thwaites examines the structure, role and philosophy of trade unions. Thwaites explores the origins of trade unionism, with emphasis not only on key elements in the past, but also on the future direction of trade unionism in the 1980s and 1990s (Chapter 4).

In Chapter 5, Rogow examines collective bargaining structures and broad environmental influences that affect this structure, including political and legislative interventions and national economic policies.

In Chapters 6 and 7, Sass and Kervin examine styles and techniques of negotiation, behavioural considerations and strategies that parties can use at the bargaining table, and the role of intra-organizational strategies in negotiation effectiveness. The recent research on the science of negotiation is also covered.

In Chapter 8, Downie examines the role of third-party processes in collective bargaining.

Strikes and strike threats are essential parts of the total industrial collective bargaining process. In many segments of the economy, a strike is the most severe form of labour/management dispute. In those parts of the economy providing essential services, strikes have, or potentially can have, a disastrous effect on the community. Ponak and Falkenberg discuss the strategies and techniques for resolving interest disputes in this section, focusing on both traditional and innovative ways of dispute resolution (Chapter 9).

In Chapter 10, Quinet proposes a cost-benefit methodology for costing collective agreements.

In Chapters 11 and 12, Sethi and MacNeil examine the process of grievance management and grievance arbitration in applying justice at work. This section discusses the impact of recent human rights legislation on grievance management and grievance arbitration.

In Chapter 13, Gandz and Beatty outline innovative strategies for changing the union–management relationship.

Swimmer focuses on the special issues facing public-sector collective bargaining (Chapter 14).

Sass and Stobbe examine, in Chapter 15, the importance of health and safety issues in collective bargaining, and proposes strategies for effective resolution of these issues.

In Chapter 16, Lemelin analyzes the key question: can quality of worklife and collective bargaining co-exist?

Crispo draws some lessons from abroad for Canadian collective bargaining (Chapter 17).

Sethi analyzes the impact of information technology on collective bargaining, and the need for unions and management to respond creatively to handle the effects of new technology that is revolutionizing the workplace in the emerging Information Society (Chapter 18).

SUMMARY

The focus of this book is on developing the subdiscipline of the field of collective bargaining. The framework within which the contents of this book are presented is based on three characteristics: (1) the structure of collective bargaining (i.e., the design of the relationships that exist between workers, unions, management and government), (2) the transactional elements and processes, including perceptions of parties within that structure which are in turn influenced by their strategic choices and decision making involved in negotiation, administration of contracts and resolution of disputes that make a given collective bargaining system work and give it life, and (3) the transactional environmental influences on collective bargaining.

BIBLIOGRAPHY

Mills, D. Q. and McCormick, J. (1985), *Industrial Relations in Transition.* New York: John Wiley.

Arthurs, H. W., Carter, D. D. and Glasbeek, H. J. (1981), *Labour Law and Industrial Relations in Canada.* Toronto: Butterworths.

2

Collective Bargaining and Industrial Relations Theory*

Amarjit S. Sethi and Stuart J. Dimmock

The aims of this chapter are (1) to examine the evolution of industrial relations theory, (2) to highlight the significance of values in industrial relations, and (3) to analyze research issues in the development of future conceptual frameworks. Throughout the chapter we will point out the importance of industrial relations theory for collective bargaining. In addition to providing a critique of existing models, we will propose a transactional model of industrial relations (TMIR) that can be used for future research in industrial relations and collective bargaining.

To understand collective bargaining, we need to pay special attention to values and strategic choices made by parties in shaping the process and outcomes of collective bargaining. In addition, internal and external forces from legal, economic, and sociopolitical subsystems exert significant influences on collective bargaining, such as the broader political power of the trade union movement, the health of the economy, changing technology, attitudes of management and unions toward collective bargaining arrangements in the private and public sectors, the Canadian Charter of Rights, and public opinion. The attitude and authority of government towards organized labour and its institutions reflect changes that have occurred within these environmental influences.

Consideration of the way in which internal and external factors influence collective bargaining requires the development of a broader industrial relations perspective. In examining and analyzing collective bargaining in the immediate past, and in exploring likely future trends and developments, it is desirable to identify the mechanisms within the structure of collective bargaining, the factors that shape the parties' decisions in collective bargaining, and the environmental influences that impinge upon the structure and its decision-making processes either

*This chapter draws upon and expands on Dimmock, S. J. and Sethi, A. S. (1986), "The role of ideology and power in systems theory: Some fundamental shortcomings." *Relations industrielles—Industrial Relations* 41 (4): 738–755, and Sethi, A. S. and Dimmock, S. J. (1987), "A Transactional Model of Industrial Relations." *Labour and Society* 12 (2): 177–195.

directly or indirectly. We will therefore examine in detail industrial relations theory and its impact on collective bargaining.

INDUSTRIAL RELATIONS THEORY: AN OVERVIEW

Dunlop's Model

Collective bargaining takes place within the context of an industrial relations framework which in turn is influenced by the external environment. One of the pioneering attempts in outlining and analyzing the basic elements of an industrial relations framework was developed by Dunlop and later followed by other authors (Dunlop, 1958, 1972; Hagburg and Levin, 1978; Craig, 1986). Dunlop's model incorporated some of the Parsonian concepts and broadened industrial relations by placing it not as a subsidiary of an economic system but rather as an identifiable eclectic system of society comprising actors, contexts, ideology which binds the system together, and a body of rules generated to manage the factors in the workplace and work community. The industrial relations system is modified by such constraints as the technological characteristics, budgetary factors, and the locus and distribution of power in the larger society.

Craig's Model

Craig (1986) has modified the systems model by emphasizing the notion of open systems and the specification of input and output variables in the framework itself. The links between industrial relations to a variety of environmental systems (ecological, economic, political, legal, and social) are emphasized within a structural functionalist framework.

To overcome the charge of "indiscriminate multi-causality" in the systems model, modifications were made by Blain and Gennard (1970) by identifying the rules of the industrial relations system which are to be explained theoretically in term of technology, market factors, power, status and ideology (Poole, 1984).

One of the key criticisms of the systems approach is that it does not give adequate attention to conflict. Poole (1984:44) explains:

> ...although it is mistake to assume that there is any underestimation of the significance of conflict and instability in Dunlop's formula, equally there is evidence that priority is given to explaining how conflict is handled in rule making to create and sustain order rather than to the question of conflict generation. And this in turn supports the claims of interalia Hyman, Margerison, and Laffer that the nature of, and the forces shaping, conflict should have a more prominent role in industrial relations research and theorizing than is ever likely from the deployment of social system models.

The British "Oxford School"

The British "Oxford School" has defined industrial relations by focusing on job regulation—a commitment to the voluntary reform of industrial relations and an association with manifold varieties of pluralism. Flanders (1970), the chief architect of this approach, included certain analytical concepts from the Dunlop model (such as rule making, technology, and market constraints) but gave greater importance to power and values and departed from a purely structural functionalist framework.

The Marxian School

The Marxian and neo-Marxian approaches have put forward their own frameworks of industrial relations. According to Hyman (1975), Marxian analyses fall broadly into two categories: (1) the "optimistic" tradition of Marx and Engels, in which a radical potential for unions was recognized, and (2) the "pessimistic" interpretations of Lenin, Michels and Trotsky, where no such role for unions was identified. As Poole (1984, 11) points out, there remain essential differences in Marxist perspectives concerning "the relative causal significance of structural variables (such as economic and technical movements) in shaping union development and of the role of consciousness in determining the economic, political and social action of trade union members themselves."

Kochan's Strategic Choice Model

Kochan et al. (1984a) have provided a "strategic choice" matrix to explain industrial relations by focusing more on behavioural decisions made by actors including government, unions, and employers. The need is to explain industrial relations by integrating systems approach with strategic choice matrix and to pay adequate attention to the role of values, culture, conflict, power, and subjectivity—the type of variables that have been mentioned in systems, British and Marxian frameworks but have not been given the prodominant role that they deserve.

According to the strategic choice model, industrial relations behaviour is seen as an interplay of strategic decisions made by actors (employers, unions, government). These decisions are made at different levels and may affect the entire industrial relations system. Kochan et al. (1984b, 22) explain it as follows:

> Our approach to strategic choice in industrial relations is defined by two conditions....First, strategic decisions can only occur where the parties have discretion over their decisions; that is, where environmental constraints do not severely curtail the parties' choice of alternatives. Examples of where government policies serve as environmental constraints and leave little room

for strategic choices to determine outcomes would be regulations that limit new entrants and/or control prices, limitations on the rights of certain groups to unionize, or limitations on the scope of bargaining. Alternatively, where the parties operate in a perfectly competitive product and labor market there is little room for discretion in the pricing of the product or the compensation of labor. Discretion is in part a by-product of the goals themselves. For example, the parties' decision-making range could be enhanced in cases where goals change over time or are formulated so vaguely as to be open to multiple interpretations. This is particularly so for unions (whose goals reflect those of a changing membership), but it is also the case for management confronting specific business decisions (such as the choice of products and markets). Even where goals are stable and clear, discretion arises because of the creativity of individual decision makers, who may envisage new strategies for reaching similar goals.

Second, within the set of decisions over which the parties have discretion, strategic decisions are those that alter the party's role or its relationship with other actors in the industrial relations system. . . .

THE SEARCH FOR AN ALTERNATE INDUSTRIAL RELATIONS PARADIGM

Most industrial relations behaviour, including collective bargaining, takes place in a social context charged with power and conflict. This environment is highly turbulent, characterized by human rights and women's movements, the growing impact of foreign (especially Japanese) competition, the deregulation of industries, and the rapid spread of information technology, including advances in telecommunications and super-computers. In the face of declining union membership, the turbulent economic environment has led major unions (such as the Autoworkers, Steelworkers and Teamsters) in the United States to accept concession bargaining as a valid mode of industrial relations strategy (Strauss, 1984). Add to this the tremendous development in human resource management practices being pursued by management—not necessarily as a strategy for countering unionism, but reflecting a determination on the part of employers to operate and run organizations on more productive lines in order to gain competitive advantage in a climate of technological change.

Owing to rapid changes entailing major union concessions and tradeoffs in the private sector in the United States, and to a lesser extent in the United Kingdom and Canada, industrial relations as a discipline is being reviewed toward developing a more relevant framework to account for dynamism and change (Cappelli and McKersie, 1983). The previous paradigms stem from the assumptions of a relatively stable environment in the United States, and do not adequately account for change and conflict (Derber et al., 1982; Kochan et al., 1984a and b).

There has been a radical transformation of the Canadian industrial relations environment—equally turbulent, characterized by repeated use of back-to-work legislation, adoption of the statutory incomes policy in 1975 and continuing pressure for economic restraints to contain global budget deficits, the jailing of prominent union leaders for the first time in the post-war era, and limitations on the right to strike. This had led some experts to state that the new era of Canadian industrial relations goes beyond a series of ad hoc coercive measures by the state, and involves the design and implementation of "a new ideology to generalize the state's new coercive role to the working class as a whole" (Panitch and Swartz, 1984). The various pressures and conflicts in industrial relations have led to a search for alternate paradigms.

A review of previous paradigms reveals a trend toward broad macro approaches. The Dunlop model concentrated on environmental variables that included the characteristics of the actors and their interactions, resulting in a "web of rules" governing employment relationships. Kerr et al. (1960) developed a global model converging toward a common set of formal arrangements and rules.

Further refinements made by Craig (1983) to the systems model expanded the framework by using a whole series of input–output components such as: (1) internal inputs as summarized by goals, values and power of actors; (2) the complex of private and public mechanisms for converting the inputs to outputs; (3) the outputs, comprising the economic and non-economic rewards to employees; and (4) a feedback process through which the outputs affect the industrial relations system.

Kochan et al. (1982) have proposed middle-range interdisciplinary models that explain variations in the structure and results of collective bargaining.

As Kochan et al. (1984b) have emphasized, neither systems nor middle-range theories explain change in union membership, managerial values in endorsing a "union free" approach, experiments with quality of worklife programs, managerial initiative in introducing innovative human resource management practices, and changes in the role of government from that of neutral party regulating the process of rule setting to one of direct intervention in industrial-relations bargaining strategies and outcomes. To quote Kochan et al. (1984b, 20):

> We believe that a more realistic model of industrial relations should recognize the role played by management in shaping industrial relations as opposed to the traditional view, which sees management as reactive, responding to union pressure. The new model should also recognize the different levels of decision making that occur within business, labor, and government organizations and their independent effects on industrial relations outcomes. This is why we believe that the concept of strategy, or strategic choice, will

add a more dynamic component to systems theory, and in so doing will help explain changing patterns in U.S. industrial relations.

TRANSACTIONAL MODEL OF INDUSTRIAL RELATIONS (TMIR)

The basic postulate of a strategic/transactional approach is that industrial relations behaviour including collective bargaining is a function of multiple and complex transactions between the structural factors in the environment and value-beliefs held by the actors in that environment; and that value-beliefs and factual factors together, rather than separately, account for formulation of strategic decisions in an industrial relations system. Value-beliefs can also be traced back to the environment, e.g., Dunlop's concept of "locus and distribution of power in the wider society" and his use of term ideology as "cement" binding actors in the industrial relations system. The effect of ideology is to create reciprocal values between actors as to their respective roles and legitimacy within the industrial relations system.

The transactional approach is based on the adaptional definition of "transaction" as given by Lazarus (1978):

> Why emphasize the term transaction rather than interaction? Interaction connotes a partitioning of variance, as in analyses of variance, implying the causal interplay of two sets of variables such as a stable property of the person (trait) and a property of the environment (e.g. a demand, a constraint, or a resource). Transaction, on the other hand, contains two special kinds of meaning. [First], a transaction means that not only does the environment affect the person, as in a S-R sequence, but also that the person affects the environment, both influence each other mutually in the course of an encounter. The interaction goes both ways. The model is no longer a linear, one-way street, but transactional. . . .[Second], in interaction, the causal, antecedent variables still retain their separate identities, whereas a transactional concept describing a relationship offers a new level of discourse in which the separate variables are now lost or changed.

The continual process of transactions within what is defined as the industrial relations system, between it and the environmental influences, and within and between the environment influences, constitute the essential dynamic of labour relations and collective bargaining.

Figure 2.1 depicts the matrix and variables in the proposed framework. The columns of the matrix refer to strategic decisions that are made by three key actors: employers, unions and government. These decisions are arrived at through a strategic value-formation process involving cognitive appraisal, perception, and creativity of individual actors. These strategic decisions are made at both the macro level, affecting broad

Figure 2.1
Transactional Model of Industrial Relations (TMIR)

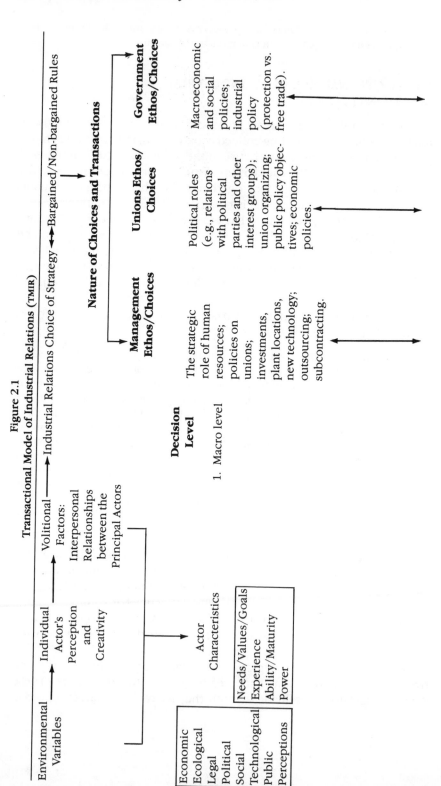

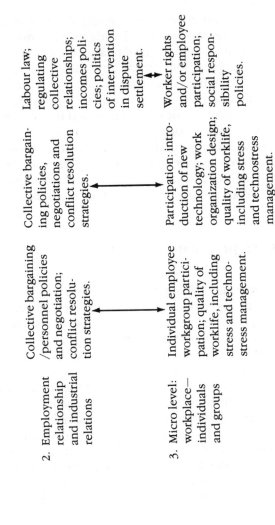

2. Employment relationship and industrial relations	Collective bargaining /personnel policies and negotiation; conflict resolution strategies.	Collective bargaining policies, negotiations and conflict resolution strategies.	Labour law; regulating collective relationships; incomes policies; politics of intervention in dispute settlement.
3. Micro level: workplace— individuals and groups	Individual employee workgroup participation; quality of worklife, including stress and technostress management.	Participation: introduction of new technology; work organization design; quality of worklife, including stress and technostress management.	Worker rights and/or employee participation; social responsibility policies.

Source: Adapted from Kochan, McKersie and Cappelli, 1984, p. 23.

social and economic policies, and at the micro level, affecting work groups and the public policy rules that govern their rights pertaining to work environment. The macro-level decisions relate to each actor's participation in decisions regarding investment, introduction of new technology, controls over outsourcing or subcontracting, and organizational design. Examples of links between micro and macro systems include links between trade unions executives and rank-and-file activists; links between senior/middle/supervisory levels of management; and government with its backbench opinion. The role of public opinion is another example of macro-level/environmental value-belief. There are discrepancies in public opinion polls, where trade unionists are generally opposed to strikes but will take strike action when they are personally affected by issues.

THE CONCEPT OF STRATEGIC CHOICE AS USED IN TMIR

Kochan et al. (1984) recognize that "strategic choice" is a term used with increasing regularity in both economics and organizational research. They cite Chandler's (1962) work on the relationship between strategy and structure and theories of administrative behaviour (Simon, 1957; Braybroke and Lindblom, 1970; Cyert and March, 1963) that have sought to integrate strategic choice into their models. The notion of strategic choice has been introduced into organization theory over the last decade as a counterweight to the contingency approach. Contingency theory rests upon the assumption that organizational characteristics have to be shaped to meet situational circumstances. The extent to which any organization secures a "goodness of fit" between situational and structural characteristics will determine the level of organizational performance (Greenwood et al., 1975). Arguments against this approach have concentrated on decision making within organizations that have chosen a particular structure.

One of the most influential critiques of contingency theory has come from Child (1972) who has argued for the need to understand the essentially political process whereby power holders in organizations decide upon courses of strategic action and shape organizations accordingly. The power holders within an organization are termed the "dominant coalition," normally the senior executives of a company who often have considerable influence over decisions and changes. Kochan et al. (1984) imply that this process has been taking place, at corporate levels, within United States companies.

In our view, strategic choice can be defined as the aim(s) (sometimes broadly conceived) of a dominant coalition in the collective bargaining process in particular or industrial relations in general. These aims are shaped by a coalition's internalized values and perceptions of power, mediated by transactions between it and the environment. Strategy is a process in which a dominant coalition proceeds to plan, shape and/or exploit (either systematically or opportunistically) circumstances or events within the environment in ways that it perceives will bring it nearer to its aim(s). The element of choice lies in determining what circumstances or events to exploit. In deciding what choice to make, a coalition will be immediately influenced by its internalized values and perceptions of power and its transactions within the environment. (See Figure 2.1.)

The TMIR approach integrates the strategic choice framework to a transactional process model involving cognitive perceptions and creativity of the individual actors, with the assumption that decisions are formulated according to values, power, and other characteristics of the various actors as influenced by various subsystems in the environment.

Figure 2.2 presents key transactional elements within an industrial relations system.

In the TMIR model, there are three transactional elements which exercise a critical influence on the overall conduct of the parties and subsequent outcomes. These are: (1) Management Ethos, (2) Union Ethos and (3) Volitional Factors. The attitudes and values held by the parties have significant implications for their collective bargaining behaviour—a point that has been recognized by Dunlop and Flanders. Moreover, as theirs is a transactional relationship, the actions of one can cause multiple complex changes in the attitudes, values, and actions of the other.*

Management and Union Ethos encompass the characteristic spirit of the parties towards:

1. The degree to which they accept collective bargaining as a legitimate means of resolving differences; and
2. Their general conduct of collective bargaining.

Management ethos in collective bargaining has not been consistently in favour of collective bargaining, emphasizing instead the "sovereignty doctrine," that the will of the people as represented by state and federal governments could not be shared with employees' representatives. The fact that management ethos can change over time is illustrated by the rapid development of collective bargaining in the public sector in Canada and United States since the 1970s. By contrast, union ethos in the United

---

*For a detailed account of values see the section entitled, "The Role of Value Theory in TMIR" in this chapter.

Figure 2.2
Transactional Elements within Industrial Relations

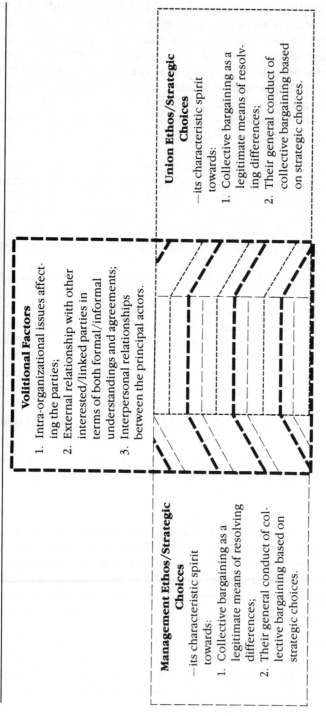

Volitional Factors

1. Intra-organizational issues affecting the parties;
2. External relationship with other interested/linked parties in terms of both formal/informal understandings and agreements;
3. Interpersonal relationships between the principal actors.

Union Ethos/Strategic Choices

—its characteristic spirit towards:

1. Collective bargaining as a legitimate means of resolving differences;
2. Their general conduct of collective bargaining based on strategic choices.

Management Ethos/Strategic Choices

—its characteristic spirit towards:

1. Collective bargaining as a legitimate means of resolving differences;
2. Their general conduct of collective bargaining based on strategic choices.

Note: Shaded area shows transactional overlap between management and union ethos and volitional factors.

States traditionally has tended to favour collective bargaining rather than other forms of behaviour.

The nature of these Volitional Factors defies attempts to capture them within a comprehensive list. They encompass such things as intra-organizational differences within both management and union(s) that are immediately involved in a collective bargaining relationship, e.g., differences of opinion over whether or not to make an offer (management) or to accept one (union). In addition, both management and union sides within a relationship may also be influenced by "political relationships" with other parties who will be affected by the outcome of decisions arrived at either separately or jointly. Thus, management in one organization may be in contact with management in other organizations and may reach informal or formal understandings with them which affect their immediate relations with unions with whom they collectively bargain. Similarly, unions too may have to take account of political factors in the wider trade union organization.

Both unions and management need to take into account technological change, its resultant uncertainties and impact on productivity and quality of worklife.

The personal relationships between the bargainers cannot be dismissed. Structural models can act to de-personalize collective bargaining. The simple fact that the process of bargaining rests on such concepts as shared trust, mutual respect and integrity between the bargainers themselves can easily be overlooked in examinations of bargaining procedures. Thus within the Volitional Factors the principal actors share a transactional relationship with each other in an interpersonal sense within the collective bargaining procedures.

Figure 2.3 shows the relationship of transactional variables to collective bargaining.

COLLECTIVE BARGAINING AND THE ROLE OF ENVIRONMENTAL INFLUENCES IN TMIR

Collective bargaining in both the public and private sectors in Canada are subject to a wide range of transactional influences whose sources are outside the relatively narrow confines of the structural and procedural forms of collective bargaining. Some of these influences are shared (although they may have different impacts and outcomes); others are separately experienced.

Figure 2.4 identifies some of the key influences that affect the process and behaviour of collective bargaining.

It is difficult to arrange the environmental influences on collective bargaining in terms of their hierarchical order or importance. However, it can be observed that a number of these influences (such as the state of the

Figure 2.3
Relationship of Transactional Variables to Collective Bargaining

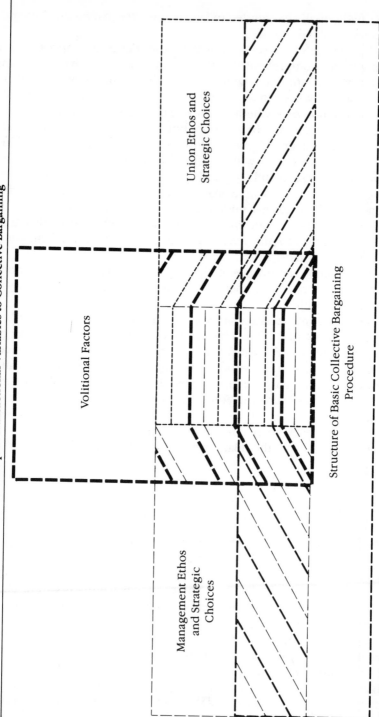

Note: Shaded areas show transactional overlap between the three transactional elements and the structure of basic collective bargaining procedures.

Figure 2.4
Transactional Environmental Influences on Collective Bargaining

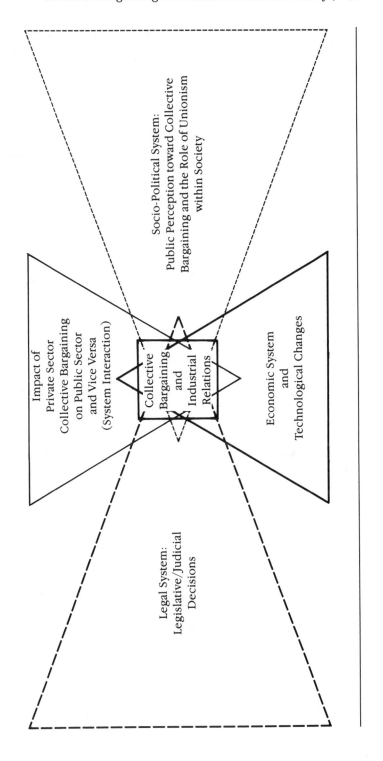

Canadian economy, changes in public opinion, and technological changes) form an essential background to the internal transactional elements—the ethos and strategic choices made by management and unions. Moreover, the dynamics generated in industrial relations out of behaviour are linked to transactional relationships formed between the environmental influences.

The following are the key influences affecting collective bargaining:

1. **Influence of public and private sector collective bargaining on each other (system interaction).** As depicted in Figures 2.1 and 2.2, a transactional model of industrial relations (TMIR) can be used to describe the structures and basic procedures available to management and unions in both private and public sectors. Within this general model are found three key variables: Management Ethos, Union Ethos and Volitional Factors. In the past the structure and procedures within the private sector formed the foundations of the model for public sector collective bargaining. The present transition in private sector labour relations seems in part to have been a consequence of a change in management ethos. The dramatic shift away from its previous commitment towards a relationship with unions, centred on distributive collective bargaining, towards union avoidance and concession bargaining may have significant implications for the public sector.

2. **Legislative/judicial policies and decisions (legal system).** Within this category are contained those influences whose immediate source is within the executive and legislative system. As such they encompass broad aspects of legislation as they affect both the conduct of management and labour within collective bargaining, the way parties settle their disputes, decisions emanating from legal bodies such as the National Labour Relations Board, recent court cases interpretating Charter of Rights provisions on equality and on fundamental freedoms, and (in the case of the public sector) specifications of designated employees who cannot go on strike in the event of a strike.

3. **Public perceptions and attitudes towards collective bargaining and the role of trade unions within society (sociopolitical system).** While the decline in union numbers in the private sector is more sharply marked in the United States than Canada, there seems little doubt that public attitudes towards trade unions have been subject to change over the past decade. Public attitude has become more hostile, and this is particularly the case in regard to public sector trade unionism where the major sanctions employed by trade unions are more immediately and acutely felt by the populace at large.

4. **The Canadian economy and international economic policies (economic system).** The changes within the economy and national economic policies are major factors in shaping collective bargaining in

both public and private sectors. While the Canadian economy is still dominated by the United States, the latter's position of absolute strength has declined as many of Canada's major industries face competition from those of Japan and the developing countries of the Far East. As a result, public sector managements have been pressured to identify and implement new methods to reduce costs. Given the labour-intensive nature of many public services, such pressure will influence the ethos of both management and unions, with consequent effects upon collective bargaining decisions. Incomes policies in general exert significant impact on the strategies employed by parties in the process of collective bargaining.

5. **The impacts of information technology on the working environment.** The strategic choices of unions and management will be influenced by changes in telecommunications, robotics and computerization. Emerging issues will include productivity, monotony, work redesign, job security, technostress, and quality of worklife in general.

THE USE OF TMIR IN COLLECTIVE BARGAINING

Collective bargaining is a continuing process of interactions ranging from free strategic choice to complete environmental determinism. This view allows both proactive as well as reactive behaviours on the part of actors (workers' unions, management, and government) in the collective bargaining process. The issue is not that of strategic choice versus environmental determinism but rather understanding a continuum that ranges from determinism to voluntarism. As explained by Hrebiniak and Joyce (1985, 337), "choice and determinism are not at opposite ends of a single continuum of effect but in reality represent two independent variables, and...the interaction or independence of the two must be studied to explain...behavior." Collective bargaining is viewed as a dynamic process, revealing several options to parties, that may involve a number of possibilities in a given situation (Hrebiniak and Joyce, 1985).

The most obvious implication of this approach is that the interdependence and interactions between strategic choice and environmental determinism define collective bargaining behaviour. In order to explain change and conflict within collective bargaining, we need both variables: strategic choice and environmental determinism. Collective bargaining thus needs to focus on interactions and interdependence between the two in varying degrees, thus signifying the dynamic nature of bargaining transactions (Miles and Snow, 1978). Our theoretical premise is to emphasize that models relying on the conceptual construction of competing explanations of cause and effect may not be sufficient to capture the complexity and spirit of collective bargaining. The transactional model, it is hoped, emphasizes multiple and often competing assumptions, foci, and explanations of cause and effect.

IDEOLOGY AND ITS TREATMENT IN SYSTEMS THEORY

In conceiving systems theory, Dunlop's treatment of ideology and power was radically different from that of early and contemporary theorists. Drawing on the work of Talcott Parsons, Dunlop adopted the structural functionalist view of ideology, "that, at root, societies are characterized by the possession of an integrated set of norms and values—or 'culture'—common to all except a possible minority of 'deviants'." (Hyman and Brough, 1975, 150.) Thus Dunlop placed ideology within the industrial relations system as "a set of ideas and beliefs commonly held" whose primary function was to bind the system together. As ideology was a factor of the different elements within an industrial relations system in this formula, it could be applied across different cultures. It therefore fitted North America's legally prescribed form of industrial relations and Britain's voluntarist system.

Dunlop's treatment of ideology also suffered from his tendency to give confusing definitions of its nature. Thus ideology was conceived as the "philosophy, values and beliefs of the actors in the industrial relations system" and "the integrative norms of the system itself" (Goodman et al., 1977, 18). This formulation is problematic, not least because the integrative norms of the system are in part a product of the ideologies of the actors. In Parsons's (1951) formulation of social systems, compatibility and congruence between "system" and "actor" ideologies is taken as given. Dunlop (1958, 16) too seemed to accept this: "An industrial relations system requires that these ideologies be sufficiently compatible and consistent so as to permit a common set of ideas which recognize an acceptable role for each actor." However, as he also discussed how the actors tend to adopt intellectuals and special agencies to create fairly explicit sets of ideologies, Dunlop seems to accept a degree of ideological dissonance. If total ideological harmony were assumed, intellectuals would not be needed for the functions that Dunlop ascribed to them.

Kochan's (1985) concern about the unpredicted developments in the United States mirror Poole's (1984) comment that any treatment of ideology must explicitly allow for its role both to reflect and to predict changes which can be traced explicitly to the patterning of outlook and perception amongst actors (e.g., government) in the larger society as well as the workplace. Continuation of relative stability in the United States, until recently, added credence to the idea of a reciprocal understanding between the actors over their respective roles within the industrial relations system. However, the structural functionalist conception of ideology does not allow for the sharp reversal in the United States government's role as a "neutral" in regulating the process of bargaining since the inauguration of the first Reagan administration. Nor does it allow for management activities aimed at reducing the influence of trade unions and collective bargaining. These changes appear to challenge assumptions of ideological reciprocity. Moreover, they could not have been predicted by a definition of ideology that conceived it as a unifying factor within industrial relations. By comparison, the "voluntarist ideology" of the United Kingdom can be said to have been consistently undermined as British governments have become increasingly concerned since the 1960s to legislate in the area of industrial relations. In Britain, Prime Minister Thatcher's Conservative government's incremental legislative policy aims to redress perceived inequalities in power between unions and management (in favour of the latter) and has been vociferously supported by organizations representing senior management and chief executives. Moreover, a process of de-centralization in pay bargaining, together with forms of concession bargaining, is also being pursued by British- and Japanese-backed indigenous management.

The recent trends in Canada include a growing militancy on the part of public sector employees to protest unjust laws, as perceived by them. This was illustrated by a province-wide strike of Newfoundland public sector employees in 1986, the growing emergence of women trade union leaders with Shirley Carr as the head of the Canadian Labour Congress, the drive for independence from American trade unionism, with UAW taking the lead and a concerted proposal by the labour movement to evolve an alternative system to current Canadian capitalism based on free trade that takes into account internal and external conflicts in collective bargaining.

Emphasis on stability via ideology in original systems theory and its subsequent adaptations (e.g., that an actor's choice of goals must be "consonant with established value orientations" (Craig, 1983) argues that management's present strategy is non-legitimate, as the values which underlie the strategy, as suggested by Kochan et al. (1984), appear to be disintegrative rather than integrative to the industrial relations system—a theoretical absurdity within structural functionalism (unless management are to be categorized as a deviant minority!).

As Wood (1978) has observed, ideology is not an element within the social system but a crucial mechanism that assists in the explanation of the creation, stability, development and instability of different patterns of industrial relations. Rejection of Parsons's formulation of ideology with its narrow function, in favour of a broader concept of values and beliefs inhabiting and interacting in both the industrial relations systems and the wider society, enable examination of a much wider collection of subjectively felt forces which affect the pattern of both management and trade union activity.

THE POWER INGREDIENT

Systems theory's treatment of power is another major factor in its inability to interpret recent events, and this too is a function of its structural functionalist base. Dunlop (1958) saw power as an ingredient of the wider social system and not in terms of an endogenous relationship between unions and management themselves (Poole, 1984). Thus, in borrowing Talcott Parsons's concept of social system order, Dunlop introduced a different conception of power into the study of industrial relations. The structural functionalism of Parsons viewed power as the property of the social system (Giddens, 1968), i.e.: "the generalised capacity to get things done in the interests of system goals" (Parsons, 1961, 187). Thus in Dunlop's (1958, 11–13) system, power in the wider society "to a degree... reflected in the industrial relations system, but it was not a direct determinant of the interaction between the actors." It was rather "a context which helps to structure the industrial relations system itself." Thus, by treating power as the property of the system or one party in it, rather than as shared (with varying degrees of equality) between different parties within a system, Dunlop avoided the issue of power within union–management relations.

Subsequent developments in systems theory encounter the same difficulties in the treatment of power. In this regard, Craig's work (1983) provides a useful illustration; for in addition to the inclusion of "the ecological context" in the environmental subsystem and a "feedback loop" in an attempt to create a dynamic, he has incorporated "goals, values and power" inside the industrial relations system. In Craig's structural functionalist scheme, power is defined as the "ability of an actor to achieve goals despite the resistance of others." Craig claims that his framework assumes neither harmony nor conflict. Nevertheless, basic harmony appears to be present. This can be seen in his reference to Barbash (1980, 87) that collective bargaining "is a co-operative form of conflict in which the parties...or for that matter the partners . . . seek to exchange what they want from each other. Unlike competitors who seek to oust one another, bargainers seek a mutually agreeable exchange." This is, of course, a restatement of Dunlop's notion of a shared ideology which acts to perpetuate the system and which Kochan et al. (1984) identify as a major difficulty for existing systems theory in explaining recent developments in industrial relations.

Moreover, Craig's definition of "goals" and "values" is similar to Dunlop's view of ideology as both the philosophy, values, and beliefs of the actors and as the integrative norms of the industrial relations system.

Thus "goals" are defined (Craig, 1983, 4–5) as "the objectives or needs which an individual or group seeks to achieve or satisfy" and "values" as "the norms or standards which an actor observes in establishing the relative importance of objectives and the means of achieving them." But for Craig, values also have an integrative function, as they dictate that the satisfaction of goals must be "consonant with established value orientations."

As "goals" and "values" are juxtaposed with "power" on the same analytical plane, Craig appears to have conflated "power" with Dunlop's notion of ideology. The effect of Craig's fusion of power and ideology within the industrial relations system (which in Dunlop's framework were viewed respectively as exogenous and endogenous elements) maintains the general sense of structural functionalism while partially departing from its Parsonian form. Hence power—"the generalized capacity to get things done in the interest of systems goals" (Parsons, 1961, 18)—is now envisaged as a property of the industrial relations system itself. This also acts to reinforce the notion of stability.

Craig's explanation of the exercise of power is therefore constrained to actions taken within the system which are perceived to be legitimate, i.e., not directed against the system itself. In this context, strikes and lockouts—which are characterized as the most extreme form of institutional conflict—are not seen as a threat to the continuation of the industrial relations system, because they are generally regarded as a temporary cessation in union–management relations rather than a permanent schism.

By contrast, some of the recent actions of management that Kochan et al. (1985) have identified do seem to be based on decisions to remove their business organizations away from the influence of organized labour, by creating conditions that overcome the requirement to participate in the rule-making process which lies at the centre of systems theory. The effect of management's strategy (particularly relocation to low union environments and the attrition and closure of unionized operations) is to take sanctions against the industrial relations system itself. And in a strictly theoretical sense, the use of power by actors within a system against the continuation of that system cannot be incorporated into a structural functionalist model. It is not surprising, therefore, that Kochan et al. (1984b) find that systems theory cannot interpret recent events.

As previously stated, Dunlop's conception of ideology and power was fundamentally different from that which had been expressed by earlier and contemporary labour theorists. Given that these did not ignore strategy as an important theoretical concept (as Kochan et al. [1984] recognize), it is important briefly to re-state traditional views of the nature of power both within and without the "industrial relations system." We believe this to be necessary for understanding collective bargaining because their analysis is crucial in shaping a clearer under-standing of the concept of strategic choice. It also serves to re-emphasize the inadequacy of systems theory as a basis for interpreting the changes identified by Kochan and his colleagues.

Power and Ideology in Traditional and Non-Systems Theory: The Webbs

In their interpretation of the significance of trade unionism in nineteenth-century England, the Webbs (1902) clearly saw power as an intercursive element in union–employer relations. This is demonstrated in their definitional example of collective bargaining—one of whose unique functions was to achieve more equitable arrangements for the sellers of labour when confronting the power of the employer. Thus, collective action by workers at the time of hiring reduced the power of the buyer of labour (Hyman, 1971).

Marxian Analysis

Both the "optimistic" and "pessimistic" traditions within Marxism saw union–employer relations in terms of power as they reflect the nature of capitalist society (Poole, 1984). For the "optimistic tradition," trade unions would act as the instruments for training the working class in the methods of struggle as a preliminary to the wider political conflict. The subsequent inability of trade unions as perceived by Lenin (1961) to be more than "centres of resistance against the encroachment of capitalism" led the "pessimistic tradition" to the belief that transcension of narrow trade union consciousness could come about only through the interven-tion of the intelligensia. However, for both traditions the true nature of capitalism and the role it ordained for labour was (in the first instance) most likely to be experienced by the working class in their struggles against the power of the capitalist employer.

Early American Writers

Early writers on the labour movement in the United States also perceived a similar relationship between workers and employers (albeit many of them drew different conclusions than the Marxists). Thus Adams (1891), Commons (1919), and Hoxie (1917) all depicted power as a critical factor in the struggle for labour to assert influence over employers. These views were echoed by Chamberlain (1951) and Selig Perlman (1949) less than a decade before Dunlop published his systems theory.

Alan Flanders

In the United Kingdom in the 1960s, Alan Flanders was one of the principal theorists in a period largely dominated by descriptive and evaluative researchers. Cappelli (1985) has been dismissive of Flanders's inductive approach to theory development in the workings of productivity agreements. However, the significance of Flanders's later work has been described by Poole (1984, 60) as "a crucial junction point... between the Webbsian tradition of inductive generalization, the strategic and more deductive conceptual scheme of Durkheim and Dunlop, and the American contributions to labour theory of Chamberlain, Derber and Ross." Flanders never formulated a precise framework, but one may be readily identified from his work. Again, as Poole (1984, 60) has observed, it constituted "a multi-causal theory in which the principal explanatory dimensions could include organizational or institutional variables...the internal political processes within trade unions and the wider labour movement, a series of 'volitional' factors which may be crucial in shaping actual bargaining encounters, the wider economic environment...technology and production...and the accepted norms and cultural values which obtain in a given society at specific points in time."

While Flanders (1975) accepted a number of Dunlop's contentions—that industrial relations was concerned with a system of rules and was influenced by technological and economic factors—he avoided the teleological aspects of structural functualism. Power operated not only in the actual bargaining relationship, but also within trade unions and management, the wider labour movement, and in the socio-cultural environment. Thus, in his critique of the Webbs' definition of collective bargaining (the predominant form of union–management interaction in North America and the United Kingdom by the 1960s), Flanders (1968) asserted that collective bargaining is primarily a *political* institution because it is a rule-making process and involves a power relationship between organizations.

Flanders also treated ideology differently from systems theory. In place of ideology with its binding properties, Flanders (1969) used his framework with some effect to explain the *instability* in British industrial relations as a combination of economic factors influencing the balance of *power* within trade unions and employers' organizations with consequent changes in the *normative* order. And his prescription for the means to create a new form of stability contained a clear recognition of the relationship between ideology, power, and strategy.

AN OVERVIEW OF NON-SYSTEMS THEORIES

In their separate ways, the "optimistic" Marx, the Webbs, and Commons (to a lesser degree) conceived trade unions as instrumental in the evolution of economic and political values within society. The Webbs (1897) discussed the role of values and beliefs in their vision of a collectivist society and identified arguments of union as reflecting the ethical and moral principles that were developing in the wider culture. The relationship between the role of unions in establishing workers' rights in the workplace and their subsequent extension into society as a whole were examined by several theorists, notably Commons (1918) and Chamberlain (1951). And these ideas were reflected in Flanders's (1969) view of the moral force of trade unions within the wider society. Albeit from a different standpoint, Marxist writers (Hyman, 1975; Hyman and Brough, 1975; Allen, 1971) have emphasized the relationship between values and beliefs in the workplace and their location in the social and political forces within capitalist societies. It is clear, therefore, that non-systems theorists have taken a much broader view of ideology—locating values and beliefs both within and without the "collective bargaining system" and depicting a constant interplay between the system theory's conception of the "philosophy and beliefs of the actors" with wider social values.

SYSTEMS VS. NON-SYSTEMS THEORIES

Given this fundamental difference in perception of ideology and power in systems and non-systems theory, how can Dunlop's original treatment be explained? His seminal contribution was produced at a time when empiricism was the dominant intellectual force and his specific objective was to shift the industrial relations perspective away from the study of collective bargaining as it first developed in Britain to the full spectrum of contemporary industrial relations (Poole, 1984). This objective reflected the divergence in academic circles in North America immediately after World War II between the political and economic interpretations of union policy. In one sense, Dunlop's decision to use Parsons's structural functionalism as the basis of his theory was a rejoinder to Ross's (1948) earlier criticism of Dunlop's economic view of wage determination. However, it would be merely tautological to ascribe systems theory treatment of ideology and power to structural functionalism. A more fruitful explanation seems to lie in the historiography of industrial relations theory. Early writers interpreted events from the perspective of their particular time in history, as witnesses to the excesses of economic and industrial exploitation experienced by workers in the period of "entrepreneurial capitalism." From different theoretical standpoints they came to broadly similar conclusions about the nature of ideology and the existence of power within union–employer relations.

By comparison, Dunlop viewed events from the standpoint of the United States in the mid-twentieth century. The bitter and often violent confrontations between unions and employers which had been a persistent feature of industrial relations in the United States during the earlier part of this century had faded. Relative stability had been achieved, largely by government intervention in the form of a legal framework designed to reduce the excesses—initially of employers and then subsequently of unions. A sense of stability was also present in both economic and political spheres, reflecting the national sense of security based on the United States' economic, industrial and technological ascendency. Thus, when Dunlop's systems theory is seen in its historical context, his assertion that "exterior power relations or exterior political systems are given" is understandable. The task which Dunlop (1985, 21) set was "to depict the industrial relations arrangements established by each political system and the characters of the dynamic interaction between external political power and labour–management–government relations," and his choice of structural functionalism as the basis of his theory was largely conditioned by the contemporary circumstances of United States industrial relations. Unfortunately, in breaking away from the traditional conceptions of ideology and power, systems theory has been far less able to explain the dynamic character of collective bargaining and industrial relations as a whole. The incorporation of strategic choice into systems theory requires careful scrutiny, lest industrial relations theory continue to suffer from ill-considered eclecticism.

THE POLITICS OF COLLECTIVE BARGAINING

Many writers have pointed to the lack of agreement within management over objectives and the process of internal negotiations to establish priorities within as well as outside collective bargaining (Pfeffer, 1981; Pettigrew, 1975; Stephenson, 1985). According to this political perspective, management within organizations can be seen as a process of negotiated order rather than a single group committed to a unified goal. In this sense Flanders's (1968) analysis of collective bargaining as a political process, vitiated by a range of internal and external factors, provides a more accurate conceptual tool than systems theory. Too great a commitment to the political perspective can lead to the view that even the corporate board is merely another interest group pursuing its own goals to the best of its ability (Lee and Lawrence, 1985). Child (1972) guards against this fragmentation within organizational decision making by arguing that the purpose of using such a concept as that of the "dominant coalition" is mainly to distinguish those who normally have the power to take initiative on such matters as the design of organizational structure from others who must respond to decisions. The concept relates to what Mann (1970) labelled "pragmatic acceptance" by lower-level participants.

The concept of a "dominant coalition" opens up systems theory to a view of distribution of power and the process of strategic decision making. It provides a stark contrast to the sociologically determined notion that behaviour within an industrial relations system can be understood in relation to the functional imperatives of "system needs," which in some way transcend the objectives of the principal actors. In studying the history of American industrial enterprise, Chandler (1962) wrote that strategy could be defined as the determination of the basic long-term goals and objectives of an enterprise, the adoption of courses of action, and the allocation of resources necessary for carrying out these goals. Decisions to expand the volume of these activities, to set up distant plants and offices, to move into new economic functions, or become diversified along many lines of business, involve the definition of new basic goals. The environmental stress referred to by Khandwalla (1970) which is experienced by decision takers when facing a hostile or indifferent environment can be depicted as a trigger to the strategic choices taken by dominant coalitions at corporate levels across North American industry. Shifting attention towards the role of choice leads us to account for industrial relations behaviour through reference to its sources rather than to its supposed consequences. This underlines the validity of the long-expressed criticism of systems-based industrial relations theory, that it tends to dwell on conflict resolution rather than the forces that generate conflict (Bain and Clegg, 1974; Hyman, 1975; Margerison, 1969; Laffer, 1968). Thus, the introduction of strategic choice seems likely to call for a fundamental re-appraisal of existing attitudes of North American scholars towards systems theory.

THE ROLE OF VALUE THEORY IN TMIR

Industrial relations "is the study of values arising in the minds, intuitions and emotions of individuals" (Brown, 1952, 6). As Barbash (1980, 9) points out, "the business of industrial relations is more than technique and know-how. It is also the values which technique and know-how are directed to. Equity, due process, fairness, rights, reasonableness, participation, incentive, alienation, privacy, democracy, self-determination, good faith, mutual survival, incrementalism, pragmatism, job satisfaction, order—these are some of the values which our field has embedded into the practice of industrial relations."

Given such a significance of values, it is imperative that the role of values should be classified in both systems and non-systems industrial relations theory. The word "value" is defined as a belief-orientation signifying the interest and desirability of an event, decision or a phenomenon that we label as industrial relations. Values are relevant only when interests emerge, because without an interest in an object, event, or phenomenon a value element does not arise. Values are basically to be understood as conceptual beliefs about the "oughtness" of a situation (Kluckhohn, 1967; Perry, 1967; Rescher, 1969).

The word "desirability," which gives a significant meaning to the definition, owes its origin to Kluckhohn, who states that values have cognitive and affective dimensions. "Values are never immediately altered by a mere logical demonstration of their invalidity" (Kluckhohn, 1967, 388).

The words "belief-orientation" permit the establishment of a mechanism through which industrial relations values can be classified and studied. The combination of the words "value-beliefs" provides the integration of reason and feeling. "Industrial relations, as a field of study...needs to liberate itself from obsessive reliance on mechanistic counting and theorizing, and return to the values of the founding fathers of industrial relations who tried to get at...the *spirit* of industrial relations" (Barbash, 1980, 10).

According to the TMIR, neither the Parsonian (consensus) nor Marxian and neo-Marxian (conflict) approaches are adequate to capture the role of values in industrial relations. The main reason is that values converge in a modern capitalistic society. It should be noted, as was emphasized by Dahrendorf (1959), that "conflict" and "consensus" approaches are mutually complementary rather than alternative aspects of the structure and process of an industrial relations system.

Dahrendorf's analysis of conflict is particularly useful in explaining assumptions about change in industrial relations. We concur with Dahrendorf's view that societies create out of their structure the conditions of social autogonisms, and that therefore, by implication, industrial relations is not a competitive system, but a relatively integrated system of conflicting structural forces (Dahrendorf, 1959). Both integrative and disruptive factors need to be explained in an industrial relations framework.

TRANSACTIONAL VALUE THEORY

The following three key propositions are proposed in ascertaining the role of values in industrial relations theory. First, values are not Parsonian dichotomies, but rather continuous processes. They are not to be understood as static entities, but as changing characterizations of a continuous industrial relations system, which historically as well as currently subscribes to both consensus and conflict. The "image of industrial relations" is that of a "transactional" process unlike that of Parsons, who established that a system of co-operation does prevail, but like that of Dahrendorf, who concluded that conflict is ever present and will be part of any future industrial relations behaviour.

Second, strategic choices in industrial relations are not grounded in the "either/or" approach, but in the ultimate analysis are transactional. They are so because the principal rate of change in technology, resource utilization, and other industrial relations events have become more and more dependent on the inter-connectedness of various parts of industrial relations and its contextual environment.

Third, the realistic value-choices exist among various actors in industrial relations (government, management, unions) that constitute a climate or an environment. Collective bargaining, for example, may be developed in one model embedded in a free play of various forces, but another model may be completely subjected to the threats of incomes policy, wage restraints and compulsory arbitration. Choice is then between varying types of climate (and techniques) that may embrace and cut across several seemingly opposing ideologies (Sethi, 1986).

The hypotheses of a transactional value theory, which may become an integral part of an industrial relations theory, may be stated as follows (Sethi, 1986):

1. The use of new climatic techniques in a given industrial relations environment depends to a great extent upon the emphasis one puts on their rationality and relevance.
2. In this equation of climate–output interaction, values play a significant role in the actual implementation of available choices for needed reform.
3. The nature of strategic choices rests upon the values that management, unions, and government hold about human beings and their institutions. This is the central thesis of the hypothesis: that the values of bargainers influence the utilization of various old and new social techniques available in a given climate.

The question is not to judge whether "systems theory" is better than "non-systems" theories—the question is that of identifying critical variables in the interactional process of industrial relations action and behaviour. "Behavior is taken transactionally (or bisocially) as of organism-in-environment, not as of the organism construed as separate from its environment, and it refers to all of the adjustive processes of organism-in-environment" (Handy, 1969, 190).

The transactional value theory recognizes four basic difficulties in explaining industrial relations output:

1. Gap between a value held, and choice made;

2. Gap between a choice, and execution of that choice;
3. Human preferences over time and situations that are not always consistent;
4. Many individuals and decision makers do not maximize, but rather achieve new levels of "satisficing" (Simon, 1958), that is, achieving what is considered desirable at the time in a limited rather than optimal sense.

These four difficulties are basic to any theory that attempts to explain industrial relations behaviour from a value perspective. The transactional value theory may perhaps provide a synthesis of systems and non-systems theories for explaining industrial relations behavioural outcomes. Transactionalism, to some extent, attempts to overcome the above-stated difficulties by emphasizing valuations that a person makes in the context of a given climate or environment, where the criteria of strategic choice are regulated by the interactional process of facts and values.

The transactional theory strikes a balance between Parsonian and Marxian perspectives. Changes in industrial relations behaviour, theoretically speaking, cannot merely be explained by resorting to "factual" changes in the industrial relations system brought forth by some fatalistic Marxian law of historical inevitability. Likewise, it cannot be explained by resorting to idealistic transcendental Parsonian values held by the individual. An alternate view is that industrial relations change and the associated confict may be construed as interactional, combining two sets of variables in a given situation: transcendental values as well as factual (structural) variables—the industrial relations behaviour results from varying transactions among these sets of variables. Values change through a process of interactional accommodation (rather than linear accommodation) between a system of existing values and the technological and social changes that impinge upon this system. The incorporation of value theory into industrial relations theory is a major task of contemporary social and political criticism.

The values of the emerging industrial relations systems do not seem to fit in either the "systems" (conservative) or "Marxian" (radical) schools of thought because the values of the modern information society are in a constant flow, ever changing its base and goals, and yet firmly retaining the idealism of the values of the past. The issues of creativity, diversity, difference, conflict, and integration in industrial relations have assumed a complex, deeper, and democratic posture.

CONVERGENCE OF VALUE THEORIES

The two recognized models of value theory, namely the consensus approach led by Parsons and the conflict approach led by Marx, treat values and their impact on industrial relations from relatively different assumptions about the nature of human beings. From a Parsonian perspective, industrial relations is viewed as a social system where members share common dominant values, and where conflict is viewed as "dysfunctional"; conflict theorists such as Coser and Dahrendorf look upon society as the stage for struggles over power and privileges (Coser, 1956; Dahrendorf, 1959). Parsons emphasized integration and system maintenance; for conflict theorists every society displays dissension and is constantly subject to change. The two approaches in turn may be viewed from a third angle: that is, a transactional approach for studying industrial relations. The TMIR approach emphasizes both the role of consensus and conflict, and is basically a convergent approach, which states that there is a convergence of Marxist (or conflict) and capitalistic (or consensus) value theories in explaining industrial relations behaviour. Neither theory is sufficient to explain the *real* situation, but we propose that a transactional theory based on the convergence of "systems" and "non-systems" theories is a sound approach for the development of future industrial relations theory. Barbash (1984, 134–136) emphasizes the need for further theoretical development along transactional lines when he states:

1. The wage relationship under collective bargaining is species of exchange in which human effort is exchanged for a wage.
2. The labor transaction under collective bargaining involves both congruence and incongruence—congruence because one side wants something from the other, incongruence because the sides invariably differ on the relative values which should prevail.
3. In order to generalize validly as to whether the exchange relationship in the case of the labor transaction is generating *undue* conflict the following intermediate theories are required:
   a) A theory of the universe of conflict which takes into account not only strikes but turnover, absenteeism, sabotage, indiscipline or latent tendencies with these results.
   b) A theory of latent and overt conflict.
   c) A theory of conflict pathology; that is, when does conflict become dysfunctional?

   No industrial relations problem of any importance turns on capitalism versus socialism. . . .Motivation, alienations, low productivity, poor supervision, the deteriorating work ethic, absenteeism—all of what we think of as dysfunctions of industrial relations, and indeed, the adversary principle as such—are problems of *all* modern industrial societies. This must be because the dysfunctions are a consequence of the industrializing process as such and not alone of the juridical system under which it operates.

RESEARCH ISSUES IN DEVELOPING FUTURE INDUSTRIAL RELATIONS FRAMEWORKS: IMPLICATIONS FOR COLLECTIVE BARGAINING

The first and perhaps most fundamental issue is whether systems theory has any continuing relevance as an explanatory vehicle. In so far that it rests on structural functionalist assumptions it is, as we have tried to show, largely out of theoretical alignment with the necessary treatment of ideology and power in terms of strategic choice. Notions of systems maintenance appear inappropriate when applied to industrial relations in the face of managerial strategies (receiving tacit, or open support from government) of the type depicted by Chandler. For the logic underlying the strategic choices among dominant coalitions within management is one that distances their operations from union influence. If the structural functionalist base is dispensed with, systems theory seems little more than a representation of social phenomena in the form of a system suggested by Schienstock (1981).

The second re-appraisal is in regard to the tendency of popular theories to perceive management as playing a reactive role in collective bargaining and industrial relations. The failure to examine management attitudes and values in collective bargaining is not a recent phenomenon in the development of industrial relations theory. Indeed, it could be said to have commenced with the Webbs, whose *History of Trade Unionism* (1902) included only one oblique reference to employers' attitudes towards combination. However, the reference is particularly intriguing as it suggests that in certain trades in Britain in the 1830s employers saw the need to restrict competition over labour as a commodity. This was a key consideration for Commons (1910), who identified that the motivation for employers in entering into collective bargaining was the degree to which wages and labour costs were taken out of competition. Systems theory fails to recognize, in any real sense, that industrial relations is just one area of concern for management. In certain periods, such as that which pertained in Britain in the 1960s and 1970s, a combination of situations may dictate that for many managements the maintenance of industrial harmony is a predominant concern—to the degree that management's corporate strategy can be described as being "driven" by industrial relations (Brewster and Connock, 1985). The evolving pressures from Japan and Far Eastern economies on the West, but particularly on the United States, Canada, and Britain, gradually re-introduced wage and labour costs to corporate managements' agendas. The perspective offered by the pessimistic tradition of Marxism (Trotsky, 1977) has much to offer in terms of an interpretation of events in industrial relations since the 1930s, particularly the notion of incorporation of trade unions into capitalism.

The third re-appraisal requires a re-consideration of the contribution made by early writers on collective bargaining and industrial relations. As we have tried to show, their treatment of power and ideology demonstrates that strategic choice is not a new idea (to be incorporated into systems theory). The works of the Webbs, Commons, and Hoxie demonstrate that the concept of dominant coalitions and strategic choice was a recognized feature within industrial relations developments. Over-concentration on the role of management and strategic choice should not lead us to neglect that unions too have options to take strategies. In short, we want to warn against an over-compensating swing of the pendulum. The concentration on trade union activities within systems theory is in part a result of Dunlop's decision to elevate the industrial relations system to the same analytical plane as the economic and political systems (Poole, 1984). (This was not, of course, in accord with Talcott Parsons's construct of social systems theory.) Realization that management activities may in reality provide the framework to reactive behaviour of trade unions, and not vice-versa, should not obscure the fact that in a system where management and unions can be represented in adversarial roles, both are able to make strategic choices. Indeed, what many classical writers and non-systems theorists have recognized is that parties within the system have made strategic choices based on their assessment of the circumstances as they perceived them. In this manner, dominant coalitions within trade unions in nineteenth-century Britain exercised sufficient influences to ensure the establishment of a legal status for themselves based on immunities from the common law (Webb and Webb, 1902) rather than the form of comprehensive labour legislation introduced over sixty years later in the United States by the Wagner Act and subsequent labour legislation in Canada. Further, by comparison with its British counterpart, North American unionism set its face against the formation of a political party with ideological aims.

The present behaviour by managements in North America and Britain is not a new phenomenon. At various times, employers have sought to regain or re-assert their managerial prerogatives (Clegg et al., 1964). In examining and interpreting recent developments, it is important to re-evaluate the insights of earlier writers, who themselves witnessed more turbulent periods within industrial relations and whose concepts were more fitted to present circumstances than those of structural functionalist systems theory.

The fourth issue relates to the development and "more specific modeling of the interactions among environmental forces, values, and strategic choices" (Kochan et. al, 1984b, 23). Further research is needed to specify the distinguishing features of private and public sector collective bargaining in light of more flexible, value-oriented transactional models of industrial relations.

SUMMARY

The study of industrial relations theory is of paramount importance for understanding and changing a collective bargaining system. There are alternate industrial relations frameworks drawing up systems and non-systems concepts. A critique of these systems shows that a structural functionalist approach needs to be reformulated, as it does not adequately explain industrial relations and collective bargaining behaviour. A transactional model of industrial relations (TMIR) is suggested, and future issues are examined in the development of research in industrial relations and collective bargaining.

BIBLIOGRAPHY

Adams, H. C. (1981), "An interpretation of the social movements of our time." *International Journal of Ethics* II, 32–50.

Bain, G. S. and Clegg, H. A. (1974), "A strategy for industrial relations research in Great Britain." *British Journal of Industrial Relations* 12 (1): 91–113.

Barbash, J. (1980a), "Collective bargaining and the theory of conflict." *British Journal of Industrial Relations* 28 (1): 82–90.

_____ (1980b), *Values in Industrial Relations: The Case of the Advisory Principle*. Presidential Address, Industrial Relations Research Association, Denver.

_____ (1984), *The Elements of Industrial Relations*. Madison, WI: University of Wisconsin Press.

Blain, A. N. J. and Gennard, J. (1970), "Industrial relations theory: A critical review." *British Journal of Industrial Relations* 8 (3): 389–407.

Braybrooke, D. and Lindblom, C. E. (1970), *A Strategy of Decision*. New York: Free Press.

Brewster, C. and Connock, S. (1985), *Industrial Relations: Cost Effective Strategies*. London: Hutchinson.

Brown, J. D. (1952), "University research in industrial relations." *Proceedings of the Industrial Relations Research Association*, Madison, Wisconsin. (Quoted in Barbash, 1980.)

Cappelli, P. (1985), "Theory construction in IR and some implications for research." *Industrial Relations* 24 (1): 90–112.

_____ and McKersie, R. B. (1983), "Labor and the crisis in collective bargaining." Paper presented at an MIT/Union Leadership Conference, Boston, MA.

Chamberlain, N. W. and Kuhn, J. W. (1951), *Collective Bargaining*. New York: McGraw-Hill.

Chandler, A. D. Jr. (1962), *Strategy and Structure*. New York: Anchor Books.

Child, J. (1972), "Organisational structure, environment and performance: The role of strategic choice." *Sociology* 6 (1): 1–22.

Clegg, H. A., Fox, A., and Thompson, A. F. (1964), *A History of British Trade Unionism since 1889*, Vol. 1. Oxford: Oxford University Press.

Commons, J. R. (1910), "American shoemakers, 1648–1895: A sketch of industrial evolution." *Quarterly Journal of Economics* xxiv: 39–84.

——— (1918), *History of Labor in the United States*. New York: Macmillan.

——— (1919), *Industrial Goodwill*. New York: McGraw-Hill.

Coser, L. (1956), *The Functions of Social Conflict*. Glencoe, IL: Free Press.

Craig, A. W. J. (1986), *The System of Industrial Relations in Canada*. Scarborough, Ont.: Prentice-Hall.

Cyert, R. M. and March, J. G. (1963), *A Behavioural Theory of the Firm*. Englewood Cliffs, NJ: Prentice-Hall.

Dahrendorf, R. (1959), *Class and Class Conflict in Industrial Society*. London: Routledge and Kegan Paul.

Derber, M., Strauss, G., Keer, C., and Cummings, L. L. (1982), "A review of symposium." *Industrial Relations* xxi: 73–122.

Dunlop, J. T. (1958), *Industrial Relations Systems*. New York: Holt.

——— (1972), "Political systems and industrial relations." *International Institute for Labor Studies Bulletin* 9: 99–116.

Durkeim, E. (1947), *The Division of Labor in Society*. Glencoe, IL: Free Press.

Flanders, A. (1968), "Collective bargaining: A theoretical analysis," *British Journal of Industrial Relations* 6 (1).

——— (1970), *Management and Unions: The Theory and Reform of Industrial Relations*. London: Faber & Faber.

Fox, A. and Flanders, A. (1969), "The reform of collective bargaining: From Donovan to Durkheim." *British Journal of Industrial Relations* 17 (2): 151–180.

Giddens, A. (1968), "Power in the recent writings of Talcott Parsons." *Sociology* 2: 257–272.

Goodman, J. F. B., Armstrong, E. G. A., Wagner, A., Davis, J. E., and Wood, S. J. (1977), *Rule Making and Industrial Peace*. London: Croom Helm.

Hagburg, E. C. and Levine, M. J. (1978), *Labor Relations: An Integrated Perspective*. St. Paul, MN: West Publishing Co.

Handy, R. (1969), *Value Theory and the Behavioural Sciences*. Springfield, IL: Charles C. Thomas.

Hill, S. and Turley, K. (1974), "Sociology and industrial relations." *British Journal of Industrial Relations* 12 (2): 147–170.

Hoxie, R. (1917), *Trade Unionism in the United States*. New York: Appleton.

Hrebiniak, L. G. and Joyce, W. F. (1985), "Organizational adaptation: Strategic choice and environmental determinism." *Administrative Science Quarterly* 30: 336–349.

Hyman, R. (1975), *Industrial Relations: A Marxist Introduction*. London: Macmillan.

_____ (1971), *Marxism and the Sociology of Trade Unionism*. London: Pluto Press.

_____ and Brough, I. (1975), *Social Values and Industrial Relations*. Oxford: Blackwell.

Kerr, C., Harbison, F., Dunlop, J. T., and Myers, C. (1960), *Industrialism and Industrial Man*. Cambridge, MA: Harvard University Press.

Khandwalla, P. N. (1970), Environment and the organization structure of firms. Faculty of Management working paper, McGill University, Montreal.

Kluckhohn, C. (1967), "Values and value orientations in the theory of action: An explanation in definition and classification." In Parsons, T. and E. A. Shils (eds.), *Toward a General Theory of Action*. Cambridge, MA: Harvard University Press, pp. 388–433.

Kochan, T. A. (ed.) (1985), *Challenges and Choices Facing American Labor*. Cambridge, MA: MIT Press.

_____ , Daniel, J. B., and Mitchell L. D. (1982), "Appraising a decade's research: An overview." In *Industrial Relations Research in the 1970's: Review and Appraisal*. Madison, WI: Industrial Relations Research Association, pp. 355–375.

_____ , McKersie, R. B., and Katz, H. C. (1984a), "U.S. industrial relations in transition: A summary report." Paper presented at the Annual Meetings of the Industrial Relations Research Association, Dallas, Texas.

_____ , McKersie, R. B. and Cappelli, P. (1984b), "Strategic choice and industrial relations theory." *Industrial Relations* 23 (1): 16–39.

Laffer, K. (1968), "Industrial relations, its teaching and scope: An Australian experience." *International Institute for Labour Studies Bulletin* 5: 9–26.

Larouche, V. and Déom, E. (1984), "The systems approach in industrial relations." *Relations industrielles—Industrial Relations* 39: 114–116.

Lazarus, R. S. (1978), "The stress and coping paradigm." Paper presented at conference organized by Drs. Carl Eisdorfer, A. Kleinman, and Donna Cohen, Department of Psychiatry and Behavioral Sciences, University of Washington, Seattle.

Lee, R. and Lawrence, P. (1985), *Organizational Behaviour: Politics at Work*: London: Hutchinson.

Lenin, V. I. (1961), "What is to be done?" In *Collected Works*, Vol. 5. Moscow: Foreign Languages Publishing House.

Mann, M. (1970), "The social cohesion of liberal democracy." *American Sociological Review* 35: 423–439.

Margerison, C. F. (1969), "What do we mean by industrial relations? A behavioural science approach." *British Journal of Industrial Relations* 7 (2): 273–286.

Miles, R. E. and Snow, C. E. (1978), *Organizational Strategy: Structure and Process.* New York: McGraw-Hill.

Panitch, L. V. and Swartz, D. (1984), "From free collective bargaining to permanent exceptionalism: The economic crisis and the transformation of industrial relations in Canada." In Mark Thompson and Gene Swimmer (eds.), *Conflict or Compromise: The Future of Public Sector Industrial Relations.* Montreal: The Institute for Research on Public Policy, pp. 441–465.

Parsons, T. (1951), *The Social System.* Chicago: Free Press.

――― (1961), *Structure and Process in Modern Societies.* Chicago: Chicago University Press.

Perlman, S. (1949), *A Theory of the Labor Movement.* New York: Kelly.

Perry, R. B. (1967), *General Theory of Value.* Cambridge, MA: Harvard University Press.

Pettigrew, A. (1975), "Towards a political theory of organizational intervention." *Human Relations* 28 (3): 191–208.

Pfeffer, J. (1981), *Power in Organizations.* Marshfield, MA: Pitman.

Poole, M. (1984), *Theories of Trade Unionism* (rev. ed.). London: Routledge and Kegan Paul.

Rescher, W. (1969), *Introduction to Value Theory.* Englewood Cliffs. NJ: Prentice-Hall.

Ross, A. M. (1948), *Trade Union Wage Policy.* Berkeley: University of California Press.

Schienstock, G. (1981), "Towards a theory of industrial relations." *British Journal of Industrial Relations* 19 (2): 170–189.

Sethi, A. S. (1986), "Interactional value theory." *Journal of Value Inquiry* 20: 1–21.

Simon, H. (1958), *Administrative Behaviour.* New York: MacMillan.

Somers, G. G. (ed.) (1969), *Essays in Industrial Relations Theory.* Ames, IA: Iowa State University Press.

Soskice, D. (1984), "Industrial relations and the British economy, 1979–1983." *Industrial Relations* 23 (3): 306–322.

Stephenson, T. E. (1985), *Management: A Political Activity.* London: Macmillan.

Strauss, G. (1984), "Industrial relations: Time of change." *Industrial Relations* 23 (1): 1–15.

Trotsky, L. (1977), "Marxism and trade unionism." In Clarke, T. and L. Clements (eds.), *Trade Unions Under Capitalism.* Glasgow: Fontana/Collins.

Walton, R. E. and McKersie, R. B. (1965), *A Behavioral Theory of Labor Negotiations.* New York: McGraw-Hill.

Webb, S. and Webb, B. (1897), *Industrial Democracy.* London: Longman Green.

_____ and Webb, B. (1902), *The History of Trade Unionism*. London: Longman Green.

Wood, S. J. (1979), "Ideology in industrial relations theory." *Industrial Relations Journal* 9 (4): 42–46.

PART 2

THE PROCESS AND FRAMEWORK OF COLLECTIVE BARGAINING

3

Collective Bargaining Law

ROBERT ROGOW

INTRODUCTION

Collective Bargaining and Public Policy

This chapter deals with the law of collective bargaining. More broadly, it deals with public policy concerning collective bargaining. Collective bargaining is the determination of terms and conditions of employment through negotiations between employers and representatives of groups of employees. It also includes other aspects of the entire employer–union relationship, for example, the administering and interpreting of the collective agreement in which the agreed terms and conditions are contained. Collective bargaining is a subset of industrial relations, which deals with the whole of the relationships among the participants in the world of work. It is one of a number of mechanisms through which those terms, conditions, and relationships can be determined.

By public policy we mean the combination of what statutes and underlying constitutional documents say about collective bargaining, what they are interpreted as saying by administrators, judges, and arbitrators, and how they are applied and enforced. We also include the goals, priorities, perceptions and values that appear to underlie and explain statutes and other government actions.

This chapter begins by explaining the general character of public policy toward collective bargaining. It then proceeds to look at successive stages of the bargaining relationship: how the relationship is established, how its terms are negotiated and written into a labour contract, how those terms are lived with during the period that contract is in effect, and how the long-term relationship survives. The chapter concludes by speculating on the future of public policy toward bargaining. It suggests answers to three questions:

1. What is public policy's position regarding the desirability of collective bargaining, compared to alternative ways of determining wages and working conditions?
2. How does public policy balance the interests of employers, employees, unions, and other parties?

3. How much, and in what ways, does public policy restrict employers and unions in the use of their power?

Objectives and Strategies of Public Policy

Public policy in most democratic and economically developed countries probably pursues generally similar objectives, but it often follows very different strategies in that pursuit. For example, Canadian emphasis on collective bargaining law versus other industrial relations law is an important distinguishing feature of the Canadian industrial relations system, compared to most other countries. Within collective bargaining law, Canadian law's emphasis on whether collective bargaining will come into existence and on the procedures and behaviours, rather than the outcomes, of bargaining, differs from the emphasis in most other comparable countries. Canada's imposition on employers of a duty to bargain with majority unions and its extensive machinery for the enforcement of this duty generate a degree of intervention and of legal complexity in public policy that few countries can match.

The objectives of a country's public policy can shift over time. Initially, Canadian public policy was concerned primarily with trying to delay, prevent, or resolve strikes, especially those affecting the country's more crucial industries. Thus, this earlier strand in Canadian public policy was based much less on a belief that employees' efforts to unionize should be supported than on a view that strikes should not be permitted to impose costs on the country, at least not until every effort had been made to resolve the issues in dispute peacefully. By the 1940s, public opinion and government policy makers were more concerned about the difficulties many employees desiring unionization had in the face of employer opposition. A unionization support objective was added to the earlier strike control objective. A tension between these two objectives in public policy can still be seen in collective bargaining legislation and in its application and enforcement.

Constitutional Considerations

Constitutional considerations influence the level of government at which policy is properly applied and the consistency of that policy with basic rights guaranteed Canadians.

Federal/Provincial Division of Authority

Canada displays a geographic and jurisdictional decentralization of authority over collective bargaining that is higher than in most comparable countries. The earliest federal law of major significance was the 1907

Industrial Disputes Investigation Act, which provided for compulsory delay of strikes in transportation, communications, mining, and public utilities, while a government-appointed tripartite committee investigated the dispute and issued a report recommending settlement. Acceptance of the report was not compulsory, but it was hoped that the prestige of government and the power of public opinion would induce the parties to accept it. Such compulsory conciliation legislation was to be the only major theme in Canadian public policy for the following three decades.

The British North America Act, 1867 did not explicitly refer to labour relations, but judicial interpretation of more general language helped shape the dividing line between jurisdictions. Until 1925 it was generally believed that the federal government had the predominant authority over collective bargaining matters. In that year the decision of the Judicial Committee of the Privy Council in the case Toronto Electric Commissioners vs. Snider held that the 1907 Act infringed upon the provinces' authority over "property and civil rights." The constitutional basis for the predominance of provincial authority over collective bargaining was established, and has prevailed to this day.

Federal jurisdiction today covers only about one-tenth of the private sector labour force. It is mainly limited to industries with an international, interprovincial, or defence character. Aside from the federal government's own employees, it has authority over all or part of employment in such industries as railway and airlines, radio and television, banking, federal government Crown corporations, telephone and telecommunications, interprovincial pipelines and trucking, feed and grain, longshoring and shipping, and in the Northwest and Yukon Territories.

Despite such limited scope, there are circumstances in which federal predominance comes into play. The federal government's constitutional authority becomes truly national in the event of a national emergency. Wartime circumstances would be a clear example. Interestingly, the Supreme Court of Canada held that the inflationary conditions of the mid-1970s constituted a national emergency sufficient to legitimize the federal government's Anti-Inflation Act, the coverage of which went far beyond the federally administered industries. Should similar generosity in defining national emergencies be followed in the future, the federal government's role in labour relations matters may expand.

The Charter of Rights and Freedoms

A constitutional subject of even greater potential impact on collective bargaining law and policy than the federal–provincial jurisdictional split is the 1982 Charter of Rights and Freedoms. Because so little of this impact has yet emerged, this interesting topic is discussed in the final section of this chapter, which speculates on future public policy toward collective bargaining.

The collective bargaining law discussed here is mainly private sector law. This somewhat limits its generality of application, especially because public (and quasi-public) sectors account for a large and rising proportion of all Canadian collective bargaining. One or more pieces of separate legislation deal specifically with the public sector or subsets thereof in almost all jurisdictions. Much of this legislation has borrowed heavily from private sector public policy, but there are important differences, especially regarding the use of the strike weapon. (See Chapter 14 for more detail.)

PUBLIC POLICY PRINCIPLES AND THEIR IMPLEMENTATION

This section explains the principles underlying public policy toward collective bargaining, how those principles may conflict with one another, and the main strategy used to implement them.

Principles Regarding the Creation of the Bargaining Relationship

Individual Choice as Cornerstone

All Canadian statutes declare that every employee is free to join the trade union of his or her choice and to participate in its lawful activities. From this the right to collective bargaining, the paramount activity of unions, is inferred. Individualism thus is the basic building block for support of collective bargaining, which is in an important sense a rejection of individualism in relations with the employer.

The absence of a policy is also a policy. Canadian public policy makers had, until the last half-century, refrained from attempting to protect this right to bargaining. Such neutrality amounted to a policy of leaving to the relative power of employers and unions the question of whether a bargaining relationship would be entered into. Under this regime only a small proportion of the labour force succeeded in entering into collective bargaining relationships with their employers. Many other employee groups attempted to secure recognition, often via work stoppages. Such strikes and lockouts over recognition were often protracted and fiercely fought. Public concern about such stoppages was one reason for the adoption of the "employee free choice" route. It is not surprising, therefore, that the recognition strike was forbidden when this route was enacted.

This freedom of choice for the individual employee reflects at least a benevolent neutrality of public policy toward collective bargaining. Public policy can and probably should be interpreted as going beyond neutrality, however, to a preference for collective bargaining (as opposed to such alternatives as unilateral determination by the employer of terms and conditions of employment, or determination of such terms directly by statute) as the socially superior mechanism governing employer–employee relations.

There are tensions between the statutes' exalting of individual choice and the collective nature of the choice available. This tension between individual and group interests is a recurrent theme, and one differentiating Canadian public policy from that of most comparable countries. It may reflect the higher priority of individualism in North American value systems and a related ambivalence concerning trade unions' legitimacy.

Another tension within Canadian collective bargaining law arises from contradictory attitudes regarding the work stoppage (the strike and the lockout). Public policy is designed to encourage a primarily adversarial relationship (although hopefully an intelligent and reasonable one) between unions and employers. Resort to the strike or lockout, or at least the realistic possibility of it, is seen as essential to such independence. At the same time, extraordinary efforts to prevent unnecessary or avoidable work stoppage from occurring are built into the law. Overt conflict, then, is seen as completely lawful but perhaps not completely legitimate.

The Need to Support Individual Choice

Canadian public policy makers have entertained considerable doubts about how free individuals were to arrive at a decision regarding collective bargaining, to express that decision, and to effectuate it in the face of employer opposition. Underlying these doubts has been a perception of the work organization as a place of substantial hierarchical imbalance in power, influence, skills, status, feelings of security and self-confidence. Given the decision to protect the individual's right to choose, such a perception implies the necessity of protecting this democratic right against the contrary preferences of structurally powerful and influential individuals and organizations. Because of these doubts, Canadian law contains a vigorously administered set of regulations protecting that right against improper pressures, arising mainly from management, but also from unions.

Principles Concerning Later Stages of the Bargaining Relationship

Canadian public policy's concerns go beyond its presiding at the birth of the bargaining relationship. It also has some concerns about the character and the viability of the relationship thereafter. Because these concerns reflect objectives that are sometimes inconsistent with one another, much of public policy regarding the established bargaining relationship is an exercise in balancing and trading off among objectives.

For example, the law imposes the bargaining relationship on employers, but does not impose the outcome of that relationship on them. They (and unions) are free to use their skills, resources, and their abilities to impose costs on one another in the event of a work stoppage to determine the content of the collective agreement and thus the terms and conditions of employment. Related is the tension between public policy's extensive procedural restraints on when, how, for what purposes, and against whom the parties can use their power and its recognition of such power as the ultimate determinant of such terms and conditions (Weiler, 1980, 288–289).

A second example is the tension between the private and public character of bargaining. The above freedom of the parties to suspend operations for however long it takes to persuade the other side to concede is central to the adversarial scheme designed into public policy. At the same time, public policy makers are concerned about the impact of the work stoppage on third parties and on society in general, especially if the supply of essential goods or services is cut off.

A third example arises from the tension, mentioned above, between individuality and collectivity. Public policy attempts to balance the union's need to present a united front of employees in dealing with the employer against some minimum level of individual and minority rights to pursue their own interests and preferences.

Commonality of Principles among Canadian Jurisdictions

All Canadian jurisdictions share the major principles, and tensions among principles, mentioned above (G. Adams, 1985,16–17). Important differences exist in procedures and in the balance struck among principles, but these are not fundamental enough to deny the existence of a common public policy across Canada.

One reason for the existence of this major common core of public policy is the common genealogy of current Canadian statutes. Beginning in the late 1930s, considerable public pressure from trade unionists and many other people urged Canadian governments to imitate the United States' National Labor Relations Act of 1935, a statute generally reflecting the principles mentioned above. Most provinces enacted variants of the American statute at the end of the 1930s, but these early versions lacked effective enforcement mechanisms. It was during World War II that Ontario and British Columbia provided more formidable versions of the statute, and these in turn were superceded in 1944 by the federal government's Order in Council P.C. 1003, which laid down the characteristics that have become standard in all Canadian legislation since then. The federal Industrial Relations and Disputes Investigation Act of 1948 repeated the major features of P.C. 1003, and formed the model for provincial legislation of the period. Another reason for commonalities is the considerable scrutiny of innovating jurisdictions' experience that appears to take place, with selective imitation of those innovations seen as successful.

Other, perhaps more fundamental, reasons for commonalities in the underlying principles in Canadian statutes are no doubt to be found in the underlying commonalities in culture, values, economies, experience, and institutions across the various jurisdictions within Canada.

Quebec has perhaps the most distinctive Canadian collective bargaining legislation, despite its sharing with other jurisdictions a commitment to all of the above basic principles and policies. Among its distinctive features are the abolition in 1969 of its Labour Relations Board (an institution common to other Canadian jurisdictions). A Labour Court and, below it, government employees known as investigation commissioners, assumed the Board's duties.Another distinctive feature is the power of the Minister of Labour to impose on non-union employers in an industry terms and conditions negotiated by the unionized sector of that industry. Substantial limitations on employer attempts to operate during work stoppages go beyond anything found in other Canadian jurisdictions. British Columbia also shows some significant variations from other jurisdictions.

The Strategy to Implement Those Principles

Crucial to Canadian public policy is the creation of an administrative body usually called a labour relations board. Every Canadian jurisdiction except Quebec establishes such a body to administer, interpret and enforce its private sector collective bargaining law. Although the boards differ in such matters as composition, workload, and speed of processing applications (Task Force on Program Review, 1986, 44–45), they function in general in a very similar manner. The law generally confines itself to stating general principles and rules, leaving to the labour relations board the discretion of applying those rules to specific circumstances. Although some of the law's enforcement, especially outside the area of employees' right to unionize, is shared by the courts or others, the role of the labour board is central to Canadian collective bargaining law.

Why Labour Relations Boards?

Alternatives to making the labour boards the core of implementation strategy certainly existed. The statutes could have left interpretation and enforcement exclusively to the general court system. Relatedly, they could have spelled out sufficient detail to permit government ministry officials to administer policy directly, subject to challenges in the general courts. Public policy recognized the factual complexity and variability inherent in industrial relationships among large numbers of employers, unions and employees at many thousands of employment sites. This, plus the recognition that encouragement of the continuous, long-term relationships in a productive and reasonably co-operative manner might be even more important to the public good than the merits of a particular legal dispute between the parties, suggested the creation of a specialist body with sensitivity to such relationships, one that would deal with nothing but industrial relations matters. Giving such bodies a substantial degree of freedom from ministerial and Cabinet supervision, major discretion to apply and even to modify the application of provisions of the legislation, and, in the case of most such bodies, a tripartite character (with representatives of the employer and union communities as participant members) was seen as adding to their effectiveness, their legitimacy and acceptability in the eyes of those over whom they would exercise authority.

Specialized competence could have been achieved without departing as far from the court system as Canada did. For example, why did the statutes generally not go the "labour court" route, as has been done in many countries (and in Ontario in a short-lived law of the mid-1940s and in Quebec today)? Courts have legitimacy and respect; judges are as capable as other people of accumulating specialized knowledge of industrial relations. Public policy makers recognized that differences between employers and employee organizations, although they often took the form of disputes over rights under the statutes, were at a more basic level differences of interests, disputes, for example, over how the economic "pie" was to be split between the two groups. Interest disputes are best handled by negotiation and compromise rather than by adjudication. The new quasi-independent bodies could do things that even specialist courts could not do: administer, investigate, advise, educate, mediate, take past history of the relationship into account, and consider future consequences of decisions on industrial relations. Further, they could avoid the common law's suspicion of collective action and its exaltation of individual rights, an important consideration in a statutory scheme whose essence was that some subordination to majority employee wishes of individual employee rights and employer freedoms would be required.

All Canadian boards have substantial authority over the establishing of collective bargaining relationships and over violations of the collective bargaining statute. They have some authority over illegal strikes, lockouts, and other matters. The British Columbia board "is the labour relations board with the most comprehensive jurisdiction over labour relations matters. Indeed it is probably a prototype of the kind of labour board that will evolve in the other Canadian jurisdictions" (G. Adams, 1985, 224). For example, its authority to regulate picketing and grievance arbitration is more substantial than is that of other boards. In addition, it has more authority over public sector employee relations than do its counterparts in other jurisdictions, where separate government employee labour boards exist. "In British Columbia, the labour relations board has reached its fullest flowering and enjoys plenary independent authority over conciliation, strikes, picketing and grievance arbitration, *inter alia*. Other labour relations boards enjoy some, but not all, of these responsibilities" (Arthurs et al., 1984, 51). It has been argued that this is superior to the older Canadian practice of splitting authority over different stages of industrial relations among different tribunals and limiting board authority mainly to the initial establishing of the relationship. All stages interact, and decisions made in any one affect the others. A labour board with a comprehensive jurisdiction can bring a more co-ordinated policy to bear on labour relationships. Some movement in the direction of the British Columbia model is observable in the years since enactment of the British Columbia Labour Code in 1973.

Labour Relations Boards and Voluntarism

Boards prefer encouraging voluntary resolution of disputes that come before them to adjudicating on them (Ontario Labour Relations Board, 1982–83, 63; Canada Labour Relations Board, 1984–85, 14; British Columbia Labour Relations Board, 1986, 34–35). Aside from supporting the voluntarist and long-term relationship emphases of public policy, such voluntary settlements lessen the adjudicative workload of labour boards. With thousands of complaints and applications each year reaching some of the boards, the high voluntary settlement percentages achieved help considerably in economizing on limited board resources.

Even when boards perform their court-like functions they attempt to do so in a less legalistic and formal manner, and are encouraged to do so by the collective bargaining statutes, which permit them, for example, to admit evidence that might not be admissible in a court of law. One reason for this flexible approach is a widespread board desire to make its hearings more comprehensible to the individuals directly involved in the controversy. Unfortunately, there are limits (imposed by principles of natural justice, by the complexity of the statutes, and by the accumulation of involved precedents in board decisions) on such informality. The use of specialists, usually lawyers, as representatives at board hearings is therefore quite common.

Labour Relations Board Powers

There has been an expansion since the 1970s in labour board powers to remedy violations of the collective bargaining statutes, and in board willingness to use those powers. Before then, labour relations boards were mainly limited to ordering violators to stop violating the statute, and to awarding reinstatement and back pay to employees discharged in violation of the statute. Since then, a much wider range of remedies has been imposed. Unions have been compensated for wasted organizing expenses and the legal costs of complaints about employer statute violations. Employees has been awarded damages for the benefits they would probably have obtained in negotiations, had employee unfair labour practices not prevented good-faith negotiations. Offending employers have been required to inform employees that they have been found guilty of breaking the law, and that they will comply with the law in the future. Access to employee names and addresses, to company bulletin boards, and even direct access to employees on company time have sometimes been ordered (G. Adams, 1985, 600–606).

Labour relations boards do not themselves initiate actions; they respond to applications (for example, for certification) or complaints (for example, of unfair labour practices). There may well be many instances of violations of the statute that do not for some reason lead to such actions by employees, unions, or employers. Board orders are ultimately enforceable through the courts. Individual choice, the obligation to bargain, and freedom to use one's power to determine the outcome of bargaining are among the principles underlying public policy. The labour relations board is the main social invention devised to implement these principles.

ENTERING INTO THE BARGAINING RELATIONSHIP: IMPLEMENTING THE RIGHT TO DECIDE

Converting the Individual Decision into a Decision about Group Representation

Within a work group it is impossible to implement every individual's preferences, except in the unusual circumstance that all members of the group agree. Therefore, the individual's right to choose becomes transformed into the majority's right to choose. Two issues then arise: the possibility of the individual's or minority's interests being overridden by the majority, and the reduction of each employee's right to negotiate with the employer.

Minority vs. Majority Rights and Interests

The overriding of minority interests by the majority is not necessarily seen as an evil thing. The law recognizes interest heterogeneity among employees (at the same time as it recognizes what it believes to be an even stronger interest homogeneity among them). It recognizes that hard choices must be made by such collectivities as unions and "bargaining units" (to be explained below), and that not all interests can be achieved simultaneously. Public policy's concern is more with the manner in which majority views get implemented than with the content of those views or of the views of the losing side.

Reduction of the Employee's Right to Negotiate with the Employer

The granting of exclusive bargaining rights to the union demonstrating majority support means that individual bargaining is forbidden, except to the (usually limited or non-existent) degree that the collective agreement permits it. Even bargaining for terms that are superior to those of the collective agreement is illegal. This right to bargain individually is a right that many employees, and perhaps even the large majority of employees, have found difficult to implement. This difficulty of implementation, in fact, has been a major employee motive for seeking a collective contracting relationship to replace it. Nevertheless, some individuals possess sufficient resources (scarce and valued work skills, bargaining ability, knowledge of alternatives, and knowledge of employer's ability to pay) that they would have done better for themselves, or at least believe that they would have, in the absence of collective bargaining. Such employees may see the enhancement of majority rights and interests as being achieved at their expense.

Who May Participate in that Decision?

Only people regarded as "employees" by the collective bargaining statutes receive the benefits and protections of the statutes and may participate in certification decisions. The statutory definitions are both broader and narrower than the usual dictionary meaning of "employee." A broader example is the considering of "dependent contractors" to be employees. Such individuals sell services to the employer, usually own- ing and operating their own equipment, but tend to share with employees a number of important characteristics, for example, economic depen- dency on the employer and close direction of their work by it.

An example of lesser breadth than the dictionary meaning would be a managerial employee, a category excluded from the "employee" defini- tion by every Canadian statute. The exclusion of managerial employees arises from a perception of collective bargaining as a polarized relation- ship. The need for an arm's-length relationship leads statutes to deny "employee" status to those employees carrying out significant manage- ment functions. Managerial exclusion also reflects a concern for the employer's interests. The employer is seen as entitled to the loyalty (and hence, presumably, the economic dependency) of those to whom mana- gerial responsibilities have been delegated. In large, complex, multi- level organizations a substantial number of such employees may exist. Like other employees, they may feel a need to be collectively represented in at least some of their dealings with their employer. Public policy does not illegalize such activities, but it denies them the protection of the statute.

In many modern work organizations, determining the dividing line between managerial and non-managerial employees is a difficult task. The clear-cut division of the workplace originally envisioned by some boards, into a handful of all-powerful policy makers completely free to give orders as they wished, and a mass of employees whose sole function was to carry out instructions precisely as given, has had to be modified as boards gained more experience with complex organizations. For exam- ple, the power to hire and fire, once seen as the minimum condition for managerial status, is often limited even for fairly senior managerial employees. Consultative and collegial management styles further blur the dividing line. It is sometimes difficult, in work situations in which several levels of authority are occupied by people sharing professional and technical qualifications, to distinguish between leadership based on expertise and leadership based on exercise of managerial functions. Several statutes distinguish between supervisors and managers, permit- ting the boards to consider the former to be employees, and even to be included in the same bargaining units as people they supervise.

Other categories of employees than managers may be excluded from "employee" status. Employees with confidential access to the employer's industrial relations information are normally excluded. In some jurisdic- tions members of such professions as medicine and law are excluded. A few jurisdictions exclude domestic workers and agricultural workers. Teachers, firefighters and police officers are excluded in about half the jurisdictions because separate legislation covers their collective negotia- tions. Interestingly, the existence and even the predominant existence of a relationship other than the employer–employee relationship need not prevent "employee" status from being found. Graduate student teaching assistants and interns and residents are two groups held to be employees despite the presence of a stronger educational and training relationship than the employer–employee relationship. Prisoners participating in a rehabilitative work program have also been found to be employees.

Who or What May They Select as their "Bargaining Agent"?

Not all employee organizations meet the law's standards for being a "trade union," and only a trade union may be certified as bargaining agent. The usual requirements are as follows:

1. The organization may not be employer-influenced or supported. It may not include managerial employees as members.
2. It must have as one of its purposes the regulation of relations between employees and employers (Arthurs et al., 1984, 183). It need not, however, be affiliated to national or international unions; independent, single-establishment organizations can and do qualify as trade unions. Employee organizations with other purposes than employee–employer relations, even with such purposes being of more importance, can qualify as "trade unions."
3. It must have some degree of formality and responsibility toward its members. It must have a formal constitution that is approved by its members, with officers elected in accordance with it. Organizations lacking this degree of formal regularity are seen as not viable enough to carry out the substantial representational obligations that the statutes impose on exclusive bargaining agents, including the obligation of being accountable to the employees it bargains for.

In Newfoundland and British Columbia it must be an organization located within the province. There, national or international unions cannot secure bargaining rights, although their intra-provincial units can.

"A Majority of What?"

Because majority support is a prerequisite to a union's being certified, the decision on the employee grouping within which that majority is calculated is important. Bargaining statutes give labour relations boards the exclusive right to determine the boundaries of such bargaining units. Because union support is often unevenly distributed among employees, the board's unit determination decision can affect the achievement of the required majority. In Chapter 5 we explain how boards make unit determination decisions.

How and When Majority Support is Determined

The probability that a certification application will be successful is affected by the method and timing used by a board to determine whether the union enjoys majority support. Generally speaking, success is much more likely if the method used is written evidence of union membership rather than a vote, and is much more likely the shorter the time period after the date of application that anti-union employees, recanting union supporters, and the employer have to mount opposition to certification.

Evidence that a majority (55 or 60 percent in some jurisdictions) of employees in the bargaining unit have joined the union and have paid some minimum amount (usually from one to five dollars) to it is sufficient to determine the applying union's representative character in all but two Canadian jurisdictions, Nova Scotia and British Columbia. A vote is normally required in the latter two provinces (Wood and Kumar, 1985, 118–121). Votes are also required in the "membership evidence" jurisdictions in a minority of cases, usually when the union's evidence of membership is above the 35 or 45 percent commonly required by statute for the making of an application, but below the percentage required for certification without a vote. When votes are held, the usual practice is to certify if the union obtains a majority of those voting, rather than the more stringent requirement that the support of a majority of the bargaining unit be obtained.

Where the vote is not relied on to establish majority support, boards are particularly careful to check that signatures and monies were collected in strict conformity to the collective bargaining statute. Intimidation, fraud, gross misrepresentation, forgery, or other irregularities can invalidate some or all membership evidence, lead to a vote being ordered, or even to the rejection of the certification application. Payment of the statutory minimum amount to the union must be unconditional and non-returnable.

The vote requirement is sometimes advocated on the grounds that it permits the individual employee, through the secrecy of the ballot, some protection against social pressures from peers, and permits anti-certification employees an opportunity to rebut union arguments and factual claims in the interval between the application date and the vote date. Canadian public policy has, in general, rejected the vote despite these possible advantages. The main reason is its fear that the employer will make use of the time interval to influence bargaining-unit employees improperly. The example of the United States, where the vote is required, and where the record of employer impropriety is well documented during this time interval, is often cited. The ability of employers there, by various legal strategies, to delay substantially the date of the vote appears to have added considerably to the difficulties unions have had in winning such elections when they are finally held. Understandably, trade unions generally prefer that the vote not be the major means of determining majority support. Even in the absence of any employer interference, it is common for some shrinkage of support to occur between the initial membership evidence submitted to the board and the later vote. The two Canadian provinces requiring the representation vote attempt to limit the time interval between application and election.

The date as of which the union's majority support is determined is important not only when the vote is the mechanism used. It is also important when the "membership evidence" mechanism is used. Half of Canada's jurisdictions use the certification application date for the date as of which majority support is determined. This means that employee statements of opposition to the certification application must be received by the board by the application date. The employer and the anti-certification employees may not even be aware of the certification campaign until official notice from the board that an application has been received. In practice, then, little or no opportunity for opposition or change of mind exists.

Even those jurisdictions that do not use the application date restrict the time period within which a petition withdrawing support for certification may be filed. Because of the risk of surreptitious employer influence, boards tend to scrutinize employee recantations of membership support very carefully. The burden of proof is on those presenting such evidence to show that they reflect a free change of heart uninfluenced by management. In the absence of clear evidence that they are untainted by employer influences, "most petitions would appear to founder" (Arthurs et al., 1984, 190). In any event, the withdrawal of majority support is not used to cancel the certification application, but only to require a vote.

Influences, Permitted and Forbidden, on Group Decision Making

Statutes contain both general and specific prohibitions on behaviour interfering with the individual employee's right to decide on collective representation. Given the wide variety of situations in which employees and employers find themselves, and given the ingenuity of some employers and others in discovering tactics not explicitly prohibited, general categories of banned actions are often stated, leaving to the boards the determination of which, if any, general category a protested action falls within.

Prohibited Employer Behaviours

(See G. Adams, 1985, 484–485, 498, 544; Arthurs et al., 1984, 165–167).

Management may not discriminate against an employee because of union membership or union activity. Discharge of union activists can be a powerful discouragement to employee free choice in a unionization drive. Even the subsequent reinstatement with back pay of such improperly dismissed employees may not suffice to revive a unionization campaign so discouraged. Plausible bases for discharging employees often exist without necessarily being acted upon. The employer who seizes upon such a reason for discharge during a certification campaign can nevertheless be intending to send a message to other employees, influencing their decision on union representation. Canadian labour relations boards and courts see such actions as illegal, even if the anti-union motivation is only a minor part of the reason for discharge, and even if the major reason for discharge is one that would in the absence of such motivation be completely justified. Because employers firing employees for anti-unionization reasons would rarely admit to this motivation, and because plausibly legitimate reasons for discharge are often found by such employers, the statutes presume that protested discharges during the unionization campaign are for anti-union reasons. It is then the employer's obligation to overcome this presumption with evidence to the contrary. Aside from discharge, lesser forms of discrimination against union supporters are also forbidden.

The employer may not interfere with the formation or operations of a trade union. Not only is management forbidden to interfere in a hostile manner (for example, by spying on the union's activities or interrogating employees regarding their support for the union) in the creation or administration of a union (and therefore, by inference, a bargaining unit). Interference in a non-hostile manner is also forbidden. Financial support and assistance in organizing are banned.

This policy reflects the widespread belief that the collective bargaining relationship has, cannot avoid having, and should have, an important degree of adversarialism, of conflicting employee and employer interests. Only fully independent unions, at arm's length from management, can fulfil the statutory duty of representing employee interests. Public policy makers have recognized the mixed character (both common interests and conflicting interests) of employer–employee relations, but feared that an employer-dominated union could not honestly represent the latter interests.

The employer may not change, without board permission, employment conditions while the board is deciding whether to certify an applying union, or during the negotiation of a first contract. These "freezes" are designed to discourage employer efforts to buy off employee interest in unionization, or to convince employees that dealing directly with the employer will yield better results than dealing through a union.

Other Protection of Employee Right to Decide

Employee vulnerability is seen as much greater before than after a collective agreement is in place. Boards therefore hold employers to more restrictive standards in new relationships than in established ones. Coercion and intimidation intended to influence employees' exercise of their right to decide on joining and being active in a union is also an unfair labour practice, whether engaged in by management, union, or others.

Employees are not legally free to respond to employer unfair labour practices by taking strike actions or picketing. Public policy reserves to boards and courts the remedying of such offences.

In addition to the remedial powers mentioned earlier, four Canadian statutes give their labour relations boards an extraordinary remedy. In spite of the seriousness with which the majority principle is regarded, they provide for the certification of a union that lacks majority support where unfair labour practices of the employer have destroyed that majority, or in some cases prevented a majority from arising. The intent here is to deter employer unfair labour practices by denying the offending employer the benefits of its misconduct.

Protection of Employer Interests

Employer interests—for example, in the efficient and orderly operation of the workplace—receive some recognition from public policy, even under some circumstances that do limit unionization activity.

Union Activity on Company Property

The employer has a right to reasonable restriction of actions—including unionization efforts—that would substantially interfere with the efficient and safe operation of its business. At the same time, the workplace during working hours is perhaps the most useful setting in which to contact, and attempt to persuade, employees to unionize. Public policy generally tries to balance these competing interests. A reasonable "no solicitation" rule that is uniformly enforced would probably be upheld as a bar to union activity during working hours but not during breaks, lunch hours or other non-working times. Similarly, the employer may reasonably limit access to company property by non-employees, including union organizers. Special statutory provisions permit access in remote locations where employees live on employer property.

"Employer Free Speech"

Managers, like other people, have a general right to free expression. The employer can expect to be affected, probably adversely, by employees' choice of unionization. Further, managers often honestly believe that employees are being misled by union supporters. But the employing organization's economic control over the livelihood of the employee can convert statements that would be unobjectionable outside the work relationship into threatening interferences with employees' right to join and participate in unions. Drawing the line between permissible and impermissible employer speech is, understandably, not an easy task.

Several statutes attempt to draw that line (for example, guaranteeing employer free speech in the absence of coercion, promises, or undue influence), but the variations in where the line is drawn appear to owe more to differences in the philosophy of individual boards than to specific statutory language. Several boards insist that employer speech be limited to normal business communications or that the employer adopt a neutral "interested bystander" position; others are more permissive. Employers normally are free to correct union misstatements of facts and even to state their views on issues raised by the union, provided the manner and context within which such statements are made (for example, the presence of other employer actions violating the statute, or the making of the statements in a "captive audience" setting) do not interfere improperly with employee freedom of choice (Arthurs et al., 1984, 170–171; G. Adams, 1985, 530, 536, 537).

Obligations Imposed on the Parties

The union certified as exclusive bargaining agent is legally obliged to represent all employees in the unit, whether or not they are members of the union and whether or not they supported certification. A number of statutes add an explicit "duty of fair representation" requiring the union to avoid gross negligence, discrimination, and bad faith toward unit members.

The employer is legally obliged to recognize and bargain in good faith with the certified union. It is forbidden to bargain with any other union, even one that may enjoy significant minority support among bargaining unit members. It is forbidden to bargain directly with employees.

Voluntary Recognition

The strike to compel employer recognition is banned by Canadian law. However, voluntary recognition is accepted as alternative to certification in all jurisdictions except Quebec. Among its advantages are that it is quicker and easier (important in evanescent relationships like construction) and that it permits parties to decide their own bargaining unit, perhaps more co-operatively. Among its disadvantages are that it provides no assurance of majority support, and has a higher possibility of employer support, of the union. Because of public policy concerns about the possibility of voluntary recognition's exploiting employees and denying them their rights of free choice, a variety of safeguards are used by various boards. In general these safeguards make challenges of the voluntarily recognized union easier (G. Adams, 1985, 368–70).

As discussed above, a substantial legal effort is made to support the creation of a collective bargaining relationship where a majority of employees desire it. Once that relationship is entered into, the parties must meet periodically to agree on the terms and conditions of employment of bargaining-unit employees.

NEGOTIATING THE COLLECTIVE AGREEMENT

Collective agreements are written by employers and unions, not by government. Government, however, does much to encourage and even compel employer and union observance of appropriate negotiating procedures.

The Preference for Non-stoppage Settlements

Public policy permits and indeed recognizes the use of the strike or lockout in settling differences between employers and unionized employees. But peaceful, rational discussion is much preferred as a means of settling such differences. For this reason, legislation attempts to guarantee that conflict is not engaged in unnecessarily. It has emphasized dispute avoidance (through compulsory conciliation and investigation while use of the strike and lockout is postponed) for many more years than it has emphasized employee free choice and compulsory recognition. Conflict is legal only after every reasonable effort toward accommodation by the negotiating parties, and after government has had the opportunity of bringing about a meeting of minds. Expiration of the collective agreement, exhaustion of good-faith bargaining efforts, conclusion of government conciliation efforts, serving of strike or lockout notice, and a strike authorization vote are among the common requirements. These requirements may result in slowing the pace of negotiations and of delaying the process of negotiators moving from preferred bargaining positions to merely acceptable ones, but these are regarded by public policy makers as a modest price to pay to guarantee that the avoidable work stoppage be avoided.

The Duty to Bargain

Canadian statutes impose a duty to bargain collectively "in good faith." Most also impose a second bargaining obligation, to "make every reasonable effort to enter into a collective agreement." The first is a subjective obligation requiring an honest intention of arriving at an agreement, the second an objective one involving the presence or absence of appropriate behaviours.

The employer must respect the union's exclusive bargaining authority during contract negotiations. It may not attempt to bargain directly with bargaining-unit employees or attempt to undermine the bargaining agent's authority. Direct communications to employees during negotiations that do not run afoul of these prohibitions, however, are permitted; the employer, for example, may explain its bargaining position. In some jurisdictions the statutory freeze on employer changes in terms and conditions of employment during first contract negotiations also applies to all later renewal negotiations (G. Adams, 1985, 556; Arthurs et al., 1984, 210–212).

The substance of contract demands and the contents of the collective agreement are predominantly a topic on which laws and boards are silent. There are some exceptions, however. Agreements must generally include recognition clauses and language providing for the peaceful resolution of disputes arising from the agreement, and in some jurisdictions must include language requiring "just cause" for discipline or discharge and provisions for handling technological change. In general, collective agreements may contain whatever topics the parties agree to, even if such topics go beyond the usual definitions of "terms and conditions of employment." More importantly, the parties are, upon impasse, free to strike or lock out over almost any issues, including issues conventionally seen as exclusively within management's domain. Contract demands that violate wage control or anti-discrimination statutes are illegal. Some behaviours may be held to violate the "reasonable effort" requirement, even absent bad faith. Grossly unreasonable bargaining positions might, in addition, lead a board to suspect that bad faith was present.

Although Canadian statutes have existed in roughly their present form since the 1940s, it was only in the 1970s that the bargaining duty was vigorously enforced and expanded. Part of the explanation for this was the limited armory of weapons made available to boards by the statutes until the '70s. Another explanation was an earlier fear that negotiations might be made too formal and legalistic by such enforcement and expansion. The negotiation process was already seen by some observers to be difficult and anxiety generating; further constraining negotiating parties to look over their shoulders at what was being said and done for fear of how a labour board might interpret their behaviours would be counterproductive. In addition, the temptation of the weaker party to attempt to obtain by litigation what it could not obtain by bargaining power might divert energies from the difficult but necessary task of negotiation and compromise to the legal arena. Also, it was hoped that the use of conciliation and mediation by governments would discourage bad-faith behaviours (G. Adams, 1985, 573, 574; Carter, 1983, 53).

Some tension is possible between the principle of voluntarism—that the bargaining power and bargaining skill of the parties should determine the outcomes of bargaining—and the principle that bargaining should be conducted in good faith. In recent years Canadian boards, with Ontario leading the way, have given greater weight to the latter (Carter, 1983, 51, 52, 39). The stronger party may not refuse to discuss fully the substantive issues raised by the other party. The stronger party may not press to impasse any illegal substantive demand—and the boards have been interpreting illegality more and more broadly, in their increasing concern about good-faith bargaining.

The Ontario board has been especially vigorous and innovative in expanding and enforcing the bargaining duty. Its reasoning starts from the obligation of the parties to engage in full and informed discussion. Such discussion better enables them to understand the other's position, and guarantees that, if impasse is reached and economic conflict occurs, it will be over real and not imagined differences. A number of separate strands of the employer obligation to contribute to meaningful negotiations have emerged (G. Adams, 1985, 577–586 Arthurs et al., 1984, 224, 225).

First is the obligation that information necessary to the union's understanding of the basis and fairness of the employer's position be supplied to it. For example, a refusal to supply a union with existing wage and job classification data, and a refusal to divulge information regarding budgetary restraints imposed on a public sector employer, were each held to violate the duty to bargain. Second is that "misinterpretations" (lies) violate the good-faith obligation because they destroy the rational basis upon which informed collective bargaining decisions are made. Third is that union negotiators must be able to communicate their positions and concerns to management figures with the power of decision over them, or at least people who are close enough to the decision makers to communicate those concerns effectively. Thus, sending of powerless and uninformed junior people to negotiate may be a violation of the bargaining duty. In a hospital bargaining case, the board held that some access should be provided to the Ministry of Health officials who influenced the size of the hospital's budgetary resources. Fourth is that parties have an obligation to explain the rationale underlying bargaining positions, so that the other party can assess the reasonableness of the position. For example, a refusal to discuss the alternative interpretations of wage control guidelines, and the refusal to explain the rationale underlying a wage offer, have each been found illegal. Fifth is the management obligation to disclose those already-decided plans that would have a major impact on the bargaining unit during the life of the agreement being negotiated. For example, a company that had already decided to close the establishment in which the bargaining unit is employed would have a legal obligation to disclose such plans at negotiations.

Compulsory Conciliation

Most jurisdictions require conciliation as a precondition to a legal work stoppage. In some other jurisdictions conciliation, although not universally required by statute, is very frequently imposed, either upon request of one of the parties or on the initiative of the Ministry of Labour. Provisions for a two-stage conciliation process are common. The conciliation board used at the second stage generally must recommend settlement terms (Carrothers et al., 1986, 32n), a requirement reflecting a long-standing Canadian belief that the force of public opinion would pressure parties into modifying their positions. Perhaps because of declining faith in the power of the public opinion, there has been a decline in the use of conciliation boards. During conciliation and for a brief period thereafter the resort to strike or lockout is prohibited. Many bargainers regard compulsory conciliation as an irksome formality to be suffered through en route to the final stage of serious bargaining. Some students of collective bargaining have criticized compulsory conciliation for its delaying of the bargaining and concession processes, but it appears firmly entrenched in Canadian legislation and cultural values.

Negotiating the First Collective Agreement

The employer's obligation to bargain is not an obligation to concede, to agree to union terms, or even to compromise. This absence of obligation to concede is necessary to the voluntarist, power-determined model and the philosophy underlying collective bargaining law. Once labour relations boards become involved in determining the reasonableness of employers' or unions' substantive bargaining positions, they become enmeshed in covert adjudication of collective agreement terms, something inconsistent with the basic policy of leaving such terms to the parties to decide.

However, there is a folk saying that one can lead a horse to water, but cannot make him drink. The law leads the often-reluctant employer to the bargaining table, but can it make him bargain? In the absence of review of bargaining offers or demands, can the employer observe the niceties of bargaining without any intention of ever arriving at an agreement? This problem may be most serious at the stage of negotiating the first collective agreement between the parties. The obligation to bargain in good faith provides a legal basis for dealing with this problem, although determining intent is often difficult.

The employer is entitled to engage in hard bargaining, to obtain the best settlement that its bargaining power will permit. This includes the making of bargaining proposals that are unacceptable, even predictably unacceptable, to the union. The same behaviours can be either legal or illegal, depending on board interpretation of the motives of the employer. Concurrent and past behaviours away from the bargaining table—for example, whether unfair labour practices have been committed—will influence such a judgment. The presence or absence of valid business reasons for positions taken is also considered.

There are serious difficulties other than employer bad faith in new relationships, difficulties that can also prevent agreement being reached. It is often difficult to decide the relative weight to assign to such factors as the inexperience of negotiators and the economic fragility of small businesses, compared to employer intransigence, as causes of failure to agree.

There have been a number of public policy efforts to do something about the problem. These include the freeze on employer changes in terms and conditions during the negotiation of the first agreement, board policing of employer bargaining via unfair labour-practice complaints, and a ban for a reasonable period after certification, even if no collective agreement has been signed, on efforts by another union to replace the bargaining agent. The most extreme weapon, however, is the imposed first agreement.

About half of Canadian jurisdictions provide that the labour relations board (in Quebec, an arbitration council) may impose a first agreement in circumstances where bargaining has failed to produce agreement. Normally the statutes contemplate the strike as the appropriate union and employee response to unacceptable employer offers, and the ineffective strike as the signal to them to accept the employer's terms. Because board-written agreements are a major departure from the principle of voluntarism, some boards have been conservative in applying this policy. They have limited the imposition to cases in which they were convinced that employer intransigence and covert refusal to bargain had caused the impasse. They appear to have tried to discourage wholesale applications under it, refusing to see it used by unions lacking bargaining power as a means of achieving the fruits of bargaining power.

Even where a first contract is imposed by a labour board, the problem of the second contract may present itself. The underlying public policy tension arises from compulsory, assisted entry of the relatively powerless into a power-determined relationship. Employee and union bargaining power may or may not improve during the life of a mandated first agreement. Employer resistance to bargaining may or may not soften over the same period. It is possible, however, that the deterrent effect on reluctant employers of such statutory provisions is substantial, and that they therefore lead to a higher proportion of first contracts being reached than would be true in their absence.

Peace and War in Contract Determination

The following section discusses how public policy affects the behaviours of the parties if negotiation fails to bring agreement and the strike or the lockout occurs. The fact that negotiation and the work stoppage are discussed in separate sections should not, however, lead the reader to conclude that they are fully separate topics. Negotiations occur in the shadow of the stoppage, and predictions of the effectiveness of the stoppage are the major determinant of the amount either side is prepared to concede in negotiations. Even when the stoppage occurs, negotiations may have substantially reduced the number of issues still in dispute. During or after the stoppage, negotiations will occur. Thus, too much should not be made of the distinction between the peaceful and the contentious stages of determining the terms of a collective bargaining.

THE WORK STOPPAGE

The work stoppage can occur at different stages of the collective bargaining relationship. It can occur over the question of employer recognition of the union, as part of the process of negotiating or renegotiating a collective agreement, or during the period when a collective agreement is in effect. This section discusses only the second of these three kinds of stoppages.

The Nature of the Strike

A strike is a concerted employee withdrawal of services. Most but not all are intended to pressure the employer to make some bargaining concessions. Partial withdrawals (slowdowns, overtime bans, "work to rule" campaigns, refusals to handle certain goods or to work with certain employees) are usually held to be strikes.

The strike is by far the most common mechanism of employee pressure on the employer, but other mechanisms are also used, either in conjunction with or as substitutes for it. The picket line, boycotts and "hot declarations," publicity, appeals to government, to other unions and even to other employers, appearances at shareholders' meetings, temporary occupations of employer premises, and the operating of temporarily competing businesses are among these other mechanisms.

The Right to Strike

The right to strike is implicit in the general language found in every Canadian statute stating that every employee is free to join and participate in the lawful activities of the trade union of his or her choice. The right to strike is also implicit in the statutes' procedural requirements that have to be met before the strike is legal. Considering the central function that the strike (or at least the plausible threat of the strike) plays in collective bargaining, it is interesting that no explicit language guaranteeing that right can be found (Arthurs et al., 1984, 236–37). This seems another suggestion that the work stoppage, although legal, is not fully legitimate. Like sexual activity to the Victorians, everyone knows it is engaged in but nice people do not refer to it unnecessarily. It is also true that most statutes, by default, leave authority over strikes and related activities (for example, picketing) mainly to the courts and the common law, although this is becoming decreasingly true.

Timeliness is the most important precondition of strike legality (expiration of the previous collective agreement, exhaustion of the various peaceful settlement efforts, notice, or strike vote, as discussed earlier). Purpose is another test; striking for recognition, in sympathy for another union, in pursuit of political objectives, or in protest of employer interpretation of or failure to observe the collective agreement are all generally illegal.

The Lockout

Some employer refusals to continue employing bargaining-unit members are called lockouts. To be a lockout, the refusal must have the intention of pressuring employees to make concessions on terms and conditions. Most employer refusals to continue employment are made for other (for example, economic) reasons, which are normally permitted by the statutes. However, where anti-union motivation is present, the employer action may be held to be a lockout, an unfair labour practice, or both.

Timeliness requirements are as important for the lockout's legality as for the strike's. These parallel the strike's procedural preconditions. The employer is as free as the union is to resort to the pressure tactic of the work stoppage to persuade the other side to make concessions after expiration of the agreement and of bargaining.

Although the lockout is in a formal sense the employer weapon that exactly parallels the union's strike weapon, it accounts for only a small minority of stoppages. Employers usually prefer to continue operating, even after impasse in negotiations has been reached. Their functional equivalent to the strike is more likely to be their ability to withstand the strike than it is the lockout.

Behaviours During the Stoppage

Stoppage outcomes are overwhelmingly, but not completely, left by public policy to the skill, nerve, and bargaining power of the parties. "In effect, modern Canadian labour legislation is seen as creating 'opportunity' or 'process' rights and not specifying 'outcomes'." The task of labour relations boards is not "to attempt to equalize the economic power available to the parties" (G. Adams, 1985, 516). This is not to say that public policy is pure Darwinism, that after it compels the bargaining interaction it is completely neutral regarding the outcome of that interaction. It is to say, though, that it is only in exceptional circumstances— those that put the relationship itself into jeopardy—that it will consider intervening to modify directly the outcomes that the relative power of the parties would produce.

To say that public policy seldom directly modifies outcomes is not to say that it has no influence on outcomes. Many statutory, judicial and administrative positions affect the degree to which the parties may deploy their economic weaponry during a work stoppage. Policy on the union use of the picketing weapon, on employer use of substitutes for striking or locked-out employees, and on strikers' rights of re-employment are examples of potentially important modifications of the parties' use of their power.

One important behaviour during the stoppage is the employer's attempt to operate. In most stoppages the employer chooses not to exercise this right. However, the right of the employer to attempt to operate during a stoppage is widely recognized by Canadian statutes, as a basic element in their voluntarist principle. An interesting exception is Quebec, where the right to operate is limited substantially via strong prohibitions on hiring of replacements, on using non-bargaining-unit employees from the struck location or others, and on continuing to employ any members of the striking bargaining unit (Arthurs et al., 1984, 238).

Some other explicit statutory limitation of the employer's use of economic weaponry exists (G. Adams, 1985, 517). Five provinces ban use of replacement employees by members of an accredited employer association. Three provinces ban use of professional strike breakers. Ontario bans such employer strike-related misconduct as intimidation, surveillance, or provocation (G. Adams, 1985, 70).

The Picketing Weapon

(See G. Adams, 1985, 631–661; Carrothers et al., 1986, 606–709.)

The Nature of Picketing

Picketing usually involves an intention to secure a sympathetic response from a person who might otherwise work for, make deliveries to, patronize, or deal in some other way with, a struck or locking-out employer. This activity is normally carried out at or near an entrance to an employer's place of business. Picketing is almost always an effort to communicate information, and as such involves some constitutionally protected rights. It also involves a constitutional right of freedom of assembly. However, picketing sometimes goes beyond mere information transmittal, to moral suasion and even to the threat and reality of intimidation and violence. In addition, even merely informational picketing may be held to limit improperly other persons' rights. The balancing of conflicting rights—for example, freedom of expression versus freedom from intimidation—has usually been decided by the courts in favour of the latter. (Arthurs et al., 1984, 248). Except in British Columbia, picketing is mainly regulated by the courts, under the common law (in Quebec, the Civil Code).

Picketing is of varying tactical importance in different stoppages, tending to be less important when the withdrawal of services itself imposes heavy costs of disagreement on the employer. Picket lines, to the extent that they are honoured, can substantially increase a weaker bargaining unit's ability to impose such costs on its employer. The union right to picket legally is especially important to it when the employer attempts to operate during the stoppage. For these reasons, picketing and how public policy deals with it are important matters.

The Courts and Picketing

There is considerable variability in treatment of picketing by the courts. Many different judges have had the occasional picketing case before them. Lacking specialized familiarity with industrial relations cases, they have tended to rely on general common-law concepts that are not known for their specificity and precision, and to apply them in accordance with their individual insights and philosophical orientations.

In the past, the courts had been quite hostile to the use of the picketing weapon and quite prone to find even relatively inoffensive variants of it illegal. In recent years the courts have tended to become more sympathetic, although they still are sometimes criticized for not being sympathetic enough, especially regarding secondary picketing (explained below).

In general, picketing tends to be held by the courts to be legal if it meets three conditions:

1. It is in support of a legal strike or in opposition to a lockout.
2. It is only an exercise in communicating information or in peacefully persuading. This requires the absence of coercion, intimidation, violence, or the implicit or explicit threat of them. Large numbers of pickets, physical interference with passage of people and goods across the line, and even a high level of verbal abuse of those crossing the line might be sufficient to illegalize it.
3. It is located at the normal place of work of the striking or locked-out employees and affects only their employer.

Conditions (1) and (2) are less controversial than is condition (3). Those who highly value the picket line as an exercise in free expression and those who dislike public policy's freeze on pressure tactics during the life of the agreement (discussed below) may criticize condition (1). Few would support coercion, intimidation, or violence by picketers, but many may disagree with the factual point at which some courts have found these activities to exist. But it is with regard to (3) that most disagreement appears.

Primary versus Secondary Picketing

Primary picketing, that which affects only the struck or locking-out employer at the employees' workplace, is normally upheld if it is in support of a legal stoppage and is peaceful. Meeting those two tests is often not sufficient if picketing goes beyond this limited focus. This latter category, usually referred to by the somewhat amorphous label of secondary picketing, can refer to many different factual situations, each involving varying interests of a number of different parties. Among the many different circumstances that are sometimes discussed under this label are the following:

1. Picketing of other, unstuck locations of the primary employer. Those other locations might or might not be producing goods and services that would otherwise have been produced by the striking employees, but are likely to be contributing income that aids the employer during the stoppage.
2. Picketing businesses that are legally distinct from the primary employer but are related to it by overlapping ownership and control.
3. Picketing other employers. Those other employers may be producing goods and services that the strikers normally produced, or may have more arm's-length business connections with the primary employer, or may even have no business connections with it. The picketing of the

latter two groups, perhaps the purest form of secondary picketing, is normally held illegal.

In addition, some primary picketing of the struck employer at the strikers' work location can have major impact on other employers, both those with some business relationship to the employer and those lacking such relationship. Picketing of a struck employer sharing a common site and a common entrance with others (in an industrial park, a shopping centre, an office building or a construction project) or a struck employer whose employees normally work at least in part at other employers' premises (installation and maintenance of equipment or utility services, delivery companies, security or janitorial companies) can raise involved issues of conflicting legitimate interests of a number of different parties.

The judiciary have made efforts to balance the interests of those involved, but consistent policy is difficult to discern. In general, the interests of uninvolved third parties have tended to be given precedence, with the effect that secondary picketing or primary picketing that substantially affects other employers tends to be modified or banned in many such situations. In addition, the refusal of other employees whose own collective agreements are still in effect to cross such picket lines would usually be illegal, and action to induce such illegality is strongly censured. The courts have been less hostile to secondary picketing where common ownership, functional integration of production, or the secondary employer assisting the struck employer are found. Picketing appeals to customers of secondary employers have been treated with somewhat more sympathy than have picketing appeals to employees.

Judges are increasingly attempting in their picketing decisions to enforce the provisions and policies of the collective bargaining statutes, although critics have complained that they lack the sophisticated familiarity with industrial relations to do this well.

Labour Relations Boards and Picketing

The British Columbia Labour Code in 1973 spelled out the limits of legal picketing and has given its board the main responsibility for supervising picketing, thereby reducing substantially the role of the courts. Because statutory language must be relatively general and picketing situations can be very varied, extensive discretion has been given the board in enforcing that language (Gall, 1984, 133, 135, 138).

The initial statutory language, passed by a New Democratic Party government, and the interpretations of it by the board, granted appreciably wider legal scope to picketing than the judiciary had tended to grant. Moderately extensive amendments in 1984 have reduced the scope of picketing to something much more closely resembling that now permitted by the judiciary in other jurisdictions. Board authority and board discretion, however, remain extensive.

Commentators in other Canadian jurisdictions have often urged a British Columbia-like shift of authority over picketing from the courts to the labour relations board. Some of this enthusiasm may have reflected their approval of the more liberal scope of permissible picketing. The 1984 conservative shift in statutory language may therefore have reduced, but certainly has not eliminated, such advocacy. The British Columbia experience suggests to many observers that boards can provide a more consistent and predictable management of the picketing weapon by an expert and experienced body sensitive to the nuances of industrial relations practice and able to relate picketing decisions to larger purposes of public policy.

Job Security of Strikers and Locked-out Employees

All Canadian statutes state that an individual does not cease to be an employee solely because he or she participated in a legal work stoppage. Therefore the employer cannot discharge on that basis, nor can it treat the striker as having resigned. This protection, however, falls short of being an unconditional guarantee of re-employment.

The prevailing judicial doctrine appears to be that the employer is not obliged to lay off employees hired during the stoppage ("strikebreakers") in order to provide re-employment at the end of the stoppage to striking unit members. The employer is required only to provide re-employment as vacancies arise (G. Adams, 1985, 517–518; Arthurs et al., 1984, 239). Critics of this limitation to job protection of unsuccessful strikers argue that employees therefore risk their jobs when they strike, and that this fear generates picket-line violence. They also argue that the limitation may be inherently destructive of the bargaining relationship. Because of concern about the limitation of such protection, some Canadian jurisdictions have attempted to provide some statutory restrictions on employer refusals to displace replacement employees in order to re-employ strikers.

Summary

The crucial rights of employers to operate, of unions to picket, and of employees to return to their jobs are dealt with by courts, statutes, and at least one labour relations board. How they are dealt with affects the outcomes of labour disputes despite public policy's general effort to leave such outcomes to the relative power of the parties.

However, virtually all stoppages end, and the large majority end with the creating or renewing of a collective agreement. The following section discusses how public policy affects employers, unions and employees during the period that the collective agreement is in effect.

LIVING UNDER THE COLLECTIVE AGREEMENT

The collective agreement freezes the rules governing the relationship among employer, union, and employee, normally for between one and three years. If the relative power of the parties shifts during that time, how free are they to try to change those rules? What protection does the employee have against employer evasion of the collective agreement? What protection has the employer against strikes and other pressure tactics? This section attempts to answer these questions.

Role of the Collective Agreement

The collective agreement is a powerful document. It displaces individual contracts and the common law. It has been described as the cornerstone of our labour relations system and as a primary source of law that defines employee, employer and union rights (G. Adams, 1985, 670; Arthurs et al., 1984, 55). The collective agreement is more like a labour relations "constitution" regulating the relationship than it is like a common-law contract. It differs from the usual contract in that, in addition to the usual statement of the rights and obligations of the two contracting parties, the employer and the union, it specifies terms and conditions of employment of others—the bargaining-unit members.

In one sense the collective agreement is an exercise in feudalism, in decentralization of law. It creates a small enclave of private law that differs, sometimes significantly, from other little duchies of private law, and from the broader statutory law made by judges, labour boards, and even arbitrators. These other sources of law, however, have considerable impact on how collective agreements are arrived at, how they are enforced, and even what their content is. There is a large potential tension between the private character of the collective agreement and the public, universal character of the more general law.

Almost all agreements contain, often at the insistence of the statute, sections providing for the recognition of the union, providing peaceful resolution of disputes about their meaning and application, and forbidding strikes and lockouts during their life. They usually contain provisions covering many other matters, both substantive and procedural, and can be of considerable length and complexity.

The Peace Obligation

The Ban on Pressure Tactics

Canadian statutes forbid the use of their power by employees, unions, or employers to compel change in the terms of the collective agreement during its life. Not only the complete withdrawal of services but more limited pressure tactics are also forbidden. Instead, and as a quid pro quo, legislation requires that a peaceful mechanism for resolving all disputes about the meaning or application of the agreement be provided. Unless both parties voluntarily agree to the contrary, the terms of the agreement are frozen for the duration of the agreement, no matter what changes in their relative bargaining power may have developed since the agreement was signed. "This requirements represents a fundamental commitment to industrial peace and stability, once an agreement has been negotiated" (G. Adams, 1985, 678).

Labour relations boards have increasingly been given powers to declare strikes or lockouts illegal and to issue orders requiring the ending of such stoppages. As in other situations, boards first try a mediative, problem-solving approach before turning to adjudication.

Employer Remedies for Illegal Stoppages

What relief or compensation is available to the employer confronted with an unlawful strike? It is not free to regard the illegal action as a cancellation of the collective agreement by the employees; it is not released from its obligations under the collective agreement by this illegal action. A variety of legal avenues are more or less available to the employer.

1. The employer may discipline leaders and participants, but such actions are subject to protest through the grievance system and grievance arbitration. Arbitrators are reluctant to uphold discharge for participating in such strike actions, but often uphold lesser disciplinary penalties.
2. If the collective agreement contains a ban on the strike (and it generally does), the employer may be able to use the grievance arbitration mechanism to secure money damages from the union. Arbitrators have authority to award damages for employer losses caused by illegal strikes. To some extent this access is a functional substitute for the court damage suit.
3. The employer may go to court. The relief traditionally sought by employers facing an illegal strike has been the injunction, usually a court order temporarily ending the action complained of. Judicial issuance of injunctions had been widely criticized for its anti-union effect and even anti-union intent. Legislation during the 1970s to

improve injunction procedures and to reduce their scope, plus judicial self-restraint, have substantially reduced these criticisms. British Columbia has gone farthest of any jurisdiction, by banning all ex parte injunctions (those issued without notice) and permitting other injunctions only where immediate danger of serious injury or actual obstruction or physical damage to property is involved. New remedial powers given to labour relations boards (including powers to issue injunction-like orders) have partially filled the gap thus created.

The courts also play a role through damage suits. Courts still have significant jurisdiction regarding stoppages, despite the tendency in recent years of legislation to reduce that role. A general, but not invariable, willingness of courts to defer to labour board expertise and authority is observable in recent years (G. Adams, 1985, 629). This is especially true regarding alleged violations of the collective bargaining statutes.

Individual strikers could be, but rarely are, sued. The union can be held financially liable for illegal stoppages it authorizes or in which its officials participated. Failure to make reasonable efforts to end an illegal stoppage may make the union vulnerable to suit.

4. The employer may complain to a labour board. The British Columbia board can declare a stoppage unlawful and issue any related orders to the parties, or can resolve the matter through voluntary settlement and compromise. It has exclusive jurisdiction to handle such complaints, as opposed to the courts. The courts, and not the board, can award damages, but board permission to sue is required. The authority of the Ontario and Canada boards to declare stoppages illegal and to issue appropriate orders is not as exhaustive or exclusive as that of the British Columbia board, but is substantial.

Permitted Stoppages

Not all stoppages and related job actions are forbidden. Some jurisdictions protect the right to refuse in concert to work over health and safety concerns, over technological change, for non-collective bargaining purposes, or to respect outsider picket lines. Some special dispensations for unions and employees in the construction industry also exist.

Health and safety. The refusal to perform unsafe work is viewed more sympathetically than are other kinds of stoppages or violations of work discipline (Arthurs et al., 1984, 254). Employees disciplined by their employer for such action may appeal to the Ontario, Quebec or federal labour relations tribunals (G. Adams, 1985, 253). The British Columbia statute declares such stoppages are not strikes and therefore not violations of the statute. Workers' compensation boards also offer support to such employees. Generally, a good-faith belief, even if mistaken, that health and safety are in peril is sufficient to protect employees so refusing to work.

Technological change. Four jurisdictions relax the strike prohibition where a significant technological change has been introduced. The term is sometimes defined very broadly to include many non-technological changes in ways of doing business. An employer obligation to bargain and a union right to use the strike weapon during the life of the agreement are written into such statutory provisions.

Non-bargaining intent. The pre-1984 British Columbia Code, in addition to defining the strike as most other jurisdictions did, contained an additional element, a subjective test—the requirement that the purpose be to compel an employer to agree to terms and conditions of employment. Thus collective withdrawals of services engaged in for any other purpose, for example political stoppages aimed at government as lawmaker rather than at employers, honouring of other unions' picket lines, or refusal to handle struck or otherwise "hot" goods, were not strikes and therefore not violations of the statute.

Individual action. In the many jurisdictions where refusal to cross a picket line is normally held to be a strike, the absence of a "common understanding" might protect refusals to cross. If employees individually decide not to cross a picket line because each independently fears doing so or each individually believes it his or her moral obligation to refuse, the honouring fails the "concerted action" element of the strike definition. However, the simultaneous operation of a large number of individual decisions to respect a line creates a strong presumption that they are acting in concert.

Other exceptions. Although in almost all jurisdictions the parties may not legally agree in their collective agreement to permit the work stoppage during contract life because of the pre-eminence of the statutory ban on it, there are exceptions, as in the federal jurisdiction. A few jurisdictions permit clauses in construction agreements that legalize the stoppage during contract life when non-unionists or members of unions not affiliated with the construction unions' council appear on a building site.

Legal Means of Protesting Agreement Violations

The law's ban on employee use during the life of the agreement of strikes and other pressure tactics over all and any issues generates both moral and functional obligations to permit the broadest possible scope for grievances and grievance arbitration.

All statutes provide mechanisms by which disputes concerning the interpretation, administration or violation of a collective agreement may be settled peacefully. The law anticipates the informal resolution of most disputes without need to resort to arbitration. In practice, this occurs. Although only a small proportion of grievances reach the arbitration stage, that stage has a major influence on how, and whether, the employer and the union use the earlier, informal stages to resolve disputes. The emergence over time of an arbitral consensus on how to decide an issue becomes known to personnel managers and union officials, who can often agree on what the probable arbitral outcome would be, and hence agree to that outcome without the time and money investment of submission to arbitration.

The union and not the individual grievor "owns" the grievance, and can decide whether to carry it forward, accept a compromise solution, or drop it. In jurisdictions with a statutory "duty of fair representation," grievor complaints about union actions are frequent, but usually unsuccessful.

Statutes require that collective agreements contain a provision for the final and peaceful resolution of any grievances not resolved and not withdrawn after the exhaustion of the grievance procedure. Arbitrators are selected jointly by the parties, with the assistance of government if they cannot agree. Arbitration awards are legally binding, but may be appealed to the courts (in British Columbia, to the labour relations board). Awards tend to be upheld on appeal, provided a genuine arbitral effort to deal with the relevant issues exists, and provided no violation of the statutes or of the principles of natural justice is found. Grievance arbitration has less delay, lower costs, and less legalism and formalism than court proceedings have, but has enough of these features to be frequently criticized by the parties. Chapter 11 discusses the arbitration process in more detail.

The grievance procedure and arbitration are not the only legal means available to employees with complaints. For example, workers' compensation boards, human rights commissions, and other adjudicative forums are sometimes available. These deal mainly with employee rights arising from statutes rather than from collective agreements. It is nevertheless true that the same circumstances may generate both a right to grieve and a right to complain to some other source. The tactical choice among these mechanisms may thus become possible. Some violations of collective agreements are also violations of collective bargaining statutes. Labour relations boards tend to defer to arbitration, unless larger issues of policy are involved, or unless they suspect that arbitration would not be able to handle the problem (G. Adams, 1985, 698–700, 591–593). Some choice of forums exists. The question of whether an aggrieved employee can use more than one route is unclear. At the same time that competition from other forums is invading arbitration's domain, that domain is expanding elsewhere. Arbitration is increasingly taking on responsibility for enforcement of statutory rights as well as contractual ones (R. Adams, 1985, 142-144).

Collective agreement terms cannot supercede contrary language in the collective bargaining statute. Other statutes, too, might modify agreement language. Wage control legislation sometimes rolls back collective agreement-scheduled wage increases or extends the life of collective agreements, for example.

Employer Rights and Powers

Some statutory language or labour board policy limits or imposes some procedural requirements on management actions that could have major impact on the bargaining unit—technological change or plant closure, for example. Is the employer legally free, outside of these few statutorily specified areas, to make any decisions not explicitly in violation of the collective agreement until the agreement expires?

The presence and relative importance of a goal to escape from statutory obligations and engage in collective bargaining can lead labour relations boards to find that relocation or closure of the work organization, contracting out, or other management actions not explicitly contained by the collective agreement's language may nevertheless be violations of the statute. But what if such actions arise, not from a hostility to the bargaining relationship itself, but rather from the economic disadvantages that result from the bargaining relationship? The employers' rights to attempt to operate profitably, to protect the enterprise against economic pressures, to make decisions for legitimate business reasons, are recognized by public policy. Some balancing of these rights against employee rights to engage in collective bargaining is therefore attempted by labour boards. Obviously, drawing the line between permissible and impermissible actions is difficult. The same action (for example, closure of all or a part of a business) can be legal or illegal, depending on such circumstances as the existence of sufficiently powerful economic reasons for the action (G. Adams, 1985, 507–508, 512).

Specific provisions of the collective agreement limit management's freedom to make decisions on compensation, work assignment, discipline and many other matters. Beyond these specific limits, however, is management free to do as it wishes? A positive answer is given by the traditional "reserved rights" or "residual rights" approach to contract interpretation; all pre-existing rights not explicitly restricted are retained. A negative answer is given by some authorities who have argued that the onset of collective bargaining eliminated exclusive management rights and introduced a regime of joint employer–union decision making, at least insofar as major changes affecting the bargaining unit are concerned. The former has traditionally received more support than the latter. However, a gradual movement by arbitrators toward a more balanced position between the two views may be developing (Carrothers et al., 1986, 514; Arthurs et al., 1984, 275).

This section suggests that the period when the collective agreement is in effect is intended to be a period of peaceful co-existence and mutual accommodation, with voluntary and adjudicative mechanisms of the grievance process available to support this relationship. The following section considers the longer-term relationship.

PERMANENCE OF THE BARGAINING RELATIONSHIP

The bargaining relationship is governed by collective agreements of limited duration, rarely with a term of more than three years and typically shorter. Does this mean that not only the detailed terms of the relationship but the question of the continuity of the relationship itself is vulnerable to the relative power of the bargaining parties at such frequent intervals? If the corporate identity and structure of the employer changes, or if a sale of the business or its assets occurs, is the relationship ended? Under what circumstances may bargaining-unit members change bargaining agents, or even end the bargaining relationship? These questions and others (for example, the question of re-employment rights of strikers discussed above) raise important points about public policy concerning the continuity, stability and permanence of the relationship. Among the important possible changes are inter-union raids, employee requests to cancel a union's certification, contract language to extend its provisions after its expiration, unilateral employer efforts to change employment terms, and changes arising from sale of the business.

Raiding

Canadian statutes permit bargaining-unit employees to change bargaining agents by majority decision. This is a logical corollary of public policy's emphasis on individual employee choice. It may also reflect ambivalence toward the union, and concern about its possible exploitation or neglect of employees. Raiding activity (attempts by another union to supplant an existing bargaining agent) is fairly extensive.

Although the statutes recognize the right to change bargaining agents, they balance this right against other considerations. One consideration is the right of a newly certified union to have a brief grace period, free from other union rivals, in which to negotiate a first agreement and stabilize membership support. Another consideration is the legitimate interest of the employer and others in a stable, predictably conflict-free period when the collective agreement is in effect. For these reasons, raiding is permitted only during limited periods. A vote is almost always ordered in raiding situations, because membership evidence is likely to be overlapping and ambiguous. The successful raider typically inherits the existing collective agreement, but may in a number of jurisdictions give notice to the employer to begin negotiation of a new one.

Decertification

All Canadian jurisdictions provide for the possibility of decertification by a majority decision of bargaining-unit members (Wood and Kumar, 1985, 127–129; Arthurs et al., 1984, p. 206), again reflecting public policy's concern with majority employee freedom of choice. Such employee applications must be free of employer influence. Such cancellations of certification are relatively infrequent, compared to the number of new certifications granted.

After the Agreement Expires

Bridging Clauses

Agreements sometimes contain language providing that some or all of their terms will remain in effect after the expiry date, either for a predetermined term or until a renewal of the agreement is negotiated. Public policy has some ambivalence about such provisions. On the one hand, they provide some stability during negotiations in terms and conditions of employment and continued access to the grievance procedure. Thus they can reduce extraneous sources of stress during the contract renegotiation period, which is stressful enough in and of itself. On the other hand, such provisions can render the legality of the strike or lockout over contract renegotiation terms suspect, and might act as barriers to raiding or decertification efforts, which statutes sometimes tie to contract expiration dates. Such provisions are generally permitted, but limits are imposed on their interference with activities like strikes and raids.

Those who make and administer public policy also have some discomfort with the concept of a perpetual collective agreement (G. Adams, 1985, 692–694), perhaps because of its inconsistency with the obligation to bargain periodically, and the useful functions believed to be performed by such bargaining. The Supreme Court of Canada has held that continuation clauses cannot permanently bar access to the strike and lockout (Arthurs et al., 1984, 220).

Post-impasse Changes by the Employer

"It appears to be recognized that the provisions of the collective agreement relating to the terms and conditions of employment of the employees in the bargaining unit survive both the expiry of the collective agreement and the period of the statutory freeze" (Arthurs et al., 1984, 277). Whether they survive as individual contracts, enforceable in the courts, or are still enforceable through arbitration, is not as clear. In any event, the employer obligation to bargain in good faith is not ended by the expiration of the agreement. Therefore some "good faith" constraint on its freedom to make unilateral changes exists. Employer efforts to offer revised employment terms unilaterally to employees after bargaining impasse appear to be meeting with judicial disapproval. For example, the British Columbia Court of Appeal in 1986 upheld a lower court's overturning of a labour board approval of this practice. Such unilateral action may be more acceptable legally if accompanied by a lockout.

Successorship and Related Employers

(See G. Adams, 1985, 398–436.)

Successorship

When a business is sold do the collective bargaining rights of the bargaining agent survive? Do the rights of employees under the existing collective agreement survive? Does the collective agreement and the obligation to bargain with the union survive a change in the identity of the employer? Canadian pubic policy generally answers such questions in the affirmative. It recognizes the employer's right to dispose of all or part of a business, but it balances this right against the rights that employees may have accumulated. Statutes, labour relations boards and courts see the bargaining relationship as attaching to the business rather than to a specific owner.

"The possibility of sham transfers from one commercial entity to another in order to circumvent collective bargaining obligations" (G. Adams, 1985, 401) is one concern to which successorship legislation directs itself. Its concerns, however, go well beyond this need to prevent corporate evasions of the statutory duty to bargain, and may reflect an implicit theory of union and employee property rights in the bargaining relationship. "The need to protect employees from sudden changes in their bargaining rights" is recognized by public policy. Successor clauses in statutes give added stability and permanence to bargaining relationships (Arthurs et al., 1984, 201). They also relieve unions of the task of seeking new certifications. The bargaining relationship is contemplated as a relatively permanent one, endable only under certain limited conditions, such as cancellation of the union's certification following disappearance of the union's majority support or the permanent disappearance of the work situation.

Transfers and dispositions of businesses, of parts of businesses, and of assets can take many different forms, of varying degrees of indirectness or complexity. Because of concern to preserve the continuing character of bargaining relationships, "a broad and liberal interpretation" of what constitutes a sale or disposal of a business or portion thereof "has been consistently adopted by the provincial and federal boards" (G. Adams, 1985, 401). Boards look beyond formal corporate identities and the legal formats used to the underlying economic realities (Arthurs et al., 1984, 202). In general, if a substantial continuity is found in the nature of the business conducted, the work activities involved, and the operations or functions engaged in, a successorship will be held to exist, regardless of the form used to transfer or dispose of the business. Such a successorship finding means that the new management inherits the bargaining obligations of its predecessor.

Transfers need not be direct to be held successorships. The fact that a business was in receivership when purchased, for example, would not guarantee the purchaser against the possibility of being found to be a successor employer. There are even circumstances under which the receiver could be found to be successor employer. "Continuity" in a business can survive a substantial period during which the business is not operated. The sale or transfer need not be of the entire business, as long as it is of a separate and identifiable part that is a viable, functioning entity in itself.

There is some variation among jurisdictions in the extent of protection they give the bargaining relationship against changes in ownership. Quebec and the federal jurisdiction, for example, provide more extensive protection than do Ontario and British Columbia.

Subcontracting. Like disposal of a business, subcontracting can abruptly end many employees' accumulated rights and can severely reduce, and in the extreme eliminate, the bargaining relationship itself. The Quebec and federal jurisdictions have often found that successorship can arise from subcontracting. Replacement of one subcontractor by another can lead to the successful rival being held a successor employer, where similar activities are engaged in. The Ontario and British Columbia boards, however, have been more reluctant to find successorship in such situations, where substantial transfer of assets or management skills are absent.

"Intermingling." There are situations in which the employees of the business that is sold find themselves performing similar work to, sometimes side by side with, continuing employees of the purchaser. Where each group is represented by a different bargaining agent, a clash of interests can arise. Labour relations boards usually prefer to combine the former bargaining units into one, with the union representing the larger number of employees becoming the bargaining agent for the new unit. Difficult seniority problems may arise; most boards have the power to modify seniority rights in such intermingling situations. Where the purchaser's employees are not unionized, boards also consider the degree of support the previous company's bargaining agent has in the new situation, in deciding whether to cancel bargaining rights or to extend them to embrace the previously unorganized employees.

Related Employers

Statutory provisions covering related employers closely interact with those covering successor employers. Legally separate businesses may in practice be so closely related that work, assets, management, and even individual employees may be transferred easily across corporate borders. Even when no employer motive to evade collective bargaining responsibilities (for example, by shifting work to a non-unionized company it controls) exists, such interactions could have substantial consequences for labour relations. Therefore, boards usually have the authority to find that two businesses are related for industrial relations purposes. Such findings can have serious consequences for certification campaigns or for determining whether the second company can be legally picketed.

Labour relations boards, before they rule that two businesses are related, require that a number of conditions be met (Arthurs et al., 1984, 200–201). First, the two businesses should be related through similarities in product market, technology, employee skills, functional integration, or employee interchange. Second, the two should be under common control and direction (in practice, operations co-ordinated, financed, or controlled by a common individual or group). Third, there should be a sound industrial relations purpose to be served by making such a ruling. For example, boards would normally find the preservation of established bargaining rights against erosion to be a legitimate purpose, but would not normally find a union's attempt to sweep into its bargaining unit the reluctant employees of an associated employer via obtaining a related employer ruling to be legitimate.

Summary

Canadian public policy puts few obstacles in the way of changes in the identity of the bargaining parties. It does, however, subject changes that might terminate or seriously damage the bargaining relationship to searching examination. Bargaining rights and bargaining units can survive collective agreement expiration and changes in ownership; they can pierce the veil of corporate identity and persist in the face of a number of managerial initiatives. On balance, public policy's preference for collective bargaining is shown almost as much in what it does to protect it as is shown in what it does to bring it into being.

FUTURE OF PUBLIC POLICY CONCERNING COLLECTIVE BARGAINING

At the beginning of the chapter three questions were posed:

1. What is public policy's position regarding the desirability of collective bargaining, compared to alternative ways of determining wages and working conditions?
2. How does public policy balance the interests of employers, employees, unions, and other parties?
3. How much, and in what ways, does public policy restrict employers and unions in the use of their power?

With regard to the first question, the chapter suggests that a strong preference for collective bargaining exists. The answer to the second question is more complex. In general, the interest balancing reflects a strong protection of employee collective bargaining rights even when some damage to employer interests is involved. However, that balancing also reflects a serious concern that people and organizations not directly involved in a bargaining relationship should not be injured by it. With regard to the third question, public policy generally permits employers and unions to use their bargaining power to achieve favourable collective agreement terms, but restricts use of power in many other situations. Use of power to compel or prevent the creation of the bargaining relationship or to improve on bargained agreement terms during the life of the agreement are among the prohibited actions.

The public policy summarized above is not one on which everyone agrees, nor is it one that is guaranteed to survive unchanged. This last section has two parts. The first lists some areas of collective bargaining law that might be affected by court rulings under the Charter of Rights. The second speculates about various alternative directions in which public policy on collective bargaining might turn in the future.

Charter Effects

The Charter of Rights and Freedoms was an important part of the Constitution Act of 1982. Relatively few issues on collective bargaining law have yet been taken through the court system to a definitive resolution.

Section 2 of the Charter lists among its "fundamental freedoms" freedom of expression, freedom of peaceful assembly, and freedom of association. Section 15 (1) states the rights to equal protection and equal benefit of the law.

These are substantial rights, but it is difficult to say exactly how substantial they are until considerable litigation has occurred. Among the ambiguities in defining the scope and impact of Charter language are both general and specific considerations (G. Adams, 1985, 139–152). Among the general considerations are the following:

1. The Charter limits actions of federal and provincial governments, rather than of private parties. Labour relations boards, Crown corporations, and municipalities are probably to be seen as creatures of the legislature and thus included. The degree to which universities, colleges and hospitals will be included is not yet clear.
2. The above rights are limited by Section 1's clause, "subject only to such reasonable limits prescribed by law as can be demonstrably justified in a free and democratic society." The manner in which the courts interpret such reasonable limits is crucial, and reflects the major policy responsibility the Charter has imposed upon the judiciary.
3. Section 33 permits provincial governments to opt out of the limitations of a number of Charter sections. It is not yet clear how extensively this freedom will be exercised in collective bargaining matters.
4. To what extent can organizations like employers or trade unions claim the rights guaranteed to individuals?
5. How interventionist an orientation will the Canadian judiciary take in interpreting and applying the Charter? Will that orientation be closer to the United States judiciary's past activism in constitutional matters, or to the Canadian traditions of judicial self-restraint?

More specifically, labour relations considerations include the following:

1. Does "freedom of association" mean that the legality of the following is questionable?
   • compulsory membership provisions of collective agreements or compulsory dues payment provisions of statutes or agreements;
   • union expenditures of dues monies for purposes other than collective bargaining;

- exclusion of agricultural workers, professionals and domestics from the "employee" protections of collective bargaining statutes;
- wage control legislation or strike bans (on the grounds that freedom of association is an empty right without the ability of trade unions to implement that right).

Does "freedom of association" mean freedom to refrain from association? If so, would it protect unionists' refusal to work on job sites with employees of non-union contractors (Arthurs et al., 1984, 258)?

2. Does "freedom of expression" mean that statutory limitations on what an employer can say during a unionization campaign are illegal?

3. Do "freedom of peaceful assembly" and "freedom of expression" prohibit statutory or common-law limitations of the right to picket? Carrothers et al. (1986, 711–720) argue that the Charter's effect will or at least should be that judicial attitudes toward picketing in general, and secondary picketing aimed at consumers in particular, change radically, and change in the direction of legalizing picketing over a much broader range of circumstances than before. However, Arthurs et al. (1984, 249) suggest that the courts will not substantially relax their limitations on picketing. Their guess is that regulation will be seen to be "reasonable limits...demonstrably justified...," in part because they support "a legislative scheme of orderly collective bargaining" or because they appear necessary to protect the interests of neutrals to the dispute.

4. Does Section 2's "freedom of conscience...,thought, [or] belief" protect the employee who refuses to handle goods from a non-union or struck plant? Does it protect bargaining-unit employees refusing to pay union dues in accordance with a collective agreement or in accordance with statutory language?

One change seems virtually certain. The judiciary, which had been playing a diminishing role in public policy over the course of the last four decades, will be playing a major role once again. The Charter will encourage appeals to the courts from labour relations board and arbitral decisions and court challenges of statutory language. The judiciary will be compelled to give meaning to "reasonable limits...demonstrably justified..." and much other language of a general character.

Does this return of the judiciary also suggest the return of the older attitudes of the courts, attitudes that generated much criticism regarding alleged conservative bias, insensitivity toward and ignorance of industrial relations, and stretching of inappropriate legal doctrines to apply to collective bargaining? Probably not. Today's judiciary is likely to continue its practice of viewing statutes and board decisions sympathetically and deferring reasonably to boards' special competence in collective bargaining matters. Nevertheless the potential for abrupt changes in policy and for inconsistency among courts in interpretation remains.

Future Directions in Public Policy

Risky though it is to speculate on the impact of the Charter, speculating on future shifts in public opinion and in the perceptions and values of lawmakers, labour board chairs and arbitrators is still riskier. Nevertheless, the alternative possibilities of public policy moving in an anti-collective bargaining and in a pro-collective bargaining direction are explored here.

Anti-collective bargaining possibilities include the following:

1. An increased respect for and weight given to market forces, combined with a growing perception of collective bargaining as an inhibitor of efficient adjustment to those market forces. This might be associated with a new prestige attributed to the entrepreneurial and executive functions. One variant of this might be the increasing desire to encourage the new, small, innovative business, combined with a feeling that existing collective bargaining law might discourage such enterprise.
2. A higher evaluation of individual, relative to collective, rights and interests.
3. A decreased perception of the strength of intraorganizational hierarchical power imbalances. This, combined with the previously mentioned possibility, might reduce the perceived urgency of and primacy of collective representation.
4. A decreased preference for collective bargaining, versus its alternatives. This could arise from an increased concern with the large number of employees who are not covered by collective bargaining and are not likely to be covered in the future. These fall roughly into two categories: first, the white-collar, professional, technical, and managerial employees in the private sector; and second, employees in what is often called the secondary or peripheral sector—the part-time, high-unemployment, low-paid, minority-group, female, very young or very old employees of small, highly vulnerable enterprises in highly competitive industries. Increased attention might be given to the first group because of its growing political influence and to the second group because of its obvious problems and needs. By now, the earlier belief that collective bargaining would expand to embrace these two groups has weakened. If their needs are to be addressed, public policy may increasingly look to statutory enactment as the appropriate weapon.

Benjamin Aaron, an American authority on labour law, suggests that "what seems to be occurring in the United States is a secular trend away from voluntarism and toward interventionism of the kind long established in Western Europe" (Aaron, 1984, 53). The similar Canadian collective bargaining law may undergo a movement toward the Western European model at an appreciably faster rate than that of the United States (R. Adams, 1985, 126, 142, 144). The law on such matters as occupational health and safety, employment discrimination, and unfair dismissal may become more central to public policy and the law on collective bargaining less central.

Such shifts away from collective bargaining may involve a shift among union functions, rather than a decline in union functions. Unions, as in Western Europe, might play more of a political and less of a collective bargaining role, moving more toward a macro-level "representative institution" and "social partner" role. This could be associated with a change in the character of unions, in the direction of becoming larger but less workplace-focused organizations.

Pro-collective bargaining possibilities include the following:

1. A continuation of the existing trend toward more imaginative, vigorous interpretation and extrapolation of implications of existing statutory language by boards and arbitrators, with its twin corollaries of increasing employee and union rights and increasing legalism and complexity in the collective bargaining system. This could be associated with a reduced public policy commitment to voluntarism and an increasing role being seen for adjudication in guaranteeing employee and union collective bargaining rights. The initiative of the Ontario board in recent years in expanding the scope of the bargaining obligation might be a forerunner of such a trend.
2. A softening of public policy's insistence on the arm's-length, adversarial distance between union and employer. The increasing interest in employer–employee co-operation and work redesign, rising demands for statutory coverage from employee groups that include presently excluded managerial employees, and the growing respect for Japanese and other management-influenced variants of trade unionism may contribute to this.
3. A wide variety of possible shifts within the pro-collective bargaining direction are conceivable to increase the importance relative to the other two actors of unions, employers, or governments, reflecting changing views of the relative legitimacy and relative contribution to the public interest of the three. Public sector labour law may be especially volatile, with changes either toward or away from the private sector model likely to be frequent.

Whatever future public policy may be, an important part of its change is likely to be achieved through a building upon and modifying of the existing body of collective bargaining law.

SOURCES AND RECOMMENDED READINGS

Documentation, citation of statutory and decision sources, and further analysis concerning most of the matters referred to in this chapter can be found in such standard sources as G. Adams; Arthurs, Carter, and Glasbeek; and Carrothers, Palmer, and Rayner. The first is an unusually comprehensive, insightful, and well-written reference work on Canadian collective bargaining law and its application by labour boards. The second is a good, shorter treatment of the same topics. The third differs from the first two in its greater attention to statutory language and judicial reasoning and lesser attention to current board interpretations. It also provides a more extensive, more vigorous and more explicitly normative critique of that judicial reasoning, plus advice on the direction in which public policy should move.

Other useful sources include:

Butterworth's *Canadian Labour Relations Boards Reports*, containing the texts of the leading decisions of labour boards across Canada.

Some jurisdictions (for example, Canada, Ontario, British Columbia) publish the complete texts of a much larger proportion of their decisions than appear in Butterworths. Some commercial services provide summaries of published decisions as well. Annual reports of the boards are an important source of information on their operations and policy positions.

Labour Arbitration Cases, published by Canada Law Book, Inc., provides the text of leading grievance arbitration cases. *Canadian Labour Arbitration*, second edition, by David Brown and David Beatty, provides a good starting point for those using this source. Another good survey of grievance arbitration is E. E. Palmer's *Collective Agreement Arbitration in Canada*, second edition.

Labour Law News and *Labour Arbitration News* are lively newsletters of particular interest to trade unionists.

Summaries of legislative changes and of the legislative status quo appear in the Queen's Industrial Relations Centre's *Current Industrial Relations Scene* annual volumes.

BIBLIOGRAPHY

Aaron, B. (1984), "Future trends in industrial relations law." *Industrial Relations* 23: 52–57.

Adams, G. W. (1985), *Canadian Labour Law: A Comprehensive Text.* Aurora, Ont.: Canada Law Book.

Adams, R. J. (1985), "Industrial relations and the economic crisis: Canada moves toward Europe." In Juris, H., M. Thompson, and W. Daniels (eds.), *Industrial Relations in a Decade of Economic Change*. Madison, WI: Industrial Relations Research Association, 115–149.

Arthurs, H. W., Carter, D. D., and Glasbeek, H. J. (1984). *Labour Law and Industrial Relations in Canada* (2nd ed.). Toronto: Butterworths.

Baggaley, C. D. (1981), "A century of labour regulation in Canada." Working Paper No. 19. Ottawa: Economic Council of Canada.

British Columbia Labour Relations Board, *Annual Report 1986.*

Canada Labour Relations Board, *Annual Report 1984-85.*

Carrothers, A. W. R., Palmer, E. E., and Raynor, W. B. (1986), *Collective Bargaining Law in Canada* (2nd ed.). Toronto: Butterworths.

Carter, D. D. (1982), "Collective bargaining legislation in Canada." In Anderson, J. C. and M. Gunderson (eds.), *Union–management Relations in Canada.* Don Mills, Ontario: Addison-Wesley, pp. 29–45.

―――― (1983), "The duty to bargain in good faith: Does it affect the content of bargaining?" In Swan, K. S. and K. E. Swinton (eds.), *Studies in Labour Law.* Toronto, Ontario: Butterworths, pp. 35–53.

Gall, P. A. (1984), "Regulation of picketing under the B.C. labour code: Some cracks in the institutional foundation." In Weiler, J. M. and P. A. Gall (eds.), *The Labour Code of British Columbia in the 1980s.* Calgary: Carswell, pp. 133-156.

Ontario Labour Relations Board, *Annual Report 1982-83.*

Solomon, N. A. (1985), "The negotiation of first agreements under the Canada Labour Code: An empirical study." *Relations industrielles* 40: 458–472.

Task Force on Program Review (1986), *Improved Program Delivery: Citizenship, Labour and Immigration.* A study team report. Ottawa: Minister of Supply and Services Canada.

Weiler, P. C. (1980), *Reconcilable Differences: New Directions in Canadian Labour Law.* Toronto: Carswell.

Wood, W. D. and Kumar, P. (1985), *The Current Industrial Relations Scene in Canada, 1985.* Kingston, Ont.: Industrial Relations Centre, Queen's University.

4

Union Growth: Dimensions, Policies, and Politics

JAMES THWAITES

The purpose of this chapter is to furnish the reader with a basic overview of the growth and development of unionism in Canada. It is an attempt to answer some of the whats, hows, and whys of the union trajectory traced in this country, in line with the "transactional model of industrial relations" developed by Sethi and Dimmock in Chapter 2. Its primary utility, in an era of waning militancy and union-bashing, is to provide a neutral account complete with the objective data necessary to help measure and understand this phenomenon properly, depicting the dynamic strategic development of the Canadian labour movement.

The statistics cited are generally those of Labour Canada from 1911 to 1986. Most of them are to be found in the Department's publication now called the *Directory of Labour Organizations in Canada*. Its name changed slightly over the period as follows:

1911–1974/75: *Report on Labour Organization in Canada*
1976/77–1978: *Labour Organizations in Canada*
1980–1987 (+): *Directory of Labour Organizations in Canada*

One of labour's constant demands during the nineteenth century was for a reliable bank of statistics on subjects pertinent to the world of work. At the time labour looked to government as the logical body to amass, treat, and publish such information. That request seems to have been very much in the minds of the founders of Canada's Department of Labour, for its publications from 1901, or 1911 on—according to the case—were amply filled with statistics. From the *Labour Gazette*, to the *Report on Strikes and Lockouts in Canada*, and the *Report on Labour Organization in Canada*, interested readers were treated to statistics on membership, numbers of unions, affiliation, strikes and lockouts, by number and intensity (numbers involved, duration) as well as settlements, wage rates, duration of the working day, government contracts, the impact of legislation, and a variety of comparative material on the situation in other countries. (Analytical articles were also added.) The list was almost endless.

More to the point for our immediate concerns, the Department went to great pains, with the assistance of its labour correspondents, to ferret out and publish information on the labour movement, its distribution, and its composition—by union, by central, by city, by province, etc. The resulting data has enabled the analysis presented here.

Unfortunately, however, a problem came up. As labour unions appeared, disappeared, grew, diminished, affiliated, and disaffiliated, coherent statistics became harder to keep. In addition, the needs of the day—be they governmental, union, or business—evolved and likely dictated new or different policies to the Department of Labour. The result was probably comprehensible at the time, but has created a lot of confusion for us in the present. New ways of looking at subjects inevitably affected the statistics compiled, and statistical methods changed, all of which left us with a "checkered" record of the past. But a record, nevertheless.

This is a roundabout way of saying that our statistical evidence cannot be considered complete. Every effort will be made, however, to draw the maximum from what does exist, and can be strung together in an intelligible way.

Material other than statistical will be drawn from the numerous secondary sources, reference works, and occasional primary sources available. This aspect of the analysis has been immensely facilitated by the production of scholars during the past fifteen or twenty years. A considerable and varied body of research has been published, but it cannot claim to be either all-encompassing or necessarily undisputed in its findings. Where applicable, however, it will certainly be used to the fullest advantage.

There have been several attempts at model building as regards union growth, many of them by economists but not exclusively. The most recent appears in an article by Pradeep Kumar and Bradley Dow (1986). The authors come to the following conclusion:

> To understand fully "why" and "how" unions grow, further research is required using various measures of union activities...and a more thorough analysis of both external and internal environmental factors in union growth...much work remains to be done on the importance of such hard-to-quantify factors as trade union leadership, the structure of labour organizations, organizational resources, approaches, philosophies, etc., as well as the management behaviour and human resource strategies. A more clear understanding of these external and internal environmental factors in our view can be gained by micro-level research, that is by studying the behaviour and growth of individual unions; analyzing why individual workers join unions and what members expect from their unions and leaders; or by exploring the profile of union behaviour and collective bargaining relationship in individual sectors and industries.[1]

What Kumar and Dow propose is very interesting, but a hefty amount of work. It is certainly impossible in an article of general nature, and could better be tackled in a book or (with Forsey's experience behind us[2]) a series of studies that could eventually be brought together in a Mintzber-gian-style analysis.[3] One conclusion that can be drawn for present purposes is the intrinsic value of studies based on "micro-level research" and on "individual unions" in particular. The present chapter will be a modest step in that direction, rather than another model-building attempt. However, because its stated purpose is to provide a basic over-view, it will have to deal simultaneously with the specific and the general view. Its approach will be historical.

TYPOLOGY AND TERMINOLOGY REGARDING UNIONS IN CANADA

Unionism in Canada has evolved generally in a context of duality, and can be analyzed with reference to dual concepts. In this way, a series of conceptual tandems can each describe Canadian union organizations: national and international, craft and industrial, public sector and private sector, affiliated and unaffiliated (or independent), as well as confessional and non-confessional. An attempt might even be made to divide it into conventional and radical unions, but with considerably less success, for the terms are quite relative.

The first pair of terms refers to the origin and organizational links maintained by unions. On the whole, international unionism had its origins in the United States and maintained organizational links with its parent bodies in that country—a case in point is the International Associa-tion of Machinists and Aerospace Workers (IAMAW) whose Canadian locals remain linked to the federation or home office in Washington, D.C. in addition to their membership in the Canadian Labour Congress (CLC) in Ottawa. There is a major exception to the U.S. rule. British internation-als also operated in Canada for several decades, an example being the Amalgamated Society of Engineers (ASE). National unionism, by contrast, existed exclusively within Canada and had no foreign organizational links, for example the Canadian Brotherhood of Railway Employees (CBRE). In exceptional cases, national organizations were foreign "inspired," but maintained no links with foreign organizations. The best example is probably the Canadian and Catholic Confederation of Labour (CCCL) that had conceptual affinities with similar movements in Germany and Belgium, without, however, any indication of official institutional ties. The Workers' Unity League (WUL) is an isolated borderline case, because of its official links with the Communist Party of Canada, the CPC itself being linked to Moscow. National unionism, by contrast, existed exclusively within Canada, having no foreign institutional links and probably no desire for foreign expansion.

The second tandem refers to the particular skill composition of unions, craft or industrial. The first group includes organizations based initially on a single craft (trade) such as the International Typographical Union (ITU). Already evident in some early cases, craft organizations in more recent times have often turned to an associated craft formula— grouping crafts (trades) that were inter-related. Early examples include the Bricklayers, Masons and Plasterers' International Union of America, and the International Brotherhood of Blacksmiths, Drop Forgers and Helpers. Later, organizations such as the ITU, mentioned above, have evolved this way. The second group is composed of union organizations that decided to put aside reference to particular skills, and bring together workers at various skill levels. Theoretically, this combined everyone from the totally unskilled manual worker to the highly skilled craftsman (tradesman) within the same union. Two cases that come to mind are the United Autoworkers of America (UAW), and the Canadian Union of Public Employees (CUPE). Predominant in the beginning and for many decades, craft unionism would give way to industrial unionism on a grand scale after World War II. The two forms of organization were based on two different conceptions of the best—that is, the most effective—way of organizing labour in industrial society to favour labour's goals.

The third tandem pertains to the areas of the economy in which workers are employed, public or private. In reality, the first group is subdivided into two. The *public sector proper* includes direct government employees—that is, the civil service at the federal, provincial, and even municipal levels (although the last is ambiguous because of the early and continuing presence of certain private sector unions). The *parapublic sector* includes indirect government employees, and is particularly associated with the social affairs areas (hospitals, etc.) and the educational sphere. There is also another group associated with the public sector, often called the *peripublic sector*, comprising the employees of Crown corporations such Hydro Québec. The unionized employees of such organizations, however, are usually affiliated with predominantly private sector unions. The private sector then is the rest, everything that is not governmental in either the direct or the indirect sense used above. The exceptions, as indicated, are in the areas of municipal government and Crown corporations.[4] Unionism began with the private sector and thrived there. The public and parapublic sectors, however, have long been partially unionized. (In some cases, the barrier between private and public sectors was crossed by accident, as in the case of the CBRE's members employed on the Grand Trunk Railway system which went bankrupt during World War I and became the government-owned Canadian National Railway system.) Their fullest impact, nevertheless, has been felt since the mid-1960s, from the passage of legislation permitting the massive affiliation of the various civil services.

The fourth tandem is used here to indicate affiliation or non-affiliation to Canadian union central organizations. By central organizations is meant those union structures which bring together the parent bodies (or federations) of local unions. (As a case in point, local unions of the Public Service Alliance of Canada (PSAC) are affiliated to their parent body (federation), the home office of the PSAC. The PSAC in turn is a member of the union central, the Canadian Labour Congress (CLC), which also includes many other such parent bodies as CUPE and NUPGE. In the case of union members of a U.S.-based parent body (federation), the locals are members of the Canadian central. This is true, for example, of the IAMAW, the ITU, and the USWA.) The category "affiliation," on the other hand, refers to all unions that have institutionally linked themselves to Canadian centrals, regardless of their specific national or international origins. For the purposes of present analysis, therefore, international organizations affiliated to foreign centrals, but unaffiliated to Canadian centrals, have been included in the unaffiliated category—the main criterion being Canadian central affiliation. The phenomenon of non-affiliation has always been part of the union reality in Canada—the rationality of which has been explored in the present context by Delorme and Veilleux.[5] It is of particular concern today because of its current extent, as will be seen later.

The fifth tandem is particularly lop-sided because the "confessional" category has had limited application and is now strictly a thing of the past. It applies mainly to what Labour Canada first called the Confederation of Catholic Workers of Canada (CCWC) and later the Canadian and Catholic Confederation of Labour (CCCL).[6] But it also applies to the predecessors of the CCCL (or CCWC), such as the Fédération ouvrière mutuelle du nord (FOMN). The other side of the tandem covers every other union movement that the country has ever known, obviously the vast majority. Its greatest impact has been on the province of Quebec, where its militant secularized successor continues to thrive.

This brings us to the doubtful sixth tandem, which is seductive but of limited use. The problem is how to define radical and conventional.[7] If radical means merely challenging the status quo, virtually all unions were and are radical in virtue of their programs if nothing else, but also often in terms of thought and actions. If radical is seen in terms of the extreme right or left, the former has been non-existent in Canada. The latter has appeared in certain movements: the Industrial Workers of the World (IWW), active particularly before World War I, the One Big Union (OBU), active particularly after 1919, and the Workers' Unity League (WUL), active from 1929 to 1935. Other unions have passed through periods of radicalism, for example: the Canadian affiliates of the Congress of Industrial

Organizations (CIO), the Canadian Congress of Labour (CCL), the CCCL and its successor, the Confederation of National Trades Unions (CNTU). From the time of the October Crisis (1970) in Quebec until the defeat of Bourassa Liberals (1976), the bulk of the labour movement there was in revolt against the government of the day, and therefore "radical" by contemporary definition.

On the other hand, if "conventional" merely means engaging in the industrial relations process established in a given period, including the various pressure tactics permitted, the vast majority of the labour movement in Canada conforms to this definition. Even movements like the IWW and the OBU had recourse to perfectly legal mechanisms. If "conventional" means generally "not rocking the boat," and selling out to management, it has very little utility as an analytic category. In fact, perhaps the greatest use of "radical" and "conventional" as categories may be to help us define diametrically opposed forms of action—if taken in their most extreme forms—between which is situated the bulk of the union movement in Canada.

Figure 4.1 summarizes the essence of the above section, with the exclusion of the "radical–conventional" terms of analysis.

UNION STRUCTURES AND NOMENCLATURE

The first and most obvious rule about union nomenclature as used is that it cannot be taken at face value. Locals call themselves unions and assemblies as well as locals; union federations call themselves associations, unions, amalgamated societies as well as federations; central bodies call themselves unions, congresses, assemblies, and confederations, as well as centrals. To make matters worse, the provincial and municipal (or regional) units established by centrals to co-ordinate activities at those levels also can have names that overlap with other union usage.

An additional complication arises from the exact significance given to such concepts as "the union central." Gérard Dion's definition is very broad. The central, he explains, is a:

> Groupement de syndicats et autres corps syndicaux intermédiaires au niveau d'un Etat. (Grouping of unions and other intermediary union bodies at the State [Government?] level.)[8]

Dion's definition would permit us to include organizations like the Quebec Federation of Labour (QFL), the Confederation of National Trades Unions (CNTU) and the Canadian Labour Congress (CLC) in the same category, although there are clearly important distinctions to be made between the QFL and the two others. Labour Canada seems, over the years, to have varied its own definition of the central. Thus, at one point the Centrale de l'enseignement du Québec (CEQ) is considered to be a

Figure 4.1
Union Centrals and Their Classification: 1873–1987

Classification	ACCL (1927–1940)	CCCL (1921–1960)	CCL (1940–1956)	CCU (1969 +)	CCWC (see CCCL)	CEQ (1974 +)	CFL (1908–1927)	CFL (1936– ?)	CFL (1982 +)	CIO (1939 +)	CLC (1956 +)	CLU (1873–1878)	CNTU (1960 +)	CSD (1972 +)	IWW (1905– ?)	KL (1881– ?)	NTLC (1902–1908)	OBU (1919–1956)	TLC (1883–1902)	TLC (1902–1956)	Unaffiliated Locals & Federations (independent locals and federations)
	Union Centrals																				
National	X	X	X	X		X	X	X			X	X	X	X			X	X	X		X
International			X						X	X	X	X			X	X			X	X	X
Craft	X	X	X			X	X	X	X		X	X	X	X			X		X	X	X
Industrial	X	X	X	X		X	X	X		X	X		X		X	X	X	X	X		X
Public Sector	X		X			X					X		X						X	X	X
Private Sector	X	X	X	X			X	X	X	X	X	X	X	X	X	X	X	X	X	X	X
Confessional		X																			
Non-confessional	X		X	X		X	X	X	X	X	X	X	X	X	X	X	X	X	X	X	X

"central," although it was excluded previously and classified as an "unaf-filiated *union*."All this difficulty is compounded by the fact that as an adjective, "union" is used to apply to everything.

The writer has taken the liberty of imposing his own ad hoc terminol-ogy on the "union" movement to clarify the present chapter, for example, the description of affiliated and unaffiliated unions. What is proposed is to speak of the part of the organization level closest to the membership as the local, and the level above it, which brings together all locals of the same composition, as the federation. In this way, a CUPE *local*, like the one that groups Laval University's maintenance and secretarial staff, is affili-ated to its *federation*, the Canadian Union of Public Employees (CUPE). CUPE in turn is affiliated along with various other federations to a con-federal structure or union *central*, the Canadian Labour Congress (CLC).

The type of inter-union role that the CLC plays at the federal level, in large part political, can be played at the provincial and municipal (or regional) level because of the governments situated at those levels. The structure at the provincial government level can be called a *provincial federation*, and that at the municipal (or regional) level can be called a municipal (or regional) *council*. Examples, respectively, would be the Quebec Federation of Labour (QFL) and the Quebec Labour Council (QLC) for Quebec City. The role of these two levels is to co-ordinate the activities of member associations from various federations operating within the territorial limits defined, at the provincial or municipal (regional) level as required. Authority on the first side of the organiza-tions described comes from the bottom up, while on the other it goes from the top down. Figure 4.2 provides an illustration of what is being advanced.

This terminology is based on the structures of a current example, the CLC. The institution is, however, highly representative for two reasons— its substantial membership, and the conservation it has made of past, even distant past, structures and terminology. By and large the type of structure described applies to all mainstream and even secondary movements. There is some divergence on the way the structure is operated in a given central, or even between Quebec CLC practice, and that in the other provinces and territories. But that issue is not directly relevant to the present discussion.

THE CHRONOLOGICAL RECORD

From its distant origins until the present, the union movement in Canada has had its ups and downs, but the general pattern as revealed in Figure 4.3 (1911–1986) is growth, in spite of the relative leveling out of the inter-war period. Figures 4.4 and 4.5 (1921–1985) reveal that this general numerical increase is also verifiable with certain modifications when the

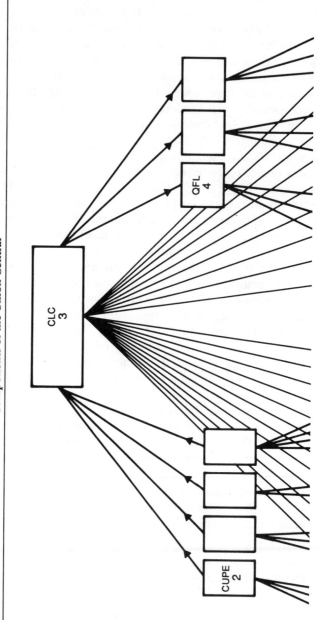

Figure 4.2
Components of the Union Central

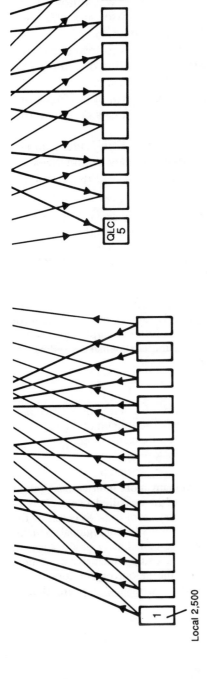

Local 2,500

QLC 5

Legend: 1 Local—example, loc. 2,500 (CUPE)
2 Federation—example, (CUPE)
3 Central (Confederation)—example, CLC
4 Provincial Federation—example, QFL
5 Municipal (Regional) Council—example, QLC
▲ Source(s) of authority

Design: **Service des ressources pédagogiques, Université Laval, Québec.**

figures for union membership are compared with those of the total civilian workforce as well as of the total non-agricultural paid workforce.

The years from 1901 to 1921, not included here, but included in other Labour Canada statistics—on the rise of the Trades and Labour Congress of Canada (TLC)—revealed a steady increase. This was followed by a percentage drop generally during the 1920s and 1930s and a renewed increase from the beginning of the 1940s. The next period of percentage drop is situated from the late fifties to the mid-sixties, followed in turn by a period of increase. The latter terminated by a leveling off after 1978 or 1979.

Those are the bare bones of the pattern of growth of unionism over the past eighty-five years. To go beyond them requires a certain knowledge of what was going on within the movement.

Labour's beginnings go back to the early nineteenth century, and for these beginnings no reliable statistics exist. Forsey summarizes the developments of these years in three sub-periods, as follows, first 1816–1859:

> ...the first period, down to 1859, may be described as that of purely local craft unions of skilled workers. But one has to add at once that the first international union, the Amalgamated Society of Engineers (British), set up its first Canadian branch in Montreal, as early as 1853, and that there were a few unions of unskilled workers, such as the Ship Labourers (Longshoremen) of Saint John, founded in 1849, and Quebec, founded in 1857. None the less, nearly all the unions down to 1859 were purely local, without any formal ties even with others in the same city or town: and nearly all of them were made up of skilled craftsmen or tradesmen, such as printers, carpenters, cabinetmakers, masons, stonecutters, painters, blacksmiths, shoemakers, sailmakers, shipwrights, caulkers, bakers, and tailors.

then 1859–1880:

> The second period...is marked by the entry of a series of international unions (both British and American), and by the setting up of the first local central organizations and the first national central organization.

and finally 1881–1902:

> The third...is characterized by the entry of many more international unions (all American); by widespread organization of the unskilled; by the effective spread of the movement all across the country, from coast to coast; by the reorganization of the old local central bodies [municipal or regional councils] and the creation of many new ones; by the establishment of a permanent national central body; and by the existence of a single inclusive movement which took in every possible kind of genuine labour organization; local, provincial, national, international, Canadian, British, American, skilled, unskilled, of one occupation or many.[9]

Figure 4.3
Total Union Membership in Canada, 1911–1986

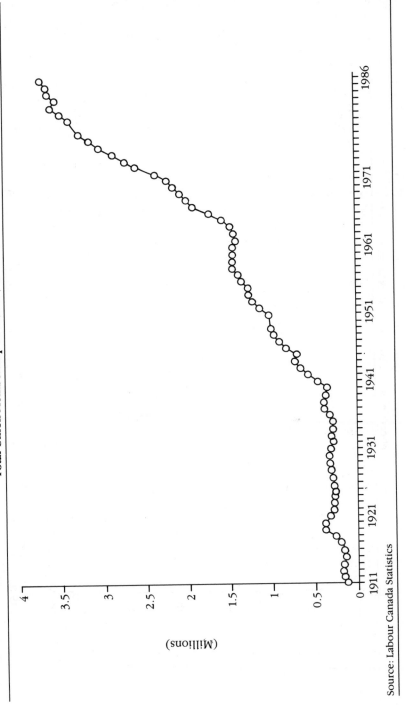

(Millions)

Source: Labour Canada Statistics

Figure 4.4
Union Membership as % of Total Civ. Workforce, 1921–85

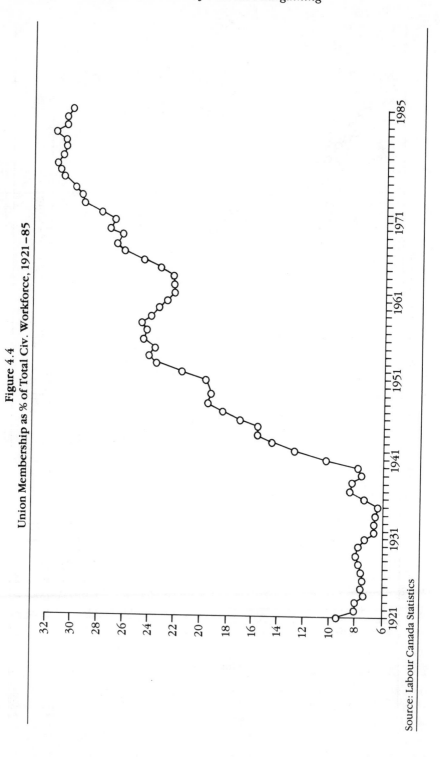

Source: Labour Canada Statistics

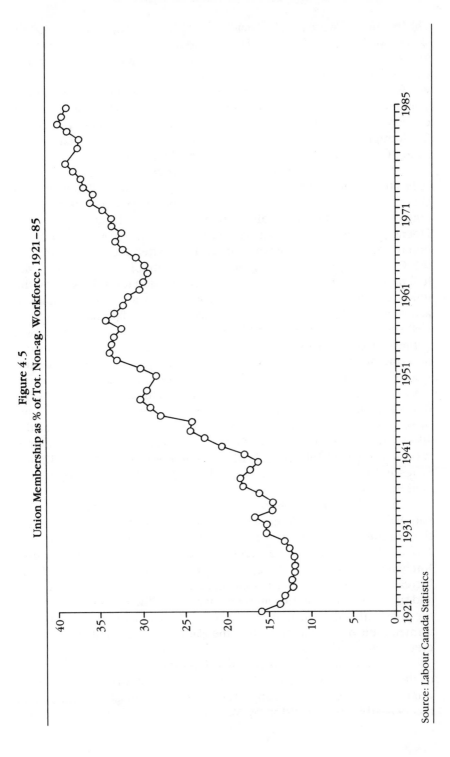

Figure 4.5
Union Membership as % of Tot. Non-ag. Workforce, 1921–85

Source: Labour Canada Statistics

The first unions were purely Canadian and purely local, formed of mainly skilled workers in craft unions. The second source drawn on by Canadians was the British craft unions, established in the Mother Country and exported or brought to Canada by British immigrants. The third source was from the United States. It included both craft and industrial unions. Thus the first two conceptual tandems were in place by the end of the last century. The second sub-period is particularly noteworthy for its successful attempt to put together a first-ever union central, the Canadian Labour Union (CLU) in 1873, subsequent to an equally important event, the first concerted effort at eliminating the legal restrictions on union activities. In fact the sequence was: a nine-hour strike by the Toronto Typographical Union—declared illegal as in restraint of trade following protests by the employer in question (who also happened to be the head of the federal Liberal parliamentary opposition, George Brown); imprisonment of the union leadership in Toronto; an irate and well-attended labour march on the Ontario Legislature; the adoption of favourable legislation by the federal Conservative Party under John A. Macdonald; followed by the union decision to launch a central organization and include political action as one of its key objectives.[10] (This may sound familiar!)

The central founded would be short lived, a victim of the severe depression of the 1870s. It would, however, reappear like the phoenix in a new, and henceforth permanent, form at the beginning of the 1880s and would be confirmed subsequently after certain initial difficulties as the Trades and Labour Congress of Canada (TLC). This latter central was the direct ancestor of today's Canadian Labour Congress, although there have been numerous changes in the composition of the organzation since the 1880s. One of the movements which had a particular impact at the time was the Knights of Labour (KL), whose central was located in the United States and whose form of action was decidedly industrial as opposed to craft.[11]

The tripartite composition of the labour movement (national; international and industrial; international and craft) would be challenged for the first time in a serious way during the years preceding the Trades and Labour Congress' Berlin convention of 1902 (Berlin was the name of Kitchener, Ontario, at the time). During the Berlin convention itself, the increasingly powerful international craft unions dominated the meeting and succeeded in expelling all their adversaries: the national unions and the international industrial unions (KL). A year later the adversaries formed their own, smaller central, the National Trades and Labour Congress of Canada (NTLC).[12]

About the same time, other forms of unionism appeared. Subsequent to the publication of a Papal Encyclical *Rerum Novarum*, which gave Roman Catholics the seal of approval to participate in labour unions, and the 1901 arbitration decision by Msgr Begin (Bishop of Quebec City), who recommended Christianizing unions to the faithful, experiments with confessional unionism began—first with the Fédération ouvrière de Chicoutimi (FOC). A few years later in 1905, a radical industrial central with its home office in Chicago launched a Canadian wing, particularly in the western provinces under the name the Industrial Workers of the World (IWW). The IWW's constituency was the immigrant worker, working in often precarious conditions on railway construction projects, lumbering, stevedoring, etc.[13]

The TLC numerically was, nevertheless, the more powerful body and was treated as such in the Department of Labour's analyses. Its growth rate for the years 1901–1921 (Figure 4.6) was impressive by any standards. Even by 1913, on the eve of World War I, it had already achieved a 700 percent thirteen-year growth rate. By 1921, that would increase to a 1,700-percent twenty-year growth rate. It is little wonder that the Dominion Government, in view of the war effort and the evident U.S. links of the TLC, invited AFL president Samuel Gompers to address a joint session of the House of Commons and Senate.

Indeed, the TLC would remain the largest single union central for most of the period from 1901 to 1956. What became increasingly clear, however, from at least the beginning of the interwar years, was that the TLC did not have a monopoly (Figure 4.7). Other centrals co-existed with it, as well as a number of unaffiliated federations.

The confessional unions of the pre-World War I years would combine to found a central in 1921, called the Canadian and Catholic Confederation of Labour (CCCL). The IWW would reappear after its wartime illegality. A new central would appear in the west subsequent to the 1919 Winnipeg General Strike, calling itself the One Big Union (OBU). The OBU was initially a western splinter group which withdrew effectives from the TLC and proposed an industrial model of organization. Later, in 1929, another industrial group would appear, the Workers' Unity League (WUL), the labour wing of the Communist Party of Canada.[14]

In fact, as Irving Abella has forcefully argued, the rest of the union movement was as considerable as the TLC during the mid-1930s.[15] In addition to the NTLC, which had changed its name in turn to the Canadian Federation of Labour (CFL) and the All-Canadian Congress of Labour (ACCL), there were in 1935 the CCCL, the IWW, the OBU, the WUL, as well as several unaffiliated national unions. The opposition to the TLC however, was decidedly disunified, and encompassed the entire ideological spectrum.

A new challenge would appear though the AFL's expulsion of the U.S.-based Committee for Industrial Organizations, which became thereupon the Congress of Industrial Organizations (CIO). After some initial manoeuvring the TLC followed suit, creating by its action a Canadian CIO. Joining forces with the ACCL, the CIO contributed to the founding of a

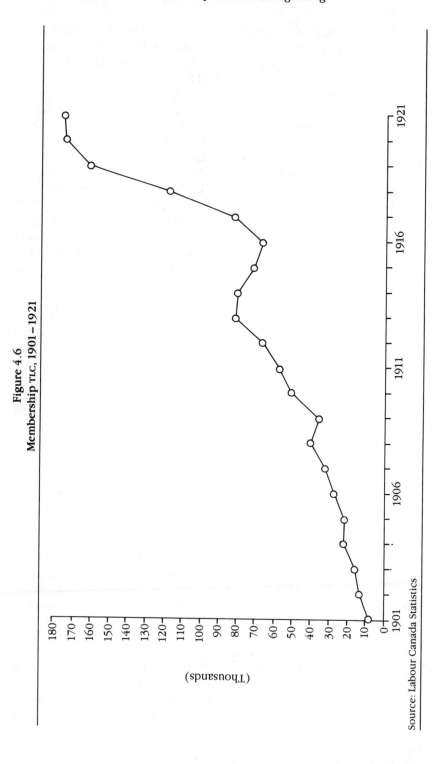

Figure 4.6
Membership TLC, 1901–1921

(Thousands)

Source: Labour Canada Statistics

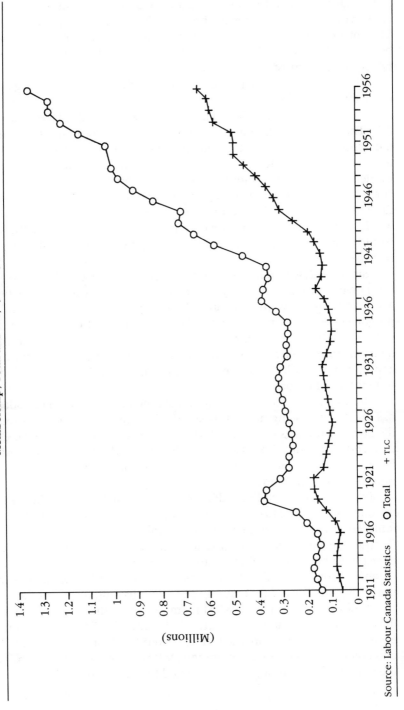

Figure 4.7
Membership, Total and TLC, 1911–1956

Source: Labour Canada Statistics   O Total   + TLC

mixed national and international central, which was also mixed regarding craft and industrial unionism, the Canadian Congress of Labour (CCL). This movement would seriously rival the TLC's membership figures between 1941 and 1948 before tapering off (Figure 4.8). It remained, nevertheless, a substantial central.

These successful challenges to the TLC's ambitions of hegemony from the beginning of the 1930s on foreshadowed the shift toward unification in the mid-1950s. The merger, which took place under the title The Canadian Labour Congress (CLC) in 1956, brought the union movement full circle to its situation before 1902. Integration, co-existence, mutual tolerance (if not respect) again became the rule. Involved in the unification movement were the TLC, the CCL, the OBU as well as certain major unaffiliated (independent) federations, the vast majority of the union movement at the time. It was even felt, then, that the CCCL would join the unification movement.[16] Ultimately, however, the CCCL would remain independent allegedly for a series of internal and external reasons.[17]

Since 1972, we seem to be entering a period of relative fragmentation ("relative" because it is not yet as extensive as that witnessed between 1902 and 1956). New union centrals have appeared at both the federal and provincial levels, in part in the wake of the internal crises at the CNTU (1972) and the CLC (1982). Another development, born also in part of the divisions of those two years, and in another sense the continuation and amplification of a longstanding trend, was the growth of unaffiliated (or independent) unionism.

Today, the CLC continues to dominate the union scene in Canada, but has to take increasing note of its smaller but significant rivals, as well as the growing number of unaffiliated federations. These include: the Canadian Federation of Labour (CFL), which is totally different in composition from its earlier namesake (now international and craft), the Confederation of National Trade Unions (CNTU) successor to the CCCL, the Confédération des syndicats démocratiques (CSD) which split off from the CNTU in 1972, the Confederation of Canadian Unions (CCU) which was founded in 1969 as a national union central in opposition to the CLC, the Centrale de l'enseignment du Québec (CEQ) which officially took the decision to become a union central in 1974 and is particularly active in Quebec province's educational system, and finally the increasingly numerous unaffiliated federations, both national and international.

As regards the current (1986) membership of these various centrals, the CLC is by far the largest with 2,164,345 members. The next two centrals by order of importance are the CNTU (218,865) and the CFL (208,822). The CEQ comes next with 91,251 members, followed by the CSD (35,967) and the CCU (35,683). Among the unaffiliated locals and federations are to be

Figure 4.8

TLC and CCL, Membership, 1941–1956

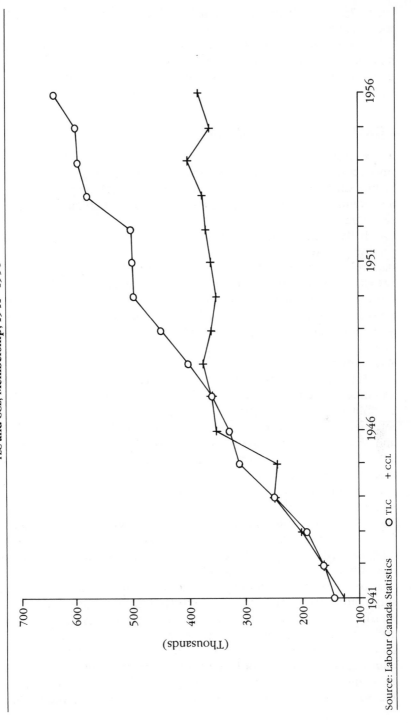

Source: Labour Canada Statistics

found 735,450 members of national and international bodies and 239,640 members of internationals. The total membership is 3,730,023.

Figure 4.9 summarizes certain of the developments discussed above and furnishes additional notes on some of the smaller centrals, as well as many of the key turning points in the development of the union movement.

CURRENT AREAS OF CHANGE

Three themes, interwoven but distinguishable, are of considerable importance to the recent development of the union movement. The first is the expansion of national unionism, the second the expansion of public sector unionism, and the third the expansion of unaffiliated (or independent) unionism.

It has already been mentioned that the total number of national union members rivalled that of the internationals during the 1930s. The national union question subsequently seemed secondary to that of the expansion of the CCL, in large part through the exceptionally successful recruiting campaigns undertaken by the industrial unions. The national unionism question resurfaced again during the 1960s, and took off to such an extent that it soon became a matter of major concern. Figure 4.10, covering the years 1948–1986, reveal its exceptional growth rate during this latter period.

The CLC itself experienced a general rise of national unionism within its ranks, particularly from the mid-1960s on as Figure 4.11 reveals. The combination of the growth rate of national unionism, and the 1982 internal CLC division which resulted in the exodus of between 200,000 and 250,000 international union members (depending on whose figures are being used) in the construction trades, resulted in a national majority from 1982 on for the first time in the history of that central.

A significant part, but certainly not all, of this national union expansion could be attributed to the boom in public sector unionism. While Joseph Rose has taken pains to show us that public sector unionism is much older than the mid-1960s, and expanded at slightly different moments from group to group,[18] its most profound impact has definitely been felt over the past two-and-a-half decades.

Rose points out that the proportion of public sector union membership compared to total union membership has risen spectacularly since the first Labour Canada statistics recorded on it in 1911. Indeed, it has grown from 0.9 percent in 1911, to 2.4 percent in 1921, 4.6 percent in 1931, dropping back to 2.9 percent in 1941 (the impact of the Depression years), rising again to 5.3 percent in 1951, 12.6 percent in 1961, 25.6 percent in 1971, and 38.6 percent in 1981. The figures for the last three years were 182,887 (out of a total of 1,447,000) in 1961; 571,834 (2,231,000) in 1971;

and 1,347,073 (3,487,000) in 1981. The author cautions us, however, that the real rate is higher still. Rose argues.

> These membership figures represent a conservative estimate of public sector unionism. They do not include membership in local independent unions, directly chartered unions, and so-called mixed unions, such as the International Brotherhood of Electrical Workers and the Service Employees International Union.....[If such additional public sector employees are added] to the 1981 membership figures...a revised membership estimate of 1,510,723, or 43.3 percent of total union membership, is obtained.[19]

The Canadian Union of Public Employees can be taken as a case in point of the exceptional rise of public sector unionism (Figure 4.12). Between 1964, when Labour Canada recorded its membership for the first time at just under 90,000 (84,800 to be exact), and 1986, when it counted just over 300,000 (304,300), CUPE had experienced a striking 358.8 percent growth rate. Formed initially by a merger of the National Union of Public Employees and the National Union of Public Service Employees, it had also shot up from fourth to first place among Canadian federations (regardless of affiliation). One of its officers, moreover, after many years as CLC vice-president, recently took over the president's role from the outgoing Dennis McDermott. Shirley Carr is at once the first public sector CLC president, as well, incidentally, as the first woman to occupy that function.[20]

CUPE's story is not unique. Other public sector federations have also registered substantial gains as witnessed by Figures 4.13 and 4.14. The Public Service Alliance of Canada (PSAC) rose from 92,800 to 182,000 for a 196 percent increase between 1966 and 1986. The National Union of Provincial Government Employees (NUPGE) rose from 101, 131 in 1977 to 254, 300 in 1986, a 251.5 percent increase in just ten years. Indeed, all three of these federations have been catapulted to the top of the listing of Canada's largest union federations. CUPE, NUPGE and the PSAC were placed first, second, and third in 1986. All, incidentally, are member organizations of the CLC.

The third theme mentioned above is the increasing rate of non-affiliation, or independent unionism, including nearly one million unionists in 1986.[21] Figure 4.15 reveals an ever-present rate of activity with an upsurge in unaffiliated national union members from 1969 on, and a lesser rise in unaffiliated international union members from 1982 on. The latter, however, is attributable in large part to the 1982 division within the CLC, three of the twelve departing construction trades federations remaining unaffiliated after the split (rather than joining the new CFL).[22] Figure 4.16 permits us to establish more clearly the pattern of international union non-affiliation, where the phenomenon actually seemed to be on the overall decrease until the 1982 split within the CLC. This detailed

Legend
1 The nine-hour strike and first efforts at legalizing the union movement, 1871–1872.
2 The TLC's Berlin Congress, 1902.
3 Papal Encyclical *Rerum Novarum* legitimizes unionism, 189 .
   Msgr. Begin's arbitration decision and recommendations regarding Christian unions, 1901.
4 Western Labour Conference, 1919.
   Winnipeg General Strike, 1919.
5 Expulsion of the CIO by the AFL, followed by expulsion of the CIO by the TLC, 1937–1939.
6 ACCL–CIO merger, 1940.
   Division within the ACCL, 1936.
7 Communist Party's decision to create the WUL, 1929.
8 Communist Party's decision to disband the WUL, 1935.
9 Massive unification effort of 1956–1957, following merger of the AFL and CIO in the USA, 1955.
10 Deconfessionalizing within the CCCL, 1960.
11 Division within the CNTU, 1972.
12 CEQ becomes a union central, 1974.
13 Division within the CLC, 1982.

Figure 4.9

Development of the Labour Movement in Canada 1816–1987

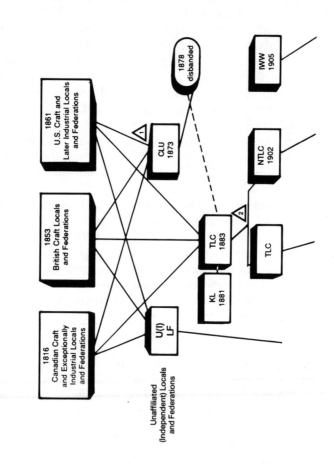

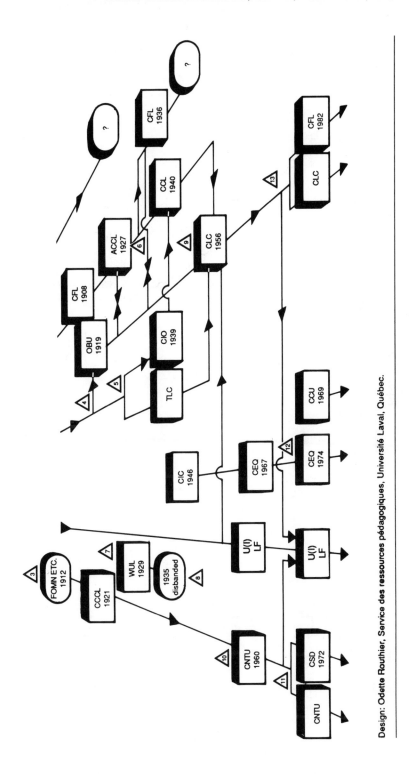

Design: Odette Routhier, Service des ressources pédagogiques, Université Laval, Québec.

Figure 4.10
Canadian Union Membership
National Unions, 1948–1986

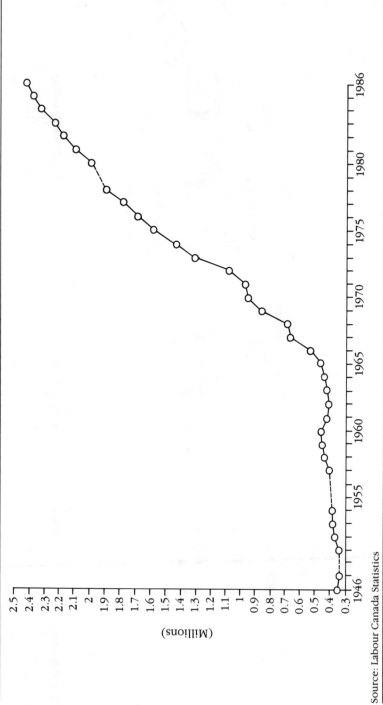

Source: Labour Canada Statistics

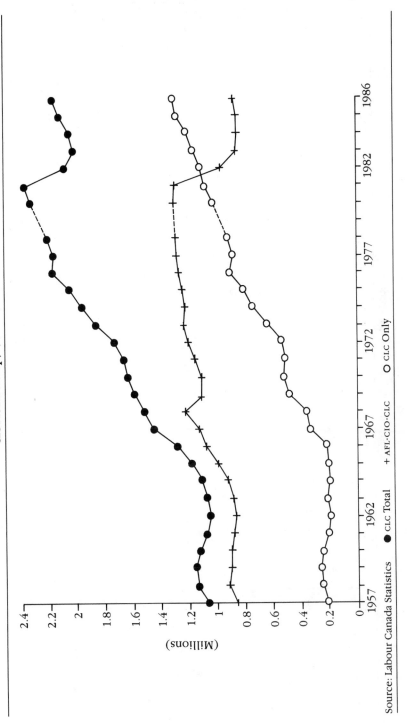

Figure 4.11
CLC Membership, 1957–1986

(Millions)

● CLC Total   + AFL-CIO-CLC   ○ CLC Only

Source: Labour Canada Statistics

Figure 4.12
Membership CUPE, 1964–1986

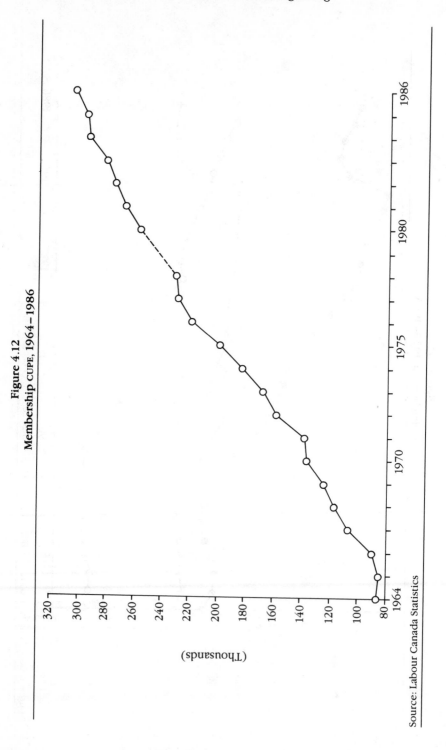

('Thousands)

Source: Labour Canada Statistics

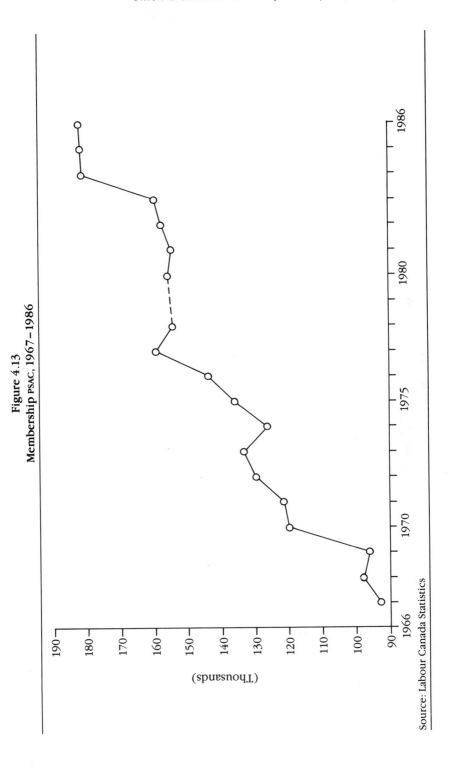

Figure 4.13
Membership PSAC, 1967–1986

(Thousands)

Source: Labour Canada Statistics

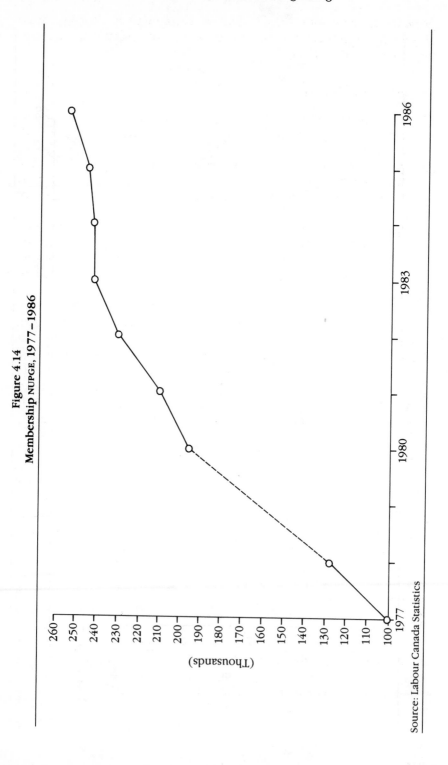

Figure 4.14
Membership NUPGE, 1977–1986

(Thousands)

Source: Labour Canada Statistics

presentation of the international case also helps focus our attention more closely on the importance of national union non-affiliation—well over the 700,000 mark in 1986, at 735,450.[23]

CONCLUDING NOTES

The initial impulse to organize labour in Canada, as has been seen, was *first* indigenous, *second* inspired by British unionism and *third* inspired by U.S. unionism. The latter two can be ascribed to a desire for overseas or foreign expansion for a variety of reasons as simple as the movement of members from one country to another, and as complex as the political and economic networks of the two countries in question—which, of course, overlapped in Canada.

From these two foreign sources came initially craft (or trade) unionism. From the United States subsequently came various types of industrial unionism—from the Knights of Labour, to the IWW, and the CIO—as well as renewed and continuous organizing waves of largely AFL-inspired craft unionism.

These were the "institutional" foreign influences, that is, the influence of structured movements that came to Canada with personnel, structures, and organizational links and obligations. There were also less structured influences, such as those which inspired the creation of confessional unionism, following earlier experiences with this type of unionism in Germany and Belgium. The various Canadian federations, such as the FOMN, and the central which later emerged (the CCCL) were, however, free from any and all overseas institutional links, as has been seen.

In part, the enthralment with international unionism could be attributed to the power it represented, or to its unique appeal. The former is likely a large part of the explanation of the success of movements like U.S.-based craft unionism in the AFL mould and the CIO. The latter recalls particularly the experience of the Knights of Labour, which survived in Canada even after their disappearance in the United States, and which survived in Quebec, as Harvey argues, even longer than in English Canada. (In fact, the early attempts to create confessional unionism in Quebec made direct reference to the ideas of the Knights, giving some additional longevity to their early fervour and moralism.) It also recalls the experience of the charismatic CIO which, if we are to believe accounts by Abella and other researchers, was virtually dragged into Canada by Canadians enthusiastic about its ideas and forms of action, and promoted at the outset by a combination of Canadian labour and left-wing political activists.

The other current, national unionism, preceded its competitors. During the opening decades, primarily of the craft type, it would eventu-

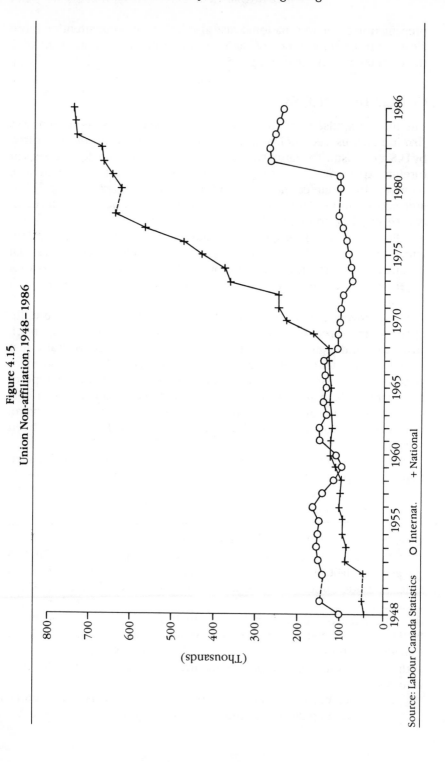

Figure 4.15
Union Non-affiliation, 1948–1986

Source: Labour Canada Statistics   O Internat.   + National

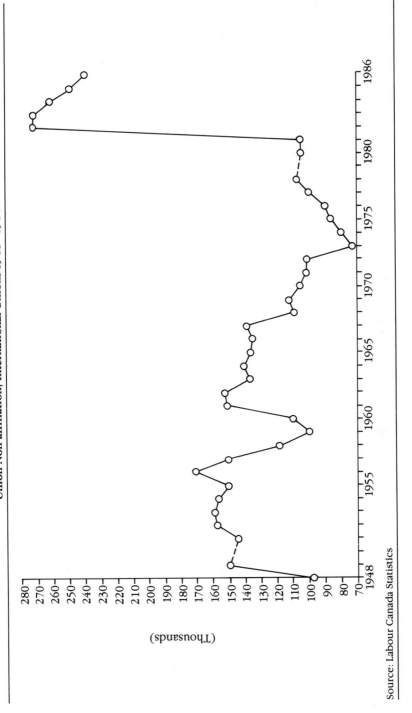

Figure 4.16
Union Non-affiliation, International Unions 1948–1986

(Thousands)

Source: Labour Canada Statistics

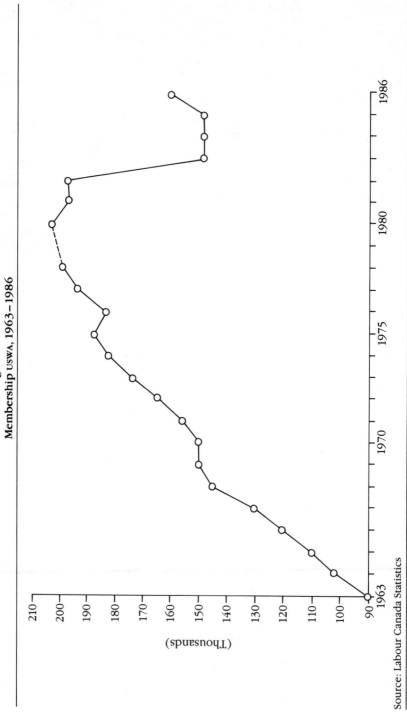

Figure 4.17
Membership USWA, 1963–1986

(Thousands)

ally produce its own industrial-type organizations. It was above all varied, including purely national centrals such as the NTLC, OBU, CCCL, CNTU, CEQ, CCU and CSD. National unionism also collaborated with international unionism in a significant way in mixed centrals like the CLU, the TLC (before 1902), the CCL and the CLC. Even during the craft internationals' dominance of the TLC(1902–1956), certain national federations were to be found in its ranks. National unionism was, in short, a constant, one with particular impact today, as has been seen.

Other observations can also be made regarding union centrals operating in Canada. Certain movements, for example, made their appeal to a particular constituency. This was the case of the IWW in its remarkable effort to organize often isolated immigrant workers, considered marginal, unorganizable or even undesirable by other forms of unionism. Quebec's CCCL, although extremely different in orientation, is another case in point, making its appeal initially to French-speaking Roman Catholic workers, and subsequently simply to French-speaking labour, primarily in Quebec province.

In certain cases, outside support for specific forms of unionism helped encourage its development (by "outside" is meant outside the union movement). This was the case of the WUL during the 1930s, founded and inspired by the Communist Party of Canada. It was also the case of the Church-inspired CCCL, at least during the opening decades.

Some movements were created through division—the impossibility of working within a given group, resulting in voluntary exodus, or the result of an internal crisis provoking an expulsion order by the central concerned. The OBU serves as an example of the former, the product of dissension within the TLC. The CSD is another example of the same phenomenon. As regards expulsion, the NTLC and the CIO are chief examples. Both were the creation of organizations expelled by an existing central, the TLC in either case. (The CFL, 1982+, also constitutes a case of expulsion, but is virtually situated at the extreme limit between expulsion and voluntary exodus because of the surrounding circumstances.)

Other movements were created through unification, through burying the hatchet, the desire to combine forces, or both. Examples are the CLU, TLC (previous to 1902), CCL and CLC. Each resulted in expansion—even in the case of the CLU, although the difficult economic times that followed its birth soon had the better of it.

Other movements, particularly in the public sector, were new creations—the result of the transformation of bona fide professional associations into union organizations (a phenomenon called "convergence" by Rose). This generally took place in the heady 1960s and 1970s, the CEQ being a case in point. It was usually guided, in that context by the conviction that unionism was a better (more effective) solution. Several organizations that took that step had already been acting as if they were union-type bodies long before, as in the case of the CEQ.

Unaffiliated (or independent) unionism constitutes another constant in the Canadian experience. It is a non-movement rather than a movement, and indicates a tendency. In recent times it has been the product of either long-established traditions or divisions within centrals such as the CNTU or CLC. Delorme and Veilleux attribute it largely to factors permitting autonomy, such as size, existing services, financial resources, etc. It may also be explained through fundamental disagreement over policy, orientations, functioning or even costs, of a given central.

All of these factors contributed to the expansion and diversity of the union movement in Canada. They are, however, only part of a full explanation of the growth and development of unionism in this country. The union movement was also influenced by such factors as general economic conditions, industrial conditions, management policy, government policy, as well as more internal questions such as the effectiveness of union leadership, the support of the rank and file, inter-union solidarity, and the effectiveness of labour political action. Thus, the key ingredients of a transactional approach (see Chapter 2), namely the "union and management ethos" and "environmental influences" are necessary components that need to be taken into consideration in tracing union dynamics. Future enquiry should direct itself to these areas.

ABBREVIATIONS

Union Centrals

ACCL:	All-Canadian Congress of Labour
AFL:	American Federation of Labor
CCCL:	Canadian and Catholic Confederation of Labour
CCL:	Canadian Congress of Labour
CCU:	Confederation of Canadian Unions
CCWC:	Confederation of Catholic Workers of Canada
CEQ:	Centrale de l'enseignement du Québec
CFL:	Canadian Federation of Labour
CIO:	Congress of Industrial Organizations
CLC:	Canadian Labour Congress
CLU:	Canadian Labour Union
CNTU:	Confederation of National Trade Unions
CSD:	Confédération des syndicats démocratiques
IWW:	Industrial Workers of the World
KL:	Knights of Labour
NTLC:	National Trades and Labour Congress of Canada
OBU:	One Big Union

TLC: Trades and Labour Congress of Canada

Specific Union Federations

ASE: Amalgamated Society of Engineers
CBRE: Canadian Brotherhood of Railroad Employees
CUPE: Canadian Union of Public Employees
IAMAW: International Association of Machinists and Aerospace
           Workers
IBEW: International Brotherhood of Electrical Workers
ITU: International Typographical Union
NUPGE: National Union of Provincial Government Employees
PSAC: Public Service Alliance of Canada
USWA: United Steelworkers of America

NOTES

1. Pradeep Kumar and Bradley Dow, "Econometric analysis of union membership growth in Canada, 1935–1981," *Relations industrielles/Industrial Relations* 41(2) (1986): 251.
2. Eugene A. Forsey, *Trade Unions in Canada: 1812–1902* (Toronto: University of Toronto Press, 1982).
3. Henry Mintzberg, *The Structuring of Organizations* (Englewood Cliffs, NJ: Prentice-Hall, 1979).
4. For a fuller definitional discussion see Allen Ponak, "Public sector collective bargaining," in J. Anderson and M. Gunderson (eds.), *Union–Management Relations in Canada* (Toronto: Addison-Wesley, 1982), p. 344; Gérard Hébert, "Public sector bargaining in Québec: A case of hypercentralization," in M. Thompson and G. Swimmer (eds.), *Conflict or Compromise: The Future of Public Sector Industrial Relations* (Montréal: Institute for Research on Public Policy, 1984), p. 233–234.
5. François Delorme and Diane Veilleux, *Les syndicats indépendants au Québec: un aperçu de leur situation* (Québec: Ministère du Travail du Québec, 1980).
6. This is true in spite of Gérard Dion's often-repeated joke that the CCCL did not shed its confessional status in 1960, but merely changed religion—from Roman Catholicism to Marxism.
7. The very use of the word "radical" recalls Frank Underhill's quip that it was unfortunate that its use was reserved for extreme forms of action only on the left of the political spectrum, while equally extreme forms of action on the right of the political spectrum had other, more neutral labels.

8. Gérard Dion, *Le Dictionnaire canadien des relations du travail* (Québec: Presses de l'Université Laval, 1986), p. 70.

9. Eugene A. Forsey, *Trade Unions in Canada*, p. 6. Reprinted by permission of the Publisher.

10. For more complete accounts of the various aspects of this question, see the following: John Battye, "The nine-hour pioneers: The genesis of the Canadian labour movement," *Labour/Le Travailleur* 4 (1979): 25–56; François Delorme and Claude Daoust, "The origins of the freedom of association and the right to strike in Canada," *Relations industrielles/Industrial Relations* 36 (4) (1981): 894–919.

    It should also be noted that an interesting case is made for a slightly earlier, but very short lived, attempt to found a central in Montreal by researchers drawing on Médéric Lanctôt's efforts to promote "La Grande association" (1867). For further information on this point see: G. Gervais, Médéric Lanctôt et l'Union nationale, Master's thesis (History), University of Ottawa, 1968; F. Harvey, "Les Chevaliers du travail, les États-Unis et la société québécoise, 1882–1902," in F. Harvey (ed.), *Aspects historiques du mouvement ouvrier au Québec* (Montréal: Boréal Express, 1973), pp 39–40.

11. For further information see: Gregory Kealey and Brian Palmer, *Dreaming of What Might Be: the Knights of Labour in Ontario,* 1880–1900 (New York: Cambridge University Press, 1982); Fernand Harvey, *Les Chevaliers du travail*, pp. 33–118.

12. For further information see: Robert H. Babcock, *Gompers in Canada: A Study in American Continentalism before the First World War* (Toronto: University of Toronto Press, 1974; Jacques Rouillard, "Le Québec et le Congrès de Berlin, 1902," *Labour/Le Travailleur* 1 (1976): 69–91.

13. For further information see: Jean Hulliger, *L'Enseignement social des évêques canadiens de 1891 à 1950* (Montréal: Fides, 1957); Ross McCormack, *Reformers, Rebels and Revolutionaries: The Western Canadian Radical Movement, 1899–1919* (Toronto: University of Toronto Press, 1977).

14. For further information see: Jacques Rouillard, *Les Syndicats nationaux au Québec de 1900 à 1930* (Québec: Presses de l'Université Laval, 1979); Jacques Rouillard, *Histoire de la CSN (1921–1981)* (Montréal: Boréal Express, 1981); David Bercuson, *Fools and Wise Men: The Rise and Fall of the One Big Union* (Toronto: McGraw-Hill Ryerson, 1978); Charles Lipton, *The Trade Union Movement of Canada, 1827–1959* (Toronto: N.C. Press, 1973), Ch. 15.

15. Irving Abella, *Nationalism, Communism and Canadian Labour: The CIO, the Communist Party and the Canadian Congress of Labour, 1935–1956* (Toronto: University of Toronto Press, 1972).

16. See the journal *Relations industrielles/Industrial Relations* for the year 1957.

17. Gérard Dion, "La CTCC et l'unité ouvrière canadienne," *Relations industrielles/Industrial Relations* 12 (1–2) (1957): 32–53.

18. Joseph Rose, "Growth patterns of public sector unions," in M. Thompson and G. Swimmer (eds.), *Conflict or Compromise: The Future of Public Sector Labour Relations* (Montréal: Institute for Research on Public Policy, 1984), pp. 121–146. Rose arrived at these additional results with the aid of a questionnaire sent to 59 private sector union federations.

19. Ibid., p. 96.

20. The rise in public sector unionism has also contributed to the rise in the percentage of female union members. Rose noted (ibid., p. 95) that the public sector unions had a female membership of 49.4 percent compared to the overall union membership (including, of course, the public sector) of 29.3 percent in 1979. It has, in addition, masked a recent downturn in private sector unionism (Figure 4.17).

21. It is important to recall that the statistics used here combine unaffiliated federations and local unions, as concerns nationals. Those dealing with internationals combine the local unions unaffiliated to any central organization in Canada or the USA and those affiliated only to their U.S.-based federation and the AFL, CIO or AFL–CIO (depending on the period). Care has been taken to exclude identifiable centrals from Labour Canada unaffiliated statistics. The only real case in point, however, is the CEQ, which has been considered as a central in spite of Labour Canada's varying position in its regard.

22. For further information see: James Thwaites, "Tensions within the union movement in Quebec: Relations between the public and private sectors in three case studies from 1972 to 1982," in M. Thompson and G. Swimmer (eds.), *Conflict or Compromise: The Future of Public Sector Labour Relations* (Montreal: Institute for Research on Public Policy, 1984), pp. 121–146; Joseph Rose, *The Building Trades—Canadian Labour Congress Dispute* (Hamilton: McMaster University, 1982). (Working Paper Series no. 193.)

23. For further information see: François Delorme, "Les Syndicats indépendants au Québec: un aperçu de leur situation," *Le Marché du travail* 1 (4) (1980): 32–36. [Full report: F. Delorme and D. Veilleux, *Les Syndicats indépendants au Québec: un aperçu de leur situation* (Québec: Ministère du travail du Québec, 1980).]

BIBLIOGRAPHY

Primary Sources

Department of Labour of Canada, *Report on Labour Organization in Canada*. Ottawa: Government Printing Bureau (subsequently King's Printer, then Queen's Printer, then Information Canada), 1912–1974/75.

———, *Labour Organizations in Canada*. Ottawa: Information Canada (subsequently Supply and Services Canada), 1976/77–1978.

———, *Directory of Labour Organizations in Canada*. Ottawa: Supply and Services Canada, 1980–1987.

Secondary Sources

Abella, Irving (1972), *Nationalism, Communism and Canadian Labour: The CIO, the Communist Party and the Canadian Congress of Labour, 1935–1956*. Toronto: University of Toronto Press.

Babcock, Robert H. (1974), *Gompers in Canada: A Study in American Continentalism before the First World War*. Toronto: University of Toronto Press.

Battye, John (1979), "The nine-hour pioneers: The genesis of the Canadian labour movement." *Labour/Le Travailleur* 4.

Bercuson, David (1978), *Fools and Wise Men: The Rise and Fall of the One Big Union*. Toronto: McGraw-Hill Ryerson.

Delorme, François (1980), "Les Syndicats indépendants au Québec: un aperçu de leur situation." *Le Marché du travail* 1 (4).

——— and Daoust, Claude (1981), "The origins of the freedom of association and the right to strike in Canada." *Relations industrielles/Industrial Relations* 36 (4).

——— and Veilleux, Diane (1980), *Les Syndicats indépendants au Québec: un aperçu de leur situation*. Québec: Ministère du travail du Québec.

Dion, Gérard (1957), "La CTCC et l'unité ouvrière canadienne." *Relations industrielles/Industrial Relations* 12 (1–2).

——— (1986), *Le Dictionnaire canadien des relations du travail*. Québec: Presses de l'Université Laval.

Forsey, Eugene A. (1982), *Trade Unions in Canada: 1812–1902*, Toronto: University of Toronto Press.

Harvey, Fernand (1973), "Les Chevaliers du travail, les États-Unis et la société québécoise, 1882–1902." In F. Harvey (ed.), *Aspects historiques du mouvement ouvrier au Québec*. Montréal: Boréal Express.

Hébert, Gérard (1984), "Public sector bargaining in Québec: A case of hypercentralization." In M. Thompson and G. Swimmer (eds.), *Con-*

flict or Compromise: The Future of Public Sector Industrial Relations. Montreal: Institute for Research on Public Policy.

Hulliger, Jean (1957), *L'Enseignement social des évêques canadiens de 1891 à 1950.* Montréal: Fides.

Kealey, Gregory and Palmer, Brian (1982), *Dreaming of What Might Be: The Knights of Labour in Ontario.* New York: Cambridge University Press.

Kumar, Pradeep and Dow, Bradley (1986), "Econometric analysis of union membership growth in Canada, 1935–1981." *Relations industrielles/Industrial Relations* 41 (2).

Lipton, Charles (1973), *The Trade Union Movement of Canada: 1827–1959,* Toronto: N.C. Press.

McCormack, Ross (1977), *Reformers, Rebels and Revolutionaries: The Western Canadian Radical Movement, 1899–1919.* Toronto: University of Toronto Press.

Mintzberg, Henry (1979), *The Structuring of Organizations.* Englewood Cliffs, NJ: Prentice-Hall.

Morton, Desmond and Copp, Terry (1980), *Working People: An Illustrated History of Canadian Labour.* Ottawa: Deneau-Greenberg.

Palmer, Brian (1983), *Working-Class Experience: The Rise and Reconstitution of Canadian Labour, 1800–1980.* Toronto: Butterworth.

Ponak, Allen (1982), "Public sector collective bargaining." In J. Anderson and M. Gunderson (eds.), *Union–Management Relations in Canada.* Toronto: Addison-Wesley.

Rose, Joseph (1984), "Growth patterns of public sector unions." In M. Thompson and G. Swimmer (eds.), *Conflict or Compromise: The Future of Public Sector Labour Relations.* Montreal: Institute for Research on Public Policy.

—— (1982), *The Building Trades—Canadian Labour Congress Dispute.* Hamilton: McMaster University. (Working Paper Series no. 193.)

Rouillard, Jacques (1981), *Histoire de la CSN 1921–1981).* Montréal: Boréal Express.

—— (1979), *Les Syndicats nationaux au Québec de 1900 à 1930.* Québec: Presses de l'Université Laval.

Thompson, Mark and Swimmer, Gene (eds.) (1984), *Conflict or Compromise: The Future of Public Sector Industrial Relations.* Montreal: Institute for Research on Public Policy.

Thwaites, James (1984), "Tensions within the labour movement in Québec: Relations between the public and private sectors in three case studies from 1972 to 1982." In M. Thompson and G. Swimmer (eds.), *Conflict or Compromise: The Future of Public Sector Industrial Relations.* Montreal: Institute for Research on Public Policy.

5

The Structure of Collective Bargaining

ROBERT ROGOW

MEANING AND SIGNIFICANCE OF BARGAINING STRUCTURE

The Meaning of "Collective Bargaining Structure"

"Collective bargaining structure" at its simplest level answers the question, "Who bargains with whom?" The numbers of unions, employers, work establishments, or employees involved are common ways of defining bargaining structure and distinguishing among them. These participants in a bargaining relationship encounter what is usually called formal bargaining structure. The industrial relations literature also commonly speaks of informal bargaining structure, a term that addresses the relationships among bargaining situations. The questions to be answered here are, "Which bargains are causally linked?" and "How strong and how stable is that linkage?"

A bargaining structure consists of a pair of employer and union bargaining groups, although the "group" often consists of a single employer or a single union. Even the single employer and single union are not homogeneous entities, and can be thought of as groupings of different components. Bargaining structure may be described in terms of successive levels (Weber, 1967, 14–15). Working from the micro level to the macro, we could label these layers the work group, the certification unit, the negotiation unit, and the unit of inter-bargain impact. Within every workplace are found several different work groups, clustered by common production activities, common skill, common work shift, or some other unifying characteristic. Such groups tend to see their group interests clearly and to assign relatively high priority to their achievement. These group interests are not always identical to or even necessarily consistent with the interests of other groups or with the interests of the employees within the workplace as a whole.

Most certification units include a number of such work groups. The certification unit is the grouping of employees designated by a government labour relations board as appropriate for collective bargaining, as discussed in Chapter 3. In a legal sense, the certification unit and not the work group is the smallest building block in the structure of collective bargaining. In a political and social sense the bargaining representative will be sensitive to the various priorities of the subgroups within the certification unit.

Although the legal obligation to engage in collective bargaining exists at the level of the certification unit, the bargaining parties can and often do agree to combine certification units into a common negotiation unit. Thus the negotiation unit can consist of more than one certification unit. When we speak of formal collective bargaining structure it is the negotiation unit that we are describing. Formal bargains may sometimes influence one another in a variety of ways. This level, the potentially broadest of all levels of structure, can be described as the unit of inter-bargain impact. It is generally to this level that we are referring when we speak of informal bargaining structure.

There is a parallel pyramid on the employer side, starting with the level of the first-line supervisor and working up to the negotiation unit. Every bargaining group is a coalition of subgroups who possess both common and conflicting interests. How well both kinds of interests are served is one of the tests we apply in evaluating a bargaining group, and is probably the main test that the subgroups within it apply.

Formal Structure

Formal bargaining structure focuses on those attributes of the bargainers and the employees covered by bargains that affect bargaining processes and bargaining outcomes, especially those attributes that are relatively stable through time. A major attribute in which structures differ is their degree of centralization.

Bargainers

The number of parties (employers, unions, and subdivisions of each) in each side is a common way of describing and distinguishing among collective bargaining structures. Thus a bargaining relationship will often be described in terms of the number and nature of the bargaining parties and the relationship of the bargaining unit to the workplace location (referred to in this chapter as the "establishment"), be it a manufacturing plant, a warehouse or an office.

Collective bargaining is both legally and functionally a relationship between employers and unions, rather than between employers and employees. Unions act as bargaining agents for certified groups of employees. Under some circumstances a group of employers, too, will be represented by a bargaining agent (perhaps the executive committee of an employer bargaining association to which they belong). A variety of combinations of single employer, multi-employer, single union and multi-union bargaining structures are possible. On the union side bargaining is often engaged in not by the union as a whole but by individual locals. The locals are often structured around one or more work establishments. Single union bargaining thus might be single local or multi-local. Multi-union bargaining is likely to be joint bargaining by some, but not all, the locals of each of the unions involved.

Employers operate at one or more establishments. If collective bargaining exists it may be structured on a multi-establishment basis, or separate bargaining may occur at each individual establishment. Single establishment bargaining may be either establishment-wide or further subdivided into smaller bargaining units by craft or skill distinctions, by distinctions between blue-collar and white-collar employees, or by distinctions between full-time and part-time employees.

Employees Covered

Even though employees are not direct parties to collective bargaining, they form an important dimension of bargaining structure in both a quantitative and a qualitative sense. In quantitative sense, numbers matter. A bargaining unit of 2,000 employees and one of 20 employees may both be single establishment, single union structures, but intuition and experience suggest that there will be important differences between the two in intra-party relationships, the nature of the bargaining process, the outcome of bargaining, and the impact of process and outcome on third parties. In a qualitative sense, the employee composition of the bargaining unit by occupation, skill, gender, age, or social background can also affect bargaining processes and outcomes.

One qualitative example is the distinction between "craft" and "industrial" units. The former refers to a single occupation unit, usually inhabited by people possessing common skills, experience, training and education of a trade, technical, or professional character. The latter refers to a multi-occupation unit, where the grouping criterion is the common work establishment. Craft units may exist at different levels. They usually are subsets of a work establishment's employees, but they can also be multi-employer units, as is common in construction, printing, or longshoring. Many writers on collective bargaining have noted the differrent effects that grouping employees by common occupation and grouping them by common work establishment can have.

The above discussion of formal bargaining structures has been stated primarily in absolute terms: the number of employers, unions, establishments, employees covered by a bargaining relationship. Structure is also important in relative terms. The proportion of a product market or labour market covered by a bargaining relationship, for example, can have profound effects on relative bargaining power of the parties, on the seriousness of non-union or other-union competition, and on many other things. The proportion of unionized employers or employees covered by a handful of the largest bargaining relationships is also of interest.

Centralization

An important characteristic in which alternative structures differ is their degree of centralization. As the previous discussion suggests, structure comes in multiple dimensions. Therefore centralization of structure, too, comes in multiple dimensions. For example, a call for more centralization could be advocating any one of the following, or any combination of them:

Multi-employer, versus single employer, structures. Multi-employer bargaining can be industry-wide or narrower in coverage. The industry itself may be small or large, local, national or international. Employer sizes may be small or large, similar or dissimilar.

Multi-establishment, versus single establishment, structures. Multi-employer bargaining is also multi-establishment, but the term is commonly used to refer to only single employer bargaining, where more than one of the employer's establishments bargain together. Some employers have only one unionized establishment; the term "single establishment bargaining" applies to them (unless they band together with other employers in joint bargaining) as well as to the multi-establishment company whose individual workplaces bargain separately from one another.

Multi-union, versus single union, structures. Either of these may exist with single establishment, multi-establishment or multi-employer bargaining. Single union bargaining is usually but not necessarily confined to a single certification unit. The same union may be the bargaining agent for a number of different establishments' or employers' certification units.

Still other meanings of centralization may include establishment-wide versus smaller structures, or multi-provincial versus intra-provincial structures, or multi-local versus single local structures.

Some suggestions to centralize bargaining go beyond formal bargaining structures in their recommendations. One suggestion is to centralize, or centralize power within, organizations that bargain. Thus transfers of power over bargaining from locals to regional or national levels within unions, mergers of unions, or transfer of power from unions to union confederations like the Canadian Labour Congress are sometimes recommended. So is the emergence of more powerful employer bargaining and non-bargaining labour relations organizations, usually at the national level.

Informal Structure

Identifying Informal Structures

Informal bargaining structure refers to interactions among negotiations; formal bargaining structure refers to the anatomy of a single negotiation. This distinction is clear enough, but the precise dividing line between the two is hard to establish. It sometimes difficult to know whether we are witnessing one or several negotiations. Some observers treat as a single formal negotiation any situation in which the parties are compelled to participate in the common negotiation, and treat any other negotiations as examples of informal bargaining structure. This is a sensible distinction, in that, compared to informal bargaining structures, formal structures do tend to be less voluntary, more difficult to leave, more difficult to change, more regulated by law. However, differences in compulsion (and its opposite, voluntarism) among bargaining structures are differences in degree, not in kind. Negotiations exist along a wide spectrum of legal and strategic pressures on the parties to enter and remain within them. Exactly where on the spectrum to draw the boundary line between formal and informal structure is a topic on which agreement is difficult.

We noted above that statutes normally compel bargaining only at the level of the certification unit. Almost all certifications are at or below the level of the single establishment. Thus multi-establishment, multi-employer and multi-union structures are in this sense often voluntary. But compulsion does not derive from statutory requirements alone. Legal obligations can arise from contractual commitments among bargainers, either within one bargaining side or between sides. These legal obligations are not absolute, and in practice are sometimes difficult to enforce. Legal compulsion, then, exists along a continuum. So do other compulsions. Many bargaining structures remain stable over time because the alternatives are economically, politically or organizationally so unattractive that participants feel compelled to remain. If the unifying forces change, so might the degree of compulsion to remain within a bargaining structure.

Differences among Informal Structures

The extent to which separate components in a bargaining group retain autonomy, possess veto power over group decisions, or have the ability to withdraw safely from the group are aspects of bargaining structure that help us determine whether we are looking at a single bargaining situation or a number of closely related ones.

All bargaining coalitions have the task of reconciling differences among their member groups and of attempting to impose discipline on dissidents, but in some coalitions these tasks are much more difficult. For example, in the construction industry during the 1950s and 1960s it was quite common and relatively easy for employer members of contractor bargaining associations to break away from the group, usually under union pressure, and to sign separate bargains with the union. Because this was seen by government policy makers as producing undesirable results (for example, excessively high wage costs), "accreditation" legislation was passed in a large proportion of Canadian jurisdictions that limited the right to break away. This legislation increased the formality of bargaining structure (Rose, 1986, 4–5).

The category of informal bargaining structure includes an array of alliances differing in coalition strength. The array ranges from the difficult-to-define border with formal bargaining structures all the way to the most limited, implicit, and temporary of interactions. The latter may be better thought of as bargaining strategies than as bargaining structures. However, some mild forms of co-ordination, such as information exchange, probably exist on a broad enough and consistent enough basis to be considered as structure.

It is also possible that even without mutual communication and commitment, fairly stable structural relations could exist. To the extent that imitative relationships exist among bargaining settlements that are formally independent of one another, there may exist an informal structural relationship among them. If the relationship were extremely strong, such that the pattern-establishing settlement was always imitated completely by the pattern-following settlement, the two sets of bargainers would be behaving (except for the time lag between the two bargains) as if they were formally included within the same bargaining structure. To the extent that such powerful relationships exist the relationship, then, is every bit as structural (in the sense of supporting and constraining behaviour) as is formal bargaining structure. Imitative relationships of this completeness and stability are rare, however.

On the union side, perhaps the strongest informal structure is intra-union. Inter-union coalitions tend to be less powerfully linked together, and therefore less stable, than intra-union coalitions. Unions in work situations sufficiently close to one another that co-operation against the employer is possible often have histories of conflict with one another. Conflict may take the form of raiding (efforts by one union to displace another as certified bargaining agent of a group of employees) or of jurisdictional disputes over which union's members have the right to perform disputed work. Craft or occupational status considerations have sometimes led to efforts by one union to "leapfrog" over the agreement its fellow unions are prepared to accept, by holding out for a better agreement.

Informal bargaining structures are often more attractive to bargaining organizations than formal ones because of the flexibility and freedom of action they permit. The degree to which an employer or union chooses to imitate or co-ordinate with another settlement is more controllable. Adapting to the special circumstances of one's own bargaining, which can vary over time, is easier. But this very flexibility for individual bargaining organizations may be a weakness of the larger interrelated group.

Structure and Collective Bargaining

"Structure" suggests an architectural and skeletal imagery. It suggests something that provides support to activities within it and at the same time sets limits to those activities. Further, it implies something that is relatively fixed through time, something difficult to change (and/or expensive or risky to change), something the collective bargaining participants may have to treat as a "given." As we will see below, this stability and inability to change is not completely true of formal structure, and is even less true of informal structure. Yet it is true enough to be useful; most of the time, in most collective bargaining situations, structure is indeed something the prudent practitioner will have to accept as beyond his or her control.

Bargaining structures could be thought of as independent or dependent variables, in that they both affect and are affected by other variables in an industrial relations system. The next section discusses the various environmental, organizational, and strategic factors that influence structure. Then we will examine structure's influence on bargaining processes, outcomes, and relationships. Perhaps the most useful way to think of bargaining structure is as semi-environment, as an intermediate or intervening variable between the various environments on the one hand and the bargaining processes and outcomes on the the other (Kochan, 1980, 25, 33).

INFLUENCES ON COLLECTIVE BARGAINING STRUCTURE

This section discusses why bargaining structures are what they are, and suggests why they differ in different circumstances. This may be useful in a policy sense. If we understand how structures have been created, we can understand how they can be changed, should change be desirable. It is useful to classify the forces affecting structures as legal, economic, organizational, and strategic influences.

Legal Influences on Bargaining Structure

Determining the Certification Unit

The most direct impact on structure is through the power given by law to labour relations boards to "determine the appropriate bargaining unit" when an application for certification has been received. These laws give little or no direction to labour relations boards concerning how appropriateness is to be determined.

Unit determination criteria. The boards have therefore developed a number of unit determination criteria, which they attempt to balance in reaching their decisions.

1. Facilitating unionization wherever a majority of employees want it:
   This criterion flows from the major objective of Canadian collective bargaining laws, the guarantee of employee freedom to choose collective bargaining. It acts to encourage the creation of smaller bargaining units than some other criteria do, because smaller units are generally more cohesive and easier to unionize (Arthurs et al., 1984, 194).
2. Community of interest:
   "Community of interest" has been perhaps the strongest single unit determination criterion among Canadian labour boards. Common interests may arise from similarities in kind of work done, interrelationships among tasks, common rules of the workplace, and common supervision. Because these similarities are never complete, collective bargains inevitably provide an imperfect fit to the interests of some individuals. The smaller the extent of such imperfection of fit, the higher the internal solidarity of the members of the bargaining unit. Like the "facilitating unionization" criterion, the "community of interest" criterion pushes labour boards in the direction of more homogeneous, and therefore smaller, certification units.
3. Encouraging harmonious bargaining relations:
   A major objective of collective bargaining legislation is the establishment and maintenance of sustainable, rational, and orderly bargaining structures. Situations where a number of production-interrelated groups of employees bargain separately from one another have often been associated with high levels of employer–employee conflict, and high levels of rivalry among bargaining units over bargaining achievements and jurisdiction over work. These rivalries limit rational wide-scale employer personnel policies, the voluntary movement of employees from one job or location to another, and the achievement of broader or longer-term bargaining objectives. Because of such "frag-

mentation" problems, boards have seen larger, all-inclusive bargaining units as desirable (Arthurs et al., 1984, 195).

This criterion often conflicts with the "community of interest" criterion because it leads to larger, more heterogeneous units. Public policy recognizes the potential for conflict among subgroup interests that more comprehensive units create, but views the common bargaining unit and the common union bargaining agent as providing a healthier forum for expression and resolution of such conflicting interests than inter-unit and inter-union relations would provide.

4. Wishes of the parties and of employees:

If both the union and the employer agree on the unit, boards will often authorize it, unless the parties' preferred unit substantially violates other unit criteria or other objectives of collective bargaining legislation. The unit preferences of the employees involved are given some weight by labour relations boards, but not a predominant one. This is especially true where employees prefer multiple small units within the establishment. More generally, boards see the unit determination responsibility as theirs, not employees'.

Impact of unit determination. It is clear, then, that there are multiple public policy objectives concerning the appropriate bargaining unit, with some inconsistency among them (Arthurs et al., 1984, 193). A unit that is ideal in permitting the maximum degree of unionization that employees want may be inappropriate in minimizing labour–management bargaining conflicts. A balancing and trading off among equally worthy objectives may be required. It is because of this, and because legislatures recognize the variability among industrial relations settings, that they have left to labour relations boards the discretion to determine the unit.

There appears to be a tendency for the above criteria to favour the establishment-wide bargaining unit at the expense of both more centralized and less centralized units. The "facilitating unionization" and "community of interest" criteria contribute to the former effect and the "encouraging effective bargaining relations" criterion to the latter effect.

The decisions a board makes in balancing among the various unit criteria can produce substantially different bargaining structures. Examples of such decisions might be choices between industrial units and craft units, choices among single location and multi-location units, decisions on whether white-collar and blue-collar employees should be in the same unit, or on whether part-time or temporary or casual employees should be in the same unit as other employees.

Boards vary in the relative weight they give to the various unit determination criteria. For example, British Columbia de-emphasizes "community of interest" in favour of " bargaining viability" and "conflict minimizing," reflecting its preference for establishment-wide units (Germaine, 1984, 77–79). Ontario and the federal board normally create separate office and production worker units, versus British Columbia's combining them. Ontario normally establishes separate units for full-time and part-time employees while British Columbia and the federal board normally combine the two groups, especially when the part-timers enjoy relatively permanent employment (G. Adams, 1985, 346–353). The implications of such differences for broadening or narrowing of bargaining structure are apparent.

The multi-establishment employer poses some special unit determination problems. Whether certification should be by single establishment or should cover more than one raises again the conflict between the unit determination criterion of facilitating unionization and the criterion of making bargaining harmonious and orderly. The difficulty of simultaneously unionizing employees at several locations means that relatively few certifications are for multi-location units. The infrequency of multi-establishment certifications does not prevent multi-establishment bargaining. As we will see later in this chapter, such negotiation units are quite common, and cover a large proportion of Canadian union members. Normally such bargaining structures are not mandated by law, but arise from the mutual agreement of the bargaining parties. Occasionally, more centralized bargaining is encouraged or compelled by law. Multi-employer bargaining in the construction industry is strongly supported by legislation in almost all jurisdictions. Under British Columbia law, related unions can be compelled to bargain jointly (Strand, 1984, 99–100).

Provincial–Federal Jurisdictional Boundaries

In addition to unit determination, another direct legal influence on bargaining structure arises from the constitutional split of authority between federal and provincial governments. Although multi-provincial bargaining is legal very little of it occurs, in part because it is technically more complex to have to observe simultaneously the procedural requirements of several different jurisdictions. The argument is often made that much more multi-provincial bargaining would exist if the federal government had legal authority over bargaining relationships, as is true in most comparable countries (Anderson, 1982, 184). The argument has merit, but economic, organizational, and cultural factors may also be important explanations of the paucity of multi-provincial bargaining.

Less Direct Legal Influences

There are aspects of collective bargaining legislation that have unintended effects on bargaining structure. The requirement of majority support has probably pushed certification unit size downward. The expense and legal complexity of actions taken under labour laws may have pushed negotiation unit size upward.

A wide variety of government policies have acted to compel, encourage, or prevent co-operative behaviours by organizations on both sides of the bargaining table, thus influencing the relative attractiveness of alternative structures. Wage controls, tri-partism initiatives, labour standards legislation, extension of bargained terms to non-unionized employers, as in Quebec, and government rules on prices and services in regulated industries are all examples of policies that encourage increased centralization. In general, government involvement seems to be positively correlated with more centralized bargaining structures (Kochan, 1980, 102).

Economic Influences on Bargaining Structure

The nature and size of product and labour markets affect bargaining structure in a variety of ways. The geographical extent of the product market affects bargaining structure. For example, local market industries are more likely to have localized bargaining and more likely to have multi-employer bargaining. An industry whose markets are national or international will tend to have more geographically extensive bargaining.

One reason for the tendency of the scope of bargaining to expand to cover the product market is the desire to reduce competition in labour costs from companies outside the bargaining structure. Unionized companies often face competition from non-unionized companies, who may enjoy lower labour costs and greater managerial freedom of action. Such competition threatens the prosperity of unionized employers and employees. Even some unionized employers may enjoy advantages relative to those unionized companies bargaining within an employer association. They could, for example, avoid work stoppages by agreeing to accept whatever settlement the dominant employer association reached. Bargaining structures that minimize such competition are often favoured by either or both of the bargaining parties.

Where bargaining is structured along occupational lines (as in construction) there is some tendency for bargaining structure to expand to take in the geographic extent of the labour market—the distance that craftsmen are prepared to travel to work, or within which employers can recruit or bid for projects.

Economic considerations are among the strongest of the influences on employer choices among bargaining structures. One important choice is between bargaining jointly with other employers or going it alone (Gladstone, 1984, 37, Davies, 1985, 85; Anderson, 1982, 80). Among the factors seen as more important influences are the following:

Product Market Characteristics

Joint bargaining is more attractive to employers the greater the degree of competitiveness and ease of entry. The nature and extent of regulation of the industry, the degree of tariff and other protection against foreign competitors, and the stage in the product cycle can also affect this employer decision. The more competition, the greater an employer's preference that competitors not be operating when it is shut down by a work stoppage. The attractiveness of more standardization of labour costs may also be higher in such circumstances.

Production and Technological Characteristics

The degree of similarity in unit costs, production methods, technology, financial condition, and composition of work force (including age and size of establishments, whether employers are or are not integrated, multi-stage producers) is also relevant. Product lines, technologies and tasks often are far from identical within a product market. Therefore, common interests may be weak. The differences in the level of wage settlements companies can afford and the differences in ability to withstand a work stoppage may be too great to permit joint bargaining. Where joint bargaining exists in such circumstances its breadth and depth of impact is likely to be limited, with formal or informal supplementary bargaining at individual company or establishment levels being more important.

Where bargaining unit labour costs are a high proportion of total costs, the incentive toward joint bargaining may be stronger.

Economy or Industry Prosperity

The level of prosperity in the company, industry, or economy affects choice. During prosperous times employers are more concerned with uninterrupted production; stoppages are less frequent under joint bargaining. Their motivation for cutting costs below competitors' is not all-powerful. During recession, lowering unit costs, preferably below those of competitors, becomes urgent. This may be accomplished through the wage bargain or through regaining the freedom and flexibility in workplace management lost during previous prosperity. Recessions are notoriously uneven in their impacts on different employers, weakening the homogeneity cement for employer solidarity. Informal as well as formal centralization tends to look less attractive to employers during harder times.

Organizational Influences on Bargaining Structure

The structure and related characteristics of bargaining organizations can influence the structure of bargaining. Such structure has both internal and external dimensions.

The internal dimension includes the locus of power, authority, expertise, and initiative within the organization and the nature of the building blocks on which the organization rests (for example, the Canadian workplace is based local, unlike the European geographic, community-based branch.) The structuring of the collective bargaining function within the employing organization can also affect bargaining structure. Decentralization of that function from the corporate headquarters level to the divisional or establishment level is likely to encourage formal or informal decentralization of bargaining. Small employers usually cannot afford to employ in-house specialized industrial relations staff, and may see multi-employer bargaining as an economical way to obtain such expertise. The degree of centralization of power and authority within one bargaining organization can affect the other bargaining organization's preferences among alternative structures.

The external dimension includes the size of the organization relative to some external measure of relevance, for example, industry, nation, labour market, or other bargaining organizations. External structure has an impact upon bargaining structure in a number of ways. Whether an industry's or company's unionized work force is represented by a single union or by a number of different unions affects the effectiveness of formal or informal bargaining structure. Whether the employer also has bargaining commitments in other industries and jurisdictions affects its willingness to engage in multi-employer bargaining. Such companies often reject multi-employer bargaining, fearing precedents and spillovers among their bargaining structures. When traditions of inter-employer co-operation are strong and long established, as in Western Europe, they also can affect structure.

The percentage of potentially eligible employees unionized—often referred to as "union density"—can influence bargaining structure. Increased formal or informal co-operation may be a response to a perception of great power on the part of the other bargaining party. High union density, often regarded as an indicator of union strength, encourages employer centralization. Union density is an indicator of union political power as well as bargaining power. Countries with high union density tend to have strong labour influence on government.

The mix of co-operation and competition among employers, or among unions, is relevant. Trust levels are crucial where less formal coalitions exist, and dependence on the good faith of allies is necessary. Low trust levels encourage formal, and therefore enforced, coalitions, in contrast to informal, and therefore relatively voluntary, coalitions. The belief that bargaining power is a function of union size is widely held in labour as well as in employer circles. This belief is an element in the frequent suggestion that the large number of small unions in Canada should merge, or should at least co-operate more closely. Many of these suggestions also have an element of "Europeanization" to them. Advocates often believe that fewer and larger unions are able to perform their political functions better. They can influence governments through lobbying, promote labour participation in national planning and decision making, conduct effective major demonstrations, mobilize membership electoral support for labour-oriented political parties, and influence public opinion better than a less centralized labour movement can.

Confederations of unions are non-bargaining bodies, but influence bargaining by encouraging information exchange, lobbying government, and advising members. They supply training and expertise to inexperienced leadership of affiliates. They mobilize support for members in bargaining difficulty, and help to resolve bargaining-related conflicts among member unions. Other, less global inter-union bodies affecting bargaining relationships also exist on either a geographic basis (for example, city labour councils) or an industry basis (for example, building trades councils). Proposals for other unifying bodies are often made. Employer confederations also exist, performing similar functions.

Strategic Influences on Bargaining Structure

Responding to the threats and opportunities perceived to be generated by all the above legal, economic, and organizational factors tends to be done by bargainers in a strategic fashion. Considerations of how better to achieve organizational goals, of how to improve the organization's institutional strength, of how to enhance its short-term bargaining power, of how to broaden its capability of responding to future circumstances, are strategic influences. They all help shape structural responses to the above factors.

Strategic influences reflect, first, these preferences of the parties; second, the extent to which those preferences differ between employers and unions; third, the relative bargaining power of the parties; and fourth, the relative priority each side gives to achieving its preferred bargaining structure, versus alternative objectives to which bargaining power could be devoted. Such preferences mainly reflect perceptions of relative bargaining power. Bargaining power may be thought of as higher in a particular structure either because it raises the other side's costs of refusing your side's terms of settlement or lowers the other side's costs of agreeing to those terms, or has the opposite effects on your own side's costs.

In general, what employers hope for from multi-employer (as contrasted to individual employer) bargaining is increased bargaining power and its consequence, better bargaining outcomes; fewer stoppages; less-damaging stoppages; scale economies in negotiation, and possibly in contract administration; reduced uncertainty about labour costs and therefore about product pricing, and non-collective bargaining advantages of membership in an employer association.

Multi-establishment employers differ from one another in their preferences for centralizing their internal bargaining structures. Factors encouraging management to prefer multi-establishment bargaining include: (1) Sequential production integration, so that stoppages in some establishments can cripple production in others. (2) Senior executive preferences for uniform corporation-wide industrial relations policies, or their fears that inept or hard-pressed establishment-level management might agree to settlements that could be used by unions as precedents in other establishments. (3) Relatively similar local labour markets across establishments, so that standardized, corporation-wide wage and benefit levels do not introduce distortions in recruitment and retention of employees or in relations with other employers.

Under what circumstances might unions prefer multi-employer or single employer multi-establishment bargaining? Multi-employer bargaining structure may be seen by unions as "taking wages out of competition," through its tendency toward increased standardization of wage levels, wage structures, wage compensation methods, and benefits. It may also be seen as providing more protection against wage cutting by marginal employers during less prosperous times. Where a strong union deals with a large number of small employers it may be willing to give up the tactical advantages of single employer bargaining for the sake of the economy, orderliness, professionalism, and speed of multi-employer bargaining. The employer association can often assist both the union and itself by persuading and pressuring less co-operative member companies, either during negotiations or during the life of agreements.

Multi-establishment bargaining can increase union bargaining power by: (1) increasing the impact of withdrawal of services, by reducing employer ability to shift struck production to other establishments and by reducing employer cash and profit flow during a stoppage; (2) achieving some negotiating economies of scale, such as being able to assign more senior and more skillful negotiators to the task; (3) enabling union negotiators to deal with more senior levels of corporate decision makers rather than with subordinate managers with less authority to make deals.

To the extent that work groups or certification units have some freedom of choice among bargaining units of different sizes, they will support the broadening of the employee coalition as long as the perceived gains in bargaining power exceed the perceived losses of autonomy and of emphasis on group-specific issues. The optimal coalition size differs among groups, and may change for a given group over time. Freedom of choice may be limited for many groups, however,

As mentioned above, some structures are more likely to induce government intervention. Organizations that believe that government intervention would improve their power position are likely to prefer them.

Bargainers prefer situations that enhance the unity, co-ordination, and discipline of their side and lessen these attributes of the other side. A favoured situation is one in which the united group can play off different subsets of the other side against one another.

Strategic decisions are sometimes influenced by non-bargaining considerations. Employer bargaining associations often perform non-bargaining as well as bargaining functions. The growth in recent decades of the importance of statutory determination of working conditions in many countries (including Canada) has increased the importance of the government relations function (Gladstone, 1984, 25–27).

Influences on Informal Structure

The above strategic considerations apply with more or less equal force to preferences within both formal and informal structures. Because informal structures are less stable than formal structures it is useful to consider separately some of the pressures contributing to the more fluid movement in and out of them.

Pattern following, for example, may be a prudent tactic. Information on what is achievable at the bargaining table is ambiguous, and is a topic about which bargainers and their principals may disagree. Well-publicized outcomes of pattern-establishing negotiations provide models of what is achievable, encourage convergence of expectations, and permit some face-saving basis for agreement. Followers have fewer stoppages than leaders have. Both employee criteria of fairness in compensation and employer criteria of staying in line with comparable companies increase the desire to follow other settlements.

On the other hand, some pattern following may be reluctant. If those unions and employees with whom members compare themselves have made attractive settlements, the union leader who fails to match them runs some political risks regarding re-election or raids by other unions. Employer labour relations managers may also have to justify their performance relative to that of companies with which senior executives make comparisons.

The forces encouraging imitation vary cross-sectionally and over time. Like formal structures, informal structures are stronger during prosperous times and where cost homogeneity is greater. They are believed to be stronger within than across industries, in the public and quasi-public sectors, and within oligopolistic industries. Information exchange is widespread, but its inter-bargain impact is neither extensive nor stable. Bargainers tend to be well informed about settlements in related situations and usually use such information selectively in their arguments across the bargaining table, but usually assign lesser weights to such settlements in their decision processes than they assign to considerations of relative bargaining power.

Compared to the relative rigidity of formal bargaining structures, the flexibility of informal structure can be an advantage to individual bargaining organizations, although probably not to the interests of the broader bargaining coalitions. This flexibility is not only in greater ease of entering and leaving of coalitions, but also in judging just how much of another bargaining settlement one wishes to incorporate into one's own.

Non-strategic Preferences Regarding Bargaining Structure

Not all organizational preferences are strategic and calculative; some are principled, per se preferences. Some trade union leaders and activists believe, as a matter of moral and ideological principle, that maximizing labour unity is a worthy end in itself, as distinguished from being a means to some other desired end. They would therefore prefer broader, more centralized bargaining units even if no increase in bargaining power would result. Some employers oppose joining multi-employer bargaining groups as a matter of principle, self-image, and preferred operating style. Even when convinced of the economic advantage of joining, some employers value their autonomy and freedom of action highly enough to refuse. On the other hand, some employers may be motivated by a sense of class, community, industry, or societal responsibility in their multi-employer bargaining activities.

Structures and Stability

Structures that are traditional within a nation, industry or region will often have an attractiveness to bargainers beyond their objective merits. In the world of collective bargaining, where cause and effect are often difficult to unravel, the familiar can be the safe, attractive option. Before the prevailing structures gelled there may have existed a number of more-or-less equally attractive alternative structures. But as soon as one structure becomes prominent, the organization, policy, interests, and perceptions of bargaining organizations and of government bodies concerned with bargaining are all shaped to some extent by that structure.

For reasons that go beyond comfort with the familiar, bargaining structures tend to be relatively stable. They vary less than do the legal, economic, organizational, strategic and ideological influences on them, although they respond to such environmental forces when such changes are large, and are moving in mutually consistent directions. This moderate degree of non-responsiveness, or of lagged responsiveness, can have both good and bad effects.

The above section suggests that a number of forces account for the existence of different bargaining structures. The section below deals with the effects of those structures on bargaining processes and bargaining outcomes.

CONSEQUENCES OF COLLECTIVE BARGAINING STRUCTURE

It is widely believed that different bargaining structures produce different effects on negotiation processes, work stoppages, bargaining outcomes, relationships within organizations that bargain, and third parties and the public interest (Thomson, 1981, 301–303; Anderson, 1982, 173; Kochan, 1980, 184). The most common discussion of structure's consequences is the comparison of the effects of centralized versus decentralized structure. As noted earlier, centralization is a multi-dimensional concept. Given the unavoidable variability in usage of the term, the reader is well advised to ask when reading the discussion here or elsewhere, "Which meaning is being discussed now?" In this section we will discuss first the effects of centralized structures, and then the research evidence supporting those beliefs.

Effects of Centralization

The major consequences of more centralized bargaining structures to which academics and practitioners usually refer are the following:

Fewer Work Stoppages

More centralized bargaining almost by definition reduces the number of negotiations. If these opportunities for stoppages are reduced, and there is no offsetting increase in the proportion of negotiations leading to stoppages, the number of stoppages must decline. Other reasons sometimes cited for a reduction in stoppages are the improvement in skill and professionalism of negotiators and their greater freedom from the control of the perhaps more emotional or more poorly informed perceptions and wishes of those for whom they negotiate. Stoppages arising from "whip-sawing" and "leapfrogging" tactics (discussed below) are believed to be eliminated by structures that compel joint bargaining by employers and unions respectively.

Some observers are doubtful about the stoppage-reducing effect of centralized bargaining. They argue that the proportion of centralized negotiations leading to stoppages should indeed be higher than the proportion in decentralized negotiations. They point to the increased heterogeneity among interests, real or perceived, covered by centralized bargaining, and the greater consequent difficulty of reaching internal agreement. They also point to the greater likelihood that centralized negotiations will be pattern establishers rather than pattern followers; the stoppage propensity of the former is believed to be much higher.

Lower Outcome Levels

Multi-employer bargaining is generally seen as reducing inter-employer competition. The employer's competitors are more likely to be stuck with similar settlements. They are more likely to be shut down when it is, thus being unable to service, and perhaps steal, its customers. For both these reasons centralized bargaining is often considered to enhance employer bargaining power.

Centralization is believed to reduce union bargaining power by reducing union "whipsawing" and "leapfrogging" opportunities. Union whipsawing arises where a union faces a number of employers who are attempting to maintain a voluntary united front through some variant of informal bargaining. Whipsawing refers to the union's attempts to break up the united front by pressuring, persuading, or rewarding one or more of the employer members of the bargaining group to break ranks and settle early on or closer to the union's preferred terms. The return to work of employees of the settling employers strengthens the union's financial resources during the stoppage. The possibility of the returned employer taking business away from its hold-out competitors pressures them to settle.

Union leapfrogging occurs where a number of unions in an interrelated work situation (interrelated in the sense that a stoppage by any one union idles the others) bargain more or less simultaneously with one or more employers. Here one union leapfrogs over the settlements achieved by other unions by holding out until all other unions have settled, and then demanding an improvement on that settlement as the price for its agreement. Leapfrogging tactics can stimulate an increase in the frequency and duration of stoppages.

This analysis makes the usual assumption (for example, Riddell, 1985, 57; Gladstone, 1984, 38) that centralization reduces union whipsawing opportunities. This is one part of the argument that multi-employer bargaining, on balance, raises employers' bargaining power and lowers unions'. This is often, perhaps usually, true, especially in those industries where large numbers of small employers face one or more large unions. Union whipsawing opportunities are probably greater during periods of prosperity. But it is important to note that employer whipsawing is also possible, and may be more common than union whipsawing in times of economic recession or industry-specific hard times. Where establishments perform the same operations and therefore might be substitutes for each others' outputs the multi-establishment employer with separate single establishment bargaining structures may be able to whipsaw by threatening to transfer work from, or even close down, higher-cost establishments. In these cases more centralized bargaining may give unions more bargaining power rather than less. Concessions demanded and won by marginal firms in single employer bargaining structures may lead to stronger competitors being able to obtain the same benefits. This suggests another characteristic of more centralized structures: they may be more stable and less responsive to cyclical economic forces. Thus there can be circumstances in which multi-employer bargaining or multi-establishment bargaining might lead to higher, rather than lower, outcomes.

Slower Negotiations

Negotiations are believed to take longer in centralized structures. This is partly because the settlement process is made more complex and delicate by the greater size, heterogeneity, and unmanageability of the bargaining coalitions. It is politically desirable that time be taken to consult, persuade or involve representatives or members of the various groups. To some extent minorities within the coalition can use their limited veto power to delay negotiations, as a bargaining tactic. The bargaining process (use of negotiating skills, offers and counter-offers, comparisons of costs of agreement versus costs of disagreement, etc.) will sometimes take more time within negotiating coalitions than between them.

In addition to these internal problems, external pressures on negotiations are likely to be greater from government and from other economic and bargaining groups, because centralized settlements have greater visibility and broader economic impact. These problems often slow negotiations.

Greater Involvement of Senior Levels of Leadership

Unions have often expressed concern about the absence of senior employer decision makers at the bargaining table in decentralized bargaining structures. A belief that management representatives are mere "messenger boys" with no power to appreciate union arguments or to accede to them sometimes leads to feelings of frustration. Such employer negotiators might be local plant- or affiliate-level management of a multinational employer or local hospital or school board management where a provincial government decides on financing levels and therefore affordable settlement levels. In this case the work stoppage may be an attempt to attract the attention of more senior management and therefore a means of informally centralizing structure. Small employers confronting large and centralized unions will sometimes opt for more bargaining centralization for similar reasons.

Greater Similarity of Terms and Conditions of Employment

Centralization is believed to lead to a substantial movement toward similarities in wages, benefits, and other terms and conditions of employment, and therefore to similarity in unit labour costs (Riddell, 1985, 57). The standardized wages and benefits may be below what the most efficient producers would otherwise have paid, and above that which the least efficient producers would have paid. The viability of a multi-employer coalition is likely to be greater the smaller inter-employer differences in ability to pay are. The status of the marginal firm in the employer coalition is a crucial one (Gladstone, 1984, 39; Thomson, 1981, 309).

Some Shift of Power Upward in Bargaining Organizations

Observers have commented that the locus of power within bargaining organizations is influenced, and perhaps even determined, by the structure of bargaining (Clegg, 1976, 40–54). Where bargaining structure is relatively decentralized, power within unions also tends to be decentralized. This may be because leadership positions in unions are filled by electoral contests, and voters give high priority to collective bargaining performance in deciding where to place their support. On the employer side a similar, but perhaps weaker, tendency exists.

This greater freedom of action of senior negotiators when bargaining is centralized is seen as desirable by those observers who want such negotiators to behave more "reasonably," more "rationally," and in a more "statesman-like manner"—that is, to give more weight to the interests of the public and the other side and less weight to the interests of those they represent. The same freedom is seen as undesirable by observers who want such negotiators to represent faithfully the preferences of those they represent.

More Suspicion toward Negotiations and Negotiators

Distance (geographic, organizational, or social) from negotiations, recognition by subgroups that they represent only a minor proportion of their side's grouping, the slower pace and perhaps the more sophisticated tone of negotiations can all contribute to feelings of alienation. It is possible that such feelings can lead to an increase in local illegal and unauthorized stoppages that reflect such frustration or that are intended to pressure central negotiators to give more attention to the striking group's interests. Political careers can sometimes be built by aggressive local union leaders capitalizing on such feelings. The individual firm's executives in multi-employer negotiation units and local workplace management in multi-establishment negotiation units are also more likely to feel distant from and even suspicious of the bargaining process.

Centralized negotiators are less likely to have backgrounds in or extensive knowledge of specific local situations; they also may for these reasons lack legitimacy in the view of lower level observers. Centralized bargaining can also generate problems during the life of the agreement, to the extent that the latter possess power covertly to sabotage the administration of agreements of which they do not approve.

Some Upward Shift in the Nature and Impact of Issues Negotiated

Some narrowing of the range of workplace issues negotiated, and of their depth and specificity of impact, appears to be associated with centralized bargaining. Given heterogeneity of workplace and workforce characteristics, the broader the bargain the less precise its fit to any one workplace or employee group can be. Issues that have variable content and variable impact in each separate work establishment are difficult to negotiate on a multi-establishment basis. Therefore they tend not to be negotiated, or to be negotiated vaguely or in least common-denominator terms. Sometimes a second tier of formal or informal negotiation over such establishment-specific issues supplements the broader bargaining. Tensions between the two levels of bargaining may result, however. For example, strong local groups may attempt to use local bargaining as a means of compensating for modest achievements at the centralized bargaining level. Problems of relative priority between central and local level bargaining may also arise. For example, strikes over local issues may occur, and may affect signing of the central agreement.

Some issues are more likely to be negotiated under centralized bargaining. Smaller companies may be better able to afford and to efficiently administer a pension or health plan through multi-employer bargaining. Retraining and re-employment provisions in the event of layoff or even of establishment closure may also be easier to negotiate under centralized bargaining. Multi-establishment bargaining may permit negotiation over corporation-wide benefit programs.

Greater Likelihood of Government Involvement

Centralized negotiations are more visible and better publicized. They affect larger numbers of employers and employees. They often suggest patterns of settlement to other bargainers. For these reasons governments are more likely to be interested in the settlement terms of such negotiations. They are more motivated in some cases to influence those settlement terms in desired directions. The centralized work stoppage has greater effects on third parties and the larger economy than do other stoppages. Further, it may be more intractable, more difficult to resolve, because it may reflect large, intra-party differences of interest that are difficult to satisfy simultaneously. For these reasons, government involvement to end centralized stoppages is more likely than in the case of other stoppages. Conciliation and mediation, fact finding, compulsory delay, arbitration, behind-the-scenes pressures, and other government intervention mechanisms are more likely to occur.

Lesser Union Workplace Impact during the Life of the Collective Agreement

In nations where multi-employer bargaining predominates, unions tend to have less of a workplace presence. They perform less of a monitoring and protesting role regarding employer observance of collective agreement terms. Such other entities as works councils assume some of these roles, but often in a less adversarial fashion. Centralized bargaining intrudes less on employer freedom of action, and often applies less wage pressure on it than does decentralized bargaining. As a consequence there is less employer resistance to unionization of their employees in centralized-bargaining countries.

On balance, the arguments above appear to suggest that centralization raises the bargaining power of employers relative to that of unions. Reasonable contrary arguments are possible, however. The "employer whipsawing" argument above is one. Another is that employer costs of agreement are lower (and therefore wage increases tend to be higher) when competitors must match wage increases (Swidinsky, 1979, 8).

In general, the anticipated consequences of centralized structure are similar whether it is formal or informal structure we are discussing. There is a special fascination, though, that some academics and policy makers have with the consequences of informal structure. Their hope is that such structural effects will be found to be widespread, powerful, and consistent. Under such conditions government, by influencing a mere handful of pattern-establishing bargains, could influence the entire bargaining system. The tremendous leverage effects of such modest intervention have great appeal to policy makers.

Evidence on Effects of Centralization

Rigorous, unambiguous and generalizable empirical verification of the above list of commonly held beliefs about the different consequences of centralized and decentralized structures is difficult to obtain. Not surprisingly, students of structure note and lament the limited extent of such verification (Kochan, 1980, 102; Anderson, 1982, 188, 190). A good recent summary of the research on the effects of structure, to which I am indebted for much of the material below, appears in Davies (1985, 235–51).

Effects on the Bargaining Process

The limited relevant research supports the general view that centralization slows negotiations, reduces flexibility and autonomy of local management and employee representatives, and increases their feeling (along with that of their bargaining-unit employees) of alienation from the negotiations and their negotiators.

Effects on the Work Stoppage

It is useful to consider separately the impacts on stoppage frequency, size, and duration, the three contributors to total time lost from stoppages.

Frequency. Centralization tends to reduce the number of work stoppages. Countries with more centralized bargaining structures tend to have fewer stoppages than do those with less-centralized structures. So many other factors are correlated with centralization of bargaining structure, however, that it is difficult to conclude that centralization by itself leads to reduced time lost. For example, unions tend to have more political influence and to enjoy more legitimacy in the eyes of government and employers. A higher proportion of terms and conditions of employment tend to be settled by political than by collective bargaining mechanisms.

Within Canada larger bargaining units are more stoppage-prone than smaller units are. This higher probability of negotiation leading to a stoppage at least partially offsets the other forces reducing the number of stoppages. Thus, evidence for the superiority of centralized bargaining using the stoppage-frequency criterion is relatively weak.

In one study, multi-plant manufacturing units in Canada were found to have the highest strike incidence and single plant units the lowest, with multi-employer units at an intermediate level. These findings appear to give modest support to the thesis that centralization increases strike proneness.

Some Canadian students of the work stoppage have recommended against efforts to centralize bargaining because the greater stoppage proneness of more centralized units appears significantly to offset the effect of the reduced number of negotiations (and therefore of opportunities for stoppages to occur). However, as Davies points out, the frequency of stoppages is only one of the important effects of structure, and recommendations should be based on a balancing of effects.

Size. Centralization normally increases the size of those stoppages that do occur because size refers to the number of employees striking or locked out, and most meanings of centralization imply larger numbers of employees in the negotiating unit. For example, centralization in the construction industry during the 1970s has been associated with a large increase in stoppage size (Rose, 1986, 8–9).

Duration. Centralization appears to be usually associated in Canada with shorter stoppages. This may reflect the greater visibility and greater likelihood of disruptive consequences, especially in public and quasi-public bargaining. Also, the difficulty in imposing financial costs of disagreement on public sector employers makes such stoppages take on more of the characteristics of brief demonstrations than of exercises in attrition. In construction, however, centralization has been associated with an increase in stoppage duration (Rose, 1986, 8–9).

Thus the limited Canadian research evidence suggests that centralization increases working time lost because of stoppages through its tendency to increase stoppage frequency and stoppage size, and decreases working time lost through its tendency to reduce stoppage duration. It seems likely that the former effect is the stronger of the two.

Transitional effects. Whatever the steady-state stoppage characteristics of centralized bargaining, substantial and rapid movements toward them have been associated with increased levels of conflict frequency, size, and duration. To be fair, it might be true that substantial changes in the reverse direction would be equally disruptive, given the stake that participants often build up in any bargaining status quo and the uncertainties that rapid change introduces.

On balance, then, the evidence does not give major support to the argument that centralization of bargaining structure would substantially improve Canada's work stoppage performance. The evidence may even suggest the contrary. This is not to deny, however, that specific situations exist in which more centralization would indeed improve stoppage performance. Railways, shipyards, and construction are examples of traditionally strike-prone industries associated with relatively large numbers of occupationally defined bargaining units, high production interdependence among units, and separate bargaining by unit. Experience suggests that centralization can be useful in reducing conflict in such circumstances.

Effects on Outcomes of Bargaining

United States and United Kingdom evidence on whether multi-employer bargaining is associated with lower wage and benefit outcomes is mixed. Most studies have suggested that it is so associated (Anderson, 1982,191), but several recent studies have produced contrary results. The very limited Canadian research generally supports the more traditional belief that multi-employer bargaining is associated with lower outcome levels than single employer bargaining is. In construction, however, wage increases following centralization were as large as before it. This, plus the sharp downturn in construction wage settlements during the recession of the early 1980s, suggests that economic factors had outweighed structural factors in their impact on settlement size (Rose, 1986, 10, 17).

Effects on Bargaining Organizations

There is some evidence that employing organizations within multi-employer bargaining structures develop less of a collective bargaining staff complement and less individual and less sophisticated personnel policies than they otherwise would. Some reverse causality also exists; companies with stronger collective bargaining and human resource management capabilities are less likely to join multi-employer bargaining groups.

As the brief survey above suggests, rigorous, generalizable testing of the hypothesized consequences of alternative bargaining structures is quite limited in extent. Many of the suggested effects of structure have not been examined. The examinations that have occurred have, as their authors are the first to agree, limitations in methodology and in generalizability beyond their specifics of time and place. To a substantial extent we still must base our beliefs on case studies, casual observation of many bargaining structures by practitioners and academic specialists, and our underlying assumptions about the goals and perceptions of bargainers—

for example, this chapter's unstated assumption that calculation of bargaining advantage is the most powerful determinant of bargainer preferences among structures. We feel strongly that bargaining structure matters, and we think we know how it matters, but we are still a long way from being able to prove these relationships conclusively.

CANADIAN COLLECTIVE BARGAINING STRUCTURE

Formal Structure in Canada

Previous sections have discussed the nature of collective bargaining structure, the factors believed to shape it, and the consequences believed to flow from it. This section summarizes the actual nature of bargaining structure in Canada. Among other purposes, it attempts to answer the question, "How centralized is Canadian bargaining structure?"

Direct information on Canadian bargaining structure is limited in quantity and uneven in quality. A useful exception is a Labour Canada study of 1982 data (Psutka, 1983) cited extensively by Davies (1985, 211–255), and referred to below. Indirect information is available through the federal government's annual Corporations and Labour Unions Returns Act (CALURA) reports. These reports were designed to produce reliable information on the membership and finances of international and other unions in Canada rather than to produce bargaining structure information, but they do fill some gaps left by the more direct data. Three categories of unions are used. International unions are those headquartered in the United States, and almost always having a majority of their members in that country; government employee unions are those unions headquartered in Canada that represent provincial and federal government employees; national unions are all other Canada-headquartered unions.

CALURA reported that in 1983 there were 23,406 collective agreements in effect, covering a union membership of 3,391,245. This suggests a mean number of union members per agreement of 145. Because it has been estimated that perhaps between 9 percent and 14 percent of those covered by collective agreements are not union members (R. Adams, 1984, 659–661), the number of employees per agreement might be 11 or 12 percent higher. The inclusion in the union membership figures of some people who are not currently employed (Chaison, 1984, 113, 117) may partly offset this. But however we fine-tune the average number of employees per agreement, this modest size, plus the large number of agreements, creates a strong impression of a country with a remarkably high degree of decentralization in collective bargaining structure.

This impression, although essentially correct, is an exaggerated one.

There are also important elements of centralization in Canadian structure: a small number of collective agreements cover the large majority of Canadian unionized employees. For example, Psutka's 1982 data report on the 1,850 bargaining units with 200 or more employees within them. These units were only eight percent of the 22,022 collective agreements in Canada that year (CALURA, 1982, p. 57)* but included 2,430,256 employees, a number that is 80 percent of the 3,054,444 union membership total for reporting labour organizations in 1982 (CALURA, 1982). This suggests a rather high degree of centralization. (However, the suggested existence of 20,352 other collective agreements covering 624,188 union members, with a mean of 31 members per agreement, simultaneously indicates the existence of a large number of very small bargaining situations.)

The 1982 Labour Canada data provide another, and more direct, measure of bargaining structure. Information (both on numbers of negotiating units and on numbers of employees within them) is given for various categories of units with over 200 employees. The proportions of units and employees under single employer structures can be contrasted with the proportions under multi-employer structures. Within the single employer category the proportions under multi-establishment structures can be contrasted with those under single establishment ones. Information on whether bargaining is single union or multi-union is also available for each of the three above structural categories.

The first impression we get from the data is one of decentralization. Single employer, single union bargaining (the least centralized combination of parties) accounted for 85 percent of the 1,850 bargaining units and for 69 percent of the 2,430,3656 employees within them. Adding single employer, multi-union bargaining to these figures would only modestly increase them, to 91 percent and 75 percent respectively. As these figures suggest, single union bargaining is much more extensive than multi-union. It accounts for 93 percent of all Canadian units with over 200 employees and for 84 percent of all employees within them. Thus the union dimension of structure, like the employer dimension, suggests that

---

*More than one collective agreement can be involved in a single negotiation. For example, a number of separate agreements may be signed in a bargaining structure that consists of the combining by the parties of a number of certification units. Because of this, using agreements (about which the CALURA reports give us information) to approximate the number of negotiation units gives a somewhat exaggerated impression of decentralization of bargaining. The 1982 Labour Canada study, however, has combined such multiple agreement situations into a single bargaining unit wherever possible, so that this problem is reduced in the data it uses.

formal multi-party bargaining coalitions are not widespread. This in turn implies a high degree of decentralization.

Much of the single employer bargaining referred to above, however, is multi-establishment. Multi-establishment structures accounted for 49 percent of all single employer units and 75 percent of all employees in single employer units. Multi-establishment structures accounted for 44 percent of all Canadian units with 200 or more employees in them, and for 56 percent of all employees within such units. Thus they, and not the single establishment units, are the predominant Canadian bargaining structure.

Multi-employer bargaining, the most centralized of formats, and the predominant format in most industrialized countries (Gladstone, 1984, 35), exists in Canada and is important in a few industries and regions. It is not, however, a predominant form. It accounts for only nine percent of the over-200 bargaining units and for only 25 percent of the employees included therein. Such units, however, are relatively large ones, as the comparison of the two above percentages suggests. On average, they are half again as large as the multi-establishment units, which in turn are several times as large on average as the single establishment units.

Multi-union bargaining units are even less common than multi-employer units, accounting for only seven percent of bargaining units and for only 17 percent of employees within them.

The data exclude the construction industry. Because construction unionists are about one-tenth of Canadian trade unionists, exclusion of construction data mildly overstates the degree of decentralization prevailing in Canada. It should be noted that the construction industry exemplifies the multi-dimensional character of the concept of decentralization. The industry's bargaining is centralized in that it is multi-employer, but is decentralized in that it is predominantly single union.

The Canadian information presented so far has dealt with the macro aspects of bargaining structure. We do not know the extent of multiple bargaining units within single establishments, although that extent is sometimes believed to be great (Riddell, 1985, 54). A somewhat contrary impression is derivable from the 1982 Labour Canada study, which shows that, for the over-200 employee group, single establishment/multi-union units were only 0.9 percent of all units and only 0.4 percent of all employees included. This suggests either that multi-union bargaining within a single workplace is relatively uncommon, or that, if common, it is a small-unit phenomenon, or that multiple units within establishments are predominantly represented by the same union. The last of these seems unlikely.

In summary, the relatively minor role played by multi-employer units suggests decentralization; the relatively major role played by multi-establishment single employer units suggests centralization. The large number of single establishment units (about 47 percent of the 1,850 unit total), plus the probability that most of the many smaller-than-200 employee units are single establishment units, is another suggestion of decentralization. Perhaps the most reasonable generalization possible is that Canada's bargaining structure is moderately decentralized. By international standards, however, a moderately decentralized bargaining structure is very decentralized indeed.

Formal Structure—Disaggregated Information

Important though the Canada-wide information is, it fails to reflect the diversity of structures across the country's industries, occupations, and geographic and political areas. Structure varies considerably among industries. Almost all major industry categories have predominantly single employer bargaining units, but in manufacturing, mining and forestry these tend to be single establishment; elsewhere they tend to be multi-establishment. Intra-industry variation is also substantial. For example, Anderson (1982, 180) reported that in half of Canadian industries the predominant bargaining structure (usually single establishment, single union) accounted for less than 60 percent of all negotiations.)

Geographic variations in bargaining structure are also substantial. British Columbia, for example, shows half its "above-200" employees in multi-employer units, roughly double the Canadian average. Quebec shows an unusually high proportion of single establishment units, 70 percent, although they account for only 20 percent of the Quebec employees. Multi-union bargaining covers one-third of Quebec employees, double the Canadian average. Collective bargaining appears to be a largely urban phenomenon. In 1983, 24 metropolitan areas accounted for 66 percent of all collective agreements, 53 percent of all union locals, and 71 percent of all union members (CALURA, 1983, Table 20).

The occupational characteristics of employees covered by collective agreements provide further insight into bargaining structure. Labour Canada's annual volume, *Working Conditions in Canadian Industry*, provided useful information on occupational coverage, with some cross-classification of occupation by industry. For October 1, 1983 it reported coverage by collective agreements of 38 percent of office employees and 73 percent of non-office employees. These figures indicated the much greater degree of bargaining among blue-collar than among white-collar employees.

Industry and occupation interact strongly, especially regarding white-collar employees. For example, 85 percent of office employees in public administration in 1983 were covered by collective agreements, compared to only 10 percent in manufacturing and mining, and still lower percentages in trade and finance. Professional and technical occupations in the public and quasi-public industries also reflected high collective agreement coverage. Ninety-eight percent of firefighters and police officers and 83 percent of hospital nurses and technical staff were covered.

The industry in which bargaining occurs affects more than the occupational composition of bargaining units. It appears to affect the degree of centralization of bargaining structure as well. The information supporting this argument is indirect, but plausible. The 1983 CALURA data showed that Canada-headquartered unions predominated in the public and quasi-public industries. There the international unions had little membership (only 2 percent of employees in public administration, for example, were international union members). The international unions had much more membership than the Canada-headquartered unions did in the private sector industries such as forestry, mining, manufacturing, and construction. Therefore we can use CALURA's information on union types as an approximation to structural differences between the private industries sector and the public and quasi-public industries sector.

The two Canada-headquartered union types give the impression of greater bargaining centralization than does the United States headquartered type. The larger mean number of members per collective agreement (894 for government employee unions, 148 for national unions, and 109 for international unions) and the smaller mean number of agreements per local (0.2, 1.2, and 3.6 respectively) both suggest greater bargaining centralization. Both differences are large for national unions and very large for government employee unions. Since the former are substantially and the latter are almost exclusively in the public and quasi-public area, the data suggest appreciably greater centralization of bargaining structure in this industry sector.

Informal Structure

Formal bargaining structure may convey too decentralized an image of Canadian bargaining, to the extent that informal bargaining is extensive and powerful. We know less about the extent of informal than of formal structures. We know that the milder forms of informal bargaining are quite extensive. Direct evidence that more powerful degrees of informal bargaining are important is generally situation-specific and does not encourage generalization.

Indirect and inferential evidence also seems consistent with the impression that informal relations among negotiations are not powerful enough or stable enough to lead us to conclude that the data on formal structure substantially understate the true extent of bargaining centralization. Employee representation within industries tends to be multi-union; well over half of the 29 industry groups for which Labour Canada information is given had at least four different unions representing employees within them (Wood and Kumar, 1985, 261–263). Union and management confederations appear to have only moderate influence on the bargaining of their member organizations, and neither type includes all bargaining organizations within its ranks. Few unions have large enough Canadian membership or financial resources to be able to exert massive influence on individual locals' bargaining outcomes (Directory of Labour Organizations, 1985; CALURA, 1983, Table 46).

In general, the available information suggests the existence of extensive, but not very powerful, informal relations among bargaining situations in Canada.

Structure over Time

How stable had Canadian bargaining structure been over time? This question is of some theoretical interest. The more stable structure is, the better its claim to pre-eminence as a determinant of bargaining processes, bargaining behaviour, and the nature of labour–management relations. Data on this are limited to the largest bargaining units, those with over 500 employees. The small number of such bargaining units (432 in 1965 and 848 in 1982) and their atypically large size limits their value as indicators of bargaining structure in general. Such information, cited by Davies (1985, 220–221), suggests that between 1965 and 1982 single employer bargains became a modestly larger proportion of both units and employees. Within the single employer category, however, a substantial shift from single establishment to multi-establishment took place, both in proportion of units and in proportion of employees. These changes suggest that a moderate degree of centralization of Canadian bargaining structure had occurred. This has resulted largely from the increasing numerical importance of public and quasi-public sector collective bargaining, in which this format predominates, more than from consolidation of pre-existing units in other industries. In 1982 the Public Administration and Service industry categories accounted for three-fifths of multi-establishment units and employees. The public and quasi-public sector also appears to be more centralized by another measure. It accounted for only 14 percent of collective agreements covering 500 or more employees in 1967, but 55 percent of such agreements in 1984. The latter percentage is well above the public and quasi-public sector's proportion of all Canadian employees covered by collective agreements (Wood and Kumar, 1985, 387). Bargaining structure, especially within industries, had not undergone radical change over time, as far as this limited statistical information can show. The general belief that its essential characteristics are retained over time (for example, Anderson, 1982, 180; Kochan, 1980, 96) is not seriously challenged by the available data. Davies concludes, based on his examination of the Canadian data, that "once a bargaining structure is established, it tends to remain fixed over a relatively long period" (1985, 223). Bargaining structure's theoretical standing as semi-environment, then, appears to survive empirical testing.

Summary

Available information suggests that Canadian bargaining structure is moderately decentralized even when the centralizing effect of informal bargaining is considered, is quite variable by industry sector, occupation, and geographic area, and is moderately stable over time. The concluding section of this chapter briefly discusses the extent to which changes in that structure are possible (within the framework of our earlier analysis of the influences on structure) and the extent to which changes are desirable (within the framework of our analysis of the consequences of structure).

ISSUES IN COLLECTIVE BARGAINING STRUCTURE

This concluding section attempts to state some of the bargaining structure issues about which controversy is likely, issues that have been at least implicit in the previous sections. It then suggests some logical and informational tests to which proposals for change in structure might be subjected. It concludes with some suggestions on structural change.

Some Issues in Dispute

Three issues regarding structure have been implicit in the prior discussion:

1. How much, and what kind of, centralization of structure do we want?
2. To what extent do we wish to leave the choice of bargaining structure to the joint decision of the bargaining parties, as opposed to imposing choices upon them through government action? If the parties are to be free to choose, to what extent do we want their relative bargaining power to be the determinant of that choice?
3. How do we choose between stability and adaptability of bargaining structures? How responsive to such outside forces as changes in economic conditions, or changes in the political and social views of the electorate do we want them to be?

Underlying those issues and shaping our positions on them are the value positions we hold regarding:

The work stoppage. Do we want it to be less frequent, shorter, less influential on third parties, more "political" and less "economic," of greater or less impact on the employer?

Unions. Do we want them to be more or less responsive to their membership's perceptions and preferences? More or less "businesslike" and efficient? More or less responsive to the larger social and economic implications of their actions? Devoting more of their resources to achieving their objectives by political means and less by collective bargaining means?

Employers and employment. Do we want to increase or decrease employer control over the workplace, employer ability to change work assignments, job classifications, work methods, and work locations to adapt effectively to market changes? Do we want to increase or decrease unionized employees' security of employment, pay, and status?

Collective bargaining and its alternatives. Would we like to see collective bargaining more important or less important, compared to alternative ways of determining employment-related matters?

Society and government. Do we want social, political and economic decisions now made exclusively by government to be shared to some degree (ranging from mere consultation to some form of sharing or delegation of authority) with national or provincial representatives of labour and employers? Do we want to see government performing a larger or smaller role in employment-related matters?

There are inconsistencies and incompatabilities among and even within these five underlying value positions, requiring us to decide their relative importance, and which of them we are prepared to give up in order to achieve others.

Some Tests for Change Proposals

The case for any proposed change would be stronger the more strongly the following were believed to be true:

1. Undesirable present features or results of collective bargaining can be identified.
2. Collective bargaining structure is the (or is at least an) important cause of such undesired features.
3. It is possible to change bargaining structure to a format that will not contribute to these undesired features.
   a) The costs of such change will be less than the anticipated benefits.

b) Changing structure is preferable, on balance, to changing some other factor also contributing to the undesired features.

Some Suggestions Regarding Change

Earlier we discussed the various forces influencing bargaining structure. This discussion reminds us that we should consider the fit of proposed changes to those various environmental and organizational forces. Some changes will be desirable even though they are not fully consistent with one or more of those forces, but we should be aware of the possible problems involved. One of those forces, the strategic preferences of bargaining parties, should be considered with special care. There is nothing wrong with changes that injure the power position of some or all of the bargaining parties. In fact, few important changes can completely avoid doing so. Advocates of change, however, might consider the choice between compensating losers or compelling them. If the latter option is chosen, some tactical problems should be faced. Bargaining parties facing power loss can be expected to seek other, perhaps indirect, means of avoiding or offsetting this. Change advocates may wish to anticipate such manoeuvres and decide on their strategy of legally forbidding them, and the costs thereof.

We then discussed the impacts of different structures on the various processes and outcomes of bargaining. Two implications of that discussion should be considered by change advocates. The first implication is that any structure has multiple consequences, some desirable and some not. Tradeoffs among desired and undesired consequences will therefore have to be considered. The second implication is that our evidence regarding those consequences is not very strong. We are less than certain, for example, about the impact of centralized structures on the work stoppage or on the size of bargained outcomes. This lack of certainty could influence change advocates in contrary ways, depending on their risk preferences. The cautious among them might see, in the difficulty in predicting consequences of change, a reason to avoid change. The confident among them might argue that the evidence of harmful effects of change is weak and therefore change should be instituted.

This writer's preferences in changing structure lean in the direction of gradualism, consensus, and specificity of targets. A cumulation of small changes in the same direction is preferable to a single large change. As a result, labour relations boards are probably the best change agents, because they are able to fine-tune the relative weight to assign to different criteria in unit determination and unfair labour practice decisions, and because they are in constant contact with employers and unions. Expanding board discretionary powers over such matters as the merging or splitting up of existing units might also be desirable. Informal bargaining structures may be even better targets for fine-tuning than formal ones. Labour boards, with or without specific statutory changes, can adjust the positive and negative incentives associated with co-operative or imitative bargaining activities in a consistent and cumulative fashion. Attempting to persuade and even to compromise with representatives of the bargaining parties might prove more effective than imposing changes upon them. Avoiding global changes and concentrating on specific structures with identifiable problems may also be desirable. The interrelated occupational multi-unit bargaining situations in such settings as construction, the grain trade, newspaper publishing, or railways might be examples of such specific targets.

Whether one opts for milder changes, as above, or for more heroic measures, it appears clear that bargaining structure is at least a moderately important influence on bargaining processes and outcomes, and that improving structure is one useful way of improving those processes and outcomes.

BIBLIOGRAPHY

Adams, G. W. (1985), *Canadian Labour Law: A Comprehensive Text*. Aurora, Ont.: Canada Law Book.

Adams, R. J. (1984), "The extent of collective bargaining in Canada." *Relations industrielles* 39: 655–667.

Anderson, J. C. (1982), "The structure of collective bargaining." In J. C. Anderson and M. Gunderson (eds.), *Union–Management Relations in Canada*. Don Mills, Ontario: Addison-Wesley, pp. 173–195.

Arthurs, H. W., Carter, D. D., and Glasbeek, H. J. (1984), *Labour Law and Industrial Relations in Canada* (2nd ed.). Toronto: Butterworths.

Chaison, G. N. (1984), "A note on the limitations of union membership data." *Industrial Relations* 23:113–118.

Clegg, H. A. (1976). *Trade Unionism under Collective Bargaining*. Oxford: Basil Blackwell.

Davies, R. J. (1985), "The structure of collective bargaining in Canada." In W. C. Riddell (ed.), *Canadian Labour Relations* (Research Volume 16, Royal Commission on the Economic Union and Development Prospects for Canada). Toronto, Ontario: University of Toronto Press, pp. 211–255.

Germaine, R. (1984), "The structure of bargaining under the Labour Code." In J. M. Weiler and P. A. Gall (eds.), *The Labour Code of British Columbia in the 1980's*. Calgary, Alberta: Carswell, pp. 77–98.

Gladstone, A. (1984), "Employers associations in comparative perspective: Functions and activities." In J. P. Windmuller and A. Gladstone (eds.), *Employers Associations and Industrial Relations: A Comparative Study*. Oxford: Oxford University Press, pp. 24–43.

Kochan, T. A. (1980), *Collective Bargaining and Industrial Relations.* Homewood, IL: Irwin.

Labour Data Branch (1984 and 1985),*Directory of Labour Organizations in Canada, 1984, 1985.* Ottawa: Labour Canada.

—— (1984), *Provisions in Major Collective Agreements, July 1984.* Ottawa: Labour Canada.

—— (1984),*Working Conditions in Canadian Industry, 1983.* Ottawa: Labour Canada.

Minister of Supply and Services Canada (1984 and 1985), *Annual Reports under the Corporations and Labour Unions Returns Act, Part II— Labour Unions, 1982 and 1983* (CALURA reports). Ottawa: Supply and Services Canada.

Psutka, S. (1983), "The structure of bargaining units: Issues, patterns and implications." Ottawa: Labour Canada, Economics and Industrial Relations Branch. (Mimeographed.)

Riddell, W. C. (1985), "Canadian labour relations: An overview." In W. C. Riddell (ed.), *Canadian Labour Relations.* (Research Volume 16, Royal Commission on the Economic Union and Development Prospects for Canada). Toronto, Ontario: University of Toronto Press, pp. 1– 99.

Rose, J. B. (1986), "Legislative support for multi-employer bargaining: The Canadian experience." *Industrial and Labour Relations Review* 40: 1–18.

Strand, K. (1984), "Altering union bargaining structure by labour board decision." In J. M. Weiler and P. A. Gall (eds.), *The Labour Code of British Columbia in the 1980's.* Calgary, Alberta: Carswell, pp. 99–125.

Swidinsky, R. (1979), *The Effect of Bargaining Structure on Negotiated Wage Settlements in Canada.* Discussion paper no. 139. Ottawa: Economic Council of Canada.

Thomson, A. (1981), "A view from abroad." In J. Stieber, R. B. McKersie, and D. Q. Mills (eds.), *U.S. Industrial Relations 1950–1980: A Critical Assessment.* Madison, WI: Industrial Relations Research Association, pp. 297–342.

Weber, A. R. (1967). "Stability and change in the structure of collective bargaining." In L. Ulman (ed.), *Challenges to Collective Bargaining.* Englewood Cliffs, NJ: Prentice-Hall, pp. 13–36.

Wood, W. D. and Kumar, P. (eds.) (1985),*The Current Industrial Relations Scene in Canada, 1985.* Kingston, Ontario: Industrial Relations Centre, Queen's University.

6

The Art of Collective Bargaining

BOB SASS

While students of industrial relations tend to focus their research on empirical studies pertaining to labour relations and collective bargaining in particular, they generally acknowledge that collective bargaining is too complex a process to be a science circumscribed by levels of validity and things that can be known—for instance, deriving an economic range of indeterminates,[1] or limits of "coercion"[2] regarding bargaining power. Varied bargaining models have become part of our industrial relations language, from the marketing concept known as the Hick's analysis,[3] which defines bargaining power as the ability to exploit and impose costs, to the Chamberlain model, where a union's bargaining power at any one point in time is management's willingness to agree to the union's terms.[4] These approaches also take into consideration non-economic behaviour of the parties—union and management tactics and the role of government as a pressure group.

The literature of industrial relations is replete with other concepts of collective bargaining. There is the government concept,[5] which views collective bargaining as a constitutional system in industry and stresses the political relationship where the union shares sovereignty with management over workers. There is also the industrial relations concept,[6] which views collective bargaining as a system of industrial governance and emphasizes the functional relationship between the two major actors in the system.

Analytical frameworks of the negotiating process that describe the complex and continuing human relationship of the negotiators are equally part of the systems approach to industrial relations. The behavioural approach recognizes that the emotional and political problems in bargaining are just as inevitable and important as economic problems. In this regard, Walton and McKersie[7] outline four subsystems of negotiation activities each with its own function, logic, and identifiable set of acts and tactics. In addition to the orthodox or "horse-trading" approach,[8] continuous bargaining approach,[9] and what has become known as Boulwarism,[10] where management competes with the certified bargaining agent for the loyalty of the workers in the certified bargaining unit,[11] the authors make an important additional contribution to the literature on the tactics of collective bargaining.

In all of the tactical approaches, the bluff, for instance, plays a large role in the parties' coming to an agreement. The bluff is generally accepted as a standard tactic by which each player attempts to gain a little more than he is actually willing to settle for, since we do not know what is a fair price or a reasonable profit in any scientific or absolute sense. Because this is the case, bluffing as a tactic and bargaining ritual as a rule become integral parts of the game of collective negotiations. It is because of this development that Sanderson categorizes collective bargaining essentially as an art[12] rather than a science.

Albert Blum, in support of this proposition, further states that

> ...a large share of collective bargaining is not conflict but a process by which the main terms of the agreement, already understood by the negotiators, are made acceptable not to those in charge of the bargaining but to those who will have to live with its results.[13]

Blum asks, "How much of the collective bargaining process has any real meaning? How much of it is empty ritual?"[14] The author suggests that "to accomplish the bargaining task properly often requires co-operation, even if surreptitious co-operation is what we frequently find if we look below the surface of collective bargaining."[15]

George Brooks has devised a spectrum describing four types of union–management relations (Figure 6.1).[16] This chart indicates the character of both collaborative and collusive arrangements. Bryan Williams further elaborates on this:

> Labour management negotiations have often been described as only ritual and ceremony. That is, the parties often know from the outset what an acceptable settlement is likely to be but engage in ritualistic tactics and the ceremony of threats and compromise in order to meet the expectations of union members and top management shareholders.[17]

This description indicates that the ritual and ceremony are engaged in by both management and union negotiators. It also suggests that the negotiation process essentially based upon the exercise of power may not universally hold true or adequately describe all or even most sets of negotiations. Although it is not possible to get a numerical or percentage breakdown of the occurrences of non-collaborative, collaborative or collusive negotiations, it is nonetheless certain that some measure of ritual and ceremony is part of the negotiation process. It is this aspect of the negotiations that many describe as the "art" of collective bargaining, as well as the negotiator's ability to "smell the ball-park figure" or what is possible with regard to the outcome of the process.

While the collective bargaining process has been the subject of scholarly study from a variety of perspectives, there is relatively little analysis or description of the art of collective bargaining or, for that

Figure 6.1
Spectrum of Union Representative's Relations with the Management Counterpart

Non-collaborative
1. Never meets or talks with management except when accompanied by an *elected* committee or at a bargaining session.
2. Talks privately with management but reports all transactions to a committee or at a meeting. (Rare.)

Collaborative
3. Talks privately with management for the sole purpose of testing management response to union positions. Reports to membership committee at own discretion. Activists know that their union representative engages in such talks. (Rare and unstable.)
4. Negotiates privately in advance with management (not always to a conclusion) without the knowledge of the workers. Would be embarrassed if this were known to the local activists. Is convinced that the bargain is better than it would be without these private negotiations.
5. Arranges the formal negotiations with the management counterpart, including definite terms of settlement which each believes will be acceptable to all principals. Each representative keeps in touch with a counterpart during negotiations to suggest responses that will be needed to elicit desired responses from one's own team. Membership control is asserted as a principle and will in fact be exercised in critical situations. Negotiations are highly ritualized.
6. Alternative: The bargaining relationship may follow a traditional pattern so rigidly that prior consultation with management representatives is superfluous. Private talks will take place only as a result of unexpected developments within either the union or management organization.

Collusive
7. Routinely arranges all settlements in advance. Normally considers the members incapable of playing any useful role in bargaining. Decision making deliberately limited to smallest possible number, although the appearance of participation may be maintained. Requires intimate relations with company representative, and is easiest to achieve when an association of employers has delegated authority to a lawyer or other consultant.

Corrupt
8. Accepts money or other bribes to make a settlement that will be attractive to the employer. Participation of members negligible, usually without any pretense to the contrary. Other bribes may mean no more than a union shop and check-off, and the attraction to the employer *may* be no more than contract-bar insulation from a less compliant union.

matter, the ritual and ceremony as part of the process.[18] This chapter is an attempt to address this lack.

First, one should ask what are some of the likely factors that encourage or promote the possibility of a collusive relationship between the professional negotiators on both sides of the table. According to Brooks, the two most critical factors are (1) the age of the bargaining relationship, and (2) the location of decision-making authority in the negotiations.

THE AGE OF THE RELATIONSHIP

To a large extent the behaviour of a union depends upon employer attitudes. If an employer strongly resists unionization there is greater likelihood that a more militant and ideological union leadership will emerge. This situation is more characteristic of the early or formative years of union organization, when management has little or no experience with a trade union and is therefore distrustful and suspicious of both the union leadership and activists. Management is therefore reluctant to give unions the institutional or organizational security that union representatives and leaders believe they "need" (as opposed to what they "want"). The most important type of union security provision is a union-shop provision ensuring that all employees in the bargaining unit pay dues as a condition of employment. Thus, the "green years"[19] are characterized by distrust between the two major industrial relations actors. Their early agreements are more likely to reflect the non-collaborative stage of the relationship. The union bargaining committee is apt to be enthusiastic and actively involved in the negotiations so that the possibility of collusion between the chief negotiators is minimal, as well as risky or dangerous.

This relationship is likely to change over time, especially with management settling down and "living" with a trade union. Management's initial fears of a union lessen, and it begins to appreciate the grievance procedure, realizing that unionization does not result in the loss of management's right to manage; rather, management can no longer make unilateral decisions. This period may be characterized as the "middle years" of the relationship.

The middle years also see corresponding changes in the character of the union staff. For instance, with institutional security and check-off the union is more likely to rely on public relations experts, lawyers, and outside consultants. The relationship between the negotiators correspondingly changes from one of suspicion to one of familiarity. After all, they have been meeting over grievances and arbitration matters from time to time, as well as negotiating agreements.

In time, the middle period inevitably evolves into the post-middle years, a period often referred to as one of "maturity."[20] It is during this latter period that the possibilities of collusion emerge, since both negotiators or professional bargainers are equally concerned with industrial stability. It is even probable that they "swap" jobs—the union enforces the collective agreement while the head of industrial relations makes the union representative look good in a grievance case or in negotiations.

After all, each is in a position to do for the other what one cannot do for oneself. In other words, each of the "pros" can make the other look good before his or her respective constituency.

Richard A. Lester describes this process as follows:

> As the parties accumulate experience with collective bargaining, their relationship usually becomes more stable and negotiations are likely to be more amiable and factual. A number of factors help to account for such a change. The longer they negotiate, the better they come to know and understand one another and, consequently, surprises are less frequent. Also collective bargaining tends to lead to common problem-solving and the establishment and use of joint machinery for such endeavours.[21]

These scenario illustrates for Brooks and Lester the evolution of bargaining from an earlier to a later period. It results not only in the accommodation of union leadership with its counterpart in negotiations, but also in ritualization of the collective bargaining regime where the chief negotiators or "pros" keep their respective principals ignorant about the accommodation. Such tactics preserve the myth of conflict and ensure appropriate psychological pressures on each team to encourage or promote a softening of bargaining positions.

Donald E. Cullen recognizes this aspect of the negotiation process. Although unable to assess how widespread it is regardless of the stage or history of the bargaining relationship, he states that

> there are clearly no easy answers to these ethical and practical problems posed by labor negotiations. The line between "cooperation" and "collusion" can be exceedingly fine, just as is the line between "exercising leadership skills" and "manipulating people."[22]

Professor Cullen suggests that "collusion" represents bargaining in its "starkest possible form."[23] When professional negotiators get to know one another over time, there is an obvious and natural pressure to remove the risks and uncertainty in the negotiating process to minimize embarrassment or serious error of judgment at the bargaining table by private meetings, as well as the working out of an "advance agreement." The ritual thereafter merely gives the appearance of conflict necessary for the bargaining teams to adjust their respective positions.

Professor Lester, in his analysis of the evolution of union–management relations, describes this trend in collective bargaining:

> In essence, the bargaining process is part conflict and part cooperation for the purpose of arriving at solutions to problems. In its early years, the union and its leadership may have stressed hostility toward the employer and even toward the capitalistic system. But with continued joint dealing and successful negotiations, psychological changes are prone to occur on both sides.

...When unions are really accepted by management, a shift in company objectives and perspectives in labour relations tends to take place....Collaborative aspects of the relationship play a more significant role. They are: (1) increasing professionalization of the bargaining process, (2) more attention on administration and enforcement of the agreement, and (3) less use of the strike weapon.[24]

Lester suggests a natural tendency of the negotiators to meet privately in advance in order to remove the risks so as to protect their intra-organizational interests. Cullen sees the "political" aspects of negotiation as more characterized by bluffing than collusion:

...most negotiators are inclined to bluff and haggle for straightforward tactical reasons; that is, simply to get a better deal, even if they have never sensed or heard of the psychological values claimed for this process.

...On the other hand, even when negotiators are persuaded of the non-economic values of bluffing, their co-operation (or collusion) seldom needs to be as explicitly planned....Two experienced negotiators, for example, might never have to exchange a word to know beforehand that they will eventually agree, for a variety of good reasons, to follow a particular industry or area pattern.[25] Yet, they may plod together through the whole bargaining ritual because each is aware that his job is to do more than sign a contract. Again, action taken by tacit agreement seems less offensive than the same action agreed upon in secret meetings.[26]

Cullen, unlike Brooks, believes the bargaining ritual serves a useful and necessary function:

...the antics of the average union or management negotiator may be termed comic or outrageous or unethical—but they can hardly be called irrational.[27] At the least, the long-winded speeches, absurd demands, and fake threats serve the tactical purpose of concealing one's own true position while probing for that of the other side, a maneuver as ancient as bartering among men....The question facing most negotiators is not how to keep emotions and personalities and politics out of collective bargaining, for that is both impossible and undesirable. Rather, how can negotiators meet the inevitable psychological as well as economic needs of their parties? In this respect, the bargaining ritual also serves important, though highly controversial, functions: as a safety valve for accumulated frustrations, and as a way for non-negotiators to gain a sense of having participated, if only vicariously, in the job decisions with which they must live for the next two years.[28]

The above represents the conventional wisdom pertaining to the "political" aspects of negotiation often referred to by some as the "art" of negotiation. This is not to discount the importance and prevalence of the hard economic facts that often dictate the solution to the bargaining problems.

LOCATION OF DECISION MAKING IN
COLLECTIVE BARGAINING

While there is no single prescription applied to all negotiations, or in the formulation of bargaining demands and goals, the structure of the bargaining unit and location of decision making are important factors in influencing the type of relationship that emerges between the union leadership and the industrial relations officer representing the employer.

The structure of the bargaining unit is largely determined by the extent of union organization and the market. In a national product market industry, such as steel and automobile production, the bargaining unit is company-wide. In the building and construction trades (such as plumbing or electrical), which are characterized by a large number of contractors, bargaining is on a local level, or at a provincial level if there is accreditation.[29] In the public sector, provincial public employees bargain a provincial contract for the majority of their workers. In the federal public service, bargaining units tend to be national in scope.

The structure of the bargaining unit—whether a national unit in oligopolistic industries leading to company-wide bargaining, or a multi-plant unit, or a multi-employer unit, or plant-centred bargaining—influences the type of relationship between the parties. A plant-centred bargaining unit obviously offers greater possibilities for rank-and-file activity or involvement in the negotiations since the negotiations are "closer to home." As the locus of bargaining becomes more centralized—such as a multi-plant bargaining unit—the location of the bargain may shift away from the area of the local to accommodate the other plants. At the same time, each local union sends representatives or delegates to the bargaining committee with some loss of local rank-and-file determination of the outcome of the agreement as well as loss of initiative in affecting the outcome of the bargain.

This tendency towards centralization of the bargaining unit may promote, to some degree, a widening of the gap between the chief union negotiator or union leadership and the local union activists and rank-and-file membership, not withstanding the ratification process. It increases the possibility of private meetings between the negotiators and the ritualization of the collective bargaining process. At the same time, this tendency is often promoted by the union leadership and the employer for a variety of reasons. If the relationship has matured over time, then of course both parties prefer centralization as a means of creating greater industrial stability: they put greater trust in the negotiators to work out a settlement removed form the rank and file, who are likely to be less compromising with the terms of the settlement, since they have to live with it. For this reason, George Brooks believes that the structure of the bargaining and the location of the decision making are the two most important characteristics of collective bargaining[30] and the basis for developing the ritualistic and ceremonial scenarios.[31]

Other students of industrial relations view the centralizing tendency in collective bargaining as a natural response to economic factors—more specifically, to the way industry is organized and operates. The survival of the union depends largely upon its capacity to adapt itself to these conditions.

It is not the purpose of this chapter to examine the pros and cons of the effects of centralization of bargaining units, but rather to suggest that there is greater probability of ritualization where the locus of decision making is removed from the plant or local union. But first we must ask what is meant by the "ritual."[32]

THE RITUALIZATION OF COLLECTIVE BARGAINING

While the idea of collective bargaining as art requires further research and analysis of the ritualistic and ceremonial scenarios, one generally accepts the view that the age of the bargaining relationship and management attitudes have an enormous effect on shaping the behaviour of the union and the possibilities of a collaborative or non-collaborative relationship. Further, as the collective bargaining process is removed from plant-centred bargaining, the negotiations tend to become more of a pageant or drama,[33] and the respective roles of the union and management negotiators undergo subtle changes. For instance, Brooks states that there is the "swapping of jobs" by the union negotiator.

> In his efforts to bring about an agreement, he frequently finds that it is the local union and not the company which is the stumbling block. His role changes, therefore; he becomes more and more a mediator. Collective bargaining itself becomes a kind of sociodrama enacted to convince the membership that the results were "fair" or at least "all that could be gotten." This is called "statesmanship."[34]

The above quotation suggests that the labour movement has also undergone a change over time in the character of its leadership.

The second assumption put forth by Brooks is that the union leader or negotiator "sells the agreement," which role requires some dramatic ability. The transformation of character between the inspired founders of unions and those who administer collective agreements is then complete. The negotiators have a keen sense of mutual interest with their counterparts and their desire to avoid conflict, contrary to their reputation and image necessary to maintain member loyalty. This scenario, in effect, requires a re-definition of "power" as the bottom line or common denominator in collective negotiations. While the strike and lockout

Figure 6.2
Conventional vs. Collusive Models of Collective Bargaining

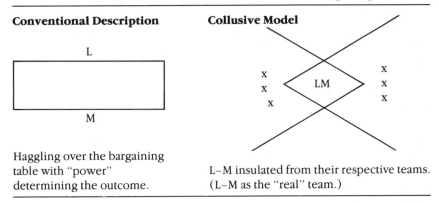

Conventional Description	Collusive Model
Haggling over the bargaining table with "power" determining the outcome.	L–M insulated from their respective teams. (L–M as the "real" team.)

legally define the process as adversarial, the ritualization and collaborative nature of "mature" bargaining require further re-examination.

Erving Goffman, in his seminal study on human behaviour in social situations, has employed a framework using the metaphor of the theatrical performance.[35] His study deals with the varied techniques used by "actors" or negotiators in everyday social intercourse to control or guide impressions of how they appear to others—the "audience."

Goffman's chapter "The Art of Impression Management" describes the "attributes that are required of a performer for the work of successfully staging a character":[36]

> ...in current management–labour relations, we know that a team may enter joint consultation meetings with the opposition with the knowledge that it may be necessary to give the appearance of stalking out of the meeting in a huff....In other words, while teams in our society are usually obliged to suppress their rage behind a working consensus, there are times when teams are obliged to suppress the appearances of sober opposition behind a demonstration of outraged feelings.[37]

The author is referring to negotiations between teams, for instance labour and management. Collusion, on the other hand, implies a secret arrangement between the labour and management negotiators insulated from their team-mates or colleagues. In other words, the "pros" work out a deal and sell it to their respective teams. This shifts the focus of collective negotiations from inter-team relations to intra-team relations, where the real bargaining goes on in the negotiation process.[38] A more precise picture of the collusive relationship, however, would be as shown in Figure 6.2.

Once the "real" team works out the "ball-park" money settlement and other important terms of the agreement, they then go through the "motions" of the negotiating process necessary to legitimize the collective bargaining process and the selling of the agreement to their respective teams. In this regard the following scenario may unfold with the opening remarks by the union negotiator: "This year we are asking for 16 cents an hour. I don't mean 17 cents an hour, nor do I mean 15 cents an hour, but 16 cents an hour." The negotiator for the union then spends half an hour or more justifying an increase of 16 cents an hour. Here, cost-of-living data and other economic factors are recited while the management team, of course, remains attentive to these statements. Needless to say, each side respects the need for each member of the team to maintain "face," since it is clear to all that humiliated subjects are more likely to retaliate with greater severity than those who receive favourable feedback. After a coffee break, management's chief negotiator begins his or her introductory remarks. They may go something as follows:

> I want to thank the union for their enormous research in support and defence of their bargaining position. We on the management team will, of course, take this information into consideration. I, too, would like to state from the outset that the workers in our plant have been most productive and loyal to this firm. There can be no doubt in my mind and the minds of senior management that they deserve the increase put forth regarding the wage package by the union. While I wholeheartedly concur with the justice of such an increase, especially for the sacrifice demonstrated by all the workers in the operation during the last set of negotiations, I regret that our operation is economically unable to afford the demands put forth today.

The management negotiator, while in sympathy with the union demands, then begins to justify a modest or relatively small increase, or as in recent years, concessions. During the "lean years" of negotiations, the collaborative model is more likely to break down; the mature relationship, as characterized by the "later" years of collective bargaining, deteriorates into hard bargaining more characteristic of the early years. On the other hand, many would argue that this situation does not represent a "deterioration" in the bargaining relationship, but rather a bargaining relationship that is non-collaborative and one without the deceptions inherent in the ritualization of the bargaining process.

After the introductory remarks by both negotiators, the teams either break into caucuses or may go to lunch, at which time the chief negotiators begin to bargain with their respective teams as outlined by Erving Goffman.[39] Consequently, the bargaining negotiations as observed by the team or the media represent the ritual, while the "real team," composed of the chief negotiators for the company and the union, have already worked out a tentative settlement during their private meetings. By doing so, they take the risk and uncertainty out of collective bargaining. The bargaining thereafter can only enhance their reputations as negotiators.

This ritual, as practised by the chief negotiators, makes the settlement look good to both teams. The negotiators come out of the bargaining with enhanced positions in their respective organizations. The real team can also judge how long the negotiations have to take in order to soften their respective teams so that they come to a mutually satisfactory agreement. Private meetings or secret telephone calls between the actors on the real team ensure a controlled and predictable outcome to the negotiations.

In selling the agreement, the union leader during the ratification process can come forward and reject the final offer of the company, knowing full well that the rest of the team believes that the final offer represents the best possible settlement without a strike. The union leader may make a presentation to the membership in the following manner:

> Brothers and sisters, this year we have gone through one of the toughest negotiations in the history of the bargaining relationship between this union and the firm. We have put down on the table fair demands. The company, on the other hand, has rejected our proposal for 16 cents an hour and is prepared to offer only 5 cents an hour. I have no doubt that if we want to increase that offer we will have to go out on strike. This year has been one of the toughest sets of negotiations that I have ever been involved in. I am unhappy with the company's final offer and I cannot in good conscience recommend that you accept this final offer. At the same time, the decision is all yours, since a strike will bring hardship on *your* families. After all, it is the bank that *you* will have to deal with regarding your mortgage payment or your auto payment. Consequently, it is you, the members of this union, that have to make up your minds whether we accept the company's final offer, or strike!

The above would be part of the ritual of negotiations. There is no general description pertaining to ritualization of collective bargaining or the varied ceremonies that have become part of it. One can readily extend these aspects of negotiations beyond ratification to both the mediation and arbitration processes so that they become part of the tactics and strategy of the two major actors on the real team. This assertion remains conjecture, since we haven't adequately or satisfactorily studied the role of ritual in grievance handling and in the arbitration process. The conventional wisdom regarding this process is that arbitration gets the parties "off the hook" regarding a contentious issue and releases frustration and tension between the major actors and the union membership and management.

CONCLUSION

This chapter emphasizes the possible ritualistic aspects of the negotiation process. The scenario is wholly hypothetical and conjectural. It is presented merely to stimulate imaginative thinking about the "art" of negotiation. Unfortunately, the empirical or descriptive literature regarding this aspect of our industrial relations system is almost non-existent. This does not mean that ritual is not a part of negotiation. On the contrary, the analysis put forth in this chapter provides a framework for both research and discussion regarding the art of negotiation. Further, we have not passed moral judgment regarding ritual. There can be no doubt that students of industrial relations find certain features of collaboration between the major actors deceptive and antithetical to the democratic features of collective bargaining and our industrial relations system. On the other hand, there can be no doubt that such tendencies exist, and that ritualistic aspects of negotiations are a reality. Although we cannot know with certainty the extent of such ritualistic behaviour, we believe that the majority of bargains fulfil the aims and objectives of collective bargaining as prescribed by legislation, reflecting the underlying assumptions of our liberal democratic society; that self-regulation is preferable to state-imposed regulations of wages, hours, and working conditions; and that decentralized decision making is a virtue.

At the same time, one must also be cognizant of contrary tendencies within our industrial relations system. Public policy must at once promote the right of workers to join unions of their own choosing and insist that trade unions be democratic organizations. The policy of industrial stability—"peace at any price"—should not override the democratic objectives served by the right of workers to join unions of their own choosing and to engage in collective bargaining.

NOTES

1. Chamberlain, Neil W. and James W. Kuhn, *Collective Bargaining*, 2nd ed. (New York: McGraw-Hill Book Company, 1965), p. 162.
2. Ibid., p. 165. This is a reference to the theory put forth by John R. Commons.
3. Hicks, J. R., *The Theory of Wages* (London: MacMillan Co., 1932). Also, Chamberlain and Kuhn, op. cit., p. 167.
4. Chamberlain, op. cit., p. 170.
5. Ibid., p. 121. See Chapter 5 for a fuller account.
6. Ibid., p. 130.
7. Walton, Richard, and R. McKersie, *A Behavioral Theory of Labor Negotiations* (New York: McGraw-Hill, 1965).
8. For an excellent discussion of this aspect of bargaining see John T.

Dunlop and James J. Healy, *Collective Bargaining, Principles and Cases*, rev. ed. (Homewood, IL: Irwin, 1955).

9. Ibid. Also Donald E. Cullen, *Negotiating Labour–Management Contracts*, Bulletin 56 (Ithaca, NY: New York State School of Industrial and Labor Relations, Cornell University, September 1965), p. 28. Also James J. Healy, ed., *Creative Collective Bargaining* (Englewood Cliffs, NJ: Prentice-Hall, 1965).

10. "Boulwarism" is derived from the bargaining strategy of Lemuel Boulware, Vice-President of Industrial Relations for General Electric Company in the U.S. in the mid-1950s. Mr. Boulware believed that a "firm but fair" offer by the company did not represent a failure to bargain in "good faith." The company would alter its position only upon appropriate union argument and evidence. This was ultimately viewed by the U.S. Supreme Court as unfair labour practice.

11. For a sympathetic account of General Electric's labour relations policy, see Herbert R. Northrup, *Boulwarism* (Ann Arbor: Bureau of Industrial Relations, University of Michigan, 1964).

12. Sanderson, John P., *The Art of Collective Bargaining* (Toronto: Richard De Boo, 1979).

13. Blum, Albert A., "Collective bargaining: Ritual or reality?" *Harvard Business Review*, November-December 1961: 64–65.

14. Ibid., p. 60.

15. Ibid., p. 65.

16. Brooks, George W., Spectrum of union spokesman's relations with his management counterpart, December 5, 1968. (Unpublished.)

17. Williams, Bryan, "Negotiating the union–management agreement." In Anderson, John and Morely Gunderson (eds.), *Union–Management Relations in Canada* (Don Mills, Ontario: Addison-Wesley Publishers, 1982), p. 200.

18. I am indebted to Professor George W. Brooks for bringing this matter to my attention, and for his insights regarding both his analysis of this development and how the practice of ceremony and ritual reveals itself. Brooks had been Director of Research and Education of the International Brotherhood of Pulp, Sulphite and Paper Mill Workers for over fifteen years before joining the New York State School of Industrial and Labor Relations Faculty at Cornell University in the early 1960s.

19. A phrase used by George Brooks to categorize the formative years of the bargaining relationship.

20. Lester, Richard A., *As Unions Mature: An Analysis of the Evolution of American Unionism* (Princeton, NJ: Princeton University Press, 1958), pp. 119–123. The author refers to union leaders during this period as labour "statesmen."

21. Ibid., p. 41.

22. Cullen, op. cit., p. 13. (See note 9.)
23. Ibid.
24. Lester, op. cit., pp. 119–120.
25. The reference is to pattern bargaining which seems, on the face, to promote more readily the ritualization of collective bargaining since the senior negotiators already have in their hands a copy of the "pattern" negotiated elsewhere. I realize not all students of industrial relations would agree with this assessment. I have nonetheless observed this phenomenon and have been told about such incidents by the negotiators themselves.
26. Cullen, op. cit., p. 14.
27. I doubt if Brooks would agree with this statement.
28. Cullen, op. cit., p. 14.
29. Accreditation is the process used to specify an organization of employers as the bargaining agent for a unit employees. The parallel term for employee organizations is "certification."
30. Brooks, George W.,"Unions and the structure of collective bargaining." In Arnold Weber, *The Structure of Collective Bargaining: Problems and Perspectives* (New York: The Free Press of Glencoe, 1961), pp. 123–147.
31. Brooks, George W. *The Sources of Vitality in the American Labour Movement* (Ithaca, NY: New York State School of Industrial and Labor Relations, Cornell University, Bulletin 41, July, 1960).
32. My views are based in part on the personal associations of my work. In the early 1960s, I was a representative and organizer for the American Federation of State County and Municipal Employees (AFL–CIO) for Region 2 (New York and New Jersey), which is the equivalent of the Canadian Union of Public Employees, CLC. I was also Education and Research Director for Local 91, International Ladies Garment Workers' Union. From 1972 to 1982 I held the following positions in the Saskatchewan Department of Labour: Director of Mediation and Conciliation, Executive Director of the Occupational Health and Safety Branch, and Assistant and Associate Deputy Minister of Labour. I should at least acknowledge that these experiences with the major industrial relations "actors" while in government only reinforced my views regarding "mature" bargaining relations, or my appreciation for the "art" of collective bargaining and the degree of ritualization of the process.
33. Brooks, George W., "Management–union relations: Observation on the changing nature of American unions." Paper presented at the Institute of Labor and Industrial Relations, University of Michigan— Wayne State University, July 6–11, 1958, p. 4.
34. Ibid.

35. Goffman, Erving, *The Presentation of Self in Everyday Life* (Garden City, NY: Doubleday Anchor Books,1959).
36. Ibid., p. 208.
37. Ibid., p. 245.
38. For a description of this process see "Intra-organizational bargaining tactics," in Walton and McKersie, *A Behavioral Theory of Labour Negotiations*, op. cit., Chapter IX.
39. Goffman has further developed his views on face-to-face interaction and communication in his book *Strategic Interaction* (Philadelphia: University of Pennsylvania Press, 1969). He uses the term "strategic interaction" to describe the game-like events applicable to both inter- and intra-organizational tactics.

7

The Science of Bargaining

JOHN KERVIN

Is bargaining an art or a science? The answer is "a bit of both." For those who take part in collective bargaining, the art lies in knowing the right thing to say and do, and when to say and do it. For negotiators, bargaining is a finely honed skill, as much art as any theatre performance.[1]

On the other hand, those who study bargaining adopt a scientific approach using theories, hypotheses, careful measurement, and empirical tests to understand why and how things happen in negotiation. For them, the science of negotiation is a set of findings about the causes and effects of different factors related to the bargaining process and outcomes. In addition, these findings can often be used by negotiators to help them better understand, and control, what happens during collective bargaining.

Interest in the scientific study of negotiation has blossomed in the last two decades. With the realization that all bargaining situations have important aspects in common, from international trade and disarmament talks to marriage counselling to labour relations, the search has quickened for concepts and theories to account for the process and outcomes of negotiation.[2]

The purpose of this chapter is to review the results of behavioural research on negotiation, and to apply them to shed light on union–management collective bargaining.[3] We will identify what appear to be important factors and, where appropriate, draw on bargaining theory to suggest how these factors operate to affect the bargaining process and settlements. To make the material more relevant to the student of industrial relations, we'll adopt the point of view of one of the parties (union or management) making decisions relevant to the conduct of negotiations, or an individual negotiator deciding what actions to take. In addition, the appendix to this chapter contains a short case study of a real collective bargaining situation in which the reader is invited to account for the process and outcomes.

We'll begin by looking at the dependent variables: four aspects of collective bargaining we want to explain and understand. We'll then identify the six categories of independent variables or "causes" we'll use to organize our examination of relevant bargaining research. Then we'll look in detail at variables within each category to see how research can help us better understand collective bargaining processes and outcomes.

DEPENDENT VARIABLES

Behavioural studies of negotiation have tended to focus on explaining four dependent variables relevant to collective bargaining:

1. The relationship between the parties (more specifically, the amount of conflict or co-operation between them);
2. The moves each party makes in the course of bargaining;
3. Whether a strike or other sanctions are used; and
4. The content of the settlement.

The Relationship

The attitudes of the parties towards one another and the nature of the relationship between them affects both the process and the outcomes of collective bargaining. The most important aspect of their relationship is the amount of co-operation or conflict. Following research by Deutsch and Krauss (1962), we can identify three positions on the co-operation–conflict continuum:

1. In a *highly co-operative* relationship, the parties work together to maximize joint outcomes on as many of the issues as possible, recognizing that at least some (most particularly, wages) are less likely to be amenable to this approach.[4]
2. In a *moderately competitive* relationship, each party seeks to maximize its own gains without any particular attention to the other side's gains or costs.
3. In a *highly competitive* relationship, each party seeks to maximize the other's losses, with less attention paid to its own gains. The objective is to punish the other party; management may try to break the union.

The type of relationship has important implications for the parties. Those with a co-operative association are likely to find mutually agreeable solutions to some of the problems facing them at negotiations; those with a highly competitive relationship are likely to view everything in win–lose terms and to miss the opportunity for reaching settlements with benefits for both parties. In addition, highly competitive negotiations are more likely to be hampered by the presence of *intangible issues*: concerns with fairness, face-saving, and appearances of toughness and competence. Such concerns become as important to the bargaining as wages, benefits, and other tangible issues.

The terms we use to describe the relationship between union and management also apply to each party's own orientation towards bargaining, and to the orientation of each individual negotiator. As part of his or her personality, each individual has a given propensity to approach negotiations in a particular manner: co-operative, moderately competitive, or highly competitive. This orientation is modified by situational factors, including the other party's actions. A party's orientation is determined by the approach of its chief negotiator, its mandate, and attitudes in the constituency (head office for management; the membership for the union).

When both parties adopt similar orientations, the relationship is likely to correspond; for example, two parties with co-operative orientations will have a co-operative relationship. When their orientations differ, as we shall see, the result is likely to be either a moderately or a highly competitive relationship, depending upon whether there is a significant power imbalance, and whether it is exploited by the more powerful party to gain a one-sided settlement. It is unlikely that a party would remain highly co-operative in its approach in the face of a competitive opponent.

Bargaining Moves

The actual course of bargaining can be seen as the sequence of moves made by the parties. For the study of collective bargaining, we can group all moves into five categories:

1. Concession: taking a new position closer to (or identical with) the latest position of the opposing team;
2. Trade-off: making a concession on one item in return for the opponent's concession on another;
3. Promise: offering some benefit to the opponent in return for a move on its part, usually offering a concession on one item in return for the opposing party's concession on another (on occasion, parties make unconditional promises);
4. Threats: suggesting some action that will harm the opponent, if (or unless) the opponent makes a particular move (parties sometimes make unconditional threats);
5. Procedural move: suggesting or making a change in the procedures of bargaining (such as meeting or agenda schedules, requesting mediation, caucusing, etc.).

Many researchers have been particularly interested in *matching* of moves. Moves are said to match when the actions of one party (especially concession rates) correspond to the moves of the other in content, magnitude, or frequency. We will examine some of the circumstances under which matching is likely to occur, as well as the determinants of different moves and rates of concession making.

Strikes

Because of their importance for collective bargaining, research on the use of strikes or lockouts (or other sanctions involving work performance) is of interest to both students and practitioners of industrial relations. Unfortunately, in the bulk of behavioural bargaining research, strikes are dealt with only indirectly. Studies have focused on two approximately equivalent situations: the breakdown of negotiations, and deadlines reached without settlement. Both of these can be treated, with caution about their generalizability to collective bargaining, as approximately equivalent to strikes. On the other hand, a number of case studies and some surveys of strikes have been carried out, but these have not always paid attention to the bargaining process and behaviour.[5]

The Settlement

Settlements can be viewed from a number of perspectives. One is the point of view of a single party, and the value of a particular settlement to that party. Research with this perspective examines the degree to which a particular characteristic or move affects the outcomes for the party possessing or making use of it. A second perspective is the total value of the settlement to both parties, or the joint outcome. Research adopting this perspective investigates the degree to which the parties are able to maximize their joint outcome by finding solutions that take into account the needs of both parties. In Walton and McKersie's terms, how much "integrative bargaining" do the parties achieve? Although behavioural research has examined both aspects, the one of more interest has been the latter.

A third aspect of the settlement is the degree to which it is one-sided, or particularly favourable to union or management, given the economic situation and other settlements in the industry and area. One-sided settlements usually indicate the exploitation by one party of substantial power differences between the parties, and have implications for the relationship and process of bargaining in future rounds.

Researchers have studied other aspects of settlements which we will not examine here. For example, an important dependent variable has been whether two negotiators actually reach an agreement. Although the occasions on which no agreement is ever reached are highly significant for the parties involved, and usually indicate a greater loss to the union than to management because of the probability of subsequent de-certification and loss of bargaining rights, the incidence of non-settlement is too low to merit our attention.

Finally, note that the first two of these dependent variables—relationships and moves—are also independent variables with respect to the second two. Thus, relationships and moves can be treated as causes of strike incidence and duration, and of the content of a settlement. In the discussion that follows, we'll treat "moves" as one of our categories of independent variables. In several instances we'll use the bargaining relationship as an intervening variable to explain why a particular factor has a particular effect.

INDEPENDENT VARIABLES

Let us now turn to the six categories of independent variables we will use to organize our discussion of the science of bargaining:

1. Characteristics of negotiators;
2. Context of negotiations;
3. Composition of the bargaining team;
4. The chief negotiator's relationship with his or her constituency;
5. Bargaining procedures; and
6. Moves the parties make in the course of bargaining.

Research involving variables in these six categories can help us understand variations in our dependent variables: the union–management bargaining relationship, the moves each party makes in the course of negotiations, whether bargaining might involve a strike before settlement is reached, and the content of the settlement. This research can also help explain many of the differences we see between different sets of negotiations, or even between rounds of negotiations involving the same two parties.

Negotiator Characteristics

Research has focused on two general types of negotiator characteristics: social and personality. The former includes visible features such as sex and socio-economic status; the latter includes such personality traits as risk-seeking, need for achievement, and need for power.

Both social and personality characteristics affect the ways negotiators behave and their effectiveness in different types of bargaining situations. Most of the research relates negotiator characteristics to their orientation to negotiations (co-operative or competitive). Knowing the characteristics of both negotiators would help an observer to predict their orientations, as well as the relationship between the parties that is likely to emerge in the course of bargaining. Other research relates characteristics to the bargaining moves negotiators make, the likelihood of stalemate, and the content of the settlement, particularly the degree of jointly beneficial outcomes.

Sex

In their review of over 100 experimental studies of the role of sex in bargaining behaviour, Rubin and Brown (1975) advance an interesting explanation for the conflicting observations that women negotiators appear sometimes to be more co-operative, and at other times more retaliatory and less co-operative, than males. They suggest that females generally have higher levels of *interpersonal orientation* (io), that is, a higher sensitivity to, and a greater likelihood of responding to, interpersonal cues and others' behaviour. They are more aware of others' expectations, intentions, and approach. They are more likely to attribute another's behaviour to his or her personality, rather than situational constraints and opportunities the other is facing. Low-io negotiators, on the other hand, tend to ignore others' acts and outcomes and to concentrate on achieving their own goals.

In bargaining, Rubin and Brown suggest, high-io negotiators are more likely to respond to the other negotiator's co-operativeness by being co-operative themselves, and to respond to what they perceive as too much competitiveness, or attempts at exploitation by a more powerful opponent, by becoming much more competitive and retaliatory themselves. We can also infer that high-io negotiators would be more likely to become involved in long, emotional strikes. In other words, with a female negotiator the bargaining relationship is likely to be more unstable and to range from extremes of co-operation to bitter competitiveness. On the other hand, it must be noted that the correlation between io and sex is far from perfect, and that many of the women who advance to positions of responsibility in collective bargaining may well have much lower levels of interpersonal orientation than the college students with whom the majority of studies have been carried out.

With respect to the content of agreement, interpersonal orientation also helps to explain why different studies have found both males (Shomer et al., 1966) and females (Borah, 1963) to have more co-operative settlements and higher joint outcomes. The difference appears to be the orientation and behaviour of the opposing negotiator. When the opponent is co-operative, females achieve better joint outcomes, but when an opponent is inclined to be competitive, female negotiators are more likely to become highly competitive in retaliation and to achieve lower joint outcomes.

One other aspect of interpersonal orientation has significance for collective bargaining. Research by Slusher et al. (1974) and others suggests that the degree to which negotiators anticipate future interaction will raise their levels of IO. This suggests that negotiators drawn from the local management and workforce will be more likely to bargain like high-IO individuals than a labour lawyer bargaining with an official from the union head office, and thus have a greater potential for co-operative problem solving and settlements with higher joint benefits.

Socio-Economic Status

A number of factors contribute to a negotiator's socio-economic status (SES), including occupation, income, education, and race or ethnicity. Research has found that status differences between negotiators can affect their bargaining relationship.

Status differences are often present between chief negotiators and between negotiating teams, particularly in negotiations involving small employers and bargaining units. Union negotiators drawn from the bargaining unit are likely to have lower income and educational levels, and less occupational status. On the other hand, public sector bargaining involving units of scientific and professional employees often reverses the situation, and leads to an interesting discrepancy: the side that has higher status may have lower power. (It is important not to confuse status differences with bargaining-power differences: a low-status negotiator may have more, less, or the same amount of power as his or her higher-status opponent.) This kind of status discrepancy can lead to intangible issues clouding the bargaining as each side attempts to redress the status inconsistency (Ridgeway, 1983).

Research shows that there is some tendency for negotiations involving pairs of high-SES negotiators to be more co-operative than negotiations in which both negotiators have lower SES. Gahagan and Tedeschi (1968) found this result in their research with college students from varying SES backgrounds. Things are more complicated when status differences exist across the table. Swingle (1969) reports that high-SES negotiators (anglophone students) continued to make co-operative moves even in the face of hostile moves on the part of francophone opponents (whom they perceived as having lower SES), as a way of maintaining "psychological distance" by not emulating their behaviour. However, with respect to bargaining outcomes and the content of settlements, research by Faley and Tedeschi (1971) with ROTC cadets of different ranks suggests that exploitation (taking advantage of greater power to achieve a one-sided agreement) is more likely when high-status negotiators are faced by low-status and less powerful opponents. Rubin and Brown (1975) suggest that lower-SES negotiators, bargaining with higher-status others, act with heightened interpersonal orientation, leading them to be either more co-operative or more competitive, depending on their opponent's bargaining behaviour.

Risk Seeking

The effect of risk-seeking personality on a negotiator's propensity to co-operate and his or her choice of bargaining moves is, at first glance, ambiguous. In many cases to initiate co-operation is risky, since it leaves the negotiator open to exploitation. The opponent may accept the initial offer, but give little or nothing in return. On the other hand, to act in a highly competitive fashion and threaten a strike is also risky since, if the threat is rebuffed, a strike or other costly sanction is likely. Thus there is risk in both co-operative and competitive moves: trying to co-operate to attain a higher joint outcome risks getting a poor settlement, and attempting to be highly competitive to attain the best possible individual settlement risks the costs of a strike.

The research in this area suggests, however, that risk seekers avoid both these options. Sherman found that, using variations of the Prisoner's Dilemma game, high risk takers were more likely to seek to maximize their own gains rather than to attempt to maximize joint outcomes (Sherman, 1967, 1968).[6] Rubin and Brown (1975) note that risk takers behave like negotiators with low interpersonal orientation, focusing on their own gains rather than the other side's behaviour. This implies that they also avoid highly competitive moves that try to "beat" their opponents. Since a moderately competitive orientation is the approach that appears to be most successful in the majority of collective bargaining situations, risk taking is likely to be a desirable quality in a chief negotiator. However, if the situation requires problem-solving approaches by both parties, low risk takers will likely achieve better solutions.

With regard to concession making, high risk takers in a Bilateral Monopoly experiment were found to make fewer concessions than risk avoiders under situations of poor information about the opponent's payoffs (Harnett et al., 1968).[7] Although this appears to be cautious rather than risky bargaining behaviour, it is consistent with the greater interest in own rather than joint benefits among high risk takers.

Need for Achievement and Need for Power

Need for achievement (Nach) is the drive to excel in personal endeavours; need for power (Nepo) is the drive to dominate and exert control over other persons (Terhune, 1968). These two psychological traits would both appear to be related to an individual's success in climbing either the union or management hierarchy; thus both are likely to be found at the negotiation table or behind the scene. However, they appear to lead to very different kinds of bargaining orientations and behaviour.

In a study by Terhune (1968) with subjects who scored highly on only one of these characteristics, high-Nach individuals were much more co-operative in their orientation and much more inclined to take advantage of the possibility of opportunities for maximizing joint payoffs. High-Nepo subjects, on the other hand, were much more competitive, more likely to make ambiguous statements, and sought to exploit power differences to gain advantageous outcomes. In an "international relations" game, high-Nepo subjects did the most lying. Rubin and Brown (1975) suggest that individuals with a high need for achievement bargain like persons with low interpersonal orientation, ignoring the other's outcomes and concentrating on maximizing their own returns, co-operating when this appears to be beneficial to themselves. Those with a high need for power, on the other hand, bargain like individuals with high interpersonal orientation and a highly competitive approach, exploiting the opponent wherever possible. The implication for collective bargaining is that, in most circumstances, negotiators high on need for achievement, but low on need for power, make the most effective negotiators.

In summary, negotiators' social and personality characteristics appear to affect how co-operatively or competitively they approach negotiations, and their sensitivity to interpersonal cues and opponents' behaviour. The results suggest that the choice of negotiator should fit a party's objectives and the known characteristics of the opposing negotiator. If problem-solving issues have high priority, then characteristics consistent with high interpersonal orientation and a co-operative approach should be sought in a chief negotiator; if the opposing negotiator is tough and highly competitive, a low-io negotiator would appear to be the best choice.

The Context of Negotiations

The general situation and specific context in which negotiations take place affect both process and outcome. Many aspects of the situation and context are economic in nature (such as markets for the employer's products or services, unemployment, the general health of the economy, and inflation) and will not be dealt with here. Other situational factors for which research results are available include the attitudes of the negotiators' constituencies (particularly on the union side), the degree of stress under which the parties are negotiating, and the bargaining power available to each side.

Constituencies

Each negotiating team has a constituency for whom it negotiates. For management, the constituency includes upper management and, indirectly, the board of directors and shareholders. For the union, it includes members of the bargaining unit and the union head office. The nature of constituencies is that they have a stake in the outcome, and can reward or punish their negotiators, at the very least by granting or withholding approval. Constituencies vary in three important respects:

1. The immediacy of the feedback they provide to negotiators;
2. Their attitudes about the opposing party (militancy);
3. The degree to which they can be divided into subgroups with competing interests.

In general, constituency effects are felt to a greater degree on the union side, since the election of union officers by the membership adds a substantial political component to bargaining.

Most research attention has focused on the immediacy of the constituency's feedback to negotiators, or in collective bargaining terms, the degree to which they are aware of what is happening at the negotiating table. When members of the constituency can observe bargaining sessions (Carnevale et al., 1979), and are thus in a position to offer immediate feedback, negotiators are more reluctant to make concessions.

Other research has examined the consequences of the constituency's attitudes towards the opposing party for the behaviour of its own and the opposing negotiator. Brown's research (1968) suggests that when negotiators believe their constituency desires hard bargaining, they are more likely to be concerned about image loss (Pruitt, 1981) and less likely to make concessions. When negotiators perceive their opponent's constituency to be tough and demanding, their concessions are more likely to match their opponent's as the bargaining progresses (Wall, 1977).

Less empirical research has been undertaken on the effects of intra-constituency conflicts. The evidence from case studies, however, suggests that such divisions hinder effective decision making by the chief negotiator (Kervin et al., 1984) and the bargaining team (Colosi, 1983). Negotiators are more likely to have trouble "selling" the settlement, particularly on the union side which lacks the hierarchical decision-making structure available to management, and it appears that strikes may be more prevalent under such conditions. Kochan (1974) found in a survey of municipal collective bargaining that intra-constituency conflicts (among politicians on the management side) led to actions on the part of certain constituency members that affected negotiators' bargaining power.

Stress

Many of the environmental circumstances surrounding negotiations can be interpreted in terms of the degree of stress they place on negotiators. For example, many economic factors (such as unemployment, inflation, and layoffs) contribute to the stress experienced by one or both parties. Other sources of stress include those that affect negotiations as a whole (public attention and publicity), the union as an organization (raiding or de-certification pressures and membership unrest), the individual union members (technological change affecting employment and job content), and individual members of management (organizational restructuring, corporate takeovers).

Research by Kelly et al. (1965) suggests that under conditions of high external stress, the members of a bargaining team will have greater difficulty co-ordinating their behaviour. This would make it more difficult for the team to decide on positions and to judge the quality of a potential settlement. The effect of stress can be partly mitigated by good interpersonal relationships within a cohesive team (Shils and Janowitz, 1948), but very high levels of team cohesion can lead to poor decisions under stressful conditions—a situation known as "groupthink" (Janis, 1972). Groups in this situation tend to do two things that greatly hinder the quality of their decision making. First, they tend to look at only a limited number of options, focusing far too early on a single choice and excluding potentially better alternatives. Second, they suppress negative opinions and ignore problematic aspects of this choice. The result is often premature "closure" on a poor decision.

High levels of stress also affect relations between the parties, since the level of trust declines (Kelley et al., 1965). Overall, the effect of high stress will be to hinder the development of a co-operative relationship between the parties, for which trust is an essential component. In addition, we can expect high levels of stress to lead to both poorer joint settlements, since the best options will never be fully explored, and possibly a higher incidence of strikes as solutions that would have avoided strikes won't be examined.

Bargaining Power

Perhaps the most important situational factor in collective bargaining is bargaining power. Economists have focused on the relationship of bargaining power to outcomes; behavioural scientists have concentrated on the effect of bargaining power on the bargaining process. Two aspects of bargaining power have received attention in experimental studies: the relative amounts the parties possess, and the total amount or sum of the parties' power. Power has most frequently been operationalized in terms of the reward structure of payoffs and costs to the parties for certain agreements, which corresponds reasonably closely to the common industrial relations definition of power in terms of the cost to self of imposing costs on the other party.

Research suggests that when the power balance is approximately equal, the negotiators jointly behave more co-operatively (e.g., Sheposh and Gallo, 1973), achieve higher joint outcomes (Deutsch and Krauss, 1960), and make larger concessions (Komorita and Barnes, 1969). Rubin and Brown (1975) suggest that an exception occurs when the two parties are competitively disposed towards each other. In such situations, the level of conflict is likely to be extremely high, and to be expressed in disputes involving intangible issues.

When power is unequally distributed between the parties, the more powerful party, as expected, is likely to be less interested in co-operation (Johnson and Ewens, 1971) and to use threats more frequently (Kelley et al., 1970). On the other hand, negotiators with less power than their opponents have been found to be more willing to compromise (Hermann and Kogan, 1968) and more willing to match their opponent's concessions (Michener et al., 1975). The greater the inequality, the more pronounced these bargaining behaviours (Aranoff and Tedeschi, 1968).

The total amount of power available to the parties has also been found to affect their behaviour. A low-power situation corresponds to a bargaining relationship in which the right to strike or lockout is curtailed. A high-power situation would be one in which, through co-ordinated bargaining, a number of locals employing a large number of employees and affecting most of a firm's productive capacity could strike (or be locked out), or a threatened strike or lockout in a time of high unemployment would seriously affect an employer's share of the market. In general, research such as that of Deutsch and Krauss (1960) suggests that when the total power is low, joint outcomes are higher, and negotiators are more willing to bargain co-operatively (Berkowitz et al., 1970).

In summary, research has shown that many aspects of the bargaining situation can affect the parties' orientations and moves and the possibility of a strike. Constituency characteristics appear to affect most the negotiators' moves, particularly concession making. External stress hinders the development of trust between the parties, and reduces the quality of intra-team co-ordination and decision making. The balance of bargaining power, as well as affecting the settlement, determines the likelihood of co-operative problem solving. Similarly, the total amount of power available to the parties also affects the likelihood of a co-operative relationship.

Composition of the Bargaining Team

The composition of the bargaining team has two components with importance for the collective bargaining process. The first is the bargaining structure: how many distinct bargaining units or employers are represented on each team.[8] The second is team characteristics: its size and composition in terms of homogeneity of members, and the extent to which sub-groups within each bargaining unit or employer are represented. For example, a union team may include female and unskilled workers, or a management team may include production and planning department heads.

Bargaining Structure

We can expect that the more complicated the bargaining structure, the more difficulties in co-ordination negotiators must deal with, and the more time must be spent on the bargaining and decision making within each team (Colosi, 1983). Perry and Angle (1981), in a study of 28 public transit organizations, found that negotiations did take longer and union–management relations were less co-operative among more complex bargaining structures. Mudge (1982) found that union negotiating teams comprising librarians and support staff were likely to be in conflict over bargaining goals.

The intra-team conflict and decision-making and co-ordination problems associated with more complex bargaining structures have several implications for collective bargaining. First, they suggest that third party intervention (particularly mediation) may be required to help settle both intra-team differences and inter-team complications arising from more complex structures. It also seems likely that settlements with problem-solving solutions to mutual problems are less likely as structures become more complicated.

Bargaining Teams

Research on the dynamics of small groups is highly suggestive for indicating the effects of team size and composition on bargaining performance. A bargaining team's task involves a wide range of components: preparing for negotiations by identifying issues and finding data to support arguments and positions, problem solving to find solutions and wording that will meet the objectives of both sides, and judging the likely reaction of the other team (and of their own constituencies) to possible settlements. Aside from the obvious need for effort, knowledge, and skills to attain a successful settlement, the strategies the group adopts for its own work and decision making will determine its effectiveness (Hackman and

Morris, 1975). Using Herold's (1978) typology, the group's task has both high technical demands (evaluating complex information) and high social demands (resolving the conflicting interests of group members and sub-constituencies). In such situations, a balance between task emphasis and attention to relationships among group members in the group's working and decision-making strategies is crucial for effective performance (Ridgeway, 1983).

An important aspect of group composition is whether the bargaining team's status structure matches the members' abilities: do the persons on the team with the most expertise and knowledge also have the highest status? Because high-status group members control the flow of communication, and have more importance attached to their ideas and opinions (Maier and Hoffman, 1960), a bargaining team is likely to be more effective, and produce better settlements, if status and abilities are consistent.

The best size for a bargaining team is an issue with no easy answers. Steiner (1972) suggests that the effectiveness of a group increases with size up to a point, and then levels off and eventually declines. The optimum group size largely depends on the complexity of the issues. The more complex they are, the more each group member can contribute to their understanding, particularly if the members are heterogeneous in background, experience, and ability. However, increases in size engender two difficulties: it takes more time and energy to organize group activities and co-ordinate discussion, and there are more competing points of view that have to be dealt with in reaching a decision. The research suggests that the more directive the team's leader, the larger the size of group that can be handled; and the more complex the issues, the larger the group should be (Ridgeway, 1983).

Finally, heterogeneous groups are likely to do better than homogeneous ones. Differences in level of ability, type of ability, and personality have been found to contribute to group performance (Goldman, 1965; Hoffman, 1959). These differences contribute both to the resources available to the group, and to a multiplicity of approaches to the team's problems. It would seem that in collective bargaining, heterogeneous teams would perform better in both co-operative and high-conflict situations by generating more strategies and solutions.

In summary, the composition of the bargaining team appears to affect most strongly the effectiveness of the team's deliberations and, indirectly, the content of the settlement. Innovative solutions to joint problems would appear to be less likely when the team reflects a complex bargaining structure. The most effective bargaining is likely to occur when there is a range of backgrounds represented on the team, and when differences in ability are consistent with differences in status. Finally, the size of the bargaining team should take into account both the chief negotiator's leadership style (directive or participatory) and the complexity of the issues on the table.

The Chief Negotiator, the Team, and the Constituency

Each negotiator has a relationship with both his or her constituency and with the opposing negotiator. As he or she attempts to represent the views and positions of the one to the other, each negotiator occupies what Walton and McKersie (1965) call a "boundary role." Factors that affect one of the boundary-role relationships also affect the other. Thus, the relationship of the chief negotiator to the constituency, and to the team, will have repercussions for his or her relationship with the opposing negotiator, and ultimately for the process and outcome of bargaining.

Negotiator–constituency relationships vary in the amount of authority the negotiator has to reach a settlement for the constituency, and the degree to which the negotiator is personally committed to the constituency's objectives. In addition, as the usual leader of the bargaining team, the chief negotiator's leadership style will also affect the team's group dynamics and decision making.

Negotiator's Authority

The discretion that a chief negotiator may exercise in advancing new positions, or accepting a tentative settlement, ranges widely in collective bargaining. Some negotiators, particularly in public sector situations, have very little authority and must constantly consult with their constituency (union officials or a bargaining committee on the union side; upper management or elected officials on the employer side). Such negotiators are high in *accountability*: their actions are closely monitored by the constituency, which can reward or punish their negotiator for behaviours during bargaining or for the settlement achieved. On the other hand, there are bargaining situations in which the negotiator has almost absolute power; in the extreme case settlements are not even submitted to the constituency for ratification. In general, the two most common situations are the negotiator who has the power to enter agreements subject to ratification, and the negotiator who must consult a bargaining committee (as distinct from the bargaining team that appears at the table) before committing to an agreement on any issue.

Research has shown that variations in the chief negotiator's authority and accountability have an impact on the bargaining process and outcomes. Gruder (1969, 1971) found that negotiators who have to justify their settlements to a constituency bargain harder and make smaller initial concessions than those who don't. The more power a constituency has over its negotiator, the larger the demands and slower the concessions of that negotiator (Bartunek et al., 1975). However, it appears that if the relationship between a negotiator and the constituency is temporary (as would be the case when lawyers or other "outsiders" are hired to conduct negotiations), these relationships do not hold (Klimoski, 1972). This is also the case for negotiators whose status is higher than that of their constituents (Kogan et al., 1972).

High levels of accountability also appear to lead to more problems in reaching a settlement. Daniel (1976) found that managers who were highly accountable were more likely to be involved in strikes or similar sanctions involving withdrawal of labour.

Elected representatives (such as a chief negotiator selected by ballot) are likely to feel highly accountable to those who elected them. Such representatives apparently are more likely to believe that their constituencies are "tougher" than they would be themselves. Lamm and Kogan (1970) showed that elected representatives were slower to make concessions than other team members.

Research reported by Pruitt (1981) is particularly interesting because it calls into question one of the taken-for-granted procedures found in collective bargaining. Pruitt and his colleagues, using male subjects in buyer–seller negotiations, found that negotiators who bargained without a specific resistance point obtained more favourable settlements than those who made a conscious resistance-point decision. The implication for collective bargaining is that negotiators who are *not* given resistance points (and thus have authority to move as far as they like) may do better. This finding is more applicable to management than union negotiators; the latter usually work with more informal and "intuitive" resistance points based on estimates of what the membership will ratify.

Negotiator's Commitment

Negotiators vary in the degree to which they feel emotionally or ideologically committed to the objectives of their constituencies. Blake and Mouton (1961) observed that negotiators who strongly identified with their constituencies found it difficult to concede to the opponent, and difficult even to perceive accurately the other side's position. Hornstein and Johnson (1966) confirmed that such negotiators bargain more competitively and encounter more difficulties in negotiations. Rubin and Brown (1975) conclude that the most effective negotiators may be those who are not too highly committed to their constituencies' positions. They will be better able to see alternative and innovative solutions, and to achieve better settlements. The research also implies that strikes will be less frequent when chief negotiators are not too highly committed to constituency positions.

Leadership Style

Research in group dynamics suggests two possible leadership styles for a bargaining team. Participative leaders are those who encourage a great deal of group-member involvement in decision making; directive leaders tend to structure the group's activities and make most decisions themselves. Research by Fiedler (1967) shows that participative leadership works best when the group's situation is neither very favourable nor very unfavourable. Since bargaining is generally a stressful and competitive activity, Fiedler's research suggests that most bargaining teams perform better under directive leadership, particularly when issues are complex. However, if the bargaining issues are fairly simple and straightforward, there is little external stress, and competing interests among bargaining team members are minimal, a participative leadership style may be more effective for obtaining a good settlement.

Colosi (1983) believes that intra-team group dynamics are more important to the process and outcomes of bargaining than the more ritual behaviour that occurs at the bargaining table. In particular, he sees the leader's task as convincing the more reluctant members of the team that the time has come to settle (and to a lesser extent, preventing other team members from settling too soon). According to Colosi, the most effective chief negotiators are those who are able to play the role of "quasi-mediators" among their team members, and who are able to raise doubts in the minds of reluctant members about the wisdom of holding out for a better settlement.

In summary, the chief negotiator's relationships with the constituency and the team have important implications for the bargaining process and outcomes. Negotiators who have been granted little authority will make smaller and slower concessions, be more likely to be involved in strikes, and may reach less advantageous settlements. Negotiators who are highly committed to their constituencies may reach poorer settlements and be more involved in strikes. Finally, negotiators with directive leadership styles are likely to bargain more effectively and attain better settlements.

Bargaining Procedures

The results of experimental bargaining research can help us to understand the effects of different procedures on the process and outcomes of negotiations. Two procedures in particular seem applicable to collective bargaining: the selection of a site for negotiations, and the imposition of deadlines by the parties. In addition, research evidence from case studies suggests that changes to customary bargaining procedures and practices can substantially hinder the bargaining process.

Bargaining Site

The site that negotiators choose for bargaining may offer both symbolic and practical advantages to one side. The options in collective bargaining are either to negotiate on the employer's territory, such as a meeting or board room, or to meet on neutral ground, most commonly a hotel. The symbolic aspects of negotiating on one's own territory can lead to more aggressive bargaining. Martindale (1971) had pairs of students bargain in the residence of one of the students in each pair. Tape recordings of the negotiations showed that students bargaining on their "home" territory spoke significantly longer and gained significantly more favourable outcomes. Further, he found that territoriality contributed far more than personality characteristics to both dependent variables; in particular, site accounted for 50 percent of the variation in talking time! While the differences are likely to be more muted in collective bargaining, especially for experienced negotiators, bargaining site may nevertheless have subtle but substantial effects. Since the bargaining site carries symbolic importance for negotiations, Rubin and Brown (1975) suggest that if site issues are not dealt with prior to, or in the early stage of, negotiations, they may emerge as intangible issues which hinder settlement later on.

The choice of bargaining site will also determine how open the negotiations are to constituency pressures. A hotel site surrounded by television cameras and newspaper reporters will clearly provide more information to the constituency and heighten the effects of the negotiator's authority and commitment to the constituency's position. On the other hand, a secret or inaccessible location (or time, such as late at night), will likely reduce constituency effects.

Deadlines

Each round of collective bargaining has a number of potential deadlines. Some are inherent in the legal context of the situation, such as the contract expiry date, and the first date at which a strike or lockout may be called following compulsory conciliation, waiting periods, or other legal requisites. Others may be imposed by the parties themselves, either bilaterally as when they agree to a negotiation "schedule," or unilaterally as when one side insists that agreement be reached by a specified date. Still other deadlines are imposed by third parties, particularly mediators. Deadlines may be downplayed by the parties, or made more salient by drawing attention to them, using them in communications with constituents, and attaching threats of various magnitude to them.

Experimental research is suggestive on the question of the consequences of approaching deadlines. A study by Pruitt and Drews (1969) utilizing pairs of subjects playing Bilateral Monopoly found that as deadlines neared negotiators made more modest demands and did less bluffing. However, Smith et al. (1979) found that time pressures have less effect on a negotiator's concession rate when his or her resistance point offers little leeway for concessions. Komorita and Barnes (1969) and others have found that, as the cost of not meeting deadlines (i.e., the cost of a strike or lockout in collective bargaining terms) increases, concession rates increase. Rubin and Brown also note that agreements are often not made until deadlines are imminent, and attribute this to the parties' needs for information about the opponent which are never satisfactorily met, and which discourage "true" position offers until time pressures are considerable.

Strikes can be viewed as missed deadlines: the parties fail to reach agreement despite a strike deadline. Rubin and Brown (1975) suggest that the failure of deadlines to operate is due to countervailing intangible pressures. Examples of such pressures in collective bargaining are the need to appear strong to one's constituency in the face of an exploitative opponent, the desire to "punish" the other party, ideological commitment to one's position, or a desire for distributive justice.

Procedural Changes

There is some research evidence that procedural changes unilaterally instigated by one of the parties are more likely to lead to stalemates and strikes (Kervin, 1977; Kervin et al., 1984). The uncertainty that a procedural change creates for the other party appears to reduce its confidence both in estimates of its opponent's true resistance point, and that its own concessions will be matched. Both result in a reluctance to make concessions, and delay settlement. In extreme cases, procedural changes and the accompanying uncertainty they generate appear to have been largely responsible for strikes.

In summary, both the content of, and changes to, bargaining procedures can affect the bargaining process. The choice of site can lead to more aggressive bargaining by the party on its "home" territory; it can also magnify or decrease the effects of constituencies. Imminent deadlines lead to increased concession making and less bluffing, an effect that escalates as the costs attached to the deadlines increase in magnitude.

Moves

A negotiator needs information about his or her opponent in order to decide what moves to make and whether and when to settle. In particular, he or she needs to know the opponent's target and resistance points, issue priorities, bargaining power, weak points, and perceptions. One major source of this information is what the opposing negotiator does and says at the bargaining table, in other words, the opponent's moves. Each move is interpreted in terms of information content and the degree to which it is only bluffing. In this way, moves by one party affect subsequent moves of the other; this sequence of related moves influences both the process and outcome of negotiations.

Opening Positions and Initial Moves

As might be expected, opening moves often set the tone of negotiations, such as how hard the bargaining will be, and the amount of trust between the parties. Interestingly, however, negotiators appear to be more tolerant of early hostile moves, compared to threats and hostile acts later in negotiations (Teger, 1970). Rubin and Brown (1975) suggest that negotiators regard early hostile moves as part of the acceptable ritual of testing the other's limits and reactions, whereas later hostile acts in an otherwise "businesslike" set of negotiations are more likely to be regarded as betrayal or attempts at exploitation.

Research with the Bilateral Monopoly game (Hinton et al., 1974) suggests that parties that begin with extreme initial positions and use gradual concessions achieve higher outcomes than those that begin close to the target point, or use large concession rates. The reasons, according to Rubin and Brown (1975), are that (1) such a strategy avoids too generous a settlement that goes beyond the opponent's resistance point, (2) it provides more time for gathering information, and (3) it communicates to the other that the negotiator has a high target point, and thus likely a resistance point as well.

Benton et al. (1972) found that the opposing negotiator felt more satisfied when a negotiator used an extreme opening and small concessions. The reason appears to be that the opposing negotiators believed they achieved more in terms of changing their opponents' position during the course of negotiations. Negotiators who are unable to bring about change in their opponents' offers feel frustrated, and may be more likely to interject intangible issues into negotiations.

The beneficial effects of an extreme opening position are more likely to be negated, however, the more information the opponent has about a negotiator's own situation (Liebert et al., 1968). Extreme opening positions in these situations appear to be unreasonable, and are likely to generate intangible issues. The implication for collective bargaining is that opening positions should be as extreme as one can reasonably defend, given the information the other party is likely to have at hand.

Newcomers to collective bargaining often wonder why so much time is "wasted" in unrealistic offers and counteroffers when both sides know at the outset what the final settlement is likely to be. This lengthy process of arriving at a settlement is sometimes described as an irrational "ritual." Bargaining research suggests some important reasons for the ritual, and the consequences of circumventing it. The pattern of slow moves and concessions has two important consequences, according to Rubin and Brown (1975). First, it helps negotiators to convince their own constituencies that bargaining was "tough," and that they achieved all that was reasonably possible. It avoids the "winner's curse" of a quick settlement that raises doubts about whether an even better settlement could have been obtained (Brazerman, 1983). The second consequence is that slow concession making from an extreme opening position allows the opposing negotiator to feel that he or she has had some influence on the process and is not powerless. One of the problems with a single "take-it-or-leave-it" offer (often known as Boulwarism) is that it ignores this important aspect of interpersonal relations: the need both to appear and to feel competent.

Concession Making

Some sequences of moves are more likely than others to move an opponent towards co-operation (and thus the possibility of problem-solving approaches to certain issues). There is evidence that moves reflecting conditional co-operation ("tit-for-tat") are more likely to elicit co-operation than a purely co-operative strategy (Oskamp, 1974; Axelrod, 1984). Likewise, changes in concession rates also have an effect on the opponent's bargaining behaviour. Negotiators who shift from a competitive to a co-operative approach in the course of bargaining are more likely to elicit co-operation from their opponents (Deutsch et al., 1967), as are negotiators who start "tough" and make gradual concession (Druckman et al., 1972). Interestingly, Schenitzki (1963) found that pairs of negotiators instructed to be co-operative in a Bilateral Monopoly game actually achieved lower joint outcomes than pairs instructed to be concerned only with maximizing their own outcomes without regard for their opponent's profits. This suggests that in collective bargaining an overly co-operative attitude may lead to unsatisfactory outcomes (if one's own needs are downplayed), or at worst, exploitation.

Research reported by Willis and Joseph (1959) and Joseph and Willis (1963) suggests that negotiators have a tendency to settle at "prominent" settlement points, i.e., those which have some special character compared to other settlement points because of precedent, symmetry, simplicity, obviousness, or even round numbers. In collective bargaining, pattern settlements fall into this category, and in negotiations which follow a pattern set elsewhere, the wage outcome is often known to both parties prior to negotiations. A settlement proposed by a mediator may also serve as a prominent solution (Eisenberg and Patch, 1976). There is some evidence that prominent settlement points are more likely to be used by male negotiators in a situation with a high level of conflict.

Threats and Promises

Making threats is not an uncommon move in negotiations ("If you can't add another 10 cents to the offer, there's no point in continuing discussions"), and promises are implicit in all conditional moves ("If you concede on the sick leave issue, we'll consider dropping our demands on job posting"). Threats and promises vary in magnitude and credibility. A threat (or promise) has low magnitude if the cost (gain) to the other is relatively low, such as the threat to turn negotiations over to a tougher negotiator. The threat magnitude of a strike is usually seen as high. A threat or promise has low credibility when there is some doubt that the negotiator has the ability and willingness to carry it out.

Not surprisingly, research shows that the impact of threats is related to their size and credibility. Faley and Tedeschi (1971) found that an opponent was more likely to comply when the threat had greater magnitude and credibility. On the other hand, threats are likely to evoke hostility and hinder co-operation, particularly as threat magnitude and credibility increase (Bonoma et al., 1970). In general, the use of threats tends to decrease joint outcomes (Deutsch and Lewicki, 1970), and to lead to counterthreats (Smith and Anderson, 1975). For this reason, according to Morley (1979), more experienced negotiators are less likely to use threats.

Research varying the credibility of a promise has shown conflicting effects on compliance ranging from significant to none (Lindskold and Bennett, 1973). However, promises do have an effect on the opponent's perceptions of the promisor: negotiators who make promises are perceived to be more trustworthy and co-operative (Lewicki and Rubin, 1974).

Procedural Moves

Among the procedural moves open to parties in collective bargaining for which there is some research evidence are the linking or packaging of issues so that they are dealt with more than one at a time, and calling for mediation.

An important part of effective negotiation, according to Rubin and Brown (1975), appears to be the ability to manipulate issues: "sized up or down, hooked together, broken apart, or stated in different language—in order to alter their initial importance rankings and thereby bring a wider range of alternatives into view." As well as leading to agreements with greater joint benefits, issue manipulation is also important for overcoming the effects of intangible issues.

Research carried out by Kelley (1966) involved negotiations over five issues in a variation of the Bilateral Monopoly game. He found that, as negotiators gained experience in repeated rounds of the game, they were more likely to combine the issues in making offers and counteroffers. Those who made offers based on all five issues were more successful in reaching settlement. Froman and Cohen (1970) discovered that negotiators who "logrolled" issues (dealt with concessions on two or more issues simultaneously) achieved better joint outcomes than those who bargained by successive compromises on one issue at a time. Following an agenda of issues in strict order appears to be both inefficient and to lead to higher levels of conflict.

The decision to go to mediation has important consequences for subsequent moves by the parties, according to research on the functions of third parties. As a number of researchers have noted, mediators are able to encourage concession making by allowing negotiators to save face and not appear weak. They permit negotiators to blame the mediator for any concessions (Pruitt and Johnson, 1970), and thus remove both the intangible issues involved in being "the first to blink," and the negative evaluations from constituency members over concession making.

Opponent's Moves

The moves a negotiator makes can, and are often intended to, affect subsequent moves by the opposing party. In particular, an opponent's reaction can be characterized in terms of whether it matches the previous move in terms of the magnitude of the concession or the amount of co-operation or conflict it represents. Mismatching, on the other hand, occurs when large concessions by one negotiator are met by large demands by the other, or a threat by one leads to acquiescence by the opponent.

Pruitt (1981) suggests that matching by a negotiator's opponent is more likely when the opponent is more confident about the negotiator's resistance point or ultimate demand. Thus, matching is more frequent when there is an obvious and prominent settlement point, such as a pattern settlement in the same industry (Michener et al., 1975). Matching by an opponent is also more likely if a negotiator suddenly offers concessions when, up to that point, his or her position has been firm and concessions have been resisted.

However, there is some evidence that in the final stages of hostile negotiations, matching behaviour that could reach a settlement may be avoided. Brown et al. (1973) found that negotiators bargaining on behalf of a constituency, with an exploitative opponent, were likely to refuse a final offer that would have avoided a loss to both themselves and the other party. It appears that the highly competitive orientation that emerges under exploitation leads to a desire to punish the opponent, even at a significant cost to oneself. In general, the presence of intangible issues seems to inhibit matching moves, except for the use of threats under conditions of relatively equal bargaining power.

In summary, the moves that negotiators make in the course of collective bargaining have important effects on the subsequent moves of their opponents. A tough opening position, combined with gradual concessions, appears to lead to effective negotiation and settlements that benefit both parties. Concession making often converges to a prominent settlement point, of which industry patterns are the most obvious example. While making threats can often bring some benefits, threats also hinder co-operation and produce settlements with less than the maximum joint benefits. Issue manipulation and mediation, as procedural moves, can improve bargaining effectiveness. In general, an opponent's moves will be affected by the prior move a negotiator makes, subject to bargaining-power differences and intangible issues.

CONCLUSION

Our objective in this chapter has been to demonstrate the wide range of topics applicable to collective bargaining in which behavioural research has been carried out. There is, without doubt, a "science" of bargaining, and it is continually adding to our understanding of why and how things happen as they do in negotiations.

No negotiator would base his or her entire strategy and tactics on the results of bargaining research. For one thing, there are too many additional variables and factors that affect the process and outcomes. For another, the strict generalizability to collective bargaining of many of the results discussed above has yet to be demonstrated beyond question. However, it is clear that the results of the science of bargaining, when combined with the art of negotiation, can contribute to improved and more effective bargaining—for both parties.

NOTES

1. In this chapter we make no distinction between "bargaining" and "negotiation," nor will we attempt a universal definition of what "negotiation" is. Our focus is collective bargaining between union members and employers over the terms and conditions of a collective agreement. We shall, however, draw on research carried out in a variety of bargaining settings, some of it involving single issues, no constituencies, and limited options for the negotiators. All of it is interpreted in terms of what it can contribute to our understanding of collective bargaining.

2. As evidence of this recent interest, there is a now a journal devoted

solely to bargaining: the *Negotiation Journal,* published by Plenum Press.

3. Many economists have studied collective bargaining, but their attention has largely been limited to wage outcomes and the incidence of strikes, rather than bargaining behaviour. We will not include such economic research in this chapter.

4. Even wages, however, can be approached co-operatively. For example, an end-loaded contract with a larger wage increase towards the end of the term might provide a more politically attractive settlement for the union, while costing management the same as a slightly smaller increase applied at the beginning of the contract.

5. Partly because a strike imposes additional costs on the parties over and above those of negotiating, they have been studied more by economists than behavioural scientists. Nevertheless, the repercussions of a strike for the parties' relationship and subsequent negotiations would seem to merit more attention to this form of industrial conflict in behavioural bargaining theory and research.

6. The Prisoner's Dilemma is a game in which persons are confronted with a choice between co-operative moves that carry a risk of loss, or competitive moves that risk poorer individual and joint outcomes. While the game doesn't have many of the characteristics of collective bargaining, it is very useful in studying individuals' orientations to bargaining under different situations.

7. Bilateral Monopoly is a two-person buyer–seller simulation in which individuals negotiate both price and quantity to be sold. Variations of Bilateral Monopoly are frequently used in negotiation experiments.

8. A somewhat related concept is the level of bargaining, the degree to which it is centralized, usually on a regional or industry basis. When two-tier bargaining occurs (wages at higher levels, local issues at the local level), there is some evidence that union–management relations at the local-level negotiations improve because a major contentious issue, wages, is removed from the table (Gallagher and Wetzel, 1984).

BIBLIOGRAPHY

Aranoff, D. and Tedeschi, J. T. (1968), "Original stakes and behavior in the prisoner's dilemma game." *Psychonomic Science* 12: 79–80.

Axelrod, R. (1984), *The Evolution of Cooperation.* New York: Basic Books.

Bartunek, J. M., Benton, A. A., and Keys, C. B. (1975), "Third-party intervention and the bargaining of group representatives." *Journal of Conflict Resolution* 19: 532–557.

Benton, A. A., Kelley, H. H., and Liebling, B. (1972), "Effects of extremity of offers and concession rate on the outcomes of bargaining." *Journal of Personality & Social Psychology* 24: 73–83.

Berkowitz, N. H., Hylander, L., and Bakaitis, R. (1973), "Defense, vulnerability, and cooperation in a mixed-motive game." *Journal of Personality & Social Psychology* 25: 401–407.

Blake, R. R., and Mouton, J. S. (1961), "Loyalty of representatives to ingroup positions during intergroup competition." *Sociometry* 24: 177–183.

Bonoma, T. V., Schlenker, B. R., Smith, R., and Tedeschi, J. (1970), "Source prestige and target reactions to threats." *Pschonomic Science* 19: 111–113.

Borah, L. A., Jr. (1963), "The effects of threat in bargaining: Critical and experimental analysis." *Journal of Abnormal & Social Psychology* 66: 37–44.

Brazerman, M. H. (1983), "Negotiator judgment: A critical look at the rationality assumption." *American Behavioral Scientist* 27: 211–228.

Brown, B. R. (1968), "The effects of need to maintain face on interpersonal bargaining." *Journal of Experimental Social Psychology* 4: 107–122.

_____, Garland, H., and Freedman, S. (1973). "The effects of constituency feedback, representational role, and strategy of the other on concession-making in a bilateral monopoly bargaining task." Paper presented at the meeting of the Eastern Psychological Association [cited in Rubin, J. Z. and Brown, B. R. (1975), *The Social Psychology of Bargaining and Negotiation*. New York: Academic Press].

Carnevale, P. J. D., Pruitt, D. G., and Britton, S. D. (1979). "Looking tough: The negotiator under constituent surveillance." *Personality & Social Psychology Bulletin* 5: 118–121.

Colosi, T. (1983), "Negotiation in the public and private sectors." *American Behavioral Scientist* 27: 229–253.

Daniel, W. W. (1976), *Wage Determination in Industry*. London: PEP.

Deutsch, M., Epstein, Y., Canavan, D., and Gumpert, P. (1967), "Strategies of inducing cooperation: An experimental study." *Journal of Conflict Resolution* 11: 345–360.

_____ and Krauss, R. M. (1960), "The effect of threat upon interpersonal bargaining." *Journal of Abnormal & Social Psychology* 61: 181–189.

_____ and Krauss, R. M. (1962), "Studies of interpersonal bargaining." *Journal of Conflict Resolution* 6: 52–76.

_____ and Lewicki, R. J. (1970), " 'Locking-in' effects during a game of chicken." *Journal of Conflict Resolution* 14: 367–378.

Druckman, D., Zechmeister, K., and Solomon, D. (1972), "Determinants of bargaining behavior in a bilateral monopoly situation: Opponent's concession rate and relative defensibility." *Behavioral Science* 17: 514–531.

Eisenberg, M. A. and Patch, M. E. (1976), "Prominence as a determinant of bargaining outcomes." *Journal of Conflict Resolution* 20: 523–538.

Faley, T. and Tedeschi, J. T. (1971), "Status and reactions to threats." *Journal of Personality & Social Psychology* 17: 192–199.

Fiedler, F. E. (1967), *A Theory of Leadership Effectiveness.* New York: McGraw-Hill.

Froman, L. A., Jr. and Cohen, M. D. (1970), "Compromise and logroll: Comparing the efficiency of two bargaining processes." *Behavioral Science* 15: 180–183.

Gahagan, J. P. and Tedeschi, J. T. (1968), "Demographic factors in the communication of promises." *Journal of Social Psychology* 76: 277–280.

Gallagher, D. G. and Wetzel, K. W. (1984), "Local employer and union perceptions of two-tier bargaining." *Relations industrielles* 39: 486–507.

Goldman, M. (1965), "A comparison of individual and group performance for varying combinations of initial ability." *Journal of Personality and Social Psychology* 1: 210–216.

Gruder, C. L. (1969), "Effects of perception of opponent's bargaining style and accountability to opponent and partner on interpersonal mixed-motive bargaining." *Dissertation Abstracts* 29: 4555–4556-A.

———— (1971), "Relationships with opponent and partner in mixed-motive bargaining." *Journal of Conflict Resolution* 15: 403–416.

Hackman, J. R. and Morris, C. C. (1975), "Group tasks, group interaction process, and group performance effectiveness: A review and proposed integration." In L. Berkowitz (ed.), *Advances in Experimental Social Psychology* (Vol. 8). New York: Academic, pp. 57–66.

Harnett, D. L., Cummings, L. L. and Hughes, G. D. (1968), "The influence of risk-taking propensity on bargaining behavior." *Behavioral Science* 13: 91–101.

Hermann, M. G. and Kogan, N. (1968), "Negotiation in leader and delegate groups." *Journal of Conflict Resolution* 12: 332–344.

Herold, D. M. (1978), "Improving performance effectiveness of groups through a task-contingent selection of intervention strategies." *Academy of Management Review* 3: 315–325.

Hinton, B. L., Hamner, W. C., and Pohlen, M. F. (1974), "The influence of reward magnitude, opening bid and concession rate on profit earned in a managerial negotiation game." *Behavioral Science* 19: 197–203.

Hoffman, L. R. (1959), "Homogeneity of member personality and its effect on group problem solving." *Journal of Abnormal and Social Psychology* 58: 27–32.

Hornstein, H. A. and Johnson, D. W. (1966), "The effects of process analysis and ties to his group upon the negotiator's attitudes toward the outcomes of negotiations." *Journal of Applied Behavioral Science* 2: 449–463.

Janis, I. L. (1972), *Victims of Groupthink: A Psychological Study of Foreign-policy Decisions and Fiascos*. Boston: Houghton-Mifflin.

Johnson, M. P. and Ewens, W. (1971), "Power relations and affective style as determinants of confidence in impression formation in a game situation." *Journal of Experimental Social Psychology* 7: 98–110.

Joseph, M. L. and Willis, R. H. (1963), "An experimental analog to two-party bargaining." *Behavioral Science* 8: 117–127.

Kelley, H. H. (1966), "A classroom study of the dilemmas in interpersonal negotiations." In K. Archibald (ed.), *Strategic Interaction and Conflict: Original Papers and Discussion*. Berkeley: Institute of International Studies.

_____ , Condry, J. C., Jr., Dahlke, A. E., and Hill, A. H. (1965), "Collective behavior in a simulated panic situation." *Journal of Experimental Social Psychology* 1: 20–54.

_____ , Shure, G. H., Deutsch, M., Faucheux, C., Lanzetta, J. T., Moscovici, S., Nuttin, J. M., Jr., Rabbie, J. M., and Thibaut, J. W. (1970), "A comparative experimental study of negotiation behavior." *Journal of Personality & Social Psychology* 16: 411–438.

Kervin, J. (1977), *The 1975 Metro Toronto Teacher–Board Negotiations and Strike*. Toronto: University of Toronto, Centre for Industrial Relations.

_____ , Gunderson, M., and Reid, F. (1984), *Two Case Studies of Strikes*. Toronto: Centre for Industrial Relations, University of Toronto.

Klimoski, R. J. (1972), "The effects of intragroup forces on intergroup conflict resolution." *Organizational Behavior and Human Performance* 8: 363–383.

Kochan, T. A. (1974), "A theory of multilateral collective bargaining in city governments." *Industrial & Labor Relations Review* 27: 525–542.

Kogan, N., Lamm, H., and Trommsdorff, G. (1972), "Negotiation constraints in the risk-taking domain: Effects of being observed by partners of higher or lower status." *Journal of Personality and Social Psychology* 23: 143–156.

Komorita, S. S. and Barnes, M. (1969), "Effects of pressures to reach agreement in bargaining." *Journal of Personality & Social Psychology* 13: 245–252.

Lamm, H. and Kogan, N. (1970), "Risk taking in the context of intergroup negotiation." *Journal of Experimental Social Psychology* 6: 351–363.

Lewicki, R. J. and Rubin, J. Z. (1974), The effects of motivational orientation and relative power upon the perception of interpersonal influence in a non zero-sum game. Unpublished manuscript cited in Rubin, J. Z. and Brown, B. R. (1975), *The Social Psychology of Bargaining and Negotiation*. New York: Academic Press.

Liebert, R. M., Smith, W. P., Hill, J. H., and Keiffer, M. (1968), "The effects of information and magnitude of initial offer on interpersonal negotiation." *Journal of Experimental Social Psychology* 4: 431–441.

Lindskold, S. and Bennett, R. (1973), "Attributing trust and conciliatory intent from coercive power capability." *Journal of Personality & Social Psychology* 28: 180–186.

Maier, N. R. F. and Hoffman, L. R. (1960) "Quality of first and second solutions in group problem solving." *Journal of Applied Psychology* 44: 278–283.

Martindale, D. A. (1971), "Territorial dominance behavior in dyadic verbal interactions." *Proceedings of the 79th Annual Convention of the American Psychological Association* 6: 305–306.

Michener, H. A., Vaske, J. J., Schleifer, S. L., Plazewski, J. G., and Chapman, L. J. (1975), "Factors affecting concession rate and threat use in bilateral conflict." *Sociometry* 38: 62–80.

Morley, I. E. (1979), "Behavioural studies of industrial bargaining." In G. M. Stephenson and C. J. Brotherton (eds.), *Industrial Relations: A Social Psychological Approach*. Chichester: Wiley, pp. 211–236.

Mudge, C. R. (1982), "Bargaining unit composition and negotiation outcomes: A study of library personnel in Ontario." *Proceedings of the 19th Annual Meeting of the Canadian Industrial Relations Association*, pp. 167–178.

Oskamp, S. (1974), "Comparison of sequential and simultaneous responding, matrix, and strategy variables in a prisoner's dilemma game." *Journal of Conflict Resolution* 18: 107–116.

Perry, J. L. and Angle, H. L. (1981), "Bargaining unit structure and organizational outcomes." *Industrial Relations* 20: 47–59.

Pruitt, D. G. (1981), *Negotiation Behavior*. New York: Academic.

_____ and Drews, J. L. (1969), "The effect of time pressure, time elapsed, and the opponent's concession rate on behavior in negotiation." *Journal of Experimental Social Psychology* 5: 43–60.

_____ and Johnson, D. F. (1970), "Mediation as an aid to face saving in negotiation." *Journal of Personality & Social Psychology* 14: 239–246.

Ridgeway, C. L. (1983), *The Dynamics of Small Groups*. New York: St. Martin's.

Rubin, J. Z. and Brown, B. R. (1975), *The Social Psychology of Bargaining and Negotiation*. New York: Academic Press.

Schenitzki, D. P. (1963), "Bargaining, group decision making and the attainment of maximum joint outcome." *Dissertation Abstracts* 23: 3528–3529.

Sheposh, J. P. and Gallo, P. S., Jr. (1973), "Asymmetry of payoff structure and co-operative behavior in the prisoner's dilemma game." *Journal of Conflict Resolution* 17: 321–333.

Sherman, R. (1967), "Individual attitude toward risk and choice between prisoner's dilemma games." *Journal of Psychology* 66: 291–298.

_____ (1968), "Personality and strategic choice." *Journal of Psychology* 70: 191–197.

Shils, E. A. and Janowitz, M. (1948), "Cohesion and disintegration of the Wehrmacht in World War II." *Public Opinion Quarterly* 12: 280–313.

Shomer, R. W., Davis, A. H. and Kelley, H. H. (1966), "Threats and the development of co-ordination: Further studies of the Deutsch and Krauss trucking game." *Journal of Personality & Social Psychology* 4: 119–126.

Slusher, E. A., Roering, K. J., and Rose, G. L. (1974), "The effects of commitment to future interaction in single plays of three games." *Behavioural Science* 19: 119–132.

Smith, D. L., Pruitt, D. G., and Carnevale, P. J. D. (1979). "Matching and mismatching: The differential effects of one's own limit." Paper presented at the annual meeting of the Eastern Psychological Association, Philadelphia. [Cited in Pruitt, D. G. (1981), *Negotiation Behavior*. New York: Academic.]

Smith, W. P. and Anderson, A. (1975), "Threats, communication, and bargaining." *Journal of Personality and Social Psychology* 32: 76–82.

Steiner, I. D. (1972), *Group Processes and Productivity*. New York: Academic.

Swingle, P. G. (1969), "Ethnic factors in interpersonal bargaining." *Canadian Journal of Psychology* 23: 136–146.

Teger, A. I. (1970), "The effect of early co-operation on the escalation of conflict." *Journal of Experimental Social Psychology* 6: 187–204.

Terhune, K. W. (1968), "Motives, situation, and interpersonal conflict within prisoner's dilemma." *Journal of Personality & Social Psychology Monograph Supplement* 8: 1–24.

Wall, J. A., Jr. (1977), "Intergroup bargaining: Effects of opposing constituent's stance, opposing representative's bargaining, and representatives' locus of control." *Journal of Conflict Resolution* 21: 459–474.

Walton, R. and McKersie, R. B. (1965), *A Behavioral Theory of Labor Negotiations*. New York: McGraw-Hill.

Willis, R. H. and Joseph, M. L. (1959), "Bargaining behavior: I. 'Prominence' as a predictor of the outcome of games of agreement." *Journal of Conflict Resolution* 3: 102–113.

Appendix 7A

Case Study: Negotiations at Canadian Switch*

"There's got to be a better way! Damned if I want to go through that again!"

The speaker is George Fuhrman, general manager of the Canadian Switch plant, discussing the most recent negotiations involving his plant and Local 1234 of the United Electrical Workers. Fuhrman and the casewriter are making their way up the sidewalk to the plant offices. In the summer sun, the quiet lawns and shade trees belie the fractious negotiations of last year, negotiations that included a ten-week strike.

Canadian Switch is located just outside Hamilton, Ontario, in a pleasant suburban area zoned for light industry. It is the branch plant of an American multinational firm. It has been in production for 26 years, and last year had sales of about $30 million.

The plant employs about 270 persons, of which approximately 215 are hourly-paid workers. They assemble a variety of mechanical and electrical switches used in trucks and automobiles. The plant normally works two shifts (day and afternoon), with ten foremen running six different departments. All workers are on a five-day week except maintenance and tool-and-die employees who also work Saturdays. However, when the plant has a rush order, as many as 40 or 50 additional employees work overtime.

The workforce of Canadian switch is about 90 percent female, of whom the vast majority are immigrant women, predominantly Polish (the largest group), Italian, and Yugoslavian in background. There are smaller numbers of Ukrainians, Koreans, Hungarians, and Jamaicans. The large proportion of immigrants is probably due to the company's wage scales, which are lower than similar firms in the area. The majority of the women are unskilled assemblers who put together switch components. A few work as primary inspectors, checking incoming material, or line inspectors who check the switches produced in the plant. There is no evident friction between the ethnic groups, and they appear to get along well together.

The plant has 27 male employees. Of these, 13 work in relatively high-paying skilled jobs: two electricians, six toolmakers, and five main-

---

*This case is based in large part on a true set of negotiations. To protect the anonymity of those involved, all names have been changed.

tenance mechanics. The other men work in shipping or on presses, doing the heavier work in the plant. Their wages are relatively low.

Employees at Canadian Switch have been represented by the United Electrical Workers since the plant was unionized 18 years ago. Over 90 percent of the eligible employees are union members. The Canadian Switch bargaining unit is the largest of 12 units (representing seven other employers) in local 1234. The local has a total membership of about 1100 members. The members of all 12 units vote in each biennial election for officers of the local. The local's full-time president, Rick Sarto, worked at Canadian Switch before taking office. Prior to the negotiations, one of the other five members on the local's executive, Abe Cunningham, was also from the Canadian Switch bargaining unit. The union rep responsible for the local is Bill Edwards, an older and experienced negotiator respected by the members.

In the Canadian Switch plant, employees are represented by a chief steward and five shop stewards. Two union members serve on the Safety Committee. Elections for all these positions are also held every two years.

LABOUR RELATIONS PRIOR TO NEGOTIATIONS

Both sides agree that labour relations at the plant had generally been fairly good. For the past decade the grievance rate had been low, averaging about four or five a year; most problems were solved through informal discussions between the chief steward, Don Ames, and the plant manager, Frank Fitzgerald, who handles personnel and industrial relations matters.

There had been very few arbitrations. Fuhrman, the general manager, recalls two in the 18 years he has been there. Ames remembers only one case going to arbitration in his seven years as chief steward. Ames: "Management prefers to talk things out, which is good. It settles a lot of problems." Fuhrman echoed this sentiment: "We put a lot of emphasis on informal discussion, and not using the 'letter of the contract.'" However, Ames notes that most of the immigrant women employees are reluctant to grieve. For his part, Fuhrman thinks that informal discussions can create political problems inside the union. "Their stewards get criticized. I've heard one union official claim that the problem around here is that there aren't enough grievances."

Up until the most recent round of negotiations, there had been only one strike. It occurred ten years ago, six years after certification of the bargaining unit, and lasted about four weeks. Since then, there had been six rounds of trouble-free negotiations. Fuhrman thinks that the first strike was largely due to union politics and management insensitivity.

"We dropped the ball. They were using a novice negotiator, and we didn't pick up on his problems."

UNION BARGAINING TEAM

The bargaining committee for the union consisted of seven members. Three were ex-officio members: Edwards as union rep, Sarto as local president, and Ames as chief steward. The other four were elected at a meeting held about two months before the notice to bargain was sent to management. The meeting was attended by about 40 employees, about evenly divided between males and females. At this meeting the men, mostly skilled tradesmen, elected three of their number to the negotiating committee: Eddy Moore, Mike Camilleri, and Don Pearson. However the women, mostly Italian and Jamaican, supported Susan Fisher, an assembler, ensuring her election to the committee. A fifth candidate, Joe Johnson, also a skilled employee, placed out of the running but was later added to the committee when Pearson left his job at Canadian Switch after the first two bargaining meetings. The most influential persons on the union bargaining team were Edwards, Sarto, Ames, and Fisher, the only woman member.

Bill Edwards, the union rep, acted as spokesman for the union team. He had been the union representative responsible for Local 1234 for the past nine years, taking over the local just after the previous strike at Canadian Switch. Edwards had the most negotiating experience of all those on the union team; his approach to bargaining is to be fairly low key and businesslike at the table.

Rick Sarto, president of the local, had occupied that position for nine years, and had been a chief steward at Canadian Switch prior to that. He had been opposed in only one of his four local elections. The most recent election had taken place almost a year before negotiations began. Because of the number of bargaining units in the local, Sarto had regularly been involved in three or four sets of negotiations at any given time, and therefore had a great deal of negotiation experience with a variety of opposing management teams. He had been through five strikes prior to this round of negotiations at Canadian Switch, four of them through his position as local president.

Don Ames had been chief steward for seven years at the time of negotiations. He had been at Canadian Switch for ten years, and was a maintenance mechanic millwright, one of the 13 skilled employees at the plant. He had taken part in four previous rounds of negotiations. For the first two of these he had been elected to the negotiating committee, but then the rules had been changed to include the chief steward automatically on the union's bargaining team. Ames also had been a member of the plant's Safety Committee since its inception three years previously. He was familiar with the employees' problems and concerns, and had a good working relationship with Fitzgerald, the plant manager. "My major job as chief steward is to talk over problems with the foreman involved, and then if we can't resolve it between us I take the problem to Fitzgerald, which happens about 90 percent of the time."

Fisher was an assembler who, despite holding no previous office in the union, had been elected to the negotiation committee. Both her fellow committee members and the members of the management team saw her as a radical Marxist, and according to them she tended to interpret events from a strongly ideological point of view. She was articulate and active in federal politics, and had run as a Marxist-Leninist candidate in two recent federal elections. She had moved to Canada from the States with her boyfriend during the Vietnam war. She refused to give the personnel clerk her home address, providing only a post office box number. Her support, according to Sarto, was largely among the Italian and black women workers. She had opposed Ames in the previous union election for chief steward, but the Polish and Yugoslavian workers, who were fairly anti-communist in their political views, did not support her.

The other members of the union team at the beginning of negotiations were Moore, Camilleri, and Pearson, all skilled male employees. They said very little at the table, and did not have a great deal of influence or input during caucuses and team meetings.

MANAGEMENT BARGAINING TEAM

Negotiations for management were conducted by Fuhrman and Brian Long, a Hamilton labour lawyer, who acted as management's chief spokesman. They were accompanied at the table by Fitzgerald and Herb Bannister, the chief engineer. Behind the scenes, the company's controller prepared statistics and, once negotiations were well underway, costed potential packages.

Fuhrman had come to Canadian Switch as general manager six months before the union was certified, when the plant had only 100 employees and sales were one-tenth what they are today. He believes that staff changes at that time led to uncertainty among employees, who unionized as a result. He has been involved in every set of negotiations since then. He prefers "the old-fashioned, gentlemanly approach to negotiations." His policy is that only the spokesman should speak at the table. Fuhrman limited himself to answering questions, and pointing out errors in the union's presentations and arguments. The parent company did not send any representative to the meeting. According to Fuhrman, he was given a great deal of autonomy by the head office, and allowed to run his own show as far as collective bargaining was concerned.

Fitzgerald had been at Canadian Switch for 24 years, starting as an hourly employee and coming up through the ranks to spend the last 17 years as plant manager. He is responsible for purchasing, industrial engineering, traffic, and all other aspects of production, as well as personnel and industrial relations. A secretary helps with routine hiring and personnel matters, and an assistant helps Fitzgerald with personnel problems and IR-related matters. "My background is administration rather than engineering. I think that this helps me with the people-related problems at the plant, and in fact it was specifically because of my administrative background that George (Fuhrman) chose me for the plant manager position. It's part of his philosophy not to have an engineer in charge, and I think it pays off in better labour relations and better productivity. The personal contact is important, especially when you've got a good working relationship. In fact the union won't deal with my assistant; they want my word on matters." Fitzgerald knows Ames well as a result of their frequent meetings in the plant. Fitzgerald is much less familiar with Sarto and Edwards, with whom he doesn't have much contact.

Long was a fairly senior partner in a respected Hamilton law firm specializing in labour law. He had negotiated the previous two rounds of bargaining on behalf of management. Edwards described Long as "pretty tough" at the bargaining table, but "straight, no tricks." His strong point was contract language rather than bargaining strategy and tactics.

Herb Bannister, the chief engineer at Canadian Switch, also sat on the management bargaining team. He had relatively little to contribute to strategy or putting together proposals.

THE NEGOTIATIONS

In preparation for negotiations, the union committee distributed questionnaires to the employees, asking for their suggestions and complaints. They received about a hundred responses. Using the results as a guide, together with their own experiences, they put together the union's proposals.

The major issues in negotiations, from the union's point of view, were wages, cost of living, and seniority rights. Also of importance were a dental plan, a pension plan, and a plan to provide prescription glasses. Many of the union members were aware of better wages and benefits earned by women doing comparable work at other plants in the neighbourhood.

A troublesome issue, according to Sarto, was the weakness of the existing seniority clause. Shifts, particularly the less-desirable afternoon shift (since many of the women had children coming home from school in mid-afternoon), transfers, and being excused from the heavy lifting work of once-a-year inventory were not assigned on the basis of seniority.

The existing contract allowed management to consider skill and ability as well as seniority in work assignments, leading to arbitrary assignments and favouritism, according to Sarto and the stewards.

At least one intangible issue not on the table underlay some of the dissatisfaction of the women employees. According to Sarto, a particular foreman at the plant aggravated the workers and played favourites with some of the women, assigning to those he liked the preferred jobs where the women could sit down while they worked, and giving his favourites more opportunities for overtime. Sarto said that some women had come complaining to him in tears about their treatment by this one foreman. He mentioned specifically some single mothers afraid of losing their jobs if they complained to management. The issue of the problem foreman was also mentioned by two of the women stewards. This same foreman was later to cause some disturbance on the picket line. Fitzgerald finally stepped in to curb his taunting of the picketers.

From the union point of view, the company came to the table with almost overwhelming bargaining power. Ames: "Most of their bargaining power was the threat of closing down the Canadian operation and shipping switches from their plant in Ohio. In all, they have six plants in the States, so we're faced by the loss of jobs here if we ask for too much."

Management's preparations for the negotiations were all done locally. Fuhrman: "We kept things pretty much to ourselves. Nobody was there from head office, and we did all our own costing. We don't rely on an employers' association. As always, we checked out the rates our competition is paying. We exchange information with M (a major competitor)—they gather extensive data and do exhaustive comparisons, but only some of of their data are useful for us. We compete only in a small area. And they're not unionized. We also rely for information on *Canadian Labour Views*, and the Canadian Manufacturers' Association."

Negotiations got underway in mid-October, well before the contract expiry date of December 31. Five meetings took place before the strike. All meetings were held at a Ramada Inn on the outskirts of Hamilton. Each began around 10:00 in the morning, and most ended at 3:00 or 3:30, with the parties taking an hour and a half off for lunch. For both teams it was the practice to meet in caucus to review strategy and other points before each negotiation session.

At the first and subsequent meetings between the parties, most of management's points were made by Long, with Fuhrman expanding on particular topics. Fitzgerald and Bannister said little at the table. On rare occasions they might be called upon to explain some particular point. Although Edwards acted as chief negotiator for the union team, others, particularly Ames and Fisher, were also likely to speak up. The amount of their participation increased as the meetings continued.

Asked about the first meeting, Fitzgerald remarked, "Negotiations didn't start off right this time. At the beginning of the first meeting, we (the management team) fooled around and pretended to take a tough line and raised our voices in jest. It just wasn't a good thing to do, especially with Fisher there. She wasn't used to negotiations. She started in on her political stuff, capitalist pigs and all. Then Long got upset, even though we'd warned him about Fisher before the meeting." After things quieted down, the balance of the first meeting was spent with the union committee presenting their proposal in detail, and advancing their initial arguments for each point.

At the second meeting, November 22, the management team checked over the meaning of each union proposal and clarified ambiguities. The teams then began discussing the non-monetary issues, with no moves made by either side. At a union caucus during this meeting, Fisher berated the other members of the committee and accused them of being ready to sell out the membership by considering concessions. She appeared to regard the bargaining, and the possibility of union concessions, as a betrayal of her ideology and her commitment to her fellow employees. When the committee returned to negotiations, she refused to sit with the other members of her committee at the bargaining table, and moved her chair to a corner of the room. The management team were puzzled and upset by this development.

From this point, according to Sarto, union caucuses became difficult and tension-filled as it was difficult to achieve consensus on positions and tactics as union teams had done in the past. Ames said much the same, and added: "You could see at the table that Long and Fuhrman were nervous about Fisher. I think she was the reason they stonewalled on our demands. Management couldn't trust her. They didn't know what the hell was happening."

At the third meeting, the discussion on monetary issues continued, with management agreeing to some demands, and giving a definite "no" to others. Fisher continued to sit apart from her fellow committee members, but still took part in the discussions. Joe Johnson replaced Don Pearson on the union committee for this and all subsequent meetings; Pearson had quit his job at Canadian Switch.

The fourth meeting, December 18, was a long one, concentrating on the key non-monetary items. Fisher returned to the bargaining table, but continued to take a hard line on any concessions or dropping of the union's demands. Towards the end of the day, management put together a complete offer on the remaining non-monetary issues and presented it to the union.

The fifth and final meeting was held January 3, three days after the contract expiry date. At this meeting, the management team presented a complete offer including monetary issues. The company had conceded on some insurance and sick-benefit items, but refused to move on a dental plan, COLA, pension plan, and prescription glasses. Fitzgerald: "It was an offer that we knew they couldn't accept. We expected it to be the basis for further bargaining, but we couldn't afford a better offer until we knew they were close to accepting it. Otherwise we're caught out on a limb with nothing more to give. As we expected, they rejected it and called for conciliation. Maybe one of the problems is that no one really does anything, we all know just about where the settlement is going to end up, and we just have to make sure we don't get to that point before they do."

After a brief caucus, the union team returned to the table to tell Long that they rejected the offer, and were requesting conciliation.

Conciliation took place on February 26 at the Ministry of Labour offices in Toronto, with John Wellman acting as conciliation officer. It was treated as a brief but necessary exercise the parties had to endure to get to mediation. They had only a five-minute face-to-face session at the beginning, and no movement was made. Wellman filed a "no board" report, and started the clock ticking towards a strike. The legal strike date was March 22.

Fuhrman was not happy with conciliation. "It doesn't seem appropriate, although I think that mediation is okay. The conciliator didn't have enough experience, and the whole exercise fortifies the parties' positions. It breeds further ill feeling."

The union's negotiation committee met with the stewards on March 13 to talk about the possibility of a strike and the necessity for strong and united support. The committee and stewards agreed to call a membership meeting for the afternoon of March 22. An announcement of this meeting, to be held at the nearby hall of another union, was distributed to employees. The announcement also contained an appeal that "no one take any action prior to the membership meeting." The union planned to use the meeting either to ratify a settlement, or to vote to strike.

Conciliation was followed by mediation with mediation officer Ian Turner from the Ontario Ministry of Labour's Conciliation and Mediation Service. The meeting was set for March 21, the day before the union could legally strike. According to Fuhrman, the management team entered the meeting hoping that, as in the past, this would be the point at which the teams got down to the nitty-gritty of negotiations and reached a settlement. Fuhrman: "The pattern for the United Electrical Workers is to do eleventh-hour bargaining. Therefore, our strategy is to hold back at the table until the eleventh hour. That's why we didn't make any move during conciliation, and waited until the mediation just prior to the strike deadline."

However, the mediation ended in failure. Fuhrman felt that neither side was ready to settle. Fitzgerald: "We blew it. We didn't listen enough to what was happening on the other side of the table. We underestimated how much disruption Fisher and Ames had caused. Their disagreements interfered with the signals, and they had more support among the employees for a hard line than we recognized. Ames talked strike both in public, which we expected, but also in private, which was unusual. And Fisher is pretty good at swaying people. Since we had to give a final offer, and we weren't sure what the hell was going on, we put an unacceptable one on the table."

On the mediation effort, Fuhrman remarked: "Turner has been doing our mediation for a long time. I've got a lot of respect for the guy, he does a fine job. He told me that at the eleventh hour our spokesman, Long, didn't pick up an important move, he dropped the ball. But, in the confusion with Fisher there, Edwards was reluctant to do any "corridor talk" (private conversation) with him (Turner), for fear that Fisher would make a fuss about being sold out. Also, something else was different this time. Traditionally, Sarto and Edwards don't make the final deal. They bring in Andrews, the union president, so he can get some of the credit for the deal. For us, when we see Andrews, we know that we've got a settlement. But this time Andrews didn't show up. We didn't know it at the time, but Andrews wasn't coming in at the last minute any more. But when we noticed that Andrews wasn't there, we figured that meant trouble, that the union committee wasn't serious about getting a deal, probably because of internal problems in their committee, likely with Fisher. It was a serious misunderstanding."

MANAGEMENT REACTIONS TO NEGOTIATIONS

The union willingness to strike surprised the management team. Fuhrman: "Before negotiations started, Ames was talking about a strike. I don't know why, maybe his personality, but we didn't attach any importance to it. I didn't think it was pressure from the membership. Also, we had heard that the union coffers were thin, and that this would prevent a strike. This local had just had a four-week strike with another plant."

Another reason for their surprise was the low level of animosity across the table. Fuhrman: "In general, the negotiations were fairly peaceful. There were no voices raised, and no shouting matches."

But the management negotiators were aware that things were very different on the union team. Fitzgerald: "Ames and Fisher despised each other, and provoked a lot of dissension in the union ranks—the traditionalists versus the radicals. She's very bright, and was able to keep the unrest going in the committee. She pushed Ames to a more militant posture." Fuhrman: "As we read it, Edwards was under some pressure to settle, because the union couldn't afford a strike. However, Sarto would go along with whatever the majority wanted. For him it's a political question."

Fuhrman raised another possibility for the failure of negotiations: "Another problem is this eleventh-hour bargaining. This forces us to take the strategy of holding back at the table until the eleventh hour, otherwise we'll be forced to give too much. Therefore, we don't budge during conciliation, but we wait for mediation just prior to the strike deadline. As I see it, the problem with this strategy, for both sides, is that it reinforces the adversary system. Also, inexperienced negotiators get hostile. Now, this is no problem for Sarto and Edwards—they know what to expect. But the others on the union team didn't understand the poker game. Whenever any of them spoke up, you could just see Edwards flinching. He was unhappy, but he didn't discipline them at the table. Sometimes I had the feeling that Sarto and Edwards weren't in control."

Fuhrman again: "Another thing I didn't like about this round was the composition of the union committee. Three skilled and one unskilled, when the general pattern is one skilled and three unskilled members. The last time we had a rough round of negotiations was also a departure from that pattern: two of each."

Fuhrman also indicated that management held back a better offer than the one they took into the strike because he felt that they could not trust the union team in general, and Fisher in particular, to accept a reasonable offer.

UNION REACTIONS TO NEGOTIATIONS

Sarto thought that management strategy had backfired: "Management came in with a very low first offer at the fifth meeting, but I wasn't too worried. I expected about six or seven more meetings. But the committee members were very upset. They thought the company had too many "no's"—management gave an outright flat "no" to too many of our demands. They were very discouraged. Also, early on the management team caucused and kept us waiting for four hours, which I think was a deliberate attempt to discourage the committee. But the first time I really began to expect a strike was when we were into conciliation. During conciliation management tried the same strategy, keeping us waiting. But it backfired, and the union committee got very angry."

Edwards, the union rep, thought that part of the problem during negotiations was that Canadian Switch was receiving bargaining guidelines from its American owners. When asked about union members' militancy, Edwards remarked, "I don't think that the previous strike, ten years ago, had any effect on the employees' militancy. It was a long time ago, and there's been a big turnover in the plant since then, I'd say about ninety percent. A much bigger reason was the poor wage increases in previous contracts."

Fisher, according to Ames, was a real thorn in the side of the union team. The other team members, he said, could not tell her to "shut up and stop her heavy ideological 'fascist-capitalist stuff' because their union ostensibly held to the same ideological and philosophical position, although it was not usually evident during bargaining, which tended in normal circumstances to proceed much like negotiations for any other union. Sarto commented, "She gave us trouble."

Ames had expected a settlement without a strike, but this time turned out to be very different from previous rounds of negotiations. "It seemed like the company wanted a strike. There was very little movement on their part, they just juggled the issues. By the fourth meeting, I knew we'd be in for a strike." Ames also thought that Long, the lawyer and management spokesman, was part of the problem. "He was sarcastic and loud. Fuhrman pulls the strings and Long does the work. He's out to beat us."

THE STRIKE

At a morning meeting of the union bargaining committee on Thursday, March 22, the day after mediation under Turner had failed, the committee decided to recommend a strike at the union meeting to be held that afternoon. The decision was supported by Moore, Camilleri, and Johnson, the three skilled male workers on the committee. Skilled workers at Canadian Switch had the most to lose in a strike, since they would have done relatively well under management's last offer. Nevertheless, the three felt they had to support the women.

Ames said later that he felt "iffy" about the strike. "I didn't think we could afford it, but I was willing to go along with the majority. I think that the other skilled guys on the committee felt the same." Fisher, however, felt strongly that a strike was necessary. According to Ames, Sarto was disappointed and upset at management's behaviour and last offer, and felt a strike was necessary because the company appeared unwilling to move otherwise. Edwards was also upset, but not as much as Sarto.

That afternoon the union held its membership meeting. About 96 percent of the members showed up. Sarto described the negotiations to date, and what the company had given so far. He concluded, "I'm going to leave it up to you in a secret ballot vote. You can vote for it, or against it (the last management offer)." Of the 288 members voting, 247 or about 85 percent voted to reject the offer and strike. After the results were announced, it was moved and approved that they strike immediately. Workers then signed up for picket duty and registered for strike pay. Picket captains were selected. The meeting lasted about four hours. Ames, feeling ambivalent, left the meeting early. The afternoon shift did not go in to work, thus marking the beginning of the strike. The next morning, Friday, workers were gathering outside the plant by 6 A.M., and by 9 o'clock organized picketing had begun.

Fuhrman: "On Thursday afternoon the union had a membership meeting. We're sitting around the office, waiting for a phone call. Then we see Ames walking up and down in front of the gate, picketing without a sign. About an hour later, Fitzgerald gets a call from Edwards saying that our last offer has been rejected. The strike is on."

The Canadian Switch management had advised the police earlier of the possibility of a strike, and two detectives who specialize in labour relations showed up on Friday to keep an eye on things. They advised both sides of their rights.

The strike was quickly approved by the union's national president. Such approval is almost automatic if more than 70 percent of the members vote to strike, and is necessary in order to authorize strike pay. The amount of strike pay an employee received was determined by the number of dependents, and participation in picket duty.

Picketing was carried out six days a week, with five shifts each day. The first began at 6 A.M.; the last ended at 10 P.M. Each shift lasted four hours, and the first three shifts overlapped to provide "double strength" picketing between 8 A.M. and 12 noon. Standard picket duty was three shifts a week. The early-morning shift was popular with mothers with young children, who could get their picketing over with and have the rest of the day with their children. Strike pay began at $25 a week for single workers, $30 for those with dependents. After four weeks each category was raised by $5 a week. Strikers were encouraged to get part-time jobs (as long as they still continued to picket), and many did.

The union received some help from other locals, including one $9,000 donation. Most of the help took the form of picket-line participation and food for picketers. According to Sarto, the level of outside support was "typical" for a strike of this size.

During the strike, the company allowed Sarto to keep a trailer parked on company property—the executive parking lot in front of the plant. Fitzgerald agreed to let Sarto hook up an extension cord for power. The trailer provided picketers a place to rest and warm up on cold days, and served as a meeting room and a place to make coffee. Collections were taken among the strikers to pay the costs of coffee and the trailer.

The union organized regular Monday-morning meetings of Sarto and Edwards with the picket captains. This allowed them to keep track of the "pulse" of the membership. About 12 to 14 picket captains (of the 20) usually showed up at these meetings. During the strike the picket captains and bargaining committee issued occasional bulletins to the membership to help keep up their spirits.

Management maintained some semblance of operations during the strike. Trucks continued to move materials in and out of the plant, through the picket lines. Fitzgerald was responsible for deciding how and when to use the staff persons in the plant. Mostly they worked on packaging local orders, and filling in the gaps the U.S. plant couldn't fill, such as some particular switch units the U.S. plant couldn't produce. Fitzgerald: "We didn't get a heck of a lot of production during the strike. Frankly, it was more of a reason to give the staff something to do, so we could continue to pay them. Productivity was really low, although we were able to take care of a couple of rush-order situations. Mostly, the U.S. plants filled our orders. The trucks brought in finished goods from the States, we packaged them for shipment in the plant, and sent out the orders. There were 62 non-hourly staff persons not on strike, and about 35 of them worked for us in the plant during the strike. The rest maintained the necessary office functions."

The company had stockpiled about two months of production prior to the strike, mostly in the period from January to mid-March. Fitzgerald remarked, "In retrospect, it was stupid of us not to ship out the entire stockpile to a warehouse on the first day of the strike."

The company stopped paying employee benefits during the strike, and the union arranged temporary benefits and insurance. Normally, according to Edwards, a company continues to pay the benefits and bills the union for them. Edwards believes that the decision not to pay the benefits was a hard-line moved dictated from the U.S. head office.

UNION REACTION TO THE STRIKE

At the start, events on the line were relatively peaceful. Later on, a few relatively minor incidents marred the calm, but no concerted violence occurred, and the strike remained fairly amicable. Some of the women picketers expressed indignation at being watched from the plant windows by the security guards hired by the company, but the strikers took no action against the guards.

One union concern in any strike is whether management will make an effort at, or succeed in, maintaining production. Sarto: "We couldn't stop them from using office workers to keep up production, and working with supervisors and management. The company tried to hire scrabs, but we didn't let them get away with it." None of the union members continued to work during the strike. One young woman worker apparently wanted to, but she was stopped by angry picketers.

One problem for the union members was the trucks moving in and out with materials and finished products. According to Sarto, this led to the only incident of violence during the strike. In the first week of the strike, a woman broke a truck tail light with a piece of pipe, and was arrested. Sarto claimed that the driver couldn't have seen who did it, but he picked her out of the crowd when the police came. She was taken to the police station and booked, but the case was later dismissed.

Sarto: "About the third week of the strike, a bunch of us in our cars one night followed a truck and discovered a warehouse in Guelph they were taking finished switches to. The warehouse belonged to a different company, but Canadian Switch was using part of it for the duration of the strike. We found out that the Teamsters represented the warehouse employees. I got on the phone to the Teamsters the next day, and with their help we did some informational picketing at the Guelph site. We also heard a rumour that one of their office employees was using his own van to pick up materials in Ohio and bring them to the struck plant."

There were also some minor picket-line incidents involving the "problem" foreman harassing women picketers as he crossed the picket line into and out of the plant. In the final days of the strike, an elderly driver of a delivery truck sent to pick up an order of switches crashed through the picket line, injuring one of the women picketers and sending her to hospital. According to the picket captain, the driver was charged.

Much of the strike was a waiting game for the union. Ames: "A lot of our strike strategy involved waiting for management to get stocks down to the point where they were hurting and would make concessions to end the strike."

Among the committee members, the amount of influence they wielded shifted as the strike progressed, as did their feelings about the strike. At the beginning of the strike, the most influential persons were Sarto and Edwards, the only ones with much strike experience. No one else knew what to do, or how to organize the strike. In addition, Edwards was responsible for deciding which workers received what level of strike pay, based on need and participation in the strike. Fisher was able to influence many of the women, while Ames was strongly backed by the skilled tradesmen in the plant.

As the strike progressed, attitudes changed. Eddy Moore, one of the skilled tradesmen on the negotiating team, was the first to waver. As Ames put it, "Eddy just got tired of waiting around." Edwards spoke with Moore and the rest of the committee, telling them that they had to pull together and help out the women. Ames himself gradually lost interest in continuing the strike, and also lost his influence on the committee and with the workers. He withdrew from the conflict and took a part-time job in the last few weeks of the strike. At about this time, Johnson, the committee member who replaced Pearson, began to get much more involved in the day-to-day business of the strike. Despite the fact that she was suffering financially more than the other members of the committee, Fisher remained strongly in support of the strike throughout.

Among the union members, according to Sarto, reactions to the strike divided the women into three groups. "A large group, composed mostly of Italian and Polish women workers, definitely wanted to stay out on strike. The really young members, without family responsibilities, didn't really care, but seemed ready to stay out. A mixed group of women, not very many, wanted to return to work." According to Sarto, many women with pre-school children brought them to the picket line, while some older workers brought chairs and knitted. Others, including the men, tossed a baseball or played cards, and some drank beer.

Opinions varied as to the core of the strike support among union members. Ames felt that the group most in support of the strike were the Italian women, but one of the women stewards said that it was the Yugoslavs who most strongly supported the strike. On the management side, Fitzgerald said that he thought a core group of about 50 women workers influenced all the others and dictated the strike.

On the picket line, many of the women complained that they didn't know what was happening in negotiations, or even whether negotiations were occurring. According to one of the stewards, the leaflets that were printed were just left lying around the trailer, and most workers never saw them. In general, the women were unsure of what their union was doing, and of how long the strike would last. One steward remarked, "After four weeks, I just didn't know how long it would go on. After eight weeks, I thought it might last until the holidays." (The plant normally closed for holidays in the last three weeks of July.)

The picketers also wanted to see the union officers on the picket lines more often. They especially resented the fact that Fisher didn't take part in picketing (she was working in a federal election campaign). Fisher did, however, show up to distribute her election material (Communist Party) to the picketers. According to two of the shop stewards, this action alienated some of the workers, particularly with Polish, Hungarian, and Yugoslavian roots. One electrician threatened to punch her in the mouth. After the strike, according to Fitzgerald and one of the stewards, a group of women employees approached Fitzgerald and asked to have Fisher fired.

MANAGEMENT REACTION TO THE STRIKE

Management appeared to have two objectives during the strike: to keep it relatively peaceful, and to maintain some productive capacity to meet regional and local orders. Fitzgerald: "We were determined not to close down entirely!"

To keep the picket line peaceful, Fitzgerald spoke to the foreman who had been harassing the women on the line and ordered him to stop. During the third week of the strike, after the truck tail-light incident, Fuhrman shifted most of the trucking to the hours of 3 to 4 A.M. in order to avoid picket-line incidents and reduce hostility among the strikers.

THE END OF THE STRIKE

Sarto: "Towards the middle of May, after about seven weeks of the strike, I was getting a lot of pressure to call it off. Some of the members were running out of money. The men had had enough. My own opinion at the start was that the strike would last about five weeks longer than it did. This wasn't a clean, simple strike over wages. I feel that three weeks is about the right length for a good, clean strike, long enough to make a point without doing real lasting damage to either side. Basically, I think it was the trucks continuing to go through the picket line that did it. It really discouraged the workers, and made them wonder if Canadian Switch was going to hold out forever. The picket captains were also getting very discouraged, and this came out strongly at their weekly meetings.

"Because of this I called Turner, the mediator, and asked him to resume mediation, but not to tell the company that I had called. Of course, if they knew I had called Turner, it would be game over, and we wouldn't get a cent more. But I could trust Turner. And technically, if the company improved its offer, I'd have to take it to the members for a vote on whether to accept the new offer and end the strike. And that would be a quick and clean way to end it."

Sarto did not tell all the others on the committee about his call to the mediator. Ames did not know; he thought that Fuhrman sought an end to the strike when he became convinced that "the union had learned its lesson."

Turner, the mediator, called the parties and arranged a meeting for May 17. That meeting produced no settlement. The company offered a COLA payment in the second year of the contract; the union demanded a first-year payment. The company offered 35 cents an hour wage increase; the union asked for 60 cents. Fuhrman: "Turner called us up to see if we wanted to get together with the union and resume mediation. At the first session we saw that Andrews* wasn't around, so we figured the union wasn't serious about a settlement and so we didn't accomplish much."

Turner arranged a second meeting for May 29. This one lasted from 10 in the morning until 11 at night, and resulted in a tentative agreement. Fuhrman: "At the second mediation session we decided to heck with Andrews, we'll settle without him. Turner narrowed down the issues. We missed dinner but had the idea we were getting closer. Finally I made the decision to move and we got the deal. We're lucky that we've got a lot of autonomy here. Many multinationals don't; they're "nurse-maided" from the head office, which makes for problems when the parent company is only interested in the bottom line and return on assets. But in our case,

---

*The president of the union who had, in fact, retired about two months earlier.

the CEO has been here only three times in seven years. They left us alone to reach the settlement that was right for us."

THE SETTLEMENT

The settlement called for an immediate increase of 45 cents (15 cents more than management's position at conciliation), and a further increase of 35 cents on January 1, in the second year of the two-year agreement. Skilled employees got more, with corresponding maximum increases of 91 and 61 cents. The agreement also specified quarterly COLA payments of one cent for every 0.4 rise in the consumer price index, with caps of 10 cents a quarter and 20 cents per calendar year. Other issues settled were improved vacations; two holidays; and increases in the shift premium, sick pay, and life insurance.

Management had more problems with the seniority issue. Fitzgerald: "Fuhrman wanted to maintain the practice of allowing supervisors to move employees across job classifications as they saw fit. He feared that any change in the agreement would be the thin edge of the wedge. We finally settled for a letter of intent changing the transfer procedure. It was a token win for the union." Long took no part in shaping the agreement, other than to alert management to potential pitfalls in the wording.

On the union side, decisions had to be made about priorities. According to Ames, Bill Edwards traded off demands for a better dental plan in order to get more on the COLA issue. Of the committee members, only Fisher opposed the settlement. She refused to sign the agreement. Sarto: "She wanted the strike to continue indefinitely, even though she said she only wanted another five cents an hour added to the raise." Edwards: "It would have taken at least another month of striking to get any improvement in the offer."

THE RATIFICATION PROCESS

The next day, May 30, Sarto and Edwards met with the picket captains and stewards. After the captains and stewards had read over the tentative agreement, Sarto and Edwards explained why they should accept it. Both said that it was very unlikely that they could get anything more out of the company. Four of the captains opposed the settlement, arguing that they wanted more money, as well as the dental plan, pension plan, and provision for prescription glasses. As one said, "It seems like all we got from the strike was a COLA, and not a very good one."

The following day, May 31, 222 employees showed up at the ratification meeting to vote on the tentative settlement. The meeting lasted about two and a half hours, and was described by one of the stewards as "rough." First, Sarto read out the contract, and explained that he didn't think they could get anything better by staying out longer. He then asked if there were any questions, which provoked an outcry from the employees. In particular, the women complained about the poor COLA, and asked why they weren't getting a dental plan. Others complained that they still didn't have a pension plan, and that the contract still didn't provide decent seniority rights. Edwards and Sarto answered their questions, and explained that a longer strike wouldn't achieve anything.

The men then spoke up from the floor, in favour of returning to work. "They got a good raise; they were satisfied," complained one of the women shop stewards. Fisher spoke out against it, but there was some feeling among the workers who had earlier supported her, according to Ames, that they had "grown tired" of her radical politics. Most of the women stewards were in favour of staying out, although they didn't particularly support Fisher. The few black employees, however, continued their support for Fisher and her position. According to Sarto, "Some employees got mad. They wanted to stay out. They wanted 50 cents (instead of the 45 offered) and a better COLA. The company had only agreed to a later COLA payment." According to several of the women shop stewards, the biggest division in the unit was not between ethnic groups, nor younger and older employees, but between men and women, or the skilled and the unskilled workers.

The discussion was followed by a secret ballot vote. During the voting, Mike, one of the male workers, got into an argument with several of the women who were reluctant to end the strike, shouting, "What's the matter with you? It's time we should go back!" The argument lasted about 10 minutes, and ended when Sarto told Mike to keep quiet.

The result of the secret ballot was that, of 222 votes cast, 134 (about 60 percent) were in favour of accepting the offer and ending the strike.

AFTERMATH

In the few days between the ratification on May 31, and the return to work of employees on June 4, Fitzgerald had the staff clean up the plant and remove all traces of their presence. "I wanted it to look exactly like it had when they left, so there would be no hard feelings and everybody could be happy about getting back to work." In an effort to get things back to normal as soon as possible, and put the strike behind them, Fuhrman ordered the staff not to talk about the strike.

Management felt that it had lost no customers, and none of its customers had been forced to lay off their own employees because of lack of production at Canadian Switch. There had been no strain on the U.S. plant, which was happy at the time to get the extra work. Management made no effort to calculate the dollar cost of the strike. According to

Fitzgerald, relations with the hourly employees have been excellent since the strike, as have his relations with Sarto and Edwards.

Sixty-six employees quit during the strike and found jobs elsewhere, not returning to work at Canadian Switch. A number of the remaining women employees felt some lingering resentment towards the union. One steward said, "We would have gotten more if we had held out for one or two weeks more." Another remarked, "We feel we were sold down the river by the union."

Ames resigned his position as chief steward shortly after the strike. "I didn't have much influence any more, I'd lost interest. It was pointless to continue." Fisher expressed a strong interest in being elected the new chief steward. However, she was opposed by the male workers and many of the women in the plant, several of whom consulted Fitzgerald on how to prevent Fisher from winning the post. Fitzgerald: "My advice was simply to nominate somebody popular for the job." As a result, Johnson, the tool-and-die maker who replaced Pearson on the union negotiating committee, and who had taken an active role in the later stages of the strike, was elected at a sparsely attended Sunday meeting.

Fisher was later elected recording secretary for the local. Sarto had hoped that the experience would make her become "more practical," but he says that she has missed many meetings. It appears that she hasn't become more integrated into the union leadership of either the local as a whole, or the Canadian Switch bargaining unit in particular.

About a year after the strike, the local raised union dues for members in all 12 units. About two-thirds of the Canadian Switch unit members signed a petition against the raise, but they weren't enough to prevent its going through.

A couple of hours after his conversation with Fuhrman, the casewriter was talking with Sarto. "It's a funny thing," said the local president, "Sometimes I get the feeling that the strike should never have happened, but I'm damned if I know how I could have stopped it."

8

Third-party Assistance in Collective Bargaining

BRYAN M. Downie

INTRODUCTION

Often in collective bargaining there is a breakdown in discussions between the parties, and outside intervention is required in the form of conciliation and mediation, fact finding and conciliation boards, or interest arbitration (conventional and final offer).

In mediation and conciliation the third party is not a decision maker. Rather, the neutral is a catalyst who tries to help the parties with their dispute. On the other hand, fact finders and conciliation boards investigate collective bargaining disputes, make findings of fact with respect to the dispute and usually issue formal, but advisory, recommendations on terms of settlement. In interest arbitration, after holding a hearing, the neutral makes a decision on terms of settlement which is binding on the parties.

While mediation and conciliation continue the collective bargaining process between the parties, fact finding and conciliation boards interrupt negotiations, and in interest arbitration the parties' decision-making powers are pre-empted. In light of this, it is not surprising that union and management are more favourably disposed to mediation than to fact finding and arbitration (Herman and Leftwich, 1985). Therefore, mediation and conciliation are the most intensively used types of third-party intervention. Craig (1983) alludes to this.

> Conciliation officers and mediators are used in the private sector and in many parts of the public sector, including the federal and provincial public services. Most statutes giving collective bargaining rights to provincial public employees, who may not legally strike, contain a provision which requires conciliation or mediation before the appointment of an arbitration board. The same is also true in the case of many parapublic employees (hospital workers, teachers, etc.).

In terms of function, mediation and conciliation are identical, and the skills exercised are the same. The difference between mediators and conciliation officers has more to do with the time period, or the stage, of the collective bargaining process at which they are appointed than with their purpose or behaviour (Craig, 1983). The function in each case is to help the parties reach their own agreement. In short, the task of both conciliators and mediators in Canada is accommodative rather than normative. Thus reference is made hereinafter only to mediation.

Mediation plays a vitally important role in Canadian labour relations. However, it is not only a popular form of third-party assistance with labour and management but also one that is little discussed or understood. There are few good descriptions of precisely what mediators do. For example, one of the leading texts on Canadian industrial relations (Anderson and Gunderson, 1982) devotes just half a page to mediation. With respect to the literature on mediation, Kielly and Crary (1986) have noted:

> ...We are left with a view of mediation that is discouragingly complex and we are overwhelmed by long lists of things a mediator might do....what is needed is not massive research into all the thousands of things a mediator might do, but instead into what the mediator should do to be effective.

The focus of this chapter, therefore, is on the mediation process from the standpoint of practice and behaviour rather than theory. Its purpose is to set forth in some detail the strategy and tactics used by labour mediators and to portray how the process generally unfolds in collective bargaining in Canada. In discussing mediation I will rely on the literature and my own experience both as a third party and as one who currently trains and appoints mediators for a government agency. Let us begin with an examination of mediator style and then look at the mediation process as it evolves from appointment to settlement.

MEDIATOR STYLE AND QUALITIES

Much of the literature on third-party work centres on mediator style (Folberg and Taylor, 1984; Robins and Denenberg, 1976; Kolb, 1983). Some of this literature tends to be confusing and, unfortunately, the reader sometimes goes away with the feeling that mediators are godlike. For example, in a frequently quoted passage, William Simkin,[1] who was Director of the U.S. Federal Mediation and Conciliation Service, listed the following requirements for a mediator:

- the patience of Job;
- the sincerity and bulldog characteristics of the English;
- the wit of the Irish;
- the physical endurance of a marathon runner;
- the broken-field dodging abilities of a halfback;
- the guile of Machiavelli;
- the personality-probing skills of a good psychiatrist;

- the confidence-retaining characteristics of a mute;
- the hide of a rhinoceros;
- the wisdom of Solomon.

While there is an element of truth in the above, few seem to fit Simkin's mold. Instead, mediators seem to be of two types. Some mediators are perceived by the parties as having the following qualities:

- good facilitative skills;
- a good and an empathetic listener;
- an accurate conveyor of information and messages;
- trustworthy;
- objective, honest and fair.

This type of mediator sees himself or herself as a reliable go-between, an individual whom the parties trust and through whom they can communicate to each other. This view or style of mediation we can entitle the honest-broker model—an approach that sees the third party's role as facilitative rather than forceful.

A second set of mediators seem to be perceived very differently. They are seen as:

- powerbrokers;
- "readers" of behaviour and of the parties' true negotiating positions;
- manipulative and persuasive;
- savvy;
- tenacious.

Individuals in this category see themselves as action-oriented risk takers. The parties often see them as manipulative. We can call this the power-broker model of mediation.

All mediators obviously do not fall neatly into these two camps. Nevertheless, other observers of the process have noted similar stereotypes. Gerhardt and Drotning (1980) in a U.S. study of public sector bargaining note that there are "passivists" and "activists." Kolb (1983) classifies mediators as "orchestrators" and "dealmakers." Orchestrators are concerned almost exclusively with process and facilitative skills and little, or not at all, with substance, i.e., the terms and conditions of the agreement. Dealmakers get actively involved in the issues as well as with the process of negotiations.

For many years labour mediators, albeit with some exceptions, tended to be of the first type (i.e., orchestrators). In Kolb's study, for example, the orchestrators were trained and employed by the Federal Mediation and Conciliation Service—one of the oldest labour relations agencies in the United States. Certainly, one of the distinguishing features of labour mediators is that historically they have been concerned almost exclusively with process rather than issues (Susskind and Ozawa, 1983). Today this has changed and, in labour relations, many more mediators are tending to be dealmakers or a mix of the two styles. One reason is that this type of individual, perhaps surprisingly, is in demand by the parties, particularly in public sector bargaining. The experience of the Education Relations Commission, for example, is that the parties themselves most often ask for a mediator of the dealmaking variety.

The dealmaker often "makes things happen" in a dispute and, in the public sector (where there is little pressure on the parties to settle), the parties often look to this type of individual to generate some movement in the negotiations. A dealmaker becomes much more than a facilitator or catalyst; hence the term "activist" is most appropriate. Henry Kissinger, in his role as mediator of international conflicts, typified this type of inter-ventionist. Susskind and Ozawa (1983) note that, as a mediator, Kissinger:

- directly controlled all communications between the disputing par-ties;
- actively persuaded the parties to make concessions;
- acted as a scapegoat and deflector of the parties' anger and frustra-tion, rather than allowing the parties to express their emotions to one another;
- co-ordinated the exchange of concessions, and by so doing, masked the bargaining strengths of the parties to one another;
- made his own proposals for possible resolution; and
- created and maintained the momentum of the talks.

Unfortunately, there is little research on the efficacy of the two styles, and the research conducted thus far appears to be inconclusive. For example, Brett et al. (1986) conducted research on third-party style in grievance mediation. They classified the styles as "dealmaking" and "shuttle diplomacy" and found there was no significant relationship between settlement rate and mediator style. On the other hand, they did find a relationship between mediator style and the type of settlement the mediators achieved. Some mediators, for example, were more successful than others at facilitating compromises, while other mediators were more successful at getting one party or the other to capitulate, and these differences were related to style. Also, anecdotal evidence from the parties does suggest that "activists" or "dealmakers" are more effective in most situations. At the same time, they may lose the acceptance of the parties more rapidly.

The issue may be one that will never be answered definitively. Not only do mediators' styles vary but also mediators may vary their approach on a case-by-case basis, depending on perceptions of their role and their beliefs about the most effective techniques in a particular situation. In any case, when this chapter describes mediator behaviour, it will do so from the activist or dealmaker perspective.

Finally, it is frequently asked regarding style whether mediators are, or should be, concerned with the terms of settlement worked out with the parties. In Canada, some mediators are permanent government employees while others serve on an ad hoc and freelance basis. Most, if not all mediators, however, would respond that their task is to attain a settlement regardless of what they personally might think about the terms of agreement. This view corresponds with the adversary system of labour relations in Canada that the parties have the capacity and responsibility to protect and advance their own interests. Peach and Kuechle (1975) note:

> ...mediators have no vested interest in the outcome of negotiations. The company and the union must live together with the product of their agreement. Consequently, the mediator's interest in helping secure a settlement extends no further than in his pride in doing a job well done.

The task of the mediator, then, is to facilitate and not regulate or evaluate the merits of the agreement. We turn now to the requirements of a mediator who is about to enter a dispute.

MEDIATOR REQUIREMENTS: A CASE EXAMPLE

There are at least two difficulties in describing precisely how mediators conduct themselves. First, it is difficult for a mediator to articulate what is effective technique. When the mediator meets with the parties, he or she generally is faced with (1) two sides who have taken rigid positions, (2) intransigent and sometimes bitter attitudes, and (3) a view by both parties that it is the other's turn or responsibility to move in the negotiations. If this were not the case, it is unlikely that the parties would need the third party to assist them in the first place. At a point in time, and often to the surprise of the mediator, the parties begin to exhibit or to declare a certain degree of flexibility on the issues. After the fact, however, it is often difficult for the mediator to express precisely what it was that he or she did to move the parties to settle.

Second, when we consider mediators who have been successful, a clear set of traits and abilities does not stand out. As we have seen, mediators have different styles and approaches. Successful mediators may be introverted or extroverted, charming or direct, verbose or quiet, academically inclined or action oriented, and so on. Therefore, to illustrate what mediators do and how they tend to operate, it is useful to start with a concrete situation that a third party might face.

Consider a set of negotiations between a school board and a teachers' union in Ontario. The mediator will be confronted with two major problems—"attitudes" and "issues." At some point he or she must deal with both dimensions. With respect to the first (i.e., attitudes), it may be that there is mistrust between the parties. For example, the teachers may fear that the school board is concerned only with costs and may attempt to control costs by, say, laying off teachers. The school trustees my fear that the teachers do not care about the quality of education but only about job security and the size of their salary increase. Also, the trustees may be trying to discourage and force out "problem teachers" by transferring them to less desirable schools or to schools that require substantially more travel time for the transferee. Some of these relationship problems the mediator may not hear about directly from the parties. For example, there may be an incompetent principal in one of the schools but the teachers may be reluctant to raise this at the bargaining table or in direct talks. Thus the mediator often must deal with a "hidden agenda," problems that hold up settlement but which are not overtly discussed.

On occasion, specific issues or demands on the table reflect the hidden agenda. For example, the teachers may demand a new job posting system because they do not trust the administrators with the board. This demand may have arisen because of favouritism in assigning new positions. Sometimes a mediator can resolve the issue through verbal assurances (say, by the board's negotiator to the teachers' negotiator) that the school trustees now recognize there has been a problem and that steps will be taken to rectify the situation. In any case, it is the task of the mediator to determine which issues on the table are "real" and which reflect a hidden agenda or negative attitudes between the parties.

In addition to attitudes, the mediator, of course, has to deal with the substantive issues. Let us assume the following eight issues are outstanding: salary, a dental plan, OHIP premiums, salary allowances for positions of responsibility such as department head, salaries for principals and vice-principals, a job posting system, board transfer policy, and the number of teachers relative to the number of students in the system or pupil–teacher ratio (PTR). Figure 8.1 shows the hypothetical position of the parties on each of the issues. As can be seen, a substantial distance separates the parties on each issue and in total.

It is often assumed that the mediator will be able to resolve, fairly easily, one of the non-monetary issues (e.g., job posting or transfers) and by so doing develop some credibility with the parties and build some momentum. Unfortunately, the situation is rarely this simple. At least one of the parties is likely to insist (1) that it is the other party's move, and (2) that all items remaining on the table are equally important. Hence, it may be difficult to get the parties to prioritize the issues. If the mediator tries to push the parties to consider and resolve one particular item, he or she is likely to lose their confidence.

Faced with such items on the table and the negative attitudes between the parties, the mediator is, therefore, faced with the question, "Should I be concerned with the issues or with the process?" The effective mediator, at least in the early stages, thinks almost exclusively in terms of the process he or she will use rather than the issues to be resolved. This view was expressed by a third party interviewed in a study on mediation (Kressel, 1971):

> I find—and this is the key to mediation as far as I am concerned—I find at the outset of a mediation I spend *all* of my time gaining the confidence of the parties. And somebody would say, "Well, what are the issues?"...I couldn't be less concerned what the issues are. I'll find out what the issues are. There's no point in knowing what the issues are and having them not talking to you.

In another study on mediation (Susskind and Ozawa, 1983) the same point has been made:

> In collective bargaining situations, the mediator is assumed to be preoccupied primarily (if not exclusively) with *process*. In contrast, it may be preferable for the mediator in environmental and other public disputes to assume the additional responsibility of attending to certain key qualities of the *results* of the resolution process (i.e., fairness, efficiency, and stability).

It is not that the labour–management mediator is totally unconcerned with the issues. However, in order to help the parties reach an agreement, the mediator as illustrated in Figure 8.2 must achieve four essential requirements—credibility with the parties, fate control, an understanding of the hidden agenda, and movement on the issues. The mediator can achieve these only through the power of personality, through the co-operation of the parties and through use of the process. Process, therefore, is uppermost in the mediator's mind. By process is meant the procedures followed by the mediator, and the configuration, sequencing, and timing of meetings that he or she sets up.

Let us consider the requirements the mediator must try to obtain. First, he or she must have credibility with the parties. That is, they must view the mediator as having the ability and professionalism to carry out an effective mediation session. Without this they are unlikely to work with, or confide in, the individual. The parties may not like a particular third party. This is relatively unimportant, but they must respect and have confidence in him or her. In some cases, the mediator may have worked with the parties previously and therefore may have their confidence. If not, the individual's credibility must be developed through effective use of the process.

Second, and related to the above, the mediator must develop what we can refer to as fate control. That is, at some point the parties must be willing to place the dispute in the mediator's hands and allow him or her to communicate messages between the parties. In an easy case (a rarity in

Figure 8.1
Hypothetical Position of Bargaining Parties

	School Board	Teachers' Union
Attitudes	Hardline re: costs of education Hardline and intractable re: managerial control over school system—manning, job posting and transfer issues	Fearful of layoffs Militant re: day-to-day treatment of teachers by administrators Mistrustful of administrators and trustees
Issues		
• Salary	2% increase offered	8.5% increase demanded
• Pupil–Teacher Ratio	Status quo—20.1 students per teacher (20.1/1); set by board policy	Reduce PTR to 19.5/1 and put the ratio in the collective agreement (subject to grievance and arbitration)
• Dental plan	No plan offered	Demand for a plan 100% funded by board
• OHIP	Status quo offered; board's contribution will cover 75% of the premium	Demand board's contribution cover 100% of the premium
• Salary Allowances	No change offered	8% increase demanded
• Job Posting	No offer	New positions internally posted for 3 weeks

• Transfer Policy   A unilateral decision by the board   Transfers by seniority

• Principals' Salaries $500 offered (an increase of 1%)   8% increase demanded

Figure 8.2
Mediator Requirements in Collective Bargaining

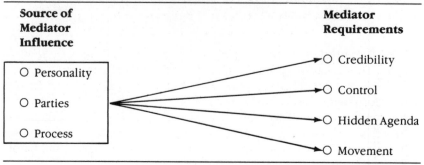

labour–management mediation), developing fate control may not be necessary. But in most cases the parties must come to the realization that only through the mediator will they be able to reach an agreement. Again, the mediator brings the parties to this position through the use of process.

Third, the mediator must gain insight into the hidden agenda. The hidden meanings and problems behind certain positions can be discovered only through procedural devices. For example, the mediator may provide opportunities for the parties to "let off steam" so that catharsis and an open discussion of the issues can take place. Thus the hidden agenda may come into the open and be resolved.

Finally, the mediator must obtain a new position or an indication of specific flexibility on the issues from one or both of the parties. This is essential: without movement on the issues there is little that can be done to assist the parties. As soon as the mediator achieves movement, the parties have taken a major step towards settlement. However, because they are unlikely to convey a new position or concrete flexibility to the mediator early in the session, he or she must use the process in subtle ways to elicit this from them. Such use of the process by third parties is the subject of the remainder of this chapter.

THE PROCESS

Meeting the Parties

A procedural matter confronts the mediator as soon as the individual is appointed. The first issue is: "Should I meet with the parties in a joint session or should I meet each party alone?" Most mediators will meet the parties at the beginning in joint session. Indeed, the classic mediation process is as follows:

1. A joint meeting with the parties;

2. Separate meeting(s) with each party;
3. Shuttle diplomacy in private caucuses;
4. One-on-one meetings with the chief negotiators;
5. A joint session once there is a settlement.

Most mediators, then, will begin by meeting the parties in joint session. There may be disputes when one of the parties will *not* want to meet with the other in the presence of a third party but, when the mediator first goes into a dispute, he or she will generally insist that the parties meet jointly. There are two reasons for this. First, when the mediator so insists it is a matter on which the dissenting party generally will capitulate. This makes it an ideal issue to establish that the mediator, and not the parties, is in charge of the process.

Second, there are numerous advantages to a joint meeting, at which the mediator can establish a number of important things. For example, the sense of formality can convey the message that the mediator is in charge and in control of the process. In a formal setting it is much easier to establish the mediator's credibility. While not as formal as an interest or a rights-arbitration hearing, a formal mediation session clearly establishes who is in charge. Also, by making the room arrangements for a joint session (generally in a hotel) before the meeting, the mediator can ensure that there is an appropriate negotiating table, seating arrangements, and general environment. By all parties' meeting jointly, the mediator can take the "power" position at the head of the table. While this may seem a minor point, such subtleties are extremely important in the collective bargaining process. Starting in this way establishes the mediator's influence.

A joint session also allows the mediator to set out ground rules for the mediation session which both parties hear at the same time and in the same way. The mediator can indicate that, as a neutral, he or she will keep confidences and press *both* parties for flexibility on the issues. The first session may go beyond ground rules and take on an educational dimension, as Robins and Denenberg (1976) have noted:

> Many mediators make it a practice at the beginning of the first session to explain what the process is and what will be asked of the negotiating committees in sessions to come.

As well, by meeting jointly it is possible for the mediator to listen and observe as the parties address the neutral's questions and interact with each other. The mediator therefore can learn something about the issues as each party articulates its position, as well as something about the personalities at the table. Kressel (1971) quotes one mediator:

> As a general rule, when I walk into a labour dispute I will typically meet with the parties jointly around the conference table....[One of the purposes] is to

become familiar with the parties, to get some idea of an approach I may use to influence them when the time comes.

One of the arguments for *not* meeting jointly is that the meeting can get out of control. The parties, particularly when the relationship is poor, may start to argue and become openly hostile towards each other. Many mediators would argue this is simply an additional reason for insisting the parties meet in joint session, viz., that the earlier catharsis takes place the better. One of the mediators in Kressel's sample noted the efficacy of this approach:

> Hostility must come out, the anger must come out; the resentment must come out; misconceptions if they've harboured must come out. Well, the only way there can be clarification is in battle.

Not only may catharsis occur, but also each party will be sure to inform the mediator of the weaknesses in the other party's argument and stance. Questions will be raised in joint session that the third party may never think of raising if meeting with each party alone. In short, the parties play off one another and reveal to the mediator the weaknesses or consequences of the other side's position.

There are other advantages to meeting jointly. For example, it is possible for the third party to start determining who are the important players on each side of the table. The joint session allows the mediator to observe and assess before meeting with each party alone. He or she may begin to discover that the key decision-makers are behind the scenes and not at the table.

The mediator has the option of keeping the talks exploratory and general, or of encouraging the parties to make tradeoffs on the items right at the table. In such a setting it is almost assured that such tradeoffs will not occur. This may appear to be dysfunctional but, in fact, it is important in establishing, or beginning to establish, the second essential ingredient, i.e., fate control. The mediator needs to bring home to the parties the fact that they cannot reach an agreement on their own. He or she does this by ensuring that each side sees how inflexible the other party is. This sets the stage so it becomes apparent that the third party is the only mechanism through which a settlement can be reached. Kressel quotes a mediator on this point:

> Unless he [the mediator] trains them at the very outset to rely on him, he is a dead-duck as a mediator.

By meeting in joint session the mediator has a better chance of moving the process, the parties or both over time from formality to informality, from hostility to catharsis, from rigidity to flexibility and, perhaps, from disagreement to agreement. That is, there should be an unfreezing as time goes on. A joint session at the beginning allows such an evolution.

Private Meetings

Whether the mediator adjourns after meeting jointly will depend on a variety of factors, e.g., the timing of the strike deadline, the relationship of the parties, the number and type of issues on the table, the disposition of the parties, and so on. In any case, once the joint session is exhausted the next meeting will be a private one with each party. A debatable issue is whether the mediator should first meet with management or the union. While this is of some relevance, the purpose of the private meetings is more important.

In this stage, the shrewd mediator is unlikely to push the parties for flexibility or a new position. Instead, this process allows the mediator to continue to listen and observe, but now under very different circumstances. In such meetings the mediator will gather additional information with respect to issues and personalities, and may begin to develop an understanding of the hidden agenda. As noted, some of the issues on the table indicate an underlying, and sometimes hidden conflict. Private sessions allow the parties to speak confidentially about such matters, and occasionally they do. In other instances, the mediator may be able to discover the hidden agenda only through more circumspect and, in some cases, clandestine meetings with the chief negotiator.

As well, in separate meetings the mediator may obtain a clearer indication "where the parties actually are" on the issues. At this point, by probing, he or she can assess whether an agreement is possible. Robins and Denenberg (1976) describe the process.

> In the separate sessions with full bargaining committees, mediators continue what they began in the first joint session. They seek to find out what the proposal is aimed at, what problem it is meant to cure, if what the party is seeking is attainable or even reasonable. They ask such questions as, "If you had to give up this demand, what would be the effect on employees? (Or on the operations.)" "What has occurred which makes this demand important enough to hang on to when you could perhaps buy something else if you withdrew it?"

In separate sessions the mediator also will be looking for cues to the parties' flexibility. In the teacher–school board example outlined earlier, the teachers may have a specific demand on the table with respect to job posting. When discussing their demands, however, the union negotiator might say, "We are looking for a fair and workable solution." The mediator, sensing flexibility on the issue, may ask the negotiator what the specific problem is and what the teachers' needs are with respect to the problem. He or she may then ask whether the negotiator had considered solutions to the problem that the mediator had worked out elsewhere. By this approach the mediator begins to unfreeze the thinking of the parties (Robins and Denenberg, 1976).

> The tools are continuing dialogue, exploration and suggestion; and not the least valuable tool is the mediator hearing properly the sophisticated language and nuances sometimes employed by the parties.

During this phase, the mediator is also able to develop a closer relationship with, and empathy for, the parties. The intensity of feeling of the various members on particular issues can be assessed. It is important to evaluate how much support a position has within the committee and how unified the committee is. The identity of the real decision makers on each side of the table may also be ascertained in this setting. Both parties will know who on the other side of the table has influence. The mediator can simply ask, say, the union committee who on the other side of the table must be "sold" or dealt with.

Early in the process mediators try to probe and explore both parties. They will ask open, non-directive questions such as, "Do you have any feelings on this issue?" or, "How important is it that this clause be inserted in the collective agreement?" or, "Are there other ways of meeting your concerns besides your current position?" This keeps the situation fluid, allows the parties wide scope for their answers and may also start them thinking in new directions. During the latter part of these sessions, however, the mediator also may prepare the parties for ultimate compromise by referring to other relevant or benchmark settlements. He or she may confront the parties with tough questions and observations such as, "Your chances of getting such a provision, in my opinion, are very low. I want you to consider some modification of your position on that item."

In private meetings, therefore, the third party educates himself or herself and softens up the parties.

Corridor Talks

The mediator may move back and forth between the parties several times in separate sessions. If a new position is not forthcoming from at least one of the parties the mediator must switch tactics. He or she might suggest to the chief negotiators that they consider a private "one-on-one" or "two-on two" meeting in the presence of the mediator.

Such a suggestion may reduce formality, particularly when there are many people at the bargaining table. The mediator can make it clear to the two sides that discussions in such private talks will be confidential and "off the record." Any positions taken will be private and, therefore, can not be referred to or publicized should the negotiations collapse or the parties ultimately wind up in interest arbitration. In most cases, the meeting will be held in an informal setting, often the mediator's room in the hotel or at some other suitable location.

Some negotiators in Canada, particularly on the union side, will not participate in "one-on-one" or "corridor" talks. Most chief negotiators will, however, and such talks tend to be invaluable in the settlement process. Some mediators introduce them later in the process while others use them before and during the next stage of mediation, i.e., shuttle diplomacy. Whenever private talks are suggested by the mediator, each party is left to decide who will represent them in a "one-on-one" session.

Once the parties agree to this type of meeting, either they will be successful in gaining some movement towards settlement because of the more informal and exploratory atmosphere or, alternatively, absolutely no progress will be made. The mediator can use lack of progress to highlight a fact that should by now be absolutely clear to both parties, viz., that only through the mediator's efforts will they be able to reach agreement.

As noted, corridor talks may be used later in the process. For example, if misunderstandings arise, the mediator may meet together with the two negotiators. Also, at the end of the process, if the parties are close to a settlement but unable to bridge their differences, the mediator may invite them to a one-on-one session. The meeting may break the deadlock or, alternatively, will at least ensure that the parties have had every opportunity to understand clearly and completely the differences still separating them before they break off talks.

Shuttle Diplomacy

After the potential of "one-on-one" talks is exhausted, the mediator is likely to keep the parties separated and begin shuttle diplomacy, carrying messages and positions back and forth to them. By this time in the process, a mediator must make it absolutely clear that he or she will not reveal a position to the other party unless given permission to do so. Not only must this be stated but also unequivocally practised. If not, the third party's credibility and trustworthiness is quickly eroded.

By this time the mediator has established some important psychological, substantive and procedural points even though little real progress may have been achieved. In the case of the teacher–board example outlined earlier, the mediator is likely to know by this time who has influence on each side of the table, what the hidden agenda is, and how strongly various members feel about the issues. The mediator also will have softened up the parties by asking them tough questions and by confronting them with facts. By this time, as well, he or she will have a good understanding of what issues the parties are soft on and how much "cushion" (i.e., flexibility) they have put on each item.

Removing Bottlenecks and Finding Flexibility

In addition to the fact that there may have been little movement on the issues, an additional problem may confront the mediator at this point. One of the parties may make, or may have already made, what is referred to as a "boulder in the road" demand. They may refuse to discuss any issue until a specific demand or problem has been resolved to their satisfaction. In the teacher–school board case, the union may demand a resolution of the pupil–teacher ratio issue before any other item is discussed. This demand does not invariably occur but, when it does, it creates difficulties for the mediator, by pushing the other party to take the opposite view, i.e., that *no* pre-conditions be placed on the negotiations, and that no discussion occur until this is agreed.

Faced with this dilemma the mediator may suggest that the issue be set aside for the moment but be the subject of problem solving or fact finding by a special subcommittee or joint committee outside the immediate negotiations. A specific deadline could be placed on such deliberations, at which point the committee could be required to report back to the parties. The mediator, instead, may suggest that a technical expert be brought in to share outside expertise on the issue. Or, he or she may persuade the other party to participate in a thorough discussion of the issue, hoping that once this has been done, the party who introduced the "boulder" will agree to proceed with normal negotiations. As a fourth strategy, the mediator may suggest that the issue be discussed but, should agreement be reached on it and if it is a monetary issue, the cost of the item be a part of the monetary package. Finally, the mediator may simply wait out the parties and let the pressure build until one of them backs off.

The "boulder in the road" problem is a difficult one. However, the more prevalent problem is that the parties will imply to the mediator that it is the other party's turn to move. Both may convey the message that they are flexible and will put out a new position but only *after* the other party moves. "Whose move is it?" is generally the most vexatious problem facing the mediator once this stage of mediation is reached.

There is an additional problem suggested earlier. Those not familiar with collective bargaining assume that a mediator can tackle one item at a time and start with the easiest items, say OHIP premiums or job posting in the teacher–school board example. This usually is not possible, however, once the parties get down to the hard-core issues and to those issues that cost money. By the time a mediator joins a dispute these are usually the only issues remaining. Or, if there are minor issues on the table they will be resolved easily, leaving the mediator with the same problem, as addressed many years ago by one mediator (Peters, 1952):

> When there is a large number of issues in dispute, the process of reflecting the real pressures in the situation becomes much more complicated. . . . Very rarely is it possible to dispose of the issues one at a time. The process can usually be facilitated by wrapping up various forms of packaging.

Because it is necessary to work in terms of packages, a good mediator will never force a single issue on the parties. If he or she raises an issue which is, let us assume, monetary in nature and the management negotiator indicates that the employer does not want to deal with it on an isolated basis, most mediators will not force the matter. It is an established pattern of the process that the parties will follow package bargaining. Therefore, because experienced negotiators understand the norms of the process, a mediator will lose credibility with the parties by trying to deal with one item at a time or by forcing the parties to deal with particular issues.

Sequencing, packaging and the norms of the process, therefore, are critically important. The mediator must understand that the issues that invariably fall into place last are the hard-core issues—almost always salary (or wages), job security, and working conditions (e.g., in the teacher–school board case, pupil–teacher ratio). Putting together a package that includes hard-core items may be, of course, extremely difficult. For example, what the school board offers with respect to a salary increase is likely to depend on what the teachers' position will be on pupil–teacher ratio. The union will operate in the same way. The Education Relations Commission (1983), in a report on mediation, highlights the problem.

> The parties are invariably faced with a strategic dilemma. . . . On the one hand, they are trying to explore the receptivity of various offers and counteroffers, yet on the other hand, they do not want to do anything that would jeopardize their bargaining posture.

The difficulty in this regard is that the mediator cannot ask the parties for their bottom-line position and thus directly discover the parties' flexibility. No negotiator would reveal that position, and a mediator would lose credibility by asking for it. Nevertheless, a mediator can be useful in breaking through the above dilemma. For example, he or she can use what is referred to as "supposals" or "what if's" to ensure that the negotiator's response is conditional and therefore protected, while at the same time protecting the position of the other party. The mediator might say to the management negotiator, "Suppose the union drops its demand with respect to putting the pupil–teacher ratio in the collective agreement. Would you consider possible solutions to their job posting problem?" Any answer management gives is conditional upon specific union concessions and leaves their bargaining posture intact. On the other hand, the mediator has not revealed the union's position to management. Peters (1952) describes a variation on this approach.

> . . .the parties were deadlocked on some nine issues. Both the business agent and the industrial relations director were determined not to make the first move, and were stubbornly trying to outwit each other. Finally, the conciliator in separate discussion with the industrial relations director said, "I realize that you feel quite strongly about all nine of these issues and are not disposed to concede any of them. However, can you indicate to me which of these issues you are especially concerned with? This does not mean that you are not also greatly concerned with the other issues, but can you segregate for me some of the issues which are the most important to you?"
>
> The industrial relations director was too cagey to respond. Undoubtedly, he felt that the issues he did not mention would give the conciliator too definite an impression of willingness to concede them. The conciliator then said, "Well, if you are not inclined to differentiate between the nine issues, as to which ones are more important to you, can you give me some idea of which of them you think the union feels most deeply about?"
>
> This he was willing to do, and he noted a number of issues which he thought the union would hold to most tenaciously. The conciliator then took the same approach to the business agent, and got him to give his opinion of which issues he thought that the management would be least inclined to concede. It developed that with one or two exceptions, the issues which the industrial relations director thought that the union would be most adamant about, were issues that he thought his own side might have to concede. The issues which the business agent thought the management would feel most strongly about were, with a few exceptions, those that the union felt it might have to concede. Through this method the conciliator was able to locate the few issues that really were in doubt, thereby considerably reducing the area of difference between the parties.[2]

There are other subtle strategies the third party can use to unfreeze the thinking of the parties (Moore, 1986). For example, the issues can be "reframed" so that the underlying interests and needs of the parties are exposed and discussed. While the teachers are asking that the PTR be lowered and a specific clause be put in the collective agreement, their underlying interest may be protection from unilateral board action on the issue which might result in teachers being laid off. There may be a number of ways of meeting that particular interest in addition to the method suggested by the teachers. The mediator may also attempt to join the interests of the parties. Management may be concerned with controlling its costs while the teachers want to increase the relative position of their salaries. The mediator can ask the parties to think of ways to "increase salaries so that they move closer to the provincial average while at the same time the board's costs are controlled at a reasonable level."

Negotiating with the Parties

It is critical, of course, for the mediator to get some specific movement to report to each side. In the early stages the wise mediator rarely argues with the parties. This often changes, however, once the mediator becomes involved in shuttle diplomacy. New positions cannot be carried to each party if these positions do not materialize. Therefore, at this stage, in order to induce some movement, the third party may have to take on the mantle of a negotiator with the parties.

The mediator must decide with which party to negotiate first in order to obtain concessions. There are different views with respect to this. Some feel it is best to go to management first, while others feel the union generally should be approached. There is, however, one compelling reason to go to the union for concessions in most cases, viz., management is dealing with real money whereas the union is dealing with paper demands. For that reason the union may have more cushion in its bargaining position. Each situation is different, however, and there are no fixed rules.

Let us assume the third party decides to press the union for a specific proposal. He or she may indicate to the union that there now is a definite possibility for movement from the other party but that the union is unlikely to see the employer's position until the union moves in a specific and significant fashion. If the mediator made the statement to the parties early in the process neither side would listen but, at this point, both parties are likely to consider such a request seriously. They know the mediator has a great deal of information by this time and would not convey the message unless relatively certain that he or she could deliver. As Robins and Denenberg (1976) put it:

> In either situation the mediator is able to say, "I have an assurance of an offer from the other side if you change your position. I do not know how much change you think you need in the other side's position as a result of your offer...but it is the time to start.

Robins and Denenberg also suggest that the negotiators may be more than co-operative.

> Thus, an employer's negotiator who is preparing an offer might ask the mediator which area would be best addressed: Is there a serious need, in the mediator's judgement, for obtaining something, however minor, on a specific contract change? A union negotiator preparing a counterproposal may ask the mediator what kind of movement will be most likely to produce an employer offer and perhaps, whether the mediator knows the kind of movement the employer expects in the counterproposal. And where the parties do not ask, the mediator sometimes volunteers that information.

Once a new position is attained it may set in motion a dynamic which carries the parties to settlement. When the mediator makes some progress he or she will try to keep the momentum going by scheduling future meetings, reviewing successes to date, and finalizing any movement agreed to. Also, the dispute now resides entirely in the hands of the third party who now may do all the communicating between the parties.

This new role allows the individual to use the following techniques and behaviours in order to drive the parties to settlement: the mediator can increase or decrease the pressure on the parties (for example, by indicating that he or she is going to, or not going to, leave); prevent each side from making irrevocable commitments which could result in the collapse of negotiations or require face-saving efforts later on; indicate there is no hope for settlement or that both sides have revealed considerable flexibility; bring new life to the negotiations by suggesting, for example, that technical experts be brought in, if necessary, to examine complex issues.

There is evidence (Gerhart and Drotning, 1980) that "active" or "intense" mediators are more effective than "passive" mediators. In the latter stages of mediation one can understand why this might be so. In order to achieve significant movement the mediator often must have a power base in order to negotiate with the parties. For this reason the mediator may also use the media in subtle ways. Often the individual will control access to the media by establishing that only the mediator may contact the press. Robins and Denenberg (1976) note:

> Frequently, mediators suggest a ban on public statements by the parties. Sometimes the parties will designate the mediator as the only person authorized to talk publicly about the negotiations.

Regular press contacts and releases, if used judiciously and diplomatically, can put pressure on the parties by informing outsiders of the progress or lack of progress at the table. The mediator may simply indicate to the media at a particular time that talks are being adjourned and that the parties have been asked to re-think their positions. By letting the public and the parties' constituents know in very general terms the status of negotiations, external pressure may be exerted on the table teams. Those affected by the talks (such as the public and employees) are unlikely to remain silent in such circumstances.

The mediator is also likely to use a power approach when meeting with the parties. In private caucuses the mediator may sit opposite the party to whom he or she is talking, as a negotiator would. The mediator may take issue with the party to whom he or she is talking in order to pressure them to change a position. The individual may indicate that, as a neutral, he or she feels the party's position is wrong on a particular issue. At times, as well, the mediator may support the other party. In short, even though shuttle diplomacy is taking place, the activist mediator becomes much more than a message carrier.

Pressure Tactics

As the deadline approaches (set by one of the parties or the mediator) a number of developments occur. The hard-core issues surface and the issues truly separating the parties become apparent. It also is more difficult to obtain additional flexibility from the parties as the cushion is reduced between their new negotiating positions and their bottom-line positions. Overall, however, deadlines force both sides to be realistic about their prospects and often force the parties to make necessary compromises.

The issue often facing a mediator is that a deadline (such as a strike deadline) does *not* exist. This is particularly true in the public sector where employees may not have the right to strike. Therefore, in many cases, it is necessary for the mediator to create a deadline or a specific time frame. To put the parties under pressure of deadline, the mediator may refer to plane reservations that have been made or to appointments that must be kept. For the same purpose, the mediator may also use time lines, if any, contained in the labour legislation governing the negotiations.

While the most effective mediators are extremely tenacious and will give up on a dispute only reluctantly, a mediator must not want to achieve a settlement more than the parties do. He or she always must be willing to pull out of a dispute and may threaten to do so as the deadline approaches in order to induce the parties to make further concessions. Such a threat may be enough to push the parties to settle.

At the same time, in this difficult stage of mediation the third party may use marathon sessions to maintain progress and to wear the parties down. However, some negotiators will oppose such sessions, and there is no point in pushing for a marathon session unless the parties agree to one. Robins and Denenberg (1976) comment:

> There is no merit to working 36 or 48 hours continuously—no mediator needs that test of endurance. But if progress is being made, if the mediator senses that the parties are ready to settle, he or she will not want to adjourn the session, concerned that momentum may be lost.

Tenacity and the use of marathon sessions often do pay off. A mediator in the Kressel survey describes the effect on the parties of a marathon session:

> Four o'clock in the morning is much more conducive to a settlement than four o'clock in the afternoon. A different sense of proportion appears at that

point as to what the meaning of these unsolvable problems are; what the value, what the significance is of all these demands. People are much more ready to abandon their principles at four o'clock in the morning. And if they are willing to sit until that time—I can't force them to sit—they're sitting there for a purpose: to get their differences resolved. And that investment of time they put in can't be squandered too easily in their own opinion. It isn't that people are tired. . . .but, you begin to get a different sense of proportion as to what the significance of these. . .points [is].

But it may be that towards the end of a marathon session the parties cannot reach agreement or make further progress. In these circumstances a question frequently asked of mediators becomes relevant, viz., "What role should the mediator play in shaping the settlement?" There seems to be a belief that a mediator often comes up with a creative solution to a problem dividing the parties. This is rare in the real world of collective bargaining. The parties know, far better than the mediator, the nuances and operational or administrative repercussions of a problem. The third party may make informed suggestions and open up new lines of thought along the way, but must avoid making any specific proposals for settlement with respect to the substantive issues in dispute. The reason for this is obvious; once the mediator makes a recommendation, he or she may no longer be viewed as neutral or objective by one or both of the parties.

"Mediators' proposals," therefore, are used very rarely and, generally, only after it has become evident in marathon sessions that the parties cannot achieve an agreement in any other way. This technique is used more today, however, perhaps because it was found to be effective some years ago. Maggiolo (1971) reports that in 95 percent of the FMCS cases where a mediator made recommendations they were accepted by the parties. Nevertheless, mediator proposals should be made judiciously. He suggests the following criteria should be satisfied before a formal proposal is made:

1. A threatened strike or the prolongation of an existing strike is having a major impact on the community involved.
2. The parties are deadlocked and no negotiated solution appears possible in the immediate future.
3. The parties have rejected alternative methods of solving the issues.
4. The mediator has a thorough knowledge of the issues in dispute.
5. The mediator has, by judicious explorations in joint or separate conferences, obtained a feeling for the issues and believes a middle ground exists.

There are two types of mediator proposals—informal and formal. In the first instance, the mediator will orally recommend to the parties the terms he or she feels would resolve the issues equitably. The process is non-coercive and the proposal may be thoroughly discussed with the parties. The proposal may be made with the clear understanding from the mediator that it is a *possible* area of settlement and subject to further negotiation and discussion. Also, informal proposals may be made to assist one of the parties politically with its constituents. That is, the proposed terms of settlement may be more acceptable to constituents if they have been proposed by a third party. The parties can blame the mediator for the terms if that is necessary in the circumstances.

If a formal proposal is used, much more coercion is involved. The mediator's recommended terms of settlement are placed in writing before the parties, generally in joint session. In the case of the teacher–school board dispute discussed earlier, the mediator's proposal might take the form of a detailed memorandum of agreement and contain the following terms for a one-year agreement:

- *Salary increase to teachers*—5.0%;
- *Salary increase to principals and vice principals*—$1,000 (or approximately 2.5%);
- *Pupil–teacher ratio*—a letter of intent to the teachers from the board indicating there will be no change in the current ratio over the period of the collective agreement;
- *Transfer policy*—a joint (teacher–board) committee to study the problem;
- *Salary allowances*—no change;
- *Job posting*—no change;
- *Dental plan*—no change;
- OHIP—no change.

It is usually made clear that the terms are *non-negotiable* because the mediator does not want the parties agreeing to only those terms which are to their liking. The parties may be given a specific period of time, say 24 hours, to report to the mediator acceptance or rejection of the total package. After presenting the proposal, the mediator may not stay for any discussion of it but, instead, may simply ask the parties to consider its merits and to call with their response. If the terms are rejected by one or both of the parties, the mediator may release to the media the proposal and the parties' response to it. Maggiolo (1971) notes the force this can have on the negotiators:

Each party to a labour contract negotiation is keenly conscious of its public relations position. Each is seeking to elicit public support for the alleged fairness and reasonableness of its offer or demand. At the minimum, each seeks sympathetic neutrality; at the maximum, each seeks the exertion of public pressure which will impel the other party to either accept the offer or demand or to modify its position.

Normally, neither party desires to have a public exposure by a neutral of the true differences between them. Nor generally speaking, do they desire to have the public know that the neutral suggested a solution and they have rejected it.

Recognizing these facts, when mediators do make recommendations, in most cases, they will reserve the right to make such recommendations public.

Experience indicates that the mere threat to do so at a later day compels each party seriously to consider the recommendations and, if unacceptable in whole or in part, to re-evaluate their position and find a new approach to the solution of the unresolved issues.

An examination of the disputes in which mediators have made recommendations shows that it has seldom been necessary to make the recommendations public. Apparently, they stimulated further thinking which led to a breaking of the log jam in the negotiations.

If the parties do accept the mediator's recommendations, the preferable practice is to announce publicly that recommendations have been made but not to disclose the specific terms pending the ratification meeting.

If the proposal is rejected, the mediator no longer may be acceptable to one or both of the parties. This is not inevitably the case but, in most situations, the mediator must withdraw. Therefore, while a powerful tool, a mediator's proposal should be used only rarely and with great care. In most cases the mediator will be able to bridge the differences between the parties through the techniques outlined earlier.

In the final stages of negotiations one other problem may face the third party. On occasion, one side or the other will make statements to the mediator implying that a new position is "final" and that they expect the mediator to convey that to the other party. Or, they may ask the mediator to convey a strike or lockout threat.

Most mediators will ignore such statements and threats and will not communicate them to the other party. If such a message is conveyed, the mediator may lose credibility with the parties because a "final offer" may turn out not to be final. Also, by conveying this type of message the mediator is undertaking the task and role of the negotiator who has asked that the mediator carry the message. Obviously, this is not the mediator's role. To deal with the situation, the mediator may simply refuse to convey the message or invite the party to make the statement to the other side at a meeting arranged by the third party; in essence, the mediator will arrange a joint session so that the party can convey the message personally. When given this option, the negotiator generally drops the request, and no more is heard of it.

The only exception to the above is if one of the parties has very clearly indicated that a position is a final one and the mediator independently has come to the conclusion that the offer does represent the party's final position. At this point most mediators would convey the message. However, the mediator would not state that the party is making a final offer; rather, he or she would offer an opinion that the party "has come as far as they are going to come" in the negotiations.

The Wrap-up

While all phases of mediation are delicate, extreme care is required at the end of the process. The possibility of misunderstanding and miscommunication is high because the parties have been separated for some time. Once a verbal agreement is attained, it is essential to bring the parties together in joint session. Robins and Denenberg address this matter.

> To avoid communications errors which may have occurred in conveying offers and counter-offers, most mediators will convene a joint session when agreement has been reached. The terms of the settlement are restated, so that any problems or misunderstandings will be aired before the session is closed. The principal negotiators may ask the mediator to write a memorandum of agreement which they and their bargaining committee will sign before the conference adjourns. At other times the parties are content merely to make notes as the terms of settlement are reviewed. In most negotiations, the final language of the agreement is not developed at that time. However, the parties may insist upon writing the precise language of contract modification before they consider that agreement has been reached and this is done whether the time of settlement is 3 P.M. or 4 A.M.

Long before the mediator reaches this stage it is essential that he or she have a clear understanding from both parties of what is still "on the table," i.e., the issues that remain unresolved. At the end of the process, and just as settlement appears likely, one party may raise an issue that the mediator had thought was no longer in dispute. Or, in reviewing the terms of settlement with both parties one party may indicate that a particular issue had been resolved in their favour sometime earlier and it is not reflected in the tentative agreement. Total control of the agenda by the mediator and a clear understanding from the parties of what issues are unresolved is necessary. The wise mediator, therefore, periodically reviews with the parties "where we are" in the process.

Finally, mediators handle the wrap-up session in a variety of ways. Some leave the meeting as soon as there is a handshake and a verbal repetition of the settlement by the chief negotiators; others stay and help the parties draft the written memorandum; still others actually draft the memorandum of agreement themselves and present it to the parties for their signature. Whatever approach is used, two things are desirable: (1) that the parties immediately meet jointly and review the terms, and (2) that the mediator not leave until the memorandum has been signed by both teams.

CONCLUSION

This paper sets forth the methods used in labour mediation or, perhaps more accurately, the methods often employed. The techniques used in settings outside labour relations may vary considerably from the labour relations approach. For example, models suggested for marriage mediation seem to be quite different and are still evolving (Stuart and Jacobson, 1987; Saposnek, 1987). In Canadian labour relations, however, the adversary system confronts the mediator. The norms and behaviour that are a part of that system are well established and, with a few notable exceptions, apparently intractable. The techniques and processes used by labour mediators, therefore, are unlikely to change substantially in the future.

NOTES

1. Simkin, William E., *Mediation and Dynamics of Collective Bargaining* (Washington, D.C.: Bureau of National Affairs, 1971).
2. Copyrighted material reprinted with permission of E. Peters, *Conciliation in Action: Principles and Techniques*, p. 397 and Bureau of Business Practice, 24 Rope Ferry Road, Waterford, CT. 06386.

BIBLIOGRAPHY

Anderson, J. and Gunderson, M. (1982), *Union–Management Relations in Canada*. Don Mills, Ontario: Addison-Wesley.

Brett, J., Drieghe, R. and Shapiro, D. (1986), "Mediator style and mediator effectiveness." *Negotiation Journal* 2(3).

Craig, A. (1983), *The Systems of Industrial Relations in Canada*. Scarborough, Ontario: Prentice-Hall Canada.

Education Relations Commission (1983), *The Bargaining Process and Mediation*. Toronto: Education Relations Commission.

Folberg, J. and Taylor, A. (1984), *Mediation: A Comprehensive Guide to Resolving Conflicts without Litigation*. San Francisco: Jossey-Bass.

Gerhart, P. and Drotning, J. (1980), *A Six-state Study of Impasse Procedures in the Public Sector*. Washington, D.C.: U.S. Department of Labour.

Herman, E. and Leftwich, H. (1985), "Mediation and fact-finding under the 1983 Ohio Public Employee Collective Bargaining Act." Madison, WI: *Proceedings of the Industrial Relations Research Association*.

Kieley, L. and Crary D. (1986), "Effective mediation: A communication approach to consubstantiality." *Mediation Quarterly* 1(12): 37–49.

Kolb, D. (1983), *The Mediators*. Cambridge, MA: MIT Press.

Kressel, K. (1972), *Labor Mediation: An Exploratory Survey*. Association of Labor Mediation Agencies.

Maggiolo, W. (1971), *Techniques of Mediation in Labor Disputes*. Dobbs Ferry, NY: Oceana Publications.

—— (1985), *Techniques of Mediation in Labor Disputes*. Dobbs Ferry, NY: Oceana Publications.

Moore, C. (1986), *The Mediation Process: Practical Strategies for Resolving Conflict*. San Franciso: Jossey-Bass.

Peach, D. and Kuechle, D. (1975), *The Practice of Industrial Relations*. Toronto: McGraw-Hill Ryerson.

Peters, E. (1952), *Conciliation in Action: Principles and Techniques*. Waterford, CT: Bureau of Business Practice.

Robbins, E. and Denenberg, T. (1976), *A Guide for Labor Mediators*. University of Hawaii, Industrial Relations Centre.

Saposnek, D. (1987), "Aikido: A systems model for maneuvering in mediation." *Mediation Quarterly* 1(14/15): 119–136.

Simkin, William E. (1971), *Mediation and Dynamics of Collective Bargaining*. Washington: Bureau of National Affairs.

Stuart, R. and Jacobson, B. (1987), "Principles of divorce mediation: A social learning theory approach." *Mediation Quarterly* 1(14/15): 71–85.

Susskind, L. and Ozawa, C. (1983), "Mediated negotiation in the public sector." In L. Susskind and J. Rubin (eds.), *American Behavioral Scientist*, Nov./Dec. (Negotiation: Behavioral Perspectives), pp. 255–279.

9

Resolution of Interest Disputes

ALLEN PONAK AND LOREN FALKENBERG

Beginning with the country's first labour minister, William Lyon McKenzie King, Canadian labour policy has emphasized the prevention of work stoppages. The 1907 Industrial Disputes Investigation Act (IDIA) encouraged this approach with its compulsory two-stage conciliation process as a pre-condition to a legal work stoppage. The IDIA incorporated what were to become the two major underlying themes of Canadian interest dispute resolution policy: (1) requiring the parties to overcome a variety of hurdles prior to being permitted to engage in a work stoppage; and (2) during the inevitable delay period, assisting the parties to achieve a negotiated settlement through various third-party procedures. More recently, in many parts of the public sector, the obstacles have been replaced by an outright ban on strike and lockout activity.

How successful has Canadian policy been in this regard? On one notable measure, time lost due to work stoppages, this policy has not been effective. Canada has had one of the highest rates of work stoppages in the industrial world. It is at least arguable that Canadian policy, designed to prevent work stoppages, has managed to accomplish the reverse.

The purpose of this chapter is to examine critically Canada's experience with respect to interest dispute resolution. Included will be a review of the record with respect to work stoppages, an assessment of conciliation approaches under right-to-strike/right-to-lockout systems, and an examination of dispute procedures where work stoppages are prohibited.

THE CANADIAN STRIKE RECORD

The Canadian experience with respect to work stoppages is detailed in Figures 9.1 through 9.5. Since the mid-1960s Canada has averaged close to 800 strikes per year (see Figure 9.1). The worst year was 1975, with close to 1,200 work stoppages; in "better" years (1965, 1967, 1970), the total was close to 500 strikes.

In terms of time lost, strikes translate into slightly more than six million work days lost per year. While this total is substantial (and certainly higher per capita than many other countries), it is important to realize that the total time lost due to strikes in any given year accounts for

Figure 9.1
Strikes and Lockouts in Canada

Year	Number	Person-days Lost	Percentage of Estimated Working Time Not Worked
1960	274	738,700	0.06
1961	287	1,335,080	0.11
1962	311	1,417,900	0.11
1963	332	917,140	0.07
1964	343	1,580,550	0.11
1965	501	2,349,870	0.17
1966	617	5,178,170	0.34
1967	522	3,974,760	0.25
1968	582	5,082,732	0.32
1969	595	7,751,880	0.46
1970	542	6,539,560	0.39
1971	569	2,866,590	0.16
1972	598	7,753,530	0.43
1973	724	5,776,080	0.30
1974	1,218	9,221,890	0.46
1975	1,171	10,908,810	0.53
1976	1,039	11,609,890	0.55
1977	803	3,307,880	0.15
1978	1,058	7,392,820	0.34
1979	1,050	7,834,230	0.34
1980	1,028	8,975,390	0.38
1981	1,048	8,878,490	0.37
1982	677	5,795,420	0.25
1983	645	4,443,960	0.19
1984	717	3,871,820	0.16
1985	825	3,180,710	0.13

Source: Labour Canada (1987), *Strikes and lockouts in Canada*, 1985. Ottawa: Supply and Services Canada.

a tiny proportion of the total time worked by the labour force. Time lost due to strikes has never exceeded one percent of total time worked. Even in the two worst years, 1975 and 1976, strikes accounted for barely more than one-half of one percent of estimated working time of the labour force. Absenteeism and work accidents produce far more lost time in our economy than do strikes.

Further perspective on Canada's strike record is provided by examining the proportion of negotiations in which a work stoppage occurs. The data in Figure 9.2 support the observation that the relatively high inci-

Figure 9.2
Settlement Rate[1]

Year	Private Sector	Public Sector	Total
1967–71	80.5%	98.6%	82.9%
1972–76	81.1%	95.7%	88.5%
1977–81	86.3%	96.9%	92.4%

[1]Proportion of negotiations settled without a work stoppage. Based on all collective agreements applying to over 500 workers and a high proportion applying to 200 or more workers. Construction is not included.

Source: Adapted from R. Lacroix (1986), "Strike activity in Canada." In W. C. Riddell (ed.), *Canadian Labour Relations* (Toronto: University of Toronto Press), p.176. See Bibliography.

dence of strikes in Canada is due in part to the large number of negotiations that occur annually. The 800 strikes and lockouts that take place each year represent a small fraction of overall collective bargaining activity. As Figure 9.2 demonstrates, the parties come to an agreement without engaging in economic combat more than 90 percent of the time. This tendency is even more pronounced in the public sector. The small proportion (less than 10 percent) that are not peacefully resolved, however, translate into a large number of strikes because the collective bargaining system is so decentralized (Lacroix, 1986).

Variation in strike activity by industry and jurisdiction is summarized in Figures 9.3 and 9.4. It can be readily seen that the traditional, heavily unionized blue-collar sectors such as construction, forestry, mining, and manufacturing have reasonably similar records with respect to work stoppages and account for most of the strike activity (see Figure 9.3). Recalling that the average annual time lost between 1981 and 1985 for the entire economy was 0.22 percent, the time lost in these industries was more than double the national average. A comparison of the time lost across the different jurisdictions shows somewhat more variation than that found among industries (see Figure 9.4). British Columbia had by far the highest level of time lost (0.45 percent), with Newfoundland, Quebec, and the federal sector in the next highest group (0.26–0.32 percent). The Maritime provinces and the three Prairie provinces experienced lower rates of time lost due to strikes in the period under review.

Whatever the internal components and explanations for the Canadian strike record, Canada clearly loses more time due to work stoppages than most other industrial, democratic nations (see Figure 9.5). From 1960 to 1984, only Italy had a consistently worse record in this regard than Canada. In the most recent period for which data were available (1982–84), Canadian workers lost five times the days per capita compared to French workers, forty times that of Japanese workers, and 500 times the

Figure 9.3
Work Stoppages by Industry

Industry	Percentage of Time Not Worked (Annual Average) 1981–1985
Forestry	0.45
Mining	0.49
Manufacturing	0.47
Construction	0.44
Transportation and Utilities	0.31
Trade and Commerce	0.17
Services	0.09
Public Administration	0.15

Source: Labour Canada (1987), *Strikes and Lockouts in Canada, 1985*. Ottawa: Supply and Services Canada.

amount of time due to strikes than did their German or Swedish counterparts. There is little doubt that, compared to its major trading partners and competitors, Canada is a strike-prone country.

To summarize, Canada has averaged 800 work stoppages a year since the mid-1960s. These strikes entail a loss of more than six million working days a year. Though only a very small proportion of total time worked, Canada still loses far more work days per capita than other comparable nations. The next two sections examine the array of techniques used by various Canadian jurisdictions to reduce or eliminate labour-management disputes.

Figure 9.4
Work Stoppages by Jurisdiction

Jurisdiction	Percentage of Time Not Worked (Annual Average) 1981–1985
Newfoundland	0.32
Prince Edward Island	0.07
Nova Scotia	0.15
New Brunswick	0.09
Quebec	0.26
Ontario	0.18
Manitoba	0.07
Saskatchewan	0.16
Alberta	0.07
British Columbia	0.45
Federal (excluding civil service)	0.27

Source: Labour Canada (1987), *Strikes and Lockouts in Canada, 1985*. Ottawa: Supply and Services Canada.

Figure 9.5
International Work Stoppage Record

Country	Average Annual Days Lost Per Thousand Employees		
	1960–1970	1971–1981	1982–1984
Canada	547	912	500
France	176	200	100
West Germany	14	49	1
Italy	1,185	1,189	815
Japan	144	104	13
Sweden	20	147	1
United Kingdom	187	549	566
United States	591	274	129
Canada's Rank (out of 8)	6	7	6

Source: Pradeep, K. (1986), *The Current Industrial Relations Scene in Canada, 1986.* Kingston, Ont.: Queens University Industrial Relations Centre, p. 435.

DISPUTE PROCEDURES UNDER RIGHT-TO-STRIKE SYSTEMS

Canadian policymakers have historically relied on two major mechanisms for resolving interest disputes prior to a work stoppage: (1) conciliation; and (2) conciliation boards. Conciliation is a process, usually conducted by a single individual, in which a neutral third party (the conciliator or conciliation officer) attempts to persuade and assist the parties to reach an agreement. The conciliator's role is one of a facilitator, a counsellor and a catalyst, with special emphasis on communications to help the parties with their dispute. Woods (1973) characterized conciliation as an "accommodative process" in which effort is directed toward "bringing the parties into an agreement of their own making, without reference to any objective standards by which the agreement is justified. . . . The intervenor shows no concern with what is right or fair or proper" (pp. 158–159).

In contrast, a normative process, which is characteristic of the concil-iation board approach, "relies on standards supplied either in law or by experience. The intervenor judges the issues in dispute against certain rules or criteria" (Woods, 1973, 159). Conciliation boards generally act in a formal, quasi-judicial manner, eliciting presentations and arguments from the disputing parties and then making formal recommendations. Depending on the jurisdiction, these recommendations may be publi-cized. In other words, "the board is expected to do much more than mediate. . . .in the event of failure to produce agreement, it is required to drop its attempt to conciliate and to judge the issues and make a report with recommendations" (Woods, 1973, 167).

There are variants of these two basic processes, as well as differences in terminology, and this has created some confusion. One particular source of confusion has been with mediation, which may or may not be the same procedure as conciliation. In some cases, as in Alberta, it involves a process indistinguishable from that of conciliation. In Ontario, on the other hand, mediation appears to be an intermediate step between conciliation and a conciliation board, taking on some of the characteristics of both (Craig, 1986). The point is, use of the term "mediation" varies from jurisdiction to jurisdiction and from statute to statute. Whether or not it is the same process as conciliation depends on the jurisdiction.

The same comments can be applied to another dispute process used in several Canadian provinces—fact finding. Fact finding is most similar to a conciliation-board mechanism in that it tends to be an investigative, normative procedure (see Chapter 8). Again, use of the term varies depending on the jurisdiction, statutory definitions, and actual practice.

To avoid confusion, the following discussion will focus mainly on conciliation and conciliation boards. Conciliation will serve as a convenient proxy for the accommodative process which it most frequently resembles. Conciliation boards, analogously, will serve as a proxy for the various normative approaches currently in use across Canada. The reader is cautioned that the conciliation and conciliation-board approaches may exist under different labels in different jurisdictions.

Policy Development

The IDIA approach adopted by most Canadian jurisdictions was the dominant mode of dispute resolution until the late 1960s. Under this system, labour and management were obliged to undertake two levels of third-party assistance whether they wished to or not, with their respective rights to strike and lockout suspended in the interim. Conciliation took place first, and if it failed to produce an agreement, a conciliation board was appointed. A work stoppage could not occur until the conciliation board made its recommendations.

There were a number of criticisms of this approach and it gradually fell from favour. First, it was a rigid system that permitted little opportunity for deviation from the pre-ordained steps. Even if the neutrals had little optimism for a successful resolution of an impending dispute, the procedures still had to be undertaken and completed. The parties thus had no choice but to go through what at times they saw in advance as a futile exercise.

Second, the two-step procedures were time-consuming. Built-in time limits for each stage ensured that a considerable period passed before the two sides were in a position to undertake economic sanctions.

Such delay, if a strike ultimately occurred, sometimes proved to be a heating-up rather than a cooling-off period.

Third, serious questions arose about the effectiveness of the two-stage procedure itself. This particular criticism centred on the efficacy of the first stage of the conciliation process when the parties knew that a second step (i.e., the conciliation board) awaited them should conciliation not succeed. It was suggested that the parties did not make concessions at conciliation in a belief that such concessions might be used against them by the conciliation board. Consequently, it was argued that the parties did not take conciliation seriously (Cunningham, 1958).

Whatever the veracity of these criticisms (a subject discussed below), they resulted in the abandonment of the IDIA approach in favour of more flexible arrangements. The compulsory two-stage procedure is no longer used in any jurisdiction. The most common replacement is a system that allows for conciliation followed by a conciliation board, but which makes both processes discretionary. For example, in the federal sector, the Minister of Labour is empowered, in the event of an impasse, to: (1) appoint a conciliation officer; (2) appoint a conciliation officer followed by a conciliation board; (3) appoint a conciliation board directly without first appointing a conciliation officer; or (4) undertake neither conciliation nor a conciliation board, in which case the parties are free to strike. In the event that a conciliation officer, a conciliation board or both are appointed, however, the right to strike or lockout does not become operative until all procedures have been completed.

Approaches similar to the federal procedure are in effect in Ontario, New Brunswick, Nova Scotia, Prince Edward Island, and Newfoundland. Essentially, they all provide for some discretion as to whether conciliation or a conciliation board will be used but prohibit work stoppages once third-party assistance is provided. In practice, it is common for at least conciliation to be attempted. Should conciliation fail to resolve the dispute, a conciliation board is not usually appointed. Conciliation boards are restricted mainly to high-profile situations, where the potential for disruption is substantial. Negotiations involving Canada Post or the major air carriers are obvious examples. On the other hand, it is relatively rare for conciliation not to be used.

In these jurisdictions, therefore, the IDIA two-stage compulsory conciliation/conciliation-board model has been replaced, for practical purposes, by a much more flexible one-stage system in which conciliation, though discretionary, is often used and still has the effect of delaying a work stoppage. British Columbia, in fact, makes this approach explicit, providing for conciliation (or mediation, as it is called) with no provision for a second stage. The use of conciliation is not a precondition to a strike in British Columbia, but should the procedure be invoked, a work stoppage cannot occur until such time as the conciliator has withdrawn.

The second major policy currently in place is even less constraining. Though conciliation, conciliation boards, or both still are available, their use or non-use has no affect on the ability of the parties to exercise economic sanctions. In other words, even if a conciliator or a conciliation board is appointed, the right to strike still remains operative. Discretionary use of either of these procedures, unlike the model described above, does not suspend temporarily the right of either party to initiate a work stoppage. Alberta, for example, which adopted this approach in 1981, provides only for conciliation (called mediation in Alberta) in the event the parties desire third-party assistance. A strike or lockout may occur with or without a conciliation attempt and may occur even in the midst of a conciliation effort. Saskatchewan, Manitoba, and Quebec have variants of this approach.

To reiterate, the old IDIA compulsory two-stage conciliation/conciliation-board model has been replaced by two more flexible dispute resolution approaches. Both provide for discretionary use of conciliation and conciliation boards. Under one approach, third-party assistance, when invoked, suspends the right to strike or lockout until the process has been concluded. For convenience in further discussion, this model will be labelled the "hybrid" approach. The other approach differs from the hybrid one in that third-party assistance, even where provided, does not delay, temporarily or otherwise, the legal right of the parties to engage in a work stoppage. This will be referred to as the "voluntaristic" approach.

Based on a review of the general labour acts (as distinct from the public sector statutes) in the ten provinces and the federal sector, the Canadian jurisdictions can be categorized as follows:

Hybrid	*Voluntaristic*
Federal	Alberta
British Columbia	Saskatchewan
Ontario	Manitoba
New Brunswick	Quebec
Nova Scotia	
Prince Edward Island	
Newfoundland	

Dispute Resolution Effectiveness

In light of the historic importance attached to dispute resolution procedures and the abundance of policy alternatives, it is remarkable how little systematic attention has been directed to measuring policy effectiveness. Although dispute resolution approaches have been widely debated, particularly the IDIA model, most discussions have been based on descriptive and anecdotal evidence. For the most part, specific measures of policy effectiveness have been absent. Only four studies were found that attempted to examine the impact of compulsory conciliation through some type of quantitative analysis; only one of these studies used advanced statistical procedures.

In one of the first major studies of conciliation procedures, Cunningham (1953) evaluated the effectiveness of the compulsory two-stage model (IDIA approach) by reviewing each dispute that required government intervention in New Brunswick between 1947 to 1956. For each case the following information was examined: (1) applications for conciliation with supporting information about the issues in the dispute; (2) official appointments of conciliation officers and boards; and (3) officer and board reports to the Minister of Labour. He found that in 56 of the 146 disputes (38.4 percent) involving a conciliation officer, an agreement occurred at meetings with an officer or shortly after.

It is difficult to determine whether a 38 percent success rate indicates the effectiveness or ineffectiveness of conciliation. During the period under review, unions were less established than currently is the case and the level of negotiating expertise on both sides generally was underdeveloped. This may have produced a greater need for third-party assistance and a greater number of issues in dispute. On the other hand, it may have increased the chances of conciliation success, since disputes may have been due to inexperience rather than irreconcilable differences. Unfortunately, Cunningham presented no data on the ability of conciliation to narrow the differences. Finally, conciliation officers were working under the IDIA model, so that their efforts were affected by the impending appointment of a board.

With respect to conciliation boards, Cunningham analyzed their impact in terms of accommodative and normative functions. He found that conciliation boards were not very successful in an accommodative role in that they rarely facilitated an agreement. Of the 67 conciliation boards appointed between 1947 and 1956, only 12 disputes (17.9 percent) were settled before a board report was issued. To analyze the boards' normative impact, Cunningham compared board recommendations on wage, hours, union security, and vacations with the clauses that eventually appeared in the collective agreement. The analysis showed that board reports formed the basis of 18 of 32 settlements in which the agreement and board report could be compared, suggesting a positive impact in 60 percent of the cases. However, Cunningham noted that in five of the 18 settlements the conciliation board itself was not primarily responsible for the final settlement, reducing the success rate of conciliation board reports to 40 percent.

The study's findings do not lend themselves easily to interpretation, particularly with respect to the effectiveness of conciliation officers. Cunningham was not willing to give unqualified approval or condemnation of the influence of conciliation officers. He was more explicit in terms of conciliation boards, in that he concluded they were ineffective in producing an agreement and that they hampered the efforts of conciliation officers.

Woods (1973), in one of the most comprehensive reviews of Canadian conciliation practices, expanded on Cunningham's analysis of the two-stage system. He identified conditions associated with success, defining success in terms of reaching a collective agreement. He found that the effectiveness of conciliation was a function of bargaining-unit size. Between 1958 and 1968 the average membership of the units settling at the conciliation officer stage was 104, while the average size of all cases that used conciliation officers was 205. At the board stage, settlements were in units twice as large as those that settled at the officer stage. The size of the units settling at the board stage, however, was still much smaller than those where boards were involved but a settlement was not attained, 208 versus 374 respectively. Woods suggested conciliation procedures were less effective with larger employers and unions because: (1) they were setting new patterns while smaller units were following patterns; and (2) larger units were serviced by skilled staff and consultants, thus requiring less assistance from conciliation than the smaller units.

Woods did not share Cunningham's view that the required second-stage conciliation board thwarted the efforts of the first-stage conciliation officer. He suggested that the ineffectiveness of the two-stage process was not, in fact, well documented, and was based largely on Cunningham's work. Woods contrasted Cunningham's findings with his own review of Ontario. In Ontario there was little difference in the proportion of agreements reached at the officer stage when a board was compulsory compared to when the conciliation-board stage was discretionary. Woods preferred to stress the Ontario results as they involved a comparison of 10,000 cases, a much larger data base than that used by Cunningham. Unfortunately, Woods did not systematically report the data or their sources; nor did he perform standard statistical tests.

In his conclusion, Woods downplayed the positive impact of eliminating the board stage; at the same time, he suggested there was a need to compare the two-stage IDIA model to a totally voluntaristic system. Misick (1978) was the first to take up Woods' suggestion. Working from an economic model, he hypothesized that compulsory conciliation could be justified only if it fostered industrial harmony at a lower cost than other options; and that the public was often paying for unnecessary conciliation services. He cited the negotiations between the Autoworkers Union and the Big Three Automakers, where serious bargaining is delayed until the compulsory conciliation procedures are completed, as examples of the public paying for needless interference in labour-relations practices.

In an attempt to analyze this hypothesis quantitatively, Mistick com-

Figure 9.6
Annual Strike Days Lost per Union Member, 1960–75

	Nova Scotia	Saskatchewan	New Brunswick	Alberta
Annual Strike Days	1.29	0.85	0.81	0.61

Source: Misick, J. D. (1978), "Compulsory conciliation in Canada: Do we need it?"
   Relations industrielles, 33:193–204.

pared the number of strike days per union member over a 16-year period, 1960–75, in Saskatchewan, Alberta, Nova Scotia, and New Brunswick. He suggested these provinces were a good basis for comparison because during the interval studied: (1) Saskatchewan had always had voluntary conciliation procedures; (2) Alberta relied heavily on the two-stage procedure; and (3) New Brunswick and Nova Scotia had conciliation procedures that fell between those of Saskatchewan and Alberta. Misick also suggested that the four provinces were not dissimilar in population, age distribution, size of work force, number of union members, and degree of unionization.

Contrary to Misick's conclusions, the data did not support his hypothesis. There was no systematic relationship between the type of dispute resolution system and strike activity (see Figure 9.6). In fact, if anything, the data suggest low strike incidence is most closely associated with the IDIA approach used in Alberta. Saskatchewan, with its voluntaristic system, had a higher strike incidence than Alberta and was almost identical to New Brunswick with its hybrid model. Even if the data are "massaged" to exclude certain years that might be considered anomalous (e.g., 1974 in Saskatchewan), there is still little support for Misick's proposition that compulsory conciliation is ineffective. Indeed, the data suggest just the opposite.

The trend in Misick's study is confirmed by Gunderson et al. (1985; 1986) in the most thorough statistical analysis of strike incidence and dispute resolution procedures undertaken in Canada to date. Gunderson et al. hypothesized: (1) strikes are more likely to occur in situations of uncertainty, imperfect and asymmetric information, and divergent expectations; and (2) policy variables that raise the cost of using the strike mechanism relative to other mechanisms reduce the likelihood of a strike's occurring. Two logit analyses were employed to test these hypothesis. The first analyzed the impact of twenty-seven explanatory variables, classified into four categories, on strike incidence. The four categories of variables were: (1) season; (2) region; (3) specific unions; and (4) policy variables. A strike-incidence equation was generated on the basis of 2,437 private sector contract negotiations for the period of 1971 to 1983. As Gunderson et al. predicted, a significantly lower strike probability was associated both with the requirement of a conciliation officer and the requirement of a conciliation officer and a board.

The second analysis involved examining the impact of nine different policy variables (conciliation officer, conciliation officer and board, cooling-off period, mandatory strike vote, employer-initiated vote option, dues checkoff, prohibition of replacement workers, negotiated re-openers, and automatic re-opener) while controlling for industry, season, region, the five largest private sector unions, the Anti-Inflation Board, risk, deficient-demand unemployment and the size of the bargaining unit. Again, as in the first analysis, both the compulsory one-stage conciliation officer and the two-stage conciliation officer or conciliation board were found to reduce strike incidence significantly. However, Gunderson et al. reported no significant difference in terms of strike probability between the one-stage and two-stage approaches.

On the basis of these results, Gunderson et al. concluded that compulsory conciliation acted to reduce misinformation, divergent expectations and intra-organizational bargaining problems, and increased the cost of a strike. They noted that even in the case of asymmetric information, a conciliator familiar with the parties and the industry may be effective in eliciting "truth-telling" from the party with the greater information. The increased cost of striking occurs because: (1) the government subsidizes conciliation procedures, thereby increasing the cost of not using them; and (2) going against the public recommendations of a conciliation officer or board can be costly in terms of public pressure. They suggest that the success of conciliation in their analysis is consistent with the reservations of many practitioners about the process. The very annoyance with the process may serve to encourage the parties to settle at the direct bargaining stage.

Summary

Existing empirical studies (Cunningham excepted) argue against a completely voluntaristic dispute resolution system. Both compulsory conciliation on its own and the conciliation/conciliation-board two-stage approach reduce the incidence of strikes. The two-stage approach provides only a marginal (and non-statistically significant) reduction of strike probability compared to a one-stage procedure and thus, the move by most jurisdictions to make conciliation boards discretionary would seem justified.

The results make further sense within the context of Woods's accommodative-normative distinction. An accommodative approach facilitates reaching an agreement in that it reduces information uncertainty, misinformation or divergent expectations. Conciliation boards, by adopting a normative stance, do not increase the flow of information, particularly after a conciliation officer has already been involved. Any additional benefit would derive from public pressure. In most cases, this pressure is negligible, especially in the private sector.

These conclusions notwithstanding, it is clear that substantially more empirical work is necessary. The availability of so few rigorous studies on one of the most fundamental pillars of Canadian labour policy is difficult to understand. For example, little attention has been directed to how one measures dispute resolution effectiveness. Strike incidence is one obvious dependent variable (and the one adopted by Gunderson et al.) but other possibilities such as strike duration and closure on disputed issues also make sense from a policy perspective. Furthermore, process variables like the acceptability of the conciliator and timing of the appointment need to be included to enhance whatever conclusions ultimately are drawn.

INTEREST ARBITRATION SYSTEMS

The rapid growth of public sector collective bargaining in the late 1960s and throughout the 1970s presented policy makers with a new dilemma. While the right to strike was well entrenched in the private sector, substantial reservations existed about permitting public employees to withdraw their services (Goldenberg, 1979; Ponak, 1982). The basis for these reservations was essentially twofold: (1) a belief that public sector work stoppages, involving irreplaceable and in some cases essential services, would place an intolerable burden on the public; and (2) a perception that the combination of political and economic pressure generated by public sector strikes would place too much power in the hands of public employee unions.

The dilemma arose in finding substitutes for the right to strike. A number of American states had prohibited public sector work stoppages but had failed to provide mechanisms for the final resolution of impasses. This approach simply resulted in illegal strikes (Wolkinson and Stieber, 1976). Most Canadian jurisdictions, on the other hand, opted for some form of compulsory arbitration when the right to strike was removed by statute. By and large, arbitration accomplished the objective of eliminating work stoppages (Thompson, 1981). Illegal strikes have occasionally taken place in the face of arbitration (a well-publicized example is the Montreal police strike in 1969), but such occurrences have constituted rare exceptions. Canadian public employees, albeit with great reluctance in some cases (Werlin, 1984), have accepted the prohibition on strikes where arbitration is available as a substitute.

Unfortunately, compulsory interest arbitration, while alleviating concern about public sector work stoppages, presents a number of problems of its own. Industrial relations systems in virtually all democratic countries place a high premium on permitting labour and management to negotiate their own collective agreements through the give-and-take of the bargaining process. Almost all available evidence suggests that compulsory arbitration systems reduce the likelihood that the parties will in fact be able to reach an agreement at the bargaining table. As will be discussed in more detail below, settlement rates under public sector strike systems approach 95 percent; under arbitration systems settlement rates decline to approximately 75–80 percent, depending on the arbitration process.

Three major reasons have been advanced to explain why compulsory arbitration reduces the likelihood of negotiated settlements (Kochan, 1979; Ponak, 1982). First, interest arbitration generally produces a lower cost of disagreement than does a strike. Put another way, the fear of going to arbitration is usually less than the fear of a work stoppage. Part of the reason parties settle in negotiations under right-to-strike systems relates to the substantial consequences of not settling. Strikes are usually expensive and painful propositions for the worker, the employer, or both. The same is less likely to be true in an arbitration system where the consequences of actually using an arbitrator may not be particularly onerous. In short, the threat of a strike is a powerful inducement to settle; arbitration systems lack such an inducement.

A second factor that is thought to inhibit negotiated settlements under arbitration systems is the fear that concessions made during bargaining may prove harmful if an arbitrated settlement is eventually required. Whether well-founded or not, a widespread perception exists that arbitrators "split the difference" between the two parties' positions in arriving at their decisions. Accordingly, negotiators are reluctant to make bargaining concessions that might narrow the differences to their side's detriment; thus, there is a tendency to adopt extreme positions and maintain them. The inhibiting impact of arbitration on compromise activity is frequently referred to as the chilling effect.

The third major reason advanced for the reduced incidence of settlement under arbitration systems is that arbitration is habit forming. It is suggested that negotiators become accustomed to rely on arbitration as an easy way out of making difficult decisions and eventually lose the ability to settle in negotiations. This tendency has been referred to as the narcotic effect, with negotiators becoming "addicted" to the arbitration process. As time passes, fewer and fewer settlements are achieved at the bargaining table as the temptation to rely on the "quick fix" of an arbitrated agreement becomes irresistible.

Table 9.7
Dispute Procedures[1] by Jurisdiction, 1986

Jurisdiction	General Municipal	Police	Fire Fighters	Hospitals	Teachers	Civil Service	Government Enterprises
British Columbia	RTS	COP	COP	COP	ARB	RTS	RTS
Alberta	RTS	ARB	ARB	ARB	RTS	ARB	RTS
Saskatchewan	RTS	COP	COP	RTS	COP	RTS	RTS
Manitoba	RTS	RTS	ARB	RTS	ARB	RTS	RTS
Ontario	RTS	ARB	ARB	ARB	RTS	ARB	ARB
Quebec	RTS	ARB	ARB	RTS	RTS	RTS	RTS
New Brunswick	RTS	RTS	ARB	RTS	RTS	RTS	RTS
Nova Scotia	RTS	RTS	RTS	RTS	RTS	ARB	RTS
Prince Edward Island	RTS	ARB	ARB	ARB	ARB	ARB	ARB
Newfoundland	RTS	RTS	RTS[2] or ARB	RTS	RTS	RTS	RTS
Federal	n.a.	n.a.	COP	COP	COP	COP	COP[3] or RTS

[1] RTS—Right to strike; COP—Choice of procedures; ARB—Compulsory arbitration.
[2] Fire fighters in St. John's, the provincial capital, must submit disputes to arbitration.
[3] Choice of procedures under the PSSRA (e.g., National Film Board); right to strike under the Canada Labour Code (e.g., Air Canada).

Source: Table compiled as of September 1986 through a statutory review of each jurisdiction.

Use of Arbitration in the Canadian Public Sector

The degree to which interest arbitration is used across major public sector groups in the eleven Canadian jurisdictions is detailed in Figure 9.7. Arbitration is most likely to be obligatory for fire fighters, police, and civil servants. At the other end of the spectrum, it is not mandated in any jurisdiction for general municipal employees (i.e., inside and outside workers, local transit).

The most commonly used form of interest arbitration in Canada is the traditional or conventional form of arbitration. Under conventional arbitration procedures, the arbitration board is free, after receiving submissions from the union and the employer, to fashion its solution to the issues in dispute. The board is permitted to accept the union or the employer position, it can split the difference down the middle, or it can derive its own compromise position on the issues. Subject to very broad constraints of reasonableness, the arbitration board can issue the award it feels is most appropriate under the circumstances and that award becomes the new collective agreement.

Although rarely used in Canada, many jurisdictions in the United States use a form of arbitration called final offer selection (FOS). Final offer selection differs from conventional arbitration in that the arbitrator is required to choose the position submitted by management or by the union, without alteration. In other words, the arbitration board is not free to fashion its own solution by adopting a middle position; it is forced to choose one side's proposal or the other's. Depending on the jurisdiction, a total package format or more flexible issue-by-issue format is used. In Canada, FOS is occasionally used by mutual agreement of the parties. At the University of Alberta, for example, the faculty association and university have agreed to use FOS, by issue, to settle their bargaining impasses. This procedure was worked out between the parties and was not mandated by the Universities Act.

A third type of arbitration system, choice of procedures (COP) was pioneered in the 1967 Public Service Staff Relations Act, which granted collective bargaining rights to federal civil servants. It continues to be used in the federal sector as well as British Columbia, Saskatchewan, and some American states (Ponak and Wheeler, 1980). Under a choice-of-procedures system, one of the parties (in Canada, the union) can specify at some point prior to or during negotiations whether an impasse will be resolved through a work stoppage or arbitration. The choice made by the choosing party is binding on the other side. For example, in the Canadian federal system, the union must specify prior to negotiations whether arbitration or a strike will be used in the event of an impasse; the employer must abide by the union's decision. Experience has shown that arbitration is chosen much more frequently than the strike. A study of more than 1,000 arbitration/strike choices in four jurisdictions indicated that arbitration was preferred by a three-to-one margin (Ponak and Wheeler, 1980). Thus, in many situations, a choice-of-procedures system differs little from a standard arbitration system.

Settlement Rate

There is little disagreement that arbitration systems reduce the incidence of negotiated settlements compared to strike-based systems. The most meaningful comparisons in this regard are among public sector jurisdictions. These data are presented in Figures 9.8 and 9.9.

The major variable of interest in these two tables is settlement rate, defined as the proportion of negotiations that are settled by the parties without resort to the final mechanism of dispute resolution. Under arbitration systems, this would be the proportion of negotiations in which no arbitration award was issued; under right-to-strike systems, settlement rate means the percentage of negotiations where settlement was achieved without a work stoppage.

It should be noted that settlement rate, as herein defined, is not affected by various intermediate steps, such as mediation or fact finding, in which the parties may have engaged. A negotiation would be denoted the same way whether the parties achieved settlement with the help of a conciliation officer, after fact finding with recommendations, or in direct negotiation without any third-party assistance whatsoever. As long as the parties did not resort to the final impasse step (be it arbitration or a work stoppage), the negotiations would be recorded as "settled."

The advantage of defining settlement rate in this manner is that it permits meaningful comparisons to be made across systems on the key variable of interest—namely, were the parties able to settle the matter themselves without a work stoppage or the imposition of an outside binding decision? Ignoring the use of intermediate steps in the calculation recognizes that: (1) different systems provide different intermediate steps, especially in the public sector; and (2) the whole purpose of intermediate steps is to encourage settlement and to avoid the ultimate dispute mechanism, whether a work stoppage or arbitration. Focusing on settlement rate thus provides one crucial measure of the success of the system.

Data for various public sector right-to-strike systems are provided in Figure 9.8. Settlement rates range from a low of 88 percent for federal public employees (those bargaining units that chose the strike route under the cop system) to 98 percent for Montana government workers. Unfortunately, many of the studies listed in Figure 9.8 cover only one- or two-year periods, reducing their reliability. The broadest data set is for the province of Ontario and covers over 600 negotiations during a four-year

Figure 9.8
Settlement Rates[1] under Public Sector Right-to-Strike Systems

Study	Settlement Rate	Total Number of Negotiations	Period	Type of Employee	Jurisdiction
Dunham (1976)	91%	800	1970	Public Sector	Pennsylvania
	99%	519	1973	Public Sector	Oregon
	98%	60	1973	Public Sector	Montana
Swimmer & MacDonald (1985)	93%	611	1979–1982	Teacher, Hydro, Municipal	Ontario
Ponak & Wheeler (1980)	88%	137	1967–1979	Federal Civil Service	Canada
Anderson (1977)	93%	58	1976–1977	Inside and outside workers	Municipal, Canada

[1]Settlement rate defined as proportion of negotiations where settlement was reached without a work stoppage.

period for teachers, hydro-electric utility workers, and municipal employees (including mass transit). The Ontario data show a settlement rate of 93 percent, a figure that appears to be a reasonable median rate for public sector strike-based systems.

Settlement rates for arbitration systems are significantly lower (Figure 9.9). Under conventional arbitration, the ability of labour and management to settle without the help of an arbitrator ranges between 65 and 82 percent. The average settlement rate would appear to be approximately 75 percent. The settlement rate goes up to the 85-percent range under final-offer selection, but still falls short of settlement rates achieved under strike-based systems.

The data, therefore, unequivocally support the proposition that arbitration systems reduce the likelihood of negotiated settlements compared to strike-based dispute procedures. The gap between the two systems is approximately 18 percent under conventional arbitration and eight percent under final-offer selection procedures.

The data cannot answer the policy question, however, of whether the settlement rate difference between strike and arbitration systems is acceptable or not. Arbitration is imposed in situations where it is believed the consequences of a strike are too high—fire fighters and police are obvious situations where such sentiments prevail. It may be that the lower settlement rates which result from the imposition of arbitration are an acceptable tradeoff, from a public-interest perspective, for the prevention of work stoppages. After all, even under the least productive arbitration systems, negotiators still manage to settle without arbitration two-thirds of the time. The fact that one out of three negotiations requires an arbitrator's intervention may well be a price that has to be paid for the overall public good. Such tradeoffs might be less palatable, however, in situations where settlement rates are much lower or where the groups involved are arguably less essential.

The Chilling and Narcotic Effects

The theoretical underpinnings of the perceived inadequacies of interest arbitration rest on two related concepts, the chilling and narcotic effects. Accordingly, they have been the subject of numerous studies (see Appendix 9A). Figure 9.10 reports the various definitions and measures that have been employed in research on the chilling and narcotic effects. It can be seen that most researchers are in agreement as to the theoretical definitions of these concepts. Chilling is assumed to occur when one or both parties are unwilling to compromise during negotiations in anticipation of an arbitrated settlement; the narcotic effect is an increasing dependence of the parties on arbitration, resulting in a loss of ability to negotiate.

Although studies generally concur on the delineation of these effects, there has been little consistency in their measurement. A major problem has been the use of the same variables to evaluate both concepts. This duplication of measurement procedures can be partially attributed to a lack of recognition of the interrelated nature of the chilling and narcotic effects. According to the conceptual description of each effect, chilling should eventually produce a dependence on arbitration. That is, if the parties continually fail to compromise they lose their ability to negotiate and become dependent on arbitration. Only two researchers have noted that chilling can be properly viewed as a sub-component of the narcotic effect (Feuille, 1975a; Olson, 1978). This confusion in measurement has led to inconclusive findings with respect to the actual impact of the chilling and narcotic effects on the negotiation process (see Appendix 9A).

Chilling Effect

There are three measures that have been previously used, and are closely aligned with the generally accepted definition of chilling. The first is the number of issues settled during negotiations versus the number of issues left for arbitration (Feuille, 1975a; Olson, 1978; Stern et al., 1975; Weiler, 1981). This measure is based on the rationale that an inability of the two parties to resolve almost any issues at the negotiation table indicates an unwillingness to compromise in anticipation of an arbitrated settlement.

With respect to this variable, research indicates that chilling is more likely to occur with conventional than with final-offer arbitration. One study investigating the behaviour of parties under conventional arbitration found a large number of issues (between six and 30) going to arbitration (Weiler, 1981). In contrast, three investigations of final-offer arbitration found an average of only one or two issues still unresolved at the arbitration stage (Feuille, 1975a; Olson, 1978; Stern et al., 1975). These results are consistent with the predicted benefits of FOS. Each party wants to appear to have taken a reasonable position in the hope that the arbitrator will then choose their offer. Therefore, more compromising occurs during negotiations.

A second measure of chilling involves the comparison of management's initial and impasse offers with the union's initial and impasse proposals to determine the degree of discrepancy and movement between the two parties (Wheeler, 1978). Chilling is said to occur when the two parties take extreme positions, and are not willing to compromise. Relatively little movement between the opening and impasse positions, or a major discrepancy between management's offer and the union's demand at the point of impasse, indicate a chilling effect. Wheeler (1978) analyzed the degree of discrepancy and movement in

Figure 9.9
Settlement Rates[1] with Conventional and Final-offer Arbitration

Study	Settlement Rate	Total Number of Negotiations	Period	Type of Employee	Jurisdiction
			Conventional Arbitration		
Hines	81%	565	1966–1970	Hospital	Ontario
Stern et al. (1975)	79%	359	1969–1974	Firefighters Police	Pennsylvania
Lipsky & Barocci (1977)	78%	152	1974–1976	Firefighters Police	New York
Thompson (1981)	65%	1660	1960–1980	Teachers	B.C.
Mitchell (1982)	82%	1035	1969–1982	Federal Civil Service	Canada
Blouin (1982)	73%	1054	1973–1981	Firefighters Police	Quebec
Swimmer & McDonald (1985)	70%	979	1979–1982	Firefighters, Police, Hospital, Public Service	Ontario

Study	Settlement rate		Period	Employee group	State
Final Offer by Package					
Lipsky & Barocci (1977)	86%	266	1975–1977	Firefighters Police	Massachusetts
Olson (1978)	88%	971	1972–1977	Firefighters Police	Wisconsin
Ashenfelter (1985)[2]	62%	n.a.	1978–1980	Police	New Jersey
Final Offer by Issue					
Stern et al. (1975)	84%	650	1970–1973	Firefighters Police	Michigan
Gallagher & Pegnetter (1979)	96%	707	1975–1977	Public Service	Iowa

[1] Settlement rate defined as proportion of negotiations where settlement was reached without resort to arbitration.

[2] Both FOS or conventional arbitration are used. Three-quarters of the arbitration are of the FOS variety.

Figure 9.10
Narcotic and Chilling Effects: Definitions and Measures

Study	Definition[1]	Measures
	Narcotic Effect	
Anderson (1981)	• Once the parties use a procedure they are likely to become reliant on it in future rounds	• Trend in use of procedure over time • Number of times units went to arbitration after the first award
Thompson (1981)	• Reliance on arbitrators to write agreement	• Comparison of number of negotiated settlements with arbitration awards
Weiler (1981)	• Dependence on arbitration rather than settling	• Number of weeks spent in negotiations before requesting arbitration (compared voluntary with compulsory arbitration)
Mitchell (1982)	• Anderson's (1981) definition	• Percentage of agreements settled through arbitration
Gallagher & Pegnetter (1979)	• Extent to which parties depend on arbitration repeatedly	• Number of arbitrated settlements in second round of negotiations
Olson (1978)	• Failure to reach an agreement in successive negotiations	• Number of arbitration awards for each bargaining unit
Finkelman & Goldenberg (1983)	• Habit forming	• Number of arbitration awards for each bargaining unit
Anderson & Kochan (1977)	• Repeated use of procedure	• Individual bargaining units' repeated use of arbitration
Wheeler (1975)	• Parties failing to reach agreement in large proportion of cases, therefore	• Number of arbitrated settlements

relying on compulsory arbitration with great frequency

Chilling Effect

Olson (1978)	• Parties less willing to make compromises at the pre-arbitration stage in case of prejudicing their respective positions • Chilling could lead to narcotic effect	• Number of issues going to arbitration • Percentage of disputes settled through arbitration
Lipsky & Barocci (1977)	• Withholding of concessions during negotiations and presenting extreme positions to arbitrator	• Percentage of negotiations going to impasse • Percentage of negotiations going to arbitration award
Stern et al. (1975)	• Parties taking extreme positions rather than compromise	• Percentage of cases with arbitration awards • Number of issues in dispute in each case • Degree of difference between proposals
Anderson & Kochan (1977)	• Same as Anderson (1977)	• Proportion of units going to arbitration • Stage of impasse at which parties settled
Feuille (1975a)	• Clinging to excessive or unrealistic outcomes in the hope of tilting the arbitration outcome in its favour • Chilling leads to narcotic effect	• Frequency of use of arbitration procedures • Proportion of arbitration awards • Number of issues going to arbitration

Figure 9.10 cont'd
Narcotic and Chilling Effects: Definitions and Measures

Anderson (1981)	• Holding back concessions during bargaining in an anticipation of arbitration	• How many times settlements occurred without going to impasse • Number of times a bargaining unit went to arbitration
Thompson (1981)	• Lack of concessions in bargaining	• Comparison of number of negotiated settlements with arbitration awards
Weiler (1981)	• Parties come to arbitration miles apart on their proposals and dump large number of issues on arbitrator's table	• Number of issues going to arbitration
Mitchell (1982)	• Reduction of good-faith bargaining prior to terminal step in impasse	• Comparison of number of negotiated settlements with arbitration awards • Number of times a bargaining unit went to arbitration
Gallagher & Pegnetter (1979)	• Withholding compromises in anticipation of a neutral's recommendation or award favouring one party	• Extent of compromise at negotiating table • Number of times parties went to impasse • Stage at impasse at which parties settled • Reduction in the number of unresolved issues at each step

[1]As much as possible, the definitions follow the author's own wording.

negotiations with fire fighters under both compulsory arbitration and fact finding, assuming that a chilling effect was more likely to occur with arbitration. His results showed that management moved less under arbitration than under fact finding, while the union displayed the same degree of movement in both situations. When the gap between the impasse positions was analyzed, there was a greater discrepancy between the parties under arbitration than fact finding. Although Wheeler suggested a need for caution in interpreting these results (because of the variables not controlled for), he concluded that his findings indicated the presence of a chilling effect.

Chilling has also been evaluated by the stage at which the parties finally settled. While this approach was not specifically identified in the literature, a number of studies have analyzed the stage of settlement (Anderson and Kochan, 1977; Finkelman and Goldenberg, 1983; Gallagher and Pegnetter, 1979; Lipsky and Barocci, 1977; Mitchell, 1982). Generally, these studies assume that any third-party intervention indicates an increasing dependence on outside help and an inability to negotiate (or a narcotic effect). Another rationale for this measure, however, is that if the negotiating parties are not making compromises because of impending arbitration, third-party intervention should have little impact. In terms of this rationale, FOS appears less likely to induce a chilling effect than conventional arbitration. Gallagher and Pegnetter (1979) and Lipsky and Barocci (1977) found parties under FOS were most likely to settle in the intermediate stages of third-party intervention rather than at the last stage of arbitration. Under conventional arbitration, Finkelman and Goldenberg (1983) and Mitchell (1982) noted that when parties in the Canadian federal public service required any third-party intervention, they tended to go all the way to arbitration.

Narcotic Effect

The most common method of assessing the narcotic effect is the proportion of units going to arbitration over time. It is assumed that if arbitration is addictive, more and more units will resort to it with each round of negotiations. Unfortunately, researchers using this measure have relied on the eyeballing of trends and an arbitrary blocking of years, often reaching conflicting conclusions. The debate between Thompson and Cairnie (1975) and Feuille (1975) is an excellent illustration. Assessing teachers in British Columbia between the years of 1960 and 1973, Thompson and Cairnie (1973) concluded that compulsory arbitration did not produce a pattern of increasing reliance on arbitration. Looking at the same data, Feuille (1975b) suggested that a trend of increased reliance was apparent if the data were organized into five-year averages. In reply, Thompson and Cairnie (1975) asserted that five-year averages hid (1) large fluctuations in the number of arbitrated settlements across years, and (2) cycles of arbitrated settlements interspersed with negotiated settlements. Differing conclusions have also been drawn from the same Canadian public service data. Anderson (1981) and Anderson and Kochan (1977) used different standards regarding dependence than did Finkelman and Goldenberg (1983) and Mitchell (1982). The former interpreted their data to show a narcotic effect, whereas the latter did not.

A more appropriate measure of the narcotic effect is the number of times an individual unit returns to arbitration over a series of negotiations. Three different investigations have used this variable (Finkelman and Goldenberg, 1983; Gallagher and Pegnetter, 1979; Olson, 1978). All three indicate that only a minority of parties becomes dependent on the process over time. These studies strongly suggest that there is little evidence to support a narcotic effect under either conventional or final-offer arbitration.

Gallagher and Pegnetter (1979) found that in the second year of FOS legislation in Iowa, none of the nine parties who used arbitration in the first round required it in the second. Olson (1978) found that only five out of 97 units in Wisconsin went to arbitration three times in a row. In the Canadian public service, Finkelman and Goldenberg (1983) found that only 12 units used arbitration repeatedly, while 95 did not use it on a continual basis.

In summary, the empirical research suggests that: (1) a chilling effect may occur with conventional arbitration but is less likely with final offer selection; and (2) while some parties may become dependent on arbitration (narcotic effect), the majority does not repeatedly use the process. These conclusions notwithstanding, there remains considerable confusion among studies in terms of inferences drawn with much of the confusion relating to a lack of clarity over appropriate measures. In addition, further work needs to be done in several areas.

First, more attention should be directed to the satisfaction of parties with contracts that have been negotiated versus those that have been attained through arbitration. Two measures of satisfaction with arbitration contracts have been previously suggested. Thompson (1981) concluded arbitrated settlements were probably not unsatisfactory to B.C. teachers because there had been no major strikes owing to union refusal to accept an arbitration award. He also suggested satisfaction could be measured by the number of times courts were asked to review arbitration awards. Another indication of satisfaction that has not been previously used is the number of grievances during the life of the contract. If contracts reached through negotiations are more satisfactory, there should be fewer grievances (especially those involving language interpretation) than with arbitrated settlements.

A second direction for future research is to compare parties who seem to rely repeatedly on arbitration and those who repeatedly engage in work stoppages. It is possible that in some relationships the parties are simply incapable of resolving their differences. These parties would go to the final stage of the conflict resolution process regardless of whether the system culminates in arbitration or a work stoppage. Anderson and Kochan (1977) concluded that across the first four rounds of bargaining in the Canadian public sector there was an increasing trend to use arbitration. Their data also indicated, however, that during the same period there was an increase in the number of units involved in work stoppages. Thus, the narcotic effect may not be restricted solely to arbitration procedures.

Finally, in terms of both the chilling and narcotic effects, little attention has been given to the type of issues that labour and management are leaving to arbitration. It has been suggested that arbitration is often used as an escape mechanism to resolve politically difficult issues (Finkelman and Goldenberg, 1983; Thompson, 1981). Although it is generally assumed that such behaviour occurs, there is relatively little research to support it. One method of analyzing whether arbitration is used as an escape mechanism would be to examine the nature of the issues that repeatedly find their way into arbitration.

CONCLUSIONS

This chapter has examined Canadian interest-dispute resolution policy under two types of conditions: (1) where a right to strike prevails; and (2) where work stoppages have been replaced by interest arbitration. The context for the analysis was provided by the Canadian record with respect to work stoppages—one of the worst among industrialized, democratic nations.

Given this context, it is not surprising that the prevention or elimination of work stoppages has been a preoccupation of Canadian labour policy since the beginning of the twentieth century. The surprise, however, lies in the equivocality of conclusions regarding the effectiveness of such policies. Clearly, Canada's high strike record cannot be blamed on the use of one conciliation process over another or the imposition or lack of imposition of compulsory arbitration. Nevertheless, given the long history of concern, there remains a considerable lack of consensus among both policy makers and researchers as to which procedures might produce the best results. This is true despite relative certainty with respect to the desired ends—namely, the fostering of negotiated settlements without the need for either a work stoppage or an arbitrated settlement.

Some explanation for this lack of consensus may lie in the nature of the available research, which suffers from a combination of methodological, definitional, and measurement problems. Moreover, with respect to empirical work on conciliation procedures, it is surprisingly porous. Taken as a whole, the body of research does not make a persuasive argument in favour of any discernible policy approach. Future research efforts, therefore, should focus on policy effectiveness and should attempt to provide clear alternatives with respect to policy initiatives. Some suggested avenues for such research have been raised in this chapter, but it is clear, especially with respect to conciliation, that much work remains to be done.

BIBLIOGRAPHY

Anderson, J. C. (1977), Union effectiveness: An industrial relations systems approach. Doctoral dissertation, Cornell University, Ithaca, New York.

――― (1981), "Arbitration in the federal public service." In J. M. P. Weiler (ed.), *Interest Arbitration*. Toronto: The Carswell Company Limited, pp. 43–78.

――― and Kochan, T. A. (1977), "Impasse procedures in the Canadian federal service: Effects on the bargaining process." *Industrial and Labor Relations Review* 30: 283–301.

Ashenfelter, O. (1985), "Evidence on U.S. experiences with dispute-resolution systems." In D. W. Conklin, T. J. Courchene, and W. A. Jones (eds.), *Public Sector Compensation*. Toronto: Ontario Economic Council, pp. 13–35.

Blouin, R. (1982), "Arbitration of bargaining disputes in Quebec." *Proceedings of the 19th Annual Meeting of the Canadian Industrial Relations Association*. Ottawa: University of Ottawa, pp. 209–238.

Chelius, J. R. and Extejt, M. M. (1983), "The impact of arbitration on the process of collective bargaining." *Journal of Collective Negotiations* 12: 327–336.

Craig, A. W. J. (1985), *The System of Industrial Relations in Canada*. Scarborough, Ontario: Prentice-Hall, Inc.

Cunningham, W. B. (1953), *Compulsory Conciliation and Collective Bargaining: The New Brunswick Experience*. Montreal: McGill University, Industrial Relations Centre.

Dunham, R. (1976), "Interest arbitration in non-federal public employment." *The Arbitration Journal* 31: 45–57.

Feuille, P. (1975a), "Final-offer arbitration and the chilling effect." *Industrial Relations* 14: 302–310.

――― (1975b), "Analyzing compulsory arbitration experiences: The role of personal preferences." *Industrial and Labor Relations Review* 28: 432–435.

Finkelman, J. and Goldenberg, S. B. (1983), *Collective Bargaining in the*

Public Service: The Federal Experience in Canada. Montreal: McGill University, The Institute for Research on Public Policy.

Gallagher, D. G. and Pegnetter, R. (1979), "Impasse resolution under the Iowa multistep procedure." *Industrial and Labor Relations Review* 32: 327–338.

Goldenberg, S. (1979), "Public sector labor relations in Canada." In B. Aaron, J. Grodin, and J. Stern (eds.), *Public Sector Bargaining.* Madison: University of Wisconsin, Industrial Relations Research Association, pp. 259–291.

Gunderson, M., Kervin, J., and Reid, F. (1985), *The Effect of Labour Relations Legislation on Strike Incidence.* Toronto: University of Toronto, Centre for Industrial Relations.

———, Kervin, J., and Reid, F. (1986), "Logit estimates of strike incidence from Canadian contract data." *Journal of Labor Economics* 4: 257–276.

Hines, R. J. (1972)., "Mandatory contract arbitration: Is it a viable process?" *Industrial and Labor Relations Review* 25: 533–544.

Kochan, T. (1979), "Dynamics of dispute resolution in the public sector." In B. Aaron, J. Grodin, and J. Stern (eds.), *Public Sector Bargaining.* Madison: University of Wisconsin, Industrial Relations Research Association, pp.150–190.

Lacroix, R. (1986), "Strike activity in Canada." In W. C. Riddell (ed.), *Canadian Labour Relations.* Toronto: University of Toronto Press, pp. 161–209. Published in co-operation with the Royal Commission on the Economic Union and Development Prospects for Canada and the Canadian Government Publishing Centre, Supply and Services Canada (Study Pt 16).

Lipsky, D. B. and Barocci, T. A. (1977), "Final-offer arbitration and public-safety employees: The Massachusetts experience." In B. D. Dennis (ed.), *Proceedings of the Thirtieth Annual Winter Meeting of the Industrial Relations Research Association Series.* Madison: University of Wisconsin, Industrial Relations Research Association, pp. 65–76.

Misick, J. D. (1978), "Compulsory arbitration in Canada: Do we need it?" *Relations industrielles* 33: 193–202.

Mitchell, L. (1982), "Interest arbitration in the federal public service." *Proceedings of the 19th Annual Meeting of the Canadian Industrial Relations Association.* Ottawa: University of Ottawa, pp. 239–258.

Olson, C. A. (1978), "Final-offer arbitration in Wisconsin after five years." In B. D. Dennis (ed.), *Proceedings of the Thirty-first Annual Meeting of the Industrial Relations Research Association.* Madison: University of Wisconsin, Industrial Relations Research Association, pp. 111–119.

Ponak, A. (1982), "Public-sector collective bargaining." In J. Anderson and M. Gunderson (eds.), *Union–Management Relations in Canada.* Toronto: Addison-Wesley (Canada) Limited, pp. 343–378.

———— and Wheeler, H. N. (1980), "Choice of procedures in Canada and the United States." *Industrial Relations* 19: 292–308.

Stern, J. L., Rehmus, C. M., Loewenberg, J. J., Kasper, H. and Dennis, B. D. (1975), *Final-offer Arbitration: The Effects on Public Safety Employee Bargaining*. Toronto: D. C. Heath and Company.

Subbarao, A. V. (1977), "The impact of two-dispute resolution processes in negotiations." *Relations industrielles* 32: 216–232.

Swimmer, G. and MacDonald, A. (1985), "Dispute resolution in the Ontario public sector: What's so wrong about the right to strike?" In D. W. Conklin, T. J. Courchene, and W. A. Jones (eds.), *Public Sector Compensation*. Toronto: Ontario Economic Council, pp. 154–178.

Thompson, M. (1981), "Evaluation of interest arbitration: The case of British Columbia teachers." In J. M. P. Weiler (ed.), *Interest Arbitration*. Toronto: The Carswell Company Limited, pp. 79–97.

———— and Cairnie, J. F. (1973), "Compulsory arbitration: The case of British Columbia teachers." *Industrial and Labor Relations Review* 27: 3–17.

———— and Cairnie, J. F. (1975), "Reply." *Industrial and Labour Relations Review* 28: 435–438.

Weiler, J. M. (1981), "Interest arbitration in British Columbia: The Essential Services Disputes Act." In J. M. P. Weiler (ed.), *Interest Arbitration*. Toronto: The Carswell Company Limited.

Werlin, D. (1984), "Labour's view of arbitration." In C. L. Rigg and A. Ponak (eds.), *Proceedings of the First Labour Arbitration Conference*. Calgary: University of Calgary, pp. 9–17.

Wheeler, H. N. (1975), "Compulsory arbitration: A 'narcotic effect'?" *Industrial Relations* 14: 117–120.

———— (1978), "How compulsory arbitration affects compromise activity." *Industrial Relations* 17: 80–84.

Wolkinson, B. and Stieber, J. (1976), "Michigan fact-finding experience in public sector disputes." *The Arbitration Journal* 31: 228–247.

Woods, H. D. (1973), *Labour Policy in Canada* (2nd ed.). Toronto: Macmillan of Canada.

Appendix 9A

Selected Major Empirical Arbitration Studies

Appendix 9A.1
Selected Major Empirical Arbitration Studies

Study		Type of Arbitration System	Impact of Arbitration		Type of Employee	Jurisdiction
			Chilling	Narcotic		
Hines	(1972)	Conventional	—	—	Hospital	Ontario
Wheeler	(1975)	Mixture[1]	—	Yes	Fire Fighters	21 States
	(1978)	Mixture	Yes	—	Fire Fighters	21 States
Stern et al.	(1975)	Conventional	Yes	Yes	Public Safety	Wisconsin Michigan Pennsylvania
Lipsky & Barocci	(1977)	Conventional Final Offer	No	—	Fire Fighters Police	Massachusetts New York
Anderson & Kochan	(1977)	Conventional	Yes	Yes	Federal Civil	Canada
Olson	(1978)	Final Offer	No	No	Public Safety	Wisconsin
Gallagher & Pegnetter	(1979)	Final Offer	No	No	Public Service Teachers	Iowa
Subbarao	(1977)	Conventional	—	—	Federal Civil Service	Canada

Study	Year	Type			Sector	Location
Ponak & Wheeler	(1980)	Conventional Final Offer	—	—	Public Service Public Safety	Canada British Columbia Wisconsin Minnesota
Anderson	(1981)	Conventional	Yes	Yes	Federal Civil Service	Canada
Thompson	(1981)	Conventional	No	No	Teachers	B.C.
Weiler	(1981)	Conventional	No	—	Essential Services	B.C.
Blouin	(1982)	Conventional	—	—	Public Safety	Quebec
Mitchell	(1982)	Conventional	No	No	Federal Civil Service	Canada
Finkelman & Goldenberg	(1983)	Conventional	—	No	Federal Civil Service	Canada
Chelius & Extejt	(1983)	Final Offer	—	Yes	Teachers	Indiana Iowa
Swimmer & MacDonald	(1985)	Conventional	—	—	Hospital Public Safety	Ontario

[1]This study combined conventional arbitration and both types of final offer selection in its analysis.

PART 3

ADMINISTRATION OF THE CONTRACT

10

Cost-benefit Analysis of Collective Bargaining Outcomes: An Emerging Approach

Félix Quinet

INTRODUCTION

This chapter explores the changing manner in which the institutions of collective bargaining and of labour relations are viewed, as reflected in selected writings. A definition of cost-benefit analysis is proposed, followed by a brief explanation of the significance of cost-benefit analysis in collective bargaining. Then, a review is made of several recent Canadian governments' responses (at both federal and provincial levels) to the problem of inflation, and of their potential significance for collective bargaining in a cost-benefit analysis perspective. The areas of potential applicability of the cost-benefit approach to collective bargaining outcomes, and its importance, are reviewed in various dimensions: informational, managerial, timing, public policy, academic, research. The chapter concludes that the institution of collective bargaining and its outcomes are worthy of further cost-benefit research.

CHANGING NATURE OF COLLECTIVE BARGAINING AS REFLECTED IN RECENT WRITINGS

Some of the recent literature in the field of labour relations seems to reflect a changing assessment, at least in some quarters, of labour relations, collective bargaining and, consequently, some of the roles of the labour movement. This literature blends measured praise with equally measured criticism, neither blindly advocating nor dogmatically rejecting collective bargaining or the labour movement. The diverse works cited in this chapter and other studies[1] have a common dimension in that they encourage a sympathetic, but lucid, assessment of the labour relations system and the labour movement, an assessment that keeps its distance from the dogmatic, if not doctrinaire pro-or-con positions of the past.[2]

Lépine and Cormier (1984,173) provide a noteworthy and interesting account of union and collective bargaining experiences in the Québec educational sector. The authors do not succumb to easy cynicism or defeatism, yet they criticize what they view as an excessively adversarial approach which, they observe, drives too many unionists into the belief that the only proper behaviour vis-à-vis "the boss" is a perpetual bad mood. The authors call for rejuvenated union and labour relations approaches which would be based on greater membership involvement and fewer bureaucratic procedures, and which would stress satisfying the important needs of employees rather than spending much often-futile time negotiating overly complex collective agreement clauses. Their study strongly advocates a more effective role for labour unions, not only in the workplace, but in society.

In France, the labour relations system allows at least as much room for ideological battles between employers and employees (and employers' associations against unions) as for collective bargaining. Bodman and Richard (1971), who expound the thinking of Jacques Delors, one of the strongest advocates of collective bargaining in France, recommend a larger role for collective bargaining (*politique contractuelle*) within the French labour relations system. The authors do recognize areas where ideological divisions between management and labour will likely remain; they also identify areas of common interest (*convergences*) between labour and management:

> ...*Areas of possible joint interest (convergences).* It is the area concerning fundamental problems of life in society where the ideological weight (*pondération idéologique*) is relatively light. *It is therefore possible to organize within that area a certain co-operation, a common action between employers and wage earners to the extent that these problems, concerning daily life, cannot be neglected by the unions, as movements defending the moral and material interests of workers.* This permits the avoidance of confusion between union demands, the amalgamation of situations, and steers the unions away from their argument for refusing any proposal: integration into the system....The joint interests (*convergences*) between the two or three parties (the State, employers and unions) concern the problem of employment, of health (*hygiène*) and safety, of work organization, of vocational training....(p. 104; emphasis added.)

Last but not least, Freeman and Medoff (1984) have provided one of the most solidly documented and well-articulated re-appraisals of the role of unions and collective bargaining in a market economy:

> ...According to our analysis, in most settings the positive elements of the voice/response face of unions offset or dominate the negative elements of the monopoly face. As a result we come out with the following assessment— generally positive though not uniformly so—of what unions do to the three major outcomes about which debate has raged: efficiency, distribution of income, and social organization.

- Efficiency. Our analysis has shown that unionism does three things to efficiency: on the monopoly side, it reduces employment in the organized sector; on the voice/response side, it permits labor to create, at no extra cost to management, workplace practices and compensation packages more valuable to workers; and in many settings it is associated with increased productivity. Although it is difficult to sum up these three effects, our evidence suggests that unionism on net probably raises social efficiency, and if it lowers it, it does so by minuscule amounts except in rare circumstances. This conclusion contradicts the traditional monopoly interpretation of what unions do to efficiency.
- Distribution of Income. On the question of distribution, we have found a definite dominance for the voice/response face of unions, with unions reducing wage inequality and lowering profits, which generally go to higher-income persons. For readers to whom greater economic equality is a plus, what unions do here is definitely good. For readers to whom greater equalization of incomes is undesirable, what unions do is definitely bad.
- Social Organization. Our analysis of the internal affairs of unions has dispelled some of the negative myths about undemocratic practices and discriminatory and corrupt behavior. It has shown that unions, for the most part, provide political voice to all labor and that they are more effective in pushing general social legislation than in bringing about special interest legislation in the Congress.

...While our research suggests that unionism generally serves as a force for social and economic good, it has also found that unions benefit labor at the expense of capital. Unions reduce the profitability of organized firms, particularly those in concentrated sectors where profits are abnormally high. In addition, while some nonunion workers lose from unionism, our investigations indicate that many nonunion workers, especially those in large firms, benefit from the threat of organizing and from the information about workers' desires that comes from unionism. (p.246.)

A SUGGESTED DEFINITION OF THE
COST-BENEFIT ANALYSIS PROCESS, AS APPLIED TO
COLLECTIVE BARGAINING OUTCOMES

For the purpose of this chapter, the cost-benefit analysis of collective bargaining outcomes is defined as the determination of costs, and of cost savings to management, through the introduction, modification or withdrawal of collective agreement provisions, such contractual changes having not infringed upon the welfare and well-being of employees.

Two important observations must be made regarding this definition. It should be noted that the "welfare" dimension has been enshrined in it. This reflects the author's view that the cost-benefit assessment of bargaining outcomes should contain an ethical component: firstly, in consideration of the prime purpose for which collective bargaining was instituted, i.e., ensuring a proper balance between the bargaining power of employers and unions in order to achieve the best possible working conditions for employees; secondly, for the broader reason that the institution of collective bargaining, which owes its existence to a civilization that values the freedom of the individual,[3] cannot escape that civilization's value judgments. The prime purpose of collective bargaining is not greater economic efficiency; rather, it seeks the greatest possible measure of welfare for individual employees. The objective of this chapter is simply to suggest, on the basis of existing and continuing research, that collective bargaining can in specific contexts ensure greater welfare by encouraging more effective use of human and financial resources.

Another important observation concerning the definition has to do with the limitations of cost-benefit analysis stated earlier. Firstly, the definition has what might be termed a bias toward private sector bargaining; it might be seen to shortchange the public interest in the context of public sector bargaining. By way of example, consider the following: could there not be danger, in certain situations, that the quality of services rendered to the public might suffer, by the parties' agreeing to cut costs while simultaneously trying to protect the welfare and well-being of employees? This question must be addressed. It suggests that implementation of cost-benefit analysis in certain areas of the public sector deserves more scrutiny. On the other hand, cost-benefit analysis, as defined, may also acquire an added dimension in certain contexts of the public sector: by ensuring the protection of the welfare and well-being of public employees, it can ensure the continuation, and even improvement, of the quality of services rendered to the public.

The terms "welfare" and "well-being of employees" require clarification. Again, by way of example, questions must be raised: does the notion of preserving the welfare and well-being of employees necessarily mean that existing levels of income must be maintained? Could it be interpreted to mean that wage increases might be granted to match the increase in the cost of living, while savings realized by the employers due to other contractual changes may do little more than cover the increased wage costs to the employer?

FOCUS AND SIGNIFICANCE OF COST-BENEFIT ANALYSIS

This chapter limits its discussion of cost-benefit analysis to collective bargaining outcomes per se; it does not consider collective bargaining tactics, procedures or strategies as important as these are. For a stimulating exploration of the cost-benefit approach (for example, the costs and benefits to employers of taking, or not taking, a strike), see Lau and Nelson (1981). In concentrating my discussion on collective bargaining outcomes, I feel that I am treating an aspect of collective bargaining that has received relatively little attention.[4] I do not wish to make the cost-benefit analysis of the outcomes of bargaining into a panacea for reforming our labour relations system.[5] Rather, I view the cost-benefit approach as only one of several approaches to the study of collective bargaining. There are a variety of approaches, including the systems approach, the legal approach, the behavioural approach, and the (more purely) economic approach; each of them has demonstrated merit.[6] I do feel, however, that given current economic circumstances, Canada as a trading nation should give greater prominence to the cost-benefit approach to bargaining outcomes.

RECENT CANADIAN GOVERNMENTS' RESPONSES TO THE PROBLEM OF INFLATION AND THEIR POTENTIAL SIGNIFICANCE FOR COLLECTIVE BARGAINING IN A COST-BENEFIT ANALYSIS PERSPECTIVE

This chapter will not attempt to review the circumstances, economic and others,[7] that led to the enforcement of the three wage control (and in two of the three instances, price control) programs that will be cited below, nor will it discuss the merits of the three legislations. The 1975 (Federal) *Anti-Inflation Act* and the 1983 Ontario *An Act to provide for the Review of Prices and Compensation in the Public Sector and for an orderly transition to the Resumption of full Collective Bargaining* had as their major declared purposes the control (or containment) of wages and prices; the 1982 British Columbia compensation stabilization program was (and continues to be), as its title suggests, aimed at the control of compensation. While the 1975 federal act covered both public and private sectors, the Ontario and British Columbia legislations applied to the public sector only.

There are striking resemblances between the three legislations. This discussion will focus on two such similarities. The first lies in the definitions of "compensation" that were used under the three programs, and the fact that the concept of total compensation was retained in the three legislations as the basis for the calculation of permissible increases. The second deals with the benefits and conditions of employment whose costs were specifically excluded from the calculation of the permissible compensation increases under all three legislations.

The federal act (Section 2 (1); Canada, 1975, 2) contains the following definition of compensation: "...all forms of pay, benefits and perquisites paid or provided, directly or indirectly, by or on behalf of an employer to or for the benefit of an employee." The Ontario Act (Section 1(d); Statutes of Ontario, 1983, 1) defined compensation as follows: "...

all forms of wages, salary remuneration, benefits, perquisites, and any other payments or benefits whatsoever that are paid or provided, directly or indirectly, to or for the benefit of a person in respect of any office, employment or position in the public sector, but compensation does not include reimbursement of any person for expenses actually incurred by him...." In "Compensation Bulletin No. 3" (Province of British Columbia, 1982, 8) issued in March 1982 by the Ministry of Finance (Honourable H. Curtis, Minister) of the Province of British Columbia, and providing details on the stabilization program, the "calculation of compensation for group" is defined in the following terms:

PART III—CALCULATION OF COMPENSATION FOR GROUPS

32. Employers are required to file compensation plans that include all employees for both years they are subject to the guidelines.
33. "Compensation plan" means the provisions, however established, for the determination and administration of compensation of an employee or employees, and includes a collective agreement, provisions established between an employer and an employee or employees, provisions established by an employer, or provisions established in accordance with or pursuant to any Act or law.
34. For the purposes of the Program, "benefit" means,
    a) pay for time not worked, including pay for vacations, statutory and other holidays, sick leave, travel time, cleanup time, rest periods and personal leave;
    b) premium pay, including overtime premiums, shift differentials, callback pay, stand-by pay and premiums for work performed under hazardous or unpleasant conditions;
    c) any payment made by an employer in respect of contributions payable by an employee under a provincial hospital and medical insurance plan, pension or superannuation plan, new increment or new job evaluation;
    d) a payment by the employer to the employee in lieu of a payment or contribution under any of the plans referred to in sub-paragraph (c);
    e) a benefit under a supplementary unemployment benefit plan or other income maintenance plan;
    f) a benefit under a superannuation, pension or other retirement benefit plan, including a deferred profit sharing plan as defined in the Income Tax Act;
    g) banked overtime, accumulated time off, or any other form of compensatory time off based on attendance at work;
    h) payments by an employer:
        (i) to employees in a group on final termination of employment;
        (ii) in a guideline year in respect of the first year expenditures of a new registered pension plan in circumstances where no pension plan had existed previously;
    i) any other compensation generally classified as a benefit.

Whatever the merits of the legislations to which reference has been made, it can be said from the standpoint of the cost-benefit analysis of collective bargaining outcomes that they have helped to lay some of the foundations of such analysis by (1) developing a total labour-cost awareness, i.e., an accounting pre-requisite for the eventual cost-benefit analysis of the total settlement or the total agreement package;[8] (2) retaining the concept of the bargaining unit as the basis for the calculation of compensation increases;[9] (3) introducing the practice of excluding the costs of certain specified terms and conditions of employment from the calculation of compensation costs subjected to the legislation.

It is interesting to review specifically those terms and conditions of employment whose costs were not to be part of the calculation of increases in compensation subject to the criteria prescribed by each of the three legislations. The relevant extracts from the respective legislations (or from related documents) are outlined below.

(Federal) Anti-Inflation Guidelines, Schedule II, s. 51 CRC 1978 (291–366)

For the purposes of section 49, "benefit" means...but, for greater certainty, does not include
h) wages and salaries;
i) cost of living allowances;
j) payments under a direct or indirect incentive plan;
k) contributions made by an employer under the Canada Pension Plan, the Quebec Pension Plan, the Health Insurance Act of Quebec, the Unemployment Insurance Act, 1971 and workmens' compensation legislation.
l) special payments made under a superannuation, pension fund or plan for the purpose of
    (i)   liquidating an experience deficiency, as defined in paragraph (2)(e) of the Pension Benefits Standards Regulations,
    (ii)   liquidating an initial unfunded liability, as defined in paragraph (2)(g) of the Pension Benefits Standards Regulations, incurred prior to October 14, 1975,
    (iii) increasing the accrued regular retirement pension benefits under a plan up to a level that is not in excess of the value of the future service benefits of the plan, or
    (iv) extending accrued pension benefits under a plan to include any prior employment service;
m) payments by an employer
    (i)   in respect of measures taken to reduce the adverse effects of technological change on employees, including training and relocation costs and redundancy payments,
    (ii)   to implement procedures and techniques to reduce the risk of injury to, and to safeguard the health of employees while at work, including the provision of safety equipment.
    (iii) under an employee suggestion and safety award plan,

(iv)   under an employee education assistance plan,

(v)   to maintain benefits under an employee benefit plan in a guideline year at the level of benefits available during the base year under the plan where the plan has not been amended to increase the level of benefits,

(vi)   to employees in a group on final termination of employment,

(vii)   in a guideline year in respect of the first year expenditures of a new registered pension plan in situations where no pension plan had existed previously,

(viii) to eliminate differences in benefits based on the sex, marital status or age of employees; and

n)   payments by an employer in respect of benefits that are not readily amenable to monetary valuation, including the provision of physical facilities for recreation or credit union operations, and for the serving of food.

The Ontario Act

For reporting purposes compensation does not include:

a)   expenses actually incurred by an employee that are reimbursed by the administrator;

b)   benefit improvements required by statute (e.g. changes in Canada Pension Plan, Unemployment Insurance, Workers' Compensation and administrator-paid OHIP);

c)   changes in expenditures incurred by an administrator due to premium or price changes during the Restraint Year to maintain, without change or improvement, benefits which existed during the Base Period;

d)   changes in the minimum wage;

e)   awards under the Human Rights Code or Section 33 of the Employment Standards Act;

f)   changes in expenditures made by an administrator to implement procedures and techniques to reduce the risk of injury to, and to safeguard the health of, employees while at work, including the provision of safety equipment but not fixed allowances paid irrespective of expenses actually incurred;

g)   amenities that cannot be readily allocated to individual groups of employees such as the provision of facilities for recreation, credit unions or food operations.

Changes in group compensation plan in respect of any matters described in clauses (a) to (g) above, need not be reported to the Inflation Restraint Board.[10]

Attention should also be directed to Section 6 (4) of the Ontario legislation where it is provided that:

(4) Where, in the opinion of the Board, the documents and information filed with the Board under subsections (1) and (2) do not adequately set out the

particulars of the changes to the group compensation plan and the cost or saving attributable to such changes. . . .

Here the word "saving," as distinct from "cost," is also significant.

British Columbia Stabilization Program

For the purposes of the Program, "benefit" means. . .but, for greater certainty, does not include

    j)   wages and salaries;

    k)   cost of living allowances;

    l)   contributions made by an employer under the Canada Pension Plan, the Unemployment Insurance Act, 1971 and the Workers' Compensation Act;

    m) payments by an employer

        (i)   to implement procedures and techniques to reduce the risk of injury to, and to safeguard the health of, employees while at work, including the provision of safety equipment.

        (ii)   under an employer suggestion and safety award plan,

        (iii) to maintain benefits under an employee benefit plan in a guideline year at the level of benefits available during the base year under the plan where the plan has not been amended to increase the level of benefits.

Computations

35. Payments not to be included in calculating changes in compensation are as follows:

    a)   Payments in respect of an increase in compensation made in recognition of savings in costs realized by an employer as a result of an agreement to reduce or eliminate restrictive work practices.

    b)   Payments in respect of an increase in the compensation of an employee that results from the elimination of differences in compensation based on matters prohibited under the Human Rights Code.

    c)   Payments in respect of compensation to an employee who is registered in an apprenticeship training program under the Apprenticeship Act.

    d)   Increment and job classification plans in place prior to the coming into effect of the Program.[11]

The above exclusions suggest that, in the cost-benefit analysis of bargaining outcomes, significant jurisprudence presumably accumulated through their implementation. The key issues that emerge are: what has been the overall degree of frequency of implementation? What were the specific items subject to exclusion, and in what frequency?

Responses to these questions (among others) could provide a body of data that would lay the basis for the cost-benefit analysis of bargaining outcomes. Of course, a labour cost does not cease to be a cost to the employer by virtue of simple exclusion from calculation under anti-inflation guidelines. But the nature[12] of many of the terms and conditions of employment whose costs are excluded from calculations necessitates the following question: what cost-decreases or savings (if any) to employers did some of these excluded terms generate, while not interfering with the welfare and well-being of employees?[13]

DIMENSION OF THE COST-BENEFIT ANALYSIS OF COLLECTIVE BARGAINING OUTCOMES

Implementation of the cost-benefit analysis of bargaining outcomes requires further research. In this conclusion to our chapter, we hope to show that the process we have been discussing is worthy of that research. However, a number of dimensions can be suggested as approaches to cost-benefit analysis.

The Informational Dimension

If it is judged useful by practitioners and researchers knowledgeable of actual cases where cost-savings have been achieved without sacrificing the welfare and well-being of employees, then the circulation, in appropriate form, of such relevant collective bargaining cost-benefit analysis data would have to be stepped up. However, some employers might be understandably reluctant to let other employers—possibly their competitors—know of these positive cost-saving experiences. Efforts would therefore have to be made to protect the sensitivity of such data while allowing their circulation. For this reason, cost-benefit bargaining information may more easily be made available in the public sector because of the generally less competitive climate.[14]

The Managerial Dimension

Cost-benefit analysis is worthy of exploration as a potential factor in the remuneration of negotiators and contact administrators. If cost-savings are identified, a fraction of these savings could be set aside as performance pay for those personnel who were instrumental in reaching a settlement.[15]

The Timing Dimension

Some cost-savings will be evident soon after the introduction of certain collective agreement provisions. But there are instances where the cost-savings and benefits will be apparent only after a considerable length of time has elapsed since the agreement. Training provisions are one example.

Swinton (1983) makes some fundamental observations regarding the area of health and safety, potentially fertile ground for cost-benefit analysis:

> ...As well, the reluctance to bargain over health is sometimes explained by the lack of worker interest in health and safety demands. When it comes to the eleventh hour at the bargaining table, wages are said to take priority over all other items. Berman has suggested that this view of worker priorities is inaccurate and reflects the misguided opinions of the bargaining committee, rather than their constituents' views. Union leaders, as political animals, feel that another dollar in the pocket will be a more tangible measure of successful bargaining than a dollar invested in protective equipment or a double locker system, and therefore, more conducive to future political success. As a result, health and safety items tend to be traded off...(pp. 48–49)

There may be political considerations on the side of management as well: "if the 'now buck' makes our workers happier, let's give it to them" might be the thinking.

But management may have other considerations. Some firms, because of their limited financial resources, might not be able to sustain the costs of implementing certain agreement clauses, without concurrently cashing in the savings resulting from these provisions. While from the unions' standpoint, educational efforts among members might contribute over time to improved realization of health and safety issues, management might see that cost-benefit information passed on from large, resourceful firms to smaller firms might go *some way* at least toward avoiding some of the costs inherent in the smaller firms' administering certain agreement clauses.

The Public Policy Dimension

As suggested earlier in this chapter, research and cost-benefit analysis of bargaining outcomes may provide information relevant to planning future income policies, should these be deemed necessary. In particular, a credit system might assign to well-identified provisions of the labour contract a value that would enable a given group to exceed by a specified amount the established guideline limiting compensation increases. Such a credit system would acknowledge the positive value of contract clauses, thereby ensuring that collective bargaining outcomes are no longer subjected to controls only but are promoted as well in income policies. By way of example, grievance procedures, having proven to be cost-saving, might allow compensation guidelines to be exceeded by, say, 0.25 percent.

The Academic Dimension

Conducting a cost-benefit analysis of collective bargaining outcomes requires a good grasp of agreement costing methods. Cost-savings deserve to be costed as accurately as cost increases. Labour relations personnel, be they labour, management or a third party, have much to gain by mastering at least the basic principles of contract costing. They, in turn, with their knowledge of agreement content, can inject into existing accounting procedures (often developed by non-labour relations personnel) the required degree of precision and detail that will make costing reliable, and cost-benefit analysis possible. Short of surveying current labour relations programs and courses in our universities and community colleges, we must raise the question: is collective bargaining costing (and cost-benefit analysis) receiving sufficient attention as part of current labour relations teaching? By the same token, is the process of collective bargaining currently receiving sufficient attention as part of accounting courses and programs? A cursory examination by the author of accounting textbooks (both Canadian and U.S.) in several university bookstores revealed scant reference to the process of collective bargaining and its cost (and cost-benefit) implications.[16] Much to our regret, references to agreement costing in otherwise sound industrial relations textbooks are, even today, very rare.

The Research Dimension

Although interest in agreement costing and cost-benefit analysis has increased in the last decade and a half in Canada (owing largely to intensified public discussion of income policies, followed by wage and price controls), much research remains to be done on costing methods, and particularly on costing assumptions. Because reliable costing is a prerequisite to sound cost-benefit analysis of bargaining outcomes, I cite here a research proposal on costing assumptions that I formulated on an earlier occasion:

> ...A survey—prepared in a context protecting the anonymity of participating organizations—might be conducted of: 1) what type of agreement costing assumptions are made within organizations; 2) the reasons why costing assumptions are made in the manner in which they are; 3) the degree of experienced accuracy of costing assumptions in the light of actually incurred costs; 4) the factors that may have led to inaccurate costing assumptions in the light of actually incurred costs. Care will of course have to be taken in designing the sample for the study so that a broad spectrum of market and operational contexts are covered by the study for the purpose of gaining as representative a picture as possible of the range of factors that can have an impact on the nature of the costing assumptions made as well as on the degree of their demonstrated accuracy.[17]

In terms of potential new research, the key topic would be a study of the impact of the costing and cost-benefit analysis function on the process of negotiation itself. How would the negotiating parties react to data that are the product of collective bargaining costing and cost-benefit analysis?[18]

CONCLUSION

The cost-benefit analysis of collective bargaining outcomes is worthy of further research not only because it is a process that would provide the parties to bargaining with a balanced and factual assessment of such outcomes, but also because it would gradually make available a body of data and information that would assist those in charge of managing the economy; last but not least, it would play an important role in strengthening the institution of collective bargaining in democratic societies.

NOTES

1. A number of the publications listed in the bibliography to this chapter, although generally of a narrower focus, can be considered part of these "other" writings.
2. A note of caution: the author abstains from assigning a universal value to the changing assessment of labour relations and of collective bargaining. For one thing, the writings cited here emanate from industrialized countries. In other social and political contexts, a more adversarial labour relations stance may currently be required. Also, in the course of the history of labour relations, assessments of the function of labour relations have no doubt occurred, dictated by circumstances. The point is that changing assessment, now observed, is noteworthy for several reasons. One is that it is a natural base for conducting balanced research on the outcomes of collective bargaining.
3. A simple illustration—if indeed it is necessary—of the underlying existence of that ethical dimension in the workplace is the 1986 circular prepared by the Union of National Defence Employees (UNDE). With regard to the right of employees to refuse work they deem to be dangerous, the following sentence appears prominently: "You have the right to avoid danger." This sentence is one of many indications within our labour relations system of the recognition by our civilization of the integrity of the individual. (The sentence, as well as the explanation following it, refer to the recently amended Part IV of the Canada Labour Code, dealing with health and safety at the workplace.) See *Circlet*, UNDE, May 16, 1986. How many thousands (if not millions) of workers in less fortunate lands crave— consciously or unconsciously—the right to refuse dangerous work?

4. Bargaining outcomes research (not only in a cost-benefit context), as distinct from bargaining procedures research, may be expected to inject a breath of fresh air into the study of our bargaining system: after all, the reasons why specific agreement provisions work well, work half well, or don't work at all can usually be explained in comparatively simple language. That simplicity in findings might also be expected to be translated into straightforward proposals for change. This might be a particularly welcome development in the administration of our collective bargaining system in view of the expected legal and convoluted debates that might, for example, be brought about by the impact of the Charter of Rights and Freedoms on collective bargaining (see, in this regard, the valuable but somewhat worrisome study by Professor Don Carter on *The Changing Face of Canadian Labour Relations Law*, Reprint Series No. 54, Industrial Relations Centre, Queen's University at Kingston).

5. Canada's collective bargaining system, decentralized and operating in a vast country, sets in motion a variety of attitudes that reflect, at any given time and location, a mosaic of specific circumstances and situations. While in one corner of the system, a co-operative labour-management approach may work wonders, a raw adversarial approach may, at the very same time, pitch people against each other in another corner of the system. Such a bargaining system which, at any one time, mobilizes thousands of human intelligences, imaginations and sentiments on its thousands of bargaining tables needs a plurality of alternate problem-solving approaches. It is in that perspective that we discuss the cost-benefit approach in this chapter. Any "blanket" approach designed to offer cure-alls to the Canadian collective bargaining system would soon, under the pressure of the diversity of local factors, look like the cracked clay bed of a dried-up Australian river.

6. See, for example, D. Carrier, *La Stratégie des négociations collectives* (Paris: Presses Universitaires de France, 1967), and A. Craig, *The System of Industrial Relations Canada* (Scarborough, Ont.: Prentice-Hall Canada, 1986). The vigorous intellectual leadership by Professor Gérard Hébert, as a leader of a group of scholars looking into the current "state of the art" in industrial relations, must also be mentioned.

7. In view of the importance, both in terms of its scope and model-setting value, we have appended to this chapter an extract from Dr. Roy Adams's article, "Industrial relations and the economic crisis: Canada moves towards Europe (see H. Juris, M. Thompson, and W. Daniels (eds.), *Industrial Relations in a Decade of Economic Change*, IRRA Series, pp. 123–124, in which the author provides both statistical information and comments on aspects of the economic

environment that surrounded the imposition, in 1975, of wage and price control by the Canadian Government. (See also Figure 10A.1.)

8. This being in turn a prerequisite for the reliable cost-benefit analysis of individual collective agreement provisions.

9. The (federal) Anti-Inflation Act (Part 4, Section 38) states that "... 'group' means (a) a bargaining unit..." (among other possible meanings, as applicable); the Ontario Act (Section 1 (d)) provides that "compensation group" means "an individual or group of persons to whom Part I of this Act is made applicable by section 3 including a unit of public sector employees established for collective bargaining..."; The British Columbia program provides that a "compensation plan" means "the provisions, however established, for the determination and administration of compensation of an employee or employees, and includes a collective agreement, provisions established between an employer and an employee or employees, provisions established by an employer, or provisions established in accordance with or pursuant to any Act or law." (See *The Stabilization Program—Program Details*, circular issued by the Ministry of Finance of British Columbia, March 1982, page 8.)

10. Extracted from *Guide to Forms IRB-06, IRB-07, and IRB-08: Group Compensation Plan Reports*, (Ontario) Inflation Restraint Board, January 1984, pages 4 and 5.

11. See *The Stabilization Program—Program Details*, British Columbia Ministry of Finance, March 18, 1982, page 9.

12. Subject to confirmation, many of these items can be described as welfare-oriented and/or productivity-oriented, etc. (for lack of more specific terms).

13. The following speculation might be offered : could it be argued that the fact that the costs of a safety plan have been excluded from the calculation of compensation costs subject to guidelines, may have stimulated the parties to negotiate such a safety plan—a plan that might have, over time, reduced the incidence of injuries (and resulting absences) costly to both employees and employers? An equally speculative, but larger, point: to what extent (if any) did the negotiation of such fringe benefits lead the parties to realize more concretely that there exist terms and conditions of employment that serve their joint interests?

14. In an earlier paper, I had more generally discussed the point covered in this section: "When we speak of examining the implementation of collective agreements it seems to me that we touch on one of the fundamental characteristics of our competitive system, a characteristic which may reasonably lead us to suppose that an employer in the private sector would hesitate—and with good reason—to divulge in detail to other employers, and especially to his competitors, the

reasons why certain of the provisions negotiated have succeeded admirably in, for example, maintaining the morale of his employees and promoting the efficient utilization of his staff. I feel, however, that for the good of our entire economy it is desirable that the results of research into positive achievements in labour relations should be widely disseminated. Should it not be one of the tasks of the researcher in industrial relations to contribute to the development of a body of information—if necessary, without divulging the source—dealing with certain experiences in labour relations? Should this information not be widely disseminated, in view of the fact that, by bringing the experiences of others to the attention of firms and other organizations, costly mistakes might be avoided and positive experiences—from the point of view of both the employers and employees—duplicated? Should the attempt not be made, in the field of labour relations, to reconcile as far as possible the demands of normal competition and the need for knowledge relating to practical situations? I raise these questions because it seems to me that, in the context of the current economic situation, we should think increasingly in terms of what is in the interest of the Canadian economy as a whole...." see "Costs and benefits of collective agreements," notes for a Seminar on Administration organized under the auspices of L'Ecole des Hautes Etudes Commerciales, Universite de Montréal, November 20, 1973, by Félix Quinet, page 3.

15. For other potential managerial dimensions of cost-benefit analysis as applied to collective bargaining, see my earlier article, "Cost-benefit analysis and experience banks in labour and staff relations," in *Collective Bargaining in the Canadian Context*, CCH Canadian (1974), pages 64–75.

16. Professor Roger Tang in an interesting article, "Taking a more active role in collective bargaining," suggests that "CAS can be key players on the management team" (see CA *Magazine*, November 1985, pp. 56–61). I would balance Tang's suggestion by adding to it: CAS can be key players on the union team.

17. *Two Papers on Collective Bargaining Costing and Cost-benefit Analysis* (Pay Research Bureau), by Félix Quinet, page 6. (N.B.—The currently receding inflation levels should not generate complacency in costing and cost-benefit research. After all, hospitals not experiencing appendectomies for a while are not expected, nor allowed, to lay to rust the surgical tools likely to be again required at some future date.)

18. I am indebted to Professor Joel Amernic, of the Faculty of Management Studies of the University of Toronto, for raising this particular dimension for research. His study "The roles of accounting in collective bargaining" (1985, 227) describes and assesses "the roles that

accounting information appeared to play in the negotiations between a not-for-profit organization and the association representing its professional employees...."

BIBLIOGRAPHY

A Guide to Forms IRB-06, IRB-07 and IRB-08: Group Compensation Plan Reports. Ontario: Inflation Restraint Board, January 1984.

Amernic, Joel H. (1985), "The roles of accounting in collective bargaining." *Accounting Organizations and Society,* 10(2): 227–253.

Argus-Journal (April/May 1986), "Employee fitness cuts health costs." Public Service Alliance of Canada.

Bequele, Assefa (1984), "The costs and benefits of protecting and saving lives at work: Some issues." *International Labour Review,* January–February, pp. 1–16.

Bodman (de), Eric and Richard, Bertand (1971), *Changer les relations sociales—La Politique de Jacques Delors.* Paris: Les Editions d'Organisation.

Canada, *The Anti-Inflation Act* (1985), Chapter 75 and Regulations; *An Act to provide for the restraint of profit margins, prices, dividends and compensation in Canada.* Ottawa: Queen's Printer.

Carrier, Denis (1967), *La Stratégie des négociations collectives.* Paris: Presses Universitaires de France.

Clark, Kim B. (1980), "The impact of unionization on productivity: A case study." *Industrial and Labour Relations Review,* July, pp. 451–469.

Closets (de), François (1985), *Tous ensemble, pour en finir avec la syndicratie.* Paris: Les Editions du Seuil.

Craig, Alton W. J. (1986), *The System of Industrial Relations in Canada.* Scarborough, Ontario: Prentice-Hall Canada Inc.

Delors, Jacques (assisté de Jacques Baudot) (1971), *Contribution à une recherche sur les indicateurs sociaux.* Paris: Futuribles.

Dewey, Martin (1980), "Managers urged to consider benefit of healthy employees." *The Globe and Mail,* September 11.

Dion, Gérard (1986), *Dictionnaire canadien des relations du travail.* Québec: Les Presses de l'Université Laval.

Duclos, Denis (1984), *La Santé et le travail.* Paris: Editions La Découverte.

Ellenbogen, J. (1980), "Costing of contracts in the 80s: The computer revolution." Paper presented at the Annual Convention of the Eastern Economic Association, Montréal, May 8.

England, Geoffrey and Lermer, George (1983), eds., *Essays in Collective Bargaining and Industrial Democracy.* Don Mills, Ont.: CCH Canadian Limited.

Finkelman, Jacob and Goldenberg, Shirley B. (1982), *Collective Bargaining in the Public Service: The Federal Experience in Canada*, Vol. 2. Montreal: Institute for Research on Public Policy.

Freeman, Richard B. and Medoff, James L. (1984), *What Do Unions Do?* New York: Basic Books.

Ginnold, Richard E. (1980), "A view of the costs and benefits of the job safety and health law." *Monthly Labour Review*, August, pp. 24–26.

Granof, Michael H. (1973), *How to Cost Your Labor Contract*. Washington, D.C.: The Bureau of National Affairs, Inc.

Harvey, Barron H., Rogers, Jerome F., and Schultze, Judy A. (1983), "Sick pay vs. well pay: An analysis of the impact of rewarding employees for being on the job." *Public Personnel Management Journal*, May, pp. 218–224.

Igalens, J. and Peretti, J.-M. (1980), *Le Bilan social de l'entreprise*. Paris: Presses Universitaires de France (Collection Que Sais-Je?).

Juris, Hervey, Thompson, Mark and Daniels, Wilbur (1985), eds., *Industrial Relations in a Decade of Economic Change*. Madison, WI: Industrial Relations Research Association Series.

Lau, C. T. and Nelson, M. (1981), *Accounting Implications of Collective Bargaining*. Hamilton, Ont.: The Society of Management Accountants of Canada.

Lépine, Ginette, Cormier, Pierre (1984), *Vous autres au syndicat...* Montréal: Editions Québec/Amérique.

Mishan, E. J. (1971), *Cost-benefit Analysis*. New York: Praeger Publishers.

Moore, Wilbert F. (1946), *Industrial Relations and the Social Order*. New York: The MacMillan Company.

Portigal, Alan H., "Current research on the quality of working life." *Relations industrielles* 28(4):736–762.

Province of British Columbia, Compensation Bulletin No. 3, *The Stabilization Program—Program Details*. Ministry of Finance, March 18, 1982.

Quinet, Félix (1983), "Meanings of an apprenticeship training provision for management, the union, graduate apprentices, school officials: Laying the basis for a balanced approach to, and the cost-benefit assessment of, collective bargaining outcomes." *Dimensions of Canadian Collective Bargaining*, CCH Canadian, pp. 35–56.

────── (1974), *Collective Bargaining in the Canadian Context*. Don Mills, Ont.: CCH Canadian.

Sheifer, Victor J. (1980), "The use of assumptions in costing labor agreements." Paper presented at the Annual Convention of the Eastern Economic Association, Montréal, May 8.

Statutes of Ontario, 1983, Bill 111 (Chapter 70), *An Act to provide for the Review of Prices and Compensation in the Public Sector and for an orderly Transition to the Resumption of full Collective Bargaining.*

Swinton, Katherine (1983), "Regulating occupational health and safety: Worker participation through collective bargaining and legislation." In *Essays in Collective Bargaining and Industrial Democracy* (Don Mills, Ont.: CCH Canadian).

Tang, Roger (1985), "Taking a more active role in collective bargaining—CAS can be key players on the management team. *CA Magazine*, November, pp. 56–61.

Thériault, Roland (1982), *La Gestion de la rémunération.* Chicoutimi: Gaetan Morin, Editeur.

Université du Québec à Rimouski (1982), *Evolution de la vie au travail et efficacité des organisations: quelques expériences concrètes (Les Actes du Colloque, 7–8 mai 1981).* Rimouski (Québec), Départment des Sciences de l'administration de l'Université du Québec à Rimouski.

Weiss, Dimitri (1980), *Relations industrielles: le travail et l'organisation, l'individuel et le collectif.* Paris: Editions Sirey.

Appendix 10A

"...The high level of militancy contributed to wage settlements from the late 1960s to the mid-1970s which substantially exceeded the rate of inflation (see Figure 10A.1). This development led some professional economists, many quasi-economists, and a gaggle of pundits to conclude that prices of goods and services were being pushed up by excessive wage increases. Organized labor generally claimed that it was merely trying to (1) make up for past losses, (2) insulate its members against price increases expected to occur during the life of the collective agreement, and (3) make sure its members got a fair share of the increasing economic product."

"...The high level of industrial conflict and the wage-price spiral associated with it in the private and institutional mind became a prime focus of debate and policy during the 1970s and early 1980s. Several approaches were tried by governments to control or influence the outcomes of collective bargaining. In 1969–1970 a wage-price guideline policy was tried, in 1975–1978 mandatory general wage-price controls were in effect and in 1982–83 public-sector compensation was controlled by law in the federal and several provincial jurisdictions (Wood and Kumar, 1976; Swimmer, 1984). The unilateral imposition of controls on wages and prices in 1975 gave rise to a good deal of opposition from both labor and management. As a result, the federal government entered into a series of discussions with representatives of labor and business in hopes of achieving a voluntary, tripartite agreement on restraint. Although no agreement could be reached in the 1975–1978 period, the process of consultation in search of consensus would be used with increasing frequency...."

Adapted from Dr. Roy Adams (1985), "Industrial relations and the economic crisis: Canada moves toward Europe," in *Industrial Relations in a Decade of Economic Change, IRRA Research Series, pp. 123–124.*

Figure 10A.1
Settlements in Major Collective Agreements and Inflation,
Selected Years 1967–1983

	Wage Settlements[a] Average % Change	CPI[b] Average % Change	Net Change in Real Wages
1960–64 (average)	8.0	1.4	6.6
1965–69	8.0	3.7	4.3
1970	8.6	3.3	5.3
1971	7.8	2.9	4.9
1972	8.8	4.8	4.0
1973	11.0	7.5	3.5
1974	14.7	10.9	3.8
1975	19.2	10.8	8.4
1976	10.9	7.5	3.4
1977	7.9	8.0	−0.1
1978	7.2	9.0	1.8
1979	8.7	9.1	−0.4
1980	11.1	10.1	1.0
1981	13.3	12.5	0.8
1982	10.0	10.8	−0.8
1983	5.9	5.8	0.1

[a]Data refer to wage settlements in collective agreements covering 500 or more employees which do not contain a cost-of-living adjustment clause. Data were collected by Labour Canada and are reported in *Economic Review* (Ottawa: Canada Department of Finance, annual).

[b]CPI = consumer price index. Data from *Consumer Price Index* (Ottawa: Statistics Canada, annual).

11

Issues in Contract Administration and Human Rights

Amarjit S. Sethi and Michael MacNeil

INTRODUCTION

A collective agreement is a basic document governing the employment relationship of employers and workers. The different values and interests of workers and organizational managers complicate the application and interpretation of this important contract. In this chapter we will outline the basic process of contract administration, the use of grievance procedures, and the role of decision making in grievance management. Some of the key issues in contract administration will be addressed, including the impact of the Canadian Charter of Rights and Freedoms, human rights legislation, new information technology and modified expectations in an emerging industrial relations system.

THE PROCESS OF CONTRACT ADMINISTRATION

A collective agreement is a contractually binding document that culminates the bargaining process.[1] It usually represents the agreement of the employer and the union although it is sometimes imposed on the parties through the binding award of an interest arbitrator. There is great diversity in terms of collective agreements, reflecting the range of structures through which bargaining is conducted. Negotiations may occur between a single employer and a single union or between the employer and several unions jointly at one location. The negotiations may cover all the locations of an employer in a region, a province or in the whole country. Groups of employers may join together in an association to negotiate for the whole industry, and unions may join together to bargain in a common front. Despite this diversity, there are certain statutory provisions that must be adhered to in every collective agreement. For instance, each collective agreement must include a clause that prohibits strikes or lockouts during the period the contract is in force. Contracts normally have a recognition clause by which the employer recognizes the union as the exclusive bargaining agent for a defined group of employees called the bargaining unit.

The collective agreement binds not only the employer and the union who are the formal parties to the contract, but all employees in the bargaining unit as well. As a binding contract between the union and the employer, the collective agreement promotes the managerial interest in industrial peace by the union's undertaking not to strike during the term of the collective agreement. As a legal code, it has a normative rule-making function, serving to ensure that the agreed conditions are applied to the workplace (Davies and Freedland, 1983, 154).

The promotion of these two interests requires, however, that a process be established for administering the agreed-upon terms. The collective agreement must be implemented, and a mechanism for resolving disputes arising while the contract is in effect must be established. Since one of the goals is to achieve this without disrupting the work process, this creates the need for a mechanism whereby the parties can settle their differences or whereby a neutral third party can resolve the dispute. Thus, the process of contract administration can be conveniently divided into two phases.

Phase A

Differences are settled through the use of grievance procedures. The collective agreement will normally set out a procedure whereby the parties will meet to discuss and negotiate a dispute concerning the interpretation, application, or administration of the collective agreement. Occasionally the grievance process may be used to deal with disagreements over issues that do not arise from the collective agreement.

Phase B

If the parties are unable to resolve their differences, they may resort to arbitration.[2] The arbitration decision is binding upon the parties. Collective agreements in all jurisdictions except Saskatchewan are required to contain a clause for final settlement without stoppage of work of all disputes arising during the term of the collective agreement. Even in Saskatchewan, given that strikes during the term of the collective agreement are prohibited, the parties normally provide for arbitration. In other jurisdictions, if the collective agreement fails to specify a means for resolving disputes, then the legislation sets out a model arbitration clause which is deemed to be part of the collective agreement.

Although statutes do not stipulate that a grievance procedure must be invoked in an attempt to settle a dispute before it is submitted to arbitration, the parties almost always include such a procedure in the collective agreement. This recognizes the desirability of a resolution to which the parties agree rather than one that is imposed upon them.

There are many reasons why the employer and the union have

disagreements concerning contract administration. These include the inherent difficulties of interpretation given the ambiguities of language, and the differing perceptions each party may have of the nature of the collective agreement and of specific provisions in determining rights and duties.

When the employer and employee agree to particular clauses in collective agreements, it is not necessarily true that they are agreed on the application of the language to particular contingencies. They may not have been able to foresee all matters that would arise, and hence have not really turned their minds to the most desirable outcome. Furthermore, the parties may deliberately choose to employ vague terminology, with the knowledge that future adjustments will have to be made. For example, it is extremely common to prohibit dismissals and discipline except for just cause. The exact content of just cause is worked out through grievances and arbitration following employer disciplinary action.

There are two contexts in which one's view of the nature of rights and duties under a collective agreement is extremely important. In one situation the collective agreement may be silent with respect to a particular issue. If one adopts a residual rights theory, a collective agreement establishes the framework outlining the rights of the union and the employees. All other rights reside with the employer, and in the absence of specific limitations on these rights spelled out in the agreement, the employer is free to make decisions. Given that unions and employees have agreed not to strike during the term of the collective agreement, this means the employer is free to act unilaterally on these issues without consultation or need for union agreement. A competing view, the status quo theory, argues that a collective agreement puts a freeze on the rights and duties of the parties. The parties have only such rights as are expressly stipulated in the collective agreement. As a result, the employer cannot make unilateral decisions unless such power is conferred by the collective agreement. Only through negotiation and agreement with the union can the status quo be altered.

This divergence of viewpoints leads to quite different results. This is well demonstrated by the situation in the 1960s when railways sought to modify their operating practices as a result of new technology by having train crews make longer runs. It was claimed that the companies had the right to make these changes without obtaining union agreement (Freedman, 1965, 88). Given that Canadian arbitrators have generally approved of the residual-rights approach, it is normally incumbent on the union to point to specific language in the collective agreement that limits the rights of management to undertake such unilateral action. Limited exceptions to this rule exist pursuant to some statutes that may require the employer to bargain with the union before implementing technological changes which have a significant impact on the workforce.

Even when the collective agreement specifically grants the employer the discretion unilaterally to make a particular decision, the union may grieve, claiming that the employer has exercised such discretion unfairly, unreasonably, arbitrarily, or discriminatorily. Again, one's views on the nature of rights and duties under the collective agreement will be very important in determining what limits, if any, are placed on the exercise of unilateral discretion. The different values and interests of unions and employers lead to different perceptions on whether limitations do or do not exist.

GRIEVANCE PROCEDURES

A grievance may be defined as anything that the parties agree to treat as a grievance. It may include the charge that the union–management contract has been violated, or it could go beyond the confines of a contract (Slichter et al., 1960, 694). For example, it could be a complaint that the employer has removed or extended a privilege without consulting the union in circumstances where it would be very difficult to construe any violation of a collective agreement. Nevertheless, there may be a good reason to have the matter addressed through the grievance procedure, even if the matter is not considered to be arbitrable.

The grievance process may involve three key stages: (1) investigation stage; (2) intelligence stage; (3) decisional stage. In the investigation stage, the charges are researched to determine their nature and cause. In the intelligence stage, alternative solutions are designed, and in the decisional stage, decisions are reached either resolving the dispute between parties, or referring them to arbitration. Thompson and Murray (1976) have provided an extensive analysis of the various stages involved in the grievance handling process, covering the following six stages: (1) triggering event; (2) cognitive effect; (3) deciding whether to act; (4) making grievance known; (5) information gathering; and (6) managerial action. A good grievance procedure has been accepted as the "life blood of a collective bargaining relationship" (Elkouri and Elkouri, 1981,106).

A number of issues may cause a particular grievance:

- Violation of the agreement;
- Violation of federal or provincial law;
- Violation of human rights recognized in the Canadian practice of contract administration;
- Violation of past practice;
- Disputes over the meaning of clauses in the agreement;
- Dispute over the method of applying those clauses;
- Disagreement about whether a disciplined employee actually committed the offence for which he or she is being disciplined.

A grievance procedure is entirely a creation of the parties, and hence there can be considerable variation. It is quite normal to have a more complicated procedure in larger employer organizations with more complex hierarchies of decision making.

A typical grievance procedure follows certain pre-defined steps:

Step 1. A worker and union steward together formulate a grievance and contact the supervisor.

Step 2. The grievance, if unsettled at the supervisor level, is sent in writing to the manager by the union steward, who expects a written response normally within five days.

Step 3. If the grievance still remains unsettled, it may be sent to the director of the unit or the department. A meeting between union executive and top management will occur.

If the grievance still remains unsettled, union grievance committees will reassess it and may decide to move to arbitration (step 4), which provides the final and binding decision on the settlement of the grievance. Figure 11.1 exemplifies these steps.

The steps outlined in Figure 11.1 are only suggestive and can vary from organization to organization. General Motors (GM) and United Automobile Workers (UAW), for example, have four basic steps which are similar to the steps outlined above, but differ in their application:

1. Meeting between the employee and his or her supervisor. If a grievance remains unsettled, it is taken to the "step and a half," i.e., the employee's union committee member and another member of the shop committee meet with the employee's supervisor and the general supervisor.
2. A meeting between the shop committee and the labour relations department.
3. A meeting between regional director of the Union, the chairperson of the shop committee, the personnel director, and the director of labour relations.
4. The final step is the appeal to an impartial umpire, whose decision is binding on the parties (Bureau of National Affairs, 1983; Gideon, 1979).

The decision whether to drop an unsettled grievance or continue to arbitration will be influenced by a wide variety of factors. These include the financial resources of the union, the seriousness of the grievance, its precedent value, the degree of co-operation between management and union and the legal duty of the union to represent fairly the numbers of the bargaining unit.

Figure 11.1
Steps in a Grievance Procedure

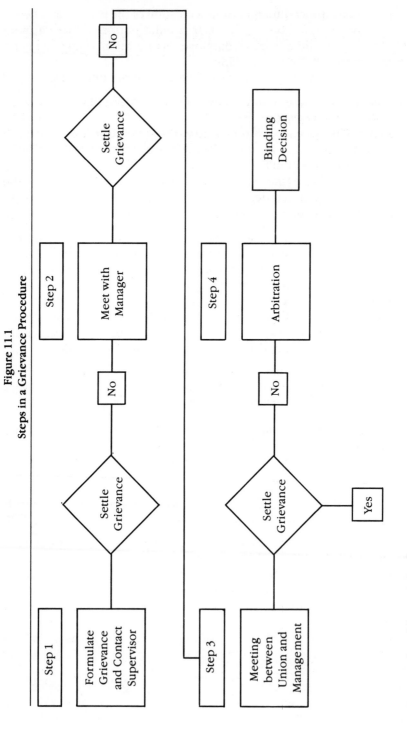

FUNCTIONS OF GRIEVANCE MANAGEMENT

The purposes of a grievance procedure are manifold. The purposes for which it is used by one of the parties to the collective agreement may conflict with the purposes for which the other party may wish to see it used. In many instances the procedure may lead to co-operative problem solving; however, if the parties perceive their values as too divergent, the grievance procedure may serve as yet another locus of struggle. The grievance procedure may be seen by the union as a relatively inexpensive way for unions to put pressure on management (Getman, 1979). In particular, the grievance procedure can be flooded if the union is particularly dissatisfied with management practices or as a negotiating tactic as collective bargaining approaches (Repas, 1984). One study has noted a tendency towards an increase in the number of grievances filed just before contract expiry (Rogow et al., 1975). Carrell and Heavrin (1985) suggest that most formal grievance procedures perform the following functions:

1. Conflict management resolution;
2. Agreement clarification;
3. Communication: Provide a vehicle for employees for expression of their problems;
4. Provide a due process, containing binding arbitration as a final step;
5. Strengthen employee loyalty and trust.

According to Mills (1986), a grievance procedure fulfils several functions:

1. It provides a mechanism to adjust employee's perception of the environment and clarify disputes over the rights and obligations of the employer;
2. It applies the problem-solving psychology to resolve the dispute;
3. It provides a structure of meeting between union and management to settle disputes, thus utilizing group dynamics of each situation.

GRIEVANCE MANAGEMENT EFFECTIVENESS

The success of a grievance procedure is a critical element in the peaceful resolution of disputes, and may serve to validate the rule-making process of an industrial relations system. However, it is very difficult to assess the success of a grievance procedure. One commonly studied variable is the frequency of grievances and the number which the parties are able to settle for themselves compared to the numbers that are submitted for arbitration. Schlicter et al. (1960) found that between 10 to 20 grievances per 100 workers per year was the norm, whereas Rogow et al. (1975) found an average of eight grievances per 100 workers per year, with fewer grievances in public sector and quasi-public sector employment than in other sectors.

Some labour experts argue that grievance and arbitration rates by themselves are not particularly good indicators of grievance effectiveness. For instance, the financial stability of the employer or the union may influence the decision to pursue a grievance to arbitration. While different analysts and parties have different conceptions of what amounts to effective grievance procedures, the following factors are significant variables in grievance effectiveness:

1. The number of grievances;
2. Speed of settlement;
3. The level of management at which grievances are settled;
4. How often the parties resort to arbitration;
5. The perception of employees, supervisors and union officials with respect to the fairness of the outcomes;
6. The type and severity of grievances filed;
7. The reliance on expedited grievance procedures (Lewin, 1984).

Another important variable that may influence grievance effectiveness is the formal structure of the grievance process. Although normally the supervisor is considered the first level of decision making when a grievance is filed (see Figure 11.1), in many cases supervisors may not actually have the authority to allow the grievance, especially when there is a perception that the matter may set a precedent.

Hence an effective grievance procedure may well provide that certain types of grievances should start at a higher level, thereby reducing delay and allowing the essential issue to be addressed by a person with the authority to make a decision. For this reason, collective agreements not uncommonly specify that policy grievances or discharge grievances will be handled differently (Loewenberg, 1984).

In a comprehensive study of grievance behaviour of five basic steel plants, Livernash and Peach (1974, 2) reported that "differences in grievance rates among departments reflected either differences in the number of charges made or differences in the manner in which complaints, problems and charges were resolved and recorded by the parties. Grievance rates count and reflect only formal charges reduced to writing. The grievance process, however, involves informal and oral activity as well...." The authors support a transactional view that "the factors do not operate independently...the environment, union, and management variables must be seen as interdependent" (Livernash and Peach, 1974, 131).

The importance of sociological transactions in the settlement of disputes was recognized by Livernash and Peach (1974). They reported six key variables which together account for differences in grievance behaviour in different steel plants. These included: (1) task organization and work environment, (2) technological change, (3) socioeconomic conditions, (4) management and union leadership, (5) management and union organization, and (6) management and union policy. A high grievance rate may be due to an unfavourable task environment, aggressive union leadership, and ineffective managerial leadership (Mills, 1986). Both factual and value interactions within a given corporate environment determine the focus of a grievance. The theory of transactionalism states that effectiveness in grievance management results from an interaction between the formal structures and the values held by the parties. As Getman (1979) indicates, where there is a strong union, the employer has an incentive to get along with it and not make every issue a battle of wills. On the other hand, the grievance machinery may serve as an aid to management to the extent that experienced stewards or grievance committees will recognize and certify the legitimacy of appropriate employer instructions and actions.

NON-UNION VERSUS UNION GRIEVANCE MANAGEMENT

Some non-union companies may have their own models of grievance procedure. Some of these models follow an effective grievance management approach by emphasizing quality of working-life concerns, including employee involvement, equity, and a problem-solving psychology. The final resolution of disputes may be referred to a neutral arbitrator, although this is unusual. Then there are those non-union companies who do not have effective grievance procedures. This may become the source of general strife between employers and employees.

VALUES AND GRIEVANCE ISSUES

Grievances can be filed over any issue relating to the workplace that is subject to the collective agreement, or they can be filed over interpretation and implementation of the agreement itself. In the settlement of a traditional grievance, say of discipline and discharge, some of the contemporary challenges of equality, human rights, and equity pose increasing problems. They in fact represent a shift in societal and industrial relations values.

The contemporary challenges identified in the succeeding section are primarily matters of statutory or constitutional developments that will affect workplace practices. It might be suggested that the Canadian Charter is a move toward increasing emphasis on legalism and individual rights. Whether this in fact leads to substantially more fairness and freedom is debatable, as we need to wait before a firm pattern of jurisprudence is established.

Figure 11.2
Grievance Issues

Equality and Human Rights	Vacation	Tasks
Equal pay for equal work	Eligibility	Issues arising out of
Equal access to work	Scheduling	computer-mediated
Equal conditions of work	Pay	work
Equal pay for work of		Machine pacing
equal value		VDT concerns
Affirmative action		Electronic monitoring
Discrimination in general		Monotony
		Technostress

Age	Holidays	
Calculating seniority	Eligibility for pay	
Retirement	Pay for holiday work	

Time Off/Absenteeism	Wages and Hours	Discipline/ Dismissal
Paid sick leave	Incentive pay plans	Insubordination
Personal leave	Job evaluation	Misconduct
Union business	Overtime	Poor work
	Premium pay	Sexual harassment
Promotion	Pay for reporting	Layoffs
Posting and bidding	(call-in pay)	Bumping
Basis for promotion	Scheduling	
Measurement of ability	Wage guarantee and bene-	
Transfer	fit plans	

	Management Rights	Others
	Union Rights	Worksharing
	Union Security	Safety
	Rules in Administering	
	Benefits	

Figure 11.2 summarizes the nature of most common grievances found in organizations.

CONTEMPORARY CHALLENGES

The following key issues in the 1980s and beyond will influence the determination of grievances, collective agreements and arbitration.

1. Employment security;
2. Human rights;

a) Recent legislation to remove mandatory retirement requirements in the public sector, thus introducing flexibility in employment continuity and setting precedents for the private sector;

b) Protection against sexual harassment;

c) Employment equity. The range of challenges in human rights, equality and employment equity. These may include (1) equal pay for equal work, (2) equal access to work, (3) equal conditions of work, (4) equal pay for work of equal value, and (5) affirmative action.

A brief description of these challenges follows.

Employment Security

Employment security is a social and economic issue the regulation of which turns upon both the negotiated terms of collective agreements and legislative and public policy initiatives. Collective agreements have traditionally addressed arbitrary managerial action by prohibiting dismissal except for just cause. However, management often retained the right to lay off for economic reasons. Now unions are increasingly seeking to bargain over terms that would protect employees in their jobs, or give them generous benefits if they are laid off. Furthermore, employers may be required to participate in helping displaced workers find new jobs by giving long notice of impending layoff, by making severance payments, by retaining or helping workers to relocate, by offering preferences for new jobs, by aiding in job search and by providing vocational counselling.

Employees not covered by collective agreements simultaneously have other avenues of protection opened. An action for wrongful dismissal may be brought in court if the employer had no good cause for dismissal and if reasonable notice of the dismissal was not given. For these purposes, dismissal for economic reasons is not considered cause. Although workers who are successful in a wrongful dismissal action are not entitled to reinstatement, they are entitled to damages measured by the amount of earnings they would have received during the period of reasonable notice. For highly skilled, long-term managerial employees this could be between eight and thirty months. For short-term unskilled workers, reasonable notice may only be the minimum number of weeks specified in employment standards legislation.

The scope and type of damages for wrongful dismissals are increasing. This was demonstrated in three recent cases in Ontario since 1980. In Pilon vs. Peugeot Canada Ltd. (1980), Pilon was granted $10,000 for mental distress; in Brown vs. the Waterloo Regional Board of Police Commissioners (1982), the Ontario Court of Appeal recognized that damages could be awarded for mental distress, and the court stated that an application for punitive damages was appropriate, although no such damages were subsequently awarded (Hughes, 1986, 16); in oohn Pilato vs. the Hamilton Place Convention Centre (1984), the award included $32,000 in back pay, $25,000 for mental suffering, and $25,000 for punitive damages (the first such award in Canada) (Hughes, 1986, 16).

The arbitration of unjust dismissals outside of the collective bargaining process is available in two jurisdictions in Canada (1) under the Labour Standards Act in Quebec and (2) under the Canada Labour Code. The necessity for a due process based on the principles of value-oriented human resources management is clear. These values represent the willingness by employers to recognize employee rights in such matters as the right to fair discipline based on facts, the right to appeal a disciplinary decision, the right to be represented, and the right to have decisions reviewed by an impartial person (Hughes, 1986). Equally necessary is the foundation for a system that increases sensitivity and awareness of both parties in understanding mutual expectations, style, and responsibilities.

Human Rights

The issue of human rights is discussed under three headings: (1) mandatory retirement, (2) sexual harassment, and (3) employment equity.

Mandatory Retirement

Mandatory retirement is another emerging issue of the eighties. The implementation of a mandatory retirement age is often a matter of unilateral employer initiative, instituted as a means of orderly disengagement of older workers. The age 65 was often chosen because it had become the age at which public and private pensions became payable. Employers were able to implement mandatory retirement unilaterally because it was not regarded as dismissal and hence was exempt from the "just cause" provision of the collective agreement. Given the nature of residual management rights, no impediment to such action existed. Manitoba and Quebec have prohibited the practice of mandatory retirement. The federal government recently announced its agreement in principle with the concept of abolishing mandatory retirement (Government of Canada, 1986, 9), but it has not yet indicated exactly how this is to be done. Court challenges based on the Charter of Rights are underway in several provinces, but it is unclear whether the Charter will apply to relations between private sector employers and their workers. The abolition of mandatory retirement will have an impact on the administration of the collective agreement. It may motivate employers to scrutinize more closely the work of older employees since it will be incumbent on employers to demonstrate that they had just cause before letting these employees go. As well, employers may still be able to implement a mandatory retirement policy when it can demonstrate a bona fide occupational qualification. For example, the need for safety and the known increased incidence of heart attacks and other medical problems may justify retiring pilots at a set age.

Sexual Harassment

Sexual harassment refers to those sexually oriented practices that undermine a person's job or performance in that job (Backhouse and Cohen, 1978). Sexual harassment is seen as a form of sex discrimination; however, in defining it one needs to be constantly alert to changing social values. According to the Co-ordinator for the Status of Women, sexual harassment refers to:

- unwanted sexual attention of a persistent or abrasive nature made by a person who knows or ought reasonably to know that such attention is unwanted; or
- implied or expressed promise of reward for complying with a sexually oriented request; or
- actual reprisal or an implied or expressed threat of reprisal for refusal to comply with a sexually oriented request; or
- actual denial of opportunity or an implied or expressed threat of denial of opportunity for refusal to comply with such a request; or
- sexually oriented behaviour when it has the purpose or effect of creating an intimidating, hostile, or offensive environment in which the student or staff member studies or works (CSW, 1987, 1–2).

Employers should be aware of the extent to which they will be held responsible for the harassment of one of their employees by another. It is becoming increasingly evident that the prevention of such offensive conduct depends in part on the employer's willingness to help educate the workforce about the inappropriateness of such conduct. This can be done by promulgating rules of conduct, by establishing mechanisms by which such offences can be reported, and by the employer using disciplinary powers to sanction against such behaviour. Unions may be caught in a conundrum, given that they have a duty to help prevent such conduct; but at the same time, they may be called upon by a disciplined employee to represent him or her in the grievance process.

Employment Equity

Since the Charter in 1982, there have been four public inquiries that have directly or indirectly investigated the concept of human rights:

- The Royal Commission on Equality in Employment (Abella, 1984);
- The Report of the Special Committee on Visible Minorities in Canadian Society (Daudlin, 1984);
- The Macdonald Commission (1985); and
- The Report of the Parliamentary Committee on Equality (Boyer, 1985).

The overall theme of these reports is summarized by Marsden (1986, 4). The value of employment equity offers "major advantages to the employer by opening up new sources of workers in the community, overcoming past discrimination, developing an explicit human resource policy and overcoming organizational arrangements which act as barriers to women, native people, visible minorities and the disabled all of whom are likely to be present in any employer's community."

Contract administration in general and grievance management in particular will be subject to the values of fairness and employment equity in the future Canadian economy. Marsden (1986, 4) sums up the nature of this challenge for employers and unions:

A "fair share" seems to be a share of employment opportunities in proportion to the number of workers available for the occupation or the job. A "fair wage" seems to mean a wage based on skill, effort, responsibility and conditions of work rather than less relevant criteria. A "fair process" seems, to all those who have examined it, one which sets some goals and targets but which evolves over time and which is sensitive to the complex differences among groups....A "fair law" and "fair regulations" mean a clear statement of the requirements placed upon the employer, the worker and the union so that it is possible and practical for them to comply with the law. A "fair reinforcement" of the law means a predictable and practicable way of both encouraging and constraining Canadians to bring their behaviour in line with their professed beliefs.

In general, human rights and equality issues have become increasingly important and will probably continue to do so. We can, therefore, expect statutory and constitutional developments and interpretations in the coming years that will translate these changes into the process of contract administration (Abella, 1984). For instance, one common problem is the refusal of an employer to hire for discriminatory reasons. Hiring is a process that is most often unilaterally in the hands of management (the exception being closed shop/hiring hall arrangements) and is not normally the subject of grievance procedures. However, promotions and dismissals may raise questions of discrimination. Furthermore, an employer who voluntarily undertakes some form of affirmative action program may be faced with hostility from the workers themselves. The Appendix to this chapter outlines legislative provisions in Canada prohibiting discrimination in employment.

It is not clear that the Charter of Rights will apply directly to the collective agreement, especially of private sector employers. Such evidence as currently exists seems to indicate that it will not. However, a strong argument may be made that the Charter is binding on the government as employer, and hence public sector collective agreements will be subject to closer scrutiny on the grounds that equality rights are being denied. In effect, the Charter will override contrary collective agreement provisions.

The Canadian Human Rights Act is based upon the principle that grievances should be settled on the basis of a worker's ability to perform rather than external factors unrelated to job performance. Section 15 of the Charter of Rights and Freedoms specifies that every individual is equal before and under the law and has the right to the equal protection and equal benefit of the law without discrimination and, in particular, without discrimination based on race, national or ethnic origin, colour, religion, sex, age, or mental or physical disability. Section 2 of Bill C-62, "An Act respecting employment equity" (House of Commons of Canada, 1986) clearly advocates that in settling grievances respecting visible minorities in Canada, we should endeavour to use strategies for accommodation of differences.

The concept of employment equity is a complex one. It has been defined to include the following concepts: (1) equal pay for equal work, (2) equal pay for work of equal value, (3) equal access to work, (4) equal conditions of work, and (5) affirmative action. Each of these concepts is detailed below (Ondrack, 1986).[3]

Equal pay for equal work. This means that workers in the same job description should receive the same rates of pay, after allowances for seniority and performance differentials in a range of pay for a job have been taken into account.

Equal pay for work of equal value. Also known as "pay equity" or "comparable worth," the concept of equal pay for work of equal value implies that there is equal pay for different job descriptions, where job evaluation has determined that work in different job descriptions is actually of the same value to the employer. "The impact of pay equity is to force a re-evaluation of the weights and values assigned to skills and responsibilities of women's jobs so that equal pay for equivalent jobs is obtained (Ondrack, 1986, 2–3).

Pay equity legislation. The laws requiring equal pay for work of equal value are a means of implementing the goal of equality. The challenge is to introduce schemes of job evaluation that are fair, efficient, and in accord with legislative prescriptions. Equal-pay provisions are included either in human rights legislation (federal jurisdiction, British Columbia, Alberta, New Brunswick, Newfoundland, Northwest Territories, Prince Edward Island, and Quebec) or in labour standards legislation (Manitoba, Nova Scotia, Ontario, Saskatchewan, and Yukon Territory). Recent initiatives include the Employment Equity Act, 1986, the Federal Contractors Program, and Ontario's Pay Equity Act, 1987. For details see the Appendix to this chapter.

Implication for contract administration. The equal-pay issue in the context of contract administration is a complex problem. Given that pay rates have traditionally been the subject of bargaining, equal pay laws will put constraints on any bargain the parties may make. More importantly, the introduction of "equal pay for work of equal value" legislation will require the implementation of job evaluation schemes. The carrying out of this function could well provide a source of grievances unless the union is fully involved in determining the criteria on which jobs are to be evaluated and the weight to be assigned to each of these criteria. Pay equity has been criticized for the following reasons (McLean, 1986, 9):

1. "Pay equity interferes with market forces."
2. "Pay equity will discourage women from moving out of the job ghettos."
3. "Employers will stop hiring women if pay equity is implemented."
4. "An army of bureaucrats will be needed to implement it."
5. "It will interfere with collective bargaining."
6. "It will cost too much."

Walter McLean (1986, 9) the Federal Minister Responsible for Women, rejects each of these arguments:

> Unions have supported pay equity. Employers have been able to implement pay equity provisions as part of the collective bargaining process. The Minnesota state legislature started its first pay equity adjustments in 1983. It allocated funds for the purpose and the funds were assigned to the different bargaining units in proportion to the total cost of implementing pay equity for each unit. The actual distribution of pay equity increases, like other salary increases, was negotiated through the usual collective bargaining process and contracts signed in 1983 awarded these funds to those in underpaid female classes.

Equal access to work. This concept tends to eliminate systematic barriers to accesss to jobs that might affect different disadvantaged groups in the labor market.

Equal conditions of work. This refers to the provision of equal facilities in the workplace for such groups as the disabled. Indirect inequalities may exist for single-parent families where there is lack of day-care facilities or flexible hours of work.

Affirmative action. Affirmative action is an effort, either voluntary or mandatory, to provide employment equity for disadvantaged groups. Well-known examples of voluntary affirmative action in Canada are Westinghouse and London Life. In the United States, mandatory affirmative action programs require quotas or hiring targets for disadvantaged groups. In Canada, the following principles are emerging with respect to affirmative action programs, as stated by Ondrack (1986, 2):

> The federal and (Ontario) governments are in favour of an affirmative action approach to speed up natural processes and to put the onus for change on employers. Affirmative action will be mandatory for government and Crown corporation employers and strongly encouraged for private sector employers. And, targets for affirmative action will be set by individual employers themselves rather than by government agencies, but employers will be asked to report on their progress toward these targets. The result of these approaches will be to create a model of affirmative action by public sector employers, which private sector employers will eventually feel obliged to match. And, the pressures will increase on private sector employers to develop more "voluntary" affirmative action programs so that employment equity will become the norm for human resource management practices in the private sector.

The Royal Commission on Equality in Employment (Abella, 1984) found that voluntary affirmative action measures were inadequate, despite the existence of human rights laws allowing affirmative action, and the Charter of Rights and Freedoms provisions that came into being in April 1985. The Royal Commission recommended that all federally regulated employers be required by legislation to implement programs of employment equity. These requirements include facilitation and the issuing of guidelines; collecting, reviewing and assessing data; and enforcing equity (Scott, 1984, 10).

One implication for contract administration is the interaction of affirmative action programs and collective agreement rights, especially seniority. An affirmative action program is likely to be more effective where the union is consulted and involved in making the continuing necessary adjustments.

The Impact of Human Rights on Grievance Management

Three key human rights concepts will shape the management of grievances.

The concept of intent. The courts have recently recognized that some discrimination may be non-intentional. One recent example is the case of Mrs. O'Malley, who filed a complaint with the Ontario Human Rights Commission, citing discrimination on the basis of religion, as her church membership prohibited her from working on a Saturday at her full-time job as a sales clerk in a Kingston Simpson-Sears store. The Court established that the real issue lay in deciding if discrimination had created an adverse effect on an individual. It held that although Simpson-Sears did not intentionally discriminate against Mrs. O'Malley, the Saturday work rule had an adverse effect on her. This raises the issue of reasonable accommodation.

The principle of reasonable accommodation. The Court in O'Malley's case enshrined this principle into law by establishing that it is an employer's duty "to take reasonable steps to accommodate the complainant, short of undue hardship." The Court rules that the duty to accommodate applies to discrimination on the grounds of religion, physical disability, sex, and age.

The definition of a bona fide occupational requirement. In Bhinder vs. CNR, Mr. Bhinder, a CNR electrician in Toronto, refused to comply with a 1978 rule requiring all employees to wear hard hats at a specific work site. As a Sikh, Mr. Bhinder's religion disallowed him to wear anything on his head except a turban. The Supreme Court ruled against Mr. Bhinder, arguing that because of safety, the hard hat rule was a bona fide occupational requirement. The Court said: "If a working condition is established as a bona fide occupational requirement, the consequential discrimination, if any is permitted—or probably more accurately—is not considered...as being discriminatory" (Alberta Human Rights Journal, 1986, 2).

INFORMATION TECHNOLOGY (IT) AND GRIEVANCE MANAGEMENT

Figure 11.2 illustrates such traditional grievance items as seniority, absenteeism, promotion, discipline, vacation, and holidays. The two key emerging areas are equality/human rights and the impacts of new information technology on workers and their tasks. A specific issue is techno-stress—a perception of uncertainty stemming from computerization, electronic monitoring, robotics, and integrated factory and office information systems. These new developments would require retraining of deskilled workers, job redesign, strategies for coping with monotony, privacy of information, and negative psycho-physiological impacts, if any, from video display terminals (VDTS). Increasingly, collective agreements will need to include innovative clauses to deal with these issues of an information society (Sethi et al., 1986).

Information technology is a broad area encompassing various disciplines as embraced by the definition given by UNESCO: "the scientific, technological and engineering disciplines and the management techniques used in information handling and processing; their applications; computers and their interactions with men and machines; and associated social, economic, and cultural matters" (Stokes, 1985, 115). The term "information technology" thus covers the totality of dynamic and complex information technologies converging microelectronics, computers and telecommunications, including the following components: hardware and software, ergonomic work stations, expert systems, knowledge-based systems, database systems, advanced telecommunications, office automation systems, robotics, computer-integrated manufacturing systems, and development of next-generation super-computers and fifth-generation technology. According to Bell (1973), information and not capital is a strategic resource of the new age, characterized as an "information society" (Masuda, 1980; Porat, 1977; Naisbitt, 1982). The information sector accounts for between 18 and 25 percent of the gross national product of seven of the member nations of the Organization for Economic Co-operation and Development and between 27 and 41 percent of employment in these countries (OECD, 1981). It is estimated that the information economy in North America accounts for more than 46 percent of the gross national product and more than 53 percent of income earned (Porat, 1977). Out of the 19 million new jobs created in the United States during the 1970s, only five percent were in manufacturing and only 11 percent in the goods-producing sector as a whole (Naisbitt, 1982, 17). The potential impacts of IT, from the standpoint of work structure, collective bargaining, and grievance management, are far reaching, encompassing individual quality of worklife, horizontal and vertical division of labour, organizational structure, job redesign and organizational interdependence. Technostress is a dynamic state of adaptation of workers to these changes, which contain opportunities for employers to initiate strategic choices by emphasizing not only the parameters of hardware and the features of software but also the motivations, skills, incentives, and grievances of people ("peopleware").

IT may lead to job displacements as well as result in job creation. Professor Tom Steiner predicts (Forrester, 1981) that by early next century we will require only 10 percent of today's labour force to satisfy our production needs. A strong growth in robotics is predicted in the North American economy. Women are particularly affected by the new technology, as a majority of them are employed in the tertiary sector of the economy and in non-manual occupations.

Improved labour relations, proactive grievance handling, and other human resource practices are the key in coping with technostress effectively. Union and management will need to develop mutually shared strategies for adapting to the impact of IT on grievances arising from job reorganization, pay systems, promotions, electronic monitoring, and health and safety concerns. Quality-of-worklife programs, such as job enrichment, autonomous work groups, worker participation and involvement, and transactional and participative styles of contract administration will become increasingly desirable for effective performance and employee satisfaction.

STRATEGIES FOR EFFECTIVE GRIEVANCE HANDLING

Strategies for Management

Management can make some strategic choices by adapting proper strategies when taking action against an employee in such matters as dismissal and discipline or in grievances arising from equality and human rights. We suggest that management should periodically do an "equity assessment" to determine if recent Canadian legislation is being followed in grievance management. The following strategies are useful in conducting such audits:

- Ascertain if your company has "systemic discrimination." [A systemic discrimination is any employment policy, practice, procedure or system that excludes or has a negative impact on women or other target groups (whether or not that impact was intended) and which cannot be justified by job relatedness or business necessity.]
- Communicate rules to employees.
- Pay attention to facts as distinguished from values.
- Use a process of warnings, and keep records.
- Obtain union's co-operation, through developing sensitivity skills for understanding the complex dynamic involved in obtaining the respect of the union and its willingness to participate in contract administration in a positive, non-disruptive fashion.
- Examine union values, and determine tactics for accommodating differences in union and management perceptions.
- Examine past practices.
- Retrain supervisors in grievance management.
- Authority to handle grievances should be clearly defined and understood by supervisors.
- Allow time for the grievor to narrate his or her grievance in private and without interruption, and show your concern for the grievor's problem by following through promptly on any action required by a settlement (Richardson, 1977).

Strategies for the Union

The union has an obligation to respond to the interests and values of its members, by following some strategies that will assist in processing grievances, and upholding the principle of fair representation. Suggested strategies include:

- Pay attention to human rights legislation. The union cannot refuse to process a grievance because of the employee's race, sex, or his or her values.
- The union must research a grievance before its final formulation.
- The union must process a grievance to its final conclusion.
- Exercise a firm hand in screening grievances for appeal. A poor grievance results in a lost grievance, a dissatisfied union member and a loss of union time and money (Richardson, 1977).
- Focus on the job-related aspect of a grievance rather than using it for political purposes.

Strategies for Both Parties

The following strategies are recommended:

- Utilize the three phases of a problem-solving methodology, namely, complete and accurate identification of the problem; research; and generation of alternate solutions in settling grievances.
- Interpret a specific grievance in light of the specific nature of your collective agreement.
- Settle at an early stage by utilizing problem-solving process and psychology.
- Inform grievor about the status of his or her grievance.
- Focus on written proof and first-hand testimony (Richardson, 1977).
- Respect sociological exchange of power and accommodation between parties at the local level (Kuhn, 1967).
- Keep records.
- Use transactional approaches to grievance management by recognizing that grievance reflects an interaction of multiple factors—both factual and values—in a given conflict situation.
- Be creative in grievance management, but apply the various strategies and procedures with consistency, flexibility, and keeping in view recent human rights and equality legislation in Canada.
- Apply effective change strategies in resolving grievances related to the introduction of new information technology.

SUMMARY

Grievance management in the eighties and beyond requires sensitivity to contemporary challenges of equity and social justice. Existing Canadian legislation provides for a minimum level of employment standards and working conditions, the right to a healthy and safe workplace, and freedom from discrimination. Although there are legislative differences in applying this justice system, the overall values of equality, fairness, reasonableness, equity, and social responsiveness are recognized and promoted.

A transactional model of grievance management relies on studying grievances based upon interactions of structures and employee characteristics and recognizes the role of preventive strategies in grievance management.

NOTES

1. In several jurisdictions, including British Columbia, Manitoba, Ontario and federally, a first contract may be imposed by the labour relations board or, in Quebec, a council of arbitration where the parties are unable to reach agreement. Subsequent collective agreements, if any, will be arrived at through the normal processes.
2. The topic of rights arbitration is discussed in detail in Chapter 12 of this text.
3. This definition is based on the proceedings of a conference on managing employment equity, held in November 1985 under the sponsorship of the University of Toronto and the Ontario Women's Directorate, a branch of the Attorney General of Ontario.

REFERENCES

Abella, Judge R. S. (1984), *Equality in Employment: A Royal Commission Report.* Ottawa: Supply and Services.

Alberta Human Rights Journal (1986, March), Landmark Court Cases for Human Rights 4(1): 1–2.

Backhouse, C. and Cohen L. (1978), *The Secret Oppression: Sexual Harassment of Working Women.* Toronto: Macmillan of Canada.

Bell, D. (1973), *The Coming of Post Industrial Society.* New York: Basic Books.

Boyer, P., MP (1985), *Equality for All: Report of the Parliamentary Committee on Equality Rights.* Ottawa: Supply and Services.

Bureau of National Affairs (1983), *Basic Patterns in Union Contracts: Grievances and Arbitration.* Washington, D.C.

Carrell, M. R. and Heavrin, C. (1985), *Collective Bargaining and Labor Relations.* Columbus, OH: Charles E. Merrill Publishing Co.

Coordinator for the Status of Women (CSW) (1987), *Sexual Harassment: What Can I Do?* Ottawa: Carleton University Public Relations/Information Services.

Craig, A. W. J., (1986), *The System of Industrial Relations in Canada.* Scarborough, Ontario: Prentice-Hall Canada.

Daudlin, B., MP (1984), *Equality Now: Report of the Special Committee on Visible Minorities in Canadian Society.* Ottawa: Supply and Services.

Davies, P. and Freedland, M. (1983), *Kahn-Freund's Labour and the Law* (3rd ed.). London: Stevens & Sons.

Elkouri, F. E. and Elkouri, E. A. (1981), *How Arbitration Works.* Washington, D.C.: Bureau of National Affairs.

Forrester, T. (ed.) (1981), *The Microelectronic Revolution.* Cambridge, MA: MIT Press.

Freedman, S. (1965), *Report of the Industrial Inquiry Commission on Canadian National Railway Run-Throughs.* Ottawa: Minister of Labour.

Getman, J. (1979) "Labor arbitration and dispute resolution." *Yale Law Journal* 88: 905.

Gideon, T. F. (1979), "A comparison of alternate grievance procedure." *Employee Relations Law Journal* 5(2): 222–233.

Government of Canada (1986), *Towards Equality: The Response to the Report of the Parliamentary Committee on Equality Rights.* Ottawa: Supply and Services.

House of Commons of Canada (29 January 1986), *Bill C-62: An Act Respecting Employment Equity.* Ottawa: Employment and Immigration.

Hughes, B. H. (1986), "Eliminating the element of surprise." *Human Resource,* 3(1): 15–17.

Kuhn, J. W. (1967). "The grievance process." In J. T. Dunlop (ed.), *Frontiers of Collective Bargaining* . New York, Harper & Row Publishers, pp. 256–257.

Lewin, D. (1984), "Empirical measure of grievance procedure effectiveness." *Labour Law Journal* 35:491.

Livernash, E. R. and Peach, D. A. (1974), *Grievance and Resolution: A Study in Basic Steel.* Cambridge, MA: Harvard University Press.

Loewenberg, J. (1984), "Structure of grievance procedures." *Labour Law Journal* 35:44.

Macdonald, D. S. (1985), *Report of the Royal Commission on the Economic Union and Development Prospects for Canada* (3 vols.). Ottawa: Supply and Services.

Marsden, L. R. (1986), "A fair share at work: An examination of four reports at the federal level in Canada concerned with the economy and with equality." *Choices* (April): 1–4.

Masuda, Y. (1980), *The Information Society as Post-Industrial Society.* Tokyo: Institute for the Information Society.

McLean, W. (1986), "Equal pay for work of equal value is necessary and just." *The Citizen*, 9 April.

Mills, D. Q. (1986), *Labour–Management Relations.* New York: McGraw-mill Book Co.

Naisbitt, J. (1982), *Megatrends.* New York: Warner Books.

OECD (1981), *Information Activities, Electronics and Telecommunications Technologies: Impacts on Employment, Growth and Trade.* Paris.

Ondrack, D. (1986), "Managing employment equity." *Labor Relations News* (March): 2–4. University of Toronto.

Porat, M. (1977), *Information Economy: Definition and Measurement.* Washington, D.C.: U.S. Department of Commerce. OT Special Pub., 77-12 (1).

Rada, J. (1980), *The Impact of Micro-electronics.* Geneva: ILO.

Repas, B. (1984), *Contract Administration.* Washington, D.C.: Bureau of National Affairs.

Richardson, D. C. (1977), *Collective Bargaining by Objectives: A Positive Approach.* New Jersey: Prentice-Hall.

Rogow, S., Beattie, S., and Maclean, D. (1975), Grievance Handling in British Columbia—A Preliminary Report. Vancouver: Mimeograph.

Schuler, R. S. (1984), *Personnel and Human Resource Management.* St. Paul, MI: West Publishing Co.

Scott, P. (1984), "Equality in employment: A Royal Commission Report." *Currents* 2(4): 3–11.

Sethi, A. S., Caro, D. and Schuler, R. S. (1986) (eds.), *Strategic Management of Technostress in an Information Society.* Gottingen, W. Germany: Hogrefe International.

Schlicter, S. H., Healey, J. J. and Livernash, E. R. (1960), *The Impact of Collective Bargaining on Management.* Washington, D.C.: The Brookings Institution.

Srinivas, K. M. (1984), *Human Resource Management.* Toronto: McGraw-Hill Ryerson.

Stokes, A. V. (1985), *Concise Encyclopedia of Information Technology.* Hants., England: Gower Publishing Co.

Task Force on Labour Market Developments (1981). *Labour Market Developments in the 1980s.* Ottawa: Canada Employment and Immigration Commission.

Thompson, A. W. J. and Murray, V. V. (1979), *Grievance Procedures.* Westmead, England: D. C. Heath.

Willes, J. A. (1984), *Contemporary Canadian Labour Relations.* Toronto: McGraw-Hill Ryerson.

Appendix 11A

Constitutional and Legislative Provision Inhibiting Discrimination in Employment

Canadian Charter of Human Rights and Freedoms

On April 16, 1986 Canada enters an era of guaranteed constitutional equality with the signing of Section 15 of the Charter of Rights and Freedoms. The Section bans discrimination on the basis of race, religion, sex, colour, age, national or ethnic origin and physical or mental handicap. The amendment comes three years after the rest of the Charter, contained in the constitution Act, 1982 was ratified, giving federal and provincial legislatives time to amend their laws in accordance with the Constitution. Section 15 gives the Courts the official mandate to strike down any statute that does not conform with the principles of equality (Hryciuk, 1986, 1–4).

Federal

The Canadian Human Rights Act

The Canadian Human Rights Act, R.S.C. 1976–77, c.33, as amended, prohibits discrimination in employment within federal jurisdiction on the grounds of race, national or ethnic origin, colour, religion, age, sex, marital status, family status, disability or conviction for which a pardon has been granted.

Discrimination on the grounds of sex includes discrimination because of pregnancy or childbirth. Disability is defined as "any previous or existing mental or physical disability and includes disfigurement and previous or existing dependence on alcohol or a drug." Furthermore, the Act prohibits differences in wages between men and women employees employed in the same establishment who are performing work of equal value. Value is measured by a composite of the skill, effort and responsibility required in the performance of the work and the conditions under which the work is performed. Different wages may be paid if the difference is based on a reasonable factor as recognized by the Canadian

Source: Adapted from Hryciuk, M. (ed.) (1986), *Corpus Almanac and Canadian Sourcebook*, Vol. I. Toronto: Southam Communications Limited, 1-4; 11-7 to 11-11. Reprinted by permission.

Human Rights Commission in its guidelines. However, sex is not a reasonable factor.

Employers, employee organizations (including unions) or organizations of employers within federal jurisdiction are forbidden to discriminate on any of the grounds listed in the Act. The anti-discrimination provisions touch on all aspects of employment including provisions in collective agreements, recruitment and promotion practices, classification and compensation schemes and pension and insurance programs. The Act applies to all federal government departments, agencies and Crown corporations and to businesses and industries under federal jurisdiction such as banks, airlines, inter-provincial railway and trucking companies and broadcasting facilities.

Canadian Human Rights Commission,
90 Sparks Street, 4th Floor,
Ottawa, Ont. K1A 1E1
(613) 995-1151

Canada Labour Code (Part III); Fair Wages and Hours of Work Act

The Canada Labour Code, R.S.C., 1970, c.L-1, contains provisions concering Labour Standards (Part III), Safety of Employees (Part IV) and Industrial Relations (Part V). Its jurisdiction is described earlier in this text, under Division of Legislative Powers.

Employment Relations and Conditions of Work Branch,
Canada Labour Department,
2 Place du Portage,
Hull, Québec K1A 0J2
(819) 997-1645

Public Service Employment Act

This act, which came into effect in 1967, provides for the appointment to and employment in the Public Service of Canada, stressing that merit is the basis for such appointments. Among other things the Act, which created the Public Service Commission, provides for demotion or the termination of employment in certain instances, and for rights of appeal or investigation in certain situations.

Appeals and Investigations Branch,
Public Service Commission of Canada,
L'Esplanade Laurier,
300 Laurier Ave. West,
Ottawa, Ontario K1A 0M7
(613) 996-4200

Unemployment Insurance Act

This Act, which came into force on July 1, 1971, contains in Part VII, concerning the maintenance of a National Employment Service, provisions prohibiting discrimination on grounds of sex and marital status when referring a worker seeking employment to a job. Any specification or preference based on a bona fide occupational qualification, however, would not be construed as discriminatory.

Employment and Immigration Canada,
Phase IV, Place du Portage,
Ottawa, Ontario K1A 0J9

The Employment Equity Act, 1986

This Act's purpose is to achieve equality in the workplace by requiring federally regulated employers with 100 or more employees to identify and eliminate discriminatory practices and to institute positive policies and make reasonable accommodation to ensure the representation of women, aboriginal peoples, disabled persons, and visible minorities. The scheme is voluntary in the sense that the Act does not contain any sanctions for failure to achieve employment equity. However, the employee must prepare equity plans and submit information that can be used by the Canadian Human Rights Commission to determine if there has been any violation of the Canadian Human Rights Act.

The Federal Contractors Program

This program requires that federal government suppliers of goods and services with 100 or more employees bidding on government contracts worth $200,000 or more commit themselves to implement employment equity as a condition of their bid.

Failure to make a satisfactory commitment to employment equity could result in a bid being declared invalid.

Suppliers who make an employment equity commitment and who are awarded contracts will be subject to on-site reviews.

Alberta

The Individual's Rights Protection Act 1972, Amended 1980 and 1985

This Act, which replaces the former Human Rights Act, prohibits discrimination in employment on a number of grounds including sex and marital status unless based on a bona fide occupational requirement. The legislation also prohibits employers from paying their employees of one sex at a lower rate than those of the other sex for work of a similar or substantially similar nature in the same establishment. If males and females are performing similar duties in the same job location, they must be paid equally.

> Alberta Human Rights Commission,
> Room 902, 10808—99th Avenue,
> Edmonton, Alta. T5K 0G2
> (403) 427-3116

British Columbia

Human Rights Act, 1984

This Act prohibits discrimination in employment on the basis of race, religion, colour, age, marital status, ancestry, place of origin, political belief, physical or mental disability, sex (unless related to the maintenance of public decency), conviction for a criminal or summary conviction charge (unless related to the occupation or employment). The statute also prohibits an employer from discriminating between male and female employees by employing an employee of one sex for work at a rate of pay that is less than the rate of pay at which an employee of the other sex is employed by that employer for similar or substantially similar work.

> British Columbia Council of Human Rights,
> Ministry of Labour,
> Parliament Buildings,
> Victoria, B.C. V8V 1X4
> (604) 389-3877

Manitoba

The Human Rights Act, 1970, Amended 1974, 1975, 1976, 1977, 1982

This Act prohibits discrimination on a number of grounds including race, nationality, religion, colour, age, marital status, physical or mental handicap, ethnic or national origin, political beliefs, and family status, in any term or condition of employment including advertising related to employment.

The Manitoba Human Rights Commission also investigates pregnancy-related complaints on the ground of sex and family status, sexual harassment complaints on the grounds of sex, and equal pay complaints on the grounds of sex.

The Manitoba statute differs from the majority of other provincial jurisdictions in that age is not defined, therefore extending protection both upwards and downwards. As a result, compulsory retirement in Manitoba is a contravention of the Human Rights Act if termination is based on age.

As amended in 1975, Part IV of the Employment Standards Act prohibits employers from paying male and female employees different scales of wages for the same or substantially the same work performed in the same establishment.

Manitoba Human Rights Commission,
1007—330 Portage Avenue,
Winnipeg, Man. R3C 0C4
(204) 944-3007

Employment Standards Branch,
Manitoba Department of Labour,
Norquay Bldg., Room 607,
401 York Avenue,
Winnipeg, Man. R3C 0V8
(204) 945-3354

New Brunswick

Human Rights Code, 1973, Amended 1976

The Code prohibits discrimination in employment and some other activities falling under provincial jurisdiction on the grounds of race, colour, religion, national origin, ancestry, place of origin, age (19 years and over), mental disability, physical disability, marital status and sex.

The Code applies to advertisements for jobs, job application forms, job interviews, employment referrals, hiring, termination, working conditions, fringe benefits, equal pay, union membership, and racial, sexual and other harassment, as well as other aspects of employment. Mandatory retirement is prohibited except when based on a pension plan.

Certain exceptions apply. Employers who wish to be exempted from any provision of the Act because of bona fide occupational qualifications must apply to the Human Rights Commission for an exemption.

New Brunswick Human Rights Commission,
P.O. Box 6000,
Fredericton, N.B. E3B 5H1
(506) 453-2301

Newfoundland

The Newfoundland Human Rights Code, 1970, Amended 1973, 1974, 1978, 1979, 1981, 1984

This Act provides protection against discrimination in employment on grounds of race, religion, religious creed, sex, marital status, mental disability, physical disability, political opinion, colour, ethnic, national or social origin, and age between 19 and 65.

The statute prohibits differences in wages between male and female employees for the same or similar work performed in the same establishment, under the same or similar working conditions and requiring the same or similar skill, effort, and responsibility. It also provides that a female employee performing the same or similar work in the same establishment, under the same or similar working conditions as a male employee, shall have the same opportunities for training, advancement, pension rights, and insurance benefits as those applicable to the male employee.

The code was amended in 1983 to provide for protection against harassment, sexual solicitation, and the approval of special programs. It was amended again, in 1984, to provide for protection against discrimination on the grounds of mental disability.

Newfoundland Human Rights Commission,
P.O. Box 4750,
St. John's, Nfld. A1C 5T7
(709) 737-2709

Northwest Territories

Fair Practices Act, R.S.N.W.T. 1974, Amended 1978, 1980, 1981, 1983, 1984

Under this statute, as amended, it is prohibited to discriminate adversely in any term or condition of employment, in hirings or dismissals, in advertising related to employment, in employment applications and interviews, and in accommodation, because of race, creed, colour, sex, marital status, nationality, ancestry, place of origin, handicap, age, family, or because of a conviction for which a pardon has been granted.

Trade unions are prohibited from denying full membership, expelling, suspending or otherwise discriminating against any of its members, and from discriminating against any person in regard to his employment by an employer, because of the same prohibited grounds of discrimination.

Adverse discrimination in any term or condition of employment because of a person's place of residence is prohibited.

The Act provides for equal pay for females performing similar or substantially similar work to males, employed by the same employer.

Employers and trade unions are prohibited from discriminating against any person who has made a complaint or participated in any proceeding under the Act.

Head, Labour Services,
Dept. of Justice and Public Services,
Government of the Northwest Territories,
P.O. Box 1320,
Yellowknife, N.W.T. X1A 2L9
(403) 873-7486

Nova Scotia

The Nova Scotia Human Rights Act, 1969

The Act, first passed in 1969 and subsequently amended several times, prohibits discrimination in employment (including terms and conditions of employment, advertising for employment and use of application forms connected with employment) on the basis of race, colour, religion, creed, sex, physical handicap, national origin, ethnic origin, marital status or age (between 40 and 65 years of age). The Act is administered by the Nova Scotia Human Rights Commission.

The Labour Standards Code of Nova Scotia forbids an employer to pay a female employee a lesser wage than a male employee for the same work, done in the same establishment under similar working conditions and which requires equal skill, effort and responsibility. Under the Code there is also protection for a pregnant employee who has completed at least a year's service under the same employer. An employer is also forbidden to discriminate against an employee because garnishment proceedings have been or may be taken against the employee. The Code is administered by the Labour Standards Branch of the Nova Scotia Department of Labour and Manpower.

Nova Scotia Human Rights Commission,
P.O. Box 2221,
Halifax, N.S. B3J 3C4
(902) 424-41111

Labour Standards Branch,
Dept. of Labour and Manpower,
P.O. Box 697, Halifax, N.S. B3J 2T8
(902) 424-4311

Ontario

The Human Rights Code, 1981

This Act prohibits discrimination in employment on the grounds of race, ancestry, place of origin, colour, ethnic origin, citizenship, creed, sex, age, handicap, record of offences, marital status and family status.

The Employment Standards Act, 1974 provides for equal pay between male and female employees employed by an employer for substantially the same kind of work performed in the same establishment, under similar working conditions and requiring substantially the same skill, effort and responsibility.

The Act further prohibits any distinction, exclusion or preference on grounds of age, sex or marital status with respect to any fund, plan, arrangement or benefit provided or offered by an employer to his or her employees, except as provided in the Regulations.

Ontario Human Rights Commission,
Rm. M-1-59A, Macdonald Block,
Queen's Park,
Toronto, Ont. M7A 1T7
(416) 965-7931

The Pay Equity Act, 1987

Ontario passed the Pay Equity Act in June 1987, requiring employers in the broader public sector and in the private sector to adjust pay inequities. This Act requires employers to eliminate systematic gender discrimination in employment by implementing pay equity plans. These plans must provide for the selection of gender-neutral job evaluation system which will enable the comparison of predominantly female groups of jobs with predominantly male groups of jobs. Where a union holds bargaining rights for any employees affected by the plans, the employer must bargain with the union over the content of the pay equity plan. In the event of failure to reach agreement, an arbitrator can impose a plan on the parties.

A Pay Equity Commission is empowered to hear complaints, to ensure that pay equity plans comply with the Act and are properly enforced.

Prince Edward Island

The Human Rights Act, 1975

This Act prohibits discrimination in employment on the basis of race, religion, creed, colour, sex, marital status, ethnic or national origin, age, physical disability and/or mental disability, and political belief. Further, it is prohibited for an employer to pay employees different scales of wages for the same work performed with the same qualifications.

P.E.I. Human Rights Commission,
P.O. Box 2000,
Charlottetown, P.E.I. C1A 7N8
(902) 894-7797

Quebec

Charter of Human Rights and Freedoms, 1975, Amended 1976, 1979, 1983

Following recent amendments to this statute, the prohibited grounds of discrimination in matters of employment now include race, colour, sex, pregnancy, sexual orientation, civil status, age except as provided by law, religion, political convictions, language, ethnic or national origin, social condition, a handicap or the use of any means to palliate a handicap. The Charter provides for equal wages to be paid to all employees performing equivalent work at the same establishment.

Under section 18.2, "No one may dismiss, refuse to hire or otherwise penalize a person in his employment owing to the mere fact that he was found guilty or that he pleaded guilty to a penal or criminal offence, if the offence was in no way connected with the employment or if the person has obtained a pardon for the offence."

Commission des droits de la personne du Québec
360, rue Saint-Jacques,
Montréal, Qué. H2Y 1P5
(514) 873-5146

Saskatchewan

The Saskatchewan Human Rights Code, 1979

This statute prohibits discrimination in employment because of race, creed, religion, colour, sex (including pregnancy or pregnancy-related illnesses), marital status, age, ancestry, or place of origin. Discrimination is prohibited in all areas of employment, including advertising, application forms, interviews, hiring, wages, promotion, demotion, dismissal, fringe benefits and any other term or condition of employment. The provisions of the Code do not apply where sex, physical ability or age is a reasonable occupational qualification or requirement for the position or employment.

The Labour Standards Act, 1969, as amended, prohibits an employer from paying a female employee at a rate of pay less than the rate of pay paid to a male employee, or vice versa, for similar work done in the same establishment under similar working conditions and requiring similar skills, effort and responsibility, except where such payment is made pursuant to a seniority or merit system.

Although the Code takes precedence over all other Acts unless they are declared by an Act of legislature to be exempt from the Code, no provision of the Code dealing with employment may limit or enlarge upon the rights of female persons provided by the Labour Standards Act.

Saskatchewan Human Rights Commission,
Suite 802, 224—4th Avenue South,
Saskatoon, Sask. S7K 5M5
(306) 664-5952

Labour Standards Branch,
Saskatchewan Dept. of Labour,
1914 Hamilton Street,
Regina, Sask. S4P 4V4
(306) 787-2438/2486

Yukon Territory

Fair Practices Act, 1963

This Act, as amended in 1974, prohibits discrimination in any term and condition of employment by employers, prospective employers or trade unions and in advertising, based on race, religion, religious creed, colour, ancestry, sex, marital status or ethnic or national origin. The Act makes provision for filing, investigating and settlement of complaints. The investigating officer makes recommendations to the Commissioner who may issue an order to effect the recommendations. Orders are appealable to the court. Investigations are conducted by the Labour Services Branch of the Department of Justice.

The Employment Standards Act, as proclaimed in 1985, prohibits an employer from paying a female employee at a lesser rate of pay than that paid to a male employee, or vice versa, "for similar work, under similar working conditions, in the same establishment, the performance of which requires similar skill, effort and responsibility except where such payment is made pursuant to seniority, merit or production system or on a differential based on any factor other than sex.

Labour Services Administrator,
Department of Justice,
Government of Yukon,
P.O. Box 2703,
Whitehorse, Yukon Y1A 2C6
(403) 667-5312

12

Rights Arbitration: Current Practices, Problems and Innovative Suggestions

MICHAEL MACNEIL

INTRODUCTION

Legislative regulation of the collective bargaining process seeks to further a number of goals. The public interest is said to require industrial harmony and peace so that productivity and efficiency in the manufacture of goods and supply of services can be maximized. Secondly, the active participation of workers in determining the terms and conditions under which they work reflects society's commitment to democratic structures and values. Furthermore, the participation of workers leads to their moral commitment to the outcome (Arthurs, 1985). None of these goals absolutely requires that the collective agreement itself be treated as a legally binding contract. Indeed, the prevailing legal attitude in Great Britain is that the parties do not intend the collective agreement to be binding and therefore its enforceability is a matter of negotiation, power, and moral obligation, or depends on the extent to which individual contracts incorporate the terms of the collective agreement.

In Canada, a different legal regime prevails. The collective agreement is a contract binding the employer, the union, and the employees. As a result, once the contract takes effect, disagreements over terms and conditions of work are transformed into legal disputes over contractual rights which may be resolved through an adjudicative process. This is combined with a prohibition on strikes and lockouts during the term of the agreement, creating a system which in theory minimizes disharmony except during those periods when a new contract is negotiated. As well, the employer's powers are legally limited by the agreement, fulfilling employees' desire to have some voice in controlling their own workplace.

A critical element in this regulatory scheme is the means whereby disputes over rights are settled. If the process is to produce the desired goal of maintaining production uninterrupted by wildcat strikes, the employer, the union, and the employees must be willing or required to resort to and accept the results of the rights arbitration process. Rights or grievance arbitration (the terms are synonymous) is both mandated by legislation and is included as a term of collective agreements. It has become firmly embedded in our industrial relations framework. Why it has predominated, its benefits, drawbacks, and the substantive and procedural issues that form the core of rights arbitration will be analyzed in the remainder of this chapter.

JUSTIFICATIONS FOR ARBITRATION

Enforcing collective agreements through arbitration has been compulsory or quasi-compulsory in Canada since 1944 (Carrothers, 1965, 357). However, arbitration had been well-known as early as the 1920s through the agreement of the parties (Arthurs, 1985, 115). Even where statutes give the parties the option of resolving disputes through some means other than arbitration, collective agreements almost always stipulate the use of rights arbitration.

An obvious alternative to arbitration is the use of courts. They have, however, been eschewed for a number of reasons. First, the courts themselves limited their own enforcement role in the years prior to 1944 by holding that the collective agreement was not a legally enforceable contract. Second, worker perception of judicial hostility toward collective bargaining made unions extremely reluctant to have courts resolve workplace disputes. Third, a number of advantages were presumed to be inherent in the arbitration device. The parties could structure the process to their own needs, control the selection of arbitrators, and gain the advantage of speed, cost effectiveness, informality, and expertise. Two themes that continue to be the focus of analysis are whether arbitration continues to deliver on these promised advantages, and whether courts are nevertheless able to exert dominant control through judicial review of arbitral awards. These will be addressed later in this chapter.

JURISDICTION

Arbitration boards have authority to resolve disputes only when jurisdiction to so do is conferred upon them. That jurisdiction derives from either the collective agreement, a statute, or in some cases the ad hoc agreement of the parties. A matter is said to be arbitrable when such jurisdiction has been conferred. Normally, an arbitration board has the power to decide whether an issue is arbitrable. The agreement of the parties that a dispute should not be the subject of arbitral resolution may have unexpected consequences. For instance, most provinces require that all differences between the parties respecting a violation of the collective agreement be subject to arbitration. Hence, the labour relations statute may overrule the agreement of the parties.

An illustration of this is provided by a consideration of rules concerning probationary employees. Employers often wish to be able to assess the merits of new employees and to be able to let them go if they turn out to be unsuitable for the position. However, collective agreements normally contain a clause prohibiting discharge except for just cause. To meet the employer's concern for efficient evaluation of new employees, collective agreements sometimes provide that these employees will be considered probationary for a defined length of time and that they are not entitled to grieve a dismissal that takes place during the probationary period. If the collective agreement creates a substantive right not to be dismissed without just cause, but then denies any procedural mechanism by which to protect the right, it violates the statutory requirement. Hence, arbitrators and courts have held that a probationary employee under such a collective agreement is entitled to grieve a dismissal despite the intentions of the union and the employer at the time of bargaining (Brown and Beatty, 1984, 504). This result is moderated to some extent by arbitrators subjecting the dismissal of a probationary employee to a much less stringent standard of review. Furthermore, the parties can agree that a probationary employee has no substantive rights under a collective agreement or that the decision to discharge a probationary employee is solely within the discretion of management.

A different sort of problem arises where a grievance complains of some managerial action but is unable to point to the violation of any specific article of the collective agreement. Arbitrators are normally given the jurisdiction to resolve disputes arising from the interpretation, application, or alleged violation of a collective agreement. Furthermore, it is quite common to provide that the arbitrator may not amend, vary, or add to the collective agreement. Hence, the grievance may not be arbitrable. This has a number of consequences. The employer is able to implement its decision unilaterally without arbitral review. The union is legally prohibited from engaging in a strike as a means of exerting pressure because of the ban on strikes during the collective agreement. The introduction of technological change into the workplace demonstrates the dilemma. If a collective agreement was silent on the issue, it was usually held that an employer could implement technological change without obtaining union agreement, even though the change may have a drastic impact on the employees. The union's inability to challenge the decision has led several legislatures to remove the ban on strikes during the term of the collective agreement where the employer proposes to implement a technological change. This mid-contract right to strike would be permitted only if the parties have failed to include clauses in the collective agreement dealing with adjustment to technological change, and only after negotiations have failed. In practice, the right has seldom been exercised.

THE ROLE OF THE ARBITRATOR

The general problem of gaps in collective agreements has led to a sophisticated analysis of the role of the arbitrator (P. Weiler, 1969). This analysis is directed in part toward determining when and to what extent an arbitrator can be expected to intervene in a dispute over the unilateral exercise of managerial power in the absence of explicit limits contained in the agreement. It further explains how an arbitrator decides even when standards may be found in the agreement.

There are several different ways in which an arbitrator could seek to settle disputes. First, he or she could attempt to act primarily as a mediator. A mediator attempts to help the parties arrive at an accommodation rather than impose a decision upon them. Such an approach acknowledges that the employment relationship is one of continuous adjustment. The existence of a dispute indicates problems in finding consensus which can be alleviated by the intervention of a third party neutral who is able to facilitate communication, warn of the consequences of failure, and suggest innovative solutions. The prime requirement for this approach to be successful is that the parties trust the mediator. This trust in turn depends on the mediator's knowledge of the parties and issues, his or her expertise and tact. Arbitrators in Canada have rarely adopted this approach, but there is growing interest in the use of mediation techniques as a part of the process for settling rights disputes.

A second approach that arbitrators might take is that of an industrial policy maker. This would permit the arbitrator to decide disputes in a manner that best promotes sound industrial relations policy, even if this means relying on standards that do not form part of the parties' agreement. The arbitrator is perceived to have not only a responsibility to the parties but to the wider community, which is affected by the outcomes of workplace disputes. Some support for this view can be drawn from the extent to which arbitration is statutorily mandated, whether or not the parties desire it. Nevertheless, arbitrators and courts have generally eschewed this approach, as well, concerned about the consequence of making decisions on the basis of goals and values that do not emanate from the agreement of the parties.

A third and now-predominant vision perceives the role of the arbitrator as one of adjudication. The arbitrator has the task of determining the facts and applying rules and principles to those facts in resolving the dispute. These rules and principles are derived primarily from the collective agreement from which the arbitrator draws authority. Within this vision, one can differentiate between those who would limit the adjudicative role to strict construction and those who would require the arbitrator to engage in purposive interpretation. The former requires the arbitrator to find an issue not to be arbitrable unless the collective agreement contained a specific clause dealing with the matter. The latter view would require the arbitrator to go beyond the specific wording, to delve intelligently into the purposes of the parties and, from the general language of the agreement, come up with a solution to the particular problem. Even this approach, however, would leave certain disputes beyond the pale of arbitral resolution.

The complexity of purposive interpretation is demonstrated in cases where arbitrators must decide whether an employer is entitled to subcontract when the collective agreement is silent. This issue raises great concern for unions because they fear the impact of subcontracting may be to destroy the integrity of the bargaining unit by reducing the number of employees whom the employer would otherwise employ, and because subcontractors often hire non-unionized workers at lower wages. How is an arbitrator, acting as an adjudicator, to decide such a case? The collective agreement could be viewed from two perspectives. First, it could be claimed to represent the complete agreement of the parties, so that the employer and the union each have only those rights that are contained in the contract. Hence, if there is no clause specifically granting the employer the right to subcontract, it cannot do so without first obtaining the consent of the union. A second approach is to view the collective agreement as preserving for management all those rights which it had formerly exercised, except to the extent they have been limited by the collective agreement. The arbitrator is expected to determine the intention or purpose of the parties in choosing between the two alternatives. The second approach has predominated in part because many early arbitral awards permitted the practice of subcontracting. Parties are presumed to know this history so that if they wished to achieve a different result they could have negotiated a specific provision. This example illustrates the importance of reference to the whole body of arbitral jurisprudence in determining the outcome of a single case. Although no one previous decision will likely be treated as binding by an arbitrator, the predominant approach developed through a series of cases is persuasive, and will be followed except in unusual circumstances.

ARBITRATION AS ADJUDICATION

The concept of the arbitrator acting as an adjudicator has an important function in determining how a variety of disputes will be resolved. An adjudicator must apply rules and principles that are based on some ground other than what the arbitrator personally views as the best outcome, although his or her own values and views of the industrial relations process remain very important. The primary search is to determine what the parties have agreed. This may, however, be extremely difficult. The collective agreement is often vague and ambiguous, reflecting the difficulties of encapsulating agreements in the form of written words, the pressure on the parties at the bargaining table, the inability to foresee all contingencies, and the desirability of not planning for all possibilities in order to be able to conclude bargaining. While in some cases the wording of the collective agreement may clearly provide the rule that determines the outcome, many times the arbitrator is forced to engage in a more extensive search to determine the applicable rule or standard, or to determine how a known standard should be applied in the particular case. There are a number of sources from which guidance can be sought.

Where an arbitrator determines that contract language is ambiguous, he or she is put in the position of determining which of two or more plausible interpretations is to be preferred. The arbitrator is expected to determine what the parties intended, and is thus precluded from merely choosing an interpretation based on personal preference. There are a number of sources that help demonstrate the purpose of the parties. Perhaps the most important is the past practice of the employer. The parties, by their continuing relationship, will have developed implicit agreements about how things should be done in the workplace. By their actions the parties develop rules and principles that form the basis on which their future conduct can be regulated. It is sometimes said that reliance on past practice as an aid to interpretation encourages the development of a common law of the workplace. But the fact that an employer has consistently done something in the past does not necessarily prevent it from changing its practice. If there is no language in the collective agreement that can be read as a limitation on the exercise of managerial prerogatives, then the employer will be entitled to implement changes.

In these situations where the parties have failed to reflect their agreement adequately in the written words of the contract, resorting to the negotiating history may also be useful. Again, this is permitted only if the clause is ambiguous. Negotiation history consists of what the parties may have said about the issue during bargaining or notes that may have been kept. The danger is that faulty memories may provide an inadequate reconstruction of events, so that an arbitrator must carefully evaluate how much weight to give to such evidence.

A further important source of guidance derives from the extensive body of legislation in the modern state. Statutes are extremely important both as aids in interpreting ambiguous language and because there are many instances when specific terms and conditions of employment may be the subject of direct legislative regulation. An assumption is made that the parties contracted in the context of the statutory framework, so that its provisions are useful in fleshing out values and assumptions within which the parties agreed. For example, in *Re Ottawa West End Villa Ltd. and Ontario Nurses' Association*, the arbitrator had to decide whether the term "monetary benefit" used in the collective agreement included premium pay for those who worked on a holiday. To hold so would mean that part-time and relief nurses would be denied a benefit guaranteed by the Ontario Employment Standards Act. Hence, it was concluded that "monetary benefit" should not be interpreted as referring to premium pay.

A more difficult issue is whether an arbitrator can rely on a statutory provision where the collective agreement is silent or clearly contradicts the statutory standard. The consensus now appears to be that where a collective agreement provision violates a statutory standard, the arbitrator can hold the provision to be null and void. However, the arbitrator has no jurisdiction to enforce a statutory standard in the face of a gap in a collective agreement (Brown and Beatty, 1984, 80). For example, if a collective agreement provided for differential wage rates for male and female employees who were performing identical jobs, the arbitrator could declare the clause requiring that women be paid less to be void. However, if a collective agreement failed to provide for a right to vacation pay, a grieved employee would have to seek a remedy through the enforcement mechanism created by the statute, and not from an arbitrator. It is important to realize that any interpretation of a statute by an arbitrator will be subject to closer scrutiny by the courts than an interpretation given to a collective agreement.

There are some occasions when an employer or union will feel aggrieved when the other party seeks to rely on the strict wording of the collective agreement. The claim is made that the other party by its words or its actions has effectively promised not to insist on its strict rights under a collective agreement, and hence should be prevented from doing so. If it can be shown that the aggrieved party has relied to its detriment on these words or this conduct, many arbitrators will apply the doctrine of promissory estoppel in favour of the party who has so relied. For example, in *City of Kitchener* (1983), an employer had for a considerable time followed the practice of paying temporarily disabled fire fighters their full wages, although nothing in the contract required this. The city proposed a modification to its existing practice during negotiations for a new contract, but withdrew the proposal in the face of union opposition. Once the new agreement was signed, the city announced it would discontinue its practice, relying on the lack of any obligation in the contract. The arbitrator held that the employer was stopped from implementing the change because, by withdrawing its proposal during negotiation, it had represented that the practice would continue. The union had settled, in reliance on this representation, without insisting that the wording of the collective agreement be changed to reflect their understanding. As can be seen, the elements of the doctrine of estoppel require that there be a promise, either in words or conduct (or possibly through silence); an intention that the other party act in reliance on the promise; and some form of reliance and detriment resulting from the act of reliance (Brown and Beatty, 1984, 83). The significance of the doctrine is that the arbitrator supercedes the strict wording of the collective agreement to provide a resolution to the dispute. The arbitrator is, however, still acting adjudicatively because the principles upon which he or she relies have been developed in the context of ensuring that parties to a contract do not take undue advantage of their contractual rights in order to perpetrate an injustice.

One final example illustrates the difficulty in defining the role of the arbitrator. In many situations an employer is granted discretion to make and implement decisions. This discretion may be granted in a general management rights clause or may be granted with respect to a more specific matter. Many grievances arise because it is felt that management has exercised its discretion inappropriately. The issue is whether the arbitrator can review the management decision in situations where no express standards for review are contained in the collective agreement. There is no consensus on this issue. Many arbitrators believe it is appropriate for them to limit the exercise of managerial discretion by ensuring that decisions are not made in bad faith, discriminatorily, arbitrarily, or possibly unreasonably. Others, however, have held that in the absence of standards set out in the collective agreement, an arbitrator would be exceeding his or her jurisdiction by fettering managerial discretion. The Ontario Court of Appeal has held that in exercising its discretion under a managerial rights clause, management's decision was unreviewable but that in exercising its right to designate employees as permanent, management must act reasonably. It is possible to characterize such arbitral review as adjudicative, because it proceeds on the basis of proof and reasoned argument, applying standards of justice that arise as a matter of implication from the nature of the relationship (Beatty, 1984, 145).

THE ARBITRATION PROCESS

Earlier it was suggested that some of the reasons why arbitration prevailed as the primary means for dispute resolution were its informality, speed, and cost effectiveness, the expertise of the arbitrator and the ability of the parties to control the process. An examination of the mechanics of the process reveals a number of features that both distinguish it from and make it similar to judicial processes.

A fundamental difference between arbitration and courts is the ability of the parties to select their own arbitrator. This can be done in a number of ways. Frequently, collective agreements require a tripartite arbitration board to which each of the parties selects a nominee. These nominees represent the interests of the parties and are responsible for selecting the neutral chairperson for the board. Only if they are unable to agree on a chairperson does the government become involved, choosing a chairperson from a list of experienced arbitrators. The value of tripartite boards is said to lie in the ability of the nominees to assess, criticize and help shape the final decision so that it will be most acceptable to the parties. The decision is made by means of a majority, which normally means the neutral chairperson and one of the nominees. Occasionally, however, there is unanimity among the members of the board.

Arbitration boards can take other forms. The collective agreement may specify that only a single arbitrator is to be appointed, to be selected by agreement on an ad hoc basis for each arbitration. Alternatively, the collective agreement may name a list of arbitrators with rotation through the names on the list. Only one arbitrator may be named to decide all arbitrations between the parties. In such a case, the arbitrator is sometimes called the umpire. Increasing concern about the speed and efficiency of arbitration has led to legislative intervention and occasionally more innovative collective agreement provisions. These will be examined at the end of the chapter.

Once the arbitration board is selected the chairperson or single arbitrator is usually responsible, after consultation, for deciding on a date and venue. Hotel meeting rooms are often the site of hearings. The nature of the dispute is defined by the grievance wherein the grievor is expected to indicate the clauses of the collective agreement claimed to have been violated.

The parties in a hearing are usually the employer and the union. The union represents individual employees and in fact decides whether a grievance should be pursued in arbitration. In making that decision, the union is under a duty to represent fairly members of the bargaining unit.

The hearing can be divided into three phases. In the first phase any objections to the jurisdiction of the board or to the arbitrability of the grievance will be argued (Sanderson, 1985, 46). For example, collective agreements often contain provisions requiring that each step in the grievance process be initiated within a specified time. If there has been delay, it may be claimed that the matter is no longer arbitrable. An elaborate set of rules has been developed to determine whether failure to comply with time limits precludes a hearing on the merits. In some provinces, such as Ontario, this has been supplemented by a statutory provision allowing the arbitrator to proceed despite the non-compliance with time limits so long as there is good reason for non-compliance and the other party will not be prejudiced by the delay. This type of issue will be argued in the preliminary phase.

The second phase comprises the introduction of evidence. One of the major functions of the arbitrator is to decide what the facts are when these are in dispute. This is a function in which arbitrators act much like judges. The hearing is an adversarial process, which means that the responsibility for introducing evidence is left to the parties. Witnesses are examined and cross-examined, and the arbitrator hears only those witnesses whom the parties choose to call. The extent to which the arbitrator is able to obtain a clear understanding of events depends on the memory of witnesses, their ability to communicate, their credibility, and the skill of the parties' representatives in asking questions. The parties are sometimes represented by legal counsel and sometimes by a member of their own staff.

The third phase of the hearing consists of the argument. This permits the parties to summarize the evidence, to indicate the principles that each thinks should be applied, and to explain how they should be applied to the facts. Relevant previous arbitral decisions will be brought to the board's attention. A decision is usually made some time after the hearing, with written reasons supplied. This decision is binding on the parties and can be enforced in the same manner as a court order.

There are a number of features of the hearing that distinguish it from a trial in court. The surroundings are much less formal. The rules of evidence are less stringent so that an arbitrator may be able to hear some types of evidence that would be inadmissible in a court. However, the reliance on the adversarial system, the swearing of witnesses and the complex legal rules and terminology all bear resemblance to court-like proceedings.

SUBSTANTIVE ISSUES

There are a number of types of disputes that form the vast majority of cases with which arbitrators must deal. These include disciplinary cases, seniority, promotion, and layoff cases, work assignment disputes and disagreements over benefits. Increasing emphasis and awareness of human rights are bringing before arbitrators grievances concerning such matters as discrimination, equal pay, sexual harassment, mandatory retirement, and privacy. This section will investigate in some detail the substantive law that is developing in some of these areas.

The arbitrator's role in resolving conflict comes to the fore in those cases where an employee has been disciplined or discharged. Collective agreements commonly stipulate that an employer is entitled to discipline or discharge only for just cause. From this brief and pithy phrase arbitrators have erected an elaborate framework within which they work out the rules and principles that will be applied in a particular case. The arbitrators have several functions to perform. They must determine, on the basis of evidence presented at the hearing, what the facts are. They must then determine whether these facts justify employer disciplinary action. Finally, even if some disciplinary action is justified, the arbitrator must determine whether the particular discipline is commensurate with the seriousness of the conduct, given a wide range of factors such as the grievor's record, seniority, past employer practice, extenuating circumstances and so on. Arbitrators generally have the power to order a lesser penalty where some cause is found, and to order reinstatement and payment of damages (usually lost wages) where there was no cause for dismissal.

A number of important principles have been developed to regulate the disciplinary system. For instance, employers cannot introduce additional reasons to justify their actions other than those given at the time of the action. If the employer is relying on the violation of a plant rule, there are requirements that the rule be reasonable, that it not violate any terms of the collective agreement, that it be made known to the employee, and that the employee be warned of the consequences of breaching the rule. In some situations, a particular action by an employee may not be regarded, if viewed alone, as warranting dismissal. However, when viewed with regard to the employee's record as a whole, it may be seen as a culminating incident for which dismissal is justified. Employers are thus encouraged to introduce systems of progressive discipline, using discharge only for egregious cases or where the employee has demonstrated by a consistent pattern of conduct an inability to conform to the acceptable standards of the workplace.

One of the major developments in arbitral jurisprudence is the scope of remedial authority. Courts normally refuse reinstatement as a remedy for wrongful dismissals. Arbitrators, however, have resorted to the practice of reinstatement as the natural response when the employer has been unable to demonstrate just cause. Several studies have examined the success of this remedy, looking at whether the employee who is reinstated is likely to avoid further disciplinary action or discharge (Adams, 1979; Shantz and Rogow, 1984). In a majority of cases it appears that employees can be successfully reintegrated into the workforce. Arbitrators are willing to reinstate employees whose problems stem from alcohol or drug dependency on condition that they receive treatment and are in a position to resume duties with some expectation of being able to handle the problem. The employer is thus sometimes involved in the process of rehabilitation, a major goal in many of the discipline and discharge decisions.

Another central substantive right created by collective agreements that forms the focus of many disputes is seniority. Unions regard seniority as important because it protects the investment of the worker's life with the employer. It also provides an objective means of making decisions, guarding against possible arbitrariness, discrimination, or favouritism that might occur if decisions were left to the discretion of management. There are two forms that seniority takes. The first links the value of benefits to seniority: for example, length of vacation, choice of shifts, pension benefits, etc. The second involves competition for scarce work, especially where promotions and layoffs occur. The exact form that seniority takes depends on the wording of the collective agreement. For instance, seniority may be defined in terms of one's length of service merely within one division, or it may extend across the whole plant or employer's operations.

The importance of looking at the exact wording may be illustrated by examining promotion clauses. Some clauses provide that seniority is one of several factors to be considered in determining which applicant will be entitled to the job. Others stipulate that seniority will be determinative only if two applicants are otherwise of equal merit. The strongest form of protection for senior employees is given when the employer is required to grant the job to the most senior qualified applicant. The employer will initially undertake the task of assessing qualifications of applicants. One of the issues the arbitrator must face is to what extent this assessment will be subject to review. In particular, it has been held in some cases that the employer must be correct in applying the appropriate criteria, so that arbitrator can substitute his or her own judgment if it differs from that of the employer. On the other hand, some arbitrators believe that insofar as the employer acts in good faith, there should be no interference with the decision.

Arbitrators have been increasingly faced with disputes that raise human rights issues. The arbitrator's authority to deal with these cases arises from several sources. Many collective agreements contain clauses prohibiting discrimination, either generally or on a number of named grounds. As already indicated, arbitrators also rely on statutes to interpret or possibly override the collective agreement. Finally, many arbitrators are willing to invoke implied limitations on the exercise of managerial discretion, especially if the managerial action is discriminatory or in bad faith.

Arbitrators have, for example, held that the maintenance of separate seniority lists for male and female employees is a violation of human rights legislation (Brass Craft Canada Ltd., 1983); that the exercise of a managerial right to transfer is improperly exercised when based solely on the physical disability of the employee (Wentworth County Board of Education 1984); and that managerial discretion in promotions cannot be used discriminatorily (Toronto Public Library Board, 1984). It has also been held that an employee who has sexually harassed co-workers is subject to dismissal by the employer (Mourant vs. Treasury Board, 1985) and that an employer is in violation of a collective agreement provision prohibiting harassment if it fails to exercise due diligence in preventing and investigating complaints of harassment by its employees (Canada Post Corporation, 1983).

One issue that often arises is whether an employer is entitled to require employees to retire against their wishes at a specified age, even though the employee is still capable of performing the job. Employees might claim that this is discrimination on the basis of age. They are, however, precluded from relying on their protection from dismissal except for just cause, because it has been held by the courts that retirement is not a dismissal. In Quebec and Manitoba, compulsory retirement policies have been prohibited unless the employer demonstrates there is a bona fide reason for them. In other provinces, while discrimination on the basis of age is prohibited by human rights legislation, age is defined to protect only those who are younger than sixty-five years. As a result, an employer could discriminate against a person at the age of sixty-five by retiring her without violating the statute. Arbitrators have disagreed whether clauses in collective agreements prohibiting discrimination on the basis of age should be interpreted to be consistent with the definition of age contained in human rights legislation. If they do so, then the employer will be entitled to implement uniform retirement policy. It is clear, however, that unless a collective agreement provision or statute limits the right of the employer to implement a mandatory retirement scheme, the employer has the right to do so.

The introduction of the Charter of Rights may have an impact on retirement schemes and other issues. Section 15 of the Charter guarantees equal protection and benefit of the law without discrimination. Such public sector employers as governments, universities, hospitals, and municipalities may be directly subject to the Charter so that if they discriminate on the basis of age without reasonable justification, they will be subject to judicial and arbitral control. Whether the same can be said of private sector employers is more doubtful, since the Charter appears to protect individuals only against governmental action. These issues have not yet been fully determined. A more indirect method by which the Charter may apply is to prohibit provisions in human rights legislation that limit the protection of the statute to those under the age of sixty-five. Several cases are presently before the courts, and it is likely to be several years before the issue is finally settled.

The Charter may apply in a number of other contexts. For instance, an employer may discipline employees for their off-work conduct. The Charter guarantee of freedom of speech or conscience could become crucially important in some of these disputes if the employee claims to have been engaged in a protected activity. Again, the same issues of whether the Charter applies to the employment relationship will have to be determined. At this time, arbitrators' opinions on the issue have diverged.

Privacy is an important, albeit difficult-to-define concept to which workers sometimes turn in protesting employer action. Employers' demands for medical information to permit evaluation of employees' fitness to continue working or claim sickness benefits are sometimes controversial. Such requests are legitimate only if sanctioned by a statutory or contractual right. The employer must point to specific language or demonstrate that there is no practical alternative before insisting that the employee be examined by a doctor of the employer's choice.

Another privacy issue arises where an employee insists on searching the person or personal effects of employees. The employer's right to protect itself against theft must be balanced by the employee's privacy interest. Generally, unless there is an express or implied contractual right, the employer is not entitled to demand that the employee submit to a search. The existence of an implied right depends on the past practice in the workplace, on whether the person or only the personal effects or locker of the worker are to be searched, and on whether a small group of workers is singled out or everyone is subjected to the search. Again, the Charter of Rights may be invoked, since it prohibits unreasonable searches.

Arbitration is not necessarily the only forum in which many of these issues may be determined. Human rights statutes create their own enforcement mechanism to which employees may resort. In some cases, however, a human rights commission will suspend its investigation of a matter if the issue is being pursued through arbitration. Thus, the arbitration process plays an important role in enforcing human rights policy.

JUDICIAL REVIEW

The extent to which arbitral awards should be subject to court review is a complex issue. The arguments favouring dispute resolution through arbitration also support limiting judicial review. The parties' ability to shape the procedures to their own requirements, the desirability of quick, informal and relatively inexpensive hearings, the need for finality and certainty, and the expertise of arbitrators in industrial relations all strongly enhance the case for making arbitration awards final and non-reviewable.

However, a strong tradition of judicial control over contract interpretation and over statutorily authorized decision makers has predominated. Supporters of judicial review rely on concepts of the rule of law to argue that it is necessary that parties are guaranteed fair hearings, that arbitrators do not step beyond the bounds of their powers, and that any errors of law made by the arbitrators should be corrected. The source of the courts' power rests in most jurisdictions on inherent court powers. Only in Nova Scotia and Newfoundland is there a statutory Arbitration Act that applies to labour arbitration. In British Columbia, the Court of Appeal is given a limited right of review. In other provinces judicial review depends on common-law principles or their statutory equivalent.

Courts have the power to shape the standards of judicial review. They have developed a range of principles for determining when intervention is justified. Arbitrators are required to act impartially and in accordance with the rules of natural justice, to act within jurisdiction, and not to commit errors of law. The courts will, however, not quash a decision, even though they believe an error of law was made in the interpretation of the collective agreement, if the reading given to the language in dispute was reasonable. The arbitrator's interpretation of a statute, on the other hand, must accord with that which the court favours; otherwise it will be struck down. At one time, courts would refuse to set aside an error of law arising in a consensual arbitration where the specific question of law had been submitted to the arbitrator. However, this category has become of minor importance, because most arbitration boards will be considered statutory rather than consensual, and because only seldom will it be held that a specific question of law has been submitted.

Exceeding jurisdiction is an even more difficult category to define. Arbitrators can be said to exceed their authority if they seek to deal with issues that they are not authorized, either by statute or collective agreement, to decide. Alternatively, jurisdiction may be lost if a decision is made in bad faith, on the basis of irrelevant considerations, where there is no evidence to support it, or where there is a failure to consider relevant matters. Even breaches of natural justice are sometimes characterized as jurisdictional errors. The problem is that there is no clear test as to what amounts to a jurisdictional question. Although courts have warned against the danger of being too ready to brand an issue as jurisdictional, the vagueness of the standard often invites parties who have lost in an arbitration to seek judicial review. This undercuts the gains that might be made by treating the award as final.

The concept of natural justice guarantees to the parties the right to a fair hearing. This requires that the parties be entitled to call, examine, and cross-examine witnesses, to be informed of the case that must be met, and to submit arguments concerning these issues. Significantly, arbitrators generally have the right to control procedures so long as these conditions are met.

The requirement that arbitrators be impartial may create difficulties when the parties choose to use tripartite boards. Unions in particular sometimes prefer to nominate members of their staff. The requirement of impartiality, however, extends to the nominees, so that if the other party objects, another non-affiliated nominee must be chosen.

On some occasions, court decisions limiting the power of arbitrators have been modified by legislatures. For instance, the arbitrator's ability to substitute a lesser penalty than that imposed by the employer for employee misconduct is the result of statutory amendments following court decisions holding to the contrary. Similarly, the legislative right of arbitrators to extend time limits in the grievance procedure overruled contrary court decisions. Some legislatures have sought to limit judicial review by means of statutory privative clauses that state either that the arbitrator's decision is final or not subject to certiorari, the name of the writ or process of a court in overturning an award. However, courts have consistently construed these clauses narrowly, and it is unclear whether they have any significant impact on the standard for judicial review.

REFORMING THE PROCESS

Despite the advantages claimed for arbitration, there is much concern about its ability to function to promote the goals outlined at the beginning of the chapter. The development of a complex jurisprudence has increased the legalistic style of argument and reliance on lawyers. Arbitration is often very expensive, so that parties who feel they have a justified grievance may choose not to pursue it because of the costs. Delay, because of increasing formality and the tendency to rely on a small number of experienced arbitrators, can be extremely frustrating, especially in discharge cases. These concerns have led to a number of innovations, both in legislation and collective agreements, designed to expedite the process and encourage alternate means of resolving rights disputes.

In British Columbia, the labour relations board has been given an extensive role in settling grievances. The board is a permanent tribunal that has responsibility for administering many aspects of labour law, such as the certification process and prohibitions on unfair labour practices. Any party may choose to bypass the collective agreement provisions on arbitration and submit the grievance to the board. The board then appoints an industrial relations officer to investigate the dispute and, if possible, to mediate a solution. Evidence indicates that mediation is successful in about seventy percent of the cases (J. Weiler, 1984, 176). If the attempt at mediation is unsuccessful, the industrial relations officer reports the results of the investigation to the board, which can then resolve the dispute or refer the matter back to the parties to be dealt with through the normal arbitration process. If the board settles the dispute itself, it does so without holding a formal hearing, relying instead on the investigation report it receives. This major innovation allows for quick action with a minimum of procedural formality. The labour relations board also has the authority to review arbitral awards. This permits the development of a consistent arbitral jurisprudence by an expert panel that is deeply involved in administering all aspects of labour law policy. Finally, parties are encouraged in British Columbia to develop their own mediation devices by the government's willingness to pay one-third of the mediator's costs. To date, there has been little resort to this provision.

In Ontario, the labour relations board is empowered to hear grievances arising under collective agreements in the construction industry. In these cases, the board, as in British Columbia, can send out an officer to attempt to mediate, which is successful in ninety percent of the cases. However, if mediation is unsuccessful, the Board does not have the option to send the matter back through the normal arbitration process, and normally holds a full-scale hearing. The Board disposes of eighty percent of these cases within two months of application (Ontario Labour Relations Board Annual Report, 1984–85).

The Labour Relations Act also encourages another form of expedited arbitration. Either party can apply to the Minister of Labour to have an arbitrator appointed, ignoring the provisions of the collective agreement. Again, a settlement officer may be appointed to help mediate the dispute. If this is unsuccessful, the arbitrator is required to commence hearings within twenty-one days of appointment. The advantages are the use of the settlement officer, and avoiding the delays that arise from the use of tripartite boards.

In Nova Scotia, an expedited form of arbitration is employed in the construction industry. The parties are expected to name an arbitrator by midnight of the day on which the grievance arose. If they fail to do so, the Minister of Labour may appoint the arbitrator, who is expected to render a decision within forty-eight hours of appointment unless the parties mutually agree to extend the time limit.

These statutory innovations are designed to speed up the process, either by imposing time limits by which things must be done, by diverting cases to tribunals whose permanent staff and bureaucratic structure permit cases to be scheduled more quickly for hearing, or by promoting mediation of cases so that a matter need not be arbitrated at all.

Some employers and unions have, by means of their collective agreement, attempted to fashion arbitration procedures more responsive to their specific needs. These schemes focus on various aspects of the arbitration process that may delay the ultimate decision. Naming the arbitrator in the collective agreement itself saves time that might otherwise be wasted in the selection of personnel. Sometimes, agreements may provide for having an arbitrator available one or more days per month. This avoids difficulties in trying to attempt to schedule hearing dates. The parties may arrange that no legal counsel be present, that examination of witnesses be limited, relying instead on a verbal or written summary of the facts, and that the decision be rendered immediately or within a few days of the hearing. A hearing may be set up, as in the British Columbia longshoring industry, right at the worksite, giving the arbitrator a better understanding of workplace conditions and reducing the sense of alienation from the process that the workers might otherwise feel (J. Weiler, 1984, 181). In designing systems of expedited arbitration, the parties may decide that only certain types of disputes, that do not raise broad policy issues but primarily affect the grievor only, should be handled in the expedited route. Other disputes would be handled in the conventional way.

The experience of mediation through government officers in British Columbia and Ontario has caused some to advocate more extensive resort to this process as a means of avoiding arbitration altogether. As already indicated, mediation appears to be relatively successful in helping the parties resolve their dispute. What is suggested here is not that the arbitrator act as a mediator, but that mediation take place with the assistance of an experienced mediator before the matter is submitted to arbitration. For this process to result in cost and time savings, it must be capable of resolving a high proportion of grievances. It has the advantage of forcing the parties to accommodate each other, an important value in a continuing employment relationship, and one that is not so easily achieved through the adjudicative form of arbitration (Goldberg, 1982).

SUMMARY

The future of rights arbitration depends on its ability to resolve grievances in a fair and efficient manner. The process was originally perceived as primarily a private method of dispute resolution. Increasing legislative regulation of labour relations has put rights arbitration at the forefront of processes designed to promote industrial peace and guarantee worker and management rights. The adjudicative style of arbitration has the strength of enabling decisions to be made in a principled fashion, but the increasing legalization of the process may jeopardize its ability to respond quickly and efficiently in resolving grievances.

The public's interest in the process has induced legislative attempts to modify the process to improve its capacity to achieve its avowed goals. The parties' own sensitivity to the need for streamlined decision making has sparked some innovative variations from the traditional model. Increased awareness of human rights and equality issues may place the arbitration process at the forefront of dealing with these issues in the employment context. A willingness to adapt to new demands and to remedy past failures will be the benchmarks to test the future of rights arbitration.

REFERENCES

Adams, G. W. (1979), *Grievance Arbitration of Discharge Cases.* Kingston, Ont.: Industrial Relations Centre, Queen's University.

Arthurs, H. (1985)," Understanding labour law: The debate over industrial pluralism." *Current Legal Problems* (38): 83–116.

Beatty, D. (1984), "The role of the arbitrator: A liberal version." *University of Toronto Law Journal* 34: 136–169.

Brass Craft Canada Ltd. (1983),11 L.A.C. (3d), 236.

Brown, D. M. and Beatty, D. M. (1984), *Canadian Labour Arbitration* (2nd ed.). Toronto: Canada Law Book.

Canada Post Corporation (1983), 11 L.A.C. (3d), 13.

Carrothers, A. W. R. (1965), *Collective Bargaining in Canada*. Toronto: Butterworths.

City of Kitchener (1983), 11 L.A.C. (3d), 47.

Employment Standards Act (1980), R.S.O. c. 137.

Goldberg, S. B. (1982), "The mediation of grievances under a collective bargaining contract: An alternative to arbitration." *Northwestern University Law Review* 77: 270–315.

Mourant vs. *Treasury Board* (1985), PSSRB Decisions 33.

Ontario Labour Relations Board Annual Report (1984–85), Toronto: Ontario Labour Relations Board.

Ottawa West End Villa Limited (1980), 25 L.A.C. (2d), 65.

Sanderson, J. P. (1985), *Labour Arbitration and All That* (2nd ed.), Aurora, Ont.: Canada Law Book.

Shantz, E. M. and Rogow, R. (1984), "Post-reinstatement experience: A British Columbia Study." *Proceedings of the 21st Annual Meeting of the Canadian Industrial Relations Association*: 184–191.

Toronto Public Library Board (1984), 17 L.A.C. (3d). 22.

Weiler, J. (1984), "Grievance arbitration: The new wave." In J. Weiler and P. Gall (eds.), *The Labour Code of British Columbia in the 1980s*. Vancouver: Carswell Legal Publications.

Weiler, P. (1969), "The role of the arbitrator: Alternative versions." *University of Toronto Law Journal* 19: 16–45.

Wentworth County Board of Education (1984), 14 L.A.C. (3d), 310.

13

Changing Union–Management Relationships*

JEFFREY GANDZ AND CAROL BEATTY

Some exciting, innovative and creative changes in traditional union–management relationships are taking place in North America. New approaches include joint union–management committees at plant and community levels, gain-sharing or broadly based profit sharing, quality-of-worklife experiments of many different types, and the growth of relationships-by-objectives programs in both the private and public sectors (Kochan, 1980; Downie, 1982; Schuster, 1983; Gandz and Beatty, 1986). While the impact of such efforts on overall labour–management relationships may be marginal and slow, the effects on those directly involved can be dramatic.

The nature of the union–management relationship is a matter of strategic choice and can be influenced by managerial action (Kochan, McKersie and Cappelli, 1984). This chapter is based on the belief that managers who are equipped with a good working model for managing change, as well as understanding the nature of union–management relationships, will be in a better position to identify and exploit the opportunity for changing that relationship than those who lack such conceptual frameworks.

THE UNION–MANAGEMENT RELATIONSHIP

Conflict in the Union–Management Relationship

The union–management relationship is a social one, usually of long duration, in which episodes of conflict occur and must be dealt with. These episodes usually take the form of issues that must be negotiated between the parties or resolved through third-party mediation or arbitration. They may be conflicts of interest, in which the gains of one party are usually won at the expense of the other; common problems, in which

*This chapter is based partly on research done with the assistance of a grant from the Education Relations Commission, and we are grateful for the support of Dr. Brian Downie and the professional staff of the Commission.

there is the potential for both parties to gain from problem resolution, although not necessarily to exactly the same extent; and misunderstandings, in which the intentions or desires of one of the parties is misunderstood by the other (Selekman, 1947; Walton and McKersie, 1965; Gandz, 1978).

Conflicts of interest (such as a conflict over how much the base wage rate should be in the next collective agreement) are usually resolved or regulated through a process of distributive bargaining in which the parties negotiate over who gets what share of the pie. Common problems (such as the rehabilitation of a previously excellent employee who has a substance-abuse problem) are resolved through integrative bargaining, or problem solving—the process whereby the parties try to bake a bigger pie. Misunderstandings (such as an unfounded belief that a company is going to contract out its cleaning service) are resolved through communication.

The nature of the issues may not be clear to the parties in the relationship. Common problems and, of course, misunderstandings are often mistakenly approached as conflicts of interest—and sometimes vice versa! There are many reasons for this confusion. At one extreme, it is possible that one party may be ideologically motivated to destroy the other, even if it means suffering itself in the process. More likely, the continuing relationship between the parties lacks trust and is highly competitive, where each party denies the other's legitimate interests and the people involved dislike each other. In such a relationship there is a tendency to see all issues as conflicts of interest rather than as common problems or possible misunderstandings (Pondy, 1967).

Even when the issues are perceived correctly, it may be difficult to tackle them appropriately in such a climate. Problem solving requires the parties to share information, venture tentative solutions, trade ideas without prejudice, and discuss various options (Ury and Fisher, 1978). It requires trust, some acknowledgment of the other party's legitimacy, and a co-operative rather than competitive orientation. It also helps if the people like each other—at least a little. On the other hand, conflicts of interest may require tough, power-based bargaining if each of the parties is to maximize its share of the pie. This bargaining may involve tradeoffs and compromises. Realistically, such bargaining is often going to involve the use of threats, sanctions, and the traditional job actions in which unions and managements engage as each tries to wrest concessions from the other (Walton and McKersie, 1965).

The use of such bargaining tactics may leave a legacy of mistrust, fear, dislike, and disrespect that makes subsequent problem solving difficult or even impossible. This is particularly the case when the parties don't understand the complex nature of collective bargaining and react personally to the process. The issues become inseparable from the personalities.

Figure 13.1
The Bargaining-relationship Cycle

If, on the other hand, the parties try to maintain a very friendly relationship, it may become difficult to use the power tactics that might be helpful in distributive bargaining. Figure 13.1 shows how various incidents that might arise during the collective bargaining relationship are perceived and acted upon and how they influence the bargaining relationship, which in turn influences the genesis and management of subsequent episodes of conflict.

The Constructive Union–Management Relationship

For many years union–management relationships have been described as existing on a spectrum ranging from conflict through containment-aggression, accommodation, co-operation, and collusion. In popular management and mass media this has been simplified further to a simple dichotomy between conflict and co-operation.

This is not a particularly useful notion, since it ignores the reality of both joint and competing interests of labour and management and the often simultaneous needs for both problem solving and distributive bargaining. We prefer to think that relationships are either constructive or destructive. The truly constructive relationship is one in which the parties:

- can identify their common problems and opportunities and engage in the required behaviours to maximize their joint gain from resolving them;
- can engage in negotiations on conflicts of interest without personalizing the issues, maintain trust and respect for the other party,

and leave an aftermath that is conducive to subsequent problem solving;

- can communicate in an open manner so that misunderstandings either don't arise or are dealt with expeditiously (Gandz and Beatty, 1986).

The constructive relationship recognizes both joint and competing interests. It is not collusive; it might be quite adversarial in nature or have the surface appearance of co-operation. But it allows for the maximization of joint gains as well as the pursuit of self-interest.

CHANGING THE UNION–MANAGEMENT RELATIONSHIP

After many years of interaction in collective bargaining, the relationship between the parties may have become institutionalized and embedded in the culture, structure, policies, and practices of the union and management groups. Many people will have come to share common attitudes, beliefs, and assumptions. These will be reflected in the ways in which things are done, the nature and tone of communications, the venues of meetings, the seating of people at those meetings, and a thousand and one substantive or trivial dimensions of their interactions (Russo, 1967). These may be rooted in the past needs of the parties and in the past success that was associated with those behaviours. Such past success has reinforced the value of those behaviours for the parties, thereby encouraging them to carry on in the same way (Dunlop, 1955).

These behaviours and attitudes must be unfrozen. Change must be initiated and implemented, and then the new, emergent, desired behaviours and attitudes must be consolidated (Lewin, 1947; Schein, 1961). In many situations, widespread, radical, sweeping change may not be possible, and something short of this may be all that is achievable. A change in staffing procedures, problem-solving grievance meetings, the avoidance of work sanctions, the smooth functioning of a joint quality-improvement committee might all be the objects of an effort toward change. In total, and over time, such adjustments might add up to a major change in the relationship. Even if this is not the case, small changes may be valued in their own right.

Resisting Change

There is an extensive academic and practitioner literature on why it is that some people resist change (Figure 13.2). Managers need to understand the reasons why people might resent or resist change in order to develop and implement appropriate change-management strategies.

Figure 13.2
Sources of Resistance to Change

Change may be misunderstood or misinterpreted

Change may be contrary to self-interest

Change may come too quickly for people to accept

Change may be required when people lack the capacity to change

Change may violate ideals, values or norms

Change may create feelings of incompetence

Change may generate different opinions about its value to the organization

Change may result in differential benefits for different parties

Change may upset established patterns of relationships

Self-interest

Change may be contrary to self-interest (Skibbins, 1974). Some changes threaten the real interests that people have in maintaining the status quo. They may lose power or influence because of a proposed change; they may have to give up some activity that they enjoy, take on some tasks that they don't like doing, interact with people they dislike; or the nature of the tasks they do may change considerably. This is more than mere inertia—there may actually be some harmful impact or, at least, the possibility of harm. The hardened negotiator may fear losing status if there is a co-operative union–management relationship; the union official may feel unneeded if a grievance-free era is established; managers and employees may fear additional workload if joint committees are established; a negotiator may fear threats from the union to destroy the co-operative relationship that the CEO is so keen on establishing; the union president may fear challenge by a militant and influential faction within the union if he is perceived to co-operate with management.

Misunderstanding and Misinterpretation

Change may be misunderstood or misinterpreted (Kotter and Schlesinger, 1979). It is not unusual for those affected by a change to misunderstand what is happening, or to misinterpret the reasons for the change and the motivations behind it. This is very likely to happen when there is competition between parties, mistrust, dislike, and other attitudes associated with conflictual union–management relations. It is, of course, even more likely when numbers of people are misinformed about proposed change—a common occurrence in labour–management conflict.

Violation of Ideals

Change may violate ideals, values or norms (Skibbins, 1974). People have strongly held beliefs about such issues as management rights, the inherent rightness of the adversarial system, the class struggle, the rights of labour and capital; there are often established norms relating to the confidentiality of certain budgetary information, the rights of unions to be involved in certain types of decisions, the ways in which negotiations are conducted. Some changes actually threaten values, ideals, and norms that may be quite strong, especially in highly cohesive groups.

Disagreement over Change

Change may generate different opinions about its value to the organization. One group may resist change when its members assess the situation differently than another group. Apart from the question of self-interest, the resisting group may believe that the unintended consequences of a change far outweigh the proposed benefits as assessed by others. For example, a local federation affiliate in a school system may resist the proposal of an administration to try single-team bargaining because, in their view, it would be bad for the health of the school system, breeding complacency as a by-product. Or, a decision in an automotive plant to adopt a certain type of shift system may be seen as less productive by the union than it is by management. Whose view is correct is irrelevant. As long as one party disagrees with the other as to the value of change, it will tend to resist it.

Differential Benefits

Change may result in differential benefits for different parties. Both parties may benefit—but if one party benefits more than the other, and the parties are competitive, then the party that benefits least may resist the change. Where two bargaining units see themselves in competition with each other, then one may oppose a changed relationship because it feels that the other stands to gain more from it. Where a shortage of skilled tradespeople encourages management to offer a large wage increase to attract and retain people with the needed skills, the unskilled and semi-skilled employees may resist this because they are not getting as large an increase, even if they are getting some.

Social Relationships

Change may upset established patterns of relationships. People get used to interacting in certain ways, either co-operating or confronting each other, for example. It is upsetting to try to adjust to different ways of interacting, to be nice to someone with whom you have traditionally argued, or to get tough with someone you have been dealing with on a friendly and informal basis. This is most noticeable when people lapse into familiar and traditional ways of negotiating, start playing their usual games at meetings, continuing the intermittent war they have come to expect.

Feelings of Incompetence

Change may create feelings of incompetence (Kotter and Schlesinger, 1979; Tagiuri, 1973). To be successful at demonstrating new behaviours, people must have the ability to perform them, as well as the motivation to do so. Whether or not they are motivated to try them will depend, at least to some extent, on their perception of the probability of success if they do try. If they feel unable to do what is asked of them, people will resist change that calls for new behaviours. If they try and then fail because they lack the ability, they will not be encouraged to persevere. While it may seem a simple matter to ask people to solve problems instead of negotiating over who gets what share of the pie, it's not that easy! And without the appropriate training and confidence building, they may resist such urging.

Rate of Change

Change may come too quickly for people to accept. Some people may resist change, even if it is in their self-interest, because it is unexpected, sudden, or radical in their view (Stanislao and Stanislao, 1983). Inertia, or the innate desire to maintain the status quo, must be overcome. Lack of advance information and adequate preparation often seem to result in such a reflex rejection.

Incapacity to Change

Change may be required when people lack the capacity to change. Although people may agree that change is needed, at the time that new behaviours are being demanded of them they may simply be overworked and lack the capacity to respond. If the new relationship requires membership in many new committees, for example, this may be beyond the capacity of an administrator at a particular time. Or if additional training is required to deal with the change, who will get the day-to-day work done while the training is undertaken? People may lack the time, the resources, the assistance to respond to new requirements.

Perception or Reality?

These reasons why people may resist change—or may resent it when they are coerced into change—may be based in reality or may be unfounded perceptions. Someone may be too overworked to participate in a joint committee, or may simply feel overworked. The chief negotiator may actually lose status when work sanctions are only a remote possibility, or may wrongly perceive a loss in status. Someone, lacking the facts, may be mistaken about his or her new role in a changed relationship. What is important is that the perception, rather than the reality, shapes the individual's feelings and behaviour.

Changes by Unions and Managements

In his highly influential book on labour relations, Kochan (1980) summarized seven basic propositions about change in union–management relations that clearly reflect the factors associated with accepting or rejecting change, described above.

First, he suggests that unions and employers will be reluctant to embark on significant efforts to change their established practices unless there are strong external and internal pressures to do so. Inertia must be overcome; if things are running smoothly, people will not want to rock the boat.

He suggests that both parties must perceive that it is in their self-interest to change in the direction being promoted; alternatively, one party must see significant costs of failing to go along with the other's efforts toward change.

Kochan also discusses the fact that implementing any change involves major political risk to both union and management representatives. For change to be successful, these risks must be managed: the political leaders of management and union groups must be able to anticipate and overcome them. Kochan suggests that the role of union leaders is fraught with difficulties, since they must walk the tightrope between appearing to be the source of the benefits yet remaining independent and "un-co-opted" by management. This implies that either management or some third party (government, consultant, mediator, or other) will be the driving force behind change at the implementation phase so that union leaders can avoid the political risk associated with changing the status quo.

Whatever change is implemented must deliver the promised goods. People in diverse interest groups must be able to see results if they are to be encouraged to pursue further efforts toward change. The process is effectively energized or fueled by its own success. Kochan also proposes that the gains or benefits from change must be equally shared by workers and the employer, although he offers no real support for this position.

Finally, Kochan proposes that, over the long run, successful efforts must be integrated with the formal collective bargaining and contract administration processes. He views collective bargaining as too established for people to believe that it can be replaced by an alternative.

MANAGING CHANGE

People's resistance to change may show overtly, in clearly recognizable form, or it may be covert—hard to identify but nevertheless apparent through a lack of progress. The union leader might flatly reject attempts to institute a quality-of-worklife program; a supervisor may agree to recognize suggestions made by subordinates but may neglect to do so. Either the desired change is completely thwarted or its momentum is retarded, and the eventual outcomes may be far short of initial expectations or aspirations.

Managing this process involves carefully selecting the change as one which people will view as important and needed; analyzing the potential impacts of the change; choosing the appropriate strategy to gather support for the change and overcome any resistance to it; planning so that the desired strategy is operationalized; implementing it effectively; monitoring the change as it is implemented; and changing the change if it fails to produce the desired results when responses and developments indicate that it is not producing the desired results.

Selecting the Change

Since people have a limited capacity to change, and since there are many reasons why they might resist change, it seems prudent to limit the initiation of changes to those that will make a major contribution to achieving the organization's purpose. This is no more profound than saying "invest effort and energy (limited resources) where they will do the most good." The change must be one whose value is evident to most people, although not perhaps everyone, and which stands some chance of success with a good strategy and plan. Given the difficulties involved in managing change, and the energy required to drive the process, it doesn't make sense to waste it on trivia unrelated to the organization's central mission, or on changes whose value appears dubious. The odds are stacked too heavily against the initiator under such circumstances. This does not mean that small changes are bad. Indeed, it has been suggested that the small, incremental changes stand the best chance of success (Quinn, 1980). It is the irrelevant, inconsequential, time-consuming changes—which annoy and irritate people rather than energize them— that should be avoided.

The continuation of change beyond its initiation depends in large measure on perceived success. Unless early success is apparent, the chances of realizing long-range goals are slim (Greiner, 1967). This suggests that primary candidates for change are those projects having the potential to show fairly rapid success or, at a minimum, having observable and measurable benchmarks by which progress can be measured. In this context, Kochan's observation that change must "deliver the goods" needs emphasis.

Analyzing the Potential Impact of Change

Given that a worthwhile change (such as a new way of bargaining, the introduction of a Scanlon plan, or a quality-of-worklife project) has been identified, there are a series of critical questions that the initiator must ask before launching into the process of change. These are laid out in detail in Figure 13.3. They involve defining the objects for change; identifying sources of support; identifying sources of resistance, and the reasons for it; assessing whether these reasons are well-founded or are just misperceptions; estimating the shock value of the proposed change and, therefore, the potential for reflex rejection.

Developing a Strategy for Change

On the micro, group or individual levels, there are many ways in which an initiator can try to overcome resistance to change: education, consultation, facilitation, negotiation, rewarding, co-optation, manipulation or deception, and coercion (Kotter and Schlesinger, 1979; Lawrence, 1954).

Education

One strategy is to educate and inform people as to the intent and purpose of a proposed change to ensure that it is clearly understood. Such a strategy is indicated where the need for the change is not apparent or the resistance is based on unrealistic perceptions. Indeed, this strategy appears to be necessary in almost all efforts toward change if reflex opposition is to be avoided. At the same time, one must recognize that attempts to communicate in low-trust relationships frequently go awry,

Figure 13.3
Questions to be Asked Before Attempting Change

Will change be perceived as violating ideals,
norms, values?
What are these and how will they be perceived
as being violated?

Will change be perceived as upsetting
familiar pattern of relationships?
What are these?

Will they perceive themselves are potentially
incompetent to demonstrate new, required
behaviours?
Do they see themselves as lacking the
aptitude for required behaviours or just
lacking the appropriate training?

Will they perceive themselves as lacking the
capacity to change?
Is this a matter of time, money, resources,
workload priorities?

Are these perceptions acccurate? Do they
exist in fact or just in the minds of people
affected by change?

Will the change so sudden that reflex
rejection may occur?

and such a strategy might actually backfire if the climate is poisoned to
such an extent that all communication is distorted.

Consultation

Sometimes resistance to change can be overcome through the process of
consultation which, of necessity, also includes communication and,
therefore, education. Quite often, people who may initially resist change
may lower that resistance as a result of having the opportunity to make
their point of view known through a consultative process. They are able to
live with the outcome—even if it is slightly distasteful—because they are
satisfied that they had some role in shaping it. Consultation has the
additional advantage of identifying possible "glitches" and unintended
consequences of which initiators may be unaware. Consultation tends to
take time; this may be a disadvantage under some circumstances, but it

does allow for adaptation while minimizing the surprise effect that can lead to reflex rejections.

Facilitation

People may resist change because they fear being incompetent or they don't have the capacity to respond in the manner requested. The term "facilitation" covers a number of strategies that might be appropriate for resistance based on these causes. It may be necessary to provide additional resources, training and development programs, some time away from the job to prepare for a new role, or perhaps just some encouragement and social supportiveness where the fear of incompetence is unjustified.

Negotiation

Faced with strong resistance, it may be necessary to negotiate change, agreeing to something that the resistor wants in return for the resistor's going along with the change. There could be an agreement, for example, to allow a union to have veto power over the implementation of a new program in return for an agreement to try single-team bargaining. Or, a guarantee of job security may be given in return for some concession with respect to seniority in promotions or relaxation of work rules. Or, an agreement to "share the gains"—either through Scanlon-type formulas or broadly based profit sharing—may be the quid pro quo for some productivity improvement plan.

Co-optation

Another possible strategy is to co-opt resistors. This often involves making them such a key part of the change, involving them in a genuine power-sharing arrangement and extensive consultation, so that they begin to feel they "own" the change. They may also lose sight of the reality that the change may not be in their long-term interest. For example, one joint staffing committee in a community college worked so well and was such a genuine co-operative effort between federation affiliate members and board administrators that the teachers' representatives suggested a reduction in the number of teachers employed. It took a sharp reminder from others, not involved in the committee, to make these teachers realize that they were not acting in the best interest of the people they represented, at least in the short run. Such co-optation carries the risk of alienating the political leaders of an organization from the rank-and-file, making the change highly unstable.

Manipulation or Deception

Co-optation differs from manipulation or outright deception, which involves getting someone to agree to a change by convincing them that it is in their best interest, even though it might not be. For example, a teachers' federation might be induced to give up some seniority protection to allow for the retention of some teachers who are more junior but whose qualifications are better. Once this breach in seniority is made, it might be used to get around strict seniority in recalls. Needless to say, the use of manipulation or deception—apart from any ethical or moral objections—must be considered in light of the aftermath if and when it is uncovered.

Coercion

Finally, of course, there is always the option of trying to coerce people into changing their behaviour. Threats, explicitly stated or merely implied, are often made in the service of initiating or promoting change. These may include telling an administrator that she will not keep her job unless she changes the way she does things, or even threatening a union with the transfer of work elsewhere and the possible closing of an operation.

Choosing the Right Change Strategy and Tactics

Given all of these potential strategies for overcoming resistance to change, the logical questions are "Which one(s) should be used, and when?" There are six factors to be considered in selecting change-management strategies.

Basis of Resistance

If the resistance stems from ignorance or misperception, then communication and education are appropriate. If it is based on fear of incompetence, training (a facilitation strategy) might be appropriate. If it is based on real loss, it may be necessary to negotiate some compensation.

Relative Power

The relative power of the initiator over the resistors must be a key consideration, specifically whether the resistors have the ability to slow down or totally sabotage the effort if they decide not to co-operate or actively to oppose the change. If the resistors have power to resist, negotiation may be required. If there is no such power, coercion might be employed.

Information

The locus of information required to design the process of change must also be a key consideration. Realistically, much of the information that is needed—knowledge, expertise—may well be vested in people who might have reason to oppose any change in the relationship. If this information is needed, consultation and negotiation may be necessary for success.

Current Climate

The current climate within which the change is being initiated (specifically, whether there is trust and acknowledged legitimacy in the relationship, whether people respect and like one another, whether they are predisposed to co-operate) also influences the viability of certain change strategies and tactics. Where there is no trust, meaningful consultation is difficult, and any efforts toward communication or education may well be interpreted as insincere and misleading.

Desired Climate

The desired outcome in terms of the relationship between the initiator and the resistor must be carefully considered. Specifically, does it matter that there be a residue of trust, some respect, perhaps even some friendliness? If the desired outcome is a trusting relationship, the strategies of coercion, co-optation, manipulation, or deception are clearly contraindicated.

Time

The amount of time available to plan and implement the process of change will also be a major factor. Since extensive consultation and some forms of facilitation described above require great investments of time, they may be inappropriate in a crisis.

Change and Participation

A debate continues about the value of involving people in planning changes that might affect them. On the one hand, some writers argue that involvement is critical if people are to comprehend the nature of the changes and to develop commitment to them (Marrow, Bowers, and

Seashore, 1967; Vroom and Yetton, 1973). Such writers tend to view commitment as a natural outcome of involvement or participation in decision making. Furthermore, participation has the advantage of bringing more and different perspectives, views, opinions, and knowledge to bear on the issue. There is much evidence that certain types of decisions are improved when there is involvement of those affected by them. The advocates of participative change management also suggest that for true commitment to be obtained, people must be involved in all aspects of the issue, from participating in the analysis of the problem through deciding on the actions to be taken. And there must be some real degree of influence or power-sharing, a perceived opportunity to shape the nature of the change.

In part, the controversy hinges on the very different forms of participation and the ways in which people define what participation means. Participation may mean just communication, or it may mean consultation, or some degree of joint decision making. Two-way communication is almost always required, and consultation of some form is usually desirable, but true co-determination—joint decision-making—may not be as crucial in most situations.

Participative management should be used selectively. It is appropriate when those affected share similar objectives as the initiators or, at least, can subscribe to some common, superordinate goal; they are affected by the change; the nature of the change is not "cast in stone" and there is a real, meaningful opportunity for those involved to shape it in some way; there is time to engage in a participative process. If the decision has already been made or if time is not available to allow meaningful consultation, then attempts to get people involved in the process will be perceived as manipulative and insincere—as indeed they are. If people are not affected by the change, they will not become involved in the process, and may resent the time that they have to spend participating in it. And, if the people don't share common goals, they may well subvert the process and use it to pursue their own objectives.

In considering the challenge of changing collective bargaining relationships, it seems to us that there is room for both participative and non-participative change management. Clearly, any decision to change the way negotiations are conducted must be participative. (It takes two to tango!) On the other hand, a decision to improve the quality of contract administration—perhaps by hiring a full-time, experienced labour relations practitioner—can be a unilateral decision that need not involve the union. Similarly, the decision to clean up a plant, start treating employees with more dignity, and ask their views about how to improve production does not require a major co-operative endeavour with a reluctant union.

Realistically, the initial climate may be so poor that one party will refuse to participate, and some unilateral decisions have to be made to get the ball rolling. On the other hand, people may be hurting so badly as a result of the relationship that the superordinate goal of relationship improvement is attractive enough to encourage participation.

Choosing the Strategy and Tactics

The choice of strategy for change must be made looking at all of these factors. While it is intuitively appropriate to use education and communication in cases of misperception leading to resistance, this course may backfire if the current climate is one of mistrust and hostility. While attempts at coercion may be expedient, resistors may have considerable power to withstand the coercion. The aftermath, in terms of the emergent relationship, might be dysfunctional. For example, trying to coerce a reluctant line manager to change the way he or she handles grievances may be difficult for a labour relations manager if, as a result of the attempt, this line manager subsequently blocks other changes out of resentment. There may be problems with the use of negotiations, particularly where they amount to appeasement. "Giving in" to an unreasonable request in order to overcome resistance to a proposed change establishes a precedent for future changes. The costs of the change may mount to the point where it isn't worth the effort any more.

It would be tedious to go through each possible combination of strategies for change, their advantages and disadvantages, and the situational conditions under which they might be effective. These are summarized in Figure 13.4 . What should be clear, however, is that the choice of strategy is critical, requiring careful assessment of the task to be done, the individuals affected, the situation within which the change is taking place, and the desired short- and long-term outcomes (Figure 13.4). Some strategies take longer than others (education compared with coercion is one example), and this fact puts a premium on the impact analysis described above. If those affected by change are not identified early and their potential reaction to change is not considered, then the only strategies that time may permit are coercion, deception, or bribery with some major, costly concession.

Multiple strategies may be appropriate. While it may be necessary to negotiate substantively with an adversarial party in a relationship, a communications program or some consultation may be all that is required to promote and manage the change as far as other members of management are concerned, particularly if their resistance to change is expected to be minimal. A union officer may need to do some serious consultation and horse trading with members of his executive, but may be able to effect certain changes without extensive consultation with the membership. In other situations, of course, the executive might be "on-side," but extensive consultation with the rank-and-file is essential.

Figure 13.4
Changing the Union–Management Relationship

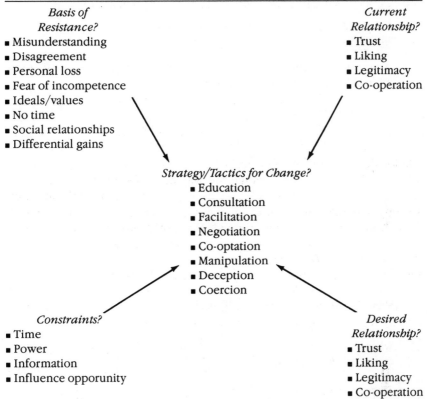

Basis of Resistance?
- Misunderstanding
- Disagreement
- Personal loss
- Fear of incompetence
- Ideals/values
- No time
- Social relationships
- Differential gains

Current Relationship?
- Trust
- Liking
- Legitimacy
- Co-operation

Strategy/Tactics for Change?
- Education
- Consultation
- Facilitation
- Negotiation
- Co-optation
- Manipulation
- Deception
- Coercion

Constraints?
- Time
- Power
- Information
- Influence opporunity

Desired Relationship?
- Trust
- Liking
- Legitimacy
- Co-operation

THE PLAN FOR CHANGE

Successful changes are managed using a plan that defines the actions to be taken, who is responsible for taking them, when they have to be taken, how they will be monitored, and so on. This should be a flexible plan, capable of changing in response to circumstances or unanticipated problems. Yet it must be there. Most changes of the type we have been talking about are complex and need thinking out ahead of time. The discipline of working out a detailed plan helps the initiator to ensure that the situation has been analyzed, the necessary choices decided, and contingency plans made. The key steps in such a plan are outlined in Figure 13.5.

Leadership Support

Successful organizational changes are characterized by the visible and stated commitment of the organization's leaders (Greiner, 1967; Beer, 1980). It is these leaders who control many of those variables that

Figure 13.5
Key Ingredients of a Plan for Change

Leadership Support
How to get support for change from top management
and union leaders.

Agent(s) for Change
Who the designated agent(s) will be.

Required Actions
The actions necessary to promote the change and
overcome any resistance identified at the impact-
analysis stage. This to include responsibilities and
timing.

Resources
The additional resources required for the proposed
change.

Training and Development
The training and development required to facilitate the
required change, including where, when, how, to whom,
and by whom this should be delivered.

Communications
What should be communicated to organizational members
concerning the change.

Measuring Success
How success is to be measured and reported.

Reinforcement
How behaviours that lead to success should be
reinforced.

Contingency Plans
What should be done if things don't work out as
planned.

determine the behaviours of others. They dispense rewards of many kinds—task assignments, promotions, pay raises, committee assignments, etc.—and control the resources that people need to do their jobs. They will decide if required resources are allocated to projects for change, if budgets for staff development and training will be made available, if adequate staffing will be provided. Particularly in the attempt to change union–management relationships, public statements of leaders will be scrutinized to assess the sincerity of their desire to effect change. If the leaders are perceived not to support the change, then others in the organization are unlikely to be enthusiastic. Even if enthusiasm is generated, it will likely be short-lived in the absence of leadership support.

Under ideal conditions, all the leaders in the relationship (including union officers, senior managers, middle managers and supervisors, as well as a few highly influential people who may hold no formal office) will support change. Yet seldom is this ideal realized. In practice, the initiator must enlist the support of as many as possible who will cooperate openly and consistently.

Many different tactics can be used to build leadership support, but all amount to demonstrating the net benefits of change relative to the costs and the feasibility of mounting the required effort. The process may require some education since, for the most part, people are unlikely to know much about bargaining relationships other than their own. There are consultants who have expertise in such techniques for improving bargaining relationships as single-team bargaining and relationships by objectives, to name just two of the more popular approaches; approaches such as those of Scanlon, Rucker, Lincoln, Improshare, and other productivity gain-sharing schemes are implemented by firms and individuals who have built up considerable experience with them.

Under ideal conditions, both union and management officials would be exposed to this educational process simultaneously so that there is some shared understanding of what it's all about. However—as is often the case—this may not be logistically or politically possible. The process of change is relatively easy to initiate in a crisis. The co-operation between Studebaker and the UAW before the car company went under; the more recent employee-involvement programs at Ford and General Motors at the height of the 1982 recession and in the face of severe offshore competition; the very successful relationships-by-objectives program at Budd Automotive during the recession and following many years of extreme union–management conflict (Lilley, 1984); and numerous other, less publicized union–management co-operation programs attest to that.

It is far more difficult to get something started without the stimulus of a crisis. Usually, one or other of the parties to a bargaining relationship will feel the need for change, either before the other or more acutely. Under such circumstances a unilateral gesture of some kind might be needed before the leadership of the other party feels secure enough to participate in joint explorations designed to assess and improve the current relationship. This need is often a major impediment to getting the process started. Many people in management and union organizations have a doctrinaire dislike of making concessions unless they are under pressure to do so. The idea that management might offer some greater measure of job security, some more favourable contract language, some degree of co-determination or power sharing without having to do so is anathema to some managers. Equally, the idea that a union should moderate its demands, or might pass up seeking modifications to every article in the collective agreement each time negotiations take place, is also incomprehensible to some union officers. But this may be the price that has to be paid to enlist the support from the leadership of both organizations.

The Federal Mediation and Conciliation Service in the United States tends to the view that its relationships-by-objectives program should be offered only in a crisis (Kochan, 1980). This position contrasts with that taken by the Ontario Ministry of Labour and the Education Relations Commission, which see their programs as a preventative measure and claim at least some success in most cases where they have been offered (Sparling, 1982).

Agents for Change

One of the most common reasons that efforts toward change fail is that such efforts either are not being managed at all or have not been assigned to the appropriate person. Management of change requires effort and skill—conceptual and analytical skills as well as action skills. The effective agent for change must understand the process and be able to communicate effectively to mediate or adjudicate conflicts that arise.

It is also important that the person responsible for the change within the party—the "champion"—is a high-status individual, clearly identified with the leadership of the organization. Nothing is more likely to convey a sense of doubtfulness in the leadership's support than assigning responsibility for change to a low-status individual. Many successful changes have involved the use of high-prestige consultants as agents, and they may be intimately involved in all aspects of managing the change. They can bring expertise, credibility, and a high profile to the process. But, in our view, they can only be temporary agents for change. At some point, whatever process is set in motion must be internalized.

Required Actions

Any good plan for change should identify the actions that will be taken to obtain support and overcome resistance. Where training and development are required, for example, they should be specified in the plan so that implementation is not held up unexpectedly while these are provided. Common techniques of managing change—such as relationships-by-objectives, preventative mediation, inter-group laboratories, role-analysis technique, or other forms of interpersonal training—require long planning horizons and, often, considerable costs. Therefore, it is important to plan them well.

It was noted earlier that an incapacity to change owing to day-to-day pressures was a key factor associated with failure to effect change. Change itself consumes energy, takes time, requires resources. If someone is to attend a training session, who will do her work? If data-based problem solving is to occur, who has the time to gather the appropriate data? If a decision is made to form a joint committee, who has the time available to sit on it?

While it is true that, over the long haul, a changed bargaining relationship might reduce workloads, that is unlikely to occur in the short run. For example, a good employee-suggestion scheme may eventually result in efficiencies and productivity increases. However, in the short run, someone has to analyze the suggestions, evaluate their practicality, report back to those who made them, and implement those that are of value. All of this consumes resources; the failure to provide them will surely result in demoralization of the suggestion plan. Therefore, the plan should explicitly recognize the need for additional resources where they are required. It is particularly important to free some resources—particularly to get well-trained people. Failure to have the right people available can inject months of delay into any project, especially if workers have to be hired from outside the system.

Training and Development

The plan for change should also include plans for any necessary training and development: courses must be prepared, personnel replacements engaged, domestic assistance arranged for those who require it—and all such efforts must be budgeted as well as scheduled. If courses are to be custom-designed, there are the associated lead times to incorporate into the plan. The type of training required depends, of course, on the objective of the process toward change. If the objective involves working together in small groups, task forces, or committees, then a program of group dynamics, group problem solving, and related areas might be appropriate. Sometimes individuals need to brush up on their interpersonal skills with such programs as active listening, giving and receiving feedback, and so on.

If the change involves adopting new styles of negotiating, such as single-team bargaining or relationships-by-objectives, these usually come packaged in courses that seek to build the required skills as well as introduce the techniques. Sometimes it is a technical skill that is needed, such as collective agreement administration or performance appraisal. Such skills may be gained through various courses offered at colleges and universities or through private consulting firms.

Communications

It is surprising how often major changes are initiated without enough thought being given to communications. A good communications plan is even more important in organizations such as school boards, where both the administration and the teachers' representatives must function in extremely political environments.

The communications plan must be thought out so that the right messages are conveyed to the right people. There will be those who will be directly affected by whatever changes take place—probably only a small number of people. Then there are all the others who will hear about the changes in one way or another, and who, in the absence of definitive communication, will read their own interpretations into what they observe or hear. There are many avenues of communication to be used: public statements, newsletters, bulletin boards, departmental and other meetings, all represent communication forums.

It is important that messages are consistent, otherwise people will become confused about the intent and nature of the changes that are being made. Confusion is a breeding ground for rumours, some of which may be very harmful to the process of change.

Measuring and Monitoring Success or Failure

Many different types of organizational change are undertaken without much prior attention to measuring its progress or impact. If the desire is to improve the relationship, how will the parties know the relationship is being improved? If the objective is more modest—perhaps just to reduce the level of personal animosity being expressed in negotiations—how will this be assessed? If the objective is to improve the ways in which joint staffing committees operate, how will this be monitored?

People are motivated to change if they see the need to do so, if there is "something in it for them." Furthermore, their motivation to change is affected by their confidence that their efforts will be fruitful. Clearly, without measurement of progress and success these required stimuli are missing and the momentum of the process may well falter.

The second reason for measuring progress is to try to influence the skeptics so that they become supportive of change—to be able to answer the question, "Where's the beef?" Many people who are skeptical about co-operative bargaining, for example, require convincing that it benefits them or, at least, that they will not suffer as a result of it.

Where additional resources have been spent, an accounting has to be made. This is the third reason for measuring the success or failure of change. There are some major difficulties in measuring the impact or progress of change but surveys, informed assessment, quantitative and qualitative measures, and other subjective and objective measures, can be used. At a minimum the plan for change should identify some objectives and suggest how their achievement, and any progress toward it, will be assessed.

Reinforcement

Closely related to the issue of measurement is that of reinforcement. hnce a change has been made—once the parties are engaging in new behaviours, a committee is working well together, a manager or administrator is doing a better job—the next challenge is to ensure that these behaviours are consolidated and established as the new norm.

In part, of course, the reinforcement will come from the success of the change. If, in fact, the change reduces hassles for a manager, lessens the amount of time spent in acrimonious discussion around the bargaining table, results in better use of staff in the plant, or allows grievances to be settled more promptly, the behaviours producing these results will be reinforced. But such outcomes may not be readily apparent, particularly if the improvements are marginal. Those responsible for managing change must be constantly aware of the various ways in which success can be highlighted and fed back to those involved, recognizing and rewarding achievements with praise, recognition, or more tangible rewards, and celebrating significant milestones along the way. This will happen if the need for positive reinforcement is anticipated in the planning stage, before the actual change is implemented. As well, the change must be institutionalized—that is, incorporated into the rules, policies, and standard practices of the organization.

Failing this, the organization may find itself in a schizophrenic state, operating by two different systems, the desired and the actual. Some research has suggested that planning appropriate reinforcement may be the most important step in ensuring the success of an effort toward change (Sorenson and Zand, 1975). Kochan's (1980) insistence that change be integrated into the collective bargaining system is to ensure that changes are stabilized and to avoid the appearance of undermining the legitimate process of collective bargaining. It is worth adding that many managers seek to establish relationships, practices, and "agreements" outside of the conventional collective bargaining forum. It remains to be seen whether these are in fact inherently unstable (Gandz and Beatty, 1986; Shershin and Boxx, 1975; Purcell, 1981).

Contingency Planning

Successful planning for change entails planning for failure. What if we try single-team bargaining and it doesn't work? What if we establish a joint committee to process sabbatical leave applications but we end up at loggerheads? What if we implement semi-autonomous work teams but they are not productive? What if we take out time clocks and workers start coming late?

Before initiating any sort of project for change, the prudent manager will have considered the possibility and consequences of failure, particularly whether such failure might leave the situation worse than it was before. One way of ensuring such prudence is to make sure the initial plan identifies a clear course of action if the objectives are not met.

IMPLEMENTING, MONITORING, AND CHANGING THE CHANGE

It is often at the implementation stage that a new project falls apart. One of the reasons is that boredom sets in. The creative part of managing change is in the early stages: thinking about what changes are needed, analyzing their potential impacts, and developing strategies and plans. The implementation often involves great amounts of detailed work and may extend over a long period. By the implementation stage the initiator—the original fount of enthusiasm and energy—may have mentally moved on to other things. Implementation may be abandoned to others who have less understanding, less commitment, and less skill at doing it.

There are other reasons why change falls apart in the implementation stage. There may be discrepancies between expected and actual results that cause people to cry "failure" even though good things have been achieved. Expectations tend to shift during the process, and they may reach unreasonable levels. Key sponsors of the change may leave or become disengaged from the process, and the original enthusiasm may not be transmitted to successors (Goodman, Bazerman and Conlon, 1980).

While great effort may go into a good, comprehensive plan for change, the probabilities of absolutely smooth implementation are remote. The assumptions that went into the plan may have been wrong in a number of respects, and there may be totally unforeseen reactions to the changes as they become apparent to more and more people.

One problem with implementation may lie in the very enthusiasm that the initiator has for the objectives and plan. While this enthusiasm is important in setting the change in motion, it can also blind the initiator to problems and make him or her defensive about the original plan. Implementation must be carried out with the same sensitivity with which a good coach implements a game plan—knowing when to stick to it and when to change it! Throughout the implementation phase, the manager must be monitoring the impact of change, seeking feedback from those affected, re-evaluating the strategies and plans. It may be necessary to change strategies, to alter time frames, to adjust objectives so that they are more realistic. Sometimes it may be necessary to abandon the plan altogether and try something else.

CONCLUSIONS

Changing a union–management relationship, whether the change is dramatic or affects only some limited aspects of the relationship, is difficult. Many efforts start as well intentioned and eventually founder; sometimes the bitter residue from failure makes the attempt harmful rather than helpful. Sometimes it is simply not possible to establish the kind of interpersonal relationships between people that are necessary to turn the larger relationship from destructive to constructive.

A first-class impact analysis is the key to designing and planning a viable approach to changing the union–management relationship. Appropriate strategies and tactics must be developed in a flexible but comprehensive plan so that support for change can be maximized and resistance to it can be overcome.

There are many obstacles in the way of changing a union–management relationship, particularly when there is no obvious crisis. However, there is reason to believe that the probability of successful change is greater when that change is managed by people who have the necessary conceptual, planning, and action skills. While there must be a confluence of certain situational factors for change to occur, good managers can be equipped to take advantage of the circumstances when they arise.

BIBLIOGRAPHY

Beer, M. (1980), *Organization Change and Development: A Systems View*. Santa Monica, CA: Goodyear.

Boxx, W. R. (1975), "Building positive union–management relations." *Personnel Journal (June)*: 326–331.

Downie, B. (1982), "Union–management cooperation." In Anderson, J. and M. Gunderson (eds.), *Union–Management Relations in Canada*. Don Mills, Ont.: Addison-Wesley, pp. 316–340.

Dunlop, J. T. (1955), *Industrial Relations Systems*. New York: McGraw-Hill.

French, W. L. and Bell, C. H. (1978), *Organization Development: Behavioral Science Interventions for Organization Improvement* (2nd ed.). Englewood Cliffs, N.J.: Prentice-Hall.

Gandz, J. (1978), "Resolving conflict: A guide for labor relations managers." *Personnel* 56 (6).

_____ and Beatty, C. (1986), *Changing Relations in Educational Bargaining*. Toronto, Ont.: Education Relations Commission.

Goodman, Bazerman, and Conlon (1980), "Institutionalization of planned change." In B. Staw and L. Cummings (eds.), *Research in Organizational Behavior*, Vol. 2. Greenwich, CT: JAI.

Greiner, L. (1967), "Patterns of organizational change." *Harvard Business Review (May–June)*: 119–128.

Kochan, T. A. (1980). *Collective Bargaining and Industrial Relations*. Homewood, IL: Irwin.

———, McKersie, R. B., and Cappelli, P. (1984), "Strategic choice and industrial relations theory." *Industrial Relations* 23(1).

Kotter, J. P. and Schlesinger, L. A. (1979), "Choosing strategies for change." *Harvard Business Review (March–April)*: 106–114.

Lawler, E. E. (1973), *Motivation in Work Organizations*. Monterey: Brooks/Cole.

Lawrence, P. R. (1954), "How to deal with resistance to change." *Harvard Business Review (May–June)*: 49–57.

Lewin, K. (1947), "Frontiers in group dynamics: Concept, method and reality in social science." *Human Relations* 1: 5–42.

Lilley, Wayne (1984), "Over the volcano." *Canadian Business* 57:9.

Marrow, E., Bowers, D. and Seashore, S. (1967), *Management by Participation*. New York: Harper and Row.

McKersie, R. B. and Shropshire, W. W., Jr. (1962), "Avoiding written grievances: A successful program." *Journal of Business of the University of Chicago* 35: 135–152.

Ontario Ministry of Labor (1982), *Preventive Mediation Relationship Improvement Program*. Pamphlet 2M/10/82.

Pondy, L. R. (1967), "Organizational conflict: Concepts and models." *Administrative Science Quarterly* 12: 296–320.

Purcell, J. (1981), *Good Industrial Relations: Theory and Practice*. London: Macmillan.

Quinn, J.B. (1980), *Strategic Change*. New York: Dow-Jones Irwin.

Rumball, D. (1982), "One way to avoid strikes: Diffuse the confrontation mood." *Financial Post*, November 8.

Russo, N. F. (1967), "Connotation of seating arrangements." *Cornell Journal of Social Relations* 2: 37–44.

Schein, E. H. (1961), "Management development as a process of influence." *Industrial Management Review of M.I.T.* 2 (2).

Selekman, B. J. (1947), *Labor Relations and Human Relations*. New York: McGraw-Hill.

Skibbins, G. (1974), *Organizational Evolution: A Program for Managing Radical Change*. New York: Amacom.

Sorenson, R. and Zand, D. (1975), "Improving the implementation of OR/MS models by applying the Lewin-Schein theory of change." In Schultz and Slevin (eds.), *Implementing Operations Research/Management Science*. New York: Elsevier.

Sparling, H. (1982), "Preventive mediation program." PAT *Reporter* 9.

Stanislao, J. and Stanislao, B. (1983), "Dealing with resistance to change." *Business Horizons* (July–August): 74–78.

Tagiuri, R. (1973), "Notes on the management of change: Implications of postulating a need for competence." In J. Glover, R. Hower and R. Tagiuri (eds.), *The Administrator: Cases on Human Aspects of Management* (5th ed.). Homewood, IL: Irwin.

Ury and Fisher (1978), *Getting to Yes.* Boston, MA: Houghton-Mifflin.

Vroom, V. (1964), *Work and Motivation.* New York: Wiley.

——— and Yetton, P. W. (1973), *Leadership and Decision-Making.* Pittsburgh, PA: University of Pittsburgh Press.

Walton, R. E. and McKersie, R. B. (1965), *A Behavioral Theory of Labor Relations.* New York: McGraw-Hill.

Watson, G. (1969), "Resistance to change." In W. G. Bennis, K. F. Benne and R. Chin, *The Planning of Change.* New York: Holt, Rinehart & Winston.

Zaltman, G. and Duncan, R. (1977), *Strategies for Planned Change.* New York: Wiley.

Zander, A. (1950), "Resistance to change—Its analysis and prevention." *Advanced Management* xv (1).

PART 4

ISSUES IN THE 1980S AND BEYOND

14

Critical Issues in Public Sector Industrial Relations

GENE SWIMMER

This chapter concerns industrial relations in the public sector. It is designed to give the reader a general overview as well as concentrate on two critical issues: politics of dispute resolution and public vs. private sector wage comparability.

DEFINING THE PUBLIC SECTOR

What is the essence of the public sector and why should it be distinguished from industrial relations in the private sector? There are differing views as to their relative importance, but most labour relations specialists point to the following criteria: ownership, monopoly, essentiality, and politics. The most obvious definition of the public sector is whether an establishment is owned by a public body. This definition is problematic because it would include commercial Crown corporations as part of the public sector, even though the employee relations policies of Petro-Canada and Canadian National do not differ from those of other oil and rail companies, respectively.

The monopoly and essentiality criteria are related, and will be discussed together. Many public sector services constitute what economists refer to as natural monopolies. The immense capital costs (i.e., roads, communication lines), together with the inability to stop public freeloading (consuming the service without paying for it), mean that the service would not be provided efficiently or at all, unless the government intervened to grant a franchise or provide the service directly. The choice between these two options usually depends on how essential the service is. Pay television and telephone services are franchised to private sector companies in most provinces while police, fire fighting and hospital services are provided by the state. The combination of monopoly and essentiality is the major justification for limiting the strike rights of public employees. Again this definition is not perfect; some essential services are provided by private sector firms (ambulance service, sanitation, and nursing homes) while at the same time, the government is the sole provider of some less-essential services, like the post office and airports.

The final factor that distinguishes the public sector is politics. Collective bargaining, which is generally an exercise in economic power, becomes an exercise in political power. Public opinion and the prospects of re-election substitute for profit maximization in the employer's calculus. A related issue is whether government policy should be decided at the bargaining table, instead of the appropriate legislature. Is bilingual air-traffic control a legitimate employee relations issue or does Parliament reign supreme? Attempts by public sector managers to develop structures of bargaining and dispute resolution to depoliticize the process attest to its importance.

What, then, is the most reasonable definition of the public sector for industrial relations? Clearly direct administration at the local, provincial and federal level should be included. In addition, protective services (police and fire) as well as education and health services ought to be included, even though the latter two groups do not necessarily work directly for a level of government (funding comes from a combination of tax levies and government grants). The issue of Crown corporations is less clear. Corporations providing services under monopoly conditions (like the post office, liquor stores, and hydro) would usually be considered public sector while commercial Crown corporations (like Air Canada and Petro-Canada) would be classified as the private sector.

THE GROWTH OF PUBLIC SECTOR UNIONS

Public sector unions represent the third wave of unionism in Canada. First came the craft unions in the 1880s, followed by industrial unions in the 1930s and then public sector unions in the late 1960s. Public sector union membership grew from 180,000 to 1.6 million between 1961–1985 (see Figure 14.1). As Figure 14.2 indicates (Rose, 1984), the growth of most public sector unions was lumpy, often coinciding with a legislative change. Municipal unions were the exception, growing steadily in the post-war period. Unlike the previous waves of union organization, membership growth did not occur as a result of militant activity. Rather, the new unions were ushered in by favourable legislation and benevolent employers. Then as now, no public entity could take a position that unions did not have a right to exist in a given jurisdiction. This is the greatest advantage of "publicness" (or "politics") to public employees. It stands in sharp contrast to the private sector, where it is considered entirely legitimate for the employer to attempt to remain "union free" (e.g., Eaton's).

"Instant Growth" has left a legacy on many public sector unions. Some authors argue that a union movement not rooted in rank-and-file militancy will not be able to mobilize its members when the bargaining environment so requires (see Panitch and Swartz, 1984). In addition,

Figure 14.1
Public Sector and Total Union Membership, 1911 to 1985

Year	Public Sector Union Membershp	Total Union Membership	Public Sector Membership as a Percentage of Total Membership
1911	1,187	133,000	0.9
1921	7,370	313,000	2.4
1931	14,304	311,000	4.6
1941	13,523	462,000	2.9
1951	54,244	1,029,000	5.3
1961	182,887	1,447,000	12.6
1971	571,834	2,231,000	25.6
1981	1,347,073	3,487,000	38.6
1985	1,616,886	3,665,688	44.1

Source: Rose (1984), p. 96; updated to 1985 by the author.

many public sector unions came into existence from previous employee associations and mergers. Not surprisingly, unions that resulted from mergers (like the Canadian Union of Public Employees) tend to be more decentralized with greater autonomy for locals. Sometimes the previous employee association was incompatible with the post-bargaining environment. For example, the predecessor association of the Public Service Alliance of Canada (PSAC) was organized along department lines in the federal government. When the Public Service Staff Relations Act was enacted, bargaining units were determined occupationally (across departments). In other words, all clerks, regardless of government department, negotiate a single collective agreement. Despite this, PSAC has maintained a component (department-based) structure that cuts across occupational lines.

The growth of the public sector unions has also changed the character of the Canadian labour movement. Given that virtually all public sector unions are national (as opposed to international), their growth is partially responsible for the declining relative importance of international unions generally and within the Canadian Labour Congress. In 1961 international unions were 72% of the total and 83% of CLC-affiliated unions. By 1985, international unions represented only 36% of the Canadian total and 40% of the CLC.

The three largest Canadian unions represent public employees. The Canadian Union of Public Employees (CUPE) represents 296,000 members in municipal, health and education sectors; the National Union of Provincial Government Employees (NUPGE) represents 245,000 members working for provincial governments (except Quebec and PEI); and the PSAC represents 182,000 federal government employees. Needless to say, the public sector unions are an important power bloc within

Figure 14.2
Public Sector Union Membership, 1946–1981

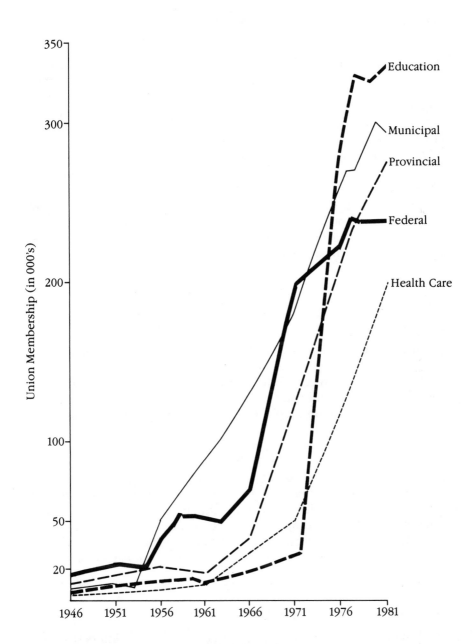

Source: Rose 1984, p. 98.

the CLC, and there have been times when tensions within the organization developed along public vs. private sector lines.

MANAGEMENT IN THE PUBLIC SECTOR

Public sector management differs greatly from its private sector counterpart. In many public jurisdictions there are two or even three sets of managers. First, there are the professional managers who are concerned with day-to-day running of the operation. Above them are the elected officials (mayor/council, school board, etc.). In addition to having a political agenda that may conflict with line management, many of these officials serve on a part-time basis (while working at other jobs). The early bargaining success of public sector unions owes much to the fact that these elected officials had neither the training nor time required for effective labour relations.

In the federal and some provincial government jurisdictions, a central agency (as opposed to departmental management) is responsible for bargaining. Here again, the goals of the central agency may diverge from other levels. For those jurisdictions without a central agency, a higher level of government often controls a large percentage of the formal employer's budget through transfer payments.

Though the structures of bargaining may occur by historical accident, they often result from specific government policy. Senior-level governments face a tradeoff between fiscal and political accountability for public sector bargaining. The more centralized the bargaining, the greater the fiscal control over the process but simultaneously the greater the risk of politicization and direct accountability for the outcomes. The Quebec government has traditionally opted for highly centralized bargaining, with a single bargaining table often determining wage increases for provincial, health and education workers. The results are extremely visible to the public, and no Quebec government has survived two rounds of public sector bargaining (see Hebert, 1984). Other provincial governments, like Ontario, have opted for decentralized bargaining. Hospital and education boards, elected or appointed locally, are the formal employer responsible for bargaining, although the province provides much or all of the funding. The province succeeds in becoming the invisible "ghost at the bargaining table," but it may find, as Ontario did in the late 1970s, that large portions of the provincial budget are no longer under direct control (see Swimmer, 1985).

THE POLITICS OF DISPUTE RESOLUTION

The legal environment of public sector labour relations differs from the private sector mainly in the areas of dispute resolution and the scope of bargaining. Virtually all public employees have the right to form unions and engage in collective bargaining (the exceptions are the military and the RCMP).

Private sector bargaining occurs in an atmosphere where the union has the right to strike and management has the right to lockout (or withstand a strike). The strike threat is the most important factor leading to concessions from both sides. In the public sector, some employees have the strike right denied or limited by legislation. In private sector negotiations any issue can be included for discussion by the parties. The scope of bargaining in many public sector jurisdictions is much narrower. At provincial and federal levels, aspects of the employee relationship that could conflict with government policy (such as the "merit system") are not bargainable. By default, those issues which cannot be negotiated become the sole perogative of management.

Chapter 9 discusses the pros and cons of interest arbitration in detail (how arbitration affects the bargaining strategy and outcomes). This chapter is concerned with the political justifications and ramifications of dispute resolution choices. If you were to read industrial relations texts from the past, you would see that there are really three broad types of dispute resolution procedures: unlimited strike, arbitration, and limited strike (some, not all, members of a bargaining unit are allowed to strike). Given that since 1975, five years of public sector compensation were determined by government fiat, wage controls must be included as a fourth basis of dispute resolution.

THE RIGHT TO STRIKE

Numerous justifications for denying the strike right to public employees have been voiced by politicians, the media, and industrial relations analysts, though many are of dubious merit. One common argument is that public sector strikes become political and not economic disputes. Politicians may give in too quickly to union demands, responding to a populace more concerned about avoiding or ending a strike than the tax ramifications of higher wages (see Cristensen, 1980). Though the political dimension distinguishes public sector bargaining from its private sector counterpart, that does not set it apart from other economic relations of public entities with interest groups. Governments bargain with corporations all the time, be it about the cost of goods and services supplied, adherence to regulatory standards, plant location, etc. Corporations routinely threaten governments with the use of sanctions that are political as well as economic. Yet there are few advocates of limitations on relocating capital (the corporate equivalent of withdrawing services) for firms that interact with governments.

A related argument for denying the right to strike to public employees is that, unlike the private sector where a strike penalizes the parties themselves, public sector strikes hurt third parties. However, as Weiler (1980, p. 239) argues:

> The general public is not an innocent, uninvolved bystander in the dispute between the government employer and its union. The public is the employer—to an even greater extent than are the shareholders of private corporate employers. It is the interests of the public that are being advanced at the other side of the table, either as the consumers of the services who want to maximize employee production, or as taxpayers who want to minimize labour cost.

When viewed in this light it is hardly surprising that Gallup polls find that the overwhelming majority of the public (73 percent in 1981) would not permit strikes by public employees.

The most legitimate justification for denying the right to strike centres on essentiality. Some government employees are the sole providers of services that are necessary for the well-being of the public. Because the denial of these services could cause irreparable damage to society, it is argued that public employees must be prohibited from organizing work stoppages. Where to draw the line between necessity and convenience is always difficult, but Adams (1981) provides a reasonable ranking of essentiality: (1) police and fire fighters; (2) hospitals; (3) utilities; (4) transportation; (5) municipal services; (6) civil servants; and (7) education.

Figure 14.3 summarizes the existing dispute-resolution policies for various public sector groupings across Canada. Although it is not shown in the table, all provinces provide for conciliation and/or mediation before the use of sanctions or interest arbitration.

It is evident, when comparing Figure 14.3 with Adams's ranking, that both high-priority and low-priority employees have been denied the right to strike. As expected, most provinces require fire fighters to resolve disputes by interest arbitration (seven of ten). By comparison, half the provinces allow police to strike (though it would have to be a limited strike in B.C.). At the other extreme, eight out of ten provinces deny or limit strikes by their own administrative employees (four require arbitration, four allow limited strikes), while workers performing identical jobs for municipal governments (clerical workers, road repair, etc.) invariably can withdraw their services.

Despite the clamour against public sector strikes, as Figure 14.4 indicates the extent of such strikes is modest. Considering that public sector unions have made up 25–38% of all union members over the period, the relative frequency of public sector strikes has been below what would be expected, averaging 18% of the total. Of course, even a short strike by essential employees could generate enormous social cost.

The one-day Montreal police strike in 1967 led to over a million dollars in damage and two strike-related deaths (Fisher and Starek, 1980).

Arbitration in the Public Sector

The use of arbitration in some public sector jurisdictions may be better understood from a public administration perspective. Interest arbitration is a form of "regulatory protectionism" that can shield governments from political accountability. As arbitration protects the public interest from a strike, it simultaneously protects the government from any responsibility for a strike. Likewise, when a contract impasse is settled by arbitration, the public authority is completely relieved of accountability for the bargaining results. Large wage settlements that could eventually lead to higher taxes must still be paid because an unbiased, wise third party has so ordained. Since provincial governments pay 100 percent of the budget of their own employees (compared to less than half of municipal and school board budgets), the shelter of arbitration would be most tempting for this sector.

Ironically, there is some evidence that arbitration may have actually imparted a positive bias to wage settlements. Auld et al. (1980) found that Canadian contracts between 1967 and 1975 determined by an arbitration award were significantly different from those determined under conventional bargaining. In particular, the degree of labour-market tightness (the rate of job vacancies) was not related to the size of arbitrated wage settlements. Another study (Auld and Wilton, 1981) found that, during the same period, Ontario public sector base-rate wage increases averaged 13.6 percent for health and 10.8 percent for provincial government (covered by arbitration) compared to 10.2 percent for both education and municipal employees (covered by strike-based legislation). However, Saunders (1982) and Swimmer (1986) found that federal government settlements negotiated under arbitration were lower than those negotiated under the strike route.

To understand these differing wage outcomes, we must discuss some of the criteria arbitrators use in making their awards. The most common criterion is private sector wage comparability. As one well-known arbitrator (Arthurs) states:

> Arbitration is made to substitute for the strike and should therefore likewise be an exercise of labour market realities. This being so, it is to relevant wage comparisons that we must look rather than abstract appeals to justice. (Quoted in Gunderson, 1983, p. 38.)

In theory, wage comparability seems to be not only intuitively fair but is consistent with labour-market efficiency concepts. Applying the rule is not straightforward. Some public employees, for instance, police and fire

Figure 14.3
Dispute Resolution Processes for Public Employees

Jurisdiction	Type of Employees			
	Police	Fire Fighters	Hospital Workers	Teachers
Federal	No Bargaining Rights	Union Choice of Arbitration or Limited Strike	Union Choice of Arbitration or Limited Strike	Union Choice of Arbitration or Limited Strike
Newfoundland	Arbitration	Arbitration	Limited Strike or Union Choice of Arbitration[1]	Strike
PEI	Arbitration	Arbitration	Arbitration	Arbitration
Nova Scotia	Strike	Strike	Strike	Arbitration[2]
New Brunswick	Strike	Arbitration	Limited Strike or Arbitration by Mutual Agreement	Limited Strike or Arbitration by Mutual Agreement
Quebec	Arbitration	Arbitration	Limited Strike[3]	Strike[3]
Ontario	Arbitration	Arbitration	Arbitration	Strike
Manitoba	Strike	Arbitration	Strike	Arbitration
Saskatchewan	Strike[4]	Strike[4]	Strike	Strike
Alberta	Arbitration	Arbitration	Arbitration	Strike
B.C.	Limited Strike or Union Choice of Arbitration[5]	Limited Strike or Union Choice of Arbitration[5]	Limited Strike or Union Choice of Arbitration[5]	Arbitration

Jurisdiction	Municipal Services	Public Administration
Federal	—	Union Choice of Arbitration or Limited Strike
Newfoundland	Strike	Limited Strike or Union Choice of Arbitration[1]
PEI	Strike	Arbitration
Nova Scotia	Strike	Arbitration
New Brunswick	Strike	Limited Strike or Arbitration by Mutual Agreement
Quebec	Strike	Limited Strike
Ontario	Strike	Arbitration
Manitoba	Strike	Strike
Saskatchewan	Strike	Strike
Alberta	Strike	Arbitration
B.C.	Limited Strike or Union Choice of Arbitration[5]	Limited Strike or Union Choice of Arbitration[5]

Notes:
1. Union can exercise right to arbitration only when more than 50% of workers are designated essential.
2. Applies to local negotiations; provincial aspects of bargaining subject to strike.
3. No strikes allowed over local or regional issues.
4. Arbitration, if union has a "no strike" clause in constitution.
5. Union can exercise choice for arbitration if its workers are designated essential.

Source: Adapted from Research Document, Labour Canada, Federal Provincial Relations Branch (1986).

Figure 14.4
Strikes in the Private and Public Sectors in Canada

Year	Public		Private	
	Number	% of Total	Number	% of Total
1972	79	13.2	519	86.8
1973	76	10.5	648	89.5
1974	167	13.7	1 051	86.3
1975	218	18.6	951	81.4
1976	202	19.5	836	80.5
1977	171	21.2	634	78.8
1978	196	18.5	861	81.5
1979	195	18.6	854	81.4
1980	218	21.2	809	78.8
1981	260	24.8	788	75.2
1982	110	16.2	567	84.8
1983	85	13.2	560	86.8
1984	103	14.4	614	85.6
Average	160	17.7%	746	82.3%

Source: Smith (1984), p. 204; updated by the author.

fighters, have no obvious comparison groups in the private sector. As a result, the comparisons are often made with other public sector groups. Unfortunately, such comparisons may rely upon wage settlements negotiated under the threat or use of arbitration, not "labour market realities."

Even when an obvious private sector employee group is available (for instance, clerical employees), questions arise as to whether to look at all employees or only union employees. A general principle of arbitral jurisprudence is that non-unionized wages and benefits should be given considerably less weight, because they are imposed by one party, while arbitration attempts to replicate the joint decision making of collective bargaining. Arbitration awards may therefore appear high in relation to the entire private sector (union and non-union wages). It should be noted that in 1983, the Alberta government amended its public sector legislation to require arbitrators to compare non-union as well as unionized private sector wages when making awards.

The most controversial criterion is the ability to pay. Historically, arbitrators have taken the view that although the employer's ability to pay wage increases is important in the private sector, it has no relevance in the public sector. Arbitrators have argued along the lines of Gunderson (1983, 41) that employees should not be required to receive lower wages

to subsidize (and thereby encourage) employers that have a low ability to pay because of mismanagement or because the service requires a subsidy to exist.

The rationale for a subsidy is a separate issue; if merited, it should come from public funds, not from specific employees.

The issue becomes particularly important for services provided locally (like hospitals and schools) but whose budgets largely depend on higher levels of government. By limiting transfer payments to formal employers (e.g., school and hospital boards), provincial governments can make the employers appear to the public and the media as unable to pay. For example, in the early 1980s Ontario and British Columbia passed legislation (in Ontario it was temporary) requiring arbitrators to apply the "ability to pay" criterion to public employers. The governments simultaneously restricted government transfers to these employers so that arbitration awards would be reduced. It is ironic that the ability of Ontario or British Columbia citizens to pay for public services was not addressed. In fact Ontario ranked last (among the ten provinces) in terms of the percentage of gross domestic product (GDP) spent on health services, ninth for education expenditure and eighth for social services. British Columbia ranked seventh on health and social services spending and last on education. In such circumstances, "unwilling to pay" seems to be more appropriate than "unable to pay."

Limited Strikes

An alternative to arbitration for essential employees is a strike by some, if not all workers. In theory, limited strikes would impose economic costs and inconvenience for the public, but would not lead to irreparable damage to public safety and property. Such a strike would generate cost upon both sides and make striking an unpleasant outcome worth avoiding through concession. In that way, we would capture the major benefit of a strike-based system, a dispute-resolution process that is rarely invoked. If and when a strike occurred and was allowed to continue until one or both parties modified their positions, neither the government employer nor the union leaders could use the arbitrator as a scapegoat, and the parties would become accountable for their decisions.

This limited-strike model has been adopted in various forms across provincial and federal jurisdictions. The crucial aspect of implementation is how essential employees who cannot strike are designated. The federal government experience is instructive in this respect. Well in advance of being in a legal strike position (before a non-binding conciliation board is appointed), the parties had to agree on those employees who were "necessary in the interest of the safety and security of the public" (see Subbarao, 1985). The employer (Treasury Board) would draw up a designation list which the bargaining agent could accept or challenge. Any disputes about the number of employees designated would be resolved by the quasi-judicial body that administered the Act. The system was accepted by the parties for fifteen years, despite the Public Service Staff Relations Board's (PSSRB) stated principle that it was less costly to society to err in favour of designating too many employees rather than too few. In 1982, the Treasury Board challenged a designation ruling regarding air-traffic controllers. The PSSRB had agreed with the union that only 10 percent of controllers should be designated to cover essential aviation (regular commercial aviation would be cancelled). The Supreme Court eventually agreed with Treasury Board that the PSSRB had overstepped its jurisdiction. Since then, designation has been virtually a management right. By 1985, fully 46 percent of the Public Service Alliance were designated, compared to 10–15 percent in the years preceding the air-traffic controllers' case. This average includes 63 percent of data processors, 68 percent of general labourers and trades, and 36 percent of clerical employees deemed to be essential.

For a system of limited strikes to work (and not represent a de facto way of removing the strike right), first and foremost, the designation process must be determined by an outside impartial third party. British Columbia fulfils this condition where the Labour Board designates employees as essential if the removal of their services would represent an "immediate and serious danger to life, health or safety" (J. Weiler, 1981, 106). In response to the designations, the union can unilaterally invoke arbitration (presumably when no pressure can be generated by non-designated strikers, e.g., fire fighters).

To retain legitimacy, the limited-strike process also requires governments to let a dispute run its course. Here, the British Columbia experience is not encouraging. In 1976, the Labour Board designated only 2 percent of Vancouver General Hospital employees as essential (and irreplaceable by other medical staff). The political heat became enormous and when the strike escalated from one to seven hospitals, the provincial government passed ad hoc legislation to end the strike. As Arthurs notes:

> ...ad hoc legislation is a dangerous business: it invites politicization of disputes; it changes the rules in the middle of the game—and is thus liable to be challenged on the grounds of basic fairness; and it does not afford the parties or the government any long-term basis for resolution of difficult, structural problems. (Quoted in J. Weiler, 1980, 105.)

The verdict is out as to whether any government has the ability to withstand media and public pressure for using legislation to end limited strikes in the public sector.

Wage Controls

Since the middle 1970s public sector compensation has been subjected to two rounds of wage control: in 1975–78 a national anti-inflation program, and in 1982–83 a series of federal and provincial restraint programs (except New Brunswick and Manitoba). A comparison of the official federal justifications for the programs found that in both periods the government was concerned with an erosion of Canada's international competitive position. Inflation rates were higher than its trading partners', and these higher rates were linked directly to high wage settlements, particularly in the public sector (see Swimmer, 1984). Whether you believe the rationale or not, the most telling feature about the two control programs is how different they were, given the similar justification. Swan argues that the 1982–83 restraint legislation reflects a political awareness of widespread animosity toward public employees:

> The latest round of legislation typically applies only to the public service, and appears to have the aim of holding down public sector wages relative to those of the private sector. While the 1975 legislation sought to deal with the inescapable inequities that arise from the application of restraints, and did not attempt to undo concluded collective agreements, current inflation-restraint legislation does not appear to respect concluded agreements, or even individual employment contracts in some jurisdictions. (1985, 65.)

The political winds have undoubtedly shifted against public sector unions in the past decade. Perceptions of their early successes at the bargaining table, coupled with their supposed immunity to layoffs, have led the media and politicians successfully to portray public employees as a privileged community within the country. The remainder of this chapter, which concerns public vs. private sector compensation, attempts to ascertain whether these perceptions are based on reality or myth.

COMPENSATION COMPARABILITY BETWEEN THE PUBLIC AND PRIVATE SECTORS

Public sector compensation is probably the most important output of the industrial relations system. Compensation not only affects worker morale, productivity and turnover, but it can also feed back on the legal, economic and political environment in which industrial relations takes place. Compensation is usually the major component in the cost of providing public services and therefore affects the service and tax levels. In turn, these factors can affect election outcomes and fiscal solvency of governments. If public sector wages become an "orbit of comparison" for private sector employees, aggregate levels of inflation and unemployment may be affected.

The compensation controversy centres on two related propositions:

1. Public employees are paid more than their private sector counterparts.
2. Public sector compensation settlements set a precedent that is emulated in the private sector.

Before evaluating the evidence for these two propositions, it is worthwhile to discuss the underlying theory that is implicitly assumed. Two reasons are generally given for the overpayment of public employees. First, the political constraint on public sector managers is not as binding as the profit constraint. Rather than adopt a tough stand on compensation and therefore risk (or actually take) a strike, politicians will tend to capitulate to union demands. This argument presumes that the political costs of a strike exceed the cost of higher wages because the public does not understand the relationship between public sector wages and future taxes. A related assertion deals with the time horizon of politicians. Unlike private sector managers who are concerned with long-run profit maximization, politicians think ahead only as far as the next election. Politicians will be prepared to offer higher future compensation in return for lower compensation during their term of office. Public sector compensation should therefore include more attractive pension plans and better job security than in the private sector. There is, however, a counterargument. Because many public employees are forbidden from bargaining certain aspects of compensation (e.g., seniority for promotion and layoffs), there should be a compensating differential in other aspects of compensation like wages or pensions. In addition, because government employers cannot be sued for breach of contract, it is always possible for governments to legislate away negotiated aspects of collective agreements (e.g., de-index federal pensions). This risk should also generate a compensating differential.

The theory underlying the second proposition, that higher public sector wages set a private sector precedent, is at best dubious. Collective bargaining is not a debating society, but rather an exercise in power. No competent employer will agree to a wage increase simply because the employees' union has made an eloquent speech that if public sector wages have increased by 10 percent, their wages must increase by 10 percent or more. The effective bargaining power of a union is composed of labour-market power (economic) and organizational power (the ability to marshall employees for a strike). For a union to raise real wages above their competitive level, both are required.

How will high public sector settlements affect wage determination? If the private employer feared that employees would quit and could not easily be replaced, it would indicate greater economic power for the union. In this case the wage expectation would be transmitted into a higher private sector wage. It is also possible that a union's organizational power would be affected. Public sector wages could be an important rallying point for private sector unions. We might expect more work stoppages (as unions wait for concessions that do not come), but not necessarily different contract outcomes. Higher private sector wage increases would require managements to be frightened into settlements that were unjustified on labour-market grounds and/or union leaders who were previously unaware of their members' economic power or unable to transmit that power into a strike. In a world of uncertainty, these scenarios are possible, but is not obvious why the signal must come from the public sector rather than another private sector industry.

Empirical Evidence

Over the past decade a number of empirical studies have been conducted, comparing individual wage levels between public and private sector employees. These studies use a statistical process known as regression analysis which estimates the average wage difference between public and private sector workers in the sample, after distinctions in individual characteristics (education, experience, etc.) have been controlled. The first such study was conducted by Gunderson (1978) using individual data from the 1970 census. He found that male public employees earned 6.2 percent more than their private sector counterparts after worker quality differences were held constant. The female advantage was substantially higher at 8.6 percent, which probably reflected less sexual discrimination in the public sector. Unfortunately, the data set did not include information on union status. Since almost all public employees are covered by a collective agreement compared to less than half of private sector employees, the wage advantage may have resulted from "publicness," "unionness" or both. In particular, it may be that unions in both the public and private sector raise wages.

Subsequent studies using data sets that capture union status have been able to disentangle these two factors. Robinson and Tomes (1982), using 1979 data, find that unionized employees in the public sector earn 6.7 percent less on average than unionized private sector employees, while non-union public employees earned 17.6 percent more than their private sector counterparts. In other words, there is a "public sector advantage" only for the small group of non-union public employees. Unionism is at the root of the aggregate public sector wage advantage. Simpson (1985), using 1974 data, and Kumar and Stengos (1985), using 1982 data, find the same result. Public sector wages of unionized employees (the overwhelming majority) are equal or below those of the unionized private sector.

Finally, Figure 14.5 presents a comparison of base-rate increases for major collective agreements without cost of living clauses (COLA clauses

Figure 14.5
Average Percentage Wage Increases in Base Rates
for Collective Agreements without Cost of Living (COLA) Clauses[1]

Annual Data Group	1972	1973	1974	1975	1976	1977	1978	1979	1980	1981	1982	1983	1984	1985	Average 1972-85
Federal Administration	8.8	12.0	11.2	13.9	11.9	9.5	6.7	8.3	10.8	12.6	8.3	5.4	5.0	3.2	9.1
Provincial Administration	7.2	10.3	14.2	25.1	11.2	7.5	7.2	8.3	11.2	13.6	11.3	5.8	5.4	4.2	10.2
Local Administration	7.6	9.8	12.6	16.5	10.4	7.9	6.4	8.7	10.4	13.2	12.9	5.7	3.3	4.7	9.3
Health, Welfare and Education	7.9	10.0	21.7	21.8	10.8	6.9	6.5	8.1	11.1	13.7	11.1	5.6	3.1	3.3	10.1
Telephone, Electric and Water	9.4	12.8	18.4	22.8	10.9	7.0	6.7	7.8	10.1	13.6	11.4	6.6	2.6	3.6	10.3
Total Public	7.9	10.6	14.5	19.7	11.1	7.8	6.7	8.3	10.9	13.3	9.9	5.6	4.0	3.7	9.6
Total Private	9.6	11.5	15.0	17.5	10.5	8.0	7.7	9.8	11.8	13.7	10.8	5.4	2.9	3.2	9.8

1. Bargaining units with fewer than 500 members are excluded.

Source: Swimmer (1984); updated by the author.

are rarely found in public sector agreements). Over the period of 1972–85 public sector agreements have increased at 9.6 percent annually compared to 9.8 percent for private sector agreements. Within public sector categories, provincial, health, education and welfare, and public utility employees' wages increased the most (10.2 percent annual average), while federal and local employees' increases were below average (9.2 percent annually). These data do not confirm general overpayment, and if public sector agreements set a precedent in the private sector, it would be one of moderation. On balance, the evidence supports the view that the outcry about public employee overpayment is really a veiled argument against unionism generally.

Before moving to the evidence regarding the precedent-setting effects, we should discuss the other aspects of compensation. The most important is job security. It has been argued that public employees are shielded from the vagaries of the labour market, and should therefore receive lower wages. Unlike the wage issue, this aspect of compensation has not been the subject of much empirical work. It is true that before 1982, layoffs at the provincial and federal governments were rare. Some provinces had negotiated job guarantees, usually in the form of downsizing by attrition. Two points about job security must be understood. In some jurisdictions, notably the federal government, job security is not a bargainable issue. Whatever rights exist for surplus employees are the result of government policy, not collective bargaining. The federal government does have a priority system that gives these employees the right to jobs for which they qualify, without a competition. Secondly, the job protection provided by the federal and most provincial governments is a luxury of a large employer (because of attrition). The question of whether public employees are more secure than private employees in establishments of comparable size has yet to be addressed empirically. The only study I am aware of focused on the seasonal variation of public employment for 1960–75 and found substantial seasonal changes in the local and provincial government employment (see Foot et al., 1978).

Finally, the issue of public sector pensions is worth discussing. Most media debate focuses on the indexation of federal government pensions, which has led to superior payouts for beneficiaries (particularly in high inflationary periods of the mid-1970s). Again, it must be stated that neither employees nor the bargaining agents have control over the pension plan. It is not negotiable, and although it clearly has been a generous benefit, the government can remove indexing at any time and attempted to do so in 1985 (though lobbying by superannuaries was sufficient to defeat the idea, at least temporarily).

At the local level there is evidence that pensions (and pension-like benefits such as a retirement bonus) were agreed to by managers without realizing the extent of their future liability. Cities and school boards have been trying to reduce these commitments in recent rounds of bargaining.

Comparisons of public and private sector fringe benefits as a percentage of payroll indicate relative equality: 37 percent for municipalities, 30 percent for hospitals, 32 percent for both education and government compared to 32 percent for all industries in 1979 (Gunderson, 1984, 24). However, if the value of job security and pensions were included, this would likely tilt the balance toward public employees. Apparently, slightly better benefits compensate for slightly lower wages for public sector unionized workers when compared to their private sector union counterparts.

The empirical evidence regarding public sector wage spillovers into the private sector was recently reviewed by Wilton (1986). Although an early study by Cousineau and Lacroix (1974) found significant spillovers, subsequent studies that were superior on statistical grounds (see Auld et al., 1976), found no evidence of public sector wage settlements spilling over into private sector settlements.

Wilton concludes:

> There is no empirical evidence that public sector wage settlements will, in general, spill over into the private sector and permeate throughout the entire economy. Any wage spillovers from the public sector would appear to be quite limited in nature, confined to specific urban areas and certain occupations. There is no empirical support for the proposition that one large public sector wage settlement, say, for Seaway workers or Toronto teachers, will affect wage settlements throughout the entire private sector. (p. 281.)

Finally, it must be noted that these results were not unknown to government policy makers. Nonetheless, the myths about public sector compensation were used as the justification of public sector wage controls. The following memorandum (obtained by the *Toronto Star*) was written by one of the architects of the federal "6 and 5" restraint program:

> There is a widespread perception in the business community that public sector wages are an important factor in the rapid rise in wage settlements. This perception is incorrect: public sector wage settlements are not "leading" the private sector. Nevertheless, the misconception remains, and there is considerable pressure from the business community for the federal government to show more restraint with respect to employee compensation. (Swimmer, 1984, 260.)

THE FUTURE OF PUBLIC SECTOR COLLECTIVE BARGAINING

Writing in 1983, Mark Thompson and I contrasted two views about the future of public sector bargaining, given the flood of federal and provincial restraint legislation. The optimistic view saw 1982–83 as an aberration, where governments attempted to respond to extraordinary circumstances of simultaneously high inflation and unemployment rates. Once the economy turned around, the collective bargaining system would return to normalcy. In addition, it was presumed that the public employers would learn the lesson that wage restraint is possible by tough bargaining without resort to changing the legislated rules of the game. The more pessimistic view (Panitch and Swartz, 1984) argued that the nature of the relationship between the "state" and public sector unions had changed from consent to coercion. Rather than negotiate industrial peace with organized labour through favourable legislative and fiscal/monetary policies, governments were using special "temporary" legislation to remove bargaining rights won over the post-war period.

Although the verdict is still in doubt, the past three years seem to support the "Doomsday view." The federal government has successfully devalued, if not removed, the right to strike via the designation process. Alberta and B.C. have permanently amended the criteria that arbitrators must employ when making awards. Although other provinces have reverted to the pre-1982 bargaining patterns, the real test will come when the economy favours the unions. Are public sector unions going to be allowed free collective bargaining in times of high unemployment and modest economic growth, and then fall subject to "temporary restraint" when the economy is booming?

An important part of the answer will come from the public sector unions themselves. The greatest challenge facing these unions will be to convince the public at large and union members in the private and public sectors that their cause is just. Are public employees really overpaid, underworked, and blessed with lifetime job security? Given the available evidence, it is possible to confront the stereotype head on and demonstrate it is mythology.

The 1980s will probably be a watershed for the public sector labour movement, as the 1930s were for the private sector. The actions of unions and governments may decide whether the benefits won by public employees over the past twenty years will wither away.

BIBLIOGRAPHY

Auld, D. A. L., L. N. Christofides, R. Swidinsky, and D. A. Wilton (1981), "The effect of settlement state on negotiated wage settlements in Canada." *Industrial and Labour Relations Review* 34: 234–44.
_____ and D.A. Wilton (1981), *Public Sector Wage Inflation in Ontario.* Toronto: Ontario Economic Council.
Adams, G. W. (1981), "The Ontario experience with interest arbitration:

Problems in detecting policy." In J. Weiler (ed.), *Interest Arbitration*. Toronto: Carswell, pp. 133–174.

Anderson, J. C. (1981), "Arbitration in the federal public service." In J. Weiler (ed.), *Interest Arbitration*. Toronto: Carswell, pp. 43–77.

Christensen, S. (1980), *Unions and Public Interest*. Vancouver: Fraser Institute.

Cousineau, J. M., and R. Lacroix (1977), *Wage Determination in Major Collective Agreements in the Private and Public Sector*. Study prepared for the Economic Council of Canada. Ottawa: Minister of Supply and Services Canada.

Deverell, J. (1982), "The Ontario hospital dispute, 1980–81". *Studies in Political Economy* 9: 179–90.

Fisher, E. and Starek, H. (1980), "Police bargaining in Canada: Private sector bargaining, compulsory arbitration and mediation arbitration in Vancouver." In Downie, B. and Jackson, R. (eds.), *Conflict and Cooperation in Policy Labour Relations*. Hull: Minister of Supply and Services Canada, pp. 35–61.

Foot, D., Scicluna, E. and Thadaney, P. (1978), "The seasonality of government employment in Canada." In Foot, D. (ed.), *Public Employment and Compensation in Canada: Myths and Realities*. Scarborough: Butterworths, pp. 93–105.

Gunderson, M. (1983), *The Economic Aspects of Interest Arbitration*. Toronto: Ontario Economic Council.

_____ (1984), "The public/private sector compensation controversy." In M. Thompson and G. Swimmer (eds.), *Conflict or Compromise: The Future of Public Sector Industrial Relations*. Montreal: Institute for Research on Public Policy, pp. 5–43.

Hebert, G. (1984), "Public sector bargaining in Quebec: A case of Hypercentralization." In M. Thomson and G. Swimmer (eds.), *Conflict or Compromise: The Future of Public Sector Industrial Relations*. Montreal: Institute for Research on Public Policy, pp. 229–282.

Kumar, P. and Stengos, T. (1985), "Microestimates of the union–nonunion wage differential in Canada, using the sample selectivity approach." Discussion paper 574, Queen's University. (Mimeo.)

Labour Canada (1985a), *Directory of Labour Organizations in Canada 1985*. Hull: Minister of Supply and Services Canada.

_____ (1985b), *Strikes and Lockouts in Canada 1984*. Hull: Minister of Supply and Services Canada.

_____ , Federal Provincial Relations Branch (1986). "Interest arbitration in the public and parapublic sectors in Canada." (Mimeo.)

Panitch, L. V. and D. Swartz (1984), "From free collective bargaining to permanent exceptionalism: The economic crisis and the transformation of industrial relations in Canada." In Thompson and Swimmer, (eds.), *Conflict and Compromise*. Montreal: Institute for Research on Public Policy, pp. 407–435.

Robinson, C. and N. Tomes (1984), "Union wage differentials in the public and private sectors: A simultaneous equation specification." *Journal of Labour Economics* 2: 106–27.

Rose, J. (1984), "Growth patterns of public sector unions." In M. Thompson and G. Swimmer (eds.), *Conflict or Compromise: The Future of Public Sector Industrial Relations*. Montreal: Institute for Research on Public Policy, pp. 87–119.

Simpson, W. (1985), "The impact of unions on the structure of Canadian wages: An empirical analysis with microdata." *Canadian Journal of Economics* xviii (1): 164–181.

Smith, D. (1984), "Strikes in the Canadian public sector." In M. Thompson and G. Swimmer (eds.), *Conflict or Compromise: The Future of Public Sector Industrial Relations*. Montreal: Institute for Research on Public Policy, pp. 201–228.

Subbarao, A. (1985), "Impasse choice in the Canadian federal service: An innovation and an intrigue." *Relations industrielles* 40(3): 567–590.

Swan, K. (1985), "Differences among provinces in public sector dispute resolution." In Conklin et al. (eds.), *Public Sector Compensation*. Toronto: Ontario Economic Council, pp. 49–75.

Swimmer, G. (1985), "Dispute resolution in the Ontario public sector: What's so wrong about the right to strike." In Conklin et al. (eds.), *Public Sector Compensation*. Toronto: Ontario Economic Council, pp. 154–178.

—— (1984), "Six and five: Part grandstanding and part grand plan." In A. Maslove (ed.), *How Ottawa Spends, 1984: The New Agenda*. Toronto: Methuen, pp. 240–281.

Weiler, J. (1981), "Interest arbitration in British Columbia: The essential services dispute act." In J. Weiler (ed.), *Interest Arbitration*. Toronto: Carswell, pp. 99–131.

Weiler, P. (1980), *Reconcilable Differences: New Directions in Canadian Labour Law*. Toronto: Carswell.

Wilton, D. (1986), "Public Sector Wage Compensation." In Riddell, W. (ed.), *Canadian Labour Relations*. Toronto: University of Toronto Press, pp. 257–284.

15

Collective Bargaining and Occupational Health and Safety

Bob Sass and Mark Stobbe

Every day that a worker reports to work, she or he is confronted with danger. Work kills more than 8,000 workers every year, making it the third leading cause of death in Canada. Every year, over one million others are injured on the job, with about one-half of these hurt severely enough that they are forced to miss time at work. An estimated 13.4 million workdays per year are lost, equivalent to the full-time year-round employment of 54,000 people (Reasons et al., 1981). These figures mean that a worker is injured in Canada every thirty seconds, and twenty-two people per day die as a result of their jobs.

The extent of occupational injury, disease, and death makes occupational health and safety (OHS) an important issue of collective bargaining. Emile Boudreau, who has served as Director of OHS for the Quebec Federation of Labour, says that

> unionized workers (and it is worse for the nonunionized) and the unions which represent them negotiate the health and safety of the workers, and they do it at every negotiation. And on an individual basis, the workers, whether they are unionized or not, negotiate their health and safety each time they report to work at most of our factories, construction sites and other places of work...let no one tell me that health and safety in the workplace are not negotiable. This idea (which plays into management's hands) is put forward seriously only by out-and-out idealists....Health and safety in the workplace are constantly negotiable (1978:82–88).

This chapter examines part of this process of negotiation. Formal collective bargaining is only one, albeit a very important one, of the ways that workers and employers negotiate OHS conditions. We will discuss the history of collective bargaining over OHS issues, the types and extent of health and safety-related clauses in collective bargaining agreements in Canada, some of the factors that influence whether health and safety will be addressed in collective bargaining, and the outcome of these negotiations.

OHS **Prior to 1970**

Prior to 1970, union response to occupational health and safety was relatively underdeveloped. While some unions had bargained over OHS issues, there had been little sustained effort using a consistent strategy by unions. The major OHS struggle of the past had been over a reduction in work hours, which had the effect of reducing workers' risk by removing them from the workplace for a greater proportion of the day. While this was an extremely important struggle for labour, the institution of an eight-hour day left unaddressed the risks faced by workers while they were still inside the workplace. In order to explain why consistent bargaining over OHS issues is a recent phenomenon, we must briefly examine the historical development of management control over the workplace and management's resulting control over OHS conditions.

Labour and employment law in Canada evolved from British Common Law. It was argued that employees voluntarily and individually entered into an implied contract with the employer under which the employee accepted the prevailing terms of labour. The employer's obligation was to compensate the worker for the time and energy expended. While this exchange was being transacted, the employer enjoyed all of the legal protection that had evolved for private property. Employees lost, for the duration of time spent at work, these legal rights since they brought no property to work and therefore had no claim to property protection (Seltzer, 1979, 1–13). Employers therefore possessed the right to use their property as they wished with only minimal regard for the health and safety implications to their employees.

This right was tempered by the possibility of civil suits for negligence. Property owners were legally liable for the consequences to others of the negligent use of their property. This enabled employees injured while at work to sue for damages in cases where they could prove that the injury was the result of negligence by their employer. However, three legal defences were allowed that greatly lessened a worker's chances of success in legal action. The first was the "assumption of risk" doctrine, whereby employees were assumed to have known about, and freely accepted, the normal risks of a job when they entered employment. The second was the "fellow servant" doctrine, which held that an employer was not liable for an injury to one employee caused by the negligence of a different employee. This doctrine was created by the Priestly vs. Fowler (1833) ruling in Britain. An employer was liable when the negligence of an employee resulted in injury to a third person, except when the injured person was another employee. To be found negligent when an employee was injured, the employer had to be personally negligent. The doctrine of fellow employment prevented successful suits in any enterprise large enough that the owner did not directly supervise every work area. The third defence was the doctrine of "contributory negligence." Under this, any negligence of the worker, however minor, eliminated or reduced any award based on the employer's negligence (Risk, 1983; Tucker, 1984).

These common-law defences against employers' liability were amended by statute in some provinces. For example, the doctrine of fellow employment was modified in Ontario in 1886 with the passage of the Employers Liability Act. Negligent actions of managers or supervisors were excluded from the protection of this defence. The legislative restriction of some of the common-law defences against employers' negligence, and the hearing of these cases before juries increasingly sympathetic to the plight of injured workers, resulted in workers having increasing success in negligence suits beginning in the late 1890s. However, only a small proportion of injured workers gained any damages for injuries suffered on the job, and the ability to sue assisted workers only after injury had occurred. Employers still retained the unilateral right to establish working conditions.

The ability of workers to act collectively to force changes to unsafe or unhealthy conditions was hindered by legal restrictions upon unions. The British Combination Acts of 1799 and 1800 outlawed any combination or concerted action by either employers or employees. These laws made unions illegal in Canada until 1872 when the Canadian Trade Unions Act declared that unions were not unlawful merely because of restraint of trade, and decriminalized peaceful picketing (Carrothers, 1965, 11). The early illegality of unions, and subsequent legal restrictions on their organization and activity, hindered the development of collective action that would restrict employers' determination of working conditions.

In response to pressure from unions and middle-class social reformers, legislatures in Canada passed a number of Acts establishing minimum terms for child and female employment; setting standards for sanitation and the guarding of machinery; and providing inspectors to enforce these standards. Under the terms of the BNA Act, jurisdiction was assigned to the provinces in most industries except rail transport, communications, and banking. Ontario passed the first Factory Act in 1884. Quebec followed in 1885, Manitoba in 1900, Nova Scotia in 1901, New Brunswick in 1905, British Columbia in 1908, and Saskatchewan in 1909. Ontario and Manitoba passed similar legislation governing conditions in shops in 1888. Nova Scotia passed the first Mines Act in Canada in 1858. All provinces with a mining industry had followed this example by 1900 (Lorentsen and Woolner, 1950). Enforcement of all of these Acts was weak and irregular. The various Factory, Mines, and Shops Acts represented at least a theoretical infringement on employers' unilateral rights to determine working conditions. They did not, however, encourage collective bargaining or worker activity to improve conditions. Instead, minimum standards were to be enforced by state officials.

By 1910, the number of injuries in industry were sufficient to force major governmental action. Employers were being subjected to an escalating number of negligence suits, and both employers and government officials were concerned that the existing system of injury prevention and compensation was radicalizing workers. The Ontario government appointed Ontario Chief Justice William Meredith to study the issue. In 1914 he recommended that the right to sue for negligence be removed and replaced by an automatic payment of a specified amount from a government-administered fund, paid for by regular assessments on employers (Meredith, 1914). Workers gained income security in the event of injury in exchange for losing their right to sue employers. Employers gained protection from legal action in exchange for the payment of a modest and predictable assessment. Despite some dispute over details, Meredith's proposals were supported by both unions and business groups (Piva, 1975), and Ontario established Canada's first Workmen's Compensation Board on January 1, 1915. Other provinces soon followed Ontario's example. Nova Scotia passed similar legislation in 1915; British Columbia in 1916; Alberta and New Brunswick in 1918; Manitoba in 1920; Quebec in 1931; and Saskatchewan in 1929.

With the passage of Workers Compensation Acts and Factory Acts, the essential features of OHS activity until the 1970s was in place. Regulations outlining minimum sanitation and safety standards existed but were rarely enforced. Compensation was paid to victims of occupational injuries and to a very small proportion of those suffering from occupational disease. There were some minor modifications in this system over the next five decades, mostly confined to improvements in benefit payments, but no substantive changes.

Within the workplace, management retained almost exclusive control over the determination of OHS conditions. Compensation laws weakened the impetus for unions to attempt to secure greater preventative powers either through legislation or collective bargaining. By providing some measure of income security to injured workers, compensation was seen to fulfil employers' obligations to those injured on the job. This was supported by the claim that workers themselves, through their own stupidity, carelessness, or foolishness, were responsible for accidents. These claims were systematized in such theories as accident proneness which blamed inherent psychological or physiological characteristics of some workers for repeated accidents (Sass and Crook, 1981). Theories of causation that blamed workers for their injuries also enabled employers and managers to argue that prevention attempts other than educational campaigns were futile. These theories gained wide acceptance with the general public, medical professionals, industrial managers, and state officials, and hindered the development of prevention strategies that might involve infringements of managerial prerogatives. It should be noted that these worker-based theories of accident causation have been scientifically demonstrated as false (Sass and Crook, 1981; Surrey, 1969).

According to Michael Nash, this system of OHS regulation and compensation resulted in some of the following problems:

> ...some workplaces or problems were covered by several statutes while others were not covered at all, there was no overall direction for research, senseless anomalies among different workforces abounded, the standards for exposure to workplace hazards were generally out of date, the penalties were ridiculously low, and workers had little access to information (1983,7).

During this period, there were attempts by unions to improve OHS conditions through collective bargaining. However, OHS rarely was of high priority. This was due to the fact that until the post-World War II era, unions were forced to devote most of their attention to survival and gaining recognition. After collective bargaining rights were obtained, other demands such as wages, union representation, grievance procedures, and job rights were a more immediate priority. Union memberships rarely coalesced around health and safety issues as major bargaining objectives. In addition, union leaders realized that OHS demands would challenge directly management's prerogatives in the operation of the workplace (Seltzer, 1979, 84). Because of this, it was realized that management and employers would strongly resist concessions in this area. The natural tendency was to attempt to achieve the attainable.

Despite the relatively low priority placed on OHS, some gains were made by unions. The most important was the reduction in hours of work. This reduced individual exposure to hazards and prevented many accidents caused by fatigue. By the 1960s, many collective agreements had some mention of occupational health or safety. Most of these simply obligated management to establish a safety program. In addition, some agreements required management to provide personal protective equipment. Although the tangible gains for unions were few, workers in the years prior to 1970 set the stage for the sudden explosion of both bargaining and legislation that was to occur subsequent to 1970.

OHS Subsequent to 1970

During the 1970s, most jurisdictions in Canada rewrote their OHS legislation. Several major strikes were conducted over OHS issues, and OHS received a higher priority in much bargaining. In the United States, major legislative reform came with the passage of the OSHA in 1970. The first legislative change came in Saskatchewan in 1972. The newly elected NDP government passed the *Occupational Health Act* which centralized OHS enforcement into one branch of the Department of Labour, and required every employer of more than ten workers to form a joint OHS committee composed of equal numbers of management and worker representatives. A year later, amendments to the *Labour Standards Act* gave legislative protection from discrimination to committee members and gave workers the right to refuse work that they believed to be unusually dangerous. The new Saskatchewan legislation and its enforcement differed from previous legislation in three major ways. First, enforcement was centralized rather than fragmented according to industry or hazard. This allowed for the development of a province-wide enforcement strategy. Second, the working theory of injury and disease causation was different. Instead of blaming workers for causing accidents, the new Saskatchewan approach blamed workplace conditions. Therefore, instead of exhorting workers to "be safe" and training managers in safety management techniques, the Saskatchewan OHS branch concentrated on improving unsafe and unhealthy workplace conditions. Finally, workers themselves were seen as intelligent, responsible people capable of participating in the process of making workplaces safe and healthy. The joint committees were to allow workers participation on a continuing basis, and the right of refusal was to allow workers to protect themselves against excessive hazards. It also came to be realized that effective participation or personal protection could not occur without knowledge of the hazards present on the job, so information-provision requirements were instituted. The Saskatchewan program was based on giving rights to workers that would enable them to better their working conditions. The trinity of the right to participate, the right to refuse, and the right to know formed the core (Sass, 1975, 1985; Reschenthaler, 1979). One aim of the Saskatchewan program was to encourage collective action by workers to resolve OHS problems.

Many elements of the Saskatchewan program were copied by other jurisdictions. Alberta, Manitoba, Ontario and New Brunswick passed new OHS Acts in 1976; Newfoundland and Canada in 1978; and Quebec in 1979. British Columbia, which administers its OHS program through the WCB, has modified its regulations so that they are similar to legislation in other jurisdictions (Nash, 1983, 8). All of the new OHS Acts provided, in varying degrees, workers with some OHS rights. Michael Nash (1983) provides the best discussion of the legal details of each program.

The new OHS legislation was partially caused by, and partially caused, collective bargaining around OHS issues. Among the more prominent conflicts were those waged by asbestos miners in the Confederation of National Trade Unions (CNTU) at Thetford Mines, Quebec; the asbestos miners in the United Steel Workers of America (USWA) at Baie Verte, Newfoundland; the uranium miners in the USWA at Elliot Lake, Ontario (Tataryn, 1979), and postal workers in the Canadian Union of Postal

Workers (CUPW) across Canada. In many other cases, OHS clauses have been written into collective agreements without the necessity of long and bitter strikes.

Collective agreement clauses dealing specifically with OHS can be grouped into five main categories. These are:

1. Premium pay clauses. In such provisions, "the employer 'buys' the right to engage employees in work that is acknowledged to be either a health or safety hazard" (Steinberg, 1978, 126). The only preventative justification for this type of provision is that premiums paid for high-risk jobs may induce the employer to attempt to make the job less risky in order to avoid the need to pay the premium. In practice, this type of clause tends to compensate risk rather than eliminate it. In recent years, most unions have rejected this approach and bargained instead for preventative measures. In a study based on a sample of 650 collective agreements covering almost 650,000 employees in all industries except construction, railways and agriculture, Charles Steinberg (1978) found that 12.8 percent of agreements covering 31.3 percent of employees contained some provision for premium pay.

2. Provision of personal protective equipment. Under the terms of these clauses, the employer agrees to provide or subsidize the purchase of personal protective equipment such as hardhats, ear muffs or plugs, safety glasses, boots, coveralls, gloves and so on. The clauses vary in items covered, the number provided and the cost to the employee. In 1982, of all contracts except construction covering 200 or more employees, 51.8 percent covering 42.9 percent of employees had some clause calling for some provision of protective equipment. In 22.8 percent of the agreements covering 24.0 percent of employees, the agreement called for the employer to pay the full cost of specified items. In only 2.4 percent of agreements covering 1.2 percent of workers did the employer agree to pay the full cost of both providing and maintaining specified items (Labour Canada, 1982).

3. Standards clauses. These clauses specify maximum exposure limits, ban or control the use of particular substances, or specify work procedures. Except to reiterate that legislative or regulative standards will apply, these clauses are rare in Canada. Management usually strongly resists such provisions since they are perceived as an infringement on their prerogatives. In addition, unions are often reluctant to impose standards at the enterprise level, since this could weaken the employer's position relative to competitors and result in job loss. Most unions therefore prefer to achieve standards legislatively.

4. Compensation and placement clauses. These provisions specify protection for workers after injury has occurred. Examples include provision for payment of wages for the balance of the workday after an injury has occurred and the provision of "bumping" rights to workers suffering a work-caused long-term disability that prevents them from performing their previous job.

5. Procedural and enabling clauses. These are the most important of the preventative contractual clauses. They provide a contractual basis for the exercise of workers' OHS rights. Procedural clauses can specify the structure, powers and terms of reference of joint OHS committees and/or call for the employer to establish and maintain an OHS program. Enabling provisions can specify information to be provided to the OHS committee, union or individual worker; enshrine the right of refusal for unsafe work; and provide protection for workers exercising their rights of refusal or participation. In 1982, of all non-construction collective agreements covering more than two hundred workers, 19.5 percent of agreements covering 22.8 percent of workers mandated a safety program; 15.2 percent of agreements covering 14.9 percent of workers established an OHS committee; and 34.1 percent of agreements covering 33.2 percent of workers called for both an OHS committee and a safety program. A total of 31.2 percent of agreements covering 29.1 percent of workers contained no procedural clauses. Education workers have the poorest coverage, with 78.2 percent of their agreements covering 82.1 percent of workers having no procedural provision. At the other end of the spectrum, 85.5 percent of agreements covering 93.1 percent of workers in the mining industry call for both an OHS committee and a safety program (Labour Canada, 1982). The contractual provision of procedural or enabling clauses can strengthen rights provided in legislation, extend these rights to workers exempt from legislation, and allow for enforcement through the grievance procedure as well as through reliance on government inspectors.

In addition to provisions dealing explicitly with OHS, other aspects of a collective agreement can have an impact on the health and safety of workers. Provisions for hours of work, rest periods and limitations on overtime reduce exposure to hazards and accidents caused by fatigue. The existence and structure of incentive payment rates can have an impact on injury rates by encouraging workers to produce at a pace or under conditions that are unsafe. Finally, the regular grievance machinery can be used to resist pressures for production or harassment of workers that can lead to accidents.

Influences on Health and Safety Bargaining

Collective bargaining around OHS issues begins in the context of employer control of the workplace. The employer is free to determine workplace conditions and procedures except to the extent that the collective agreement or legislation places limits upon the unilateral exercise of management powers. As Harry Glasbeek simply states: "Employers, by definition, have control over the enterprise" (1982, 58). When the law "by definition" grants control to the employer, the most important influence on OHS collective bargaining is immediately established. Workers and their unions are placed in the position of attempting to limit or regulate powers possessed by management. Within these confines, a number of factors influence how vigorously unions will attempt to bargain for OHS improvements, and how successful they will be.

Technological Factors

The technology used by an industry determines to a certain extent the range of hazards existing in the workplace. The existing hazards influence the motivation of employers and employees either to ignore or attempt to improve health and safety conditions (Bacow, 1980, 88). For example, the dangerous nature of mining in Canada is partially responsible for the almost universal existence of OHS clauses in mining collective agreements, while the lack of immediate or visible hazards in offices contributes to a lower priority being placed upon OHS. In addition, the technology also can influence the form of preventative measures negotiated (Bacow, 1980, 89). If workers are being exposed to a single, identifiable hazard, then negotiation for a standards type of clause is feasible. Thus, asbestos workers in Thetford Mines in 1975, and in Baie Verte in 1978, struck to demand adherence to an exposure standard for asbestos (Tataryn, 1979, 15–60). If hazards are more numerous and constantly changing, unions will likely seek to bargain for procedural clauses to establish a framework to resolve problems on a continuing basis. Despite the importance of technological factors in OHS collective bargaining, it is a mistake to describe it as the major determinant. First, the technology of an industry is not fixed, but created over time as a result of management choices and decisions. Therefore, it is not the technology that independently determines the nature of hazards and the level of risk, but rather the decisions about what types of technology to create, purchase and utilize. These decisions are made on economic and political grounds. Collective bargaining and the response of individual workers can influence what decisions are made, as well as be influenced by the existing technology. Second, the technology in place at any given moment merely sets the parameters of risk. Other factors such as speed of production, payment method, supervision style, shift scheduling, length of work day, or maintenance of equipment also contribute to the level of risk and therefore the motivation for bargaining. Finally, a focus solely on technology does not explain changes in bargaining priorities while the technology remains constant, or explain variations between work sites using the same technology.

Market Conditions

Market conditions or fiscal constraints can affect the willingness or ability of both employers and employees to bargain over OHS. The financial status or competitive position of a company can affect management decisions on compliance with union requests for changes in workplace conditions. Unions are also often unwilling to insist upon expensive changes in industries or companies that are in precarious financial condition (Bacow, 1980, 89–90). This hesitation is particularly pronounced when labour-market conditions are unfavourable to workers. In periods of high unemployment, the alternative for workers is often putting up with an unhealthy or unsafe job, or having no job at all.

Power Relationships

The overall relations of power in the workplace affect the nature or existence of OHS bargaining. Until unions are successful in establishing themselves in a workplace, negotiating a living wage level, and negotiating and enforcing a working grievance procedure, OHS concerns will not usually receive high priority. Even after a union is established, relatively strong unions will likely be more successful in negotiating OHS protection than will weaker ones. The relative strength of workers and management in a workplace depends on many factors including the level of unemployment, market conditions, the capital intensity of the industry, and the degree of centralization of bargaining. In addition, where management has the ability to transfer the location of production, the strength of the union will be much lower. Emile Boudreau (1978) tells of the case of a lead processing factory in Montreal in which 29 of 90 workers were forced to leave work because of lead poisoning in an 18-month period. Officials from the Ministry of Labour identified the situation as "unacceptable" and stated it could warrant a shutdown for renovations. When the company responded "with a thinly veiled threat to transfer production to its Toronto plant or to its furnace in Windsor," the union safety committee and workers in the plant chose job security rather that the possibility of losing their jobs in the pursuit of health. In a similar case, workers at the Inglis plant in Stoney Creek, Ontario have been unable to obtain an adequate containment system for meso-isocynates in the face of continual threats and rumours of plant closure due to a shift in production location (Martel, 1986). The threat of job transfer can be applied on an industry- or nation-wide basis as well as plant by plant. "Excessive" OHS protection has been cited by corporation officials as a reason for the transfer of some hazardous industries, such as asbestos fabrication, to the Third World (Castleman, 1983). Such explicit or implicit threats greatly weaken a union's bargaining position for improvements in OHS conditions.

Another management strategy that can shift the power relationship in its favour is the selective hiring of immigrant workers. In their study of workers' attitudes to asbestos hazards, Sally Luce and Gene Swimmer (1982) encountered one plant where language diversity prevented the dissemination of information about asbestos hazards and hindered workers attempting to raise OHS concerns as a bargaining issue. Immigrants who lack citizenship are often very difficult to organize because of fears of deportation or loss of immigration status (Bolaria, 1986). Some high-risk industries such as textiles, clothing and market-garden agriculture rely heavily on immigrant labour, as have such industries as mining, construction and some sectors of manufacturing in the past. Since management has the right to hire, it is possible to select a workforce that will be relatively powerless.

Another factor that can have a major impact upon power relationships within the workplace is government legislation and regulation. The terms of labour relations legislation will strengthen one side or the other in collective bargaining (England, 1983). Achievement of standards and procedures through legislation alters the legal basis from which bargaining begins. In the United States, most OHS bargaining revolves around union efforts to secure procedural clauses such as the establishment of joint OHS committees or the right to refuse unsafe work. In most jurisdictions in Canada, these have been achieved legislatively, allowing unions to bargain for extensions and to attempt to ensure compliance. Katherine Swinton concludes her study of OHS reforms with the conclusion that "to be effective, [they] need the support of government. Effective policing by worker auditors requires objective standards, which can be enforced, if need be, by administrative remedies and ultimately prosecution" (1983, 175). That is, the power of workers and unions in the workplace must be augmented by supportive governmental power if their basically weaker position is to be strengthened sufficiently to ensure adequate protection.

Availability of Information

Collective bargaining for OHS protection is often neglected because of ignorance of existing hazards. This is particularly true of health hazards that are not as immediately visible as traumatic injuries. Lack of information includes lack of knowledge of the effects of substances workers are exposed to, lack of knowledge of exposure levels and even lack of knowledge about what harmful substances workers are being exposed to. Much of this lack of knowledge is intentionally created. There is no national program of labelling or monitoring of toxic chemicals in Canada (Ison, 1978, 3), in part because such labels would violate trade secrets protected by manufacturers (Doern, 1977, 19). In many cases, even employers do not know the ingredients of substances to which they are exposing their employees.

The most striking example of the suppression of information involved the hazards and level of exposure to asbestos. The harmful effects of asbestos on the human lung had been observed as early as the first century A.D. In 1918, the Prudential Life Insurance Company noted the "probable harmfulness of asbestos dust" and stopped issuing life insurance policies to asbestos workers (Jangula, 1985, 141). In 1930, official recognition was given to asbestosis in both the United States and Britain. The causal relationship between asbestosis and lung cancer and mesothelioma was established soon after (Selikoff and Lee, 1978). Despite this proof, asbestos industry officials continued to deny that asbestos caused lung disease, usually by blaming cigarette smoking for asbestos-caused lung disease. Much reliance was placed upon industry-funded studies employing faulty methodology which showed minimal health effects (Tataryn, 1979, 33–37). In Thetford Mines, Quebec, dust exposure readings were kept from workers, and many workers who were developing asbestosis were not informed of the fact by the company physician conducting a medical monitoring program. In 1975, ten days after the Thetford Mines asbestos workers did receive information about the hazards they faced and its effects on their health in a report from the Environmental Sciences Laboratory of Mount Sinai Medical School, they struck to force reductions in exposure levels (Tataryn, 1979, 15–60). Since the hazards of asbestos became widely publicized in the mid-1970s, its elimination or control has become a bargaining item in workplaces across Canada, ranging from mines to libraries and from power plants to schools. Information about both the existence of asbestos in these workplaces and of its hazards was a prerequisite for bargaining to occur.

The provision of information is both a prerequisite and an objective of collective bargaining. Information must be available before effective negotiations over OHS issues can occur. Therefore, information clauses are often among the first contractual OHS provisions negotiated by unions.

Management Attitudes

Management willingness to negotiate about OHS issues will have a great impact upon whether collective bargaining will improve working conditions. To the extent that management is unwilling to negotiate, the result of collective bargaining will depend solely upon the power relationships within the workforce. Management's attitudes to collective bargaining over OHS issues are not usually based on the psychological condition of individual managers, or upon the level of concern or lack of concern for the well-being of their workers. Instead, these attitudes are based upon several political and economic factors.

A primary cause of management's resistance to negotiating over OHS issues is the defence of management's rights and prerogatives. As such, OHS issues are usually vigorously resisted on the grounds that such limitations will hinder management's ability to manage in the most efficient and profitable manner. Many managers also argue that infringements on their prerogatives would confuse lines of authority and thereby weaken managements' attempts to impose safe working practices. Some will make improvements voluntarily that they would resist in collective bargaining. This fundamental defence of management prerogatives also helps to explain the types of OHS clauses that are successfully negotiated. Provision of personal protective devices or payment of risk premiums do little to threaten these prerogatives and, as such, will only be resisted on economic grounds. Seen as more damaging to these prerogatives are negotiated standards and joint OHS committees. These have historically been resisted by management in a far more vigorous fashion. However, as long as the committees' powers remain only advisory, most managers and employers learn to live with them. Many will react promptly to the committee's suggestions, both in the interests of health and safety and to ensure co-operative and harmonious labour relations. The crucial concern is that management retain the power to decide which suggestions to accept and which to ignore. Even where managers are willing to react to concerns raised by committees or during collective bargaining, "the one area you will not get into is asking the workers to participate in making the decisions as to what is to be done to correct the problem" (Heard, 1978, 111).

In addition to their defence of their decision-making powers, employers' and managers' attitudes to OHS demands will be influenced by their net cost to the firm. The net cost to the firm is defined as the cost of an improvement minus the savings of the improvement from reduced production losses, machine damage, risk premiums, compensation assessments, and training costs of replacement workers (Manga et al., 1981). If the net cost of a measure requested by the union is positive or low (that is, if it saves money or does not cost too much), management is likely to be willing to agree to its implementation. High-cost items are more likely to be resisted. This helps to explain the tendency of most employers to be more co-operative with unions on safety concerns than upon health concerns (Kochan et al., 1977; Bryce and Manga, 1985). Safety improvements are usually relatively inexpensive, and savings are immediate and visible. Health impairments often involve expensive procedures such as installation of ventilation or isolation systems or substitution of materials. Because of latency periods, the bias of workers compensation against disease claims, and difficulties in assigning causality, the employer bears little of the costs of the disease being created. The avoidance of the fiscal costs by the employer of inadequate health protection raises the net cost of prevention to the employer and leads to a reluctance to grant improvements during collective bargaining.

The net cost of OHS demand most affects management's willingness to bargain in competitive industries. Agreeing to protective clauses and standards at a single plant or enterprise can weaken management's competitive position. This is accentuated with the decentralized nature of much collective bargaining in Canada (Gunderson and Swinton, 1981, 5.3–5.4).

Union Attitudes and Preferences

The attitudes of workers and union officials is a mix of the ideal and the attainable. Some oppose collective bargaining on moral grounds, stating that health is a right that is non-negotiable. They oppose negotiations that implicitly or explicitly balance health with wages and other benefits. Most have a more pragmatic view and see OHS as an essential bargaining item (Boudreau, 1978).

The most important determinants of whether a particular union will attempt to negotiate OHS protection, and how vigorously they will pursue these negotiations, are the level of hazards in the workplace, the extent of knowledge about these hazards, and the degree of strength of the union's bargaining position. Workers in a relatively risk-free workplace are unlikely to place a high priority on further protection, while those in a hazardous one will have strong interest in OHS collective bargaining. Suppression of information about a hazard will have the same effect upon collective bargaining as its non-existence. However, where workers discover that the existence or effects of a long-term hazard have been concealed from them, they usually react with justified anger. The hazard becomes the subject of immediate and militant bargaining (Tataryn, 1979, 15–60; Stobbe, 1984). Finally, the stronger a union's bargaining position, the more likely it is to attempt to negotiate OHS protection. Because collective bargaining in this area results in infringements to management prerogatives, resistance to demands will be greater than would be justified in strictly economic grounds. This is instinctively realized by union leaders, so unions in weak positions will often concentrate upon more easily attainable objectives.

Evidence regarding the priority that workers and unions do place on OHS in collective bargaining is mixed. One report, based on a 1977 attitudinal survey of American workers, ranked OHS as seventh in priority after increased retirement benefits, increased medical insurance, an increase in paid vacations, more promotional opportunities, a shorter work week, and greater job security (Frankel et al., 1980). Re-analyzing the same data, Thomas Kochan (1980, 167–171) ranked OHS in the middle of worker concerns, and concluded most workers felt it merited more attention than it was now given by unions. Nicholas Ashford (1976, 89) states that 70 percent of workers considered protection of health and safety as a very important objective of collective bargaining. Only inadequate income ranked higher. In a survey of worker attitudes in three Ontario asbestos brake manufacturing plants, OHS was ranked second after wages as a priority in bargaining. Sixty percent supported a ban on the use of asbestos even when told this would result in a 20 percent increase in the cost of brake products (Luce and Swimmer, 1982). Attitude surveys do indicate that OHS is a concern of workers, but fail to capture the complexity of the assigning of priorities. A worker may, in the abstract, rank OHS somewhat lower on a list of priorities. This ranking may change dramatically, even if only temporarily, when a specific hazard emerges.

The priorities of the membership are usually reflected in the bargaining priorities of the union. However, there are some factors that can result in a lower priority for OHS than is warranted by membership preference. Daniel Berman sees a split in some unions between those in traditional union offices, such as executive positions and negotiating committees, and those in health and safety committees. The former tend to be older workers with greater seniority, while OHS activists tend to be younger and working in more hazardous jobs owing to their lack of seniority (Berman, 1978, 169). The older workers tend to have more influence in the setting of bargaining priorities and are often less willing to trade off other items in collective bargaining to gain OHS improvements (Luce and Swimmer, 1982). This is in part the result of their working in safer jobs owing to the workings of seniority systems, and partly the result of differential effects of exposure to some health hazards. A young worker is more likely to suffer from exposure to a harmful substance with a long latency period than is an older one. If exposure has been a long-term problem in the workplace, preventative measures taken in the present will be of more use to those who do not yet have high cumulative exposure.

In some cases, issues other than OHS may be more politically popular for union leaders. Wage increases, improved vacations, reduced hours of work, and so on are more tangible and immediate gains than an improvement in protections for refusing work or the lowering of a standard of exposure to a carcinogen with a latency period of twenty years. There are political pressures upon union leaders, as there are upon all elected officials, to concentrate efforts to achieve immediate, concrete gains.

Government Attitudes

It is not possible to speak of a single government attitude to collective bargaining over OHS issues in Canada. Historically, most state activity, either legislative or judicial, has tended to support management prerogatives. Governments have passed legislation and regulations governing aspects of working conditions. Very often, however, this action is more symbolic than real.

> Too many provincial governments either will not or cannot enforce their own regulations. In some provinces, regulation is virtually non-existent. Prosecutions are rare, and fines for failure to comply with regulations usually amount to little more than a licence fee (OFL, 1982, 191).

The traditional regulative approach to government OHS programs provided for no role for worker and union involvement or collective bargaining. OHS was seen as a management responsibility with some enforcement of standards by government officials. The newer legislation, beginning with Saskatchewan in 1972, mandated some form of worker involvement and legislatively granted rights to make this involvement possible. Even though the provisions of legislation in different provinces are similar, enforcement varies as to the extent that collective bargaining is encouraged and workers' OHS rights actively supported. In most jurisdictions, unionists argue that enforcement is lacking. These charges are supported in studies of OHS administration (Reschenthaler, 1979; Manga et al., 1981; Reasons et al., 1981; Swinton, 1983; Martel, 1983, 1986). However, the legislative provision of basic OHS rights on paper has served to encourage many unions and workers to bargain collectively to achieve these rights in fact.

Attitudes of Technical Experts

Experts in the various fields of OHS such as industrial medicine, toxicology, engineering, industrial hygiene and ergonomics in Canada have tended to be opposed to collective bargaining in OHS. They have instead argued that protection can be best assured by the actions and efforts of well-meaning experts (i.e., themselves). In many cases, this argument has disguised biases in favour of management and management priorities (Walters, 1985; Sass, 1979).

CONCLUSION

Collective bargaining has been a major vehicle for improving working conditions in Canada. The procedural provisions (such as the right of refusal and the establishment of joint OHS committees) that have been gained both legislatively and through collective bargaining in the past fifteen years have begun to provide workers with the means to protect themselves from the hazards of work. They also represent the beginnings of a democratization of the workplace and an extension of basic citizenship rights into the sphere of production.

Important as these gains have been, they have only begun to assure workers of safe and healthy jobs. Serious gaps remain in the protection that workers have won for themselves. Collective bargaining does not even begin to address the OHS needs of workers who remain unorganized. Some indication of the importance of unionization for the exercise of even legislatively provided rights is given by the fact that more than 93 percent of refusals of unsafe work in Ontario have occurred in unionized worksites (Swinton, 1983, 168). Unionization of all workers is the first prerequisite to enabling all workers to bargain for protection from health and safety hazards.

In those workplaces where collective bargaining over OHS issues has occurred, limitations on management's prerogatives have been limited. Terrence Ison notes that:

> It has generally been accepted in Labour Relations that the location of new plants, the design and structure of new buildings, the selection of equipment, the products to be made and the selection of material are all management rights. They are questions that management usually decides without consultation with the union (1978, 5).

The OHS rights that workers have gained through collective bargaining have been both advisory and reactive. Employers and management still retain the right of decision-making power over issues affecting OHS. The procedural OHS clauses, for the most part, establish mechanisms whereby workers can make suggestions. Management then decides if and how these suggestions will be implemented. In addition, the retention of management prerogatives and rights of decision making ensures that collective bargaining will be reactive. Workers and their unions are confined to responding to conditions and procedures that have already been established by management. Unions are excluded from the long-range planning that will determine working conditions in the future. If collective bargaining is to become more effective in securing OHS protection, then it must begin to challenge the unilateral powers of management in the workplace. That this will happen is by no means assured. In a climate of high unemployment and international competitiveness, employers are in a strong position to resist union demands. Indeed, even the limited gains made by workers and their unions during the last fifteen years are under attack as efficiency and competitiveness re-emerge as higher priorities than the health or safety of workers.

BIBLIOGRAPHY

Anderson, John and Gunderson, Morley (1982),*Union–Management Relations in Canada*. Don Mills: Addison-Wesley Publishers.

Ashford, Nicholas (1976), *Crises in the Workplace: Occupational Disease and Injury*. Cambridge: MIT Press.

Bacow, Lawrence (1980), *Bargaining for Job Safety and Health*. Cambridge: MIT Press.

Boudreau, Emile (1978), "Health hazards—Confrontation issues on the job." In *Are Health and Safety Negotiable?* Proceedings of the 26th Annual Conference of the McGill University Industrial Relations Centre, 79–92.

Berman, Daniel (1978), *Death on the Job*. New York: Monthly Review Press.

Bolaria, B. Singh (1986), "Capital, labour, and criminalized workers." In Brian MacLean (ed.), *The Political Economy of Crime*. Scarborough: Prentice-Hall, 295–310.

Bryce, George and Manga, Pran (1985), "The effectiveness of health and safety committees." *Relations industrielles* 40 (2): 257–281.

Carrothers, A. W. R. (1965), *Collective Bargaining Law in Canada*. Toronto: Butterworths.

Castleman, Barry (1983), "The double standard in industrial hazards." *International Journal of Health Services* 13 (1).

Doern, G. Bruce (1977), "The political economy of regulating occupational health: The Ham and Beaudry Reports." *Canadian Public Administration* 20 (1): 1–35.

England, Geoffrey (1983), "Some observations on selected strike laws." In Kenneth Swan and Katherine Swinton (eds.), *Studies in Labour Law*. Toronto: Butterworths, 221–298.

Frankel, R., Priest, W. C. and Ashford, N. (1980), "Occupational safety and health: A report on worker perceptions." *Monthly Labour Review* 103: 11–14.

Glasbeek, Harry (1982). "The contract of employment at common law." In John Anderson and Morley Gunderson (eds.), *Union–Management Relations in Canada*. Don Mills: Addison-Wesley Publishers, 47–77.

Gunderson, Morley and Swinton, Katherine (1981), *Collective Bargaining and Asbestos Dangers at the Workplace*. Study No. 1 for the Royal Commission on Matters of Health and Safety Arising from the Use of Asbestos in Ontario.

Heard, Lorne (1978). "Can health and safety be negotiated? Coping with regulations." In *Are Health and Safety Negotiable?* Proceedings of the 26th Annual Conference of the McGill University Industrial Relations Centre, 109–114.

Ison, Terrence (1978), *The Dimension of Industrial Disease*. Kingston: Industrial Relations Centre.

—— (1979), *Occupational Health and Wildcat Strikes*. Kingston: Industrial Relations Centre.

Jangula, Gordon (1985). Occupationally related disease and injury in Canadian industry. M.A. Thesis, Dept. of Sociology, University of Saskatchewan.

Kochan, Thomas (1980), *Collective Bargaining and Industrial Relations*. Homewood, IL: Irwin.

——, Dyer, L. and Lipsky, D. (1977), *The Effectiveness of Union–Management Safety and Health Committees*. Kalamazoo: W. E. Upjohn Institute.

Labour Canada (1982), *Provisions in Collective Agreements in Canada Covering 200 and More Employees (Excluding Construction)*. Ottawa: Labour Canada.

Lorentsen, Edith and Woolner, Evelyn (1950), "Fifty years of labour legislation in Canada." *The Labour Gazette* 50: 1412–1459.

Luce, Sally and Swimmer, Gene (1982), *Workers Attitudes about Health and Safety in Three Asbestos Brake Manufacturing Plants*. Study No. 6 for the Royal Commission on Matters of Health and Safety Arising from the Use of Asbestos in Ontario.

Manga, Pran, Broyles, Robert and Reschenthaler, Gil (1981), *Occupational Health and Safety: Issues and Alternatives*. Technical Report No. 6. Ottawa: Economic Council of Canada.

Martel, Elie (1986), *Still Not Healthy, Still Not Safe*. Report of the Ontario New Democrat Caucus: Second Task Force on Occupational Health and Safety.

—— (1983), *Not Yet Healthy, Not Yet Safe*. Report of the Ontario New Democratic Caucus Task Force on Occupational Health and Safety.

Meredith, William (1913), *Final Report of Laws Relating to the Liability of Employers*. Toronto: Ontario Attorney General.

Nash, Michael (1983), *Canadian Occupational Health and Safety Law Handbook*. Don Mills: CCH Canadian Limited.

Piva, Michael (1975), "The workmen's compensation movement in Ontario." *Ontario History* 55 (1).

Reasons, Charles, Ross, Louis and Paterson, Craig (1981), *Assault on the Worker*. Toronto: Butterworths.

Reschenthaler, Gil (1979), *Occupational Health and Safety in Canada: The Economics and Three Case Studies*. Montreal: Institute for Research on Public Policy.

Risk, R. C. B. (1983), "'This nuisance of litigation': The origins of workers compensation in Ontario." In David Flaherty (ed.), *Essays in the History of Canadian Law (Vol. II)*. Toronto: University of Toronto Press, 418–491.

Sass, Robert (1985), "Saskatchewan approach to workplace health and safety, 1972–1983." In Harley Dickenson and Bob Russell (eds.), *The Politics of Work in the West*. Saskatoon: Social Research Unit.

_____ (1979), "The underdevelopment of occupational health and safety in Canada." In William Leiss (ed.), *Ecology Versus Politics in Canada*. Toronto: University of Toronto Press, 72–96.

_____ (1975), "Occupational health and safety in Saskatchewan." *Canada Labour* 20 (4): 14–16.

_____ and Crook, Glen (1981), "Accident proneness: Science or nonscience." *International Journal of Health Services* 11 (2): 175–190.

Selikoff, Irving and Lee, Douglas (1978), *Asbestos and Disease*. New York: Academic Press.

Seltzer, Curtis (1979), *Surveying and Analyzing the Field of Employee Rights Related to Occupational Disease*. Report No. ASPER/PUR-79/2220/1A. Washington: U.S. Department of Labor.

Steinberg, Charles (1978), "The scope of safety and health clauses in labour agreements." In *Are Health and Safety Negotiable?* Proceedings of the McGill University Industrial Relations Centre 26th Annual Conference.

Stobbe, Mark (1984), "Sask power: Deceit, denial and asbestos." *Canadian Dimension* 18 (4).

Surry, Jean (1969), *Industrial Accident Research: A Human Engineering Appraisal*. Toronto: University of Toronto Press.

Swinton, Katherine (1983), "Enforcement of occupational health and safety legislation: The role of the internal responsibility system." In Kenneth Swan and Katherine Swinton (eds.), *Studies in Labour Law*. Toronto: Butterworths, 143–176.

Tataryn, Lloyd (1979), *Dying for a Living*. Ottawa: Deneau and Greenberg.

Tucker, Eric (1984), "The determination of occupational health and safety standards in Ontario 1860–1980: From markets to politics to...?" *McGill Law Journal* 29 (2).

Walters, Vivienne (1985). "The politics of occupational health and safety: Interviews with workers' health and safety representatives and company doctors." *Canadian Review of Sociology and Anthropology* 22 (1).

Appendix 15A

Model OHS Provisions for Collective Agreements*

Co-operation on Safety

The union and the employer shall co-operate in establishing rules and practices which promote an occupational environment which will enhance the physiological and psychological conditions of employees and which will provide protection from factors adverse to employee health and safety.

Union–Employer Health and Safety Committee

A health and safety committee shall be established which is composed of an equal number of union and employer representatives, but with a minimum of two union and two employer members. The health and safety committee shall hold meetings as requested by the union or by the employer for jointly considering, monitoring, inspecting, investigating and reviewing health and safety conditions and practices and to improve existing health and safety conditions and practices. Minutes shall be taken of all meetings and copies shall be sent to the employer and union.

Collective Bargaining

Should the employer fail to implement the recommendations of the committee, they shall become the subject of collective bargaining.

Health and Safety Committee Pay Provisions

Time spent by members of the committee in the course of their duties shall be considered as time worked and shall be paid for in accordance with the terms of this agreement.

Health and Safety Clothing, Tools, and Equipment

The employer shall provide all employees working in any unsanitary or potentially hazardous jobs with all the necessary tools, protective equip-

---

*Source: Canadian Union of Public Employees

ment and protective clothing required. These shall be maintained and replaced, where necessary, at the employer's expense. It is recognized that such protective equipment and clothing are temporary measures. The conditions necessitating their use shall be subjected to further corrective measures through engineering changes or the elimination of the hazard.

Monitoring Equipment

The employer shall provide and maintain workplace monitoring equipment for detecting and recording potential and actual health and safety hazards.

Compliance with Health and Safety Legislation

The employer shall comply with all applicable federal, provincial and municipal health and safety legislation and regulations. All standards established under the legislation and regulations shall constitute minimum acceptable practice to be improved upon by agreement of the union–employer health and safety committee or negotiations with the union.

Disclosure of Information

The employer shall provide the union written information which identifies all the biological agents, compounds, substances, by-products and physical hazards associated with the work environment. Where applicable, this information shall include, but not be restricted to, the chemical breakdown of trade name descriptions, information on known and suspected potential hazards, the maximum concentration exposure levels, precautions to be taken, symptoms, medical treatment and antidotes.

Safety and Health Records, Reports and Data

The employer shall provide the union all accident reports and other health and safety records in the possession of the employer, including records, reports and data provided to and by the Worker's Compensation Board and other government departments and agencies.

Access to the Workplace

Union staff or union health and safety advisors or consultants shall be provided access to the workplace if required to attend health and safety committee meetings, or for inspecting, investigating or monitoring the workplace.

Time Off for Health and Safety Training

Union members of the health and safety committee shall be entitled to time off from work with no loss of seniority or earnings to attend seminars sponsored by government agencies or the union for instruction and upgrading on health and safety matters.

Right to Refuse and No Disciplinary Action

No employee shall be discharged, penalized or disciplined for refusing to work on a job or in any workplace or to operate any equipment where he/she believes that it would be unsafe or unhealthy to himself/herself, an unborn child, a workmate, or the public, or where it would be contrary to the applicable federal, provincial or municipal health and safety legislation or regulations. There shall be no loss of pay or seniority during the period of refusal. No employee shall be ordered or permitted to work on a job which another worker has refused until the matter is investigated by the health and safety committee and satisfactorily settled.

Proper Training

No employee shall be required to work on any job or operate any piece of equipment until he/she has received proper training and instructions.

Union Health and Safety Committee

In order to promote the occupational health and safety of employees, the employer acknowledges the right of the union to establish a health and safety committee and appoint health and safety representatives in each department. The union shall notify the employer in writing of the names of each representative and the department(s) he/she represents. Union health and safety representatives shall have the right to participate in the monitoring of the workplace and to accompanying government inspectors on inspection tours.

Health and Safety Expenditure Fund

The employer agrees to contribute $0.02 for each regularly scheduled hour worked by each employee in the bargaining unit to a special health and safety fund to be administered and used by the union to promote the occupational health and safety of employees.

Injury Pay Provisions

An employee who is injured during working hours, and is required to leave for treatment or is sent home as a result of such injury, shall receive payment for the remainder of the shift at his/her regular rate of pay, without deduction from sick leave, unless a doctor or nurse states that the employee is fit for further work on that shift. An employee who has received payment under this section shall receive pay for time necessarily spent for further medical treatment of the injury during regularly scheduled working hours, subsequent to the day of the accident.

Transportation of Accident Victims

Transportation to the nearest physician or hospital for employees requiring medical care as a result of an accident shall be at the expense of the Employer.

Health and Safety Grievance

Where a dispute involving a question of general application or interpretation of this article occurs, it shall be subject to the grievance procedure and steps 1, 2 and 3 of the grievance procedure may be by-passed.

16

Quality of Working Life and Collective Bargaining: Can They Co-exist?

MAURICE LEMELIN*

Quality of working life and collective bargaining: can they co-exist? A few years ago, a CLC officer addressed this question in the following words:

> The labor movement could not help but be surprised when the concept of the quality of working life was presented as if it were a totally new idea.
>
> We would respectfully note that, since its inception, the trade union movement has been intensely concerned with working conditions. In fact, unions have been created, and continue to exist, only because they contribute in a real way to the improvement of the quality of working life. In that respect, the most important accomplishment was the expansion of the collective bargaining process and the conclusion of collective agreements. (Major, CLC Executive Vice-president, "Forum de la QVT," *La Scène canadienne* 3 (4), 1980. Translation.)

Coming as it does from a union leader, such a response leaves little room for interpretation. Unions exist in order to improve the quality of life, and the quality of working life (QWL), of their members. They fulfill that mandate through collective bargaining. There should therefore be little doubt that QWL and collective bargaining can indeed co-exist.

A closer look at the labour scene, however, suggests that the answer to the question addressed here is not all that clear cut. Indeed, although labour leaders would agree that the unions' chief objective is to improve the quality of life and the QWL of their members, some unions, federations, and individual union officials have nonetheless taken positions opposing QWL programs. For instance, in 1983, the British Columbia Federation of Labour's Quality of Work Life Committee issued its report recommending that affiliates "shall not participate in QWL programs, including work improvement programs, quality circles, team work, semi-autonomous work groups, employee core groups, employee involvement in job progression or other titles formulated by consultants" (Parker, 1985, 141). This position was adopted by delegates to the Federation's 1983 convention. The following year, the Ontario Federation of Labour

* The author would like to thank Mario Giroux for his research assistance and Judith Rice-Lesage for editing the text.

also passed an anti-QWL motion. In a related development, in Quebec, one issue of *Le Monde ouvrier*, the information bulletin of the Quebec Federation of Labour, carried the headline: "Qualité de vie au travail—un cadeau empoisonné." ("Quality of working life—a poisoned gift." *Le Monde ouvrier*, Jan.–Feb. 1982.) In contrast, some unions, such as the United Automobile Workers or the Energy and Chemical Workers, do give some encouragement to QWL programs.

The current situation is therefore quite ambiguous. Certain unions are somewhat favourable to QWL programs, others are opposed, and many others have adopted a "wait and see" attitude. Whatever their position, however, all seem to share the belief that QWL is one of the ultimate goals of individual unions and of the labour movement as a whole.

There are, no doubt, many reasons to account for this wide variety of attitudes and opinions. A partial explanation for the heterogeneity of views may be found in some of the disappointing results of early QWL experiments and in the inter-union differences in membership composition and ideological perspective. Part of the ambiguity may also be a function of the fact that the QWL movement—if such a term may be used—is paying the price of its own popularity. The term QWL is currently used to cover so many types of organizational changes, so many governmental policies, and so many kinds of union demands, that it is becoming difficult to find a universally acceptable meaning. Each individual, each group, seems to have its own definition of QWL.

For purposes of this chapter, which seeks to develop a more complete answer to the question of co-existence, the QWL concept will be treated in two distinct but related ways: first, as a process, then as a result or outcome of that process. Such a distinction appears to be warranted, because it is possible for people to agree on the basic goal of improving QWL without accepting the process of co-operation proposed by QWL theorists. Moreover, by analyzing QWL as both a process and an outcome, it becomes possible to explore the issue as it relates both to the collective bargaining process and to collective agreements themselves. (For a similar view, see Greenberg and Glaser, 1980, 36.)

In the discussion that follows, the first part of the chapter focuses on QWL as a process of co-operation. Using that perspective, we then look at the history of labour–management co-operation to see what lessons may be drawn from these experiences. This will be followed by a discussion of the various types of constraints affecting co-operation—ideological, organizational and political, and legal. The second part of the chapter explores QWL and its relationship to collective agreements, and a subsequent section takes up the question of whether QWL programs should be separated from the collective bargaining process.

QWL AS A PROCESS OF CO-OPERATION

A review of the literature reveals that QWL projects are typically assimilated into a process of union–management co-operation. (See, for example, Schuster, 1984). It is important to note, however, that the existence of such co-operation does not imply either the absence of conflict or the existence of industrial harmony. Neither should it be equated with concessionary bargaining, as is often the practice today (Gray, 1984, 210). Rather, depending upon the nature of the economic situation and the degree of union bargaining power prevailing at the time, concessionary bargaining has taken place within the context of the traditional adversarial relationship. The fact that, today, many unions are obliged to make important concessions should not be construed as reflecting a desire for co-operation from either the union or the management side. More than likely, it merely indicates that current economic circumstances, and probably political circumstances as well, are less favourable to the unions, and that their ability to wrest major concessions from employers suffers accordingly.

According to Dion's *Canadian Dictionary of Industrial Relations*, labour–management co-operation could be defined as

> ...a general formula intended to represent the mutual desire of the Employer and the Union to work together to establish, maintain, and promote within the organization the best possible working climate. In practical terms, cooperation can be operationalized, on the one hand, as the Employers' efforts to assure their employees' satisfaction, security, and welfare, and to provide an interesting work environment, etc., and, on the other hand, the Unions' efforts to incite employees to reduce production costs, improve work methods, assure proper equipment maintenance, etc. (Dion, 1986; translation.)

A somewhat more specific view is proposed by the American Center for the Quality of Work Life in its working definition of QWL, which also stresses the notion of "working together":

> Quality of working life improvements are defined as any activity which takes place at every level of an organization which seeks greater organizational effectiveness through the enhancement of human dignity and growth...a process through which the stake-holders in the organization—management, the union(s), and employees—learn how to work together better...to determine for themselves what actions, changes, and improvements are desirable and workable, in order to achieve the twin and simultaneous goals of an improved QWL for all members of the organization and greater effectiveness for both the company and the union(s) (Osley and Ball, 1982, 27).

Labour–Management Co-operation in North America

Labour–management co-operation is not a recent phenomenon in the United States and Canada. Co-operation between the two, in fact, goes back a long way, although its history has been marked by a number of peaks and valleys. During World War I, the program of co-operation proposed by the U.S. government was officially endorsed by the AFL convention of 1918 (Gray, 1984, 211; Gold, 1985, 5). The following year, the AFL itself called for greater democracy in industry as well as co-operation with management in order to improve productivity (Jacoby, 1983, 21). Not only did co-operation seem possible at that time, it was, in fact, a reality, one that was brought about by the economic constraints of wartime and the necessity for unity among diverse sectors of society. As one labour leader of that era remarked:

> The union, in order to exist, must be conservative in many aspects, many times. They have to cooperate for efficiency; it is easy for one to say they should or shouldn't do it, but those in the unions know that, unless they work along those lines, very often they may be left with a fine radical union and with all their people starving in the streets and the work being done else-where. (Beckerman, 1926; quoted in Jacoby, 1983, 26.)

Once the war was over, however, these efforts toward co-operation evaporated, and unions and management moved back to their more traditional adversarial relationship. According to Dale, it seems that "... while the AFL lacked the ability to translate its broad objectives of promoting efficiency into specific action, much of the responsibility for the failure of co-operation in the Twenties must be placed on management shoulders. Employers refused to assist the frail practical efforts and generous hopes of the unions" (Dale, 1954, 361).

Not until the advent of World War II did labour–management co-operation recur on a large scale in the United States. And, once again, these co-operative efforts were encouraged by the government (Brett, 1980, 200; Gold, 1986, 6). For example, the government attempted to foster collaboration by encouraging the creation of labour–management committees at each work site (Gray, 1984, 212), and more than 5,000 such committees were actually established.

As before, most of these initiatives were abandoned once the war ended, although some projects, such as the Scanlon Plan, did outlast the war era and ultimately gained a measure of popularity. The projects that lived on, however, were more the exception than the rule and did not reflect the dominant pattern.

With the 1970s came a resurgence of co-operation, once again ignited by the recurrence of economic difficulties, such as the energy crises and the rise of foreign competition (Gold, 1976, 1986). At that time, a number of labour–management committees were set up and other joint projects were undertaken with a view toward improving QWL and productivity, among other things. As it had twice before during the war years, the government stimulated co-operation through the enactment of the Labour–Management Co-operation Act of 1978, among other things. This act was intended to encourage co-operation efforts, improve communication, explore new and innovative joint approaches to achieving organizational effectiveness, and permit increased worker participation. It empowered the Federal Mediation and Conciliation Service to provide assistance to unions and companies in this endeavour (Schuster, 1983, 416). Prior to that, in 1975, the U.S. Congress had passed the National Productivity and Quality of Working Life Act, which resulted in the creation of the National Center for Productivity and Quality of Working Life. In addition, other initiatives aimed at promoting co-operation were undertaken by various government departments and agencies (Parker, 1985, 119).

The Canadian experience with co-operation resembles the American one in many respects. As in the United States, the history of labour–management collaboration has been a relatively long one. In 1919, in its final report, Canada's Royal Commission on Industrial Relations drew attention to the urgent need for greater labour–management co-operation. As a means to this end, the Commission recommended the establishment of joint industrial councils and works committees. In the year following publication of the Commission's report, the government convened a national conference, which was attended by representatives of management, the unions, and the general public. At this conference, participants unanimously adopted a motion calling for the creation of such councils and committees (Wood *in* Economic Council of Canada, 1965, 26).

While it is true that, in certain companies, these committees were set up chiefly as a way of keeping the unions out, many meaningful co-operative endeavours did result from these initiatives. As was the case in the United States, Canadian ventures in co-operation also dissipated as the global conflict faded, remaining in hiatus until the coming of World War II.

Once again, during the war years, the Canadian government found it necessary to promote co-operation, mainly as a means of assuring the increases in production required by the war effort. Under the combined leadership of the Minister of Labour, the Minister of Munitions and Supply, and later the Industrial Production Co-operation Board, the government again pushed for the creation of labour–management committees in the workplace (Wood *in* Economic Council of Canada, 1965,

29). But, like their American counterparts, these committees did not survive on a large scale after the war.

In the 1970s, the Canadian government resumed its campaign for greater labour–management co-operation. Among the initiatives taken were those in the realm of QWL, which were seen as a way

> ...to de-emphasize the adversarial relations in this country, and to encourage new approaches that would recognize the advantages to both labour and management of working together in their common interest and in the interests of the country as a whole (Trist, 1978, 1).

So it appears that, in both the United States and Canada, the three peak periods of collaboration occurred during the two world wars and during the period beginning with the 1970s up to the present. It is important to acknowledge, however, that cases of co-operation have always existed outside these three peak periods, albeit on a sporadic basis (Schuster, 1984). Whether the goal has been responding to foreign competition, resolving a particular problem, or protecting jobs, unions and management have usually been able to adapt their modus vivendi to the prevailing economic realities. Sometimes, even in the context of a typically adversarial relationship, employers and unions have managed to find some formula for co-operating on specific issues of mutual concern, such as health and safety or better communication.

If recent history is any indication, then, there is little credible support for the view that labour–management co-operation, such as that associated with QWL, is not feasible. On the contrary, not only has co-operation existed for a very long time, it has also co-existed with collective bargaining. For example, a survey of a sample of top union officials has shown that 97 percent of them agree that co-operation is possible on specific programs designed to improve productivity (Katzell and Yankelovich, 1975, 95).

A close analysis of labour–management co-operation in Canada and the United States suggests that instances of collaboration typically emerged during periods of economic difficulty, where the stability or even the survival of an industry or corporate enterprise was threatened (Economic Council of Canada, 1965, 23; Schuster, 1984, 112). More specifically, following a study of union–management co-operation since the 1920s, Jacoby concluded that collaboration takes place within what he calls an "intermediate range of economic stress." In other words, while unfavourable economic conditions may facilitate a softening of adversarial postures, the struggle for power may reappear if there is either a radical deterioration or a marked improvement in the economic environment (Jacoby, 1983, 31). According to Gray, who concluded that instances of collaboration from the 1920s to the present are remarkably similar, the conditions necessary for successful co-operation appear to be the following. First, managers must accept the principles of collective bargaining and union security. Second, in order for management to participate fully and effectively, there must be freedom to innovate and the belief that the union is able to deliver on its commitments. Third, co-operation is normally associated with a mature relationship, one that is characterized by a relative balance of power and mutual respect. Fourth, a strong commitment to co-operation at all levels is essential. Fifth, the participation of workers depends on the existence of gainsharing and a feeling of job security. Sixth, successful co-operation calls for the kinds of personal skills typically associated with decision making and problem solving. And, finally, the results must be satisfying to all parties (Gray, 1984, 218).

Constraints Affecting Co-operation

Ideological Constraints

The union view. Although past experience has shown that union–management co-operation is not only possible but capable of co-existing with collective bargaining, there exist numerous obstacles which act to restrain it. Some obstacles are ideological.

Authors, and industrial relations specialists in general, usually agree that the labour movement in North America has not been characterized by the radical political orientations evident in many other countries. Such terms of reference as class struggle, social upheaval, or radical change in the political or economic order are not commonly part of the lexicon of North American labour organizations.

This may be an over-generalization. North American labour unions are politicized to some degree, yet these political orientations vary greatly from one union to another. The CNTU and the Teamsters, for instance, are quite different, just as certain craft unions in the construction industries and certain public sector unions hold diametrically opposing views on many issues.

It is hardly surprising, then, that opinions within the labour movement diverge widely on the issue of co-operation. For some unions and some union leaders, the very idea of any form of collaboration with management on QWL programs in unthinkable, because these programs are seen as a mechanism by which capitalists may co-opt their opponents or merely "fine tune" the system (see, for example, Parker, 1985). For proponents of this view, the interests of employers and the working class are inherently in conflict, and it is only through confrontation based on bargaining power that unions will ultimately succeed in protecting and advancing their members' interests. Union–management co-operation in general, and QWL programs in particular, are merely strategies for crippling union strength, facilitating lay-offs, inciting productivity increases, and so on.

Underlying these anti-cooperation, anti-QWL sentiments is the view that, historically, labour unions have not generally been accepted in North America. Management in North America, unlike management in many other countries, has rather been anti-union (see, for example, Freedman, 1985). As a consequence, certain union activists find it difficult to believe that times have really changed, that a new era of harmony has dawned or will come to pass. As one union leader put it:

> If the shop floor people are so vital in achieving management's goals, then why in hell hasn't management recognized our vitality until now? All of a sudden, why is it that we start sharing decisions?
>
> Our quick answer is that management has often made such a mess of things, they want to share the blame. They come to us after they've screwed up.
>
> A second answer is that management wants to make a change in production planning or process, or it wants to introduce some new technology, either or both of which will show some of us out the door onto the unemployment line, and it wants to "con" us into helping get the job done.
>
> A third answer is that management simply wants more production—more work—from the same or fewer workers. In other words, a speed up. But a fourth answer is more likely the real answer: to undercut the union, to usurp its duties and powers and responsibilities; to make it seem unnecessary and ultimately put it out of business; to take control of workers away from the bargaining agent and put it in the grip of management itself. (Poulin, General Vice-president, International Association of Machinists and Aerospace Workers; quoted in Schuster, 1984, 11.)

For some union leaders, this fear of being undercut is also grounded in lessons from the past. Some authors see similarities between union–management interaction of the 1920s and '30s and that which prevails today (Dubofsky, 1985). They are referring, of course, to the practice by many employers during those years of using company unions to circumvent or eliminate organized labour. To many, the QWL programs that have surfaced in recent years are merely "new wine in old bottles"—i.e., a modern version of earlier management tactics for curbing and ultimately eliminating union power. This concern appears all the more critical to union survival today, in the sense that many facets of current economic and political realities are now working to the detriment of the labour movement (e.g., the shrinking primary and secondary sectors, the stiff competition from abroad, the political move to the right). Indeed, as Kochan and McKersie have observed, "...the development of sophisticated non-union human resources management policies and strategies may turn out to be the most important development in the American industrial relations system of the last two decades" (Kochan and McKersie, 1983, 60).

Another problem for many trade unionists is that QWL is, at least partially, associated with the human-relations school of management theory (e.g., Goodman, 1979, 7). According to human-relations theory, although conflicts-of-interest may arise in organizational life, they are not inherent to it. Moreover, since conflict is neither positive nor constructive in its effects, it should be avoided. In order to minimize the potential for conflict, human-relations theorists argue that personal goals should be subordinated to organizational goals. Obviously, in this perspective on organizational life, unions are not seen as playing a very influential or useful role. As Kochan has written:

> Kerr and Fisher (1964) summarized the posture of the human relations theorists: unions were believed to be useful when they cooperated with management efforts and dysfunctional when they opposed management. Of course, as Kerr and Fisher note, unions would be unnecessary if their sole purpose is to cooperate with management (Kochan, 1980, 134).

The fears of many union leaders concerning QWL are also exacerbated by the fact that, very often, these programs were proposed, or at least supported, by organizational behaviourists. This is problematic because, as Strauss points out, behavioural science consultants have always provoked a degree of mistrust among unions (Strauss, 1977, 350). Another writer summarized the explanation in this way:

> Organizational behavior appears to the union commentators as an efficiency ideology disguised as an organizational science, in which trade unions and collective bargaining are largely tangential, redundant, irrelevant, and friction-inducing. (Barbash, 1974; quoted in Brett, 1980, 208.)

Stated even more pungently, Payne comments that many union leaders go so far as to categorize most behavioural scientists as "union busters" (quoted in Kochan, 1980, 135).

Given prevailing sentiments, it is evident that QWL programs, despite their laudable intentions, will continue to raise many questions within the labour movement. From the union point of view, conflicts-of-interest, at least in part, are inherent to organizational life and have historically been managed chiefly through negotiation. Many union leaders are therefore not easily persuaded to abandon traditional negotiation in favour of a more collaborative approach. It is also interesting that the more recent schools of management thought have distanced themselves, to one degree or another, from the view of the work organization as an entity where harmony reigns. Rather, organizations are coming to be viewed as political systems, in which the various groups and individuals form coalitions and attempt to manipulate situations to attain their respective ends (see, for example, Crozier and Friedberg, 1977). In the words of March:

> ...a business firm is a political coalition and...the executive in the firm is a political broker. The composition of the firm is not given; it is negotiated. The goals of the firm are not given; they are bargained (March, 1962, 672).

As management theorists increasingly view the work organization as a locus of negotiation among competing interests, it is hardly surprising that union leaders, who have historically perceived the organization in these terms, continue to give priority to negotiation as the most appropriate mode for transacting with the employer. The union stance is even less astonishing when we consider that the forms of participation envisaged by QWL programs are seen by many as offering no guarantee of greater democracy. As Elden has noted:

> Political theorists are careful to distinguish between participation and democracy (see, for example, Pateman, 1970). Participation is a means. Democracy is a value state that can be characterized either by means or ends. Democratic political theory distinguishes between participation that contributes to democratization (that is, that transforms authority structures in the direction of autonomy, power equalization, and self-management) and that which does not so contribute (that is , involvement in untransformed hierarchical authority structures, such as quality-control circles, problem-solving groups, and participative management). This distinction—essential to theories of political democracy—is overlooked, misunderstood, or completely muddled in discussions of organizational behavior.
>
> The idea of democracy is so confused and misused in planned change that most OD and QWL strategies either actively hinder power-sharing and democratization or unwittingly collude in preserving undemocratic organizational forms. The assumption in OD seems to be that an increase in participation translates automatically into increased democracy. Nothing could be farther from the truth. Why do so many of us seem to overlook how necessary participation and commitment are for quite undemocratic forms of organization? (Elden, 1985, 201.)

The management view. Ideological constraints on co-operation and participation are not the sole province of unions; the management side, too, is subject to a number of ideological biases of its own. For example, a key precept prevailing in business circles is that managers, who are legally responsible for business operations, should enjoy full and unfettered authority in reaching business objectives. Co-operation with the union—which is perceived as allowing the union a voice in business decisions—is understandably viewed by management as a threat to its authority and a dilution of its power. Of course, as Chamberlain and Kuhn have argued, "...managers' fear that co-operation will threaten their authority rises more from ideology than it does from reality" (1986, 460).

On balance, then, it is evident that the belief in co-operation and participation as hallmarks of better management is not widely shared among managers. This reality simply mirrors the ideological bent that has always characterized the dominant streams of management thought, i.e., scientific management theory and human-relations theory. For both of these schools, although they take differing, even diametrically opposing positions on many aspects, there is the shared assumption that authority in the workplace is a non-issue.

Some would argue, of course, that scientific management and human relations theories are outmoded, and to some extent, this is true. Yet their assumptions (or lack of same) about authority and participation reverberate through organizational life even today. A close look at the modern work organization reveals that Taylorism and the bureaucratic model continue to be the prevailing modes of functioning. Participation is accepted mainly when economic necessity dictates—and then to the extent that it does not interfere with traditional management rights (Chamberlain and Kuhn, 1986, 454; Rouleau, 1986, 21).

What is more, many managers still cling to the belief that workers are not really able to contribute much of value to the decision-making process, because of a lack of interest, training, or some other attribute. Even for those managers who do believe that employees are capable of participation, however, the perception that participative decision making is time-consuming, as well as the perception that getting the job done requires submitting to "popularity contests," serves to discourage many of them from giving up their traditional ways of doing things.

Political and Organizational Constraints

Union politics. A union is a political organization (Ross, 1948, 12). Union leaders are elected; they receive their mandate from rank-and-file members, to whom they are ultimately accountable. Although variations may exist from one union to another in the degree of democracy practised, most unions, with some noteworthy exceptions, satisfy the criteria of modern democracy. At least, they do so as well as any other political organization or political party.

Generally speaking, experience has shown that union officers standing for election are usually defeated for one or more of the following reasons: they are accused of either misappropriating funds, or "being in bed with the boss," or failing to represent the membership. Depending, of course, on the sophistication of the candidates involved, the list of accusations may be expressed in many different ways. However, in most cases, the political demise of union candidates can be traced to one of these three basic failings.

Therein lies a partial explanation for the unions' ambivalence toward QWL programs and co-operation with management. No matter how potentially beneficial given QWL projects may be, by their very nature they open the door to accusations of co-optation. The decision to collaborate with the employer always carries with it a measure of political risk for a union official. On the contrary, any union leader who adopts a confrontational stance in dealing with management will rarely find his or her integrity called into question. Perhaps that union leader will ultimately be less effective than another who chooses the more collaborative approach, but at least his or her integrity will be protected.

In their role as political organization, or as a simple association of workers, unions and their leaders have as their primary duty the defence and promotion of their members' concerns and demands. To date, however, QWL-related issues have not been seen as crucial by the rank and file (Strauss, 1980, 354). This may be due to a perception problem of sorts. That is, it may be that QWL-related preoccupations actually are a priority matter for the rank and file, but that unions themselves are not perceived as the appropriate instrument for dealing with these issues. This suggests, among other things, that there may be a need for unions to educate their members about QWL issues and the role the union may play in that regard. For the time being, however, it appears that "bread and butter" issues figure most prominently among the concerns of union members.

The tepid interest in QWL issues may also have something to do with perceptions about employee attitudes toward working life. For example, many have been lulled into indifference by survey data showing that, year after year, some 80 percent of workers express satisfaction with their jobs. Although some psychologists, sociologists, and organizational behaviourists may dismiss such data as dubious in value*, many others appear to accept them as a credible indication that there is no reason for alarm concerning the quality of working life. As one union official wryly observed, a close look at history would no doubt reveal that at no time were 100 percent of workers satisfied with their jobs. It is doubtful that 100 percent of the ancient Egyptians who built the pyramids, or 100 percent of the medieval craftsmen who constructed the great cathedrals, or 100 percent of the nineteenth-century Irishmen who laid the tracks for American railroads were filled with job satisfaction (Winpisinger, 1972, 154).

For the sake of argument, it may be presumed that the unions'

---

*Skeptics argue that questions on work satisfaction are subject to response bias in much the same way as the question, "How are you today?" That is, they are perceived as somewhat inconsequential and tend to elicit automatic positive responses from most people.

traditional "bread and butter" concerns and QWL issues are not mutually exclusive goals, in the sense that improvements in QWL are not purchased at the expense of something like job security. Quite the contrary. It is even conceivable that a QWL program could bring about improvements that generate productivity increases, which may in turn assure greater job security. In practice, however, unions must pursue their goals within a context of limited resources. They must therefore be prepared to make hard choices about goals and means, and they must see to it that the time, energy, and monies at their disposal are invested in the most cost-effective way possible. Very often, when faced with a choice between negotiating traditional kinds of collective agreements and opting for some QWL project whose parameters and benefits are uncertain, unions understandably tend to take the tried-and-true path, the path which their members understand and accept. In doing so, they are no doubt pursuing the path that promises the greatest payoff in political terms as well.

Management structure. On the management side, there are also a number of organizational and political constraints that hinder QWL programs. One such impediment is the fact that management systems were designed to reinforce managers' authority. Obviously, the adoption of any kind of participative management approach, which modifies the manager's role substantially, will involve not only significant changes in philosophy but alterations in organizational structure and policy as well (Schlesinger and Oshry, 1984). For many, then, QWL programs understandably signify a loss of authority and prestige in favour of the unions.

Interestingly, while most early writings on QWL pin-pointed workers and unions as the chief sources of resistance, the more recent literature suggests that this may not be the case. Significant resistance may also come from management. According to Klein (1984), the primary source of opposition comes from the ranks of middle managers, who find their authority diluted and experience difficulties in adjusting to the ambiguities of their new role. They feel cast aside and complain that they lack the organizational support, training, and skills necessary to master their new responsibilities and challenges. At times they may balk because they fear their very jobs are threatened. In other words, when middle managers ask themselves, "What's in it for me?" the answer is not always an encouraging one (Chamberlain and Kuhn, 1986, 453; Walton and Schlesinger, 1979).

Legal Constraints

The various labour codes enacted in both the United States and Canada are based on the fundamental principle of the separation of union and management. In fact, certain clauses have been expressly included in these codes to assure that this distinction will be preserved. An interesting development in this regard is noted in a study by Sockell (1984), which concludes that—in the United States, at least—employee participation programs that are not controlled by the unions would, in the event of a complaint, probably be declared illegal. The implication of this, of course, is that any union choosing to object to a QWL program would probably succeed in getting the tribunal to rule in its favour, thereby assuring the demise of the program. Of course, whether Canadian tribunals would rule similarly in such matters remains to be seen.

On the whole, the various labour codes as they now stand could hardly be said to reflect a state of labour–management collaboration; rather, they testify more to the conflictual nature of the relationship. In the current legal context, the two parties come together for a fixed period of time in order to establish the working conditions that will prevail. In the event of an impasse, each side resorts to economic pressure tactics in order to attain its objectives. The end-product of these negotiations is a written contract, which typically grows more detailed as time passes. When the two parties disagree over the interpretation of this contract, the conflict is submitted to arbitration. It is noteworthy that this arbitration mechanism, which was originally conceived as an expeditious means of settling differences, is becoming increasingly legalistic in its orientation, so that, very often, legal technicalities triumph over the substance of the problem itself.

QWL AND COLLECTIVE AGREEMENTS

As the preceding section shows, QWL is a continuous process. But it is also more than that. Even though no QWL program ever reaches a stage where the quality of life per se is truly attained, these programs obviously do have important effects on working life. Typically, QWL programs reorganize work so that employees' needs for growth and development can be met on the job. This usually entails restructuring and reorganizing tasks to make the work as interesting as possible. Generally speaking, "interesting work" is defined as activities offering variety and challenge, autonomy, appreciation and support, opportunities for continuous learning, for using skills and judgment, and for making useful contributions, as well as the expectation of a desirable future (Davis *in* Tannenbaum et al., 1985, 161; Suttle *in* Hackman and Suttle, 1977, 4; Trist, 1978, 12).

Theoretically, these job characteristics are not at cross-purposes with the clauses of collective agreements. That is, in theory, there is no reason why the employee cannot enjoy both interesting, challenging work and the benefits and privileges afforded by the labour contract. Viewed in this way, QWL and collective agreements do not stand in "zero sum" relationship to one another (i.e., a relationship in which one party's gain derives from or depends upon the other's loss). In practice, however, the relationship between the two is more complex. For example, one of the basic objectives underpinning all collective agreements is control over the content and scope of jobs, a principle based on the notion of task specificity. Ironically, this principle was not invented by the unions; rather, it is a cornerstone concept of Taylorism, long cherished by management, to which the unions have merely adapted (Upjohn, 1973, 112). Even today, collective agreements are based on the division and standardization of tasks, thereby perpetuating the dichotomy between management rights on the one hand, and the job classification and seniority rules designed to protect against the arbitrary exercise of those rights, on the other.

In contrast, QWL programs, particularly those following the socio-tech approach, are typically based on the principle of minimal critical specification and maximum flexibility, which involves changes that directly contravene the content of existing collective agreements. Specifically, this means that all clauses pertaining to job classification rules could be modified, as could those dealing with wages, seniority and everything related thereto (e.g. bumping), up to and including the clause prohibiting foremen from carrying out the duties of union members covered by the agreement. Another important clause affected by QWL programs is the one dealing with management rights. Although formulated in many different ways, this clause almost always conveys the idea that the organization of work is a management prerogative. QWL programs, on the other hand, by virtue of their insistence on employee participation in the organization of work, substantially modify the substance of that clause.

SHOULD WE SEPARATE QWL FROM THE COLLECTIVE BARGAINING PROCESS?

As we have just seen, QWL programs, in terms of both process and outcomes, inevitably pose problems for union–management relations. These problems and constraints are not, however, insurmountable. Such a conclusion is at least partly affirmed by the sheer number of QWL programs existing in unionized milieux. But generally speaking, QWL programs have been dissociated from the collective bargaining process (Strauss, 1977, 357; Gold, 1986, 9). As Lewin has observed:

> . . .it is apparent that, for the most part, the institution of collective bargaining has been kept outside the ken of those who have studied, written about, and participated in attempts to improve the QWL. The inferences to be drawn from this exclusion are that collective bargaining is somewhat separate from QWL, that collective bargaining does not encompass or is not directed toward those aspects of work that affect the QWL, and that, consequently, collective bargaining is not a vehicle for improving QWL (1981, 37).

There are a number of reasons why authors, as well as a number of practitioners, have wanted to keep QWL separate from the collective bargaining process. First of all, the two processes are seen as very different. Although QWL projects emphasize the role of collaboration in the attainment of goals, the emphasis in negotiation is often on confrontation. Anyone who is familiar with the negotiation process knows that bargaining is conducted within a framework of relationships based on power. Co-operation and negotiation, then, can be seen as two processes that operate according to two fundamentally different sets of rules. Co-operation involves a rather flexible process, having no fixed agenda and no formal rules, where exchanges require information sharing, openness, and trust. In contrast, negotiation involves a more rigid and formalistic process, characterized by the use of poker strategies and bargaining power, in which the enforcement of the signed agreement is left to a very formal, somewhat legalistic procedure known as arbitration. One AFL–CIO leader expressed the difference in these terms:

> A union demand is a negotiable demand which, if not satisfied, can be met by a strike. How do you talk about these QWL questions in terms of a negotiable demand and a possible strike? (Jenkins, 1977; cited in Strauss, 1980, 132.)

Just as the processes of negotiation and co-operation are themselves very different, so are the skills required of those who would carry them out. In this connection, Walton and McKersie have argued that those individuals who are effective at collective bargaining may not be effective at problem solving, since the latter requires many behaviours that are directly counter to those used in bargaining (Brett, 1980, 202). One set of goals and tactics is, by definition, at cross-purposes with the other, so that one role has the potential of undermining the other. For example, holding back information in order to improve one's bargaining position is wholly incompatible with divulging that information in order to resolve a problem. Once information is given, it cannot be retracted; nor can the receiver be expected to disregard it. Conversely, the refusal to give out certain information may give rise to doubts about the communicator's sincerity, intentions, or desire to co-operate. Thus, it can be argued that the skills and action premises of the crafty negotiator are not those of the successful collaborator, given the incompatibility between the trust required for co-operation and the caution required for negotiation.

As early as 1968, the Wood Commission acknowledged that the limited coverage and scope of collective bargaining impair its effectiveness as a vehicle for dealing with the problems of discontent and alienation. In its final report, the Commission had this to say on the subject:

> Collective bargaining has yet to be brought to bear on the problems of job dissatisfaction and alienation from work. Should workers begin to use their

unions and collective bargaining to demand more meaningful and gratifying employment, it is debatable whether the process would rise appropriately to the challenge. Indeed, under some circumstances, unions, if not collective bargaining itself, might prove a hindrance.....

Collective bargaining cannot be expected to accommodate all employer–employee problems equally well. Reason and experience show that its effectiveness in relation to different issues varies widely. Just as the limited coverage of collective bargaining requires that other devices be instituted to govern relations between those not covered by the process, so does its limited scope suggest the same need in relation to issues it cannot completely handle. . . (Canadian Industrial Relations, 1969, 64).

The limits inherent in the negotiation process, then, have led to the dissociation of QWL projects from collective bargaining. Even on the union side, a good many leaders have come to endorse this "dual channel" model of labour–management discourse (Parker, 1985, 47).

Despite the advantages of separating QWL programs from collective bargaining, the dual channel approach is not exempt from problems and uncertainties of its own. For instance, the distinction often drawn between "distributive" as opposed to "integrative" bargaining issues often appears to exist more in theory than in practice. A case in point would be the modification of task content. Although dealing successfully with an issue such as this probably depends more on collaboration that on confrontation, there are no doubt many union leaders and workers who would perceive such modifications as a more appropriate subject for negotiation. However, even if a given issue is amenable to integrative collaboration, this does not necessarily mean that either the operationalization of the decisions taken or their outcomes will be integrative as well. The same could also be said for such contentious issues as the productivity gainsharing resulting from a QWL program, or job classification, or workload, or even the consequences of the seniority clause. Although this has almost always been the case, some surprising research findings in this regard have come to light. In a study of union activists by Kochan and colleagues, the agenda items that typically figure in collective bargaining, including wages, were seen by respondents as *more* integrative than those associated with QWL (e.g., workload, control of work, superior–subordinate relations) (Kochan et al., 1975, 157).

In choosing to dissociate QWL projects from collective bargaining, however, the possibility must not be overlooked that QWL-related issues may eventually make themselves felt, in one way or another, in the content of labour agreements. In other words, sooner or later the parties will turn to the collective bargaining process as the forum for dealing with QWL issues, too.

It is interesting to note that many of the studies advocating separate treatment of integrative and distributive issues have cited the work of

Walton and McKersie in this regard. In the interest of precision and prudence, however, it should be pointed out that, although these authors distinguish between distributive and integrative bargaining, they also warn of the inadvisability of generalizing. Rather, in their view, even such topics as wages and salaries may, under certain circumstances, become integrative items.

> ...The existence or the extent of inherent conflict is an empirical question, in each case to be examined on its own merits....The fact that certain items often become the subject of distributive bargaining is explained as much by a party's perception as by the inherent nature of the agenda items (Walton and McKersie, 1965, 19).

It would also be unwise to idealize the dual channel model in the mistaken belief that industrial warfare is the inevitable result of collective bargaining and harmony the ineluctable by-product of discussions of integrative issues. In Brett's words:

> Parties that are unable to deal with issues in a traditional relationship, without regularly resorting to economic warfare, are unlikely to develop a successful cooperation relationship (Brett, 1980, 202).

The tendency toward dichotomous thinking in this regard may be a partial function of the fact that a number of textbooks have tended to emphasize the conflictual aspects of collective bargaining, when, in fact, the process is not wholly conflictual. It is instructive to recall the caricature of collective bargaining reported by Dunlop and Healy (1955). In their view, collective bargaining is a poker game, where the largest pots go to those who combine deception, bluff, luck, or ability to come up with a strong hand when challenged by the other side; it can be likened to a debating society, replete with the same flow of words, massing of arguments, and name-calling; it is power politics, where the strong impose their terms on the weak; it is a rational process, in which the parties are persuaded to alter their original positions by the facts and arguments presented by the opposing side (Dunlop and Healy, 1955, 3). Generally speaking, there has been a parallel tendency in the literature as well to portray collective bargaining as more of an exercise in power than a problem-solving process. On this point, Kuhn remarked:

> After all, collective bargaining is not just an adversary activity; it includes within its process adjudication, problem-solving, communications and information flows, and rule-making as well as negotiations....Moreover, not only does collective bargaining encompass a variety of processes, it displays many different emphases in different industries. Consequently, the reality of collective bargaining across the economy may allow for more innovations, more possibilities, and greater contributions than scholars usually remember. Theorists need constantly to study and observe collective bargaining as

currently practiced to see if it fits the abstracted categories to which it may be assigned (1976, 353).

Finally, it must be remembered that the legitimacy of all union activity rests, in large measure, on the collective bargaining process. Under the provisions of the various labour codes, certification obliges the employer to negotiate, and, in the event of an impasse, this same code empowers the union to use economic sanctions to persuade the employer of the validity of its arguments. For many unions, the collective bargaining regime and its legal underpinnings offer a framework for action which is reassuring, well understood, and proven effective. Venturing outside this traditional framework—i.e., abandoning collective bargaining in favour of another formula—is understandably viewed as a risky and prejudicial course of action, implying as it does a diminution in the control the union can exert over the process.

CONCLUSIONS

When confronted with the employer's plan for a QWL program, the union has a choice of three possible responses: fight it, ignore it, or get involved and try to shape it (Cole, 1984).

In the long run, ignoring such programs is an unacceptable option, because no union who chooses to bury its head in the sand can adequately fulfil its mandate. Employees form unions, after all, in order to protect and promote their interests, and a union that turns its back on a QWL program of any importance would be failing its membership badly. Of course, in strategic or political terms, it might be advantageous to step back for a time and adopt a "wait and see" attitude. However, no union with any pretentions to legitimacy would dare ignore, for any appreciable length of time, a QWL program that has, or promises to have, a significant impact on working conditions. Moreover, according to data on U.S. firms, there were in 1982 more than 700 QWL programs operating in both unionized and non-unionized companies. Equally impressive are the findings from a 1984 study of the New York Stock Exchange, which reported that 41 percent of companies employing more than 500 workers had worker–management participation programs (Gold, 1986, 3). How can unions reasonably ignore such a reality?

Fighting against these programs is also a high-risk strategy. Of course, unions could probably get away with opposing certain projects on grounds that they seem to be designed to manipulate workers or cripple union power. It would be foolhardy, however, to oppose all such projects across the board. Part of the dilemma stems from the fact that, as a concept, improving employee well-being is difficult to oppose, especially since such improvements are supposed to be the raison d'être of the labour movement. In more practical terms, there is also the risk that a union might find itself opposing a QWL program that eventually results in advantages for the employees it supposedly represents. How, then, could these employees justify supporting that union?

Clearly, the third option—involvement in the program in order to control it—is probably the most viable strategy in the long run. This, of course, begs the question: should the unions involve themselves in these projects through the traditional collective bargaining mechanism or through some mechanism parallel to it?

It is true that the collective bargaining process, by its very nature, is problematic in many respects for co-operation in general and for QWL programs in particular. Often criticized for its rigidity and other failings, the collective bargaining regime has nonetheless shown, over time, a certain capacity for flexibility. At least, sufficient flexibility to enable the process to adapt to changing economic conditions and other exceptional circumstances. Concessionary bargaining, which surfaced primarily in the early 1980s, is one such example of flexibility. Since that time, unions engaged in concessionary bargaining have shown themselves to be capable of a wide range of reactions and positions, some of which have been creative and unusual. A case in point would be the nomination of a union representative to the company's board of directors in exchange for other concessions on the bargaining table—hardly a traditional approach to negotiations, but it has occurred. It seems fair to argue, then, that the collective bargaining regime may be more supple than heretofore imagined.

It also seems plausible to presume that collective bargaining will remain, at least for workers, the vehicle of choice for attaining the labour movement's goals. It is, after all, a process that is familiar, proven, and relatively effective. Its continued existence is no doubt also reinforced by the growing tendency for representatives of diverse sectors of society— the elderly, students, farmers, homosexuals, battered wives, and others— to resort to negotiation in order to advance their group's particular interests. Would it not therefore be illogical to conclude that unions, for whom collective bargaining is the foundation of their existence, will abandon negotiation? Indeed, it would make more sense to presume that they will come to rely on collective bargaining even more as time passes.

Such a development seems all the more likely when we consider that the very legitimacy of labour union activity is rooted in collective bargaining and that the scope of bargaining itself has broadened over the years. From the union point of view, then, it would appear perfectly normal for the collective bargaining process to encompass, eventually, all the components now included in QWL programs. After all, working conditions are the focus of both the collective bargaining process and the QWL agenda.

Also relevant here is the fact that co-operation is always difficult, if not impossible, to achieve when one of the two parties feels threatened. This being the case, it is possible that assimilating the discussion of QWL issues into the traditional collective bargaining framework may offer a way to deal with these issues while, at the same time, reducing the perceived threat to the unions.

The foregoing remarks are obviously not intended to minimize or dismiss the difficulties inherent in labour–management co-operation in general or in the implementation of QWL programs in particular. However, if we are to succeed in creating projects that will stand the test of time, we are inclined to believe that they will have to be at the heart of the collective bargaining process and figure directly in their respective collective agreements. To do otherwise might probably relegate these programs to marginal status.

BIBLIOGRAPHY

Barbash, Jack (1976), "The union as a bargaining organization: Some implications for organizational behavior." *Industrial Relations Research Association, Proceedings of the 28th Annual Winter Meeting*, pp. 145–153.

Brett, Jeanne M. (1980), "Behavioral research on unions and unions management systems." In Staw, Barry M. and Cummings, Larry L. (eds.), *Research in Organizational Behavior*, vol. 2. Greenwich, CT: JAI Press, pp. 177–213.

Brossard, Michel (1982), "La stratégie syndicale face aux groupes semi-autonomes de production." *Relations industrielles* 37 (3): 670–683.

————, (1981), " Les syndicats nord-américains et les groupes semi-autonomes de production." *Gestion* 6 (1): 9–13.

Canada (1969), *Report of the Task Force on Labour Relations*. Ottawa: Queen's Printer.

Chamberlain, Neil W. and Kuhn, James W. (1986), *Collective Bargaining*, 3rd ed. New York: McGraw-Hill.

Cohen-Rosenthal, Edward (1984), "The other side of the coin: The impact of QWL programs on the union as an organization." *Labor Studies Journal* 8 (3): 229–243.

Cole, Robert (1984), "Some principles concerning union involvement in quality circles and other employee involvement programs." *Labor Studies Journal* 8 (3): 221–228.

Craver, Charles B. (1985), "The NLRA at fifty: From youthful exuberance to middle-aged complacency." *Industrial Relations Research Association, Proceedings of the 1985 Spring Meeting*, pp. 604–615.

Crozier, Michel and Friedberg, Erhard (1977), *L'acteur et le système*. Paris: Ed. du Seuil.

Dale, Ernest (1949), "Increasing productivity through labor–management cooperation." *Industrial and Labor Relations Review* 3 (1): 33–44.

―――― (1954), "Union–management cooperation." In Kornhauser, Arthur, Dubin, Robert, and Ross, Arthur M. (eds.), *Industrial Conflict.* New York: McGraw-Hill, pp. 359–372.

Davis, Louis, Sullivan, E., and Charles, S. (1981), "A labour–management contract and quality of working life." In Dorion, Raynald (ed.), *Adapting to a Changing World*, vol. 2. Ottawa: Labour Canada, pp. 87–100.

Dion, Gérard (1986), *Dictionnaire canadien des relations du travail,* 2e ed. Québec: Les Presses de l'Université Laval.

Driscoll, James W. (1979), "Working creatively with a union: Lessons from the Scanlon plan." *Organizational Dynamics* (Summer): 61–79.

Dubofsky, Melvyn (1986), "Industrial relations: Comparing the 1980s with the 1920s." *Industrial Relations Research Association, Proceedings of the 38th Annual Meeting*, pp. 227–236.

Dunlop, John T. and Healy, James J. (eds.) (1955), *Collective Bargaining: Principles and Cases.* Homewood, IL: R. D. Irwin.

Economic Council of Canada (1965), *National Conference on Labor–Management Relations.* Ottawa: Queen's Printer.

Elden, Max (1985), "Democratizing organizations: A challenge to organization development." In Tannenbaum, Robert, Margulies, Newton, and Massarik, Fred (eds.), *Human Systems Development.* San Francisco: Jossey-Bass, pp. 198–223.

Fédération des travailleurs du Québec (1982), *Le Monde ouvrier* (jan.–fév.).

Freedman, Audrey (1985), *The New Look in Wage Policy and Employee Relations.* Conference Board.

Gold, Charlotte (1986), "Employer–employee committees and worker participation." Key Issues no. 30. Ithaca: New York State School of Industrial and Labor Relations, Cornell University.

―――― (1985), "Labor–management committees: Confrontation, cooptation or cooperation." Key Issues no. 29. Ithaca: New York State School of Industrial and Labor Relations, Cornell University.

Goodman, Paul S. (1979), *Assessing Organizational Change: The Rushton Quality-of-Work Experiment.* New York: John Wiley and Sons.

Gray, Lois S. (1984), "Union–management cooperation: A passing fad or permanent change?" *Labor Studies Journal* 8 (3): 209–220.

Greenberg, Paul D. and Glaser, Edward M. (1980), *Some Issues in Joint Union–Management Quality-of-Worklife Improvement Efforts.* Kalamazoo, MI: W. E. Upjohn Institute.

Hackman, Richard J. and Suttle, J. Lloyd (1977), *Improving Life at Work.* Santa Monica: Goodyear Publishing.

Hammer, Tove H. and Stern, Robert N. (1986), "A yo yo model of cooperation: Union participation in management at the Rath Packing Company." *Industrial and Labor Relations Review* 39 (3): 337–349.

Holley, William H., Field, Huberts, and Crowley, James C. (1981), "Negotiating quality-of-worklife, productivity and traditional issues: Union members' preferred roles of their union." *Personnel Psychology* 34 (2): 309–329.

Jacobs, David (1985), "In society: New representational roles for labor and management." *Industrial Relations Research Association, Proceedings of the 1985 Spring Meeting*, pp. 624–631.

Jacoby, Sanford M. (1983), "Union–management cooperation in the United States: Lessons from the 1920s." *Industrial and Labor Relations Review* 37 (1): 18–33.

Katzell, Raymond A. and Yankelovich, Daniel (1975), *Work, Productivity, and Job Satisfaction*. New York: NYU Psychological Corporation.

Klein, Janice A. (1984), "Why supervisors resist employee involvement." *Harvard Business Review* 62 (5): 87–95.

Kochan, Thomas A. (1980), "Collective bargaining and organizational behavior research." In Staw, Barry M. and Cummings, Larry L. (eds.), *Research in Organizational Behavior*, vol. 2. Greenwich, CT: JAI Press, pp. 129–176.

_____ and McKersie, Robert B. (1983), "Collective bargaining: Pressures for change." *Sloan Management Review* XXIV (Summer): 59–65.

_____ , McKersie, Robert B. and Chalykoff, John (1986), "The effects of corporate innovations on union representations." *Industrial and Labor Relations Review* 39 (4): 487–501.

_____ and Dyer, Lee (1976), "A model of organizational change in the context of union–management relations." *The Journal of Applied Behavioral Science* 12 (1): 59–78.

_____ , Lipsky, David B., and Dyer, Lee (1976), "Collective bargaining and quality of worklife: The views of local union activists." *Industrial Relations Research Association, Proceedings of the 27th Annual Meeting*, pp. 150–162.

_____ , Katz, Harry C. and Mower, Nancy R. (1984), *Worker Participation and American Unions*. Kalamazoo, MI: W. E. Upjohn Institute.

Kuhn, James W. (1977), "Conflict resolution: Discussion." *Industrial Relations Research Association, Proceedings of the 29th Annual Meeting*, pp. 352–355.

Lawler, Edward E. and Drexler, John A. (1978), "Dynamics of establishing cooperative quality-of-worklife projects." *Monthly Labor Review* 101 (3): 23–28.

Lawler, Edward E., III and Ozley, Lee (1979), "Winning union–management cooperation on quality-of-worklife projects." *Management Review* 68 (3): 19–24.

Lemelin, Maurice (1981), "Trade unions and work organization experiments." In Dorion, Raynald (ed.), *Adapting to a Changing World*, vol. 2. Ottawa: Labour Canada, pp. 110–120.

_____ and Lamoureux, Daniel (1983), *Les changements dans l'organisation du travail: quelques tendances.* Institut national de productivité.

Lewin, David (1981), "Collective bargaining and the quality of worklife." *Organizational Dynamics* (Autumn): 37–53.

Maccoby, Michael (1984), "Helping labor and management set up a quality-of-worklife program." *Monthly Labor Review* 107 (3): 28–32.

March, James D. (1962), "The business firm as a political coalition." *Journal of Politics* 24 (2): 662–678.

Moss Kanter, Rosabeth (1982), "Dilemmas of managing participation." *Organizational Dynamics* (Summer): 5–28.

Nadler, David A., Hanlon, Martin, and Lawler, Edward A. III (1980), "Factors influencing the success of labour–management quality-of-worklife projects." *Journal of Occupational Behaviour* (1): 53–67.

Nielson, Richard P. (1979), "Stages in moving toward cooperative problem-solving labor relations projects and a case study." *Human Resource Management* 18 (3): 2–8.

Osley, Lee M. and Ball, Judith S. (1982), "Quality of worklife: Initiating successful efforts in labor–management organizations." *Personnel Administrator* 27 (5): 27–39.

Parker, Mike (1985), *Inside the circle: A union guide to* QWL. Boston, MA: South End Press, Labor Notes Books.

Ross, Arthur M. (1948), *Trade Union Wage Policy.* Berkeley: University of California Press.

Rouleau, Linda (1986), *La participation des travailleurs dans l'entreprise: un état de la situation.* Commission consultative sur le travail et la révision du code du travail, Québec.

Schlesinger, Leonard A. and Walton, Richard E. (1977), "Work restructuring in unionized organizations: Risks, opportunities, and impact on collective bargaining." *Industrial Relations Research Association, Proceedings of the 29th Annual Winter Meeting*, pp. 345–355.

Schmikman, John and Keller, Kimberlee (1984), "Employee participation plans as section 8(a) (2) violations." *Labor Law Journal* 35 (12): 772–780.

Schuster, Michael W. (1984), *Union–Management Cooperation.* Kalamazoo, MI: W. E. Upjohn Institute.

_____ (1986), "The impact of union–management cooperation on productivity and employment." *Industrial and Labor Relations Review* 36 (3): 415–430.

Shiram, Arie (1983), "Toward a theory of organization development interventions in unionized work settings." *Human Relations* 36 (8): 747–764.

Sockell, Donna (1984), "The legality of employee-participation programs in unionized firms." *Industrial and Labor Relations Review* 37 (4): 541–556.

Strauss, D. (1980), "Quality of worklife and participation as bargaining issues." In Juris, Hervey A. and Roomkin, Myran (eds.), *The Shrinking Perimeter*. Lexington, MA: Lexington Books, pp. 121–150.

Strauss, George (1977), "Managerial practices." In Hackman, John R. and Suttle, J. Lloyd (eds.), *Improving Life at Work*. Santa Monica: Goodyear, pp. 297–362.

Thacker, James W. and Fields, Mitchel W. (1985), "Joint QWL projects and some consequences for unions: An empirical analysis." In Lemelin, M. (ed.), *Canadian Industrial Relations Association, Proceedings of the 23rd Annual Meeting*, Montreal, pp. 168–179.

Trist, Eric (1978), "Adapting to a changing world." In Dorion, Raynald (ed.), *Adapting to a Changing World*, vol. 1. Ottawa: Labour Canada, pp. 10–20.

Upjohn Institute for Employment Resources, *Work in America*. Cambridge, MA: MIT Press, 1973.

Walton, Richard and Schlesinger, Leonard A. (1979), "Do supervisors thrive in participative work systems?" Organizational Dynamics (Winter): 25–38.

_____ and McKersie, Robert B. (1965), *A Behavioral Theory of Labor Negotiations*. New York: McGraw Hill.

Winpisinger, William W. (1982), "Job enrichment: Another part of the forest." *Industrial Relations Research Association, Proceedings of the 25th Anniversary Meeting*, Toronto, pp. 154–159.

Woodworth, Warner (1985), "Prometheon industrial relations: Labor, ESOPs, and the Boardroom." *Industrial Relations Research Association, Proceedings of the 1985 Spring Meeting*, pp. 618–624.

Zager, Robert, and Rosow, Michael P. *The Innovative Organization*. New York: Pergamon Press, 1982.

17

Collective Bargaining: Lessons from Abroad*

JOHN CRISPO

Periodically, Canadians become so disenchanted with their own industrial relations system that they look overseas for a better model. The author has had the privilege of studying virtually all of these models, and can appreciate why the Canadian search for a foreign panacea has proven so frustrating and futile.

This chapter begins with a brief review of the various problems within the Canadian industrial relations system, then considers the different forms of industrial democracy in Western Europe that have attracted so much Canadian attention. After a cursory treatment of Japan's much-vaunted industrial relations system, the chapter closes with some observations on what Canada may hope to learn from these foreign industrial relations experiences.

INDICTMENTS OF CANADIAN INDUSTRIAL RELATIONS

The Canadian industrial relations system usually comes under assault for one or two particular reasons. The most common criticism is that the system is too strike-prone. Sometimes it is also alleged to be too inflation-prone.

As for lost time owing to industrial conflict, Canada vies with Italy for the dubious distinction of leading the international strike league. Especially where important public services are concerned, Canadians get as fed up as anyone when lockouts or strikes cause disruptions. Their sensitivity is further heightened if any mayhem or violence accompanies the disputes.

The allegation of inflation-proneness of the Canadian industrial relations system is more difficult to accept. Collective bargaining is seldom if ever a primary cause of inflation, although it is usually integral

---

*For further elaboration and substantiation of the author's views, see John Crispo, *Industrial Democracy in Western Europe* (Toronto: McGraw-Hill Ryerson, 1978) and John Crispo, *National Consultation: Problems and Prospects* (Toronto: C.D. Howe Institute, 1984).

to any inflationary spiral once it is rolling. The fact that collective bargaining receives more than its share of the blame for inflation can be attributed to the public nature of the collective bargaining process, particularly when compared with other cost- and income-determining mechanisms. Unlike most other groups in society, unions and workers have to pursue their goals in a very public manner.

To the extent that Canadian industrial relations are strike- or inflation-prone or both, we must appreciate the underlying domestic causes before searching for foreign solutions. Apart from such influences as the normal business cycle, Canada has traditionally had a much larger resource sector than most other countries. This sector is known the world over for its more militant industrial relations. Canada has also experienced a great deal of industrial conflict in the public sector, where collective bargaining has spread at a much faster rate than in most other countries.

To understand the Canadian industrial relations system one must appreciate its highly decentralized and fragmented character, federally and provincially the most diffuse distribution of power over industrial relations in the world. Labour and management aggregations are correspondingly decentralized and fragmented. All of this helps to explain a collective bargaining process that is as decentralized or fragmented as any to be found anywhere.

Instead of focusing on such fundamental causes of industrial conflict in Canada as these, Canadians would rather consider what they might beg, borrow or steal from abroad in order to paper over their own shortcomings. This is why Canadians returning from purported foreign industrial relations meccas command such attention at home, even if no one pays any attention to them anywhere else, least of all where they have been touring.

INDUSTRIAL DEMOCRACY IN WESTERN EUROPE

Canadians first began to look abroad for an industrial relations panacea during the late 1950s and early 1960s. At that time the model was the Netherlands, where labour and management had collaborated for years to rebuild the country's devastated war-torn economy. Like other countries later on, however, Holland lost its model status after its great wage-price (or price-wage) explosion in 1965, when collaboration suddenly gave way to confrontation.

Until the recent focus on Japan, most Canadian attention was devoted to the industrial democracies of Western Europe. But there is a problem in trying to generalize about either Western European industrial democracies, or their industrial relations in general. First, there is no one system of industrial relations in Western Europe. In fact, there are at least three distinguishable types of industrial relations systems in that part of the world. The Northern countries tend to more class-collaborationist processes within relatively well-structured and stable systems. This includes West Germany and Austria as well as the Scandinavian countries. The South has had more class conflict-ridden processes within less structured and stable systems. This includes such countries as France and Spain. In between, one finds the more mixed models of Belgium and Holland. Off totally by itself is Great Britain, whose unique system, or series of systems, defies ready categorization. British industrial relations range from the relative stability and practical working labour relations found in electrical power generation to the no-man's land of confrontational class warfare in coal mining.

The North's more consensual models of industrial relations offer three distinct subsets of industrial democracy which have commanded Canadian attention: economic democracy, representational democracy, and shop-floor democracy. Since little will be said about the last form, let us deal with it at the outset. Shop-floor democracy—often referred to as quality of working life—involves a range of measures designed to make work a more participative, meaningful, and therefore more productive experience. At the simplest level this may mean little more than job enlargement and job enrichment, or even just job rotation. At its more sophisticated levels it entails such concepts as leaderless teams and stall assembly, all designed to take close supervision and repetitive routine out of work. Japanese work circles are another manifestation of this same approach. Of the three forms of industrial democracy discussed here, this is the one most prevalent in Canada.

Economic democracy raises fundamental questions about the distribution of equity ownership of business enterprises in a capitalist system. This contentious issue first arose in Sweden because of its labour movement's practice of wage solidarity within what was an extremely centralized and disciplined collective bargaining framework. Under Sweden's system, the average level of wage and salary increases was negotiated centrally between the major labour and management federations, with workers in high-paid industries subsequently taking a little less while workers in low-paid industries got a little more. The desired result was a smoothing of current income flows among workers in different industries.

One undesired side effect, from labour's point of view, was that the owners of profitable enterprises reaped comparatively larger returns than they would under Canada's style of collective bargaining, where a company's (or industry's) ability to pay is a much bigger factor in the micro-negotiations that characterize the system. Thus while Swedish unions secured what they deemed a more equitable income distribution among workers, they left much more on the table for the owners of many enterprises than would otherwise have been the case. To counter this adverse side effect of their wage-solidarity program, the Swedish unions and their social-democratic political allies proposed a very radical form of what came to be known as worker equity or capital formation. This amounted to a giant mutual-investment portfolio for workers. As originally conceived, this plan would have required companies to transfer a significant portion of their pre-tax profits in the form of new equity to a large investment fund controlled by the unions in the name of the workers.

This plan held many controversial features. First, in the case of profitable firms, so much of their ownership would have been transferred to the centralized fund that within a short span of years the fund would have controlled them. Since the fund was to be controlled by the unions, and their social-democratic allies were in control of the government, legitimate questions were raised about the future of both private capitalism and democratic pluralism in the country. Equally intriguing was the labour movement's insistence that no workers be allowed any direct control over their transferred equity capital or the dividends flowing therefrom. It was as if the unions did not trust their members to vote their shares or use their dividends as the unions might have wished.

After much debate, a deadlocked royal commission, and a couple of elections, the labour movement and its allies in the social-democratic party introduced a modified version of their original plan. To avoid the charge of centralized union control over virtually everything in Sweden, a series of employer-financed, regional worker-investment plans was introduced, with trustees drawn from both the labour movement and other sources. The notion of collective worker ownership of these funds was not sacrificed by allowing individual workers any control over their share in them.

A more modest version of the Swedish worker capital-formation funds has been in effect in Denmark for some time. The European Economic Community has also published a green paper espousing more equitable distribution of equity or share ownership in private enterprises. Thus, while this remains for the time being a back-burner issue in the rest of Western Europe, it could become a very contentious front-burner issue if, as and when economic conditions improve in the various countries.

Representational democracy claims the most attention of Canadians who believe Canada has much to learn from developments in the industrial relations arena in Western Europe. By far the most refined and sophisticated system of this type is found in West Germany, though comparisons to relevant developments in a few other Western European countries are likewise useful. At one time West Germany had a top-to-bottom system of representational democracy whose institutions were less conventional than the usual forms of collective bargaining and political action.

At the pinnacle of the West German system for some time was the Concerted Action Committee. This was a tripartite body composed of senior labour, management and government representatives who usually met quarterly to work towards a common understanding of the country's economic problems and prospects. Over the years it met with varying degrees of success, but on balance had a beneficial effect on the general climate of labour–management–government relations simply through the assurance that its constituents shared a common perception of the country's situation. Unfortunately, the Concerted Action Committee was formally dissolved when the labour movement walked out during an unrelated constitutional challenge brought by the employers against the modified co-determination system (discussed below). Apparently, meetings similar to those of the Concerted Action Committee continue, although on an ad hoc, informal, and irregular basis.

The West German Bureau of Employment—roughly the equivalent of Canada Employment—is also operated on a tripartite basis. This applies at the national, regional, and local levels, with labour and management each having one-third representation at all levels, while the government shares one-half of its third with representatives of the employees of the Bureau. This Bureau is responsible for all public retraining, upgrading and relocation programs, as well as the country's unemployment insurance system.

Much of West Germany's social security program is based on a series of industry and regional plans, supplemented by national catch-all plans for those not covered by any of the others. These plans—comprising everything from health care to pensions—are effectively run by joint bodies composed of labour and management representatives in the appropriate industries and regions.

Despite the importance of the foregoing forms of representational democracy in West Germany, most foreign attention on its industrial relations has focused on its co-determination system. Co-determination involves worker and/or union representation on company boards of directors (or supervisory boards, as they are called). Co-determination was reintroduced into West Germany after World War II by the allied occupying powers as part of a concerted attempt to democratize the country. Since then three different versions of co-determination have emerged.

The most advanced form of co-determination applies only to the coal and steel industries, and requires 50 percent union and worker representation on the supervisory boards, with a neutral chairman. At the other extreme, applying to relatively small firms, is the one-third model, which provides only for elected worker (and not union) representation. Larger firms other than those in coal and steel are subject to the 1976 modified form of co-determination, the result of an all-party compromise between labour demands for the 50 percent coal-and-steel model and management demands for retention of the one-third model. This compromise model of co-determination entails what might be termed a "50 percent less one" formula. The "one less" than the 50 percent allocated to union and worker representatives is elected by the white-collar workforce from candidates drawn from the ranks of senior management.

If this seems a strange formula it is worth noting, in passing, the current approaches to co-determination in both Austria and Holland. The latter's co-determination system applies only to relatively large firms and entails a mutual co-optation or mutual veto approach, depending on one's perspective. Under the Dutch approach all candidates for the supervisory board have to be agreed upon by the worker's half of the works council (discussed below) and the shareholder representatives. Not surprisingly, this involves a sometimes complex and cumbersome trading-off process between the various names brought forward by the two sides.

Austria also has a unique system of co-determination which applies only to its many Crown corporations. The boards of these corporations have a one-third worker component, with the other two-thirds nominated by the country's two major political parties, proportionate to their representation in the legislature. While this system may seem odd at first glance, it has two decided advantages. Because both major political parties appoint board members they resist the normal temptation to name loyal political bagmen, cronies, and hacks, through fear that the other party will name more competent people and thereby steal the show. In addition, having both political parties name the board members of Crown corporations makes these bodies more responsible to parliament and the public, rather than just to the government and party in power, as is the case with Crown corporations in Canada.

The West German system of co-determination cannot be dismissed as unworkable. West Germany has done too well under co-determination to suggest otherwise. Yet neither can one argue that West Germany's success is due to co-determination. The truth lies somewhere in between, and may be attributed to the informal compromise that seems to have been worked out between labour and management. On the one hand, union and worker representatives on company supervisory boards have demanded access to all company information and an equal voice in all company social policies that in any way affect employee well-being. In return, union and worker representatives have more or less agreed to accept management and shareholder views on accounting, financial, marketing, production, and related matters, as long as these do not jeopardize the income and job security of the workers—the bottom line equivalents, for workers, of shareholder profits.

The last form of West German representational democracy involves what are termed works councils, which are common in one form or another in most other Western European countries. Works councils in Western Europe are mandated by law in all but the smallest enterprises. The workers' halves of such councils—where they are joint bodies—in many ways play the same roles as local unions under master agreements bargained on a multi-local basis in Canada. Indeed, because of their long tradition, these works councils have for the most part supplanted the need for North American-style union locals, although union activists invariably dominate the worker components of their councils. In West Germany, for example, 90 percent of the chairmen and 80 percent of the members of works councils are union members, even though less than 40 percent of the workforce is organized.

Works councils in Eastern Europe historically have had three types of powers. In the first place they have extensive information rights usually stemming well beyond any entitlements union locals have in Canada. Second, they have far-reaching consultative rights—in which labour is now less interested because these are seen as pro forma rights, with management only going through the motions of consultation required by law. Finally, works councils have growing joint decision rights in areas where management cannot act without the agreement of labour. For example, in West Germany, management cannot introduce any change that is likely to affect its workforce adversely in any significant way, unless it first secures a social plan through the works council which addresses that effect. Failing agreement within the works council, such an issue is referred to a tripartite labour court for adjudication, a procedure not unlike Canadian grievance arbitration.

By this time it should be clear that West Germany's system of representational democracy provides far more scope for meaningful union and worker input into all levels of its socio-economic-political and especially managerial decision processes than is true in Canada. How applicable the West German experience might be for Canada remains to be seen. Before turning to that question, however, it is useful to spend some time on Japan, which has become for many Canadians the favoured foreign model of industrial relations.

JAPANESE INDUSTRIAL RELATIONS

If Japanese industrial relations has any great relevance for Canada it probably lies in the success that country has had with its aforementioned labour circles. At the micro-level of office or plant, Japanese management has fostered a style of operations that has encouraged meaningful participation by workers. This type of shop-floor democracy is not uncommon in some parts of Western Europe and especially in Sweden, where Volvo's stall assembly has received much attention. It is likewise common in North America, particularly in such successful non-union firms as IBM. The transferability of this aspect of Japanese management—if it can truly be called Japanese—is further demonstrated by the success of most Japanese subsidiaries in the United States in applying it there.

Japan's industrial relations are also widely known for such supposedly paternalistic policies as lifetime employment and seniority wages, not to mention company housing and recreational facilities. But all is not as rosy as it seems. Lifetime employment, for example, applies only within the government and very large corporations—together comprising less than 40 percent of the total labour force. The other 60 percent-plus work in a much less secure environment, leading many observers to suggest, quite properly, that Japan has both a dual economy and a dual labour market.

Further, although many Japanese workers who enjoy lifetime employment also receive semi-annual bonuses amounting to one-third or more of their earnings, these bonuses can be withheld if the employer is experiencing financial difficulties. Many Canadian employers could doubtless afford Japanese-style lifetime employment if they had this degree of flexibility in their annual payroll.

As for seniority wages, it is a fairly general practice in Japan for workers to be paid more the longer they work for an enterprise, regardless of whether they assume greater responsibility. Combined with lifetime employment, this practice can prove a very attractive package for those who benefit from such customs. Even those so fortunate, however, must reckon with a normal retirement age of 55, with no pension rights until age 65. During the interim, even the most favoured workers must often fend for themselves in the poorest part of the dual labour market.

Another reason the Japanese model may not be so attractive for Canada, if not North America as a whole, relates to the relative weakness of the labour movement within Japan. For a long time the Japanese economic miracle was largely attributed to what was known as Japan Inc. or Japan Incorporated—a catch-phrase that expresses the extremely close working relationship between business and the government. In this relationship there was virtually no place for organized labour, a situation that continues to this day.

Further witness to organized labour's relatively weak position in Japan is the prevalence of so-called enterprise unions. Most unions in Japan are confined to one company, and companies will not accept any labour representation drawn from other than their own workforce. Moreover, it is traditional for top managers in Japanese firms to have spent some time as officials in their own firm's enterprise unions. Union office effectively serves as a stepping-stone to a management career. Not surprisingly, these same unions tend toward a strong company orientation that detracts from their affiliation and loyalties to the labour movement as a whole.

RELEVANCE FOR CANADA

Although Canadians may learn much from foreign industrial relations, caution is recommended in trying to transplant or transfer such experiences. There are no panaceas, as shown by the breakdown of the Dutch post-war model that for some time attracted so much foreign attention. Sweden's so-called middle way, the next centre of attention, has become less attractive with its declining competitiveness and deteriorating labour–management relations. Even the much-touted West German system is now in considerable difficulty, as the labour movement refuses to back off from its futile drive for reduced working hours—a supposed solution to the country's continuing unemployment problem. Enough has already been said of the questionableness of the Japanese model from a Canadian point of view.

Even if there was one proven model abroad, it would be difficult to transplant or transfer it to Canada. There are usually significant attitudinal and institutional differences between any two countries. For example, in West Germany organized labour is referred to as a social partner (the other partner is management) and is treated with great respect. As a result it assumes major responsibilities in its various roles within that country's system of representational democracy. In Canada—in marked contrast— the labour movement is tolerated more as a social embarrassment than a social partner. It neither seeks nor is given many responsibilities because there is no institutional structure within which it can do so.

At best, Canada can probably only adapt some foreign industrial relations successes to its own situation, rather than adopt them. More than that would be risky, as attitudes and institutions in the industrial relations arena in Canada are far removed from those in other countries whose practices it might choose to emulate. In this cautious spirit, one can examine the prospects for adapting to the Canadian scene some of the experiences outlined above.

One can draw perhaps the most useful lessons from the two extreme ends of spectrum: shop-floor democracy and the tripartite economic and social forum. Shop-floor democracy—or whatever one cares to call it—can be applied to virtually any system of industrial relations in which management recognizes that workers who are allowed meaningful participation in their work are more productive. Any democratic country's industrial relations system can also benefit from something like a tripartite national forum, if only by discovering a common framework for understanding the country's economic and social problems and prospects.

Transplants or transfers that fall between these two extreme ends of the spectrum of industrial democracy become more difficult. Even so, there are often parallels worth exploring, such as the Swedish notion of economic democracy through collectivized worker asset-formation funds. Canada already has the potential equivalent of this approach, on a different but much wider basis than in Sweden. This is because Canada relies so much more on private than public pension plans, and those private plans involve massive amounts of funds. As unions demand and win pensions as a form of deferred wages, and a greater voice in administering these funds, they achieve a variation on the Swedish model of economic democracy that is currently much more appropriate to the Canadian environment.

What seems particularly foreign to Canadians is the West German model of co-determination. Nonetheless, there have been some token moves, with labour representatives sitting on company boards (most notably in the case of Chrysler and several American airlines, as part of a quid pro quo for recent concession bargaining). Perhaps in time these token moves will bear some positive fruit and therefore spread. In the meantime, it would be unwise to legislate any such scheme, especially since neither labour nor management has called for it. The only exception where legislation might be appropriate would be Crown corporations, where just about any form of board appointment would be preferable to the prevailing one.

Western European-style works councils seem to be no more popular with labour and management in Canada than is co-determination. Canadian unions have shown little or no interest in works councils as such because these have tended to preclude development of the local union base that is the hallmark of the Canadian and North American labour movements. Management has shown even less interest because it does not want to have to live with the power of information and co-decision associated with such councils. Insofar as labour and management may care to supplement their normal adversarial relations at the local level, there are home-grown North American approaches such as the Scanlon Plan which can serve just as well as Western European works councils.

CONCLUSION

This chapter does not seek to discourage experimentation and innovation in industrial relations in Canada. Apropos of the Scanlon Plan, there is a real need in Canada to explore more consultative and co-operative relations in order to meet the serious competitive challenge that confronts this country.

The chapter has suggested several successful foreign industrial relations experiences upon which Canada may draw. But for the most part, these can only be adapted, not adopted. Much more emphasis needs to be placed on seeking Canadian solutions to Canadian problems in the industrial relations arena rather than trying to emulate some elusive and inappropriate foreign model or panacea.

Fortunately, some attempts are being made to find new, Canadian ways of accomplishing more positive results in industrial relations. Sometimes the results have been discouraging, halting or inconclusive, but that is bound to be the case as labour, management, and government attempt to relate to each other in new ways. Two examples will suffice.

The first concerns the very troubled Canadian Labour Market and Productivity Centre (CLMPC), which was established after a series of tripartite approaches that had mixed results at best. CLMPC was created as a bipartite body at the joint request of labour and management, both of which felt that government involvement in several earlier tripartite ventures had exposed them to too much politicking. Labour and management were to control CLMPC jointly, albeit with a heavy component of federal and provincial government participation on an ex-officio basis.

Unfortunately, CLMPC has gone nowhere so far, despite the logic in its mandate to devise policies to improve Canada's performance, both in the labour market and in productivity. Canada must become more productive in order to become more competitive. Yet there will be undue resistance to improvements in productivity unless adequate measure are taken to retrain, upgrade and, where necessary, relocate and compensate workers, so that they do not bear the brunt of the changes required to make the country more productive. If labour and management in Canada cannot eventually forge some common goals, there is not much hope for the country.

Another noteworthy experiment in industrial relations is the establishment of the Canadian Steel Policy Conference, a joint effort by labour and management in that industry to come to grips with its current challenges. The Conference has come up with some constructive ideas in relation to staffing and productivity, more than the CLMPC has so far accomplished. At the same time, however, the Conference has demonstrated protectionist and self-serving instincts that could spell its degeneration into little more than a common lobby for the narrow concerns of the steel industry, its unions and workers.

In exploring new ways to conduct its industrial relations, Canada should look abroad for enduring success stories that hold some hope of adaptability to the Canadian environment. In the final analysis, however, Canadians must tailor-make their own industrial relations solutions to their own industrial relations problems.

18

The Future of Collective Bargaining in an Information Society: Strategic Choices for Management and Unions*

Amarjit S. Sethi

INTRODUCTION

The latter part of the twentieth century finds the Western world facing major problems of technological change that will require strategic responses from both unionized and non-unionized organizations in the business and public sectors. Both sectors will play major roles in the search for solutions to technological impacts within and outside of the collective bargaining framework to meet a wide range of expectations. Although there has been a tremendous growth in technology in general in the past several decades, the coming period represents fundamental shifts in a whole range of information technologies. The future challenge lies in recognizing that a range of effective joint management and union strategic choices are critical in mitigating the potential adverse impacts of information technology (IT), and enhancing the effectiveness of an operational industrial relations system.

Although the focus of this chapter is Information Technology (IT), elements of technological change have been introduced in the chapter that may not specifically be defined as IT but have been thought to be of broad relevance to it.

According to Jacques Ellul (1964, 25) technology, or technique as he calls it, "is the totality of methods rationally arrived at and having absolute efficiency (for a given stage of development) in every field of human activity." In a broader sense, technology "is the organization and application of knowledge for the achievement of practical purposes. It includes physical manifestations such as tools and machines, but also intellectual techniques and processes used in solving problems and obtaining desired outcomes" (Kast and Rosenzweig, 1985, 208).

The term IT refers to the totality of dynamic and complex information

*I would like to acknowledge the benefit of comments made by Dr. Jane Fulton, Mr. Norman Metzger, and Mr. Felix Quinet.

technologies combining microelectronics, computers and telecommunications, including the following components: hardware, software, ergonomic work stations, expert systems, knowledge-based systems, database systems, advanced telecommunications (telematics), office automation systems, robotics, computer-integrated manufacturing systems, and development of the next generation of super-computers and fifth-generation technology. Figure 18.1 shows some of the functions and applications of IT.

According to Bell (1973), information and not capital is a strategic resource of the new age, characterized as an "information society" (Masuda, 1980; Porat, 1977; Naisbitt, 1982) The actors in an industrial relations system must confront one of the chief distinctive features of an information society, namely the widening base and power of knowledge made possible by technological advances. "The productivity of knowledge has already become the key to productivity, competitive strength, and economic achievement. Knowledge has already become the primary industry, the industry that supplies the economy the essential and central resources of production" (Drucker, 1980).

Porat (1977) measured the information economy in the United States and concluded that it accounted for more than 46 percent of the gross national product and more than 53 percent of income earned. Out of the 19 million new jobs created in the United States during the 1970s, only five percent were in manufacturing and only 11 percent in the goods-producing sector as a whole, while almost 90 percent were in information, knowledge, or service jobs. As the public sector is primarily a service industry, the impact of IT on jobs in this sector will be significant (Naisbitt, 1982, 17).

In Canada, from 1931 to 1971, the proportion of Canadian workers in information-related occupations increased from 21 percent to 40 percent, and the transition is expected to continue at a rapid pace during the eighties and beyond (Science Council of Canada, 1982). According to Walter Light, President of Northern Telecom Limited, new technologies will dominate the industrial development of the world. "Without mastery of, if not leadership in these new technologies, no nation can hope for more than a peripheral existence" (quoted in Science Council of Canada, 1982, 14). Workers and managers in both private and public sectors must cope with the difference between the knowledge needed for task execution and the knowledge currently available to them. This gap emanates from two sources: lack of knowledge about how to perform a task and lack of knowledge about what to do when exceptional conditions are created (Perrow, 1967). Exceptional conditions primarily arise from variations in inputs (e.g., in the situations of clients or conditions of raw materials) and in variations in the performance of new technologies.

A comprehensive study of about 1,000 establishments across Canada

Table 18.1
Information Technologies: Functions and Applications[a]

Function	Application	Technology
Data Collection	Weather Prediction	Radar, Infra-Red Object Detection Equipment, Radiometers
	Medical Diagnosis	CAT-Scanners, Ultrasonic Cameras
Data Input	Word Processing	Keyboards, Touch-Screens
	Factory Automation	Voice Recognizers (Particularly for Quality Control)
	Mail Sorting	Optical Character Readers
Storage	Archives	Magnetic Bubble Devices, Magnetic Tape
		Floppy Disks
	Accounting Systems	Wafer-Scale Semiconductors (Still in Research Phase), Very-High-Speed
	Scientific Computation	Magnetic Cores
		Charge-Coupled Semiconductor
	Ecological Mapping	Devices, Video Disks
		Hard Disks
	Libraries	
Information Processing	Social Security Payments	General Purpose "Mainframe" Computers, COBOL Programs
		Minicomputers
	Traffic Control	Multi-User Super-Micros, Application
	Distributed Inventory Control	Software Packages
		Expert Systems
	Medical Diagnoses	Spreadsheet Application Packages,
	Engineering Design	Microcomputers

Application	Technology
Scientific Computation	Super-Computers: Multiple Instruction–Multiple Data (MIMD) Processors, Vector Processors, Data-Driven Processors, FORTRAN Programs
Ecological Mapping	Array Processors, Associative Processors
Communications	Robotics, Artificial Intelligence
Office Systems	Local Area Networks, Private Branch Exchanges (PBX), Editor Applications Packages
Teleconferencing	Communications Satellites, Fibre Optics
Factory Automation	Cellular Mobile Radios
Rescue Vehicle Dispatch International Financial Transactions	Transport Protocols, Data Encryption, Integrated Services Digital Networks (ISDN)
Word Processing (Data Output and Presentation)	Personal Computers, Printers (Impact, Ink Jet, Xerographic)
Management Information	Cathode Ray Tubes, Computer Graphics
Pedestrian Traffic Control	Voice Synthesizers

aThis list is not exhaustive; any given technology may also be used for some of the other applications mentioned.
Source: Office of Technology Assessment, 1985, 309. Reprinted by permission.

undertaken by the Economic Council of Canada (1987) concluded that "while Canadian industry has introduced much computer-based technology in the 1980s, this country is lagging in comparison with...Japan, the United States and Western Europe....Canadians must improve their performance with respect to the introduction and use of the computer-based technologies. Failure to do so will lead to a loss of prosperity and jobs as Canada's competitive position deteriorates" (ECC, 1987,2).

In order to deal with technological uncertainty, a collective bargaining system needs to consider some strategic choices that can be applied by employers and unions to improve both organizational productivity/effectiveness, as well as accommodate employees' needs for job security, flexibility, quality of worklife and self-actualization. In this process, unions have the social responsibility to make strategic preventive choices; organizations have the social responsibility to examine the long-term impact of technology on jobs, technological stress or technostress, and employee well-being.

TECHNOLOGICAL PERSPECTIVES AND COLLECTIVE BARGAINING POLICIES

Management and unions need to understand and develop perspectives to manage IT effects. There are five such perspectives that can serve as a foundation for employer policy, and union response to that policy, that can be covered as part of the technology agreement in the process of collective bargaining. These include:

1. Rational Efficiency Perspective. Organizations computerize in order to pursue long-standing goals of efficiency and cost effectiveness. In pursuing the policies of rationalization, computerization is viewed the most rational technological innovation (Attewell and Rule, 1984). Unions need to develop a proactive strategy to cope with this perspective.

2. Technological Imperative Perspective. Jacques Ellul (1964) so cogently held the view that technology is the product of a philosophy that demands its self-sustaining development. In this sense, technology becomes autonomous and a catalyst for change in organizational behaviour and thereby influences the collective bargaining system.

3. Political Perspective. Another explanation, of particular interest to unions, is that changes in information technology may be changes in power relations (Downs, 1967; Laudon, 1964; Olson, 1975). As reported by Attewell and Rule (1984), IT developments may actually be the source of satisfying management's political goals.

4. Ethical Perspective. Unions may question the ethics of technological growth not only on grounds of the job insecurity that it may cause, but also on the basis of a philosophical view that computers reduce human dignity, responsibility, and autonomy. The questions that need to be explored are: Is human thought entirely computable? What limits, for example, should be pursued in ultimate computerization of a professional worker?

5. Strategic Choice Perspective. This view holds that IT brings complex changes in the work environment and demands a strategic understanding, by both managements and unions, of the ways in which work environments are influenced by the characteristics of a specific IT so that the agenda of collective bargaining can cope with technological uncertainties, with the twin objectives of increasing productivity as well as quality of worklife.

One example of interest to bargainers relates to conclusions about the use of the Cathode Ray Tube (CRT) or Video Display Terminals (VDTS). Studies indicate that the source of psychosomatic stress is not the use of a CRT display per se, but rather the way in which office automation systems are organized (Turner, 1984a; Dainoff et al., 1981; Ghiringhelli, 1980). The implication for bargainers is to understand that simply controlling the use of the CRT display will not remedy the stressful situation but strategies will have to be negotiated to focus on the "network environment" (including job satisfaction, emotional exhaustion, absenteeism or performance) in controlling the use of computer systems. It is thus imperative for bargainers to understand the ergonomic and stress factors in formulating their positions on technology and working conditions (WHO, 1985).

We cannot provide clear evidence for the support of one technological perspective over another as cited above. The various studies have reported a mixed picture insofar as the effects of computer innovations are concerned (Laudon, 1964; Dutton and Kraemer, 1978; King and Kraemer, 1980). Advocates who argue that technology is autonomous (Ellul, 1984; Winner, 1977) state that we are caught in the inevitable struggle when we develop technology for the sake of technology. Management often takes the position that technology increases productivity and efficiency, whereas unions will argue that technology may not automatically increase quality of worklife, and may be a threat to job security.

Figure 18.2
Dimensions of Technostress

Factual Factors[a]

- Number of Technological Elements
- Rate of Technological Change
- Heterogeneity of Elements
- Clarity of Elements
- Relationship among Elements
- Predictability of Change

Value Factors[a]
(Moderating Variables)

- Relative Power
- Time Pressure
- Importance of Issue
- Individual Ability Interdependence
- Locus of Control

- Ambiguity of Tolerance
- Field Dependence
- Availability of Feedback
- Task and Group Cohesiveness

---

[a]The "factual" and "value" factors are interrelated. They are separated here for showing their importance in the experience of technostress.

Technostress and Collective Bargaining

Our view is that IT produces its own social stress, which we have identified as technostress. Technostress is a perceived state of uncertainty in the face of technological change that occurs at individual, organizational, and societal levels. The term refers to uncertainty experienced by the person in different contexts in adapting to the new technological development. In negotiating new technology-related provisions, negotiations on both management and union sides can benefit by an increased awareness of technostress at work.

Technostress is not an isolated category of mere response, but a dynamic state of adaptation combining (1) sources (e.g., technology), (2) dimensions (how the source is transmitted and perceived), and (3) responses (reaction to uncertainty). These responses are moderated by such characteristics as locus of control, individual ability, time pressures, relative power, ambiguity of tolerance, field dependence, availability of feedback, and task and group cohesiveness (see Figure 18.2).

Technostress has three key ingredients in the environment: the nature of the stressor, the reaction or response to this stressor, and results from this reaction, leading again to a cycle of new reactions and formulations at various levels of analysis including management, workers, and unions. There are two components to technostress: (1) positive stress or technoeustress, and (2) technodistress. This is based on the assumption that technology can have differential effects on its users.

Technoeustress is the stress that is beneficial or has a positive effect on the functioning of the individual and his or her contribution to the level of organizational productivity. Organizational performance and quality-of-worklife concerns are given equal emphasis jointly by management and unions. (A striking example is the sponsorship of joint Quality of Worklife [QWL] activities by General Motors [GM] and the United Automobile Workers [UAW], recognizing the positive outcomes for GM and UAW.) Technodistress is that stress having a negative impact on the individual's functions, with consequent negative effects on the overall industrial relations system. In a technodistress context, workers suffer through developing a high level of anxiety and associated psychosomatic illnesses, while management and unions experience a higher level of labour relations conflict and reduced organizational commitment.

A STRATEGIC CHOICE MODEL FOR MANAGING IT

Before we explain our model, we need to define strategic choice. Strategic choice, in our view, is (1) an awareness of the aim by a dominant coalition (such as management or union) which is shaped by existing values and transactions within the environment; (2) internalization of that aim in a given environment; and (3) proceeding to identify, negotiate and exploit (often opportunistically) events and broader circumstances within the environment in ways that, one believes, will bring oneself nearer the desired aim. The choices lie in determining what events to ignore, or exploit to achieve the aim. Essentially, what is being created is an "agenda of negotiation" through the use of strategies for achieving desired aims.

This definition of strategic choice has three key elements: vision, values and decision. The awareness of a technological aim by management and unions requires some vision about the future. Values are conceptions—explicit or implicit—of the desirable situations or states of consciousness that underlie decisions, and decisions are those negotiated choices that take management, workers, or unions nearer to the aim. Vision, values and decisions thus interact in the determination of collective bargaining aims. Strategic choice, in the context of technological change, implies internalization of the aim of managing technology effectively for both management and unions; identifying and assessing organizational and technological environments and selecting those strategies that reduce negative uncertainty (technodistress) and increase opportunity (technoeustress).

Effective coping with technostress by management and unions may help them to increase their respective power base (Pfeffer et al., 1976; Hinings et al., 1974; Goh, 1985). One of the key negotiating skills needed, therefore, is strategic planning in order to cope effectively with IT impacts. Walton (1985, 560) describes the importance of planning skills required in implementing IT changes as follows:

1. Work systems based on the new technology often require less skill and knowledge, but sometimes these new systems result in more jobs being upgraded than downgraded. System design can influence that outcome.
2. The technical system can increase the flexibility of work schedules to accommodate human preferences, or it can decrease flexibility and require socially disruptive work schedules.
3. New systems often contribute to social isolation, but sometimes they have the opposite effect. Similarly, they often separate an operator from the end result of his or her effort, but occasionally they bring the operator in closer touch with the end result. Seldom are these planned outcomes, but they can be.
4. These systems sometimes render individuals technologically obsolete because of changed skill and knowledge requirements, but they also open up new careers.
5. New technology can change the focus of control—toward either centralization or decentralization.
6. New information systems can change—for better or worse—an employee-typist into a subcontractor operating a terminal out of his or her home.

Technostress can be positive if preventive strategies are adopted. Parties in collective bargaining can display their skills and awareness in negotiating meaningful contract provisions by anticipating human effects of new technology. The proposition is that negotiating technology provisions requires the competence and skills to formulate and make strategic decisions. To quote Schönpflug (1983, 355):

> Prospective planning, clear priority of decisions, and wise renunciation of goals of low priority may help to prevent multi-demand situations. . .Lack of prospective planning, inability in setting priorities and blind fixation to various incentives may. . .serve as the *via regia* to the creation of an entangling stress situation, finally also leading to fatigue. This, at least is one of the lessons taught by the theory of action and its good companion, the theory of behavior economics.

Components of a Strategic Choice Model

The approach we have taken is that it is not technology alone that causes productivity increases (or decreases), or tends to improve (or lower) quality of worklife; rather, old and new values interact upon the impact of new technology. These values emanate from the interaction of the work environment and persons in it, requiring strategies directed not only in changing the person or the work environment but towards developing new assumptions about how the technology is to be integrated into the working environment. We call this conceptual framework a strategic choice model, as presented in Figure 18.3.

Preventive and proactive strategies are significant in increasing the competence of management and workers in coping with impacts of new information technology in promoting not only productivity and competitive edge but also quality of worklife (Turner and Karasek, 1984). When these strategic choices are considered by managements and unions, the agenda and process of a collective bargaining system can be accordingly structured to achieve organizational effectiveness, competitive edge, and quality of worklife. In the technologically renewed collective bargaining process, workers and unions have the social responsibility to make strategic preventive choices and management has the social responsibility to examine alternatives that protect job security as well as employee well-being. The government has also a critical role to play in ensuring, through responsive regulation, that the parties use the organizational and collective bargaining systems in ways that use the tremendous power and flexibility of IT that help to keep technological impacts under human control. Figure 18.3 illustrates this process at both micro- and macrolevels.

Moreover, IT can influence the process of collective bargaining by the release of timely, well-selected and well-developed information. Parties to collective bargaining may be able to use IT to deal effectively with IT's own impacts.

In a review of recent research on positive and negative impacts of technology in relation to the issue of whether technology controls workers or vice versa, Alcalay and Pasick (1983, 1980–81) came to the following tentative conclusions:

1. The use of new technologies can increase job strain, job overload and underload and can decrease the level of workers' control over work.
2. Technologically intensive work can have an impact on the individual's social support networks.
3. Workers who benefit the most from the use of new technologies are usually high-level management and/or professionals.
4. Workers who suffer the most from technology-centred tasks are in lower status, blue-collar or clerical positions.

The Use of Strategic Bargaining

Collective bargaining is a continuing process of interactions ranging from free strategic choice to complete environmental determinism. This view allows both proactive as well as reactive behaviours on the part of actors

Figure 18.3
A Strategic Choice Model of Technostress Management[a]

ORIGINS OF TECHNOSTRESS

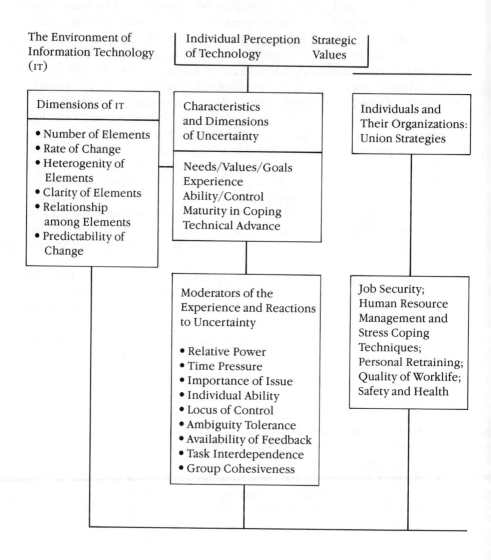

The Environment of Information Technology (IT)

Individual Perception of Technology   Strategic Values

Dimensions of IT

- Number of Elements
- Rate of Change
- Heterogenity of Elements
- Clarity of Elements
- Relationship among Elements
- Predictability of Change

Characteristics and Dimensions of Uncertainty

Needs/Values/Goals
Experience
Ability/Control
Maturity in Coping
Technical Advance

Individuals and Their Organizations: Union Strategies

Moderators of the Experience and Reactions to Uncertainty

- Relative Power
- Time Pressure
- Importance of Issue
- Individual Ability
- Locus of Control
- Ambiguity Tolerance
- Availability of Feedback
- Task Interdependence
- Group Cohesiveness

Job Security;
Human Resource Management and Stress Coping Techniques;
Personal Retraining;
Quality of Worklife;
Safety and Health

[a] The model can be applied to both unionized and non-unionized situations.
Source: Sethi et al., 1987, 21.

Technostress Responses and Strategies

Nature of Strategy Decisions

Outcomes

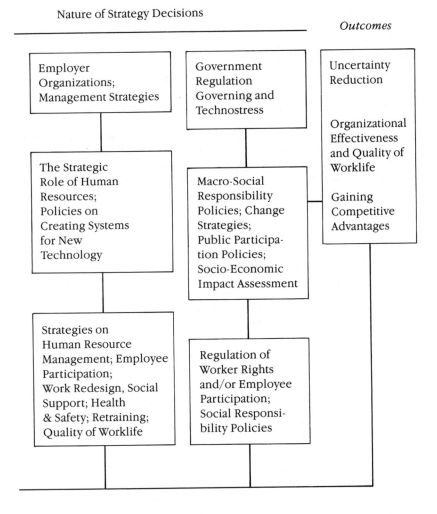

(workers' unions, management, and government) in the collective bargaining process. The issue is not that of strategic choice versus environmental determinism, but rather understanding the dimension encompassing a continuum ranging from determinism to voluntarism. As explained by Hrebiniak and Joyce (1985, 337), "choice and determinism are not at opposite ends of a single continuum of effect but in reality represent two independent variables, and...the interaction or independence of the two must be studied to explain...behavior." Collective bargaining is viewed as a dynamic process, revealing several options to parties, that may involve a number of possibilities in a given situation (Hrebiniak and Joyce, 1985).

The practical result of employing a strategic approach is the determination on the part of the parties to engage in what Kochan et al. (1984a, 17–18) have called "strategic bargaining," which includes:

> negotiations that specifically involve tradeoffs of changes in wages, benefits, or other contractual provisions in exchange for new investment or employment commitments. A recent example is the agreement between several Electric and the International Union of Electrical Workers (IUE) in Lynn, Massachusetts, in which the company agreed to build a factory of the future in Lynn, whose workers would be IUE members in return for major changes in the way work is scheduled, jobs are organized, and compensation is determined...The key feature of strategic bargains is that they build on and reinforce the sharing of information and the improved workplace relationships that have grown out of QWL processes.

The most obvious implication of this approach is that the interdependence and interactions between strategic choice and environmental determinism define collective bargaining behaviour. In order to explain conflict within collective bargaining, we need to focus on interactions and interdependence between strategic choice and environmental determinism, thus acknowledging the dynamic nature of bargaining transactions (Miles and Snow, 1978). Our theoretical premise is to emphasize that models relying on the conceptual construction of competing explanations of cause and effect may not be sufficient to capture the complexity and spirit of collective bargaining. The strategic approach, it is hoped, emphasizes multiple and, often, competing assumptions, foci and explanations of cause and effect.

The principle of redefinition of goals (and values) is clearly demonstrated in the case of technological change in the private sector where unions and managements have voluntarily negotiated the emergence of new plants, work-design systems and associated contractual relationships. Kochan et al. (1984, 18) illustrate this practice:

> General Motors and the United Automobile Workers Union have a number of...new plant agreements in place. Project Saturn (the joint GM–UAW study

group exploring alternative ways to build small cars) is of enormous scale and already has involved extensive involvement by the UAW in business decisions, thereby making it an extremely important example of such processes. Phillip Morris and the Tobacco Workers have a new plant in Alabama operating with jointly planned innovative work practices. Such agreements will test whether new plants designed with up-to-date technology and with a flexible/high participation workplace industrial relations system can match or better the performance of new nonunion plants. Evaluation of these experiments must await further time to amass significant experience and comparative data.

The Use of Information Technology Strategies in Canada

The survey conducted by Economic Council of Canada of about 946 firms representing all regions in Canada and most industries (except agriculture, fishing, construction, and public administration) revealed that three-quarters of those Canadian firms (innovators) adopted some form of computer-based technology during the first half of the 1980s. Most of the new technology introduced in the first half of the 1980s involved office automation, although it is expected that from 1986–90 process automation (such as Computer-Aided Design and Computer-Assisted Manufacturing) will take the lead. The highest users of new technology were wholesale trade (91 percent), followed by the communications and utilities sector (88 percent); business services (82 percent); finance, insurance and real estate (79 percent); manufacturing, primary industries and the health and social services sector (76 percent); retail trade (74 percent); and the lowest in transportation and storage (60 percent). (Betcherman and McMullen, 1986.)

The main factors motivating industries to adopt the new technology were increased productivity, reduced labour costs, and improved product quality. The survey showed that innovative firms had much stronger sales growth (51 percent vs. 38 percent) than those not making technological changes. This means that there were fewer job losses than what labour feared would result from new technology. The innovators were also able to come up with much bigger wage increases for their workers (40 percent vs. 32 percent).

A number of strategies were used to cope with impacts of new technology. The major ones included retraining and recruiting (see Figure 18.4). Nearly 95 percent of companies used retraining to cope with technological impacts and their resultant technostress. Other strategies included internal transfers, reduced hours, early retirement, and external transfers.

Although relatively fewer Canadian-owned firms adopted new tech-

Figure 18.4
Information Technology Strategies in Canada
(Other Than Retraining and Recruiting)

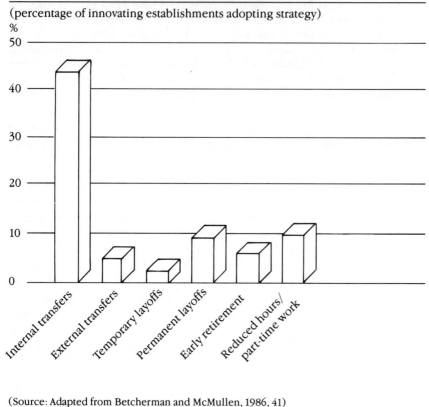

(percentage of innovating establishments adopting strategy)

(Source: Adapted from Betcherman and McMullen, 1986, 41)

nology (72 percent) than U.S.-owned firms (94 percent) and other foreign-owned companies (88 percent), this survey does establish that the climate for introduction of new technology is here to stay and will increase. Traditional reasons for restraining new technology include cost of equipment, lack of trained personnel, low return on investment, system integration difficulties, management reluctance, and collective bargaining provisions. Harris (1986, 18) summarizes the survey results as follows:

> One reason office automation has dominated so far is that it costs much less than process automation. For example, the average investments involved in introducing personal computers and word processors were $25,000 and $20,000, respectively, while $100,000 was required for CAD and $200,000 for CAM. . . . The survey shows that the introduction of new technology was most

prevalent in the West, but even in the Atlantic provinces, more than two thirds of firms got into the act. Not surprisingly, big companies were the most likely to introduce new technology, as 99% of companies with more than 500 employees did so vs 86% for those with a work force of 101–500 and 62% for smaller firms.

Collective Bargaining Strategies and IT in Canada, 1980–85

Betcherman and McMullen (1986) reported that just under half of the Economic Council of Canada survey respondents in Canada had employees covered by collective bargaining (Figure 18.5). Of these, 46 percent reported that there had been union contract negotiations over technological change since 1980. The survey results suggest that

> the bargaining concerns associated with innovation vary considerably in different situations. While a wide range of issues were raised, no single one was pervasive. The technology-related item most frequently negotiated was advance notice, followed by training, wage rates, job/income security, seniority provisions, and joint consultation. For most issues, negotiations led to contract changes just over 50 percent of the time. Where information was the concern—layoff notice and advance notice—this figure was slightly higher. On the other hand, contract amendments were less frequent where changes in decision-making—either through joint consultation or management rights provisions—was the subject of negotiations (Betcherman and McMullen, 1986, 43).

The concept of strategic bargaining emphasizes that technological impacts can be positive if preventive strategies are adopted by managements and unions in a co-operative collective bargaining system. Alcalay and Pasick (1983, 1082) state:

> Where innovations are simply adopted by virtue of their proclaimed benefits and intended functions, and where the work environment is structured around such innovations, technology may indeed be in control. However, where planning takes into account benefits, functions and possible unintended consequences, and the work environment, including new technologies, is structured around the health and well-being of workers, then technology is certainly the object of human choice.

Based on a review of several successful companies in the United States who have implemented IT, Benjamin et al. (1984, 3–10) support the proposition that IT impacts can be used by management (and unions) to gain competitive advantage through generating awareness of the potential benefits of IT, and by creating a cultural environment in which "information technology is considered an important strategic weapon."

Recent ILO-initiated research shows that the impact of micro-computers on an organization can lead to technostress where there is (1) an unco-

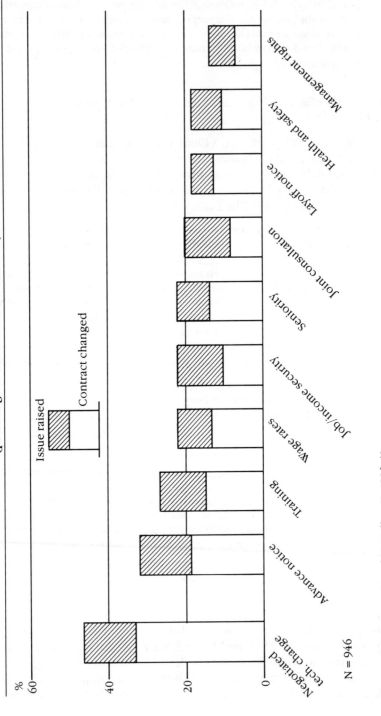

Figure 18.5
Negotiating Technological Change in Canada
(percentage of unionized establishments)

Source: Betcherman, G. and McMullen, K., 1986, 43.

operative labour–management system, (2) a lack of supportive management, (3) unclear job definitions, and (4) a high level of physical environmental stressors (ILO, 1984; Fraser, 1983; Levi, 1984; Wereneke, 1983; Rada, 1980). A recent empirical study supports the proposition that technological innovation produces a lack of fit between demands made by the technology and the needs, skills, procedures, structures, and equipment embodied in the social and technical structure of organizations. The result is that new technology raises both cognitive and motivational problems with which managers, staff specialists, and workers and their unions have great difficulty in coping (Blumberg and Gerwin, 1984).

Effects of New Technology

Some of the frequently described effects of information technology include job insecurity, monitoring, machine pacing, monetary and repetitive work environmental conditions (e.g., temperature, air quality, and ergonomic problems) and lack of worker participation and control. On effects of automation, Arndt and Chapman (1984, 32) conclude:

> The automation of offices has led to increasing concerns about new or more extreme sources of stress including increased boredom, monotony, job insecurity, job future uncertainties, lack of job control, increased monitoring, job fragmentation, alienation and job dissatisfaction. Broad statements about the effects of automation are difficult to make. It has been suggested that automation offers the opportunity to eliminate tedious, difficult and boring work. It would appear that in some cases this is indeed possible. However, management [and unions have] choices concerning how automation will be used. At one extreme the technology can be introduced under the control of workers to make their jobs easier. At the other extreme, workers are told exactly how to do the work and are closely monitored (Cyr, 1979; Meyer, 1980)...It appears that the former option is being primarily reserved for professional and managerial uses of new technologies.

Figure 18.6 summarizes the critical areas of information technology. The impacts are multi-dimensional, affecting all facets of our society. A collective bargaining system cannot escape these technological impacts, and is thus influenced by pressures from the environment to adapt to technological change.

New Technology and Health Effects

Clerical employees in both private and public sectors have been increasingly using video display terminals (VDTS) to perform their work. It is estimated that by 1990 about 40 million American workers will be using VDTS on the job (Bureau of National Affairs, 1984).

Figure 18.6
Summary of Impacts of Information Technology

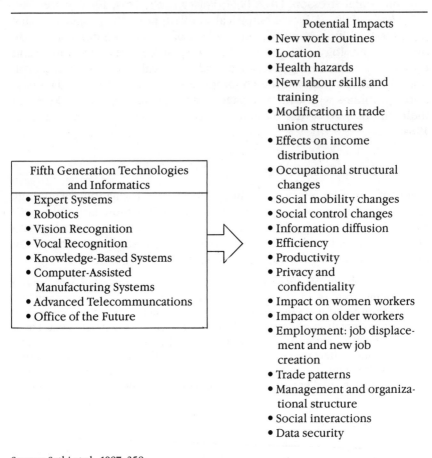

Fifth Generation Technologies and Informatics	Potential Impacts
• Expert Systems • Robotics • Vision Recognition • Vocal Recognition • Knowledge-Based Systems • Computer-Assisted Manufacturing Systems • Advanced Telecommuncations • Office of the Future	• New work routines • Location • Health hazards • New labour skills and training • Modification in trade union structures • Effects on income distribution • Occupational structural changes • Social mobility changes • Social control changes • Information diffusion • Efficiency • Productivity • Privacy and confidentiality • Impact on women workers • Impact on older workers • Employment: job displacement and new job creation • Trade patterns • Management and organizational structure • Social interactions • Data security

Source: Sethi et al., 1987, 358.

Although studies reporting health effects of VDTs are inconclusive, Sauter et al. (1982) conclude that stress does predict health complaints, job dissatisfaction and emotional states for both VDT and non-VDT work. On the positive side, the new technology has the enormous potential for increasing productivity, upgrading job tasks, and increasing employee earning power (Pava, 1985). On the negative side, the new technology may result in job displacement, machine control, resistance to change, information overload, and performance monitoring (Arndt and Chapman, 1984; Zuboff, 1982).

Further epidemiological research is needed to measure the impact of radiation from VDT on pregnant women workers (Cox, 1980; Labour Canada Task Force, 1982). A higher incidence of visual complaints among

VDT operators in comparison with traditional office workers has been reported in several studies. The VDT constitutes a hazard if the cause of complaint can be related to image quality or screen flicker. The VDT represents a risk factor if the vision complaint arises because of the more intensive and sustained nature of the VDT task.

A large number of reputable scientific surveys on radiation emissions from VDTs have been carried out in various parts of the world, investigating emission measurements for X-ray, microwave, radio-frequency, extremely low frequency, ultraviolet, infrared and visible radiations. VDTs have no components that can generate microwave radiation. Some low-frequency (up to 150 kHz) radiation has been detected very close to the surface of some VDTs. However, the levels fall off so rapidly with distance that at the position of the operator they are either non-detectable or significantly lower than the most restrictive standard in the world (Health and Welfare Canada, 1983).

The health hazards of IT relate to such environmental factors as air quality, temperature, musculoskeletal stress, visual stress, psychological stress, noise, and accidents. Figure 18.7 summarizes the analysis of potential hazard and control strategies.

A 1977 NIOSH study in the United States (Colligan et al., 1977) reported that out of 130 occupations studied, secretaries, office managers and manager-administrators were among the top twelve occupations in terms of stress-related disease. This finding was corroborated by the Framingham Heart Study, in which coronary disease rates were found to be almost twice as great among women holding clerical jobs as among housewives (Haynes and Feinleib, 1980).

The sources of technodistress for clerical workers include some traditional and some new factors, including monitoring, machine pacing, lack of promotional opportunities, low pay, monotonous and repetitive work, environmental conditions (e.g., temperature, air quality, and ergonomic problems), lack of feedback, and underutilization of skills (Arndt and Chapman, 1984).

Technoeustress can occur as a result of work simplification realized through the use of microelectronics. However, technoeustress can be converted into technodistress and decreased job satisfaction if the introduction of IT leads to fragmentation of jobs and increased repetitiveness. Research indicates that machine pacing does lead to high job tension, underutilization of abilities, frequent health complaints, and a variety of psychosomatic disorders (Murphy and Hurrell, 1979). We should, however, be cautious in assigning all negative impacts of IT on office workers. Arndt and Chapman (1984, 34–35) have assessed it as follows:

> The results of studies comparing VDT and non-VDT work tend to confirm the theory that broad generalizations about the effects of new office technologies should not be made. For example, Sauter et al. (1982) reported that "VDT

Figure 18.7

Strategies for Controlling Potential Hazards in Offices

	Potential Health Effects*	Potential Hazards	Hazard Control
Air Quality	Irritation, discomfort, outbreaks of disease sensitization	Formaldehyde, ozone, organics, allergens, micro-organisms	Ventilation, substitution, enclosure, filtering
Temperature	Discomfort	Heat, cold, humidity, air circulation	Radiant control, air circulation, different location, individual control, humidity control
Musculoskeletal Stress	Neck, shoulders, back, arm fatigue and chronic disorders	Workstation design, chair design, task repetitiveness, constrained posture	Furniture ergonomics, task redesign, job enlargement, rotation, rest breaks, exercise
Visual Stress	Eyestrain, burning or itching	Lighting, close work, quality of VDT and other viewed material, dry air, stress	Vision exams, illumination controls, equipment design, rest/exercise, work layout

			Stress management, wellness, exercise, job redesign, worker control, job enlargement, job enrichment, rotation, environmental control
Psychological Stress	Anxiety, tension, stress, boredom, headaches, job dissatisfaction, alienation, absenteeism, turnover, behavioral problems (smoking, drinking), ulcers, heart disease, diabetes and other diseases	Repetitiveness, monotony, monitoring, lack of promotional opportunity, lack of job security, lack of control, pacing, piecework, work environment	
Noise	Irritation, interference, distraction	Conversations, equipment, ventilation systems	Barriers, equipment design, enclosures, absorption
Accidents	Traumatic injuries	Work surfaces, furniture, equipment, lifting	Guarding, hazard removal, training
Radiation	None yet established	Low-level radiation	Shielding, low voltage, alternative designs, work removal, time limits

*Almost all potential hazards may affect health indirectly by causing emotional stress, especially air quality, temperature, and noise.
Source: Arndt and Chapman (1984, 123–124). Reprinted by permission.

work did not contribute to psychological distress or job dissatisfaction to any greater extent than non-VDT clerical work," among the group of workers studied. Other studies have reported similar findings (Starr et al., 1982; Dainoff et al., 1981; Coe et al., 1980). Thus, the conclusion that VDTs and related technologies do not have to increase psychological stress and job dissatisfaction seems warranted. In fact, a number of studies report some positive aspects and feelings about VDTs (Hunting et al., 1981; Starr et al., 1982; Dainoff et al., 1981; Gunnarsson and Ostberg, 1977; Cakir et al., 1978; Gunnarsson and Soderberg, 1980; Johansson and Aronsson, 1980) especially relating to making certain tasks easier. At the same time, a number of studies have clearly indicated that VDT tasks with certain characteristics are more stressful than both non-VDT and other types of VDT work (Smith et al., 1981; Gunnarsson and Ostberg, 1977; Cakir et al., 1978; Elias et al., 1980;...). The most frequently mentioned variables were monotony and boredom, monitoring, piecework, loss of control over work pace, technical problems or interruptions, and production quotas.

The overall conclusion of research studies on VDT (Smith, 1982) is that job design factors, primarily highly paced work, lack of control, and deadlines, are more prevalent in some type of VDT work than in others. These factors have been shown to be related to many of the health complaints that are reported by VDT operators and could be linked to serious health disorders.

The Issue of Privacy

One of the impacts of IT is the extent to which an individual's privacy is affected. Privacy is centred on the rights of individuals that access to and availability of information pertaining to their private lives will be safeguarded. Regulation should provide adequate protection of privacy and individual liberties.

Westin (1979, 3) explains the issue of privacy as follows:

> Privacy is the claim of individuals, groups, or institutions to determine for themselves when, how, and to what extent information about them is communicated to others. Viewed in terms of the relation of the individual to social participation, privacy is the voluntary and temporary withdrawal of a person from the general society through physical or psychological means, either in a state of solitude or small-group intimacy or, when among larger groups, in a condition of anonymity or reserve. The individual's desire for privacy is never absolute, since participation in society is an equally powerful desire. Thus each individual is continually engaged in a personal adjustment process in which he balances the desire for privacy with the desire for disclosure and communication of himself to others, in light of the environmental conditions and social norms set by the society in which he lives. The individual does so in the face of pressures from the curiosity of others and from the processes of surveillance that every society sets in order to enhance its social norms.

Collective bargaining, although not an all-purpose institution, may be used as a mechanism, possibly in addition to responsive regulation, where provisions concerning privacy may be developed.*

LABOUR-MARKET IMPACTS

Impact on Employment

IT may lead to job displacement as well as job creation. Rada (1980, 105–106) explains the consequences of IT as follows:

> It would seem that a transition is taking place from a society with unemployment to one that no longer needs its full potential labour force to produce the necessary goods and services under current conditions of work. It is doubtful whether measures such as early retirement, shorter working hours, and the creation and development of small business and new products and services will have much effect on job creation. Nevertheless, the need to meet the educational, cultural and social ends inherent in such a transition, plus cultural resistance, could lead to job creation in some fields. A transition of this nature will not be free from turmoil while the population tries to adjust to new life styles.

Servan-Schreiber, head of France's World Centre for Computer Science and Human Resources, estimates that by 1990 fifty million people in the industrialized Western world will be jobless because of high technology (Servan-Schreiber, 1981).

Professor Tom Stonier predicts (Forrester, 1981) that by early next century we will require only ten percent of today's labour force to satisfy our production needs. Choate (1982) estimates that as the American economy robotizes and domestic jobs are lost to foreign production, 10–15 million manufacturing jobs may be lost along with a similar number of service jobs.

On the other hand, Marvin Cetron estimates (Blackwell, 1986) that by 1990 industry in the United States will need 1.8 million computer software writers, 600,000 computer-assisted design production engineers, and 250,000 genetic engineering technicians. More artificial intelligence experts will be needed, as well as fibre-optics researchers and computer database managers (Blackwell, 1986).

Despite the creation of new jobs, there will, however, be some workers displaced in the process of applying technology to traditional

---

* For a model collective agreement, see "Data protection agreement between Lucas Industries (UK) and Unions APEX and ACTSS," *European Industrial Relations Review*, March 1983, 20.

industries. Blackwell (1986, 26–27) summarizes the impact of technology on employment in Canada as follows:

> There are several conflicting views on this subject, and studies of the issue are under way. In 1985, an Ontario task force on employment and technology reported that unemployment problems do not necessarily stem from the introduction of technology....The task force thought the overall effect of technology on employment would be positive, although it acknowledged that jobs in some industries will change....The details of this job shift are being studied by the Economic Council of Canada....A preliminary report, released in 1985, said that job growth in technology industries will be faster than in the economy as a whole. However, these jobs will not all appear at once, and in the meantime many people could find themselves out of a job and with no prospect of employment. The danger...is that most of the jobs will be at the top or the bottom end of the salary range, with few in between. Highly paid blue-collar workers could be put out of work, for example, while low-paying positions, such as data-entry operators and security guards, will expand. This lack of middle-income jobs could split society into those who have gained from the new technology and those who have lost.

According to the study done by the Economic Council of Canada (ECC, 1987, 8–9), "between 1971 and 1981, high-tech occupations (engineers, systems analysts, computer programmers and so on) experienced high rates of employment growth as a result of increases in the demand for those skills." On the other hand, "low-skill occupations (such as general office clerks, mining workers, labourers in construction and barbers and other personal service workers) saw the demand for their skills diminish." The net effect of technological change in Canada during the period 1971–81 was growth in employment in the vast majority of occupations. Some occupational classifications have, however, disappeared, while several new ones have been added. The conclusion is that technological change "has a wide-ranging impact on the structure of industry and occupations" (ECC, 1987, 8).

The Canadian Experience : Impacts on Skill and Wages

The study undertaken by the Department of Industry, Trade and Commerce (ITC) in 1979 showed that mass terminations, parts of which can be attributed to technological change, resulted in mobility among various manufacturing sectors, on account of de-skilling. Electrical and electronics workers, for example, may have been deskilled and thus moved to clerical jobs. Insofar as wages were concerned, the study rated wage declines among electronics and electrical industries, whereas those displaced from the clothing and textiles industries might have increased their wages. "Workers in lower paying industries such as clothing were more likely to find higher-paying jobs after layoff than were workers laid off from higher-paying industries such as electronics" (Industry, Trade and Commerce, 1978, 73).

In a review of 21 plant closures in Ontario, the Ontario Ministry of Labour (1984) pointed out a similar pattern. In 1984, 29 percent of employed respondents were earning less than they had been before the closure; 24 percent did not face any change, and 41 percent were earning more. The studies done by Hiscott (1982) and Owen (1982a, 1982b) confirm that "closures produce mobility from one sector to another and that some individuals earn more after a closure, some less....They do not deal adequately with the net effect on skills and wages" (Grayson, 1986, 9).

In an in-depth case analysis of closure at SKF Canada Ltd., CGE, Scarborough, and Black and Decker, Grayson (1986) posed the following critical questions: "What is the fate of those who are involuntarily thrown into the labour market as a consequence of plant closures (an increasing phenomenon in the contemporary world)?...Do victims undergo a net de-skilling; do they take net wage losses; are re-training schemes needed to accommodate them?" Parts of these effects may be due to information technology, or broadly speaking, technological change. Grayson (1986, 25) answers them as follows:

> In the United States and Canada, part of the answer to these questions has been supplied. As a result of closures, many employees do accept de-skilling and wage cuts. As yet, however, the net effect of closures on skills and wages has not been studied in the detail it deserves. Do the gains and losses cancel each other out? Despite losses, is the net result positive or negative? Nobody knows for sure.
>
> The analyses of the closures of the manufacturing operation SKF Canada Ltd., CGE Scarborough, and Black and Decker provided some answers.... Overall, in each case, post-closure unemployment was high. Net de-skilling was also high and increased as time wore on. Compared to wages earned at the time of closure (even if inflation is not taken into account), former employees who found new jobs were worse off than they had been before the closure.

Concerning the crucial question of de-skilling, Grayson (1986) argues that the unemployed are not to be held responsible for their fate. Grayson thinks that the MacDonald Commission (1985) implicitly assumes that the unemployed are not prepared to accept jobs that require fewer skills than their former job. According to research conducted by Grayson (1986, 17), the conclusion is that although "there are differences in the number of employees who, at various points after the closures, were prepared to take jobs at lower skill levels, the overall impression is one in which the majority of the unemployed would accept less skilled jobs were they available."

Impacts of Robotics

The three key impacts of new technology are on job displacement, new job creation, and new training requirements. One such example is the impact of robotics on industry, which is an emerging trend in the forthcoming IT developments.

Hunt and Hunt (1983) predict a strong growth in the use of industrial robots in the decade of the 1990s. They forecast that the total robot population in the United States by 1990 will range from a minimum of 50,000 to a maximum of 100,000 units, representing an annual growth of 30 to 40 percent. Although job displacement will not be a major problem according to these authors, some occupational areas such as painting and welding will need to adapt to new changed circumstances. Insofar as job creation is concerned, Hunt and Hunt (1983) estimate about 32,000 to 64,000 new jobs will be created by robots in the United States by 1990 within four broad areas: robot manufacturing, direct suppliers to robot manufacturers, robot systems engineering, and corporate robot users.

The new technical skills required by robotics technology will need a well-planned training policy by corporations in order to cope with new technical and scientific demands that will be required in the newly created jobs.

In summary, we agree with Hunt and Hunt (1983, 181) that the impacts will be evolutionary:

> Industrial robots are simply one more piece of automated industrial equipment, part of the long history of automation of production. Robots will displace workers in the same way that technological change has displaced workers. There is a possibility that this job displacement will be a significant problem, particularly in a given occupation or industry or geographical area. There is also the certainty that robots will create new jobs. Most of these will be quite different from the kinds of jobs eliminated. It is not time to panic, it is time to begin rational planning for the human resource implications of robotics.

The Canadian automobile industry has been quite progressive in introducing robotic technology. General Motors of Canada is expected to spend about $3.2 billion in 1986–87 to create a state-of-the art manufacturing centre at Oshawa, Ontario. "This plant will be the most modern plant in North America, combining computers, robots, automatic guided vehicles and work teams in one synergistic whole" (Blackwell, 1986, 24). Almost three-quarters of the robots in Canada are to be found in automobile or auto parts plants. Despite these moves, Canada still lags far behind other industrial nations such as Japan, Sweden, West Germany, France, and the United States in the number of robots installed per capita (Blackwell, 1986). "In 1984, Canada ranked ninth out of ten countries in the number of robots used per 10,000 workers employed in manufacturing—well behind Japan and Sweden, in particular. Another estimate (by the Evans Research Corporation) places Canada three to four years behind the United States in the rate of adoption of robot technology" (ECC, 1987:5).

Impact of New Technology on Women Workers

The majority of women are employed in the tertiary sector of the Canadian economy and in non-manual occupations that are affected by the new technology (Menzies 1981a, b; 1982). As is the case with United States and United Kindgom, about half of the labour force works in the information-related occupations (Porat, 1971; Bird, 1980). In the United States about one-third of all women workers are concentrated in white-collar or clerical occupations, which will be affected by the advent of Information Technology. Collective bargaining strategies need to take into account the needs of women workers who will increasingly face the impacts of IT (Wereneke, 1983).

In her analysis of a large company's head office, an insurance company, the banks in general, and supermarkets in Canada, Menzies (1981) found a consistently declining demand for clerical, administrative and related supervisory work to be done by humans, and an increasing demand for and an intensification in professional, technical and managerial work. Menzies (1981, 93–95) observes:

> Projecting from the trends that I have observed from the way it is currently being applied and comparing those from the continuing concentration of women seeking clerical type work, the unemployment rate among female clerical workers could escalate to as much as 33 per cent by 1990. In other words, one million Canadian women could be unemployed by the end of the decade. Yet, 60 per cent of the Canadian women work because they have no choice. They are single parents or married to someone whose income is such that if the wife was not working, the number of Canadian families living below the poverty line could increase by 50 percent.
>
> Industry-wide figures kept by Statistics Canada bear out the trend. Looking at clerical employment growth as a whole,...there has been a shift downwards in clerical employment growth. Between 1961 and 1975, clerical employment growth was keeping well ahead, or at least keeping pace with if not actually ahead of, growth in the female labour force. Then, in the '75 to '79 period, you suddenly saw this relative decline and...clerical employment growth during the '75-'79 period was 12 per cent compared to, for instance, 33 percent before....The professional managerial ranks...grew by 20 per cent during that same 1975–79 period....Computer technology is increasing employment opportunities in the occupations where women are least represented and is diminishing employment opportunities in the areas where women are most concentrated...Women have been socialized toward support staff, assistant and other helper-type roles. Yet, the computer is automat-

ing and de-skilling much of that work everywhere, from the factory to the office. Very simply, computer technology is automating process and procedure work.

The estimates by the Economic Council of Canada (ECC, 1987) suggest that within the high-tech sector female employment is very heavily concentrated in retail trade, finance, insurance and real estate, and services to business—all these industries employ a high proportion of clerical workers. "There are signs, therefore, that the disturbing traditional tendency towards the 'ghettoization' of women in clerical occupations is continuing in the high-tech sector" (ECC, 1987, 24). The problem of job quality is further complicated by recent increase in part-time work, where almost three-quarters of employees are women. "Our evidence suggests that the shifting locus of employment opportunities may reduce job quality...The case studies affected by technological change in the federal public service reinforce our emphasis on the instability and impermanence of many female jobs" (ECC, 1987, 25).

Impact on Unions

Information technology gives managers enormous new powers to process information and use it for achieving their goals. In so doing, this integrated control paradoxically permits production to be fragmented, affecting the international division of labour. The powerful ideology of technology makes it imperative for unions to develop coherent preventive strategies for dealing with technostress and encouraging workers to participate in the decision process.

Some of the union techniques in coping with IT practised in Sweden and shared by the United States are pertinent (LO, 1981). These include policies on advance notice, consultation, and full information on what the technological effects will be on employment, work environment, job organization and training. According to the Swedish trade union report (LO, 1981), workers are becoming more isolated and conversations are being replaced by anonymous messages on visual display units. Employees are subjected to more supervision, with computerized evaluation of individual performance contributive to new stresses. The Swedish trade union movement offers the following union strategies to cope with technostress:

- Legislated right to co-determination and the acceptance of free collective bargaining system;
- Better trade union control over the work environment regulations;
- Right to work on computerization issues during working hours without deductions from pay;
- Right of unions to consult experts.

Labour–Management Relations and IT

Improved labour relations is the key in coping with technostress effectively in the Canadian economy as a whole. In the case of Japan, for example, strategies include an improved structural base for labour–management relations, emphasizing consultation and training at all levels. Training has the dual objective of meeting human resource needs and safeguarding jobs, whereas dialogue through consultation in labour relations has the possibility of converting technodistress into technoeustress. If labour and management fail to accommodate technostress and IT changes, the stability of labour–management relations will be threatened (ILO, 1984).

The intended decision of GM to close the outdated plant at Ste-Thérèse, Québec echoed the complexity of labour–management relations, when GM of Canada president George Peapples asserted that unless worker attitude improved and unless unacceptably low productivity levels were reversed, the plant was doomed to close (McGregor, 1986).

There will be greater demand for such new general skills as planning, team working and conceptual skills, in addition to technical and scientific skills. The training system will need to make structural and attitudinal adjustments to meet new IT-related training needs. These strategies include modernization and rationalization of small and medium-sized undertakings through the promotion of the application of information technology throughout the economy. Early training in data processing and IT in secondary school curricula will need to be matched by continuous lifelong training and education.

Training and the Older Worker

Studies in the United States and Canada that have explored the impact on workers of plant closings and layoffs find that age significantly influences the success of finding another job. Unemployment resulting from IT will probably have a more serious impact on older workers between the ages of 45 and 65. Persons aged 45 to 64 numbered 4.8 million in 1986 in Canada, accounting for 24 percent of the work force (ECC, 1987).

Some employers fear that hiring older workers will add to extra costs to their pension plans, thus producing a bias in favour of hiring younger workers.

GOVERNMENT'S RESPONSES

Government responses to technological change in Canada have included:

1. The Freedman Royal Commission (1965), appointed in response to the strike over Canadian National's unilateral operation of run-throughs in two small communities. The Commission recommended that workers be given the right to advance notice of a major change. It believed that unilateral change by management represents a manifest inequity.
2. The Woods Task Force on Industrial Relations (1968), which endorsed the workers' right to a minimum of six months' advance notice of technological change (Woods, 1986).
3. Current legislation of the federal government, British Columbia, Manitoba, and Saskatchewan governments, requiring employers to give advance notice of technological changes. The relevant sections (Sections 149 to 153) of Part v of the Canada Labour Code were passed in 1972 and later amended in 1984. They contain a definition of technological change, and Section 150(1) requires the employer, where a collective agreement exists, to give the bargaining agent 120 days' notice (90 days, prior to 1984) of any changes likely to affect a "significant" number of employees. During the 1970s, the B.C. Labour Code was amended to broaden the definition of technological change, requiring that every contract contain provisions for dealing with technological change disputes. The Saskatchewan Trade Union Act (Section 43[2]) requires the employer to give advance notice of 90 days to the union, giving the union the right to reopen the contract and to bargain over technological change. Under the Manitoba Labour Relations Act, a 90-day advance notice is required, and the right to bargain technological change is automatic if a "significant" number of employees are affected.
4. The Carrothers Commission (1979) on redundancies and layoffs, which recommended "effective joint consultation" on a regular basis at the enterprise level and suggested that a standing works council be set up to process such consultation. Consequently, the Labour Adjustment Benefits Act was passed to provide for the payment of benefits to laid-off employees, and provided for the establishment of joint planning committees in both unionized and non-unionized plants.
5. The Task Force on Micro-Electronics and Employment, which was established by the federal labour minister in 1982. The Task Force called for the setting up of mandatory joint technological committees in both unionized and non-unionized establishments of 50 employees or more under the jurisdiction of Canada Labour Code. The purpose of these committees will be to negotiate appropriate strategies for coping with technological issues at the workplace. If negotiations fail, the parties can resort to arbitration. The overall emphasis of the Task Force is to change the adversarial model in dealing with technological impacts to a collaborative model. The National Centre for Productivity

and Employment Growth, with representatives drawn from labour, management and government, was expected to encourage the development of such a model. In addition, the Task Force recommended that:

- The 1972 definition of technological change in the Canada Labour Code be amended and broadened to ensure that discussion between labour and management is started as soon as management proposes to introduce any new equipment or material that could affect, either directly or indirectly, the working conditions or job security of any employee.
- Employers be required to give a minimum of 180 days' notice of a proposed technological change (instead of present 90 days).
- Disputes concerning the powers and functions of joint technological committees or the adequacy of proposed plans be settled by binding arbitration (Jain, 1983a, b; Labour Canada, 1982).

6. Ontario's 1984 Task Force on Employment and Technology, comprising three union and three management representatives. The Task Force reported in 1985, outlining its recommendations on the impact of information technology on employment.
7. Efforts have been made to introduce technological change clauses in labour legislation in Quebec, New Brunswick and Nova Scotia.

COLLECTIVE BARGAINING PROVISIONS

According to Swan (1982), collective agreements containing provisions concerning technological impacts have placed emphasis on job security. In 1982, of the 1,018 collective agreements covering 325,860 employees under Part V of the Canada Labour Code, 72 percent made no provision for prior notice of a technological change. "A much higher percentage of these agreements had no substantive provision for adjustment to change, such as training, retraining, relocation allowances, and labour–management committees (Jain, 1983b, 87).

An examination of provisions in 960 collective agreements in Canada covering 2,034,615 employees in bargaining units of 500 and more employees revealed the following results, as contained in the Labour Canada analysis (Labour Canada, 1985). As of July 1985, 38 percent of the agreements provide for advance notice and/or consultation with the employee or union prior to the introduction of new technological methods, up from 29 percent in 1978. Similarly, 45 percent of these agreements include a notice period of three to six months (35 percent in 1978). In addition to advance notice, 31 percent of the agreements contain training or re-training clauses in the event of technological change (22 percent in 1978). "These clauses facilitate the replacement and upgrading of employees' skills, thus minimizing the likelihood of unemployment" (Labour Canada, 1985, xxvii). The wage or employment guarantee is another means of responding to technological change. Twenty-one percent of the agreements contain clauses that guarantee prevailing wage rates when moving to lower-graded jobs (19 percent in 1978) (Labour Canada, 1985).

The analysis undertaken by the Economic Council of Canada shows that technology-related clauses are found in only a minority of Canadian labour contracts. The clause providing for advance notice prior to the technological change is not included in over 60 percent of the agreements. (See Figure 18.8.) "Considerable differences are found in the incidence of such clauses across industries; they are more prevalent in older industries, often with static or declining employment growth" (ECC, 1987, 23).

A recent analysis of collective agreements done by Craig (1987, 29) shows that those jurisdictions with a positive policy thrust regarding technological change have a higher incidence of collective agreements and employees covered by technological change provisions than do those jurisdictions without a positive policy thrust. (See Figure 18.9.) Craig's finding differs from that of a 1987 study of technological change done by the Economic Council of Canada, which asserts that "...the evidence does not indicate that the incidence of technology-related clauses is consistently higher in the four jurisdictions with relevant legislation that in others" (Economic Council of Canada, 1987, 23). However, as summarized in Figure 18.10, Craig's conclusion is generally supported that notice and/or consultation prior to the introduction of technological change is most prevalent in agreements under Part v of the Canada Labour Code, British Columbia, Manitoba and the Public Service Staff Relations Act (PSSRA). Although the PSSRA does not have a technological change clause, the incidence of technological change provisions in collective agreements under the PSSRA is quite high, probably owing to the presence of an elaborate technological change clause in the agreement between the Post Office and the Canadian Union of Postal Workers (Craig, 1987, 31).

DEFINITION OF TECHNOLOGICAL CHANGE

The Canada Labour Code (Section 149[1]) defines technological change as:

> (a) the introduction by an employer into his work, undertaking or business of equipment or material of a different nature or kind than that previously utilized by him in the operation of the work, undertaking or business; and

Figure 18.8

Frequency of Provisions Related to Technological Change in Collective Agreements[1], Canada, 1972–85

	Proportion of agreements covered						Proportion of workers covered					
	1972	1978	1980	1982	1984	1985	1972	1978	1980	1982	1984	1985
					(Per cent)							
Provisions for:												
Advance notice or consultation	27.4	28.5	33.5	35.5	38.1	38.0	35.5	34.9	40.2	41.6	42.7	42.1
Training/retraining	22.7	21.7	25.5	28.7	31.1	31.1	28.1	27.8	29.9	32.5	31.5	31.5
Labour–management committee (on technology-related issues)	13.9	12.3	14.9	14.7	14.3	14.6	17.3	21.0	25.6	22.3	20.8	22.2
Employment security (technology-related)	12.1	18.1	19.9	21.2	21.9	22.7	15.2	23.8	24.7	24.1	24.0	25.4

1. Agreements covering 500 or more workers; agreements in the construction industry are excluded after 1978. Estimates by the Economic Council based on data from Labour Canada.

Source: ECC, 1987, 23.

Figure 18.9
Percentage of Collective Agreements and Employees Covered
by Technological Change Provisions in Major Collective
Agreements Covering 500 or More Employees by Jurisdiction

	Percent Agreements	Percent Employees
Newfoundland	63.1	77.8
Prince Edward Island	74.4	75.0
Nova Scotia	47.4	56.3
New Brunswick	26.8	34.8
Quebec	39.6	62.4
Ontario	57.2	43.9
Manitoba	81.9	71.1
Saskatchewan	67.4	63.0
Alberta	33.2	33.0
British Columbia	83.4	75.7
Part V, Canada Labour Code	87.4	72.3
Public Service Staff Relations Act	92.2	81.6
Multi-Provincial	82.4	87.5

Source: Computer printouts and examination of collective agreements on file with Labour
Canada, Summer and Fall, 1986. The figures in this table are based on an analysis
of 980 collective agreements covering 2,052,671 employees. Adapted from Craig,
1987, 29, and reprinted by permission.

(b) a change in the manner in which the employer carries on the work,
undertaking or business that is directly related to the introduction of
that equipment or material.

Section 78 of the B.C. Labour Code defines technological change as:

(a) the introduction by an employer of a change in his work, undertaking or
business, or a change in his equipment or material from the equipment
or material previously used by the employer in his work, undertaking or
business; or

(b) a change in the manner an employer carries on his work, undertaking or
business related to the introduction of that equipment or material.

The Saskatchewan definition contained in the Saskatchewan Trade
Union Act is similar to Part v of the Canada Labour Code, with an added
clause not included in the federal Act, namely "43(1) (c) the *removal* by
an employer of any part of his work, undertaking or business." (Emphasis
by Craig, 1987, 23.)

The definition used by the Manitoba Labour Relations Act is also
similar to that in Part v of the Canada Labour Code, although it is
broadened. Per Section 72 (1) of the Manitoba Act, the impact of technological change is expanded to include "...or to alter significantly the
basis upon which the collective agreement was negotiated..." (Craig,
1987, 25).

In analyzing various legislative provisions on technological change,

Figure 18.10
Percentage of Employees Covered by Technological Change
Provisions in Collective Agreements Covering 500 or More by
Jurisdiction and Type of Technological Change Clause

	1*	2	3	4	5	6
Newfoundland	51.4	47.3	2.0	28.4	29.9	—
Prince Edward Is.	10.8	10.8	10.8	—	—	—
Nova Scotia	32.0	23.7	10.4	6.4	10.7	—
New Brunswick	11.6	9.6	22.0	8.1	2.0	2.4
Quebec	26.3	21.8	17.8	27.2	13.2	0.8
Ontario	31.1	33.5	27.5	20.0	17.1	1.7
Manitoba	76.7	59.1	—	21.1	20.7	1.9
Saskatchewan	30.0	36.3	10.1	9.2	7.1	6.1
Alberta	20.5	24.6	0.4	14.8	11.3	—
British Columbia	46.3	41.0	19.0	39.5	31.2	4.3
Federal	74.9	58.0	28.7	54.3	10.9	59.4
PSSRA	72.3	0.6	48.5	—	9.5	—

* The numbers refer to the types of clauses coded by Labour Canada.
1. Notice and/or consultation prior to introduction by Technological change.
2. Training or retraining (technological change).
3. Labour–management committee (technological change).
4. Employment security (wage or employment guarantee–Technological change).
5. Notice of layoff (technological change).
6. Relocation allowance.

Source: Special computer printout (Labour Canada), 21 May, 1986. The figures in this table are based on an analysis of 966 collective agreements covering 2,032,020 employees. Adapted from Craig (1987, 30).

the Economic Council of Canada summarized their results as follows (ECC, 1987, 37–38):

> Four jurisdictions in Canada have enacted statutory provisions aimed at encouraging collective bargaining over technological change....That the goals have been better realized in British Columbia is, in our view, at least partly the result of differences between the approach in that province and those of the other three jurisdictions. One important difference in the B.C. model is that, in contrast with the other three relevant cases, there is no opportunity for opting out of the legislation's purview. In the federal jurisdiction, for example, the parties are exempted if they have privately negotiated related clauses or if the contract stipulates that the Canada Labour Code's provisions on technological change do not apply.
>
> There are other ways in which the B.C. legislation departs from that of the other jurisdictions. These include a less restrictive definition of what constitutes technological change as well as a procedure for referring technology-related disputes to binding arbitration.

Response of the Canada Labour Relations Board

In the Ottawa–Carleton Regional Transit Commission Case (Amalgamated Transit Union, 1981, 365–399), under Part v of the Canada Labour Code involving the introduction of an automated vehicle monitoring system, the Board suggested that the interpretation of key criteria should be based on situational contingencies, namely whether or not technological change has had a substantial adverse impact and if it has affected the terms and conditions of employment of a significant number of employees. The Canada Labour Relations Board has, however, given importance to human factors in technological change. For example, in the case of Prince Rupert Grain Terminal Ltd. and B.C. Terminal Elevator Operators Association and Train Workers Union, Local 333, the major issue centred on whether the introduction of computers in the storing and shipping of grain in the new facility resulted in technological change. The Board concluded that human impacts on workers resulting from relocation and retraining were significant factors. Computerization, if it affects a substantial number of employees, should be considered technological change, although the Board "did not give any criteria by which parties may be guided in the future with respect to the meaning of 'a significant number'" (Craig, 1987, 11).

Another criterion in determining technological change is to examine if the operational process of work has changed owing to computerization. In the case of Grain Services Union and Manitoba Pool Elevators, Winnipeg, Manitoba, the Board agreed that computers did constitute technological change because it found that there was a change in the manner in which the receiving, storing, blending and shipping of grain were affected by the computer.

Craig summarizes this experience as follows:

> [Owing to] the fact that the CLRB has found that the introduction of computers into an organization constitutes a technological change, its decisions may impact on decisions made by the private parties as well as on decisions made by arbitrators in those jurisdictions which do not have technological change clauses. Should this occur, the Board's decisions may have a greater impact than was expected when the legislation was introduced in the early 1970s.

> Another question with which the Board will almost certainly be faced in the future is whether a change in "software" or computer programs constitutes a technological change. The development of new software is now one of the most important aspects of the computer revolution. A 1984 report of the International Labour Organization concluded that "software now frequently accounts for 50 percent of total costs in many systems, a percentage which is expected to reach 80 to 90 by the end of the decade..." (Craig, 1987, 14–15).

Response by Arbitrators

The overall analysis of collective agreements shows that although progress has been made since 1978, technological-change policy directions need to be strengthened in all jurisdictions in Canada. There have been, however, noteworthy initiatives made in this regard.

For example, at Bell Canada, collective agreement negotiations on technological change have resulted in provisions that include (a) advance notice of change and its impact, (b) retraining and/or relocation at company's expense, (c) transfer indemnities, (d) maintenance of benefits during layoff, (e) job protection based on seniority, (f) severance pay, (g) termination annuities, and (h) early-retirement programs (McKay, 1981). Some flexibility exists in interpreting these benefits, as was demonstrated in the case involving Bell Canada vs. Communications Workers of Canada, where the arbitrators established that the workers had the choice of electing termination of service rather than being transferred or reassigned (Picher et al., 1984).

There is an increasing emphasis by arbitrators on the quality of notice and consultation pertaining to technological change. Drawing upon a number of cases between the Canadian Union of Postal Workers and the Treasury Board (Post Office Department) and Canadian Union of Postal Workers and Canada Post Corporation, Swan (1983, 18–19) endorsed the following propositions:

> (1) The notice must be complete and must meet the test...before the consultation process begins; the purpose of the provision is to provide all of the contractually required information prior to the consultation process. (2) The notice must be sufficiently detailed in its description of the project to permit meaningful consultation to take place. (3) Each of the specific issues raised...must be addressed, even if the only answer which can be given is speculative and even if changing circumstances may alter the actual outcome by the time the change is implemented.

Although there are variations in recent arbitral awards on the meaning of technological change, we agree with Swan (1985, 28–29) that "a change in work methods only constitutes a technological change when it is related to the introduction of equipment different in nature, type, or quantity from that previously utilized by the employer." In the case of International Nickel Company of Canada Limited vs. United Steel Workers (1972), the board of arbitration found that the transfer of the work from one mill to the other, from an essentially normal and mechanical to a highly computerized system, was a technological change (Picher, 1986). The majority observed that these changes are "technological" in every sense of the term. It is not a case of substituting new and improved machinery for old, but rather of instituting a strikingly different industrial system" (quoted in Picher, 1986, 27).

Based on a review of recent arbitration awards, Picher (1986, 29–31) explains the overall response of arbitrators on the impacts of technological change:

> In considering the impact of technological change, arbitrators have taken great care to ensure some causal connection between the technological change asserted and any adverse impact on employees. In Guide des Employés de Journeaux de Montréal, Section Locale 111 et Gazette (The), Division de Southam Inc. [1983] T.A. (Clément), the Union alleged that the introduction of a computerized circulation information system to facilitate the current subscription listing of a newspaper was a technological change which reduced the volume of work and resulted in the loss of employment to a number of district managers and Swingmer employed in the bargaining unit...The arbitrator dismissed this grievance on the basis that there was no connection established between the introduction of the computer system and the layoff of any employees in the newspaper sales department.
>
> As the decisions of the arbitrator Brunner in the Benson and Hedges award and adjudicator Beatty in the Canadian Union of Postal Workers Case indicate, arbitrators are extremely cautious to avoid characterizing the adjustment or rearrangement of pre-existing equipment, systems and methods of operation as 'technological change'. This conventional wisdom is perhaps more succinctly reflected in the following passage from the award of the board of arbitration in Los Angeles Herald Examiner and Los Angeles Newspaper Guide, Local 69, 46 L.A. 51 at p. 153:

> Technological is a word whose meaning cannot be brought to include any kind of change or improvement without destroying the meaning of the whole phrase. As the word has come to be used, it has reference to the application of scientific research to the problems and processes of industry. Putting machines of common use and existence and machines which are not particularly unique or special to uses which are fairly within their intendment, but simply have not been availed of before, does not fall within the meaning of technological improvement as I understand that term.

Union Responses

In a study of union responses to technological change, Petchinis (1983) found that Canadian trade unions are not proactive in their approach to coping with technological issues. The Canadian Labour Congress, however, advocates that strategies for satisfactory adjustments resulting from information technology are negotiated in relation to adversely affected workers (Jain, 1983a, 86). The Task Force on Microelectronics and Technology and Employment (1982), established by the federal Minister of Labour, concluded that Canada must support a technological strategy. It stated that the major task of the newly recommended National Centre for Productivity and Employment Growth was to encourage a co-operative industrial relations system in order to avoid the "social unrest that would inevitably occur if management and unions repeat the mistakes made by the Canada Post Office during its early phases of postal-automation in the late 1960s and early 1970s" (Jain, 1983b, 871).

The Canadian Labour Congress has advocated the development of a consensus strategy for effective co-ordinated bargaining to cope with emerging technological issues. The overall philosophy of the CLC approach to bargaining is to ensure that quality of worklife is maintained, covering such priority bargaining items as reduced work week and early forecasts of massive job losses (Jain, 1983). The Canadian Union of Public Employees (CUPE) has been concerned with the following technological impacts: increased control over workers, job structure, monetary rewards, increased work pacing, growing skill gaps, increased sexual division of labour, a general lowering of job satisfaction and negative impacts on health and safety (Belanger, 1983). Collective bargaining is seen by the Canadian Union of Public Employees and the Canadian Labour Congress as one of the primary vehicles to deal with these issues, through advocating strong collective bargaining clauses, a comprehensive definition of technological change, advance notice of all the foreseeable effects of the technological change, access to information regarding such change, and mutual agreements ensuring job and income protections (Belanger, 1983).

One striking example of how computers can influence the union's power to strike was demonstrated in the case of air-traffic controllers in the United States. The Professional Air Traffic Controllers Organization (PATCO) walked off the job on August 3, 1981. The Reagan Administration gave the strikers forty-eight hours to return to work or face permanent dismissal. The result was that 12,000 air traffic controllers were fired and the union decertified. As Shaiken (1984, 248) reported, the government skillfully used computer technology to keep air-traffic moving, thus "gutting the striker's leverage." "The government's expanded bargaining power means it can now implement...options to increase automation more readily and is moving aggressively to do so" (Toong and Gupta, 1982, 154). According to a Rand Commission report, the critical questions are: "Should we strive for a system in which the machine has the primary responsibility of control and human expertise is used in a secondary, backup fashion...or should men, in spite of their intrinsic limitations, retain primary contact responsibility and utilize machine aids to control their activities?" (Wesson et al., 1981, 23). Shaiken (1984, 254–55) states:

> The story of the confrontation between PATCO and the FAA underscores the potential importance of computers in labor–management relations in general and strike situations in particular. On the one hand, computer technology and telecommunications make possible central direction of far-reaching

activities, concentrating enormous power into relatively few hands. The few dozen controllers in Gander, Newfoundland, for example, demonstrated their ability to halt virtually all trans-Atlantic flights for a number of tense hours near the beginning of the strike. Had a few more PATCO members joined the strike, the air traffic system of the entire country would have been tied in knots. On the other hand, complex computer systems often lend themselves to operation by a reduced and less skilled work force in an emergency situation. The leverage for the air controllers evaporated because less-experienced workers could successfully take over the job.

Another example in which computers caused a shift in balance of power was provided by an office workers' strike during a 1980–81 dispute between Blue Shield of California and 1,100 members of the Office and Professional Employees Union (OPEU) Local 3 in San Francisco. Shaiken (1984, 258–259) states:

> As the 133-day strike began, the company adopted a carefully prepared contingency plan. This plan included assigning all available supervisors to computer banks in the claims-processing area, hiring and quickly training 350 new workers, and routing some claims processing to non-union offices as far away as Los Angeles. The various offices were linked together through computers and telephone lines irrespective of picket lines. In addition, training the new workforce was made far easier because computers had been used to simplify tasks. As a result, Blue Shield asserted that it was able to maintain near-normal operations with far fewer workers. After the strike, the company refused to return 448 jobs to the main office.

Unions need to develop and make strategic choices in coping with technological change. Shaiken (1984, 263) sums up these strategies as follows:

> If new strategies are not developed by labor, its power could become increasingly eroded—first at the bargaining table, and ultimately in the society itself. The strike of the Communications Workers of America (CWA) against AT&T and the Bell System in the fall of 1983 is one more example of union leverage being sharply curtailed. While the strike disrupted certain services, such as telephone installations, the telephone company nonetheless was able to continue its core operations uninterrupted for over three weeks. Ironically, the strike occurred against a backdrop of near record profits for the telephone company and at a time when its relations with its union were among the most cordial of major U.S. industries. The company was obviously using power to protect its interest not simply in 1983 but for years to come in a deregulated market. If unions are weakened at the bargaining table in this way, then the erosion of the power of the labor movement in the society is not far behind. To the extent that power shifts in management's direction in negotiations, new industries, particularly high-tech industries, could become even more difficult to organize. None of this grim scenario for

labor is inevitable. But in an age of high technology, "business as usual" is no longer a tenable strategy for unions.

As a proactive strategy for influencing the course of technology, unions and managements can use a "Technology Bill of Rights," rooted in the concept that "the introduction of new technology is not an automatic right of management but a process subject to bargained development" (Shaiken, 1984, 270). There are four key assumptions of this concept, and three key hypotheses, as explained below:

Assumptions

The design of new technology can be strategically based upon the following assumptions:

1. The quality of worklife is as important as productivity;
2. The social aspects of technological change are as important as economic benefits;
3. Workers (and their organizations) have a right to participate in the decisions that affect their work;
4. The benefits of technology should be shared by employers and workers.

Hypotheses

The three key hypotheses include (Shaiken, 1984, 272–273):

1. New technology must be used in a way that creates or maintains jobs.
2. New technology must be used to improve the conditions of work.
3. New technology must be used to develop the industrial base and improve the environment.

The implications of a Technology Bill of Rights are explained by Shaiken (1984: 273–278) as follows:

> The implementation of a Technology Bill of Rights would obviously require profound changes at the collective bargaining table and in the political arena. Unfortunately, the swift introduction of new technology won't wait until the proper mechanisms are available to deal with it....Ultimately the issues transcend collective bargaining and their political character becomes apparent....The design of machines reflects social values as well as technical needs. The ideas and experiences of those who are affected by new designs can help ensure that computerization will be a force that aids in liberating people rather than a vehicle for increased authority and control.

A FUTURE RESEARCH AGENDA ON THE IMPACTS OF IT IN CANADA

A research strategy exploring the impacts of IT on the labour market and industrial relations can cover an extensive list of issues. This research currently under way should be broadened and can be conducted by management, unions, and government to facilitate negotiations in collective bargaining. The areas for research might include the following:

- The development of an operative model of industrial relations and the future direction of government's labour policy.
- Extent of net job loss in sectors that have rapidly adopted IT and its consequences on workers in the contemporary information society.
- Nature of specific IT technologies that are most likely to have major labour-market effects in the future.
- Extent to which workers undergo a net de-skilling and net wage losses.
- Emerging new skills and the need for restructuring education and re-training for maximum accommodation.
- Union and management strategies for adapting to IT impacts in relation to organization of work, pay systems and industrial relations for organizational effectiveness.
- Union and management strategies in human resource management for coping with qualitative effects of IT, such as part-time/full-time distribution of employment; new employment arrangements (job sharing, work-sharing, flexible hours); quality-of-worklife programs (job enrichment, autonomous work groups, worker participation and involvement) and programs based on theory Z concepts (Ouchi, 1980).
- Innovative human resource management concepts and ergonomic tools including new ways of appraising, remunerating and motivating staff.

Collective Bargaining Practices in the United States, 1980–1984

A brief examination of collective bargaining practices in the United States is provided to gain some insights for Canadian policies, wherever relevant. Ornati (1985) analyzed the contractual clauses dealing with technological change by using the data from a *Comparative Survey of Major Collective Bargaining Agreements*, issued by the Industrial Union Department, AFL–CIO (Prosten, 1980, 1982, 1984). Each of these surveys summarizes, by type of contract clause and benefit, the contents of 100 collective agreements. As summarized in Figure 18.11, there appears to be

Figure 18.11
Contractual Arrangements Dealing with Job Security

Changes in clauses in the number of companies
reporting job security provisions

		1980	1984	1984–1980
1.	No Special Provisions, Seniority Rules Apply	4	0	−4
2.	Special Provisions in Local Agreement	2	1	−1
3.	Contract Provides Advance Notice to Union	24	31	+7
4.	Contract Sets Up Special Co./Union Committee	7	9	+2
5.	Contract Provides for Negotiation of Rights	7	8	+1
6.	Attention Clause for Greater Job Security	2	3	+1
7.	Contract Prohibits Layoff	6	9	+3
	Workers Have Right to:	11	21	+10
	a. Training for New Job			
	b. Bump into Another Job/Same Plant	8	8	0
	c. Transfer to Replacement Faculty	5	5	0
	d. Preferential Hiring, Same Plant	9	8	−1
	e. Preferential Hiring, Other Plant	8	6	−2
	f. Retain Prior Seniority When Hired at other Plant	5	3	−2
8.	Layoff w/Recall Rights	10	11	+1
9.	Severance Pay	14	22	+8
10.	Moving Expenses	7	5	−2

Source: R. Prosten, *Comparative Survey of Major Collective Bargaining
Agreements.* Washington, D.C.: I.U.D./AFL–CIO, 1980, 1982, 1984 issues. Reprinted
by permission.

a clear change in contractual clauses by 1980 to provide protection from technological impacts.

Ornati (1985, 6–7) analyszes the data (contained in Figure 18.11) as follows:

> ...at least some union employees have gained job security in the language of contracts as negotiated over the last four years. The requirements of advanced notification to the union appears more frequently (+7), there is an increase in the number of contracts with an outright prohibition of layoffs (+3). Along with expanded employment protection there is a diminution in preferential rehiring by seniority (-5) and an increase in the number of companies with no specific job security clause (+4). The major development is in the expansion of workers' rights to have training for new jobs (an increase over 1980 of 10 covered companies) coupled with a major use in severance pay (+8). The changes...seem to indicate a trend in which unions and managements have

expanded the job security of workers presumably capable of acquiring new skills and knowledge, while older workers presumed not as able to adapt to the new technologies are being "phased out" with various types of severance pay.

Rights Arbitration and Technological Change in the United States

Ornati (1985) conducted an inquiry into the impact of contractual restraints, precedent and arbitrators' values as moderators of the impact of technological change. Twenty-nine cases (drawn from BNA and CCH Arbitration reports) from 1976 to 1984 were analyzed, dealing with grievances arising from staffing impacts pursuant to the introduction of new technology. In a detailed survey of sixteen cases, the researcher found that management was sustained in fourteen of the sixteen cases; the union's grievance was upheld entirely only in two and in part in two others. On the whole, 88 awards went in favour of management (Ornati, 1985). The major issues as a result of technological change included (a) job elimination, (b) assignment of work in an out-of-bargaining unit, (c) changes in wages, and (d) job classification changes.

An analysis of the arbitration awards for the period 1980–84 revealed that arbitrators followed well-established criteria, such as "the centrality of the contract viewed in its totality, the importance of the wording of the management rights clause, the parties' duty to negotiate and binding nature of precedent" (Ornati, 1986, 8). The two key considerations arbitrators have constantly considered are the parties' willingness to negotiate and the economic necessity for introducing technological change. Precedent is given "explicit weight" in decisions that "permit management to eliminate jobs or transfer duties of a position or a classification when technological developments require it" (Ornati, 1985, 9).

The researcher found that the most challenging cases were those dealing with new technologies that led to work assignment in an "out-of-bargaining unit." Ornati (1985, 10) reports:

> ...the Arbitrator is brought face-to-face with the central characteristics of the newer technologies; still a substitution of capital for labour, the machine now is a substitute for brain rather than brawn. What we see here is the compressing of control functions (as in Drano Co. Case...) where all timekeepers were displaced or in the Eaton Corporation Case...where the quality control function was removed from jurisdiction of layout craftsmen, or the enlargement of the information requirements for the control of subsidiary activities (as in the case of the Ben Secours Hospital, Inc....) where coding process of what was earlier an essentially clerical process, was enlarged requiring the operator to have knowledge of biology, physiology and medical terminology.

The rationale of the arbitrators in out-of-bargaining unit cases was based on multiple factors that included (1) management's right, (2) the time needed to phase out an employee's work before a new computer system is involved, (3) joint determination by union and company to establish exactly how much of a job is still left after automation, (4) union jurisdiction, (5) costs involved in retraining employees, and (6) union's legitimate claims.

Based on the preceding survey analysis of rights arbitration of cases involving technological issues, Ornati (1985, 16) arrived at the following conclusions:

1. While the cases surveyed clearly point to more basic, and so to speak, discontinual, changes in operating processes in the 1980s, the principles that guide arbitrators have *not* changed.
2. While arbitrators are clearly aware of the environmental changes that have been impacting our industries, these have not visibly influenced their decisions. The data deny my hunch that arbitrators in their case-by-case examination of the interaction of facts and contractual texts would have softened the employment impact of the new technologies. "It all depends on the circumstances" and "the contract is what we are guided by" is still at the core of what we do and precedent is what we follow—with care.
3. While surveys of available contracts show that new clauses increasing job security are being introduced, these do not appear to have limited management's freedom to implement new techniques.
4. The cases reviewed suggest that in the 1980s we will see an expansion of arbitral jurisprudence as to employee training rights.
5. When confronted with managerial clauses that are imprecise, and when the totality of the contract does not explicitly deny it, management is viewed as fundamentally free to assign work and pay as business need seems to require it. Indeed, recent arbitrators' obiter dicta, like in those of the past, show a broad internalization of the importance of technological change and of its related constructive/destructive influence.

Implications from Canada–U.S. Comparisons

In comparing the Canadian and American collective bargaining practices, Jain (1983b) concludes:

> In Canada, unlike the United States, there has been a recognition that collective bargaining was not capable of answering all the problems ensuing as a result of technological change. (This recognition has been brought about by greater government intervention in the collective bargaining process than in the United States, stronger unions in Canada than in the U.S., the greater politicization of unions as well as political support from the New Democratic Party at the federal and provincial levels that unions have received in Canada.) Legislation, either recommended or existing, has therefore helped to fill the vacuum....As Clarke (1983) has suggested, neither collective

bargaining nor legislation can ensure that disputes concerning the introduction of technological change are avoided. What they can do. . .is to encourage collaboration. This, is turn, may help employer, union, and employees understand the issues involved in technological change, how the costs and benefits can and should be shared, and how microelectronics technology can be adopted and advanced.

Challenges for Collective Bargaining in Canada

The introduction of new technology raises issues and thereby new challenges and choices, not only in job redundancies, but in work organization, union organization and traditional demarcation lines. Moreover, it raises the fundamental issue of the role and place of collective bargaining as a system in managing change in the new information society (Wetzel, 1986). Management representatives in Canada emphasize their right to adopt and apply new technology, whereas unions have succeeded, to some extent, in negotiating new technological provisions. In the process of change in Canada, two outcomes are clear—first, technological negotiations are shaped by the balances of power among the various social and political forces and institutions which govern those forces. Second, there is indication that IT has created a new value structure in society, in which technological change is perceived as inevitable and progressive, not only by management, government and even arbitrators, but to a significant degree unions themselves.

As Walton (1985) argues, IT is less deterministic than other basic technologies that have shaped our industrial system for two main reasons:

> First, the rapidly declining cost of computing power makes it possible to consider more technical options, including those that are relatively inefficient in the use of that power. Second, the new technology is less hardware dependent, more software intensive. It is, therefore, increasingly flexible, permitting the same basic information-processing task to be accomplished by an even greater variety of technical configurations, each of which may have a different set of human implications (Walton, 1985, 561).

Given the explosive future growth of IT, our proposition is that technology can be guided by strategic choices, developed by management, unions and government. This will require increased commitment, competence and leadership on part of industrial relations actors. The very technology that poses tremendous challenges can be used to develop these strategies.

> The challenge for Canada is to develop an effective industrial-relations approach to technological change, based on its unique collective-bargaining system. The approach must encourage joint involvement and decision making. It must also facilitate the negotiation of mutually satisfactory conditions

with respect to operational flexibility, employment security, and the sharing of the productivity dividend. Such a framework is essential if Canada is to cope effectively with the pace of change that we anticipate for the future (ECC, 1987: 24).

CONCLUSIONS

The overall conclusion is that the perception of technological uncertainty (technostress) can be the driving force of a productive opportunity and can aid in gaining a competitive edge if this uncertainty is managed strategically at both micro- and macro-levels and becomes part of an operational industrial relations system (Abernathy et al., 1983; Hill and Atterback, 1979; Abernathy and Townsend, 1975). The development of strategic choices for managing technological change both within and outside of a collective bargaining system thus becomes a fundamental challenge to an industrial relations system.

Technostress can be either positive (eustress) or negative (distress), depending upon how it is handled by individuals, organizations, and society as a whole. The ability to cope raises the issue of the competence needed by collective bargaining players to understand and manage technological complexity. At what stage technostress is harmful or dysfunctional is a determination that depends upon complex relations between product costs, markets, technology, competition, extent of maturity of the industry involved, managerial competence to manage technological impacts, and union–management co-operation.

There is evidence to show that technological uncertainty associated with information technology is disruptive, and introduces change in relation to obsolete existing capital equipment, labour skills, materials, components, management expertise, and organizational capabilities (Sabel, 1981; Abernathy, 1978; Clark, 1982). Technological uncertainty destroys the value of present competence in various aspects of production and may alter the relative position of competitors (Tilton, 1971; Abernathy et al., 1983). How this uncertainty is integrated into the production process is rooted in the basic competence of producers, including workers and managers, and their cultural attitudes towards change and instability. Bargaining skills become the critical capacity in responding creatively to environmental change in both private and public sectors.

It is estimated that information technology will become a prime stimulant to innovation and technological change (Abernathy et al., 1983). The increasing speed and integration of IT will become pervasive in all key industries and services in Canada and the United States. The overall lesson for collective bargaining is that excellence lies in understanding the complex relations among technology, production management, markets, competition, the level of an industry's maturity over time and the motivations and skills of people involved. The key ingredient in adapting to technology lies in the quality of technological adaptation, i.e., the capacity to influence how technology changes production and services in both the private and public sectors. The development and maintenance of a technology strategy as a part of an industrial relations system in Canada becomes a key process in coping with technological change.

The main feature of technological adaptation is the demonstrated capacity of management and unions to go through the painstaking sequence of managing strains that stem from exploring, introducing, maintaining and changing technological systems. The underlying assumption is that technological adaptation does not happen by itself—it needs to be strategically managed. This is the essence of the technostress imperative: technological excellence requires the skills needed to map out an entirely proactive strategic approach. Put differently, new technologies can yield their potential as competitive weapons when they are based upon strategic human resource management of impacts and technostress with a skilled and responsive workforce in a given industrial relations system in the private or public sector.

The argument is that the door to a new technological renaissance for Canada lies through dynamic, creative, and joint management–union responses. This requires renewed energy and expertise on the part of management and unions to become strategic, committed, adaptive, to transcend the old certainties and use the new technological uncertainties to gain a productive competitive edge in domestic and international markets (Rosenbloom, 1983).

New Collaboration in the Future

The future evolution of collective bargaining, as well as the overall industrial relations system in Canada, must contend with several key trends: the acceleration of change in information technology, the globalization of industry, the results of free-trade negotiation with the United States, international competition, the extent of government intervention in the industrial relations system, and the enhanced strategic importance of information systems. Canadian managers and union leaders "must recognize that they have entered a period of competition that requires of them a mastery of technology-driven strategy, of efficient and high-quality production, and of competent work-force management" (Abernathy et al., 1983, 9). Long-term success in both industry and the public sector in Canada depends on the increased competence of both managers and workers to manage the core of a business, its technology and its impacts, its technostress. The development of these competencies represents a technological and industrial renaissance in the emerging information society. Moreover, strategic management and its success are assets in increasing competitive significance of technological change as it affects the evolution of systems. Technological management is also a key to gaining a competitive edge in the national and international markets (Abernathy et al., 1983; Radford et al., 1983). Effective technological management depends on competent managers and their organizations as well as individual workers and their unions. An added impetus can be provided by governments in introducing special legislation concerning technological change in jurisdictions where they do not have such policy now, and further refining and improving current legislation to make it more flexible, equitable, and effective.

The future of collective bargaining and an industrial relations system in Canada will depend on the commitment and competence of unions, management and government, who have the opportunity to develop and negotiate strategic choices with regard to the advent of information technology. As Canada struggles to meet greater international competition and technological change, the process of collective bargaining will likewise need to undergo a fundamental change, from an adversarial system to a co-operative one. If this change is based on an analysis of strategic choices faced by management, unions, and government, then it can be beneficial for both labour and management. "As jobs change due to robotics, technology, and a surging service sector, employees demand more satisfying and challenging jobs. Workers want greater participation in the workplace through QWL, quality circles, and other techniques. They also want more leisure time and alternate work schedules to fit their lifestyles. Collective bargaining can help them realize these goals" (Carroll, 1985, 425). How well the parties can organize and bargain for new technological impacts in the information society will determine their future.

The aim is to research, develop and utilize IT strategies for both management and union effectiveness in a collaborative collective bargaining context to gain a competitive edge in the global marketplace. Proper implementation of these strategies can have the added benefit of an improvement in the overall quality of worklife.

REFERENCES

Abernathy, W. J. (1978), *The Productivity Dilemma*. Baltimore: John Hopkins University Press.

―――― and Townsend, P. L. (1975), "Technology, productivity and process change." *Technological Forecasting and International Trade*: 379–396.

―――― , Clark, K. B. and Kantrow, A. M. (1983), *Industrial Renaissance*. New York: Basic Books.

Adams, R. J. (1983), *The Unorganized: A Rising Force.* McMaster University Working Paper, Series No. 201.

Alcalay, R. and Pasick, R. J. (1983), "Psycho-social factors and the technologies at work." *Social Science Medicine* 17 (16): 1075–1084.

Amalgamated Transit Union (Locals 1502 and 279) and Ottawa-Carleton Regional Transit Commission (1981). Ottawa: Canada Labour Relations Board, di. 45.

Arndt, R. and Chapman, L. (1984), *Potential Office Hazards and Controls.* Washington, D. C.: Office of Technology Assessment.

Attewell, P. and Rule, J. (1984), "Computing and organizations: What we know and what we don't know." *Communications of the ACM* 27 (12): 1184–1192.

Belanger, M. (1983), "The work world: Wholesale deskilling and elimination of jobs." *CUPE-The Facts* 5 (7): 32–38.

Bell, D. (1973), *The Coming of Post Industrial Society.* New York: Basic Books.

Benjamin, R., Rockart, J. F., Morton, M. S. and Wyman, J. (1984), "Information technology: A strategic opportunity." *Sloan Management Review* 3: 10.

Benson, I. and Lloyd, J. (1983), *New Technology and Industrial Change.* London: Kogan Page.

Betcherman, G. and McMullen, K. (1986), *Working with Technology: A Survey of Automation in Canada.* Ottawa: Economic Council of Canada.

Bird, E. (1980), *Information Technology in the Office: The Impact on Women's jobs.* Manchester Equal Opportunities Commission.

Blackwell, R. (1986), "Manufacturing lags behind in adapting to new technology." *The Financial Post Outlook Report on the Nation* (Winter): 24–30.

Blumberg, M. and Gerwin, D. (1984), "Coping with advanced manufacturing technology." *Journal of Occupational Behavior* 5: 113–130.

Bureau of National Affairs (1984), *Special Report on VDTs and the Workplace.* Washington, D. C.

Cakir, A., Reuter, H., von Schmudt, L. et al. (1978), *Research into Effects of Video Display Workplaces on the Physical and Psychological Function of Persons.* Bonn, West Germany: Federal Ministry for Work and Social Order.

Canada Tomorrow Conference, 6–9 November 1983 (1984), Summary. Ottawa: Supply and Services.

Choate, P. (1982), *Retooling the American Workforce.* Washington, D. C.: Northeast-Midwest Institute.

Clark, K. B. (1982), *The Competitive Status of the Influence of Technology in Determining International Competitive Advantage.* Washington, D. C.: National Academy of Sciences.

Clarke, R. D. (1983), *New Technology and Labour*. Paper for International Symposium on Work and Safety, Houthalen, Limburg, September 22–23.

Coe, J. B., Cuttle, K., McClellan, W. C. et al. (1980),*Visual Display Units*. Wellington, New Zealand: Department of Health Report W/1/80.

Colligan, M. J., Smith, M. J. and Hurrell, J. J. (1977), "Occupational incidence rates of mental health disorders." *Journal of Human Stress* 3 (3): 34–39.

Cox, E. A. (1980), "Radiation emissions from visual display units." In *Health Hazards of VDTS, 1. Papers Presented at HUSAT Conference*. Loughborough: Loughborough University of Technology.

Craig, A. W. J. (1987), *Technological Change, Labour Relations Policy, Administrative Tribunals and the Incidence of Technological Change Provisions in Major Collective Agreements*. University of Ottawa Working Paper, 87–24.

Cyr, N. J. (1979), "Improved productivity through computerized memomotion." *Ind. Eng.* 11: 34–39.

Dainoff, M., Happ A. and Crane P. (1981), "Visual fatigue and occupational stress in VDT operators." *Hum. Factors* 23 (4): 421–437.

Downs, A. A. (1967), "A realistic look at the final payoffs from urban data systems." *Public Adm. Rev.* 27 (3): 204–209.

Drucker, P. (1980), quoted in a speech by N. B. Hannay, Vice-President, Research and Patents, Bell Laboratories, Northwestern University, March 5. Quoted by NAISBITT, J., *Megatrends*. New York: Warner Communications Co., 1982.

Dutton, W. and Kraemer, K. (1978), "Determinants of support for computerized information systems: The attitudes of local government chief executives." *Midwest Rev. Public Adm.* 12 (1): 19–40.

Economic Council of Canada (1987), *Making Technology Work: Innovation and Jobs in Canada*. Ottawa: Minister of Supply and Services Canada.

Elias, R., Cail, F., Tisserland, M. et al. (1980), "Investigations in operators working with CRT display terminals: Relationships between task content and psychophysiological alterations." In E. Grandjean and E. Vigliani (eds.), *Ergonomic Aspects of Video Display Terminals*. London: Taylor & Francis, pp. 211–218.

Ellul, J. (1964), *The Technological Society*. Trans. by John Wilkinson. New York: Alfred A. Knopf.

Forrester, T. (ed.) (1981), *The Microelectronic Revolution*. Cambridge, MA: MIT Press.

Fraser, T. M. (1983), *Human Stress, Work and Job Satisfaction*. Geneva: ILO.

Ghiringhelli, I. (1980), "Collection of subjective opinions on the use of

VDT." In E. Gradjean and E. Vigilian (eds.), *Ergonomic Aspects of Visual Display Terminals*. London: Taylor & Francis, pp. 227–232.

Goh, S. C. (1985), "Uncertainty, power and organizational decision making: A constructive replication and some extensions." *Canadian Journal of Administrative Sciences* 2 (1): 177–191.

Grayson, J. P. (1986), *Plant Closures and De-Skilling: Three Case Studies*. Ottawa: Science Council of Canada.

Gunnarsson, E. and Soderberg, I. (1980), *I. Eystrain Resulting from VDT Work at the Swedish Telecommunications Administration*. Stockholm: National Board of Occupational Safety and Health, Staff Conference.

_____ and Ostberg, O. (1977), *Physical and Mental Working Environment in a Terminal-based Data System. Research Report no. 35.* Stockholm: Industrial Welfare Council.

Harris, C. (1986), "Computer job toll not too painful." *Financial Post* (4 October): 18.

Haynes, S. G. and Feinleib, M. (1980), "Women, work and coronary heart disease: Prospective findings from the Framingham Heart Study." *AJPH* 70 (2): 133–141.

Health and Welfare Canada (1983), *Investigation of Radiation Emissions from Video Display Terminals* (83-EHD-91). Ottawa: Environmental Health Directorate.

Hill, C. T. and Atterback, J. M. (eds.) (1979), *Technological Innovation for a Dynamic Economy*. Elmsford: Pergamon Press.

Hinings, C. R., Hickson, D. J., Pennings, J. M. and Schneck, R. E. (1974), "Structural conditions of intraorganizational power." *Administrative Science Quarterly* 19: 22–44.

Hiscott, R. D. (1982), Plant closures and employee displacement. MA thesis, Kingston: Queen's University.

Hrebiniak and Joyce, C. F. (1985), "Organizational adaptation: Strategic choice and environmental determinism." *Administrative Science Quarterly* 30: 336–349.

Hunt, H. A. and Hunt, T. L. (1983), *Human Resource Implications of Robotics*. Kalamazoo, MI: W. E. Upjohn Institute for Employment Research.

Hunting, W. T., Laubli, T., and Grandjean, E. (1981), "Postural and visual loads at VDT workplaces, I. Constrained postures." *Ergonomics* 24 (12): 917–931.

Industry, Trade and Commerce (1978), *A Report on the Labour Force Tracking Project/Costs of Labour Adjustment Study*. Ottawa: Industry, Trade and Commerce.

International Labour Organization (ILO) (1984), *Automation, Work Organization and Occupational Stress*. Geneva: ILO.

Jain, H. C. (1983b), "Micro-electronics technology and industrial relations. *Relat. ind.* 38 (4): 869–879.

_____ (1983a), "Technological change and industrial relations: An international comparison." *IRRA Proceedings*, San Francisco, CA, pp. 85–91.

Johansson, G. and Aronsson, G. (1984), "Stress reactions in computerized administrative work." *Journal of Occupational Behavior* 5 (3): 159–181.

Kast, F. E. and Rosenzweig, J. E. (1985), *Organization and Management*. New York: McGraw-Hill.

King, J. L. and Kraemer, K. (1980), *Cost as a Social Impact of Telecommunications and Other Information Technologies*. Irvine, CA: Public Policy Research Organization.

Kochan, T. A., McKersie, R. B. and Katz, H. C. (1984), *U. S. Industrial Relations in Transition: A Summary Report*. Paper presented at the Annual Meeting of the Industrial Relations Association, Dallas, Texas.

Labour Canada (1985), *Provisions in Major Collective Agreements in Canada Covering 500 and More Employees*. Ottawa: Labour Canada.

Labour Canada Task Force (1982), *In the Chips: Opportunities, People, Partnerships*. Ottawa: Labour Canada.

Laudon, K. (1964), *Computers and Bureaucratic Reform*. New York: Wiley.

Levi, L. (1984), *Stress in Industry: Causes, Effects and Prevention*. Geneva: ILO.

LO (1981, September), Facklig data Poletic (Jönköping). Quoted in Social and Labour Bulletin 3: 261–262.

Macdonald, D. S. (1985), *Royal Commission on the Economic Union and Development Prospects for Canada: Report*. Ottawa: Minister of Supplies and Services.

Manwaring, T. (1981), "Trade union response to new technology." *Industrial Relations Journal* 1–10.

Masuda, Y. (1980), *The Information Society as Post-Industrial Society*. Tokyo: Institute for the Information Society.

McGregor, D. (1986), "Proposed GM backout packages flies in face of economic evidence." *The Citizen*, December 16.

McKay, R. (1981), "Labour–management relations." *Proceedings of a Conference on the Impact of Micro-Electronic Technology on the Work Environment*. Ottawa: Labour Canada.

Menzies, H. (1981a), "Employment impact." *Proceedings of a Conference on the Impact of Micro-Electronic Technology on the Work Environment*. Ottawa: Labour Canada.

_____ (1981b), *Women and the Chip*. Montreal: The Institute for Research on Public Policy.

_____ (1982), *Computers on the Job*. Toronto: James Lorimer & Co.

Meyer, M. W. (1968), "Two authority structures of bureaucratic organization." *Administrative Science Quarterly* 13: 211–228.

Miles, R. E. and Snow, C. E., (1978), *Organizational Strategy: Structure and Process.* New York: McGraw-Hill.

Mills, D. Q. (1986), *Labor–Management Relations.* New York: McGraw-Hill.

Murphy, L. R. and Hurrell, J. J. (1979), "Machine pacing and occupational stress." *New Developments in Occupational Stress.* Los Angeles, CA: University of California Press, pp. 17–35.

Naisbitt, J. (1982), *Megatrends.* New York: Warner Books.

Office of Technology Assessment (1985), *Information Technology and R&D.* Washington, D. C.: U. S. Congress, OTA. CIT-268.

Olson, M. (1965), *The Logic of Collective Action.* Cambridge, MA: Harvard University Press.

Ontario Ministry of Labour (1984), *Labour Market Experiences of Workers in Plant Closures: A Survey of 21 Cases.* Toronto: Ontario Ministry of Labour.

Ornati, O. (1985), *Rights Arbitration and Technological Change.* Working Paper No. 85–38. New York: New York University.

Ouchi, W. G. (1981), *Theory Z.* New York: Avon Books.

Owen, T. (1982a), *Plant Closure—Lindsay Case Study.* Toronto: Thomas Owen and Associates.

_____ (1982b), *Plant Closure—St. Catharines Study.* Toronto: Thomas Owen and Associates.

Pava, C. (1983), *Managing New Office Technology: An Organizational Strategy.* New York: Macmillan/The Free Press.

Perrow, C. (1967), "A framework for comparative analysis of organizations." *American Sociological Review* 32 (2): 194–208.

Petchinis, S. G. (1983), "The attitude of trade unions towards technological changes." *Relations industrielles* 38: 104–18.

Pfeffer, J., Salancik, G. R. and Leblebeci, H. (1976), "The effect of uncertainty on the use of social influence in organizational decision making." *Administrative Science Quarterly* 21: 227–45.

Picher, M. G. (1986), "In the matter of an arbitration between Canadian Broadcasting Corporation and Canadian Union of Public Employee." *Award,* 13 March. Ottawa: Labour Canada.

_____ , Sinclair, G. and Robbins, L. (1984), "In the matter of arbitration between Bell Canada and Communication Workers of Canada." *Award,* 8 March. Ottawa: Labour Canada.

Porat, M. (1971), *The Information Economy: Definition and Measurement,* Publication 77-12 (1). Washington, D. C.: U.S. Department of Commerce, Office of Telecommunications.

_____ (1977), *Information Economy: Definition and Measurement.* Washington, D.C.: U.S. Department of Commerce/Office of Telecommunications. OT Special Pub. 77-12 (1).

Prosten, R. (1980, 1982, 1984), *Comparative Survey of Major Collective Bargaining Agreements*. Washington, D.C.: AFL–CIO.

Rada, J. (1980), *The Impact of Micro-electronics*. Geneva: ILO.

Radford, R. et al. (1983), *The View from the Top: Executive Perspectives on the New Industrial Competition*. Harvard Business School Working Paper.

Rosenbloom, R. S. (1983), *Research on Technological Innovation Management and Policy*. Greenwich, CO: JAI Press.

Sabel, R. (1981), *IBM: Colossus in Transition*. New York: Truman Talley Books/Times Books.

Sauter, S. L., Gottlieb M. and Jones, K. C. (1982), *A General Systems Analyses of Stress/Strain in VDT Operations*. Paper presented at Conference on Human Factors and Computer Systems, Gaithersburg, MD.

Schieman, W. et al. (1984), *Supervision in the 80s: Trends in Corporate America*. Washington, D. C.: Opinion Research Corporation.

Schönpflug, W. (1983), "Coping efficiency and situational demands." In R. Hockey (ed.), *Stress and Fatigue in Human Performance*. New York: John Wiley and Sons, pp. 299–326.

Science Council of Canada (1982), *Planning New for an Information Society*. Hull, Que.: Canadian Government Publishing Centre.

Servan-Schreiber, J. J. (1981), *Un centre mondial pour le développement des ressources humaines*. Rapport à M. le Président de la République. Paris, France.

Sethi, A.S., Schuler, R.S. and Caro, D.H.J. (1987), "A strategic choice model of technostress management." In A.S. Sethi, D. Caro and R.S. Schuler (eds.), *Strategic Management of Technostress in an Information Society*. Toronto: Hogrefe International Inc., pp. 16–32.

Shaiken, H. (1984), *Work Transformed: Automation and Labor in the Computer Age*. New York: Holt, Rinehart and Winston.

Smith, M. J. (1982), *Health Issues in VDT Work*. Cincinnati, OH: NIOSH.

Swan, K. P. (1985), "In the matter of an arbitration between Canada Post Corporation and Canadian Union of Postal Workers." *Award*, 5 July, No. CPC 831-2-3-19 Ottawa: Labour Canada.

——— (1983), "In the matter of an arbitration between Canada Post Corporation and Canadian Union of Postal Workers." *Award*, No. CPC 831-2-3-19 Ottawa: Labour Canada.

——— (1982), "Union impact on management of the organization: A legal perspective." In Anderson, J. and Gunderson, M. (eds.), *Union–Management Relations in Canada*. Don Mills, Ont.: Addison-Wesley.

Tilton, John E. (1971), *International Diffusion of Technology: The Case of Semiconductors*. Washington, D.C.: Booking Institution.

Toong, H. D. and Gupta, A. (1982), "Automating air traffic control." *Technology Review*: 54.

Turner, J. A. (1984b), *Computer Mediated Work: A Comparative Study of Mortgage Loan Servicing Clerks and Financial Investment Officers in Savings Banks*. Research Report GBA#84-70. New York: New York University, Center for Research in Information Systems.

———and Karasek, R. A. Jr. (1984), "Software ergonomics: Effects of computer application design parameters on operator task performance and health." *Ergonomics* 27: 6.

Walton, R. E. (1985), "Social choice in the development of advanced information technology." In M. Beer and B. Spector (eds.), *Human Resource Management*. New York: Free Press, pp. 557–560.

Weber, C. E. (1959), "Impact of electronic data processing on clerical skills." *Pers. Adm.* 22-33 (1): 20–26.

Wereneke, D. (1983), *Microelectronics and Office Jobs: The Impact of the Chip on Women's Employment*. Geneva: ILO.

Wesson, R. et. al. (1981), *Scenarios for Evaluation of Air Traffic Control*. Monograph, Rand, R-2698-FAA.

Westin, A. F. (1979), *Privacy and Freedom*. New York: Atheneum.

Wetzel, K. (1986), "Collective bargaining target of government." *CAUT Bulletin* (May): 5–6.

Winner, L. (1977), *Autonomous Technology*. Cambridge, MA: MIT Pres.

Woods, H. D. (1968) (ed.), *Industrial Conflict and Dispute Settlement*. Montreal, Quebec: Industrial Relations Centre, McGill University.

World Health Organization (1985), *Consultation on Linkage of Occupational Exposure Information with Morbidity Data: Summary Report*. Geneva: Regional Office for Europe/World Health Organization.

Zuboff, S. (1982), New Worlds of Computer-Mediated Work. *Harvard Business Review*: 142–152.

Index

Aaron, Benjamin, 88
Abella, Irving, 106
Affirmative action, 333
Air Canada, 401
Alcalay, R., 491, 497
All-Canadian Congress of Labour (ACCL), 107
Amalgamated Society of Engineers (ASE), 94
American Federation of Labor (AFL), 107, 121
Anderson, J. C., 286
Angle, H. L., 196
Anti-Inflation Act (1975), 46, 300
  compensation defined in, 302
Anti-Inflation Board, 271
Arbitrators
  criteria used by in making awards, 407, 410-11
  and exceeding jurisdiction, 366
  jurisdiction of, 353-54
  and reinstatement issue, 362
  response of to technological change, 519-20
  role of, 355-57, 361
  and seniority issue, 362-63
Arndt, R., 502
Ashford, Nicholas, 436
Assumption of risk doctrine, 423
Austria
  co-determination system in, 476

Barbesh, J., 30, 34
Bargaining duty, 63-65
Bargaining moves
  categories of, 186
  concession making, 204
  opening, 203-4
  opponent's, 206-7
  procedural, 205-6
  threats and promises, 205
Bargaining power, 194-95
Bargaining settlement, 187-88
Bargaining site, 201
Bargaining structure
  Canadian, formal and informal, 158-63
  centralization in, 135-36, 149-55, 175
  changes recommended in, 166-67
  consequences of, 149-58
  definition of, 132-34
  disputed issues in, 164-65
  multi-employer, 144, 146, 150, 151, 154, 157
  role of employees in, 134

influences on, 139-47
Bargaining teams, 196-98
Barnes, M., 202
Barocci, T. A., 285
Begin, Monseigneur, 106
Bell Canada, 519
Bell, D., 335, 483
Benjamin, R., 497
Benton, A. A., 203
Berman, David, 436
Betcherman, G., 497
Bilateral monopoly game, 191, 201, 203, 204, 205
Blake, R.R., 199
Blum, Albert, 170
Bodman, Eric, 297
Boudreau, Emile, 422, 431
Boulwarism, 169, 204
Bourassa, Robert, 97
Brett, Jeanne M., 463
British Columbia compensation stabilization program (1982), 300
  compensation defined in, 301, 304
British Columbia Labour Code, 72
  technological change defined in, 516
British North America Act (1867), 46
Brooks, George, 170, 171, 173, 174, 175, 176
Brown, B. R., 189, 190, 191, 192, 193, 195, 199, 202, 203, 205
Brown, George, 106

Cairnie, J. F., 285
Canada Labour Code, 328, 512, 513, 514
  technological change defined in, 514, 516
Canada Labour Relations Board
  response to technological change, 518-19
Canada Post Corporation, 266, 514, 519
Canadian Brotherhood of Railway Employees (CBRE), 94
Canadian and Catholic Confederation of Labour (CCCL), 94, 96, 107, 121, 125
Canadian Charter of Rights and Freedoms (1982), 46, 85, 317, 325, 328
  applied to collective agreement, 331
  and collective bargaining, 86-88
  and workplace issues, 364-65
Canadian Congress of Labour (CCL), 97, 125
Canadian Federation of Labour (CFL), 107, 125
Canadian Human Rights Act, 303
Canadian Labour Congress (CLC), 94, 96, 99, 112, 125, 126, 135, 374, 520
Canadian Labour Market and Productivity Centre (CLMPC), 481
Canadian Labour Union (CLU), 106, 125
Canadian Steel Policy Conference, 481
Canadian Trade Unions Act (1872), 417

539

Printed in Canada